WORSE THAN WAR

WORSE THAN WAR

Genocide, Eliminationism,
and the Ongoing
Assault on Humanity

DANIEL JONAH GOLDHAGEN

PUBLICAFFAIRS
New York

PublicAffairs books are available at special discounts for bulk purchases in the U.S. by corporations, institutions, and other organizations. For more information, please contact the Special Markets Department at the Perseus Books Group, 2300 Chestnut Street, Suite 200, Philadelphia, PA 19103, call (800) 810-4145, ext. 5000, or e-mail special.markets@perseusbooks.com.

Designed by Brent Wilcox
Text set in 10.75 point Sabon

Library of Congress Cataloging-in-Publication Data
Goldhagen, Daniel Jonah.
    Worse than war : genocide, eliminationism, and the ongoing assault on humanity / Daniel Jonah Goldhagen. — 1st ed.
        p.   cm.
    Includes index.
    ISBN 978-1-58648-769-0 (alk. paper)
    1. Genocide—Psychological aspects.   2. Genocide—Prevention.   3. Racism—Psychological aspects.   4. Prejudices—Psychological aspects.   5. Hate—Case studies.
6. Group identity—Case studies.   I.Title.
    HV6322.7.G65 2009
    364.15'1—dc22

                                                                        2009028035

First Edition

10 9 8 7 6 5 4 3 2 1

For Gideon and Veronica

CONTENTS

The Choice

HUNDREDS OF MILLIONS of people are at risk of becoming the victims of genocide and related violence.

They live in countries governed by political regimes that have been and are inherently prone to committing mass murder. In some countries, such as Sudan, the killing is ongoing. In others, such as Rwanda, the killing has been recent. In still others, such as Kenya, the threat of mass murder has appeared real if not imminent. In yet others, although no warning signals suggest immediate danger, mass slaughter could begin precipitously.

Our time, dating from the beginning of the twentieth century, has been afflicted by one mass murder after another, so frequently and, in aggregate, of such massive destructiveness, that the problem of genocidal killing is worse than war. Until now, the world's peoples and governments have done little to prevent or stop mass murdering. Today, the world is not markedly better prepared to end this greatest scourge of humanity. The evidence of this failure is overwhelming. It is to be found in Tibet, North Korea, the former Yugoslavia, Saddam Hussein's Iraq, Rwanda, southern Sudan, the Democratic Republic of the Congo, and Darfur.

Individuals, institutions, and governments, in every region of the world—we all have a choice:

We can persist in our malign neglect that consists of three parts: failing to face the problem squarely and to understand the real nature of genocide; failing to recognize we can far more effectively protect hundreds of millions of people and radically reduce mass murder's incidence; and failing to choose to act on this knowledge.

Or we can focus on this scourge; understand its causes, its nature and complexity, and its scope and systemic quality; and, building upon that understanding, craft institutions and policies that will save countless lives and also lift the lethal threat under which so many people live.

How can we not choose the second?

CLARIFYING THE ISSUES

CHAPTER ONE

Eliminationism,
Not Genocide

H ARRY TRUMAN, THE THIRTY-THIRD president of the United States, was a mass murderer. He twice ordered nuclear bombs dropped on Japanese cities. The first, an atomic bomb, exploded over Hiroshima on August 6, 1945, and the second, a nuclear bomb, detonated over Nagasaki on August 9. Truman knew that each would kill tens of thousands of Japanese civilians who had no direct bearing on any military operation, and who posed no immediate threat to Americans. In effect, Truman chose to snuff out the lives of approximately 300,000 men, women, and children. Upon learning of the first bomb's annihilation of Hiroshima, Truman was jubilant, announcing that "this is the greatest thing in history."[1] He then followed up in Nagasaki with a second *greatest thing*. It is hard to understand how any right-thinking person could fail to call slaughtering unthreatening Japanese *mass murder*.

People, particularly Americans, have offered many justifications and excuses for Truman's mass slaughter. That it was necessary to end the war. That it was necessary to save tens of thousands, even hundreds of thousands of American lives. But as Truman at the time knew, and as his advisers, including his military advisers, told him *prior* to the bombing of Hiroshima, none of these was true.[2] Then supreme Allied commander of the forces in Europe and soon to be American president, Dwight Eisenhower explained: "During his recitation of the relevant facts [about the plan for using the atomic bomb], I had been conscious of a feeling of depression and so I voiced to him [Secretary of War Henry Stimson] my grave misgivings, first on the basis of my belief that

3

Japan was already defeated and that dropping the bomb was completely unnecessary, and secondly because I thought that our country
should avoid shocking world opinion by the use of a weapon whose
employment was, I thought, no longer mandatory as a measure to save
American lives. It was my belief that Japan was, at that very moment,
seeking some way to surrender with a minimum loss of 'face.'"[3]

Truman, in his press release informing the American people about
the annihilation of Hiroshima, offered the primitive logic of retribution: "The Japanese began the war from the air at Pearl Harbor. They
have been repaid many fold."[4] These justifications notwithstanding,
the best that can be said for Truman, for those Americans (in August
1945, 85 percent) and others who supported his mass slaughters, and
for those who have been duped by the drumbeat of self-exculpation
into believing that the slaughter was just (in 1995, 72 percent of Americans ages fifty to sixty-four, and 80 percent of those sixty-five and
older), is that he and they, not otherwise wicked people, perpetrated or
supported this twin horror owing to erroneous information or reasoning, to moral blindness, or to hardened hearts after years of war.[5] Even
this best face does not change what Truman did.

What if Adolf Hitler had dropped a nuclear bomb on a British or
American city? What if during the Cuban Missile Crisis Nikita
Khrushchev had incinerated Miami? Would we not call such acts mass
murder, even though in Hitler's case it would have also been done with
the veneer of a rationale that it was a military operation and not the mass
slaughter of noncombatants? In the case of Hitler, we would inscribe his
act prominently in his long ledger of evil. Why should Truman's wholesale extermination of so many men, women, and children be different?

What if the Japanese had not surrendered a few days after Nagasaki's bombing, and Truman had proceeded to annihilate another
Japanese city? And then another. And another. And another. At what
point would people stop making excuses? At what point would all people speak plainly about his mass murdering? Why would the successive nuclear annihilation of the people of, say, five or ten Japanese cities
be deemed mass murder—which undoubtedly it would be—but the
slaughter of the Japanese of *only* two cities not be?

Or what if the Americans had conquered a few Japanese cities,
stopped their advance, and proceeded to shoot 140,000 Japanese civil-

Hiroshima after the mass murder

ians, men, women, and children (the number who died immediately or from injuries in the next few months from the atomic bombing of Hiroshima), explaining to Japan's leaders and its public that only surrender would prevent more mass slaughters? Would Truman's apologists have similarly justified this more conventional mass murdering as militarily and morally necessary? What if three days later Truman ordered American soldiers to shoot another seventy thousand Japanese men, women, and children from a second city? Would we not call such slaughters mass murder? Except for the technological difference between 210,000 bullets and two nuclear bombs (the nuclear bombs destroyed also the cities themselves, and subsequently caused at least another sixty thousand deaths owing to radiation poisoning and other injuries), it is hard to see how, in deciding whether each constitutes mass murder, these two scenarios differ in any conceptually or factually meaningful way. Truman's Chief of Staff William Leahy, a Navy admiral, abhorred using nuclear weapons against the Japanese, and not only because "the Japanese were already defeated and ready to surrender." Leahy explains: "My own feeling was that in being the first to use it, we had adopted an ethical standard common to the barbarians of the Dark Ages. I was not taught to make wars in that fashion, and wars cannot be won by destroying women and children"[6]—because that is not war but mass murder.

I start with the Truman's mass annihilation of Japanese to indicate how deficient our understanding of large-scale mass murder is. The willful slaughter of more than a quarter million people, in full view of the world, should be universally recognized for what it was, causing the label *"mass murderer"* to be affixed to Truman's name. Japanese, to a degree people in other countries, and especially critics of the United States do see Truman's use of nuclear weapons this way. But in the United States and the corridors of power, it is denied or ignored. That Truman's nuclear incineration of Hiroshima and Nagasaki's people is not invariably and prominently listed among our time's mass murders points us to one of the acute problems—aside from truthfulness—confounding our understanding: the problem of definition. How should we define mass murder so that we do not misconstrue it?

Why have Truman's actions not been universally seen and condemned for what they were? For Americans the problem of facing up to the crimes of one's own country and countrymen is real. Most peoples have prettified self-images that cover up blemishes, airbrush scars and open sores on the self-drawn portraits of their nations, their pasts, and themselves. For Americans, Turks, Japanese, Poles, Russians, Chinese, French, British, Guatemalans, Croats, Serbs, Hutu, and countless others, the ugliness that they easily see in others, they fail to acknowledge in themselves, their own countries, or their countrymen. How can we establish appropriate general criteria that give people a more accurate view of themselves?

Americans and others fail to see and speak truthfully about these American crimes against the Japanese for other reasons. The difficulty of adequately defining mass murder or genocide is compounded by the common failure to keep it distinct from two other essential tasks: explanation and moral evaluation.

For many people, especially Americans, it just *feels* wrong, and offensive, to speak of Truman in the same breath as Hitler, Joseph Stalin, Mao Zedong, and Pol Pot. Why? The latter four killers were certifiable monsters. They destroyed millions because they deemed certain people human trash or obstacles to their power or millennial or imperial goals. Truman, however, was no such monster. While these monsters' mass murdering was an organic expression of their long-standing racist or ideological views and political aspirations, Truman's was accidental, owing to a confluence of circumstances that he would have preferred never came about. While these monsters planned, even lusted, to kill millions and created institutions explicitly for such purposes, Truman would have gladly had history take another course. While each of these monsters killed as an integral part of his use of power, did so over much of the time that he held power, and would have continued doing so had he stayed in power, Truman killed in a very specific setting, in the context of a brutal and extremely destructive war that Japan had launched against the United States starting with a surprise attack on the American Pacific fleet in Pearl Harbor. After destroying much of Hiroshima and Nagasaki, Truman stopped. When one looks at each of the other four, it is hard not to conclude that, if the term is to be applied to human beings, each was a monster. When one looks at Truman, one sees an otherwise conventional man who committed monstrous deeds.

Still, none of these distinctions speaks to the *definition* of mass murder. None suggests that the *nature* of Truman's acts and those of the other four are different. Each distinction, rather, addresses either differences between why the four monsters and Truman acted, or how we ought to evaluate the four and Truman morally. None makes Truman's willful killing of Japanese children in Hiroshima and Nagasaki any less a mass-murderous act than Hitler's, Stalin's, Mao's, or Pol Pot's willful killing of Jewish, Ukrainian, Chinese, or Cambodian children.

This failure to distinguish between defining an act, explaining it, and morally judging it likely leads many to recoil at putting Truman in the dock with the greatest monsters of our age. Nevertheless, that Truman should have found himself before a court to answer for his actions seems clear. How such a court's judgment and sentence would read—compared to those of the other four—can be debated. Truman was not a Hitler, Stalin, Mao, or Pol Pot. In this sense, people's intuitions are correct. But that should not stop us from seeing his deeds for what they are.

The difficulty of keeping distinct the three tasks of definition, explanation, and moral evaluation muddles considerations of mass murder. The passions of assigning guilt, blame, or moral responsibility hijack the other two usually cooler enterprises. This happens constantly in discussions of the Holocaust, the name for the Germans' annihilation of European Jews. If Truman and Hitler are not to be judged the same, then their acts, so goes the faulty and backward chain of thinking, could not be the same. Similarly, if their deeds cannot be explained in the same way, then they could not be of the same kind. Hitler killed Jews because he was in the grip of an ideology, a fantasy, that held the Jews to be the source of evil in the world. Truman, not beholden to any such fantasy, annihilated the Japanese of Hiroshima and Nagasaki for other, though not entirely clear, reasons: perhaps his belief that it was a just way to hasten the war's end (even if, as Truman knew, the slaughter was not necessary to end the war soon), or perhaps to demonstrate American power to the Soviets for the emerging cold war struggle. But these different explanations do not make one slaughter a mass murder and the other not.

We can, as a matter of fact, call Truman's annihilation of the people of Hiroshima and Nagasaki mass murder and the man a mass murderer, putting Truman and his deeds into the same broad categories of Hitler and the Holocaust, Stalin and the gulag, Pol Pot, Mao, Saddam Hussein, and Slobodan Milošević and their victims, without giving the same explanation for Truman's actions as we do for theirs, and without judging them morally as being equivalent.

As Truman's example suggests, we must put an end to a host of fallacies and self-deceptions that have clouded the facts and muddled our judgments. We must consult the corrective lenses of others. We must look at mass killings using impartial criteria. We must keep distinct the tasks of definition, which requires specifying what it is we are examining; of explanation, which requires accounts for why events occur and people act; and of moral evaluation, which requires us to judge the character of events and the culpability of the actors. We must approach the phenomenon with the willingness to think it through systematically and from the beginning.

Human Beings and Mass Slaughter

Our investigation of mass murder begins with basic questions: Is it easy or hard to get people to kill others, including children? Some say that, with opportunity, all or most people will readily slaughter others. Others say that human beings will assent to kill others merely because they receive orders to do so. Still others hold that people who find themselves subjected to social psychological pressure to kill will generally do so, or that propaganda can quickly, almost immediately, turn any people into mass executioners of any men, women, and even children. Each of these views has scholarly and "common-sense" or popular versions. Are they right?

Are all or most adults potential mass murderers, mass exterminators of children, just waiting to be asked to kill? Or must something profound happen to people for them to perpetrate mass slaughter? Are all or most states, are all or most societies, proto-genocidal, meaning they could easily be moved to commit genocide? Or are only some ready to be easily incited to slaughter? Why has our age of such technological, economic, and undeniable moral progress seen so much mass slaughter?

The foundation for answering these seemingly simple questions is an exploration of critical aspects, in turn, of the nature of human beings, modern societies and their cultures, states, and mass slaughter.

Any serious investigation of mass murder must reject two widespread notions. The first consists of several related notions: that people's actions are *determined* by external forces; that they have little or no say over how they act; that free will is an illusion. Yet if forces or pressures determined people's actions, it would not be so hard to understand mass murder, or so much about our social and political lives in general that we understand only partially or hardly at all. Some people always deviate from what the external forces supposedly acting upon them are said to push them to do; often so many do that forces, such as state orders, deemed so powerful in one setting, seem hardly relevant in another, as during rebellions and revolutions.

The second faulty notion is the first's curious analogue. It holds that internal drives impel people to commit mass murder. When civilization's restraints are lifted, the universally existing antagonism of people unlike oneself, the love of violence, the will to vent aggression, to dominate, to vanquish, and the pleasures of sadism easily awaken the darkened heart, the Caligula that is everyman. A kindred view holds that when opportunity presents itself, when the incentives are right, the universal drive for gain will move people, like so many automatons, to kill others. Either way, this notion about innate internal drives is also false. Far from everyone kills or tortures others whenever the opportunity presents itself or when it appears profitable, or kills or tortures *any* group of people, regardless of their national, political, ethnic, religious, or linguistic identities.

These various notions about human nature are often not articulated but instead embedded in the discussion of mass murder as unstated assumptions. However explicitly or baldly their proponents state these notions, they rarely investigate, examine, test, or justify them, and fail to assess them against competing views. This is true of scholarly and popular writing and (in my considerable experience) of discussions among acquaintances and friends.

The real task is not to postulate that all people have the general capacity to kill and therefore will kill anyone at any time or, still more wrongheaded, to assume that because of external circumstances or internal drives those who have killed have done so automatically, and then to declare the investigation closed. The real task is to adopt a more multifaceted and realistic view of humanity and to explain the *variation* in people's responses to the forces outside them and those (whatever they are) inside them, to understand how people mediate such influences when they move themselves to act. Why do some people kill (though not just anyone) and other people who find themselves in the same situation do not? Why do some people torture and others similarly positioned do not? On a larger scale, why do some groups of people perpetrate mass murder, including slaughtering children, and others who find themselves in *very much the same circumstances,* say of deprivation or of being at war, do not?

To answer these and the many other questions about mass murder, we must begin with several fundamental truths about human beings: People make choices about how to act, even if they do not choose the contexts in which they make them. People make these choices according to their understanding of the social world and their views of what is right and wrong, good and evil, and of their own understanding of how the world is to be shaped and governed, even if different contexts make some choices more or less plausible, or easier or more difficult to choose. And people ultimately are the authors of their own actions because humans are fundamentally beings with a moral dimension (which does not mean we endorse their moral views), and they are so because the human condition is one of *agency*, namely the capacity and burden of being able to choose to say yes, which means also being able to say no.

We must keep these facts about human beings in mind for another reason. Ignoring them depersonalizes and dehumanizes the perpetrators. It turns them into puny abstractions, fleshy automatons with internal robotics programmed by whatever theories are supplying the motor. This also means that when presenting accounts of the perpetrators' deeds, we should not omit them linguistically, as people often do who want it to appear as if some larger forces, and not human beings with human motives, are effectively doing the killing or who, for political reasons, wish to obscure the identities of the perpetrators. We should not employ the passive voice, which omits the presence of the actors—on this or that day, this or that many Armenians, Chinese, Jews, Bosnian Muslims, or Tutsi were killed—and instead use the active voice. And we should make sure to name the perpetrators, and not be afraid to call them Turks when they were Turks, Japanese when they were Japanese, Germans when they were Germans, Soviets when they were Soviets, Americans when they were Americans, Serbs when they were Serbs, Hutu when they were Hutu, Political Islamists when they were Political Islamists.

This linguistic rectitude is not just analytical but moral as well. Without human beings, without naming them properly, there cannot be moral and legal accountability. Perpetrators who want to escape culpability, foreign leaders who want excuses for inaction or to provide cover for the perpetrators, and scholars and writers who wish to hide the identity of or absolve perpetrators typically use the passive voice. For decades, Germans and many writing about the Holocaust obscured the German perpetrators' identity by using the passive voice or by falsely referring to the perpetrators as "Nazis" (the vast majority of the German perpetrators were not Nazi Party members or any more allegiant to Nazism than Germans in general) and by attacking those calling the perpetrators—as both the German perpetrators and the Jewish victims did at the time—plain and simply "Germans." A similar consideration to the Germans' and their apologists' attempts to absolve the German perpetrators, especially the many ordinary Germans among them, can be seen in the Japanese government's changes to its school textbooks in 2007 that effaced the role of Japanese soldiers during World War II in coercing or inducing 100,000 Okinawans to commit mass suicide before the American invasion of Okinawa. For the previous quarter century the textbooks rightly specifically named the Japanese's Imperial Army soldiers as the perpetrators. The new textbook version omits the perpetrators completely, asserting that Okinawans simply committed mass suicide or felt the need to do so. This change produced a howl of protest in Okinawa, including local governmental resolutions for a rescission of the textbook falsifications, and a public protest one day in Ginowan of more than 110,000 people, almost 10 percent of Okinawa's people.[7]

During mass murders, the murderers themselves, their supporters, and those who wish to stand idly by practice linguistic camouflage. In the 1980s Guatemalan murderers of leftists and Maya used the passive voice in their voluminous and meticulous document-keeping. Police do not kidnap a person. Instead a person "is kidnapped." The strange locution "was disappeared" became the standard for many Latin American mass murders. A Guatemalan supervisor wrote on one police agent's report, which used the first person singular, "Never personify—the third person must always be used."[8] Mike Habib, a high-ranking U.S. State Department official, in keeping with Secretary of State Warren Christopher's principal objective regarding the Serbs' mass slaughter of Bosniaks (or Bosnian Muslims), which was to prevent the United States from effectively acting to stop the killing, instructed Marshall Harris, the State Department's country officer for Bosnia, to conceal the Serbs' identities and therefore their responsibility for the transgressions. Habib told Harris not to write that the *Serbs* were shelling a certain town but rather that "there was shelling" or "there were reports of shelling." Harris explains that Habib "didn't want us to be seen pointing the finger when we weren't going to do anything."[9]

Taking seriously people's agency, understanding of the social world, and moral values is essential, and so too is understanding how they come to hold their views. This entails rejecting another common notion, which was for decades common to scholars of Nazism and the Holocaust, and remains the view of those seeking to exculpate Germans and others of their responsibility for their mass murdering and related deeds: that the cultures in which people have grown up and live are irrelevant for understanding their participation in mass murder. This mistaken view contains two interrelated notions: that (1) every person who has lived in any age or society is equally easily a potential mass murderer of (2) the people of any and all other groups (except possibly his or her own). Yet a person reared in a society with the uncontested common sense, such as in medieval Europe, that Jesus is the son of God is overwhelmingly likely to believe that and to feel hostility and be willing to act violently toward people considered evil—Jews, Muslims, heretics—for rejecting Jesus' divinity than toward those sharing his bedrock religious belief. A white growing up in the pre–Civil War American South was overwhelmingly likely to believe that blacks are inherently inferior and to feel more hostility and be willing to use violence toward blacks than he was against whites. A person growing up in a society or in a subculture deeming a certain group of people—whether they are Armenians, Jews, Bosnian Muslims, or Tutsi—to be evil or dangerous will be more likely to say yes to using violence to rid society of them when it is considered necessary than someone will growing up in a society or subculture deeming the same group to be good or socially munificent.

An account of mass slaughter must therefore look to how the circumstances are engendered that first make mass annihilation even thinkable and then an actual option. It must also examine why people eventually embrace or reject such action. This requires a wide range of factors to be systematically assessed, without prejudging the matter with simplifying, seemingly powerful, yet ultimately untenable assumptions about human nature. This means that we must consider what it is about societies and their cultures that contribute to the circumstances that produce exterminationist conditions, or put differently, that make mass extermination plausible as a group or national project, a project that is led by the state, supported by a good percentage of the nation or its dominant group or groups, and which employs large institutional and material resources. In many societies, groups come to be seen as deleterious to the well-being of the majority or, sometimes, a powerful minority. How this happens and the character of the pernicious qualities projected onto such groups vary enormously. In some instances people deem the group's perniciousness so great that they want to eliminate it. In some of the cases such beliefs become socially powerful and coalesce into an explicit public and political conversation about elimination. At other times such beliefs hover below the surface, never finding powerful, sustained articulation. In these instances, the eliminationist beliefs do not become the basis of a coherent political ideology, while retaining their potential to do so.

Eliminationism

The existence of eliminationist beliefs and desires, conversations and ideologies, and acts and policies has been a central feature of all eras of human history and all sorts of societies. Nevertheless, the many facets of eliminationist beliefs and deeds have not been conceptualized as belonging to a common phenomenon: *eliminationism*. Even if eliminationism's many forms are better known by their particular and spectacularly horrible consequences and names, such as genocide, the desire to *eliminate* peoples or groups should be understood to be the overarching category and the core act, and should therefore be the focus of our study.

Political and social conflicts among groups exist in all human societies, and often between societies or countries. When unwilling to come to some modus vivendi, groups, people, and polities (usually the dominant groups within them) deal with populations they have conflict with or see as a danger that must be neutralized by seeking to eliminate them or to destroy their capacity to inflict putative harm. To do this, they employ any of the five principal forms of elimination: transformation, repression, expulsion, prevention of reproduction, or extermination.

Transformation is the destruction of a group's essential and defining political, social, or cultural identities, in order to neuter its members' alleged noxious qualities. (Eliminationist transformation—which is often accompanied by violence or its threat—differs from the ordinary processes of education or acculturation because it is directed at suppressing others rather than giving them new skills or expanding their possibilities.) Groups' real or alleged features or practices—religious, ethnic, or cultural, among others—that putatively set them off from the dominant culture or group have been transformative projects' main target. Historically, conquerors and empires have commonly sought to assimilate conquered peoples and areas by destroying their distinctive identities and loyalties. It has also been frequently done in our age. The Turks have at various times suppressed spoken and written Kurdish. In the first half of the twentieth century, the Japanese, having colonized Korea, tried to destroy an independent Korean identity, including by forbidding the use of Korean. The Germans during the Nazi period, the Soviets, the communist Chinese, and many others have also sought to forcibly transform victim peoples. Many eliminationist projects animated by religion have compelled people of other religions to convert, sometimes on the pain of death. Historically, Christianity and Islam had this project at their core. Christianity focused its most fervent eliminationist project of two thousand years, the one against the Jews, on transformation through conversion, often threatening or using violence against those who would resist. Our time has seen many such forced conversions. Today, powerful strains of Political Islam maintain this transformative orientation as a high priority.

Repression entails keeping the hated, deprecated, or feared people within territorial reach and reducing, with violent domination, their ability to inflict real or imagined harm upon others. Such repression has been a regular feature of human societies. Its most extreme form is enslavement, which does have sources besides the desire to reduce a threat. Though few do today, most human societies have had slavery. Other violent forms are at least as common. Apartheid—a legal system of domination, political disenfranchisement, economic exploitation, and physical separation of a subordinate group—existed until recently in South Africa and, under the name of segregation, not so much longer ago in the American South. Political and legal segregation and ghettoization are by definition forms of eliminationist repression. Repression, including the ongoing threat of violence and its occasional or frequent use, exists against many groups—peasants, workers, ethnic groups, religious groups, political groups, and more—in many countries today.

Expulsion, often called deportation, is a third eliminationist option. It removes unwanted people more thoroughly, by driving them beyond a country's borders, or from one region of a country to another, or compelling them en masse into camps. From antiquity to today, expulsions, often by imperial conquerors, have been common. In the ancient world, victors routinely killed many among their vanquished enemies and expelled others, often into slavery. The Assyrians routinely deported conquered peoples. The Romans expelled and enslaved enemies who had rebelled or who excessively resisted them, including the Carthaginians at the end of the Third Punic War. Spaniards expelled their Muslim minority in 1502 and then again from 1609 to 1614. The English deported 100,000 Irish to North America and the West Indies from 1641 to 1652. The English, French, and others banished Romas (called Gypsies) in the sixteenth century. Americans drove Native Americans from their lands—perhaps most infamously the 1838 Cherokee *Trail of Tears,* an eight hundred–mile winter trek that killed perhaps four thousand Cherokee—and forced them onto remote reservations during the nineteenth century. During World War II, the Soviets undertook internal expulsions, forcing eight different ethnic groups, including the Crimean Tatars, from their homes in the Soviet Union's western part, scattering them hundreds or thousands of miles into the interior. Germans during World War II expelled Poles and others from various regions, and then, after the war, Czechs, Hungarians, and Poles took their turn driving out ethnic Germans. During the period of Israel's establishment in 1948, the Jews partly created the Palestinian diaspora by expelling Palestinians from their homeland. This coincided with many Arab countries expelling Jews beginning in 1948. In 1972, Ugandans expelled their ethnic Indians. In 1974–1975, Greek Cypriots and Turkish Cypriots expelled each other from their respective parts of Cyprus. From 1988 to 1991, Saddam depopulated entire areas of Iraq of Kurds, destroying their villages and their agricultural base and depositing many into camps, and then in 1991–1992 expelled the Shia Marsh people from their region of southern Iraq, in each instance as part of a broader exterminatory and eliminationist campaign. During Yugoslavia's breakup, ethnic expulsion was a constituent part of the conflicts, including the Serbs' massive expulsion of Kosovo's ethnic Albanians, also known as Kosovars, in 1999. Today, we witness the ongoing mass murder and expulsions of Darfurians by Sudan's Political Islamic government. The unfortunate term *ethnic cleansing* (the perpetrators' euphemism for deeds opposite of the beneficent act of *cleansing*) became during Yugoslavia's breakup a standard of the international lexicon to characterize expulsions, particularly when accompanied by mass slaughters or smaller terror killings.*

The most frequent victims of expulsions have been Jews. During ancient times, Babylonians drove them from ancient Israel, and during medieval times the peoples of one city, region, and country of Europe after another expelled them. Every part of Europe expelled Jews at some time. England expelled its Jews in 1290, France in 1306. Most German regions expelled their Jews during the fourteenth century. Many Arab countries did the same starting in 1948. As late as 1968, Europe saw another expulsion of Jews, this time from communist Poland, which forced out approximately twenty thousand in a supposed anti-Zionist campaign. The best-known such expulsion remains the Inquisition-inspired one from Spain in 1492. The Spaniards and the transnational Catholic Church's eliminationist campaign against the Jews is particularly noteworthy because its perpetrators employed four of the eliminationist means: transformation (forced conversion), repression, expulsion, and selective killing.

Prevention of reproduction is a fourth eliminationist act. It is the least frequently used, and when employed, it is usually in conjunction with others. For varying reasons, those wishing to eliminate a group in whole or in part can seek to diminish its numbers by interrupting normal biological reproduction. They prevent its members from becoming pregnant or giving birth. They sterilize them. They systematically rape women so men will not want to marry or father children with them, or in order to themselves impregnate them so they bear children not "purely" of their group, thereby weakening the group biologically and socially. Preventing reproduction is an eliminationist act with the longer time horizon of future generations, while the perpetrators simultaneously employ different eliminationist means for those currently living, or sometimes none at all. The Nazis forcibly sterilized many Germans

---

*Actual resettlement (as opposed to expulsions euphemistically called resettlement) differs from expulsion in two respects: The people being resettled are seen by their government, the broader society, and themselves as members of the larger national community, and second, the government attempts to create new and some semblance of decent lives for them (even if the attempt falls short). Resettlement may occur because of economic projects, such as building dams, or because of geostrategic necessities, such as resettling Israelis from settlements in Gaza to Israel proper.

suffering from real or imagined congenital afflictions, without other-wise eliminating them, and considered sterilizing Jews as an alternative to killing them. The Serbs systematically raped Bosniaks and Kosovars, while murdering many others and expelling many more.

Extermination is the fifth eliminationist act. Radical as it is, killing often logically follows beliefs deeming others to be a great, even mortal threat. It promises not an interim, not a piecemeal, not only a probable, but a "final solution" to the putative problem. The most notorious "final solution," giving this infamous euphemism worldwide currency, was the Germans' mass murder of the Jews. Hitler and those following him first employed a *variety* of lesser eliminationist measures against the Jews, until circumstances arose that permitted them to finally implement a program for their total extermination. Already in 1920, Hitler in the speech "Why Are We Antisemites" publicly declared the general eliminationist intent "the removal of the Jews from our *Volk*" and specified his preferred exterminationist solution, which he hoped the German people would "one day" implement. Hitler explained: "We are animated with an inexorable resolve to seize the Evil [the Jews] by the roots and to exterminate it root and branch. To attain our aim we should stop at nothing." This is an utterly clear *and* carefully formulated statement of an eliminationist, in this case exterminationist, ideal: According to Hitler, (1) the Jews are so evil and dangerous that (2) they must be exterminated—root and branch—that is, totally, and (3) the need to do so is so acute that Germans should let nothing stay their hand. To make it unmistakable that this was no frivolous statement either about the extent of the putative danger or the utter emergency of eliminating it, Hitler continued his declaration "we should stop at nothing" by concluding, "even if we must join forces with the Devil."[10] The devil is less to be feared than the Jews.

Extermination has also been a staple of all eras and parts of the world, though historical accounts are often so sketchy we cannot be sure that certain slaughters occurred or of the number of victims. In ancient times peoples often slew those they conquered, in some places such as ancient Greece so commonly that the discussion of the mass annihilation was an unremarkable topic. In the celebratory *Iliad*, Homer has Agamemnon, the commander of the Greek forces arrayed against Troy, speaking to his brother Menelaus about the Trojans, and through him to his assembled troops and all Greeks for all time: "They've ground the truce under their heals . . . they'll pay for their misdeed in lives, in wives and children! For this I know well in my heart and soul: the day must come when holy Ilion [Troy] is given to fire and word, and Priam [the Trojan king] perishes, good lance though he was, with all his people."[11] In the Jewish Bible, God instructs the ancient Jews to slaughter the peoples living in the "promised" land of ancient Israel. In the medieval world, mass murders were common, which the perpetrators often consecrated by invoking God. In the name of their Lord, Christian Crusaders slaughtered Jews, Muslims, and others in the eleventh and twelfth centuries. This age's greatest butchers were probably Genghis Khan and the Mongols, who killed peoples over vast terrain in Asia and Eastern Europe in the thirteenth century. In early modern and modern times imperial European peoples slaughtered many less technologically advanced peoples of other continents. In our time virtually all manner of peoples have perpetrated mass murder against virtually all kinds of victims.

Identifying these five eliminationist means of transformation, repression, expulsion, prevention of reproduction, and extermination suggests something fundamental that has escaped notice: from the perpetrators' viewpoint these eliminationist means are (rough) functional equivalents. They are different technical solutions to the perceived problem of dealing with unwanted or putatively threatening groups, to fulfilling the most fundamental desire of somehow getting rid of such groups, which Germans emblematically expressed in one of the most frequent rallying cries before and during the Nazi period: "Juden raus" (Jews out). As radically different as the various measures are for the victims, for the perpetrators the solutions logically follow their eliminationist beliefs, are substitutes for one another, and can be employed interchangeably.

Conceptualizing these forms of violence as variations of the same phenomenon of eliminationism itself suggests that when perpetrators embark on an eliminationist program they might use several of them simultaneously—just as the Spaniards during the Inquisition in the late fifteenth century used four of the eliminationist means at once against the Jews. Alisa Muratčauš, president of the Association of Concentration Camp Torture Survivors in Sarajevo, explains that the Serbs "aimed to eliminate all Bosnian people." Yet they used a variety of means: "Some people will be expelled to another country, a Western country. Some people would be killed. Some people will be [kept] alive for maybe their [the Serbs] personal needs. Who knows? Maybe like slavery."[12] Indeed, when people adopt one eliminationist measure, they frequently also employ other ones in a subsidiary or complementary manner. The Turkish leaders codified in 1915 the use of a plurality of such instruments in a preparatory document for the eliminationist assault on the Armenians. They called for extermination ("all males under 50," among others), expulsion ("carry away the families of all those who succeed in escaping"), and transformation ("girls and children to be Islamized").[13] When perpetrators use mass expulsion as the principal eliminationist policy, they typically complement it with selective killing, sometimes on a large scale. The peoples of different European countries, regions, and cities not only expelled Jews from their midst during medieval times. They also episodically slaughtered them, ghettoized them, and compelled them to convert as part of a centuries-long Church-inspired orientation to eliminate Jews from their midst.[14] And if, as with the Soviets, the expulsions do not deposit the victims outside the country, then repression, usually severe, follows to ensure the victims do not return home or rebel.

This unrecognized, yet startlingly intimate relationship among the various eliminationist means of transformation, repression, expulsion, prevention of reproduction, and annihilation is crucial to acknowledge and explore. Several questions present themselves.

Regarding mass slaughter: Is it so distinct from other eliminationist forms that it is a singular phenomenon unrelated to the others? Or is it on an eliminationist continuum of increasing violence, related to the other forms but qualitatively different? Or is it a rough functional equivalent of the others, meaning the different eliminationist options emanate from the same source so the perpetrators see them as effectively achieving the same ends, and their choice of which to use depends on tactics, practicality, expediency, and (perhaps) the perpetrators' moral restraints?

Regarding eliminationist policies' genesis: Where do eliminationist beliefs come from? Is there something distinctive about the ones of our age? How do eliminationist beliefs, or even an eliminationist ideology, get translated into eliminationist action? Put differently, what has to happen for beliefs to move people to act?

Regarding eliminationist policy's character: Whatever those mechanisms may be, why do eliminationist beliefs sometimes lie dormant and sometimes get translated into action? When such beliefs produce action, why do they sometimes lead to one eliminationist policy, transformation, sometimes a second, repression, sometimes a third, expulsion, sometimes a fourth, prevention of reproduction, and sometimes a fifth, mass slaughter, and at other times some combination of them? And if it is relatively easy for the politics of one eliminationist kind to slide and morph along the continuum into another, should we treat a regime's violent repression of peoples or groups as inherently prone to exterminationism, or proto-exterminationist?

Eliminationist beliefs have been commonly held by ordinary people throughout history. Yet such beliefs have not always led to action because *alone* they do not generate mass slaughter or elimination. Extermination and elimination programs are not inevitable. Eliminationist beliefs, though all but a *necessary cause,* are not in themselves a *sufficient cause* of mass murder or elimination. This was true, as I have shown elsewhere, even for the Holocaust. Eliminationist antisemitism among Germans was enormously widespread, deeply rooted, and potent in its demonology but lay dormant until Hitler and the state he led initiated, organized, and oversaw the Jews' mass murder.[15] To understand why exterminationist and eliminationist assaults occur in some places and times and not in others where eliminationist beliefs are also widespread, it is critical not just for the Holocaust but in all other instances to always look to the political arena, to political leaders, to, in our time, by and large, the state.

The Modern State, Transformative Power

The world of the twentieth and twenty-first centuries is vastly different from before.[16] Societies and states' ability to transform their physical environment and themselves is many orders of magnitude greater than before. The nineteenth century's capitalist, industrial, and technological revolution was not a single time-bounded revolution, as it is often portrayed, but a continually accelerating, thoroughgoing societal transformation. In the West it created vast wealth, leveled and reshuffled society, and altered politics, social relations, the nature of culture, and even human beings, with, for example, their greater education, mastery over their lives, and life spans. This revolution, eventually giving birth to globalization, continued through the twentieth century and into our own, spreading unevenly around the world. Most relevant for the discussion of mass murder and elimination is the emergence of the contemporary state.

The contemporary state has enormously greater power than ancient or medieval, or even nineteenth-century, states. Power in its broadest form is simply the capacity to transform, to change things, whether the things belong to the natural world or to human order. State power has grown mainly because wealth, communication and mobility, and knowledge and organizational know-how have increased enormously. With greater wealth the state can raise more money, mainly through taxes, and therefore employ more people with more resources to carry out its tasks. The contemporary state—which includes not just the government but also its many agencies and the military—is vastly larger than earlier states. With greater communication—radio, television, telephone, highways, air travel, and now the computer, wireless technology, the Internet, satellites, and GPS—it is easier to move, and to coordinate this greater number of state officials and employees, including the military. With greater knowledge about society and people and greater know-how about organizing people, the state has developed a greater capacity to manage its officials and employees and to monitor their tasks. The state's capacity to survey society—meaning to know what people are doing, to penetrate it, meaning to affect people's daily lives, and therefore to control it—has grown colossally. Compared to the era of the American and French revolutions, when politically the modern world began to take its form, the mid-twentieth century's state, not to mention the contemporary state's transformative capacity, its power, is a figurative million times greater.

The changes to society and state that have produced the modern world have also produced a fundamental alteration in how people, particularly political leaders, *understand* the social world and in how they *imagine* themselves, their societies, and the future. The essential difference is a new awareness that change, not stasis, characterizes the human world. The enormous growth in social power has made people, particularly those wielding political power, aware that altering the world is a matter of human control and can therefore be undertaken according to human design. The design, or redesign, can be extensive and the alteration thoroughgoing. In the modern world, man conceives of himself as the fashioner of himself, his society, and his environment, an architect and engineer of the human soul and of the cacophony or chorus of souls. This has been true among Marxists and capitalists alike, practitioners of cybernetics and readers of science fiction, past and contemporary eugenics and genetic engineering enthusiasts, and others. And the manner in which people, particularly those wielding state power, have imagined that that engineering should take place and what it should fashion has been qualitatively different from earlier eras.

The notion that society and people are not givens or only capable of being changed incrementally but instead can be transformed, even radically, has been at the heart of our age's politics. And, as never before, the capacity to act upon this notion efficaciously has also existed. This transformative vision and capacities have spawned varied and often comprehensive transformative projects. Because modernity has also mobilized all people into politics (in premodern times most people were never engaged in the politics of their countries or kingdoms), thereby making all people political concerns of the state, those governing societies must deal with people's desires to shape their own destinies and to influence their political systems. They can incorporate people into politics and accept social and cultural pluralism. Democrats do this. Or they must repress and reduce pluralism that threatens them, which has a self-reinforcing propensity to make them want to reduce pluralism further. Nondemocrats, more appropriately called tyrants, do this.

Spurred on by their transformative capacities and their need to restrict pluralism and freedom, this era's transformative dreamers typically believe that they must subject all members of their societies, and sometimes all human beings, to their extensive or comprehensive visionary projects. Power does allow people to kill. Great power does allow people to kill on a massive scale. But what great power does first is make it plausible for political leaders, and even for common people, to *imagine* massive exterminationist and eliminationist projects and to imagine them in a new way, as something doable. In no previous era have political leaders dreamed of disposing of hundreds of thousands, millions, or tens of millions of people, which the political leaders of our time—and not just Hitler, Stalin, and Mao—have routinely done, whether by killing them or by some other eliminationist means. They have the capacity: So they dream. Then plan. Then act. Because they dream their eliminationist dreams, their transformative capacities have become dangerous beyond anything the world had previously known.

Mass elimination is often part of some broader transformative or eschatological political project, including many of the principal projects that nation-states have undertaken during the past century, such as nation- or state-building itself, imperialism, economic development (whether capitalist or communist), democratic development, or the transformation of state and society according to a visionary blueprint. These projects have been wedded to ideologies that designated enemies of a size and threat sufficient to make eliminating them often a seemingly pressing consideration.

Nation-building has been an impetus for our age's mass slaughters, from the Turks' annihilation of Armenians during World War I through the Serbs' various slaughters of the 1990s. Imperialists' eliminationist onslaughts were predominantly a feature of earlier centuries, such as the Spanish depredations in the Americas and the Americans' killing and expulsion of Native Americans. Yet they have also taken countless lives in our time from its beginning to end, starting with the Belgians' mass murder in the Congo, a carryover from the nineteenth century, and the Germans' annihilation of the Herero and Nama in South-West Africa starting in 1904, to the Japanese's wholesale killings during World War II in China, to the Indonesians' mass slaughter in East Timor and the Chinese's grinding eliminationist and murderous one in Tibet. In each instance, the perpetrators violently reduced the respective country's people to subdue and colonize the territories they annexed. The desire for economic development or political transformation spurred many South and Central American governments during the past century to wage eliminationist campaigns against indigenous peoples, often called Indians. Democratic development has been less explicitly murderous or even eliminationist. The eliminationist onslaughts of the communist world's and of Nazism's apocalyptic regimes have victimized and killed the most people.

The corollary of this transformative power and its attendant eliminationist projects is that people, particularly political leaders, know they are imperiled by others who, if in the position to do so, might undertake their own transformative projects. This knowledge produces enormous insecurity and feeds leaders' suspicions or paranoiac tendencies. This can thus spur power holders to act preemptively to eliminate populations they define as problematic or threatening in order to secure their power or the order of society. Political leaders' greater awareness of existing arrangements' impermanence, including power holders' tenure, together with the knowledge that they can transform society, makes political leaders still more likely to act preemptively, in a subjective sense "defensively" to secure their well-being, and offensively to quickly realize their dreams.

All countries, groups, and people face a complex world beset by difficulties, challenges, obstacles, and problems. All develop bodies of thought, called political ideologies, to make sense of that world and how to manage it. Modern political ideologies are calls to action, often calls to arms, calls therefore for transformation. Whatever else a political ideology does, it typically answers three questions: What is the political problem? Who or what is the problem's source? What is the political solution?[17] In the modern world, political leaders and their followers have frequently answered the questions as follows: The problem is extreme, even life-threatening. The enemy is an identifiable group of people, demarcated by skin color, ethnicity, religion, class, or political allegiance. The solution to defang said enemies must in some way be "final." Hence eliminationism. The particular ideologies animating modern eliminationist politics have varied greatly, from communism to imperialism to Nazism. Some ideologies have emphasized the need to purify society. Others have called for utopia or the end of days (without God, man brings it about). Still others have glorified naked power and enrichment. Many roads lead to an eliminationist end.

The Problems Defined

Analyzing our time's mass murders and eliminationist projects requires us to clarify critical concepts and to choose an approach adequate to the task. A range of problems besets discussions of these issues. These problems include the already familiar, critical one of defining genocide. Once the definition is settled upon, the crucial issues for undertaking an *actual* study are the questions asked, and the cases chosen for investigation.

Discussions of genocide often founder over definitions, producing seemingly endless debates, and then whether one or another instance of mass killing qualifies under a given definition. Questions include whether the mass slaughter or intended slaughter must be total, as in the Holocaust (leading some to say the Holocaust is the only genocide). If not, then how many people or what percentage of the targeted group must be killed? Must killing be the principal form of assault or may it be part of a broader policy? Does the assaulted group's nature matter? The United Nations Convention on the Prevention and Punishment of the Crime of Genocide, which codifies the international legal definition of genocide, for example, does not admit groups defined politically, such as the communist Indonesias slaughtered in 1965, or economically, such as the kulaks (rich peasants) slaughtered by the Soviets. If a group is forcibly denied its ability to maintain and perpetuate its collective identity, even absent mass killing, does this qualify as genocide? The problem with these debates is not that definitions are unimportant. To the contrary, they are crucial, because definitions shape the questions asked, the research undertaken, the biases introduced, the understandings emerging, and, ultimately, the conclusions' validity. Politically, definitions critically inform whether people correctly identify events for what they are, and the policies they consider or enact to prevent or stop different kinds of assaults.

The problem with these debates is that genocide's common definitions exclude both elimination's nonlethal forms and the many instances of lethal eliminationist assaults deemed too small or partial. By restricting the universe of study to the largest mass slaughters—the Holocaust, the Turks' slaughter of the Armenians, the Soviets', the Chinese's, Cambodia, Rwanda, etc.—important questions remain unasked, such as why some people opt to commit large-scale slaughter, others smaller-scale slaughter, others nonlethal forms of elimination, and others nothing at all against hated or feared groups. Lacking a sufficient comparative foundation, the conclusions drawn are unnecessarily limited in range and deficient. The policy prescriptions that follow are inadequate.

The problem besetting the struggle over genocide's definition is threefold. First genocide is split off from kindred phenomena that are seamlessly interwoven. Genocide (however defined), smaller mass killings, and elimination's other forms are on a continuum, and perpetrators often use several eliminationist means in conjunction with one another.

So treating *genocide* as a qualitatively different phenomenon discrete from mass elimination's other forms, in addition to being conceptually untenable, violates the reality of eliminationist politics and practice.

The Holocaust has been seen as the paradigmatic genocide (though many by now have gotten away from this practice), or at least as the starting point for thinking about how to define and understand genocide. As former UN Secretary-General Boutros Boutros-Ghali betrayed, this is both common and dangerous. "I was not realizing that there was a real genocide," says Boutros-Ghali, speaking retrospectively about the Rwandan mass murder. "Because there is a definition—for us, genocide was the gas chamber, what happened in Germany. You need to have a sophisticated European machinery to do a real genocide. We were not realizing that with just a machete you can do a genocide. It takes time for us to understand."[18] Even if Boutros-Ghali was not being honest about his and others' failure to recognize the Rwandan mass murder as a colossal mass murder—as a genocide—his statement contains a truth that led him to think that it would be believed and therefore exculpate him for his failure.

Because of how the Holocaust has been understood, including the misplaced fixation on modern technology and gas chambers, and the wrongheaded insistence that the killing's comprehensiveness be used as a benchmark, its paradigm has misled people about the real nature of genocide and mass murder. Even the Holocaust itself is, in its own terms, widely misconceived. The Holocaust was not a stand-alone killing event, but part of the Germans' broad-based eliminationist assault against Jews for which the Germans used and even experimented with a wide variety of eliminationist means. It was not a genocide that began when the Germans' systematic mass extermination program commenced in 1941 and ended in 1945, but rather the culmination of an already intensive eliminationist assault by Germans upon Jews during the 1930s, which led to the elimination of two-thirds of the Jews from Germany proper before the Germans replaced one set of eliminationist policies—expulsion, segregation, repression, and episodic killing—with the most lethal and final eliminationist policy, total annihilation.

The second problem is that even when focusing only on the mass-murder form of eliminationism, the conventional conception of genocide has been too narrow, encompassing only slaughters totaling in the hundreds of thousands or millions. But these enormous mass murders are really just the largest instances of a general phenomenon of *all* large-scale mass killings—including ones that seem "small" only by comparison to those conventionally termed "*genocide.*"

The third problem is analytical. Definitions of genocide typically include elements of the factors that produce it, which are expressed by such words as "intent" and "wanted." Doing this restricts the scope of study and biases results. This is a more technical issue in social analysis, which I mention here only briefly. A basic premise of social science is that a factor that might account for *outcomes*—in this case mass murder or elimination—should not be used *to define* the phenomenon to be studied. Doing so excludes from the analysis all cases that do not conform to the preconceived notion of what is causing the outcomes, and thus promises false conclusions. Doing so is also faulty, because it prejudges that factor as critical even before the analysis begins, making the results tautological. This does not mean that intent is unimportant or that I will not discuss it. Political leaders and others often articulate their intent, and to the extent that we can identify intent, it is crucial to analyze and understand it. But this does mean that intent should not be a criterion for determining what instances qualify as genocide, or what instances of mass death or elimination should be included in the investigation.

These initial conclusions suggest several important things. Because mass killing is but one act in the repertoire of functionally equivalent eliminationist acts, and because whenever people have perpetrated genocide, they have simultaneously used other eliminationist policies, it is misleading to isolate *genocide* as a discrete phenomenon. Moreover, we should not restrict our study to only our time's largest mass slaughters, those totaling in the millions and some in the hundreds of thousands. We should instead include all instances of mass killing that are not war dead and that do not occur under conditions of anarchy or political chaos. Mass killing can be defined as the killing of more than a few hundred people, say, a thousand. War dead, which is a conceptually distinct topic, consists of military and civilian casualties caused during conventional or guerrilla war that are not outright massacres and that, according to some defensible account of military operations, occur during operations that target military forces, installations, or production while keeping civilian deaths reasonably proportionate to that purpose. These initial conclusions further suggest that the domain of study includes not just killing but also *all eliminationist outcomes*—including Serbs' expulsions of Bosniaks and Kosovars, the North Korean communists' incarceration of Koreans in concentration camps, the Indonesian government's forced conversion of communists in the mass murder's aftermath, the Germans' enslavement of millions of Europeans during the Nazi period.

Because a domain of study's definition cannot include the factor that purportedly explains it, the domain must be defined exclusively by outcomes. These initial conclusions also mandate that an explicit *intent* to eliminate, let alone to kill, a group not be a criterion of inclusion. Furthermore, because eliminationist policies are part of politics more broadly, failing to study genocide and eliminationist politics within a *political* framework misconstrues its nature. Mass murder is a political act that can be and must be analyzed with the same tools and levelheadedness we use to understand other political acts and programs, which also means that we should reject startling or reductionist conclusions (which have all too often been the norm) that violate what we know about politics.

If a large number of people, except through defensible military operations, are eliminated in any manner, why should this not be part of a study of genocide, which rightly becomes a study of mass murder, which rightly becomes a study of mass elimination? This question is particularly acute regarding famine. Famine has been used as a purposeful method of mass murder during our time, so in many instances death through famine cannot be distinguished from mass murder. Famine, or calculated starvation, has been used, or at least deliberately tolerated, by the Soviets, the Germans, communist Chinese, the British in Kenya, the Hausa against the Ibo in Nigeria, Khmer Rouge, communist North Koreans, Ethiopians in Eritrea, Zimbabwe against regions of political opposition, the Political Islamists in Southern Sudan and now Darfur, and elsewhere. In most places for most of our age, governments could have prevented famine with available food stocks, which they chose not to distribute or, in rare cases of shortage, they could have received aid from other countries and chose not to. Rithy Uong, a survivor of four years under the Khmer Rouge, explains. They "let us starve to death. They wouldn't give the plenty of food that they had, to us to eat. They wouldn't give us regular medicine to take when we got sick. They let us die. With starvation."[19] Whenever governments have not alleviated famine conditions, political leaders decided *not to say no* to mass death—in other words, they said *yes*. Seen in this light, the politics of famines and starvation resemble the politics of mass murder and elimination.

An examination of eliminationism's many forms, irrespective of means or intent, is still larger than the already large study of mass murder. So while remaining cognizant of all forms of eliminationism for drawing conclusions, the presentation here focuses systematically on mass murder—the murder of more than a few hundred in several massacres—and to a somewhat lesser extent on expulsions, discussing eliminationism's other forms and means, including famine, forced transformations, repression, and prevention of reproduction, less systematically, mainly when they accompany more conventional mass murder and expulsions.

A second set of problems goes beyond definitional matters. Studies of genocide either mainly restrict themselves to a subset of usually the most familiar and largest mass killings, devote individual chapters to narrating them, and draw some conclusions in a final chapter, or they float above the material on a general level to offer conclusions without a solid and broad empirical foundation.[20] Works on genocide also often seek its essence—sometimes found in the Holocaust together with a select few of mass murder's most notorious instances—focusing on uncovering what makes the genocides similar. This can be discerned already at the beginning of most studies, which are restricted to whatever conforms to the stated definition of genocide, or are guided by typologies that fall within that restricted definition's boundaries. Unearthing regularities and similarities among mass slaughters is important. Explaining their differences is equally important. All mass murders vary from all others. We must understand these differences if we are to comprehend both the general phenomenon and its individual manifestations. The variations become that much more multifarious and therefore important to understand, when the inquiry expands from mass murder to include eliminationism's other forms.

We must address all mass murders and eliminations from our time and consider both the similarities and differences among them. We must also examine instances such as South Africa, where mass slaughter did not occur, even though the conditions for it seemed propitious. Only by also considering such instances can we understand why some countries and not others erupt in mass murder and elimination.

A third set of problems revolves around the questions asked. Aside from the extensive discussion of definitional matters, the only question systematically addressed in the literature is why genocides occur. When someone writes or says: *How can we explain genocide?* the question typically really means: *How can we explain why genocides begin?* That question usually boils down to examining the circumstances producing genocides. Yet mass murder and elimination has a natural history. Every stage, not just the first, requires systematic investigation and explanation.

To be sure, any eliminationist assault's first feature is its initiation. Why does it occur? Yet once political leaders initiate it, many things must happen for it to be carried out. Leaders must mobilize or create institutions for the killing or expulsions. They must devise procedures for selecting and apprehending the victims. They must find people to slaughter or otherwise eliminate the targeted people. Which people become perpetrators? Why do they carry out the slaughter, or decide not to? How is the mass killing and elimination, in the end, implemented?

All annihilationist and eliminationist campaigns also end. How they stop also varies. The role of domestic and international actors is not the same in all mass murders and eliminations. Why do eliminationist onslaughts end, and why do they not end earlier or later?

Eliminationist and annihilationist campaigns produce different outcomes. The perpetrators kill different mixes of people, sometimes primarily men, sometimes also women and children. Sometimes they kill comprehensively, sometimes selectively, and the criteria of selectivity vary. The perpetrators do many other things to their victims aside from killing or expelling them, which also vary substantially in eliminationist assaults. The extent and character of the perpetrators' cruelty, aside from the killing itself, are not constant. The perpetrators' relocation and dispossession of victim groups also vary. How can these and other outcomes of eliminationist campaigns be explained?

The aftermath of mass murders and eliminations takes us beyond the horrific deeds' commission, so I do not treat its many aspects here in depth. Wounded and broken people, groups, and societies must find a way to go on. How they do so deserves its own lengthy and systematic study. In various ways and admixtures, survivors and their societies seek to engage or put the past behind them. This is also true for the perpetrators and for the peoples supporting them. The issues that victims and perpetrators alike must confront, if only to deny and suppress them, are: acknowledging and publicizing what happened, bringing the perpetrators to justice, and repairing what can be repaired, politically, materially, and morally. I have addressed these general themes in another book, *A Moral Reckoning,* and also for that reason will not take them up here.[21] A final issue victims and perpetrators must confront is ensuring that eliminationist assaults do not recur, which, as with other themes relevant to understanding their aftermath, depends also on the international community.

Laying out and explaining these various sets of themes—mass murder and elimination's (1) initiation, (2) implementation, (3) cessation, and (4) variations in outcomes—form this book's empirical and analytical core. Until now, in the general literature on genocide only the first has been treated systematically. Part I and Part II are devoted to analyzing these themes, and, by drawing together and going beyond these investigations' findings, these sections form the basis in Part III for crafting policies to substantially reduce mass murder and elimination's incidence and toll.

This book approaches the study of *genocide,* which is actually one aspect of eliminationism, in a distinctive manner. It integrates mass murder and elimination into our understanding of politics, while broadening our understanding of politics to include them. It opens up the study beyond those covered by conventional definitions to include smaller mass killings and places it within an investigation of mass elimination's other forms. In accounting for mass murder and elimination, it does not regard this as being the same as explaining *only* the circumstances setting the killing and eliminationist programs in motion but analyzes the various dimensions that form mass elimination's natural history. It also goes beyond uncovering a few similarities among some mass slaughters to systematically account for both similarities and differences among them in a host of dimensions. Drawing on the new understandings derived here, especially about eliminationism's neglected yet ultimately familiar political character, this book proposes sweeping measures to reduce exterminationist and eliminationist onslaughts' incidence and extent.

All this is predicated upon an accurate view of our age's mass slaughters.

CHAPTER TWO

Worse Than War
Our Age of Suffering

O N OCTOBER 2, 1904, General Lothar von Trotha, governor of the German colony of South-West Africa (today's Namibia) and commander of its troops, issued a public proclamation announcing his intent to annihilate the Herero people:

> I, the Great General of the German Soldiers, address this letter to the Herero people. The Herero are no longer considered German subjects. They have murdered, stolen, cut off ears, noses and other parts from wounded soldiers, and now refuse to fight on out of cowardice. I have this to say to them: Whoever turns over one of the captains to one of my garrisons as a prisoner will receive 1,000 Marks and he who hands over Samuel Maharero will be entitled to a reward of 5,000 Marks. *The Herero people will have to leave the country. Otherwise I shall force them to do so by means of guns. Within the German boundaries, every Herero, whether found armed or unarmed, with or without cattle, will be shot. I shall not accept any more women and children. I shall drive them back to their people— otherwise I shall order shots to be fired at them.* These are my words to the Herero people.[1]

So began the twentieth century, a century of mass slaughter, with "the Great General of the Mighty Kaiser, von Trotha" declaring unabashedly a policy that has since been so frequently enacted elsewhere, though rarely proclaimed openly: a program of violent elimination, including mass slaughter. The Germans' aim here was total elimination, for which they deemed expulsion and wholesale killing to be equally good solutions to the "Herero problem." Their ensuing campaign of destruction's comprehensiveness and viciousness rivals any of our age, yet it remains little known. The location, the survivors' political impotence, and the West's continuing racism often render the deaths of nonwhites invisible, thus de facto of little broader social and political consequence. Adolf Hitler's musing thirty-five years later, on the eve of launching his annihilationist war with the assault on Poland, "Who, after all, speaks today of the annihilation of the Armenians?" would have been still more apposite had he, echoing von Trotha (see below), asked, *Who now has even heard of the Herero people?*[2]

Von Trotha's and the Germans' unabashed exterminationist proclamation and deeds caused no real uproar in Germany or internationally. Presaging Hitler, von Trotha responded to the subsequent rebellion of the Nama people similarly, declaiming on April 22, 1905: "The Nama who chooses not to surrender and lets himself be seen in the German area will be shot, until all are exterminated. Those who, at the start of the rebellion, committed murder against whites or have commanded that whites be murdered have, by law, forfeited their lives. As for the few not defeated, it will fare with them as it fared with the Herero, who in their blindness also believed that they could make successful war against the powerful German Emperor and the great German people. I ask you, where are the Herero today?" The Germans slaughtered about half the twenty thousand Nama and incarcerated most of the rest in concentration camps, effectively eliminating them from the German colony. Even though the Berg Damara had not even rebelled, the Germans killed about one-third of them merely because they had trouble distinguishing them from the Herero.[3]

As is true of almost all mass murders, these annihilations' essential facts are straightforward. The best known one, though still barely known, is the Germans' obliteration of the Herero. In 1903 the German colonizers adopted an eliminationist policy of forcing the Herero into reservations as the 4,500 German settlers gobbled up the Herero's land for cattle farming. The Herero, ever more dispossessed and victimized by the Germans since their arrival in 1892, rebelled in January 1904. From the outset of the armed conflict, the vastly stronger Germans exterminated the Herero—massacring them, driving them into

Herero returning starved from the desert; two women are unable to stand.

the desert, poisoning their water holes. Jan Kubas, a Griqua, accompanied the Germans:

> The Germans took no prisoners. They killed thousands and thousands of women and children along the roadsides. They bayoneted them and hit them to death with the butt ends of their guns. Words cannot be found to relate what happened; it was too terrible. They were lying exhausted and harmless along the roads, and as the soldiers passed they simply slaughtered them in cold blood. Mothers holding babies at their breasts, little boys and little girls; old people too old to fight and old grandmothers, none received mercy; they were killed, all of them, and left to lie and rot on the veld for the vultures and wild animals to eat. They slaughtered until there were no more Hereros left to kill. I saw this every day; I was with them.[4]

Von Trotha's infamous "Extermination Order" came after the Herero, already defeated, were suing for peace. He wanted to finish them off. Seven years later, the Germans had annihilated 80 percent of the eighty thousand Herero. Having decided that the "Herero cease to exist as a tribe," the Germans appropriated the Herero's land and cattle, and subjected surviving Herero to a kind of apartheid.

The Germans offered themselves various justifications for why 4,500 Germans' economic well-being and the German empire's glory warranted the elimination of two peoples, twenty times more numerous than the small German colony. Perpetrators are always convinced that they have good reasons for killing their victims, typically the heartfelt fiction that their victims are criminals, miscreants, or impediments of such enormity as to deserve the death penalty.

Our Age's Slaughters

This mass annihilation that inaugurated our time's eliminationist campaigns was characteristic of earlier times: imperialist Europeans acting without moral restraint to secure non-Europeans' lands. As a rule, previous centuries' colonizers—Americans as they spanned their continent, Belgians in Congo, British, French, Portuguese, and Spanish in Asia, Africa, and the Americas—despoiled, enslaved, or killed people of color who resisted or were deemed obstacles to Europeans' occupation or exploitation of their lands. Europeans regularly employed murderous methods against non-European peoples that they did not use against their conventional European enemies. Racism and impunity explain the difference.

The Germans' annihilation campaign is, in a different sense, a quintessential phenomenon of our era: One group, in the name of a national or ideological project, self-consciously attempts to eliminate another unwanted or putatively threatening group, and methodically works to do so for years. The French, Portuguese, and others, also racists, were wantonly murderous in Africa during the first part of the twentieth century, killing or working to death hundreds of thousands or millions in their African colonies, yet they did not set out, as national policy, to systematically exterminate targeted peoples in whole or in large part. But since the twentieth century's beginning, states, supported by significant percentages of their people, have done just that.

Unlike colonial predations in the sixteenth through the nineteenth centuries—which include the colossally murderous trans-Atlantic African slave trade that took 15 million to 20 million Africans' lives, more than the roughly 10 million who survived to become slaves—most of our age's mass murders and eliminations have not been perpetrated by colonial or conquering powers. They have been wholly or principally within the country the perpetrators and victims both inhabit.

In this sense the Turks' mass annihilation of the Armenians during World War I—commonly if wrongly understood to be the twentieth century's first mass extermination—is typical. Under war's cover, the Turkish leaders decided to eliminate their "Armenian problem" because they considered Armenians an irredeemably non-Turkish element posing a secessionist threat. With the transparently false accusation that during World War I the Armenians had revolted against Turkey to abet the Russian enemy, the Turks "relocated" them, which meant rounding them up and quickly slaughtering the military-age men before or shortly after they sent the Armenians marching away. In a contemporary report, the American consul in Kharpert explains what relocation was known to mean and how the Turks disposed of the Armenian men: "If it were simply a matter of being obliged to leave here to go somewhere else, it would not be so bad, but everybody knows that it is a case of going to one's death. . . . The system that is being followed seems to be to have bands of Kurds awaiting them on the road, to kill the men especially, and, incidentally, some of the others. The entire movement seems to be the most thoroughly organized and effective massacre this country has ever seen."[5] One Armenian survivor relates what happened on her death march:

> They asked all the men and boys to separate from the women. There were some teen boys who were dressed like girls and disguised. They remained behind. But my father had to go. He was a grown man with a mustache. As soon as they separated the men, a group of armed men came from the other side of the hill and killed all the men right in front of our eyes. They killed them with bayonets at the end of their rifles, sticking them in their stomachs. Many of the women could not take it, and they threw themselves in the River Euphrates, and they, too, died. They did this killing right in front of us. I saw my father being killed.[6]

The Turks forced the women and children (and the remaining men) to walk for months, with no shoes, little food, no shelter, often no blankets at night. Barely living Armenians populated Turkey's byways: "At the first station, we saw a lot of Armenians who had gotten there much earlier than us, and they had turned into skeletons. We were surrounded with skeletons so much that it felt like we were in hell. They were all hungry and thirsty, and they would look for familiar faces to help them. We became terribly discouraged, so hopeless that it is hard to explain exactly how we felt."[7] Their destination was the desert where they perished in colossal numbers, and at the end of the marching, the Turks slaughtered perhaps 200,000 of those still alive. The Turks eliminated almost all of the 2 million Armenians living in Turkey, exterminating 1.2 million, expelling most of the rest. Employing a wide range of eliminationist policies, they also converted, forced into slavery, or kidnapped and raised as Turks between 100,000 and 200,000 Armenian women and children.[8] The Turks left Armenians in Constantinople, today's Istanbul, alive because eliminating them was unnecessary for solving the problem as the Turks understood it, and extending their eliminationist project to their capital city would have further exposed their predations to the world. With the Bolshevik Revolution and the Russian armies' collapse, the Turks extended the annihilationist campaign to Transcaucasia, known as Russian Armenia, which they occupied in 1918, and where 300,000 Armenians had fled. They killed perhaps 200,000.[9]

Like this mass elimination, many of our era's enormous domestic mass murders have resulted from the perpetrators' calculations that mass killing is a sensible way to destroy political opposition, to forestall secession, or to safeguard their power or their existence. Such Machiavellians have often been satisfied to kill enough of the victim people to stave off the putative danger, and then to cease. Or they have killed some significant portion of their chosen victims and disposed of the rest in some other way, such as expulsion.

Machiavellians, such as von Trotha and the Turkish leaders, have not initiated most of our age's enormous slaughters. Our time's most lethal killers—Hitler in Europe, Kim Il Sung and his son Kim Jong Il in North Korea, Pol Pot in Cambodia, Joseph Stalin in the Soviet Union, and Mao Zedong in China and Tibet—have acted from beliefs calling for their societies' or the world's thorough transformation. Several features were common to these mass murderers' eliminationist enterprises. The destruction was enormous. Hitler killed perhaps 20 million people,

Stalin 8 million or more, Mao perhaps 50 million, the dynastic Kims perhaps more than 4 million, and Pol Pot the highest percentage of the inhabitants of any country, more than 20 percent of the Cambodians, totaling 1.7 million. They each set up a new political institution, the camp system, as an infrastructure of domination, violence, and death, and a partly autonomous, if integral, system within each one's society. Hitler built the concentration camps, Stalin the gulag, Mao the Laogai ("reform through labor"), Pol Pot the cooperatives, and the Kims the Kwanliso ("special control institutions"). They killed the bulk of their victims not in a quick assault, but spanning most of their time in power, as they knew they were not subject to opposition, intervention, or punishment. And they made slaughtering people a constitutive feature of their civilizations, because their ideologies, as varied as they were, unceasingly summoned them to eliminate others to preserve the present and create a radically new future.

In the Soviet Union, mass annihilation was the midwife of the communist paradise waiting to be born. Since the birth was expected to be difficult (and was in reality impossible), mass murder became state policy's semipermanent feature, beginning shortly after the Russian Revolution of 1917 and extending until Stalin's death in 1953. The gulag was one of the largest camp systems ever constructed, with thousands of installations in which the Soviets imprisoned probably more than 28 million people over the years. The Soviets dealt with real and imagined political problems by killing people outright or, more frequently, consigning them to the gulag, where the regimen and conditions guaranteed a steady death toll. The great famine in Ukraine in 1933—whether Stalin willfully manufactured it, as some believe, or it resulted from the disastrous and brutally callous communist economic policies, as others hold—augmented the gulag's death toll by 5 million or more. Throughout his rule and especially during World War II, Stalin deported many ethnic groups in whole or in large part, including Chechens, Crimean Tatars, Karachai, and Volga Germans. Deeming these peoples disloyal or treasonous, he deported more than 6 million of them into the country's interior, including Siberia. In the process, hundreds of thousands, perhaps even more of them, died. The impunity with which Stalin could act allowed him to kill a vast array of victims: Ukrainians; so-called class enemies, Kulaks, who were (in relative terms only) prosperous peasants;

various real or alleged uncooperative ethnic groups; repatriated Soviet nationals after World War II; and political opposition, real or imagined, of any kind. The Soviets' mass murdering spanned more time, over thirty-five years, than any but that of the communist Chinese, with the regime's policies taking the lives of at least 8 million people, with many estimates placing the toll at many millions more.

In addition to the Soviets' mass murders and eliminations, World War II saw such predations by the Japanese in China, Korea, and elsewhere in Asia; by the Germans from one end of Europe to the other; by other Europeans, such as the Croats' exterminating of Serbs and others; and by the Americans in Hiroshima and Nagasaki. These constitute a spate, geographic scope, and variety of mass annihilation unequaled during our or any other time.

War can facilitate the mass extermination and elimination of hated or unwanted people. In various ways war makes people more likely to consider eliminationist initiatives. It encourages people to see violent and lethal measures as appropriate for dealing with real or imagined problems that had or would have been previously managed differently. War predisposes people to magnify threats, to believe tales of enemy crimes, and to lash out in fear or in self-righteous retribution. It provides readily believed justifications for mass slaughter, such as an enemy's insurrection or the needs of national security. War also creates new practical opportunities to act on eliminationist desires, by giving perpetrators better access to the potential victims, and by lessening the perceived cost of committing mass murder (one is, after all, already at war). It makes secrecy from the outside world easier, as operational areas become closed to media, and communication among victims to facilitate defense or evasion becomes more difficult.

Japan's mass eliminations became possible because they sought a vast empire in Asia and decided to make war to gain it. The Japanese committed mass murder at the end of the nineteenth century in Korea, a precursor of their more extensive, brutal, and deadly eliminationist subjugation of their country starting in 1910. The Japanese's murderousness increased exponentially with their invasion of China in 1937, and then during World War II. The Japanese, like the Germans in Eastern Europe, were wanton, murderous conquerors, doing anything to subjugate peoples they deemed racial inferiors. The Japanese's racism, paralleling the Germans', produced similar, vast imperial aspirations and eliminationist practices.

War can incubate existing eliminationist hatreds and provide a context for people to act upon them. But, with rare exceptions, war does not itself *create* the eliminationist animus that becomes the impetus for exterminating people. By whatever mechanism war *itself* is supposed to produce the mass annihilation of civilians—whether it is simply being at war, a real threat of being annihilated, the agony of defeat, or the euphoria of victory—each one fails to account for mass murder's basic facts.

If warfare somehow created the eliminationist mindset characterizing mass murderers, then mass murder would be still far more common. Every war, or at least most wars, would produce an annihilationist campaign paralleling the military campaign. Indeed, in all or most wars two such campaigns, one from each combatant, would occur. Yet in the overwhelming majority of wars it did not, and no evidence shows that the combatants even contemplated annihilationist campaigns. If, instead, suffering is supposed to produce the desire to annihilate the source of one's pain, then the Germans, twice, after each World War, and the Japanese after World War II, would have been destroyed by their conquerors. Overwhelmingly, mass murder's perpetrators have not been defeated people who suffered enormously during war.

The people slaughtering large civilian populations under war's cover have usually been the military aggressors, who furthermore have either exterminated peoples other than those against whom they fought or began their mass murdering before suffering major military defeats. This was true of the Turks' annihilation of the Armenians during World War I, of the Germans and Japanese during World War II, and of many others, including the Pakistanis in Bangladesh in 1971, where they killed between 1 million and 3 million people, and the Indonesians in defenseless East Timor, which started with the Indonesians' unprovoked imperial invasion in 1975 and continued with a murderous occupation that lasted until 1999 and that, all told, killed perhaps 200,000 people.

Perpetrators have slaughtered noncombatants not in reaction to wartime hardship, but as an integral part of their strategic political goals. As a high-ranking German Embassy official reported one of the Turks' eliminationist assault's masterminds, Interior Minister Mehmet Talât, explaining to him, Turkey "wanted to take advantage of the war in order to thoroughly liquidate its internal enemies (the indigenous Christians), without being disturbed by foreign diplomatic intervention."[10] Talât and War Minister Ismail Enver explained in a telegram to Turkey's ally Germany that "the work that is to be done must be done *now;* after the war it will be too late."[11] In the 1930s, Hitler was looking forward to war as an opportunity to carry out his eliminationist projects, including the Jews' extermination. Regarding his mass-murderous project, euphemistically called "euthanasia," to kill mentally ill people and other Germans deemed biologically unworthy of life, he told the Reich doctors' leader in 1935 that "in the event of a war he would take up the question of euthanasia and enforce it" because "he was of the opinion that such a problem could be more easily solved in war-time, since opposition which could be expected from the churches would not play so significant a role in the context of war as at other times." Hitler understood that war would provide the cover "to solve the problem of the asylums in a radical way."[12]

Mass murder and elimination are also not the stepchildren of the euphoria of military victory. If vanquishing an opponent creates a sense of omnipotence and a desire (not previously existing) to annihilate entire populations, then all or certainly many more victors would annihilate their enemies. In 1940 the Germans would have exterminated their bitter enemies, the French, against whom they had fought three major wars in seventy years, and would have planned to kill the British. The Israelis would have annihilated several neighboring peoples after their victories.

Our era's differing landscapes of war and of mass murder belie the common belief that war itself causes annihilationist programs. War has provided the occasion for would-be mass murderers to finally act and has therefore been an *arena* for mass murder. But that is different from war itself producing it.

Many mass slaughters have had little or nothing to do with war. Stalin's mass murdering long predated, and was most intensive before, World War II. Though Stalin deported eight national groups to the Soviet Union's interior during the war, the Soviets' general domestic eliminationist drive markedly abated. Mao's killing took its greatest toll long after the communists had an iron grip on China. This is also true of the Chinese's killing of more than half a million and perhaps as many as 1.2 million Tibetans since their imperial occupation of Tibet in 1950.

The Indonesian military's slaughter of perhaps half a million Indonesian communists in 1965 occurred during peacetime. The Tutsi slaughter of at least 100,000 Hutu in Burundi in 1972, and smaller numbers three other times, had nothing to do with war (a fifth, the most recent, in 1993, occurred in response to a Hutu uprising in which Hutu slaughtered perhaps twenty-five thousand Tutsi). Many mass killings in Latin America during the 1970s and 1980s—by Augusto Pinochet in Chile, the military junta in Argentina, José Efraín Ríos Montt in Guatemala, and elsewhere—occurred during peacetime, even if their tyrannical regimes confronted resistance (including some armed resistance).

Slaughtering foreign civilians during war has been a common feature of our age, but mass murder's principal locus has shifted from international to domestic terrain. The impetus to annihilate populations has been less the correlate of conquest or colonization, as it had been in earlier centuries, and more the desire to alter power relations within or to remake one's own society. Seldom has war created in the perpetrators novel desires they had not previously had, to slaughter large numbers of unarmed men, women, and children, or to expel them from their homes and countries. But it has often been the converse. Leaders' and their followers' common desires to eliminate or annihilate other peoples, such as the Germans' desire to create a new empire in Eastern Europe, the Japanese's wish to create an empire in Asia, and the Serbs' wish to secure theirs in Bosnia and Kosovo, have frequently *produced* the idea to initiate military conflicts, which they then use as an occasion to enact previously laid murderous plans. The evidence suggests the relationship between war and eliminationist assaults on targeted groups of people is the reverse of what is commonly held. People harboring mass-murderous and eliminationist aspirations often initiate or broaden military conflicts for those purposes, or see others' violent elimination as integral to the conquest or colonization of foreign territory.

Varieties of Eliminationist Assaults

Even if our age's eliminationist projects have shared certain characteristics, they, especially the domestic eliminationist projects, have also had varying features, which are important to understand.

The communists' colossal mass murders in the Soviet Union, China, North Korea, and Cambodia notwithstanding, either rightist or nationalist or ethnicist regimes (which the Khmer Rouge partly also was) have committed most domestic mass murders. During the 1960s, 1970s, and 1980s, many rightist dictatorships in Latin America, under the name of anticommunism or counterinsurgency, undertook campaigns to exterminate political opponents or indigenous peoples. From 1976 to 1982 the Argentinean military dictatorship conducted a secret campaign against leftists and other opponents—real or invented—murdering or, in the time's euphemistic language, "disappearing" thirty thousand people, often by dropping them from airplanes into the ocean. Mass-murderous regimes in Argentina, Chile, El Salvador, Guatemala, and elsewhere were moved by the doctrine of "national security," meaning the nation's integrity, economic order, and security required the annihilation of those deemed a threat—which often included conventional political opponents. This systematic killing of targeted political opponents was analogous to some of Stalin's and Mao's killings, but in Argentina and elsewhere the slaughter was much more selective, and not tied to a visionary transformative project. During this period, across Latin America widespread murder was part of the ordinary repertoire of forfending challenges to political power and economic benefits of the dominant groups and political regimes. The El Salvadoran rightist regime slaughtered perhaps seventy thousand people during a counterinsurgency campaign during the 1970s, though few of the victims were actual guerrillas. The Guatemalan rulers turned a campaign against a relatively unthreatening, leftist insurgency into a systematic slaughter of perhaps 200,000 Maya, mainly from 1978 to 1985, and expelling from their villages between a half million and a million more.

Such "counterinsurgency" mass murder is related to others that, at least formally, are reactions to domestic political challenges, guerrilla war, or concerted rebellions. In 1982 in Syria members of the Muslim Brotherhood (a Political Islamic movement seeking to create theocracies throughout the Islamic world), which was challenging the tyrannical rule of Hafez al-Assad and his Alawite Party, killed government officials in Hama and declared the city's 350,000 people liberated. Assad chose not to root out the few hundred lightly armed rebels. Instead, using planes and artillery, he bombarded the city for days, then sent in tanks.

Assad's forces stopped only after leveling a good part of the city and slaughtering between twenty thousand and forty thousand men, women, and children. Assad opted for a final solution to this particular city's "problem" and also to show Syrians the peril of challenging his rule. Assad's destruction in Hama made any cost-benefit analysis of rebellion a bleak one. As many others have, Assad used mass murder to produce terror and as a deterrent.

Not all of the recent decades' domestic eliminationist projects have been as restrictive as these Latin American and Syrian slaughters of "only" tens of thousands. The Rwandan genocide of 1994 had a comprehensiveness, scope, and killing rate that recalls the Germans' slaughter of the Jews. In Central Africa, Hutu and Tutsi have vied for power in adjacent Rwanda and Burundi, as well as in neighboring diasporas. Since the process of decolonization from Belgium began in 1959 and independence was achieved in 1962, each group has perpetrated several mass slaughters against the other. In 1994, after a plane carrying the presidents of both countries was blown up, in Rwanda the Hutu attacked the Tutsi with unsurpassed intensity and fury, seeking to eliminate them all. In three months, they killed about 800,000 men, women, and children. The remaining several hundred thousand Tutsi fled the country or hid in the countryside. The Hutu's individual, face-to-face butchery of Tutsi, usually by machete, stopped only when a rebel Tutsi army defeated the Hutu mass murderers and seized control of the country. A regional war among different ethnic and political groups, with forces from neighboring countries and a vast array of armed groups, ensued in the Democratic Republic of the Congo—a country of Western Europe's size (including Spain and the United Kingdom). Seemingly all sides perpetrated massacres and pursued policies that have led to rampant deaths from starvation and disease. Although the war formally ended in 2004, slaughters and death from starvation have continued on a massive scale. The death toll, estimated at more than 5 million, has engendered its regionally understandable moniker, the Third World War. Kim Il Song's eliminationist policies in North Korea, now with son Kim Jong Il at the helm, also continue, as does the Political Islamic Sudanese lethal eliminationist assault on the people of Darfur.

The twentieth century's final European eliminationist onslaught started in March 1999, as the Serbs attempted to purge Kosovo of all ethnic Albanians (or Kosovars). This full-scale eliminationist assault is a classic case of the interchangeability of killing and expulsion as solutions to putative problems. Slobodan Milošević, the Serbian ruler of what remained of Yugoslavia after the country began breaking up in 1990, considered Kosovo an integral part of Serbia, making the Kosovars, composing 90 percent of the population, a threat. The Serbs had a few years earlier made eliminationist politics, a mixture of mass murder and expulsion, their policy in Bosnia. They responded to the Kosovars' desire for more political autonomy, with a more thorough, if less lethal, eliminationist campaign. In the face of international sanctions, pressure, and eventually bombing, the Serbs forcibly expelled 1.5 million people, almost all the Kosovars, from the country. The Serbs also selectively slaughtered approximately 10,000 mainly military-age men, which diminished the Kosovars' capacity to resist Serbian onslaught. Serbs burned and destroyed at least 1,200 Kosovar residential areas, including 500 villages, and tens of thousands of homes, in the ultimately failed attempt to obliterate the Kosovar presence (NATO forced the Serbs to let the Kosovars return).[13]

From the Germans' imperial slaughter of the Herero to the Serbs' mass expulsion and murder of Kosovars, to the recent and ongoing slaughters in Central Africa and Sudan's Darfur region, and China's continuing eliminationist grip on Tibet and Kim's on North Korea, our age's mass slaughters and eliminations have different characters, facets, and features. This considerable heterogeneity makes the Holocaust's status, singly and together with the Germans' other eliminationist assaults, as our time's emblematic (which is different from its defining) mass murder, more understandable and striking—precisely because of its all-encompassing nature.

The Germans' annihilation of European Jewry is the best-known, most extensively documented and studied, and most discussed mass murder of all time. It is the only mass slaughter with an internationally known proper name. It even has two: *Holocaust* and *Shoah*. Yet the Holocaust's preeminent status owes less to a sober, comparative assessment of its features than to misguided and false understandings scholars and nonscholars have propagated.

How did Germany, a highly "civilized," educated, and modern country produce this gargantuan slaughter? To comprehend what to many has seemed incomprehensible, people have latched on to a fictional frame-work: The Holocaust represents modernity's lurking dangers. Among the many widely circulating myths and falsehoods about the Holocaust, three specific ones help compose this once all but unquestioned (but now roundly discredited) view.[14] First, the perpetrators were and are Every-men, meaning that all people are at any moment equally potential killers of anyone. Second, Germany was no different (regarding its people's at-titudes toward Jews and other "races") from other Western countries of the time (or our time). Third, modern technology and organization—conveyor-belt killing, gas chambers, trains, bureaucracy—made the Holo-caust possible.

These three myths create a superficially compelling but false univer-salism: The country, at the pinnacle of modernity, mobilized perpetra-tors of no distinctive feature, except being modern and therefore like us, to slaughter Jews. These perpetrators killed others in enormous numbers only because the modern world gave them the necessary tech-nology and organizational capacity. This strange combination of ren-dering the Holocaust commonplace and close—anyone could do it—and also abstract and distant—the technology and bureaucracy of killing replace the human beings as the central actors—has created a continuous fascination and ongoing struggle both to make sense of the Holocaust and to control emotions generated by the notion that this greatest horror can be identified with us all.

The Holocaust has modern features, but they do not distinguish it among mass murders. What is truly modern about the Holocaust, other genocides share. Why have the "civilized" Soviets' killings and camps, begun under Vladimir Lenin and Leon Trotsky, not produced a similar fascination and dread? The Bolshevik leaders were more ed-ucated, literate, and modern in outlook than the Nazi leaders. Do they "fascinate" people less because they did not create gassing factories—even though their killing, organizationally and logistically, was as tech-nologically modern? Perhaps. But far more important is that people in the West attributed the Soviets' deeds to evil beliefs—the creed of communism—that rendered the actors and their civilization *different* from us and ours.

Yet recent scholarship has demonstrated the fictive character of this previously widespread understanding of the Holocaust. Evil beliefs, namely antisemitism, moved Germans, Austrians, and other Europeans who helped them, to kill Jews—and led many others to support the eliminationist onslaught. And antisemitism and prejudice are not particularly modern (even if the Germans' particular racist brand of antisemitism is a modern variant), having moved the "civilized" and "uncivilized" alike, from the ancient world through today. Modern technology, especially the gas chambers, was unnecessary to perpetrate the Holocaust. The Germans killed masses of Jews with more conventional methods, which they easily could have employed for the rest of their victims.*

The Germans' mass murdering can be seen as the emblematic instance of our age's mass slaughters, not because of this mythologized view but because of its real character. Even though the Germans did not kill the most people, they were our age's most omnivorous killers, exterminating the greatest *variety* of victims and, upon conquering the main areas of intended destruction, they killed *the most people on average per year* of all mass-murdering regimes. Equally significant, the Germans' mass murdering encompassed virtually all facets of mass elimination and its annihilationist variant.

The Germans killed abroad as imperial conquerors, decimating the peoples living in large swaths of Eastern Europe, so that Germans could Germanify the conquered territories. And they perpetrated domestic slaughters. They killed as self-conceived apocalyptic warriors. And they killed as calculating Machiavellian overlords. They destroyed populations with the passion of fanatical belief. And they killed for cool reasons of realpolitik. For them, mass murder was often an end in itself. And they responded to rebellion with mass murder as a deterrent to

---

*Had an accurate account of the Holocaust been accepted from the beginning, then this singular fascination with and dread of the Holocaust might not have developed. It might still have been understood as the most horrific episode of bigotry and hatred's consequences, but its central place in the West's existential musings and the academy's detached, abstract theorizing would have been unlikely. Silence about other genocides, a stunning disregard of the facts (including that the Germans shot and starved millions, that antisemitism among Germans was rampant, and so on), and adherence to the paradigm described above led scholars away from fundamental questions (such as the killers' identities, patterns of choices, and motives) and helped to produce a widely held, partly mythologized view of this period that robbed the killers of their agency and humanity and that obscured central features of the Holocaust, such as the perpetrators' widespread, systematic, willful cruelty and glee.

future challenges. They killed with the most time-tested and primitive methods. And they innovated and built death factories. They slaughtered their victims in the cruelest manner. And they killed them clinically, with gas or lethal injection. They killed their victims face-to-face. And they killed them from a distance. They murdered in the most planned and organized way. And they killed in an impromptu way, with every German in Eastern Europe allowed to be judge and executioner of dehumanized people. They killed some categories of people comprehensively. And they killed others selectively. They killed people because of their putative individual biological characteristics (the mentally ill and physically handicapped), social and national identities (which they conceived of in racial terms), and political allegiances.

In these annihilationist and eliminationist campaigns, the Germans used every conceivable violent eliminationist means, from brutally repressing and enslaving, to deporting large populations, to incarcerating people in camps, to preventing reproduction by sterilizing them, to decapitating peoples by destroying their elites, to slaughtering entire populations. They invented and experimented with different killing techniques (including lethal injections, explosive bullets, and gas vans), in order to find ones that would maximize their various murderous values. They drew on professional cadres of killers, drafted citizens into the task, and employed or allowed just about any German in the vicinity to participate. Except for possibly in Cambodia under the Khmer Rouge, in no other country, certainly not in the modern era, was elimination, and specifically mass murder, such a reflexive state instrument, or internalized by so many ordinary citizens as the all but automatic solution to a vast range of real and perceived obstacles and problems.

Seeing the Germans' slaughters as our era's emblematic moment of mass annihilation and those who perpetrated them in this manner as its emblematic mass murderers is further justified by the aspect of the Holocaust that actually does make it singular: the unparalleled drive to kill every Jew, including every child, and not just in their own country but in other countries, ultimately in the world.

This partial overview of our time's mass annihilations reveals mass murder to have many facets, which the Germans' killings during the Nazi period encapsulate. It also shows the erroneousness of the simple formulae that have been foisted upon the public by theorists of modernity

and the so-called human condition and by the often blinkered and misguided scholarship on the Holocaust, which has also been a major
source of images and slogans about genocide in general. Mass elimination and its lethal variant *are* complex phenomena that take many
forms and have differing features. They defy the simpleminded, ahistorical, and reductionist slogans of "total war," "the banality of evil,"
"assembly-line killing," "bureaucratic killing," "ordinary men," slogans that had once been the stock and trade of the Holocaust's interpreters and, more generally, mass slaughters' commentators.

The Scope of Eliminationist Assaults

Surveying some salient moments and some of the many aspects of our
age's mass eliminations only suggests their frequency, scope, and character. Mass annihilations spanned virtually the entire era. Since the beginning of the twentieth century there has been no time when the
world was free from ongoing mass annihilation. The number of people who have been mass murdered is, conservatively estimated, 83 million. When purposeful famine is included, the number becomes 127
million, and if the higher estimates are correct the total number of victims of mass murder may be 175 million or more. If we take the conservative estimate, then roughly 2 percent of all people who died
during our time were felled by mass murderers. If the high number is
correct, then it is more than 4 percent, in other words one of every
twenty-five people.[15] If the higher number is correct, their number exceeds the population of all but seven countries today. And all the victims' children, and their children's children, that would have been
born, never were or will be.

The geographic distribution of our age's mass annihilations spans
the globe. The Americas, from Argentina and Chile at the southern tip,
to Brazil at the heart, up through Guatemala and El Salvador, have suffered it mostly in the 1970s and 1980s. From 1910 to 1920, the pre-
revolutionary and then revolutionary Mexican regimes killed hundreds
of thousands of people. Prior to 9/11, the United States has been spared
such ravages, though the United States perpetrated mass murder against
the Japanese of Hiroshima and Nagasaki, and during the cold war gave

covert aid and public tacit support to mass murderers in many countries, including in Latin America.

Europe has had the most victims. A higher percentage of countries there than elsewhere have fallen victim to mass murderers, who mainly served two regimes: Nazism and Soviet communism. Virtually every European country was touched by Nazism's volcanic murderousness, and many peoples, including Croats, Latvians, Lithuanians, Slovaks, and Ukrainians, themselves slaughtered the Jews of their own countries or helped the Germans do so. All peoples of the multiethnic, multireligious Soviet empire lost members to the Bolsheviks. The peoples of Central and Eastern Europe, among them Russians, Ukrainians, Poles, Hungarians, and Czechs, some of whom suffered enormous loss of life at the hands of the Germans during World War II, themselves undertook, after the Germans' defeat, retributory eliminationist campaigns against ethnic Germans, forcibly expelling roughly 10 million and killing tens of thousands. The Balkans have been a local zone of elimination. During World War II, with German encouragement, Croats slaughtered Serbs, Jews, Sinti, and Roma, then Josip Tito's communist regime during its consolidation of power after 1944 killed on the order of 100,000 to 200,000 people. With Yugoslavia's breakup in the 1990s, Serbs and Croats perpetrated mass murder and expulsions, including the Serbs' eliminationist assaults against Bosniaks and then Kosovars. Turks, whose country is geostrategically part of Europe, not only exterminated their Armenians and other Christian minorities, including Greeks and Assyrians, during World War I, but earlier annihilated 150,000 to 300,000 Armenians from 1894 to 1896, as well as nearly 5,000 Greek villagers in retribution for a 1903 revolt in Macedonia. During their war with Greece from 1919 to 1923, Turks slaughtered perhaps another 200,000 Greeks. In the 1980s and 1990s, Turks killed 15,000 to 30,000 Kurds. Not only has mass murder victimized most European countries, but the people of many of them have also been perpetrators. The European death toll (this includes the Soviets' Asian victims) to eliminationist onslaughts is in the tens of millions.

Africa has seen the most individual annihilationist assaults, even though it has had fewer victims than Europe or Asia. In the first part of the century and during the later struggles over decolonization, the European colonizers, such as the Germans in South-West Africa, the

Belgians in Congo, the French in French Equatorial Africa, the Italians in Ethiopia from 1936 to 1941, the British in Kenya from 1952 to 1956, and the Portuguese in Angola in 1961 through 1962 committed mass murder—in some places, including Congo, on a colossal scale. They also fomented enmities among different African peoples, as the Belgians did with the Hutu and Tutsi, that would eventually erupt into killing sprees. In the century's second half, the politically and ethnically fragmented African countries have suffered mainly domestic mass murders as a tool in struggles over power and economic benefit. They include the Hausa's and Ibo's killing of each other, mainly through engineered starvation, totaling 1 million between 1967 and 1970, when the Ibo seceded from Nigeria to form the short-lived country of Biafra. Idi Amin's butchery of perhaps 300,000 Ugandans between 1971 and 1979 made his name synonymous with mass murder. In 1972 in Burundi, the Hutu slaughtered about 100,000 Tutsi. Twenty years later, in 1994, the Hutu in neighboring Rwanda unleashed their total extermination campaign against the Tutsi. Between 1998 and 2004, many participants perpetrated mass slaughter in the regional war fought in the Democratic Republic of the Congo, where the mass murdering continues today. Many African countries have suffered induced or preventable famines, in which millions of people perished, famines that often coincided with other eliminationist measures. Between 1974 and 1991 the Dergue political regime of Mengistu Haile Mariam in Ethiopia slaughtered perhaps 150,000 political enemies, killed perhaps another 100,000 during a regional expulsion program of 1.5 million to 2 million people, and caused another million to die through famine.

The Arab crescent, spanning parts of Africa and Asia and composed of countries governed generally by brutal dictatorships, has suffered widespread mass murder since World War II. In a final colonial attack from 1954 to 1962, the French murdered perhaps tens of thousands, more likely hundreds of thousands, of Algerian Muslims in outright massacres and through privation in camps, in their desperate attempt to hold on to the last vestige of empire. After France's defeat, the new Algerian regime killed many tens of thousands of Algerians for collaborating with the French. In Iraq, Saddam Hussein and the Baathists slaughtered 200,000 to 300,000 Kurds from 1987 to 1991 and 60,000 Shia Marsh people in 1991–1992, as part of their overall mass murdering that numbered perhaps half a million. Syria's Assad and the Alawites decimated the people of Hama. The region's most catastrophic annihilation is ongoing. In Sudan, following on the heels of the Arab Muslim northerners' killing (mainly by inducing famine but also with extensive direct killing) of upward of 2 million black Christian southerners over twenty years, they have, in the past few years, been conducting an eliminationist campaign against overwhelmingly black Muslims in the western Sudan region of Darfur, killing more than 400,000, expelling more than 2.5 million, and burning hundreds of villages so the people will have no place to return to.

Asia has suffered the largest number of gargantuan mass slaughters, with every major country being the site of eliminationist projects. In addition to the Japanese mass murders during World War II of several million people, mainly in China, though also in Burma, East Timor, Korea, Manchuria, Philippines, and elsewhere; the Chinese communists' murdering of a mind-boggling number of people, perhaps between 50 million and 70 million Chinese, and an additional 1.2 million Tibetans; and the Khmer Rouge's lethal eliminationist system in Cambodia, the continent has seen killings of hundreds of thousands during India's partition from 1946 to 1948, and of between 1 million and 3 million during the Pakistanis' onslaught against seceding Bangladesh in 1971. The Vietnamese communists' long-term campaign of killing opponents, starting in 1945 with the war against the French and ending in the aftermath of the Vietnam War in the 1980s, have produced widely diverging estimates of the victims. They killed perhaps 200,000 to 300,000 people (it might be many more), a figure that does not include the 200,000 boat people who died fleeing the regime. North Korean communists have (not including famine deaths) killed perhaps 2 million people since the regime's inception. Indonesians have on their ledger approximately half a million communists in 1965–1966, and 200,000 East Timorese starting in 1975, when Indonesia invaded the country upon the Portuguese colonizers' departure. Other killings include those by colonizers in the twentieth century's first part; a multinational force, including Americans, in China during the Boxer Rebellion; the French in Indochina; and the Dutch in the East Indies and West Indies. Mass-murderous famines have also afflicted Asia. During their attempt from 1958 to 1961 to rapidly transform China socially and economically, known as the Great Leap Forward, the Chinese communists caused a famine that took the lives of perhaps 25 million people (included in the total above). North Korea let 2 million to 3.5 million people die owing to famine between 1995 and 1998.

In our age, mass elimination and extermination have visited all parts of the world not just geographically but also socially, with peoples of virtually every imaginable type of group falling victim: people defined by ascriptive characteristics such as skin color, by genetic endowments such as autism, by social or cultural identities such as ethnicity or religion, by sexuality, and by political identity, such as national membership, or political affiliation such as being a communist or being an anticommunist. Germans during the Nazi period slaughtered people in all these kinds of groups.

One particular category of victims has repeatedly been targeted in eliminationist and exterminationist assaults, and yet it has been barely noticed: indigenous peoples. From 1900 to 1957 Brazilians alone obliterated more than eighty Indian tribes, with the indigenous population declining from perhaps 1 million to fewer than 200,000. In Latin America, Asia, and Africa, dozens of exterminationist and eliminationist assaults against indigenous peoples have been documented, including the Paraguayans against the Aché from 1966 to 1976, the El Salvadorans against Indians from 1980 to 1992, the Tanzanians against the Barabaig from 1990 to 1992, the Filipinos against the Agta in 1988, and the Laotians against the H'mong from 1979 to 1986. More groups of indigenous peoples have likely been destroyed during our age than in any other comparable time period.[16]

Mass murder and elimination's perpetrators have come from all parts of the economic and political spectrums: Nazis, conventional rightist regimes, democratic countries, communists, nationalists, and regimes guided by no particular ideology. Nevertheless, during the past century communist regimes, led and inspired by the Soviet Union and China, have killed more people than any other regime type. Democracies have been by far the least murderous type (although as colonizers—where democracies transform themselves into tyrannies—they have killed liberally), measured in the number of mass slaughters and of victims.[17] Except the Germans' and the Japanese's killings shortly before and during World War II, and the Europeans' mainly earlier colonial predations in Africa, mass murders have been principally domestic. Perpetrators have overwhelmingly killed their countrymen.

Our time has been an age of mass murder. More so, mass murder and eliminations are among our age's defining characteristics. People understand *individual* eliminationist campaigns—the Holocaust or, more recently, the mass slaughters in Rwanda and Darfur—to be horrific. Yet only when the mass slaughters and eliminations of our age or even of recent times are seen in aggregate does the horror's true immensity become clear. Mass annihilation and elimination are not just an ad hoc problem that crops up with the latest or next instance of mass slaughter or expulsion, usually, for Westerners, in some seemingly remote place. They ought to be understood as among our time's most pressing and systematically produced political problems. They should be at the center of security discussions in the United Nations and in other international and domestic forums concerned with security, the international order, and justice. That they are not shows how skewed are our depiction and understanding of the past century and the one just begun.

Estimates for mass murders are usually imprecise. High estimates are often two or three times low estimates. For the largest mass murders, estimates vary by millions, and even, as for that of the Chinese communists, tens of millions. Most perpetrators keep few if any records, and often sequester or destroy those they do make. Many mass murders are intertwined with war and other forms of elimination, so it is hard to disentangle what deaths are murders. They have often occurred in politically closed or distant places, and against people of color, so little has become known of what has transpired, or its magnitude.

Nevertheless, it is critically important to present figures for individual mass murders and eliminations, and also aggregate figures, keeping in mind the theme is politically charged (with propagandists and partisans on all sides ready to attack those who do not accept their views). I present here the best estimates based on the figures that others have given, fully aware that any given figure may lead to vociferous criticism that it is an exaggeration or understatement. Some estimates might be wide of the actual mark, by millions.

Still, in aggregate, even mid-range estimates produce a frightening, largely unknown portrait of our time. As we have seen, since the twentieth century began, human beings have mass murdered directly or through famine a conservatively estimated 127 million people, and may have killed as many as 175 million. By the lower figure, mass murderers have killed more than twice as many people than the 61 million people (42 million military deaths, 19 million civilian deaths) dying in war. By the higher figure, mass murderers have killed almost three times as many. By any reasonable accounting, mass murder and elimination have been more lethal than war. Yet war is reflexively, and wrongly, considered *the* major problem of violence around the world, being international security institutions' and public attention's overwhelming focus.

During the past century's second half and into the twenty-first century, the vast majority of people have lived in countries victimized by the systematic annihilation of parts of their population either during their lifetimes or in their countries' recent pasts. They have themselves been such annihilation's targets or near targets, been perpetrators or sympathized with perpetrators, or been related to, or on the sides of, victims or perpetrators. For most people, mass murder and elimination have not been merely a distant problem, but integral and prominent in their mental, emotional, and existential landscapes. This was driven home to the *New York Times'* Fox Butterfield while in Beijing in 1979–1980 during the aftermath of Mao's death and the Cultural Revolution. Butterfield later wrote about the consequences of the Chinese communists' various mass murderous and eliminationist politics: "Almost every Chinese I got to know during my twenty months in Peking had a tale of political persecution. . . . From their stories it seems as if a whole generation of Chinese . . . had known nothing but arbitrary accusations, violent swings in the political line, unjustified arrests, torture, and imprisonment. Few Chinese I knew felt free from the fear of physical or psychological abuse and the pervasive sense of injustice."[18]

PART I

EXPLAINING ELIMINATIONIST ASSAULTS

CHAPTER THREE

Why They Begin

WHY WOULD PEOPLE DECIDE one day to slaughter other human beings by the thousands, tens of thousands, hundreds of thousands, millions? That someone might want to kill a person he knows, an avowed enemy, or a person who has done or explicitly threatens to do him or his loved ones injury, most people can comprehend. But that someone would wish to kill thousands or millions of people, including children, whom he has never met or seen seems unfathomable.

How could anyone want to do this? The seeming incomprehensibility of people consciously wanting so much death and suffering has led many to construct accounts that, in effect, deny that such desires exist or that they motivate mass murder. Such accounts focus not on the perpetrators but on transnational systems, such as capitalism or globalization, or social structures, such as authoritative political systems or bureaucracies, or on transhistorical forces, such as ethnic conflict or human nature. They make mass murder seem impersonal and inevitable, something beyond human control. Such accounts seem to make mass murder more comprehensible, by glossing over the essential question: How could anyone *want* to do this?

One such account is that mass murder is a consequence of nation-building, which is a complex political process that includes states consolidating and extending control over territory, and forging in a heterogeneous society a dominant national identity. It often leads to the elimination of groups that do not fit the new nation—through a combination of transformation, expulsion, and extermination. The Turks' annihilation of Armenians, the mass murders in various countries of postcolonial Africa, and others, even the Germans' slaughter of the

Jews, have been attributed to nation-building. Yet, in reality, the relationship between nation-building, which often takes place over decades or longer, and mass slaughter is, at best, indirect and complicated, as we can see perhaps best from the history of the United States.

Nation-building began during the American Revolution. Its central constructive moment was the adoption of the American Constitution in 1783. Tens of thousands of Tories, those opposing the new nation of a self-governing democracy, fled or were expelled. The former colonies, in a postrevolutionary compromise, produced a weak federal government with two incompatible political, social, economic, and moral systems: the free North and the slave South. These systems coexisted so uneasily that the South eventually contested the American state's legitimacy. The Civil War of 1861–1865, in which more Americans died than in any other war, was American nation-building's second great moment. In destroying the Southern system, it secured for the American state unchallenged authority.

The third part of American nation-building was also violent. As the nation expanded westward and inward, through and onto Native American lands, the American state and Americans sought Native Americans' general elimination from most of the country. Americans, overwhelmingly of European descent, reduced the Native American population with various policies that are sometimes hard to categorize because their effects were often indirect, if calculable. The absolute numbers of Native Americans whom Americans directly murdered is comparatively low, probably in the tens of thousands. Many more died from disease, which Americans, knowing their immunological vulnerability, sometimes purposely spread. Under government leadership or acquiescence, white Americans destroyed Native Americans' livelihood, by taking their lands and killing the bison. Americans further eliminated Native Americans by herding them onto so-called reservations, institutionalizing a spatial and social apartheid, not of exploitation but of neglect. The number of Native Americans on American soil declined from an estimated 10 million prior to the Europeans' "discovery" of the Americas (a number that would have since expanded substantially) to 2.4 million today. Not all or maybe not even most of those deaths resulted from explicit eliminationist policies and acts, but many did.

These three principal aspects of American nation-building produced three different challenges to the American state and society. The presence of Tories would have undermined the fledgling republic. From the perspective of the victorious revolutionaries, Tories had to become loyal Americans or leave. The American state destroyed the Southern slave civilization in response to a fundamental challenge to power and the country's integrity. The Americans' systematic destruction of Native American life and lives, and their spatial elimination from American society, was an imperial conquest carried out by the state with the broad support of Americans.

The violence of American nation-building exemplifies three major tasks that states and groups face during nation-building that produce insecurity, conflict, and bloodshed: removing a foreign power and its loyalists (here the colonial British and the Tories); the political, social, or cultural homogenization of society (here destroying Southern slave civilization and the repression of its adherents); and the elimination of unwanted or putatively threatening groups (here annihilating, killing, and segregating Native Americans). American nation-building's most recent phase occurred in the 1960s and 1970s, with the American South's desegregation—really the destruction of the Southern whites' post–Civil War "lesser" eliminationist option of an apartheid system. This was accomplished without eliminationist violence.

Nation-building is not a smooth process. It can proceed in alternating bursts of activity and quiescence. According to the ideals of those stewarding the national project, it typically remains incomplete, at least producing dissatisfactions and insecurities among those building the nation and those being squeezed into its image. Groups that lose out in this process are killed, leave the country (ordinarily they are expelled), or are socially transformed by having central aspects of their identity, culture, or practices denied, repressed, or destroyed. In responding to the paradigmatic challenges to them, Americans and their governments used the full range of these eliminationist means. They expelled (the Tories), transformed and homogenized, however partially (Southerners), and killed, expelled, and repressed (Native Americans) peoples who did not seem to or want to fit. There was also white Americans' eliminationist domination, killing, and repression of blacks, first by enslavement and then with apartheid.

American nation-building and its mass eliminations bring to light critical themes for explaining the initiation of exterminationist and other eliminationist assaults. States and societies often face challenges, must deal with recalcitrant groups, and often face extreme ethnic conflict or resistance to plans of expansion. How do they respond to such challenges? When the elimination of recalcitrant groups is sought, is it principally the state or groups within society that initiate it?

Why did the American state and Americans respond to the three challenges of nation-building with such different means and results? In each instance the response's severity did not correspond to the challenge. The Southern states began the Civil War, resulting in 360,000 dead and an additional 275,000 wounded among the Union. However, even though the Union's armies laid waste to swaths of the South during the war, they did not systematically slaughter or expel Southern civilians. Native Americans never inflicted nearly as many casualties or destruction upon Americans as the Southerners did against the North, yet Americans conducted thoroughgoing eliminationist campaigns against them, clearing entire regions of them, sometimes by slaughtering them, such as the almost total annihilation of the ten thousand Yuki of Northern California in the late 1850s. The Confederate army's defeated military commander, Robert E. Lee, was permitted to retire with honor. Imagine his fate, and the fate of his lieutenants and others, had he been a Native American general who killed so many American soldiers and inflicted so much misery on the American people. With the Indian Removal Act of 1830, the American government enshrined the de facto expulsion of Native American tribes east of the Mississippi River in American law and political practice.

Tories—British, white, and Christian—were treated with relative dignity, allowed to choose to take an oath to the new nation or leave for the old. *Southerners*—American, white, and Christian—were coerced into accepting the national order and, after a short occupation, were permitted to retake control of their own Southern society and to create brutal apartheid against blacks. *Native Americans*—not "real" Americans, dark-skinned, and non-Christian—were deemed barbaric and threatening, so white Americans rendered them harmless by killing them or depositing them in camps, euphemistically called reservations, or assimilating those deemed assimilable, including by forcibly removing Native American children from their families and educating them in Western ways as a means of "killing the Indian and saving the man."[1]

Why did Americans employ different eliminationist responses to different challenges? I imagine that when Americans reflect on each episode in isolation, the answer to the question—if people even see this as a question—seems obvious. But once the three episodes are seen in the light of the others—and of other countries' eliminationist projects—the answers seem anything but self-evident. Nation-building, in and of itself, could not be the principal explanation for why mass murders, or even eliminations, are undertaken. After all, many Tories who had sided against the revolutionaries were allowed to join the new nation, and they chose to do so. Likewise, white Southerners or even the rebellious elites—unlike their political system of slavery—were not eliminated, and the repression they suffered was lifted soon after the Civil War. Nation-building always faces challenges to its goals and always produces political responses to them. But the responses are of different eliminationist means, or no eliminationist means at all when nation-builders pursue, often successfully, political compromise. To understand the relationship between nation-building (or other structural or transhistorical forces) and eliminationist and exterminationist assaults, a perspective is needed that is more complex and multifaceted than one that asserts that nation-building, or anything else, *causes* mass murder.

Four Questions and Three Perspectives

Explaining the initiation of campaigns of mass elimination and annihilation begins with four questions. The first, most obvious one is the staple of the general literature on *mass murder:* Why does the machinery of destruction get set in motion? The other three are generally not directly addressed, so their answers are assumed. Question two: Why do some groups get targeted for elimination and others, even others in the same country, do not? Question three: When a group is slated for elimination, why is the annihilationist variant chosen? Question four: Why does the annihilationist assault begin when it does, and not earlier, or later?

Relevant to these four questions, and to explaining mass murder, is the issue of determinism. Are episodes of mass annihilation inevitable?

Once certain conditions are created, such as a nation-building project, acute ethnic conflict, or intensive prejudice and persecution against a group, is the path to mass extermination unavoidable? This question has been posed most famously for the Holocaust, with some people treating it as having been inevitable. Perspectives on mass annihilation generally take deterministic positions or have a strong deterministic bent.

Many general perspectives exist about why mass murders begin, which, of the four questions discussed above, is the question this chapter focuses on. Yet whatever these perspectives' substantial differences, each locates mass murder's source principally in one of three places: the character of the state, the composition of society including its culture, or the psychology of the individual. Each of these perspectives captures important elements of the entire complex, yet each, taken on its own, is inadequate.

State-centered perspectives correctly observe that annihilationist campaigns are quintessentially political acts that are almost always started by states (or entities vying to be states). Therefore, mass murder's causes are to be found in the nature of states. Most commonly, state instability is held responsible: weak and threatened states react by annihilating those perceived as an actual or potential threat. This sort of thinking is a political analog to the analytical dodge and crutch of the endlessly invented and reified "human nature"—it's just in the nature of states. Nation-building, the decline of empires, war, and, today, globalization are frequently said to cause such state instability and consequences. Proponents of this state-centered perspective routinely cite postcolonial states in Africa, as well as tottering countries such as Turkey during World War I, which was both an empire in decline and a state engaged in nation-building, and Germany during the Nazi period. A different state-centered view holds the opposite, that it is great power that leads states to slaughter people. States that completely dominate their societies, states that are not restrained by internal checks and by a vibrant civil society are able to kill people standing in their way or deemed superfluous, so they do. The colossal mass murders of Nazi Germany, the Soviet Union, communist China, and Cambodia under the Khmer Rouge are adduced as evidence that although power kills, great power kills even more.

A second perspective about the initiation of mass annihilation focuses on a country's social and ethnic composition. Where ethnic conflict is acute over power or economic benefits, or where competing mutually exclusive ethnic, religious, or linguistic visions rend a society, groups seek to exterminate their enemies. Society-centered perspectives are typically put forward for poor countries, often former colonies, composed of antagonistic ethnic groups that colonial powers threw together. Because the political and economic spoils are so meager, deadly struggle ensues. Kill or be killed—or so it seems to the protagonists. Society-centered perspectives sometimes focus less on the country's social composition and more on its dominant culture. When a culture of dehumanization removes a group from the family of humanity, and therefore from the moral order, mass murder results. In this view, acute ethnic or religious conflict may produce such dehumanization, which then induces its bearers to kill.

Individual-centered perspectives for the initiation of mass annihilation locate mass murder in the psychological mechanisms of the individual that impel people to slaughter others. One aforementioned view, typically not articulated, underlies many analyses. When the opportunity to annihilate others presents itself, the will to power, the beast within us, leads people to kill the people they see as enemies or obstacles. The view that unfettered state power allows and therefore impels states to kill relies implicitly on this notion. Variants of the individual-centered perspective propose a range of psychological mechanisms that cause people to feel mortally threatened, that remove inhibitions against killing, or that lead people to vent aggression lethally, which alone or in combination produces mass annihilation.

Abundant approaches and notions seek to account for why mass murders begin. They work at different levels of analysis—political, societal, and individual—and select cases for discussion that seem to substantiate the given view, with each one finding credence for two additional reasons. First, analyzing mass annihilation is difficult (this is also true of the all but ignored mass elimination). Much goes into producing mass murder, so the events and factors to be accounted for are complex. Yet our knowledge of most mass murders is spotty or unreliable, so the empirical foundation is insufficient for deriving robust conclusions. Accounting for such a complex phenomenon with poor data makes simplification, and focusing on only one level of analysis, tempting. This leads to the proliferation of views capturing one or another of mass murder's aspects while failing to account for the phenomenon writ large. Second, because mass murder is complex, as are the concepts used to analyze it, defining or redefining a state or a society in a manner that accords with a favored approach is easy. For example, Germany during the Nazi period is said to have been the wellspring of mass murder because of state weakness (the loss of World War I, followed by the disaster of the Weimar Republic, followed by the garrison-like situation of Nazism) and because of Nazism's enormous state power. The Jews' mass murder was initiated supposedly because of the euphoria of military victory and because of the despair of impending defeat. The Germans decided to kill Jews because of the Jews' unusual economic and cultural success in Germany, and because of long-standing prejudice, antisemitism, that was independent of the Jews' economic and cultural lives. Often the concepts used are so woolly they can be stretched to accommodate almost any reality, becoming analytically meaningless. Nation-building is a prime example. When one group seeks to eliminate another, it is easy to declare it an expression of nation-building, particularly because perpetrators typically invoke their nation (or people) to justify their deeds, heighten group conflict, and mobilize support among their compatriots. A proponent of the nation-building view can almost always see a mass murder in this light. It is not surprising that the Jews' mass murder by Germans, the "delayed nation," as their country has often been called, has also been accounted for in this way.

These general propositions about state, society, and the individual can still be assessed in light of the four questions, and in light of the evidence that, though imperfect, suggests which conclusions are valid. In doing so, we should keep in mind that each proposition, whatever its virtues, either overdetermines (suggests that mass murder is inevitable) or underdetermines (fails to account for the specific aspects of mass murder's beginning) what it purports to explain.

State-centered views correctly identify the state as mass annihilation's prime mover. But claims about why states move to kill people—nation-building's challenges, war's stress, totalitarian domination's unchecked power—fail to account for why many similarly positioned states do not initiate mass murder. State-centered views also cannot tell us why states kill certain groups and not others. Nazi Germany systematically killed mentally ill and developmentally disabled people, Sinti, and Roma, but the Soviet Union did not. Nor can such views explain why states choose to kill some groups, yet eliminate others using different means. Nor the timing of the killing. They cannot account for the possibility, which historically has in fact frequently occurred, that the causality is reversed: that eliminationist desires *produce* the nation-building project, lead to war, or create the wish for total power. These views' greatest failing, perhaps, is to explain the origin of the motive to annihilate or eliminate people. The structural condition, whether it be perceived weakness or great power, does not self-evidently generate motives of any kind to act, and certainly not according to some ironclad cause-and-effect rule. Most obvious, they do not generate the motive to destroy or otherwise eliminate specific groups, and to kill their children, groups that manifestly have little or nothing to do with state conditions—such as people deemed mentally ill, Sinti, Roma, or Jews. State-centered perspectives present the generation of the motive to kill as being precisely what it is not: self-evident, or somehow immanent in the condition of power. They treat mass murder as being determined and they fail to account for the variability and uncertainty of its initiation and of the eliminationist programs themselves.

Society-centered perspectives identify the source of an animus that can motivate people to annihilate others. Ethnic conflict, or great prejudice, can produce the desire, and a justification for slaughtering others. But society-centered perspectives otherwise suffer failings similar to state-centered views. They cannot explain why some ethnic conflicts or prejudices produce systematic mass murder, whereas others do not—such as in the American South against blacks, in South Africa against blacks and then against whites, in Western European countries against Muslims, or in most countries past and present. Societal accounts cannot explain the mass murder of groups that are *not* the object of intensive social conflict or cultural prejudice, including the victims of communist regimes. And they cannot explain the timing of mass murder, of, for example, the various phases of the Germans' eliminationist program against the Jews or of their various assaults on their other targeted groups. Society-centered views also rely on the disqualifying assumption that intensive social conflict or prejudice will reflexively provide the impetus for a state program of mass annihilation, and that the state's character (the regime type, the leaders' character, etc.) is of little or no causal importance, because the state, as an obedient servant, is a conveyor belt for powerful social groups' murderous desires.

Individual-centered views may reveal something about what moves certain individuals in the destructive process, but they do not address mass annihilation's broader political and social contexts. They tend to treat people as universal abstractions, having the same psychological properties and reaction to external stimuli. They, like the state- and society-centered perspectives, cannot explain why similar conditions only sometimes produce mass murder, why only some hated groups are targeted, or the timing of the killing.

By privileging one arena—the political, the social, or the individual—each of these views misses much that is essential to initiating mass murder. Each depends upon a causal chain that assumes steps that need explanation. (As do existing analyses that point to a confluence of causal factors.) Each has a deterministic bent to it, having not unequivocally rejected the notion that certain factors *determine* the perpetration of mass murder. And each could not possibly provide the explanation for why mass murder begins because none specifies the mechanism that unleashes it.

Whatever other factors may be present, whatever other events may occur, whatever other acts may be taken, mass killing and elimination's initiation consists of a discrete act that takes place at an identifiable moment. The many existing accounts do not explain why mass annihilation is undertaken at the time that it is—even though this act is, compared to much in the social and political world, relatively simple and straightforward. This suggests that the act of initiating mass murder does not lend itself to a systematic, causal explanation. If it did, we would know it.

A New Perspective

Explaining the initiation of mass murder and eliminations requires that we recognize that certain conditions or factors of state or society *create the opportunities* and *increase the probability* a mass annihilation or elimination will be set in motion, but that *none of these conditions, singly or in combination, inexorably produces such assaults.* We must accept that different paths lead to mass murder and that the patterns that exist are partial. We must treat politics as central in the genesis of mass murder. We must specify the source and character of people's motivation to slaughter others. Perhaps most important, we must acknowledge that *only one or a few people initiate a mass annihilation or elimination.* As I adopted in *Hitler's Willing Executioners* an explicitly multilevel and multifaceted approach with different causal components for the different aspects—state initiation, implementation, source of motivation, etc.—of mass murder and elimination as the only way to explain the Holocaust's perpetration, it became clear to me that the same is necessary for understanding eliminationist and exterminationist politics in general. Regarding the initiation of mass murder, I wrote, analyzing in detail the evolution of Adolf Hitler's eliminationist thinking about Jews into a total annihilation policy, "the most virulent hatred, whether it be antisemitism or some other form of racism or prejudice, does not result in systematic slaughter unless political leaders mobilize and organize those who hate into a program of killing."[2] This means that at some point, one or a few people consciously, willfully, and with full capacity to do otherwise, decide to slaughter other human beings by the thousands, hundreds of thousands, or millions— or to eliminate them in another way. This decision-making moment is not reducible to or determined by other factors. It is generated by the will to kill and also the forge for translating that will into a firm resolve to perpetrate the act. It is therefore the self-sufficient account for why these people perpetrate mass murder and elimination.

The Central Committee of the Turkish Committee of Union and Progress, the political party ruling Turkey, decided to eliminate, mainly to exterminate, the Armenians probably in March 1915, after, according to one of its members, "long and in-depth discussions." The Central Committee's leaders were Mehmet Talât and Ismail Enver, whose stewardship and approval of the eliminationist assault they repeatedly affirmed in Turkish documents and in discussions with foreign diplomats, including with American Ambassador Henry Morgenthau, who has copiously related the rather candid discussions they had with him about their desire to annihilate the Armenians, as they responded to his objections and arguments that they desist. The Turkish leaders opted, as part of their political remaking of Turkey, to finally solve what they and many Turks, and the previous Ottoman regime, considered an acute political problem, the existence of this substantial non-Turkic minority within an ever more aggressively Turkic Turkey. The Armenians' position had been a theme in Turkey's politics and life for decades, resulting in previous eliminationist and exterminationist assaults. Now, under the cover of war, Talât and Enver, with the other Central Committee leaders, finally decided decisively. Talât, in a letter dated May 26, 1915, announced to the head of parliament, known as the grand vizier, that deportations must begin so that Turkey could eliminate its Armenian problem. This leadership decision was coolly calculated. Talât explains: "Preparations and presentations have been proposed and considered for a final end, in a comprehensive and absolute way, to this issue, which constitutes an important matter among the vital issues for the state." He further informed Morgenthau "that the Union and Progress Committee had carefully considered the matter in all its details and that the policy which was being pursued was that which they had officially adopted. He said that I must not get the idea that the deportations had been decided upon hastily; in reality, they were the result of prolonged and careful deliberation." German consul general Johann Mordtmann reported on June 30 that Talât had instructed him "a few weeks" earlier that "'what we are talking about . . . is the elimination of Armenians.'"[3]

Hitler both created general eliminationist and exterminationist policy orientation and took the decisions for individual programs. Shortly after assuming power he issued the Law for the Prevention of Offspring with Hereditary Diseases, mandating the compulsory sterilization of Germans "suffering from a hereditary disease," including feeblemindedness, schizophrenia, bipolar disorder, epilepsy, Huntington's chorea, blindness, deafness, physical deformities, and alcoholism, if they were deemed hereditary. This first of the Germans' formal mass elimination programs destroyed more than 300,000 people's reproductive capacities. Hitler authorized the camp system's creation around the same time. Hitler, holding sterilization to be a second-best eliminationist means for the mentally ill and developmentally disabled, ordered in 1939 that such children and adults be systematically exterminated in a "euthanasia" program. He created the general contours for the eastern conquered territories' murderous subjugation, starting with Poland, in preparation for which he infamously declared that no one any longer spoke about the Armenians. And Hitler made the critical decisions to move policy forward in every stage of the eliminationist assault against the Jews, culminating in spring 1941 with his decision for systematic mass murder during the coming assault on the Soviet Union and its Jews.

Shortly after the Khmer Rouge took power, Pol Pot presided over a five-day meeting of its military and civilian leaders. He personally enunciated his transformative and eliminationist program's central contours. His second in command, Nuon Chea, elaborated on the programs' and procedures' details. Five people have testified (three were present; two received accounts from their superiors who had been there), with general consistency, about Pol Pot's orders for the eliminationist expulsion of people from cities and towns, the expulsion from Cambodia of all ethnic Vietnamese, and the establishment of the camp system, called "cooperatives." One participant explains: "It was Pol Pot who distributed this plan personally." Pol Pot declared: "Don't use money, don't let people live in the cities." He specifically singled out one group: "Monks, they said, were to be disbanded, put aside as a 'special class,' the most important to fight. They had to be wiped out . . . I heard Pol Pot say this myself." A third participant describes Nuon Chea delivering the general killing order:

> In order to achieve the construction of socialism progressively and advance all together in the set period, we must take care to carefully screen internal agents in the party, in the armed forces, in the various organizations and ministries, in the government, and *among the masses of the people* [my emphasis]. We have to carefully screen them, Nuon Chea said. He mentioned "the line of carefully screening internal agents to improve and purify, in order to implement the line of building socialism. . . . "
>
> This was a very important order to kill. Their careful screening was to take all measures so that people were pure. The line laid down must be followed at all costs. . . . If people could not do it, they would be taken away and killed. This was called the line of "careful screening." . . . The words "carefully screen" were the killing principle . . . and were stated strongly on 20 May. It was to be done.[4]

In Ethiopia, the Dergue's mass murdering and regional expulsion program was leader Mengistu Haile Mariam's brainchild. Dawit Wolde Giorgis, the commissioner of the euphemistic Relief and Rehabilitation Commission, the institution that was to carry out the deportations, relates its inception: "In the beginning of October 1984 . . . Mengistu called me into his office. He told me, out of the blue, that he was planning a massive national resettlement campaign. He planned to move 300,000 families, 1.5 million people, from Wollo and Tigray to Southwestern Ethiopia in nine months. I was amazed at these numbers. He said that this was the opportune moment to implement this project, which he claimed to have been considering for a long time, since the people couldn't refuse. They were helpless. . . . " Dawit then describes Mengistu's rationale, which Mengistu emphasized was tied to his political transformative objectives, including using the target areas as places for politically undesirable people and "to depopulate rebel areas in order to deprive the guerrillas of support." Dawit continues:

> It was one of those rare moments when he becomes relatively frank and one gets a glimpse of the real Mengistu. I told him that it would be a fatal mistake to attempt to settle 300,000 families in nine months. . . . He refused to see my points. He said that he would support my agency with the necessary manpower and financial backing. He argued that the RRC could mobilize international support. I was instructed to draw up a tentative operational plan.
>
> Mengistu was overflowing with enthusiasm as he told me all this. It was clear that he considered this project to be the panacea for all the ills of the country. Mengistu loves campaigns, and this was something he could sink his teeth into.[5]

Initiating mass murder and elimination is a quintessential act of human agency, of choice. This act is typically accompanied by the total conviction with which Talât and Enver faced down Morgenthau, Hitler so often openly demonstrated when speaking about the need for and, then coming, extermination of the Jews, that Joseph Stalin was known for, that Nuon Chea conveyed (Pol Pot was reserved), that Mengistu demonstrated, and that Political Islamists, including Osama bin Laden, regularly parade. It is sometimes—for all we know, often—accompanied by the kind of enthusiasm that Dawit describes Mengistu displaying as he, like other eliminationist dreamers and perpetrators, contemplated this "panacea for all the ills of the country."

Anyone who asserts that the initiation of violent and lethal eliminations is determined by structures or forces simply overlooks the facts of the orders and the meetings in which they were promulgated, the facts of the many other orders and meetings in which they were *not,* and the facts of decision after decision to initiate (or not to initiate) one exterminationist and eliminationist program after another. There is no mass murder or elimination I know that could not have been avoided had *one person or a few people decided to do otherwise,* which they easily could have done. There is no mass murder or elimination that could not have been avoided had other people held power. This means that the worldviews, aspirations, and moral framework, the prejudices and hatreds, and the personalities of the person or small group of people who make the eliminationist decision are crucial. These specific individuals, their ideas and personalities, require investigation.

A general framework for answering the basic questions about the initiation of mass annihilations and eliminations—why they begin, why only some groups get targeted, why certain means are chosen, and why they begin when they do—starts with the conditions that first generate the idea that mass killing or elimination may be desirable, and the conditions that then make it practical, namely thinkable as policy. Many societies contain groups that others hate or think dangerous, and would therefore like to eliminate. Why, then, do the eliminationist views around the world get transformed into actual annihilation or elimination against some of them, actually only a small percentage of such groups, but not others?

War, nation-building conflicts, extreme challenges to the state or national integrity, and intense ethnic strife increase the likelihood that eliminationist sentiment will be inflamed, brought into politics, and turned into policy, including lethal policy. They create conditions that make eliminationist, even annihilationist politics more thinkable and more practicable—but never certain, or even likely. Just as war made the Germans' annihilation of the mentally ill, the Jews, and the Sinti and Roma feasible but did not lead Germany's conquerors to annihilate Germans; just as American nation-building led to the eliminationist policies against

Native Americans but did not produce similar policies toward others threatening the national project, so too do challenges to the state and intense ethnic conflict sometimes provide the context for merciless annihilation and eliminations, and at other times do no such thing.

South Africa is an example of an intense conflict that produced protracted violence, but not mass annihilation, by either whites or blacks against the other. For decades, mutually incompatible visions of the nation and politics, ethnic conflict between blacks and whites, and military and civil fighting between the African National Congress and the white apartheid state dominated the country. Yet these overlapping and reinforcing conflicts never resulted in the whites' annihilating those they believed would destroy their society and perhaps themselves. These conflicts, and all that blacks had suffered, also did not lead the African National Congress and blacks, upon taking power, to annihilate whites or even the apartheidists (as many had feared). Few countries have had more long-lasting and intensive domestic conflicts than South Africa. According to most perspectives on mass annihilation, South Africa should have suffered one mass murder campaign, if not successive or reciprocal campaigns. South Africa's history, during and after its apartheid years, resoundingly belies structural or deterministic theories of mass murder.

Various circumstances facilitate people's choosing a path leading to mass murder or elimination, but political leaders are compelled neither to choose that path nor to reach its end. Whatever a country's stresses, whatever the real or imagined threats, however intensive its ethnic conflicts, if political leaders do not enact an exterminationist or eliminationist program, then mass murder, expulsion, and incarceration do not occur. The critical factor is the political leaders: Some move states or groups to commit mass murder. Others, where mass murder would be possible, do not.

The Centrality of Political Leaders

Mass annihilation or elimination begins when leaders are animated by an eliminationist ideology and are determined to turn broadly existing eliminationist sentiment into a state policy of extermination or elimination. The best known such instance is Germany, where Hitler, who from the beginning of his political career was determined to eliminate the Jews, tapped into Germans' widespread, already existing anti-Jewish eliminationist beliefs, and mobilized them first to support or partici-pate in the brutal eliminationist policies during the 1930s of segregat-ing Jews—removing them from most economic and professional activity, creating systematic legal and social disabilities, subjecting them to violence and murder, and driving most of them to emigrate—and then in elimination's exterminationist variant during the war. Hitler could mobilize such beliefs, which existed within many European coun-tries and within the Catholic Church and the German Protestant churches, precisely because these beliefs, whatever their variations, broadly accorded with his own and with his eliminationist project's fundamentals. This was also true, often to a lesser extent, about Hitler's various racist and biological views that led to the slaughter and despo-liation of the Germans' many non-Jewish victims.

This mechanism and pattern has characterized our age's mass mur-ders and eliminations. Talât easily mobilized preexisting anti-Armenian eliminationist views among many Turks. The political and military leadership in Indonesia in 1965 mobilized existing profound and wide-spread anticommunist hatred. The Tutsi leaders in Burundi in 1970 ac-tivated their followers to slaughter Hutu, and the Hutu leaders in neighboring Rwanda in 1994 did the same against Tutsi. In Yugoslavia, the deep-seated animosity of Serbs for Croats and Muslims was long-standing, so Slobodan Milošević easily got Serbs to support and imple-ment his eliminationist projects.

Less frequently, eliminationist leaders assume power in a society where their views are not broadly shared, and they nevertheless enact their eliminationist ideals. Cadres of like-minded followers form their vanguard for the eventual mass elimination, or over time inculcate their eliminationist views into a significant portion of society, most quickly and effectively the young. This occurred in the Soviet Union, in China, and in North Korea. Saddam Hussein similarly brought to power with him his Baath Party and then inculcated into new generations of Iraqis his murderous Baathist credo.

But most often, even in societies that harbor broad eliminationist sentiment, murderous leaders do not come to power. Because they do not, most eliminationist beliefs around the world never get transformed into eliminationist policy. Before Talât took power in Turkey, Turks widely hated Armenians and had even been mobilized twice in the previous decades in orgies of mass slaughter. However, the leadership preceding Talât chose not to bring about the Armenians' total elimination, and therefore no national-scale mass murder and expulsion program occurred—even though it easily could have. It took Talât and Enver's decision to set complete mass murder and elimination into motion. For decades prior to Hitler's ascension, a broad consensus in German society existed that Jews should be eliminated, but there was no mass elimination, let alone annihilation. When Hitler, after a victory in national elections, assumed Germany's chancellorship in January 1933 and almost immediately embarked upon a high-profile, explicit eliminationist program against the Jews, the conditions of society had not appreciably changed from when his predecessors had not undertaken any such program. In each case it was political leaders who made the difference. More recently, Serbs' long-standing wish to eliminate Muslims from their midst produced no eliminationist onslaught until Milošević activated such beliefs behind his murderous program of a purified, greater Serbia for the Serbs. Since Rwandan independence in 1962, anti-Tutsi eliminationist sentiment has widely existed among Hutu. But it has produced mass murder only when the Hutu leaders decided it should: in December 1963, from 1990 to 1993 on a sporadic and clearly preparatory scale with Hutu perpetrating at least seventeen trial massacres, and then in 1994, when the opportunity finally seemed propitious, in the intended final comprehensive annihilationist scale. At other times, the Hutu leaders allowed the powerful hatred against the Tutsi to lie dormant. Parallel though reversed circumstances between Hutu and Tutsi have existed for several decades in neighboring Burundi, leading the Tutsi political leaders to initiate five mass slaughters of Hutu over two decades.

More generally, in every instance of repeated mass murders and eliminations in a given country or region upon a targeted group after intervals of years—including various murderous assaults in the Indian subcontinent between Muslims and Hindu and Pakistanis and Bengalis, or the Muslim Arab northern Sudanese against the Christian and animist black southern Sudanese—the starts and stops are orchestrated from above and are not just the ebbs and flows of disorganized passions among the involved groups' ordinary members.

Political leaders are the critical actors setting eliminationist policies and mass annihilations in motion. They are not some faceless, abstract entity, not some bureaucracy, but one or a few identifiable people governing a country, who are typically extremely well known to followers and victims. Talât, Enver, and a handful of others decided to slaughter the Armenians. Vladimir Lenin and Leon Trotsky, and then Stalin, created the Soviet Union's eliminationist institutions and programs. Hitler decided to annihilate European Jewry and to sterilize and then kill mentally ill Germans. Together with Heinrich Himmler, the head of the SS and other security forces, and a few others, he set in motion policies that led to the deaths of millions of Russians, Ukrainians, Poles, and others, many inside the Germans' camp system and many outside it at the hands of the SS, the military, or other police forces. Harry Truman, alone, decided to annihilate the Japanese of Hiroshima and Nagasaki. Mao Zedong was the prime mover of the Chinese communists' gargantuan slaughters. General Haji Muhammad Suharto in Indonesia gave the order for the slaughter of the Indonesian Communist Party's members. General Agha Muhammad Yahya Khan, Pakistan's ruler, set his army to murder millions of Bangladeshis. Idi Amin initiated the slaughter of hundreds of thousands in Uganda. Presidents Fernando Romeo Lucas Garcia and José Efraín Ríos Montt were responsible for the mass murder and elimination in Guatemala of Maya under the guise of counterinsurgency. Mengistu masterminded and initiated the various Ethiopian eliminationist and exterminationist programs. Pol Pot and the Khmer Rouge leaders around him instituted the murderous policies that took millions of Cambodians' lives. The Argentinean junta's members started the Dirty War against their real and imagined enemies. Augusto Pinochet authorized the slaughter of thousands in Chile. Hafez al-Assad gave the order to indiscriminately slaughter people in Hama. Saddam Hussein orchestrated the annihilation of hundreds of thousands of Iraqis. Milošević enacted one Serbian murderous eliminationist onslaught after the next. After President Juvénal Habyarimana's assassination, Théoneste Bagosora, the Ministry of Defense's director of services, and a small circle of associates set in motion the comprehensive annihilative assault on the Tutsi and the targeted one on their Hutu enemies. Omar al-Bashir and the other Political Islamists ruling Sudan initiated the mass murders and expulsions first against the southern Sudanese and then against the people of Darfur. Bin Laden ordered the mass murder of the World Trade Center's and Pentagon's occupants.

Naming the people who initiated mass murders and other eliminationist assaults during the past century could go on. They had advisers and underlings who may have influenced them or who may have themselves originated the programs' parts. But in the end, these people, political leaders all, were the prime movers.

These and the other initiators of exterminationist and eliminationist programs did not have their hands forced, whatever exactly that might mean. If any leader had been somehow compelled to initiate such a program, then that would mean only that someone else was making the decision, so the onus would merely fall on that person or persons, and the analysis of the destructive program's initiation would be shifted from the titular decision-maker to the actual ones. And if somehow a mass-murdering leader were brought to power by a public bent on slaughtering or eliminating some designated enemy, explicitly to enact that public's wish, then the symbiotic relationship between eliminationist leaders and followers would differ somewhat, with the leader still critical for initiating the eliminationist program. This somewhat different relationship has not existed in our time. Almost all mass-murderous and eliminationist leaders (overwhelmingly true of domestic ones) have come to power nondemocratically. They have usually taken power without announcing their future policies, which they typically have not yet decided upon, or even so concretely conceived.

The people who moved many other people to destroy and displace still others had confidantes and needed the cooperation of followers to create the often elaborate operational plans, and then to implement them. When these political leaders decided to initiate the preparatory planning, and then the eliminationist programs themselves, they invested executive and administrative responsibilities in their subordinates. Planning has often been months, sometimes years, in the making—further evidence that mass murders do not just erupt spontaneously from uncontrollable hatred and rage, and are not responses to victims' provocations. Organizing mass murder and eliminations requires strategic and tactical preparation, including delegating responsibilities to different institutions and people, creating operational plans with sequences of actions, detailing targets, often including priority lists for killing, figuring out how to minimize resistance from the victims, determining how and when to dispose of the victim group (or groups) and the various categories of people within them, and deciding how to maintain desired levels of secrecy or publicity. Because of such planning, exterminationist and eliminationist assaults often occur simultaneously across a country or region to minimize escape. Practically every aspect of planning can be seen in the document that appears to have resulted from secret deliberations by five members of the Turkish leadership, including Talât, who probably presided, that took place in either December 1914 or January 1915 and thus preceded the eliminationist assault by several months. The document was acquired by the British high commissioner in Constantinople, which gave it the name "The 10 commandments of the COMITE UNION AND PROGRES":[6]

1. Profiting by the Arts: 3 and 4 of Comite Union and Progres, close all Armenian Societies, and arrest all who worked against Government at any time among them and send them into the provinces such as Bagdad or Mosul, and wipe them out either on the road or there.
2. Collect arms.
3. Excite Moslem opinion by suitable and special means, in places as Van, Erzeroum, Adana, where as a point of fact the Armenians have already won the hatred of the Moslems, provoke organized massacres as the Russians did at Baku.
4. Leave all executive to the people in provinces such as Erzeroum, Van, Mamuret ul Aziz, and Bitlis, and use Military disciplinary forces (i.e., Gendarmerie) ostensibly to stop massacres while on the contrary in places as Adan, Sivas, Broussa, Ismidt and Smyrna actively help the Moslems with military force.
5. Apply measures to exterminate all males under 50, priests and teachers, leave girls and children to be Islamized.

6. Carry away the families of all who succeed in escaping and apply measures to cut them off from all connection with their native place.
7. On the ground that Armenian officials may be spies, expel and drive them out absolutely from every Government department or post.
8. Kill off in an appropriate manner all Armenians in the Army— this to be left to the military to do.
9. All action to begin everywhere simultaneously, and thus leave no time for preparation of defensive measures.
10. Pay attention to the strictly confidential nature of these instructions, which may not go beyond two or three persons.

In some exterminationist and eliminationist assaults, the prime movers promulgate explicit policies and, together with their inner circles, maintain oversight and centralized control over the main contours of preparation and execution. Others set in motion a general eliminationist enterprise with broad authorization to subordinates to operationalize it. Always there is some combination of central control and local initiative. With mass murders and eliminations of the Germans', the Soviets', or the Chinese's scale, or under such poor capacities of command and control, as in Turkey, Cambodia, Rwanda, or Sudan, the political leaders naturally delegated much executive authority and decision-making to those in the killing fields.

Whatever latitude political leaders granted their acolytes, the leaders have been the prime movers of the annihilative and eliminationist onslaughts. Had each of them said *no,* which each could have, or rather had each of them chosen not to say *yes* (often where no question was being asked), then our era's many mass slaughters and eliminations would never have occurred. Even in those rare cases where it might be reasonably argued that another person or persons might have forced the hand of the then-reluctant mass murderer, or toppled him, we cannot be certain that the slaughters would have ensued anyway. And certainly not all (or perhaps even any) would have reached the magnitude of the colossal mass murders and eliminations of Hitler, Stalin, Mao, Pol Pot, Saddam, and others.

Had Talât, Enver, and others had a different vision for a more pluralistic Turkey, then there would have been no genocide of the Armenians. Had Hitler decided otherwise, then there would have been no
Holocaust. Had Stalin been opposed to mass killing and elimination,
then no vast expansion of the gulag. Had Truman listened to those urging him to adopt a different strategy, then no initial nuclear incineration
in Hiroshima, and no second one in Nagasaki. Had Mao not sought
the violent transformation of China, then no camp system, murderous
Great Leap Forward, or Cultural Revolution and other barbarities.
Had Suharto not wanted to forcibly take and then hold power, had he
not seen the Indonesian Communist Party's annihilation, a potential
obstacle to his ambitions, as a desirable preemptive measure, then there
would have been no mass slaughter in Indonesia. And had Suharto not
opted for imperial aggrandizement by invading and decimating the opposition in East Timor, then no grinding mass slaughter of the East
Timorese. Had Idi Amin not chosen to rule with licentiousness and
murderous brutality, then no mass slaughtering of Ugandans. Had
Pinochet and the generals in Chile, or the junta in Argentina, not
wanted to rule by a rightist dictatorship, or had they been willing to
tolerate opposition, then no systematic murders of those they "disappeared." Had Lucas Garcia and Ríos Montt, and the Guatemalan
army's leading generals, not defined Maya as guerrilla supporters and
had they been willing to open up political space to hear Maya griev-
ances, then hundreds of thousands of Maya would still be alive, and
many hundreds of thousands more would still be living in their towns
and villages, which would not have been obliterated from Guatemala's
map. Had Pol Pot chosen a peaceful course after taking power, then no
Cambodian killing fields. Had Assad not wanted to demonstrate that
he would brook no opposition, then no considerable leveling of Hama.
Had Saddam chosen to help Iraq flourish rather than pursue his power
and destructive dreams, then his many murdered victims would be
alive. Had Milošević been content with a smaller Serbia (or even perhaps a federated Yugoslavia), then no mass murderous and eliminationist assaults in Bosnia or Kosovo. Had the Hutu leaders not been
animated by a vision of an ethnically and politically purified Rwanda,
then no comprehensive annihilative assault on the Tutsi. Had al-Bashir

and the Political Islamists around him not been determined to remake Sudan according to their totalitarian political theological doctrine, then the millions in the south and in Darfur whom they slaughtered or expelled would still be living in their homes. Had bin Laden decided to accept that Arab and Muslim peoples should fully take part in the modern world, rather than lash out at the country and people he despises as modernity's principal agent, then the World Trade Center towers would still stand.

To understand why mass annihilations, expulsions, and eliminations begin in each instance would require lengthy investigations and excursions into each case's often complex politics, including explicating the context for the leaders' choice to eliminate real and imagined enemies rather than to deal with them in other ways—as American nation-building and so many instances from other countries show is possible. The instances from American nation-building are actually ones of extreme conflict where the targeted groups (certainly the Tories and the southerners) threatened the American political state and nation's existence. The perpetrators of many, indeed most, mass murders and eliminations act against groups that *do not pose* any such powerful threat. So why do they kill? And the overwhelming majority of political conflicts do not result in mass murders and eliminations. So why do some?

Delving more deeply into each eliminationist instance's broader political context and struggles would reveal relevant factors: In Indonesia a distemper with President Sukarno's politics led others to want to stop him; in Guatemala the Right and the military's political machinations formed a backdrop that had nothing per se to do with their leftist or Maya victims; in Rwanda a critical conflict existed not just between Hutu and Tutsi but also among the dominant Hutu parties and factions; in other instances there were other relevant circumstances, conflicts, and disposition of forces. Yet none of these constellations in themselves explains the mass murders, mass expulsions, the camp systems, and brutal incarcerations, not to mention the other cruelties, soon to be discussed, that political leaders and their followers visit upon their victims. Even after providing a fuller context of the politics of each country in which the specific antagonism for the targeted groups and peoples occurred, the critical questions would remain: Why have political leaders conceived of certain groups as noxious? Why in ways that suggest a problem so extreme as to make them consider violent, even lethal elimination as a solution? Why did they choose such violent and destructive solutions to the putative problems and not others? And in addition to needing answers to these questions in every individual case, the broader issue of whether any general conclusions can be drawn about the initiation of mass murder and eliminations remains. Some can: With rare exception, our time's mass murdering and elimination-ist leaders have been radical antipluralists, seeking purity or homogenization, or to forfend the apocalypse, or bring about their vision of utopia. The leaders all possessed beliefs about their victims and the broader social and political world that rendered their victims' killing or elimination subjectively good, necessary, and just. The leaders' beliefs that their victims, or their putative threat, must somehow be eliminated, or their allegiance to a transformative vision that would eventually mark certain peoples or groups for elimination, predated substantially their actual initiation of the eliminationist onslaught. This means that we must understand both the generation of their eliminationist beliefs and the eventual circumstances that gave the mass murderers the opportunity to act upon them.

Setting eliminationist slaughters in motion is a quintessential act of choice, freely taken, neither determined by abstract forces or structures, nor brought about accidentally by circumstances. In this case, the *great man* view of history—if "great" means *powerful*—has enormous credence in the sense that a man who can set the state in motion is necessary. Such individuals are aware of their power and of its use for furthering their political goals. They are also proud, even boastful, of their self-understood historic achievements. "I have accomplished more toward solving the Armenian problem in three months," Morgenthau reports Talât bragging to his friends, "than [the Sultan] Abdul Hamid accomplished in thirty years!"[7] The prime mover of exterminationist and eliminationist assaults is definitely not the inanimate implement of historical or transnational forces, material or other interests, classes, or his ethnic or religious group. But he is also not a lone godlike figure or warrior who, as kings were once naively thought to do, can move armies, nations, history itself. The prime mover is indispensible, and he has reasons of belief and reasons of politics, which are inherently intermeshed, to decide to use violence, often lethal, to eliminate the people he targets. But if the prime mover's demotic desires are to be fulfilled, translated into murderous action, he must speak to the aspirations, wishes, fears, hatreds, resentments, and notions of the good and necessary that are held by many others. More about *why* our era's mass murdering and eliminationist leaders set in motion these calamities is explained in later chapters. First we must examine how these self-styled godlike figures' lethal dreams and initiatives get turned into earthly hells.

CHAPTER FOUR

How They Are Implemented

Three months into the Germans' systematic annihilation of Europe's Jews, one German perpetrator, Martin Mundschütz, though a true believer in the cause, found the gruesome killing too unnerving. Like a meat eater unable to bear the gore of the slaughterhouse, he had to get out. Referring to an earlier meeting, Mundschütz wrote his commander:

> Colonel, you are under the assumption that I have succumbed to a spell of weakness which will pass again without injury. Weakness was not the cause of my regrettably unmanly behavior towards you on the occasion of our discussion, rather my nerves snapped. They snapped only as a result of the nervous breakdown of three weeks ago, as a result of which visions have haunted me day and night, driving me to the verge of madness. I have partly overcome these visions, but I find that they had bereft me totally of all my energy and that I can no longer control my will. I am no longer able to contain my tears; I flee into doorways when I am in the street and I slip under covers when I am in my room.

After explaining that he had managed to conceal his condition from his comrades and prophesying that if his commander did not transfer him, his condition would become "so obvious that my name [will be] on everyone's lips," Mundschütz continued:

If you, Herr Colonel, however, have an understanding and a heart for one of your subordinates, who wants to sacrifice himself to the very last for the cause of Germany, but who does not want to present the spectacle of one who is said to have succumbed to cowardice, then please remove me from this environment. I will thankfully return when recovered, but please allow me to leave before I succumb to the same melancholia that afflicts my mother.

How did his commander, a colonel in the SS, respond to this man's request to stop killing? With venom? With violence? Or with solicitude? The colonel wrote his superiors:

I have spoken with Mundschütz myself and tried to straighten him out. As an answer I have received from him the enclosed letter. . . . According to it, it seems all in all that a hereditary disposition of Mundschütz has asserted itself. Mundschütz is no longer fit for action. I therefore have transferred him to the rear and request that all formalities necessary for his return be completed. According to the opinion of the unit's doctor, a transfer to the SS sanatorium for the mentally ill in Munich appears necessary.

Mundschütz was transferred home and assumed other duties. An ardent Nazi, he passionately sought admittance to the SS, the institution that had brought him into the killing fields and now considered his membership application without prejudice, his refusal to kill notwithstanding.[1]

This spectacle of a whimpering, "cowardly" executioner, who approves of the killing and who is treated with understanding by the supposedly most unforgiving SS, gives lie to many misconceptions about the German perpetrators and, as we will see, about the perpetrators of mass murder in general. The most egregious misconception is that perpetrators are incapable of reflecting on the desirability of mass slaughter or their own participation in it. As this episode suggests, if we want to understand eliminationist perpetrators, then we must eschew the prevailing, thoughtless clichés about "human nature," blind obedience to authority, bureaucratic mindsets, or irresistible social psychological pressure. Instead, we must investigate the killers, asking how and why they do what they do.

Both scholars and nonscholars have assumed that when a leader orders people to be eliminated, his followers do it reflexively, and that the unhuman, so-called *machinery of destruction,* like a machine, inexorably begins to roll forward. This assumption, most prevalent in writings about the Holocaust, was so powerful that for the first several decades of the investigation of mass murder, the perpetrators and their own understanding of their actions were not topics of serious scholarly inquiry. Almost no research was done on the perpetrators and almost no actual knowledge about them existed. What substituted for knowledge was an array of false notions, some having achieved mythological status, about the Holocaust's perpetrators, the institutions of killing, and its essential features.

It was wrongly believed that the Holocaust's perpetrators were all or principally SS men, that they were relatively small in number, that they had to kill, and that modern technology itself made the genocide possible. (These notions still circulate in the popular media and unscholarly writing.) Something as basic as the number of perpetrators was therefore unknown and not even raised as a question in the central works on the Holocaust. Dehumanizing and virtually racist clichés about so-called German national character informed many. Who the killers were, how they joined killing institutions, what life was like while killing, what they thought of their victims and their deeds, what choices they had, and what choices they made about treating their victims—these and other questions were left uninvestigated. On the rare occasions that such questions were asked, they were answered with empirically barren speculation presented as settled fact.

Until my book *Hitler's Willing Executioners* directly took issue with this historical neglect, what was true about the Holocaust's investigation, which antedated the study of other mass murders by decades, has by and large been true about other mass murders. Thus, when Michael Kaufman, trying to make sense of the Serbs' onslaught against Kosovars in 1999, deemed it necessary to plumb the motives of the Serbian perpetrators, he wrote in the *New York Times* that the time had come to ask "the kinds of questions raised in Daniel Jonah Goldhagen's book."[2] Even today, untenable assumptions about why people follow orders to annihilate thousands or millions of people remain rife in the literature on mass murder. Little has been written on the institutions of mass slaughter and elimination. Few empirically grounded conclusions have been put forward about why mass murders, or eliminations, get implemented, and in the manner and with the means that they do.

This subject is explosive. Shifting attention away from monstrous, supposedly irresistible leaders, from abstractions such as a "terror apparatus," and from faceless institutions such as the German SS (or Saddam's Republican Guards, the Serbs' Arkan's Tigers, and others) forces people to confront the *humanity* of the perpetrators and their horrifying acts, and to ask difficult questions, deemed threatening by many, about the societies and cultures that bred such people. Confronting perpetrators—one man, then another, then another—also forces people to face the overwhelming, undoable necessity of bringing thousands, sometimes tens of thousands, or even hundreds of thousands of people to justice for committing murder. People on all sides would generally prefer (some are desperate) to sidestep this task, to get on with life, and so are content to blame leaders and a few unusually barbarous killers. It should therefore have come as no surprise that when *Hitler's Willing Executioners* was published, an international explosion ensued that lasted years. In being a broad and unvarnished study of the Holocaust's German perpetrators, the book made their humanity unavoidable. By forcing these themes before the public and answering these questions, it overturned misconceptions about the Holocaust, including about Germany's political culture before and during the Nazi period. Rejecting customary abstractions and the ahistorical and incoherent implication of humanity itself in the mass murder (the "anyone would have done it" refrain), it focused on the actual human beings, principally though not exclusively Germans, who actually committed and supported the mass murder and other eliminationist acts.

An in-depth study could be done on the German perpetrators, because a wealth of information exists about them—from the vast testimony of survivors and of the perpetrators themselves, collected after the war by Germany's legal authorities. Only a fraction of such information exists for other mass murderers. Generally, little is known about the killing institutions and their members. Hence, an analysis of why and how the perpetrators implemented most exterminationist and eliminationist programs relies on less voluminous and good information (substantial knowledge about the defeated Hutu killers in

Rwanda has been emerging). Overall conclusions must be provisional and tentative, until more complete information is uncovered about other mass eliminations (though it is unlikely to happen about most of them).

Mass murder and eliminations begin because, in seemingly opportune circumstances, leaders decide to address their "problems" with "final solutions" or near-final ones that usually employ a combination of eliminationist means. Yet leaders do not perpetrate the crime alone. So the analysis must venture beyond the leaders, their worldviews, and their decision-making circumstances, to a range of institutional, logistical, and human factors that map what must occur for the killing and eliminationist acts to proceed.

Mass elimination operations are often mammoth: the vast number of victims (hundreds of thousands, millions, even tens of millions) and of perpetrators (tens, hundreds of thousands, even millions); the operations' geographic size can be a country or a continent; the places to attack or comb through can run into the thousands; the coordination of the many institutions and perpetrators can be extensive and complex. It should come as no surprise, then, that substantial planning often precedes the actual murderous and eliminationist onslaughts. It should also come as no surprise that, for two reasons, this strategic planning typically focuses on killing targeted peoples' elites, the most dangerous portion of the people who are most likely to organize resistance.

The Turks carried out such detailed preparation and targeting of elites. For months they planned a coordinated lethal assault on Turkey's Armenians, raised the units that would spearhead it, and drew up lists of the Armenian elites to be killed immediately. The Germans similarly had planning offices working out the programs for the elimination of the Jews in Germany and throughout Europe, and for eliminating Poles and others from territories that Germans wished to repopulate with Germans. Before the Germans began Soviet Jews' systematic annihilation, they created and mobilized, among other units, the Einsatzgruppen mobile killing squads. Before the Germans began the assault on each country's or territory's Jews, they planned and coordinated the assault's different aspects, and in many places, starting with Germany itself, the strategy included creating a pseudolegal foundation that itself composed one facet of the eliminationist program and provided a basis for the upcoming intensified attacks.

The Khmer Rouge, anything but the embodiment of modern forward thinking, nevertheless knew what they would do upon taking power. They immediately embarked on the most thoroughgoing and precipitous expulsion in human history—emptying Cambodian cities, towns, and villages in a few days. They also proceeded to murder Cambodia's elites, slaughtering former government and military officials, doctors, lawyers, teachers, other professionals, anyone with evidence of an advanced education. The Hutu leadership similarly conducted extensive planning for the eventual annihilation of the Tutsi. The preparation may have begun four years before implementation. It included raising and training units, drawing up lists of Tutsi elites to be killed, coordinating the assaults nationwide, and undertaking more than a dozen exploratory killings. Major Brent Beardsley, the executive assistant to General Romeo Dallaire, the UN commander in Rwanda during the genocide, explains: "In the space of one day, [the perpetrators] amputated the entire moderate leadership of Rwanda; by that night, they were all dead. They and their families were dead. A lot of the leadership within the Tutsi community was dead. They had targeted all that day, and they had succeeded. So this was extremely well planned, well organized and well conducted. This was not something that was just spontaneous."[3] In each case—and this is true of many others, including in the Soviet Union, China, Kenya, Indonesia, Bangladesh, Sudan—the nature of eliminationist political leaders' planning varies, depending on a host of differences among the countries, settings, and intentions behind each eliminationist assault. Yet there are some constants.

Political leaders must find people to carry out the eliminationist program. What are the identities, recruitment procedures, and motivations of the perpetrators? The leaders must organize these people within institutions. What institutions are they? Do the leaders use existing ones or create new ones? How do the institutions function? The perpetrators must gain access to the victims. How do they choose and identify them? The perpetrators must then implement the program. What are its logistics and what means do they use?

The annihilation cannot happen instantaneously (except with nuclear weapons, massive airpower or artillery targeting civilians, or fully fueled aircraft), so at what pace and for how long do the perpetrators kill and eliminate their targets? The perpetrators often have more extensive contact with the victims than merely the instant of execution, and they are often charged with other, nonlethal tasks. What else do they do to the victims? The victims themselves are not inert. When are they able to resist their would-be murderers, and with what consequences?

The answers to these questions vary. Sometimes the best that can be done is to describe the variations and to unearth certain patterns, while seeking to account for the similarities and differences among onslaughts, and to assess how critical each of these subjects is for explaining mass annihilations and eliminations more broadly. Ultimately, we wish to know why the perpetrators kill. Why do they brutally expel people from their homes, regions, and countries? Why do they subject their victims to many other forms of deprivation and suffering? Why do the perpetrators not say *no?*

The Perpetrators

A perpetrator is anyone who knowingly contributes in some tangible way to the deaths or elimination of others, or to injuring others as part of an annihilationist or an eliminationist program. This includes people killing at close range or by protracted means, such as starvation. It includes people setting the stage for the lethal blow, by identifying victims, rounding them up, moving them to the killing sites, or guarding them at any stage of the elimination process. It includes people more distant from the deed. Leaders creating the killing and elimination programs, and those working closely with and in support of them, and lesser officials contributing to the fashioning or transmitting of eliminationist policies or orders, are perpetrators. People supplying material or logistical support to killing institutions are perpetrators. What exactly a person perpetrates, and for what exactly he should be legally and morally culpable, depends on what he does in aiding what kinds of eliminationist ends. If he orders or organizes or has a ministerial or command role in institutions that take part in the eliminationist programs, then he is a perpetrator of the overall mass murder or eliminationist program. If he kills or facilitates the killing of many people, then he is a perpetrator of mass murder. If he helps to drive people from their home and country, then he is a perpetrator of eliminationist expulsion. If he beats and tortures people but somehow manages to do nothing to contribute to people's deaths, then he is a perpetrator of assault and torture. What the minimum is that a person must do to cross the legal and moral threshold into culpability can be debated. But for those participating in eliminationist onslaughts, the need to explain why each perpetrator acts, which includes how each one understands the victims and his own deeds, applies to the person rounding up the victims, and the one organizing killing logistics, as much as it does to the person mowing down the victims or hacking them to death.

A killing or eliminationist institution is one deployed for mass murder or elimination, and its members kill or eliminate, or tangibly hasten the deaths or elimination of others. Many different institutions have been used for these purposes, and their variety is examined below. In many instances they include central national institutions, including governments and ministries, and in certain instances, there may be so many as to include virtually entire bureaucracies, if these are deeply enmeshed in an annihilationist or eliminationist program, as in the Soviet Union, in Nazi Germany, in communist China, and in Baathist Iraq.

The perpetrators of mass annihilation and elimination are not born as killers or brutes. They must be made, in two senses: by following some path that lands them in institutions of killing and elimination, and by making a transition from not imagining that they would slaughter or systematically eliminate other human beings to a point where, for whatever reason, they are mentally and emotionally prepared to do so. Whether each journey is short or long, direct or tortuous, at some point each perpetrator makes theses dual transitions.

The perpetrators enter eliminationist institutions with different identities and in different ways. Political leaders or subordinates charged with implementing the eliminationist assaults decide on some recruitment method based on their notions of which organizations and people are preferable for the task. Some perpetrators are drafted (or assigned); some volunteer. When drafted, they can be transferred from institutions identified with their country's political regime, which might suggest a predisposition on their part to participate in an eliminationist project, or they can be chosen haphazardly, without consideration of whether they are especially suited for the enterprise. The Soviet leaders staffed the gulag with NKVD troops, the regime's ideological guardians, people of demonstrated fidelity to the communist creed and the use of violence to restructure Soviet society. The regimes in Guatemala, El Salvador, Argentina, and Chile typically employed soldiers who were members of special elite units dedicated to rooting out the states' real or designated enemies. The Turkish leadership employed a combination of special units of criminals, ordinary Turkish troops, and local people who took it upon themselves to torture and kill the Armenians trudging on their death marches, and to plunder their goods. Allowing for such local participation of ordinary Turks produced more than enough volunteers who worked as de facto auxiliaries of the major killing institutions. In Croatia during World War II, the Ustasha mass murderers of Serbs, Jews, and others were mainly volunteers. Similarly during the 1990s, the Serbian perpetrators in Bosnia and Kosovo, whether organized in marauding paramilitary units or having descended impromptu locally upon their neighbors, were by and large volunteers for the unabashedly murderous eliminationist enterprise. In Rwanda, Hutu in vast numbers, of all and no governmental or paramilitary institutional membership, butchered the Tutsi around them. Eliminationist perpetrators are frequently not the special storm troopers with previously demonstrated fidelity to the mass murderous regime. They are the groups' or societies' ordinary members.

The Holocaust's German perpetrators were an unusual amalgam. Those in the SS resembled the Soviet NKVD troops. They were the regime's proud, ideological, and violent shock troops who, having earlier volunteered for the SS, were unsurprisingly sent to implement Nazism's most apocalyptic designs. Others were volunteers, soldiers, or civilians joining in when the opportunity presented itself, as one German entertainment troupe, upon learning that the units they were providing diversion for were going to kill Jews, begged to participate in the genocidal slaughter. Others volunteered to guard local camps in Germany or to join the Death's Head Unit staffing the camp system. Still others became perpetrators when the regime drafted them—without any regard for their backgrounds, ideological affinity for the regime, or martial spirit—into reserve police units that were then employed in the annihilationist program. The regime also used regular army soldiers to slaughter Jews and others, and policemen and other officials to take part in killing operations against local Jews. The German leadership used the whole range of recruitment methods, drafting those who likely had a predisposition for the task, relying sometimes on volunteers, and choosing an enormous number of German men almost at random, expecting them to participate in the annihilation of millions. Most striking about the political leaders' methods for staffing killing institutions and operations is their casualness. They believed that just about anyone was fit to become an executioner, and seemingly never considered finding willing Germans a problem. They were right. (The Germans also employed local auxiliaries of various nationalities, both organized and volunteer, whose members generally freely opted to help kill Jews.) Many more Germans and non-Germans not formally serving perpetrators in killing institutions lent their hands knowingly to the mass murder.

The number of people during our age who have participated in exterminationist and eliminationist assaults (let alone in associated abuses, violations, and crimes such as using victims as slaves or robbing them) is astronomical and unknown. It is hard to see how one could even come up with an estimate, given how little is known about the number of perpetrators involved in many eliminations, including some gargantuan ones. There may have been half a million Germans (Austrians at that time were members of the German Reich) involved in the Jews' annihilation. Across Europe, thousands upon thousands of people of other nationalities participated in the same annihilation, especially Poles, Ukrainians, and Lithuanians, who themselves killed many Jews during and sometimes, as in Poland and Ukraine, after the Holocaust. The French, Dutch, Slovaks, and others helped deport Jews to their deaths. Beyond this one aspect of the Germans' various exterminationist and eliminationist assaults on Europe's peoples, the Germans and their local auxiliaries staffed thousands of eliminationist institutions (twenty thousand camps alone). The Germans used more than 7.6 million slave laborers (many housed in the camps), all of whom had to be guarded and controlled by people using or threatening violence. If we count all the Germans (and their helpers around Europe) who fueled this economy of violent domination by servicing and doing business with these facilities, or who helped serve as the overlords for Europe's peoples against whom the Germans were conducting eliminationist campaigns, the perpetrator population becomes astonishing—probably many millions.

We know much less about the perpetrators of other annihilationist and eliminationist assaults. Yet even a quick survey suggests that an enormous number of people have lent themselves to such violence during our time. In Rwanda, Hutu all over the country and of virtually every institutional affiliation, background, and profession took a hand in slaughtering their neighbors. A study of Hutu perpetrators that employed a restrictive definition of what actions qualify someone as a perpetrator concluded that between 175,000 and 210,000 Hutu participated in the murdering or serious injuring of the 800,000 Tutsi victims. This amounts to a stunning 14 percent to 17 percent of the active adult male Hutu population ages eighteen to fifty-four.[4] But this already extraordinarily high figure is likely an enormous underestimate. The Rwandan justice system, in its traditional communal justice institution Gacaca, has convicted approximately 900,000 people of participating in mass murder (often multiple people or large groups killed a single victim or a small group).[5] More than seventeen thousand Serbs served in killing institutions in just one small part of the Serbs' attacks, the mass murder and expulsion of Srebrenica's Bosniaks. How many more Serbs perpetrated eliminationist violence during Yugoslavia's breakup? More than thirty thousand Turks served in the special units (discussed below) set up to spearhead the exterminationist assault on the Armenians. How many more tens or hundreds of thousands were there in the army and police forces who, unbidden, participated in the annihilation and expulsion? How many Soviets, how many Chinese, how many North Koreans staffed their vast gulags and other eliminationist institutions and contributed to the deaths of the millions these regimes felled? How many Japanese soldiers and civilians gave themselves to their country's colossal mass murders around Asia? Add to these all the unknown thousands, tens of thousands, or hundreds of thousands of perpetrators from one eliminationist assault to the next, and the number of mass murderers and eliminationist warriors who have peopled our era is staggering.

Mass annihilations and eliminationist programs show that leaders are knowledgeable about which people are suited to carry out the assaults on the targeted groups. Whatever initiative perpetrators take to join killing institutions or the eliminationist enterprise—from volunteers, to those who had the jobs thrust upon them, to those who chose to be their regime's shock troops—regimes have rarely used coercion to bring perpetrators to kill or commit eliminationist violence. Leaders know that coercion cannot be a principal or widespread means for getting people to make their apocalyptic visions real. After all, a political leadership cannot coerce everyone or nearly everyone because there must be sufficient people who give themselves freely to regimes, particularly those practicing eliminationist politics and mass annihilation, if the regimes are to survive. The surest way for a political leadership to destroy itself is to try to force an enormous number of armed people to commit deeds that they think evil, which is what those who disapprove of mass extermination, expulsions, or incarcerations of civilian men, women, and children consider them to be. It is safer and easier to equip willing people of like eliminationist mind, though leaders of course might compel some others to aid them.

Once political leaders decide upon mass elimination and identify the people to perpetrate it, they must turn eliminationist ideas into eliminationist projects. The designated executors must be activated, in two senses, to become perpetrators. Their minds and hearts must be animated for killing and its attendant cruelties. They must also be placed in the position to kill.

The historical record—from the Germans in South-West Africa, to the Turks, Germans, Croats, and others during the Nazi period, the Japanese, the Chinese, the British in Kenya, the Indonesians, Khmer Rouge, Hutu and Tutsi, the former Yugoslavia's various peoples, and to the Political Islamists in many movements and countries—provides every indication that perpetrators quickly comprehend an eliminationist policy's announcement. Even though the measures are radical, the perpetrators understand the policies' rationale and necessity. The perpetrators do not wonder whether the measures are those of a madman, whether the world has gone awry. They do not react with incredulity and overwhelming horror, the way Leslie Davis, the American consul in Harput, did to the Turks' slaughter of the Armenians taking place around him. He felt as though "the world were coming to an end."[6] Instead, to the perpetrators, as a Turkish reserve officer, commanding a unit of perpetrators, calmly explained, annihilating people by the tens of thousands or more makes perfect and good sense. Their purpose "was to destroy the Armenians and thereby to do away with the Armenian question."[7] The perpetrators see the imminent eliminationist onslaught as a rational means to solve severe problems, restore order to the world, straighten a badly twisted society. The record reveals virtually no shock or befuddlement, let alone horror, among perpetrators upon learning of the eliminationist enterprise. Some incipient perpetrators know that the gruesome task ahead may test their mettle. There are dissenters. But the evidence suggests they are very few compared to the legions of nondissenters readily giving themselves to violent and lethal programs.

In Rwanda, where the Hutu's demonization of Tutsi was long, firmly established in the public discourse, and taken for granted in much of Hutu culture, and where in the years preceding the full-scale annihilationist assault there had been preparatory smaller-scaled mass murders of Tutsi, the assassination of President Juvénal Habyarimana together with Burundi's President Cyprien Ntaryamira on April 6, 1994 (the culprits' identities remain unknown) roiled the country. Voluminous testimony explicitly or implicitly conveys that Rwandans immediately understood that the assassination portended a potential bloodbath, and grasped its sources. Broadcasts on the two national radio stations, Radio Rwanda and RTLM, blamed the Tutsi for the assassination and, as in one broadcast that was recorded, explained that Tutsi should be attacked:

Because of bad [Tutsi] plans we had discovered. Because before the killing of the President of the Republic, people were talking about it in rumours, saying that he was going to die, and even [Hassan] Ngeze wrote about it in *Kangura,* and others said that after they [the Tutsi] have killed the President, they will exterminate the Hutu. When the Hutu saw that they had just killed the President of the Republic, they said, "Their project is being put into practice now." They started before them. So, the first reason is that they killed the President. The second one is that they attacked and the third because they were planning to exterminate the Hutu and I think there would be no Hutu left.[8]

This all made sense to Hutu who were ready to slaughter Tutsi. Hutu inside and outside of paramilitary, military, and police institutions almost immediately were mobilized or mobilized themselves, requiring little or no explanation as to why the Tutsi would do the things that would make them necessary targets for annihilation. Hutu, led by local officials, held meetings in rural communities all over the country. A Hutu killer, Elie Ngarambe, recounts that "On [April] 10th that is when they started to call meetings of people. They were meeting in football fields, in primary schools, everywhere. So you can imagine all the people went to the meeting. They told them that things have changed, and that what was going to be killed were the Tutsi. They told them that the Tutsi are their only enemy. There was no one else that made the plane crash. There was no one else that killed the president of the republic except people who are called Inkotanyi. From this time on, fight against Inkotanyi. Fight against all their spies. Tutsi are their spies. Kill them all. That is how it is." Having received the green light, Hutu in the military, paramilitary, police forces, and mostly in no formal organization at all, then sprang into action all over the country. Ngarambe explains that the authorities told them to "'start patrols, stop the enemy, block all intersections to the point that wherever he would pass while fleeing, you will get him and kill him.' So that is what happened after we came from the meeting. We went to a place where so many people pass and we got them. Some of them managed to escape and run, others were stopped by others because roadblocks were put in place almost everywhere. That is when the plan started to be put in action from the hour and a minute the authorities said so." Ngarambe himself also killed people they stopped: "You would get him, put him down and hack him, after that you would hit him with a club, pull him and dump him somewhere and continue your journey."[9]

Many Tutsi, because they too knew how easily the already inflamed Hutu's anti-Tutsi imagination would absorb the rationale for slaughtering them, understood the peril and tried to flee before the eliminationist onslaught began. Jean Pierre Nkuranga, then twenty, and his family and neighbors convened at night shortly after the president was killed, as the local community leader had earlier that day told them, with open satisfaction, that the next day they would be slaughtered together with all the country's Tutsi. At this surreal meeting, Nkuranga's family and friends resolved to flee into the bush, splitting up in the hope that some would survive. Nkuranga did. The Hutu hunted down and butchered the others.[10]

Half a century earlier, in July 1942, Major Wilhelm Trapp, commander of Germany's Police Battalion 101, assembled his men in an emblematic moment in our age's eliminationist onslaughts. It was the night before their first of many killing operations in Poland. Kindly "Papa" Trapp, as his men affectionately called him, informed them that the next day they would exterminate Józefów's Jews, including the children. He did not give them a long speech explaining its necessity, but sought only to strengthen their resolve for the gruesome task of shooting the Jews at point-blank range (he himself was somewhat faint-hearted). How did he do it? By reminding them that their loved ones at home were endangered by bombing. Only to a Nazified mind that held the Jews to be a cosmic evil would this make sense, because Józefów's Jews had no relationship whatsoever to the bombing. Yet Trapp offered his rationale, and it was accepted at face value. The Germans needed no further explanation for the extermination order, and no further explanation as to why a threat to their own children in Germany should spur them to kill Jewish children in Poland. The vast record of the Germans perpetrators' testimony shows that the reasons for, and the subjective sanity of, the annihilation orders made sense to them, as it did to millions upon millions of other Germans. In fact, when this major, as other German commanders did for their own units, explicitly offered his roughly five hundred men the opportunity to avoid becoming mass murderers, only a few accepted the offer.[11]

Of those perpetrators not formally organized by state authorities, there can be no doubt that they assented to the mass slaughters and eliminations to which they freely chose to contribute. Voluntary participation has been a common feature of our age's mass murders. Turkish, Kurdish, and other volunteers, murderously descended on columns of Armenians dragging themselves through the countryside. Germans and non-Germans alike volunteered across Europe to participate in the Jews' mass murder. Lithuanians, Romanians, and Ukrainians voluntarily fell upon the Jews among them, often killing with a barbarism that impressed even some Germans. In the Polish town of Jedwabne, virtually the entire Christian Polish population, having received the implicit green light from the Germans, turned on the town's Jews and slaughtered them, including the Jewish children. Volunteers, including members of religious schools (as in Indonesia), the victims' neighbors (as in Bosnia and Kosovo and in Rwanda), and all manner of civilians joining paramilitary groups specifically to kill or to assist those in formal eliminationist institutions, have been integral to the mass slaughters and eliminations in Indonesia, Kenya, Burundi, Rwanda, the former Yugoslavia, Sudan, and many more.

Eliminationist assaults' front-line perpetration has been overwhelmingly men's work. Yet women have been involved, and the population broadly supporting the politics and acts of elimination, including mass slaughter, has not been a single-sex affair. In Germany women sometimes staffed camps and death marches for women. They treated their victims as cruelly and murderously as their male counterparts. One death march of 580 Jewish women took place during the war's last three weeks, departing the Helmbrechts camp in southeastern Germany. The German women and men subjected the Jews to a regime of hardship, privation, and brutality, killing between 178 and (more likely) 275 of them. At war's end the surviving women were lucky enough to be immediately treated to intensive life-saving measures by American medical personnel. The treating American physician testified that without these measures 50 percent of the 300 to 400 survivors would have died within twenty-four hours. (By contrast, it is likely that not even one of the march's 590 non-Jewish prisoners died, the German guards having deposited them in another camp after one week of marching!) The surviving Jews report that the female guards were without exception cruel to them, probably more so even than the men. The female guards even beat the starving, emaciated Jews when sympathetic Czech bystanders offered them food. The chief female guard confessed that the women serving with her were incredibly cruel, explaining that "all the 'SS' [they were SS in name only] women guards carried rods and all of them beat the girls."[12]

From the Germans' slaughter of the Herero until today, women have been in various ways deeply involved in mass eliminations, including sporadically killing or torturing victims themselves, which it appears they have done voluntarily, or doing it in conjunction with men. Women frequently have accompanied men on their eliminationist forays, or urged them on. In what number, and exactly when and how, they crossed the line from bystanders to perpetrators is, given our knowledge, impossible to say. Yet under an appropriately comprehensive understanding of what constitutes a perpetrator, the number of female perpetrators during our time is certainly enormously large. A vast number of women have been part of eliminationist colonizations, appropriating the lands and homes that belonged to the victims their countrymen and (sometimes they) have expelled or killed. A vast number of women have used elimination's victims as slaves or have supported eliminationist assaults logistically. Nevertheless, women and men become perpetrators, especially executioners, in very different numbers, but only because of the customary sexual division of labor. This is so even when mass murders, expulsions, incarcerations, or enslavements are being perpetrated amidst broader populations, with women present and, in large or small ways, involved, such as the Germans' extermination of the Jews and their eliminationist campaigns and colonizations in Poland and elsewhere, the Indonesians' assault on communists, the communists' various murderous policies in China, the Serbs' eliminations of Muslims, and the Hutu's annihilation of Tutsi.

In Rwanda, Hutu women in enormous numbers participated in and supported their neighbors' slaughter. The number or percentage of the killers, or of those hunting Tutsi, who were women is unknown. Rwandan justice officials' estimate is that the percentage of killers who were women was relatively small (under 10 percent), which, however, makes the absolute number very large—larger than some mass murders' total number of perpetrators—as hundreds of thousands of Hutu were perpetrators.[13] Many Hutu women have been convicted of killing Tutsi. Hutu women wanting to kill Tutsi in the Nyamata commune, according to the testimony of the killer Adalbert Munzigura, were "prevented by the organizers, who lecture them that a woman's place was not in the marshes." There were exceptions, including "one case of a woman who bloodied her hands out there, a too quick-tempered woman who wanted a reputation for herself." In the villages "if women happened to come upon some Tutsi hidden in an abandoned house, that was different." Léopord Twagirayezu, another Hutu executioner, confirmed this: "The women vied with one another in ferocity toward the Tutsi women and children that they might flush out in an abandoned house. But their

most remarkable enterprise was fighting over the fabric and the
trousers. After the expeditions they scavenged and stripped the dead. If
a victim was still panting, they dealt a mortal blow with some hand
tool or turned their backs and abandoned the dying to their last sighs—
as they pleased." Marie-Chantal, a local Hutu leader's wife, confirms
women's general support for their men's work:

> I don't know of any wife who whispered against her husband during
> the massacres. Jealous wives, mocking wives, dangerous wives—even
> if they did not kill directly, they fanned the burning zeal of their hus-
> bands. They weighed the loot, they compared the spoils. Desire fired
> them up in those circumstances.
>   There were also men who proved more charitable toward the Tutsi
> than their wives, even with their machetes in hand.

Marie-Chantal's conclusion about the differences between men and
women regarding the Tutsi: "A person's wickedness depends on the
heart, not the sex."[14] Little about eliminationist assaults suggests this is
not generally true, especially, as we will see, if one includes the mind
with the heart.

Eliminationist Institutions

Perpetrators have operated in a variety of institutions, some old, such
as the military and police, and some new, such as death marches, specialized mobile killing units, and camps. Leaders bent on destroying
groups of people have naturally used existing organizations that could
easily be deployed. The military is the most obvious one. Even a cursory global tour provides abundant examples. Starting with the Germans' annihilation of the Herero and Nama, militaries have
participated in mass slaughters and eliminations throughout our age, as
the lead killing institution or in a critical support role. In Asia, the
Japanese military immediately before and during World War II was the
principal agent of human destruction in China and in other countries.
Elsewhere in Asia, soldiers have been at the center of the violence, including the Indonesians' slaughter of the communists and later their

eliminationist occupation of East Timor, and the Pakistanis' assault on Bangladesh. In Uganda, in Burundi, and elsewhere in Africa, where the military has often been one of the few coherent institutions of the continent's poor countries, it has been the main instrument of mass slaughter and elimination. In Latin America, including in Guatemala, in the 1960s through the 1990s, principally soldiers annihilated the various regimes' targets. In the Middle East, the Syrian army leveled much of Hama and slaughtered its residents, and the Iraqi army killed first northern Iraq's Kurds and then southern Iraq's Shia Marsh people and lay waste to their habitat. It may be that in our age armies have killed or helped kill more people in human extermination campaigns than in military ones.

Paramilitary and police forces have also frequently slaughtered people in eliminationist campaigns. Such forces carried out much of the Serbs' killing and expulsion of Muslims and Croats, and the Croats' killing and expulsion of Serbs. Many of the Serbian murderers in Bosnia were paramilitaries, most notoriously Arkan's Tigers—the butchers Arkan, whose real name was Željko Ražnatović, organized and led—who spearheaded killings and expulsions in Bosnia and earlier in Croatia. While Arkan's Tigers came mainly from Serbia proper, such paramilitaries in Bosnia appear to have been mostly Bosnian Serbs. In Rwanda, where virtually every manner of person and organization took part in slaughtering Tutsi, the Interahamwe paramilitary force was at the slaughter's forefront.

Often the preexisting institutions of violence work in concert. Militaries have frequently acted in a collaborative, auxiliary, or support role in eliminationist programs. The German army, its leaders and soldiers, though not the lead exterminatory institution, was still a partner in the Jews' slaughter in large areas of Europe, most notably in the territories captured from the Soviet Union. It also murdered many Russians, Ukrainians, and others—most notably Soviet POWs, around three million of whom the German military's leadership purposely starved to death or shot, while delivering Soviet political commissars and Jews to the SS and other German police units to be killed as part of a formal extermination campaign. In Kosovo, the Serbian army provided the infrastructure for the eliminationist project, including the killing, and carried out much of it itself, though it left considerable dirty work to paramilitary and police forces. In many African countries, armies have collaborated with paramilitaries, police, and local gangs to slaughter targeted groups, including the Hutu in Burundi, the Tutsi in Rwanda, and Idi Amin's real and imagined enemies in Uganda, as well as in the Democratic Republic of the Congo and Sudan today.

Those leading mass eliminations, similar to many substantial national projects, often see the need for new specialized institutions. Unlike for other domestic or even international campaigns of violence, eliminationist leaders frequently create distinctive new destructive social systems: death marches, mobile killing units, and camp worlds.

Death marches are part of an eliminationist onslaught that has mass killing as a major component. The perpetrators force the victims to march for weeks or months to some distant destination, never to return. They starve their victims, expose them to the elements, privation, and suffering that cause many to die, in addition to those whom the perpetrators kill directly with guns or blows. Death marches vary in the percentage of their victims who end up lying dead along the way. Sometimes the perpetrators' explicit purpose is to kill all or most of the marchers, having chosen marches as a surrogate for guns or blades. Sometimes the perpetrators let many marchers die from starvation, exposure, illnesses, or wounds, even though mass slaughter is not intended as their principal eliminationist means. Yet, whatever the perpetrators' varying intent, and whatever the highly varying percentage of people who actually die on such marches, all these marches should be understood to be death marches because the perpetrators conduct all of them in a manner that guarantees many deaths, and from the perpetrators' standpoint, and often in actual fact, the marches are a surrogate for killing their victims, with the survivors rendered socially and politically dead.

Death marches present a pitiable sight. The perpetrators force hundreds and thousands of emaciated, destitute, exhausted, bedraggled people to trudge through the countryside. These images of people subjecting others, including children, to such cruelty defies ordinary social experience. Death marches convey to onlookers that the victims are beyond sociability's realm, vulnerable, and fair game to be attacked or robbed (of their meager possessions), tortured, or killed. Death marches have frequently provided a ready opportunity for onlookers to transform themselves voluntarily into perpetrators, as at different moments, Turks, Germans, Serbs, Sudanese, and others did.

Death marches span our age. The Germans in South-West Africa initiated the twentieth century's mass murdering with the death march of the Herero into the Kalahari Desert, where the vast majority, as planned, perished. The century ended with the Serbs forcing the Kosovars on a death march to Albania, where almost all arrived (and stayed until NATO compelled the Serbs to let them return). The twenty-first century has opened with Political Islamic Sudanese driving Darfurians into neighboring Chad.

Regimes have created death marches as principal or auxiliary eliminationist institutions. The Turks sent hundreds of thousands of Armenians, mainly women and children, on marches of hundreds of miles, lasting weeks, encouraging local people along the way to attack, brutalize, and slaughter them. In 1918, the American Consul Jesse Jackson in Aleppo reported that survivors had recounted

> the harrowing details of the separation of the grown male members of their families therefrom, or the actual killing of them before the eyes of, their relatives and friends, or of the robbing of the emigrants en route, of the unlimited suffering and death of famished women and children, the unbelievable brutality of the accompanying gendarmes towards young girls and more attractive women, the carrying off by the Kurds and Turks of beautiful girls, women, and children, and countless other atrocious crimes committed against them all along the way.

An extremely high, though unknown percentage, of the Armenians never reached Aleppo, their ostensible destination. In 1915, an American observing the deportations estimated that three-quarters of the deportees would die. In October 1916, Jackson described the Turks' treatment of one death march caravan: "For another five days they [the Armenians] did not receive a morsel of bread, neither a drop of water. They were scorched to death by thirst, hundreds upon hundreds fell dead along the way, their tongues turned to charcoal. . . . On the seventy-fifth day when they reached Halep [Aleppo] 150 women and children remained from the whole caravan of 18,000." In 1918, as the

Armenian death march victims

eliminationist assault was winding down, the American consul, Davis, reflected on the eliminationist assault of the past few years, "I predicted few of these people would ever reach Ourfa, which was all too true a prediction."[15] Yet the Turks did not spare even those Armenians who survived. According to one Turkish military intelligence officer, the Turks drove the Armenians "to the blazing deserts, to hunger, misery and death."[16]

The first march that had "death march" affixed to it as part of its proper name is the Bataan Death March of 1942, the murderous trek on which the Japanese sent American and Filipino POWs in the Philippines. The Japanese marched them in stifling tropical heat for a week, denying them food and aid, brutalizing them, and butchering stragglers and others, often in gruesome ways. The Japanese killed eighteen thousand of the seventy-two thousand on the march, a one-week mortality rate of 25 percent.

In World War II's last six months, as the Germans emptied camps that would soon be overrun, they sent the Jews and non-Jews on scores of death marches, making them a familiar sight in much of Germany and Central Europe. The Jews' death rate on many marches approximated that of extermination facilities. After the war, Poles, Czechs and others expelled millions of ethnic Germans. They sent these Germans on such marches, the local populace often treating them brutally, although the Germans often traveled on trains or other vehicles in what were, for expulsions, comparatively tolerable conditions.

The most concentrated, gargantuan death marches were created by the Khmer Rouge, which emptied Cambodia's cities of virtually their entire populations. From Phnom Penh alone they drove between two million and three million of the country's fewer than eight million people into the countryside, brutally propelling them onward, sometimes for weeks, until they reached the designated places for their camps, called cooperatives. Youkimny Chan recounts his death march. The Khmer Rouge, upon capturing Phnom Penh on April 17, 1975, announced that everyone had to leave the city, dispossessing the city's inhabitants, including, as was true of Chan's family, their cars:

Now everyone in our family had to walk, and we had to divide the remaining food among us to carry it on our backs. It was the dry season and it was very hot. There was no water. People began to get heatstroke and fall down on the road. The soldiers wouldn't let us stop to help those who were sick. I couldn't believe what was happening. We walked for days, then weeks. Pregnant women gave birth under trees by the road. Old people died from exhaustion and lack of water. Everywhere was the sound of babies screaming and people crying for loved ones who had died and had to be left on the road.

There was no time for funerals. Soldiers threw the bodies into empty ponds and kept everyone moving. Guns were pointed at us, and tanks forced us to keep moving. I saw two men with their hands tied behind their backs. Soldiers were questioning them on the side of the road. The soldiers cut off the men's heads, which fell to the ground as their bodies slumped. There was nothing I could do. People were being murdered before my eyes. These were my friends, my neighbors. The rest of us kept walking.

Finally, after almost two and a half months of walking and stopping, walking and stopping, we arrived outside the province of Battambang, where most of the small villages in the jungle had been burned to ashes during the fighting. We were told that we must live in those burned-out villages.[17]

On these marches, the Khmer Rouge intentionally killed and drove to death many tens of thousands, perhaps as many as 400,000 people. They forced the survivors to locales that could not sustain them, lacking housing, infrastructure, viable economies, and often even arable land. Thus began the Khmer Rouge's eliminationist transformation of Cambodia. A partly parallel instance occurred in Ethiopia, when the Dergue dictatorship under Mengistu Haile Mariam starting in fall 1984 sent approximately 1.5 million people from northern Ethiopia on death marches to the southwest as part of a "resettlement" program, intended to pacify Ethiopia's northern region, where rebel groups were fighting the government. The Ethiopian perpetrators killed about 100,000 people during the death marches or in their aftermath, as survivors perished in the "resettlement" camps.[18]

Among the most chaotic death marches were the many that moved more than fourteen million people between India and Pakistan during the region's partition in 1947, when the British pulled out. Although this population transfer was intended to allow Muslims in India and Hindu living in Pakistan to resettle in the other country, they became death marches that took the lives of roughly a half million people. Their transformation into mutual eliminationist assaults came about in part because the local populace in many regions, and on both sides, understood them as death marches and because those same local people were encouraged by their leaders with their killing squads to turn their conceptions of what the marches were, or should be, into reality.

Unlike camps, which are fixed in space, multipurpose installations, death marches are transitory, single-purpose institutions. Although they sometimes are revived or reconstituted, they generally come into being for a defined time and expire when their victims are gone. Most death marches are either mainly annihilatory, as the Germans' marches of the Herero and, forty years later, of Jews were, or mainly expulsive, as the Serbs' march of Kosovars, the Dergue's march of northern Ethiopians, and the Sudanese Political Islamists' driving from their homes of Darfurians have been. Whichever, all such marches are variations upon a lethal eliminationist theme.

Since expulsion marches of civilians are by definition eliminationist, they inherently tend toward lethal violence. Perpetrators who compel people to abandon their homes, or banish them abroad, convey the message that these people are dangerous or noxious, enough to deserve elimination. In the modern world, social and physical attachment to a physical place is seen as a constituent part of community membership. Being wrested from one's place suggests an abrogation of a person's full humanity. Ordinarily, societies treat only criminals in such a way. Those violently driving people from their homes, particularly families that have resided there for generations, relegate their victims to the status of outlaws—literally, outside the law—to whom virtually anything may be done. The Soviets treated the Crimean Tatars, one of the eight ethnic groups they deported for putative disloyalty, with murderous brutality:

> At 2:00 in the morning of May 17, 1944, Tatar homes were suddenly broken into by NKVD agents and NKVD troops armed with automatics. They dragged sleeping women, children, and old people from their beds and, shoving automatics in their ribs, ordered them to be out of their homes within ten minutes. Without giving them a chance to collect themselves, they forced these residents out into the street, where trucks picked them up and drove them to railroad stations. They were loaded into cattle cars and shipped off to remote regions of Siberia, the Urals, and Central Asia.
>
> People were not allowed to get dressed properly. They were forbidden to take clothes, money, or other things with them. The agents and armed troops swept through these homes, taking these people's valuables, money, and anything they liked, all the while calling the Tatars "swine," "scum," damned traitors," and so on.
>
> These people left their homes naked and hungry and traveled that way for a month; in the locked, stifling freight cars, people began to die from hunger and illness. The NKVD troops would seize the corpses and throw them out of the freight car windows.[19]

Death marches and expulsions express eliminationist beliefs' multiple potential. For the perpetrators, expelling and killing go hand-in-hand and are interchangeable. This is so for leaders creating the marches, those guarding them, and the local people jeering, brutalizing, and sometimes murdering the marchers whose banishment they celebrate. The same spirit infuses death marches and expulsions' aftermath: The perpetrators deposit the survivors en masse in distant places without physical or economic infrastructure, and so, predictably, many more die. The perpetrators know, witness, and promote this, or at least allow it to happen, with perhaps the most infamous instance being the Khmer Rouge.

The Germans' deportation plans for Jews are documented cases of eliminationist intent and of the interchangeability of eliminationist solutions. The two most comprehensive proposals receiving serious consideration were, first, to create a "reservation" for the Jews in eastern Poland's Lublin region and, second, to ship millions of Jews to Madagascar. The Germans' proposals for mass expulsion, including these two, were interim steps on the road to the Jews' extinction. Those fashioning these schemes conceived of the proposed dumping grounds as uninhabitable environments. As the district governor of Lublin suggested in November 1939, the "district with its very marshy character could . . . serve as a Jew-reservation, a measure which could possibly lead to a widespread decimation of the Jews."[20] The proposed reservations were to be enormous prisons—like walled-in ghettos that the Germans constructed for Polish Jewry—consisting of economically unsustainable territory, where the Jews, cut off from the world, would die off.[21] In Ethiopia, the Dergue expelled 1.5 million northerners, exposing them to new diseases, including malaria, which led to hundreds of thousands of deaths—especially the sick, the elderly, and children. One former Dergue member, who witnessed the Tigrayans' brutal, murderous deportation, packed into buses like Jews in cattle cars, called the resettlement a "genocide of helpless people."[22]

Another often used eliminationist killing institution is the mobile killing squad. Its function (unlike the death marches) is unambiguously recognized. It is neither some informal marauding, murderous group, nor an established institution of a normal polity, such as the military, that might kill episodically, along with other noneliminationist duties. The mobile killing institution is both formal and enduring, principally devoted to annihilation and elimination.

To spearhead and execute the Armenians' elimination, the Turkish leaders created a substantially autonomous institution, the Special Organization, which, having its own funding and organizational structure, functioned as a virtual "state within the state." Consisting of approximately thirty thousand men, mainly criminals, the Special Organization's principal task was to exterminate the Armenians. Its units went from town to town rounding up victims, shooting men, and sending the remainder on death marches, which the Special Organization's men would sometimes themselves murderously fall upon.[23]

Among the new institutions the Ethiopian Dergue created to conduct its operations were "revolutionary death squads" and the Dergue Special Forces, which early in the regime's tyranny killed fifteen to thirty youths in each of Addis Ababa's twenty-eight zones, in order to terrorize its actual and potential opposition.[24] In many Latin American countries, including Argentina, Brazil, Chile, Colombia, El Salvador, Guatemala, and Honduras, murderous regimes created shadowy death squads that struck anywhere, descending upon targeted individuals and groups, killing or abducting them (usually to kill them later), and then melting away. In Guatemala, the regime and army created a special mobile killing institution that was formally conceived of as a counterinsurgency force, called Kaibiles. Their training "included killing animals and then eating them raw and drinking their blood in order to demonstrate courage." Their Decalogue stated baldly: "The *Kaibil* is a killing machine."[25]

Among the most lethal and notorious mass murderers were the German Einsatzgruppen, which the German leadership established for the attack against the Soviet Union in June 1941. The Einsatzgruppen, in conjunction with supporting police and military units, and sometimes also with local Ukrainian, Lithuanian, and other auxiliaries, began, as planned, in the campaign's first few days to slaughter Jews. As the Germans went deeper into Soviet territory, their killing pace and scope increased. Typically, they rounded up the Jews of a conquered town or city in the city square or at its outskirts, brought the victims to anti-tank ditches or ravines, or to a location where they forced the Jews to dig large ditches, and shot them at point-blank range in wave after wave after wave. Sometimes they stood the victims at the ditch's edge to be shot in turn. Sometimes they compelled the victims to lay themselves down in the ditch upon the bleeding dead bodies of the group just killed, and then shot them. Depending on the Jewish community's size, and the Germans' operation logistics, the number of victims ranged from a few dozen to ten thousand or more. The Einsatzgruppen's most infamous killing operation was on Kiev's outskirts, at Babi Yar's ravines, where over two days they, together with other German units and Ukrainian auxiliaries, shot more than thirty-three thousand Jews. During the assault on Soviet Jewry's first wave, from June 1941 to the first part of 1942, the Germans in the Einsatzgruppen slaughtered probably more than half a million Jews, mainly by shooting them.

For their mass murdering and expulsions in Bosnia, the Serbs employed their own mobile killing units, which often went by colorful names: the Yellow Wasps, the White Eagles, the Wolves from Vučjak, and most notoriously Arkan's Tigers. Because the Serbs had opted for a mixed eliminationist solution—kill many people, expel more—these squads were not as pure a killing institution as the Germans' Einsatzgruppen were toward Jews. The Serbs' units slaughtered Bosniaks as they expunged town after town of non-Serbs. Their brutality and cruelty became legendary in Bosnia and throughout the region. Arkan's Tigers became the institution that epitomized and became almost synonymous with the eliminationist assault itself.

Infamous though they have become, the creation of such distinctive formal mobile killing institutions has not been common because most eliminationist regimes that need mobile units use the military and police. Often they rely on local police and other forces to do the dirty work against their neighbors. They sometimes raise these units, as the Germans and Guatemalans did, because they decide that specialized killing units will serve them especially well. At other times, as in Bosnia and several Latin American countries, such units operate in the shadows, providing political leaders deniability. In Latin American countries they have been appropriately called death squads.

Still more permanent and more lethal than mobile killing institutions have been camp systems, some of which are called concentration camps. More often, the perpetrators, and those wittingly or unwittingly adopting their perspectives and nomenclature, call them various euphemistic names, including resettlement camps, labor camps, reeducation camps, agricultural camps, and cooperatives. Many regimes and people have used camps as eliminationist tools, including the Spanish, British, Germans, French, Soviets, Americans, Poles, Chinese, North

Koreans, Indonesians, Cambodians, Serbs, Hutu, and more. Camps are sociopolitical systems for sequestering people, usually for broader domination, transformation, and destruction. Political leaders bent on eliminating a sizable number of people create them when existing institutions appear inadequate for their destructive or transformative goals. Eventually an integrated system of dozens, hundreds, or even thousands of camps can become an enduring, useful, and seemingly indispensable instrument in eliminationist destruction, which the regimes put to several interrelated uses.

Camps eliminate unwanted people from society's concourse, depositing them in a spatial, social, and moral netherworld. Permanent elimination may follow. Camps can be used for temporary elimination during military conflicts, as the British did in South Africa to Boers during the Second Boer War of 1899–1902 and then half a century later, at least initially, to Kikuyu during the Mau Mau rebellion in Kenya, and as the Americans did to more than 100,000 Japanese Americans during World War II. In such instances, the incarcerators released the inmates when the war or declared emergency ended. Camps can also be used in a more temporary manner, as short-lived extermination facilities, or as intermittently lethal holding tanks, awaiting the moment when the elimination process of those surviving the camp's initial killings moves to expulsion. In Rwanda, the Hutu set up ad hoc extermination camps in churches, hospitals, and other local institutions to which Tutsi had fled for sanctuary. The Hutu compelled the Tutsi to stay in these places, now camps. Daily, the Hutu brutalized and killed the Tutsi in the camp or removed them to kill them nearby. In Bosnia, the Serbs used camps as extermination facilities, mainly for Muslim men, and as way stations for Bosniak children and women— whom they often raped or otherwise brutalized—before expelling them, including on death marches.

Regimes also use camps for the semipermanent or permanent elimination of people. They can be a brutal, often lethal, temporary part of a larger eliminationist campaign, until the survivors' expulsion ensues. The Turks established such camps for Armenians. The Poles created such camps for ethnic Germans after Poland's liberation from German occupation, often using former German camps, including Auschwitz, Lamsdorf, and Jaworzno, to confine approximately

100,000 Germans suspected of being Nazis and then, having killed between 20 percent and 50 percent of them, dismantling the camps when they expelled the remaining inmates to Germany.[26] In Kenya, the British camp system, which included the barbed-wire villages of the Kikuyu "reservations," evolved into what was going to be a semi-permanent or permanent arrangement to eliminate the noncompliant Kikuyu. The Indonesians, upon slaughtering communists, created a temporary camp system incarcerating between 650,000 and 1.5 million people for shorter or longer periods. Our era's more permanent camp systems include, among others, the German camp world, the Soviet gulag, the Chinese Laogai, Cambodia's cooperatives, and North Korea's Kwanliso.

Camps, especially when they are permanent installations, are used to put people to work. The Germans during the Nazi period, the Soviets, the Chinese, the Khmer Rouge, and the North Koreans did this. But camps, and the work within, are not governed according to rational productivity's norms or even the standard of the minimal humaneness accorded to society's noncamp population. Take the camp system that was probably the most productive among all the major camp systems, the Soviet gulag. "In the fall they kept people" in Kolyma, located above the Arctic Circle, "soaked to the skin, out in the rain and the cold to fulfill norms [production quotas] that such hopeless wrecks could never fulfill. . . . Prisoners were not dressed for the climate in the Kolyma region. They were given third-hand clothing, mere rags, and often had only cloth wrapping on their feet. Their torn jackets did not protect them from the bitter frost, and people froze in droves."[27] No wonder these inmates froze: They worked outdoors regularly in temperatures as low as sixty degrees below zero. Murderous regimes and the executors of their policies work inmates under the most egregious conditions, denying them sufficient food, adequate clothing, shelter, sanitation, and medical care. Elinor Kipper, a former communist prisoner in Kolyma, explains:

> Even if the work performed is listed honestly, it is impossible for a person unaccustomed to physical labour to fulfill the quota. He quickly falls into a vicious circle. Since he cannot do his full quota of work, he does not receive the full bread ration; his undernourished

body is still less able to meet the demands, and so he gets less and less bread, and in the end is so weakened that only clubbings can force him to drag himself from camp to gold mine. Once he reaches the shaft he is too weak to hold the wheelbarrow, let alone to run the drill; he is too weak to defend himself when a criminal punches him in the face and takes away his day's ration of bread.[28]

In the massive camp systems incarcerating millions, the prisoners' overall output can seem substantial. Yet, in these socially and economically artificial environments, productivity, the real measure of economic output, is incredibly low because of the dreadful circumstances and physical condition in which the perpetrators force their victims to work, and because of the poor available plant, machinery, and tools. Camp systems' economic productivity is actually lower still, because in wresting irreplaceable people and resources from the normal economy, they disrupt it substantially. In Cambodia such economic destruction was almost total.

The camp systems that eventually return their victims to society leave lasting physical, mental, and emotional scars, and social disabilities. Like freed slaves who bear an ongoing social stigma, former camp inmates are people whom others wish to keep at arm's length. Unless formally rehabilitated, as some were in the Soviet Union who then even rose to high positions, they are marked as having been in the camp netherworld. As long as the eliminationist regime is in power, they are suspect. Getting close to such a person is potentially to court danger. Even those former inmates who are not seen in this way find that others—even sometimes in countries to which they subsequently emigrate—often define their lives by their time in the camps, mostly with pity.

Two other purposes of camps—whatever they are formally called— are well known: to kill and to terrorize a political regime's enemies, potential opposition, or future targets. The Germans' extermination camps, Auschwitz, Treblinka, and others, are the most notorious killing facilities. For Jews (and Sinti and Roma), though not for other prisoners, the Germans' camps in general—not just these death factories constructed for mass annihilation—were extermination facilities, with mortality rates often approaching 100 percent. The large Mauthausen camp's comparative death rates demonstrate the disparity.[29]

Death Rates in Mauthausen by Type of Prisoner

	November–December 1942 (percent)	January–February 1943 (percent)	November–December 1943 (percent)
Jews	100	100	100
Political prisoners	3	1	2
Criminals	1	0	1
Preventive detainees	35	29	2
Asocials	0	0	0
Poles	4	3	1
Soviet civilian workers	—	—	2

Similarly, the Germans killed, mainly by starvation, a vast number of Soviet soldiers in POW camps. Soviet, communist Chinese, Khmer Rouge, and North Korean camps were or are also institutions of colossal mass killing. Although Kolyma in Arctic Siberia, like other camps in the communist world, was formally a work camp, the Soviets "worked" its prisoners to death by the hundreds of thousands. The Soviet gulag and the Chinese camps housed and killed enormous populations. Under the most brutal communist regimes, the societies as a whole or at least many of their institutions are themselves organized like large, often murderous camps, or verge on being such institutions. Demarcating the formal camp system from a regime's other institutions of domination that house people can be difficult. Yet if we restrict this discussion to "forced labor" camps, the numbers are staggering enough. The communist Chinese built at least one forced labor camp in each of more than two thousand counties during the 1950s. During the regime's first few years, from 1949 to 1953, they eliminated ten million to fifteen million people by confining them in these lethal institutions. In central and southern China, they supplied their victims with about eighteen ounces (five hundred grams) of food a day. Estimates of the labor camp death toll during this period are, as with practically all of the Chinese's mass murdering, wildly divergent, yet a conservative estimate is more than two million.[30]

Soviets aside, the regimes, leaders, and guards who run large camp systems do not try to hide them from their societies. Such enormous systems, as those of the Germans, Soviets, Chinese, Vietnamese, Khmer Rouge, North Koreans, or even American internment camps for Japanese Americans and the British pipeline in Kenya, would be impossible to conceal. But while some seek to prevent them from being known, such as the Soviets, who sequestered them in Siberia and in the uninhabited Arctic, others publicized them, as the British colonials in Kenya did. The Germans constructed twenty thousand camps around Europe and thousands in Germany itself. Berlin alone had 645 camps just for forced laborers and the Hesse (about the size of New Jersey) had at least 606 camps—one for every five-by-seven-mile patch.[31] Germans knew full well about the camps and their basic functions of violent domination, enslavement, and killing. (The farcical notion that ordinary Germans did not know about these things taking place openly all over their country is one of the myths that Germany's apologists still propagate despite the unanimity of serious scholarship that knowledge even of the Jews' mass murder was enormously widespread in Germany.)

The broader populace's knowledge of the camps' character and murderousness varies from country to country, yet that camps exist as eliminationist institutions of great privation and violent domination is well known. Secrecy is unfeasible and is usually not even desired. Morally, the eliminationist regimes consider the camps just and, instrumentally, they often use the camps to terrorize even people outside them whom they wish to subjugate or eliminate. Everyone knows that entering a camp is to enter a circle of hell or beyond.

Political leaders typically boast about their camps. Less than two months after the Nazis took power in 1933, Heinrich Himmler, the leader of Germany's SS, convened a press conference to announce the founding of the first formal camp, Dachau, and to tell Germans and the world that it would incarcerate five thousand people. The Chinese communist leadership was proud of its Laogai camps, where leaders claimed to be reeducating people and getting them to do honest labor. The Khmer Rouge heralded its cooperatives—holding a good portion of Cambodia's population—as the authentic Khmer revolutionary community. The American government saw no reason to conceal its internment of Japanese Americans (notwithstanding the great injustice, it fundamentally differed from these others). The Indonesians were open within their country that they were incarcerating the communists they did not kill. The same was true of the British in Kenya. Regimes often announce to their followers that camps salt away putatively dangerous elements, transform them into productive and responsible people, and by implication forge the future. Political leaders often happily convey that the camps are for eliminating unwanted groups, even if they fail to specify all the means they use. The principal, often the only, reason regimes try to hide aspects of the camp system or do not publicize their existence more is the difficulties such information might cause them abroad. The Germans, the Soviets, the Chinese, the North Koreans, to whatever extent they each have, have been circumspect about their camps' existence and real character because their adversaries abroad would use the truth to mobilize peoples and countries against them.

The camp system has been one of our age's distinctive and quintessential eliminationist tools, frequently used for various goals serving one or another of modernity's visionary transformative projects. The major camp systems were produced by communist and Nazi regimes that called for radical societal transformation and, if not explicitly, then implicitly, the elimination of those they saw standing defiantly astride the path to the future. Such transformative regimes' political leaders, whether with foresight or through trial and error, came to understand that realizing their vision, murderous at its core, requires a social infrastructure of domination. They needed places for plunging into misery the designated implacable class enemies or the putative subhumans they did not kill, and for rendering them slaves in accord with the perpetrators' conceptions of the world. They had to fell or transform enormous numbers of people—in the case of the Germans, Soviets, and Chinese tens of millions or hundreds of millions—and thus created an enduring system to dispatch obstructionist people and others they, for whatever ideological or capricious reason, slated for elimination. Hence the camp system, which formed a new system of each society. Under these and other regimes, camp systems became worlds of their own, maintaining relations with normal society but governed by norms and practices that made them separate netherworlds of misery and destruction. The ways that camp systems in Germany, the Soviet Union, China, Kenya, and elsewhere were integrated into the economy and society, locally, regionally, and nationally, and the kinds of relations they had with the broader societies and their peoples, are barely explored topics.

Camp systems vary enormously, depending on the regime's character, its transformative and eliminationist goals, the prisoners' identities, and the perpetrators' conception of the victims. Death rates vary from system to system, and even within a given system. Economically irrational, some camps nevertheless are more productively organized than others. Camp systems have differing release rates. Perpetrators' cruelty differs from system to system, and within a given system depending on who the prisoners are. The guards in the German camps personally tortured and brutalized their prisoners, especially the Jewish prisoners, much more than the Soviet guards did their prisoners. Camps' proximity to and integration into the broader society also vary enormously. The people they are meant to terrorize differ markedly: The Soviet and Chinese leaders used camp systems to terrorize almost all people, while the German leaders directed the terror potential not at the German population in general but only at selected groups within Germany—Jews, Sinti, Roma, gays, so-called antisocial elements, dedicated political opponents—as well as vast populaces of putative subhumans in German-occupied Europe. The camp systems' variable character suggests aspects of the future that each regime was building.

Annihilationist and eliminationist institutions vary, then, along two dimensions: space and time. The most ad hoc one is the death march, which is created as needed and disbanded when its victims have died or reached their site of expulsion. Spatially and temporally, the death march is transitory. Those guarding the murderous marches often do so by sheer circumstance and on a one-time basis. Death marches fleetingly pass through an environment, leaving behind—except for the corpses—no visible sign. At the same time, death marches create the broadest permanent imprint on a human landscape precisely because they cover so much territory, with the dying, broken, and unwanted strewn in columns over main roads, past cities and towns, announcing to the countless bystanders unmistakably what their leaders and countrymen do in their name, and leaving indelible images in mind after mind.

Mobile killing units are spatially transitory, yet endure over time. They are used repeatedly, moving from place to place, from targets to targets. They appear to be the most conventional killing institutions, because they resemble military and police units, and sometimes are composed of them. In form, they are the most familiar major eliminationist institutions, though their activities defy conventional social and political life. Mobile killing units combine permanence with flexibility, allowing them to kill, singly or in conjunction with other institutions, and then move on to the next kill. Their activities, or at least their effects, are also not hidden from sight, and burrow deeply into a society's consciousness. Their permanence in people's minds derives from their capacity to appear at any time, and their fleetingness comes from the likelihood that they will appear in a locale but once, even if stories of their activities can be heard repeatedly.

The camp world, fixed in space and durable over time, has a destructive and lethal monumentality that escapes other eliminationist institutions, and that can become a defining feature of a regime, a society, and its human and physical landscape. As a domination and destruction system, the camp world absorbs, redirects, and reshuffles society's human and material resources. It is a social and political black hole, sucking in life and extending its gravitational field, providing a constant tug on the rest of society's consciousness and practices.

Means and Methods

Just as political leaders employ for their annihilationist and eliminationist projects existing and new institutions in varying combinations, they kill in different ways. It is worth sketching out these methods even if they are of little analytical importance. Notwithstanding that many writers about the Holocaust fetishize killing logistics and technology, organizing mass killing, and, technically, ending a life, even many lives, is easy. Survivors of the Tutsi's mass murder of Hutu in Burundi in 1972 explain: "There were many manners of killing them," said one. Another agreed: "Several techniques, several, several. Or, one can gather two thousand persons in a house—in a prison, let us say. There are some halls which are large. The house is locked. The men are left there for fifteen days without eating, without drinking. Then one opens. One finds cadavers. Not beaten, not anything. Dead."[32] Political leaders possessing the most limited capacities in organizationally and technologically simple societies, including Burundi, Cambodia, and Rwanda, have easily managed to slaughter hundreds of thousands or millions. Killing speed, methods, and implements have more to do with the perpetrators' character, their conception of the victims, the avail-

The implements of genocide, western Rwanda, July 1994

able technological means, and perceived time pressure than with fundamental logistical and technical problems in killing. All technologically and organizationally more sophisticated killing regimes could employ simpler means than they do, with the same results and often more efficiently.

Burundi and Rwanda have been among the least developed countries in the world. When the Tutsi slaughtered Hutu in Burundi, it was among the poorest countries, with a per capita yearly income hovering around two hundred dollars and an adult illiteracy rate exceeding 70 percent. When the Hutu slaughtered the Tutsi, Rwanda was only marginally better off, still one of the twenty poorest countries in the world, with an adult illiteracy rate around 50 percent. Burundi and Rwanda each had an extremely undeveloped infrastructure, with a military and police force that were outfitted with archaic weaponry and insufficient guns and munitions. Guns and bullets were so relatively rare and costly that each country's perpetrators (like Turkey's and others) used them sparingly, choosing the more primitive killing implements of clubs, knives, and machetes. They typically apprehended the victims simply by removing them from their homes, or wherever they were, and butchered or bludgeoned them on the spot or nearby. There was nothing sophisticated about these killing operations: no gas chambers, no "assembly-line killing," no advanced technology, no intricate logistical planning, no complex bureaucratic machinery moving mindlessly forward in supposed "stages of destruction," no need for massive transportation. To execute their murderous intentions, political leaders needed only: people to carry it out, basic institutional organization, simple communication, and machetes and clubs, sometimes (and only sometimes) backed up by a few twentieth-century weapons. With such simple means, Rwanda's Hutu conducted as intensive a killing campaign as any of our time. Their average monthly death toll exceeded the Germans' monthly body count of Jews.

In 1975 the Khmer Rouge took power in war-ravaged, poor Cambodia. The leadership, headed by Pol Pot, was animated by a strange ideological brew of apocalyptic Marxism and a romanticized vision of ancient Cambodian civilization. They hated modern civilization, particularly modern technology, so they destroyed the country's physical plant, mainly by neglecting it into ruin. Cities are the principal sites of modernity, of economic productivity, of technological capacity. The Khmer Rouge emptied Cambodia's cities almost entirely, forcing the people into a network of rural camps called cooperatives, to live and work preindustrially, with the most primitive means, using only their hands or cups to dig irrigation ditches or Borgesian roads that stretched onward to nowhere for no good purpose. The perpetrators, frequently just teenage boys with little training, were only somewhat better equipped, often having but poor weapons and insufficient munitions. But that didn't stop them from killing. Chhun Von, a survivor, explains that when the Khmer Rouge "executed the people they didn't shoot a bullet because they [wanted to] save the bullet. They just hit the people with a stick or like an ant. . . . Some people were not dead yet but they buried them anyway. And sometimes they just cut them to take their bladder. Or, for their medicine."[33]

The poorly equipped Khmer Rouge also managed to construct a camp system that contained the vast majority of the country's people, whom they controlled with an unsurpassed totalitarian grip. It was mainly in the camps, using primitive means, that the Khmer Rouge killed 1.7 million people. Most perished from planned, or what might as well have been planned, starvation, though the perpetrators shot and beat many to death. Thoun Cheng, a Cambodian survivor, explains:

> In 1977 and 1978 we got nothing but gruel to eat. Production was low because of flooding; the dam broke. The locals told us that you had to plant floating rice in this area. But the Khmer Rouge wanted to try something else, and it all died. So there was nothing to eat. The locals' land and houses were all flooded out. . . . In the old society, a family could get by on one hectare of land, but now under the Khmer Rouge there was nothing to eat. This was because farming was collective, or if there was enough food, it was stored away, not given to us to eat. There were eleven people in my family. None were killed, but ten died of starvation in 1977–78, and only I survived. By 1979 just over twenty families out of 500 were left in the village.[34]

Over less than four years, this technologically backward and regressing society's political leaders induced their followers to turn society into a large concentration camp, in which they steadily killed or let die through calculated malnutrition those not conforming to the leaders' immediate wishes or image of the future. They turned Cambodia into our time's arguably most murderous, brutal, inhuman small country, utterly dragooning and terrorizing, and killing the greatest percentage of a country's entire population (the sparsely populated German colony of South-West Africa aside). All without modern technology, gas chambers, or "assembly-line killing."

The Germans' extermination of the Jews is infamous precisely for the gas chambers and the so-called assembly-line killing. Yet whatever such death factories' existential horror and significance, these installations were not essential for the mass murder. This is so obvious it is astonishing that the gas chambers have been turned into the horror's central aspect, to the longtime neglect and exclusion of so much else (particularly the perpetrators and the victims), as if the gas chambers and technology themselves caused the killing instead of being the incidental implements of people who wanted to kill. Modern technology was unnecessary and the Germans knew this. They killed their victims overwhelmingly without gassing. This included their annihilation of three million Soviet prisoners of war they mainly starved to death. They just as easily could have starved their Auschwitz gassing victims. While the Germans were gassing Jews, they continued to shoot Jews by the tens of thousands, just as they had before they built the gas chambers. In the first phase of their attack on the Soviet Union, during summer and early fall 1941, the Germans shot hundreds of thousands of Jews, including 23,600 in Kamenets-Podolski over two days, 19,000 in Minsk in two massacres combined, 21,000 in Rovno over two days, 25,000 near Riga over three days, and more than 33,000 in Babi Yar over two days. These killing rates far exceeded what the death factories using gas chambers ever achieved.

Gassing, especially in camps, may offer the perpetrators aesthetic advantages, but it is inefficient—so inefficient that *no other* mass murderers have seen it economically rational or technically necessary to construct them. Shooting people on the spot is much easier and requires fewer resources than rounding them up, getting them to a train line, guarding them the whole way, diverting scarce train engines and freight cars from critical military and economic functions, loading the victims, transporting and guarding them hundreds of miles, and only then killing and disposing of them using technology that sometimes breaks down. The Germans adopted gassing for killing Jews not for efficiency but because they had a rare inventive killing spirit, were consciously planning to continue killing well into the future, wished to distance the killers from the gruesome task, and symbolically liked to think they were disinfecting the world, especially of Jews.

Only a tiny percentage of our era's mass-murder victims were felled by methods of killing invented during our time: roughly 4 million out of the 125 million or more victims—less than 4 percent. The Germans gassed most of those killed with "modern technology," Japanese exterminated 580,000 Chinese and Koreans with biological warfare weapons and experimentation, American atomic bombs incinerated or killed with radiation more than a quarter million Japanese, the Americans and British bombed German and Japanese civilians, slaughtering several hundred thousand more, Assad used artillery and tanks to shell Hama, Saddam gassed several tens of thousands of Kurds, and Al Qaeda used hijacked airplanes to murder nearly three thousand Americans. Our age's mass murderers killed more than 95 percent of their victims using technologically unsophisticated means. Starvation and attendant diseases have taken the lives of most, followed, in some order, by gunshots and various types of blades or clubs that have been available since antiquity. The Soviets killed the overwhelming majority of their victims by starvation, the cold, and predictably devastating diseases. In Turkey, China, Kenya, Indonesia, Nigeria, Sudan, Democratic Republic of the Congo, and virtually all our age's mass murders, the perpetrators murdered the vast majority of their victims by calculated starvation or bullets or some combination of the two.

Once a regime chooses its eliminationist institutions, the logistics of mass annihilation and elimination are not difficult. When the intended victims are coterminous with a city, town, or building, the municipality or structure itself can be targeted, as the Americans did with Hiroshima, Nagasaki, and Tokyo, the Americans and British did with Dresden, Assad did with Hama, and bin Laden did with the World Trade Center towers and the Pentagon (in what, strangely, is conceived of as only a terrorist attack and not also the genocidal or eliminationist assault that it was). In more conventional mass murders and eliminations, the killers easily round up the victims. Sometimes the perpetrators and victims are segmented geographically, as in Biafra and in the assault by the Political Islamists governing in northern Sudan first on black African people in southern Sudan, and now those of the large western region of Darfur (the size of France). Sometimes physical markers such as skin color differentiate the perpetrators and the victims. Generally, the killers or their local helpers know their targets and where to locate them. This was true of the Germans in South-West Africa, the Turks, the Germans, the Croats during World War II, the British in Kenya, the Indonesians slaughtering the communists, the Serbs in Bosnia and then Kosovo, the Tutsi in Burundi, the Hutu in Rwanda, Saddam's henchmen in Iraq, and in so many other instances. In Germany itself, the Germans used genealogical records to determine who they would treat as a Jew in the small percentage of cases where the quantity of a person's Jewish "blood" was in doubt (exceptions aside, the amount needed to be at least 50 percent). Outside of their own country, the Germans were far less particular, ready to slaughter just about anyone local people identified as Jews; in Poland, Lithuania, Ukraine, and elsewhere, many were happy to oblige. When Lithuanians, Ukrainians, or

Poles, such as in Poland's 1941 Jedwabne massacre, slaughtered the Jews, with German encouragement or assistance, they were murdering their own neighbors whom they knew well, a phenomenon seen recently by a virtually uncomprehending world in Rwanda and the former Yugoslavia, particularly Bosnia.

In annihilationist assaults, the perpetrators either congregate their victims at collection points, sometimes using the ruse that they are relocating them. The Germans used this standard technique to deport Jews to the death camps or to take them outside a city to be shot. The Turks earlier and the Khmer Rouge later did the same for their massive, lethal death marches. Or, as the Germans also often did and the perpetrators did in Indonesia, Burundi, and Rwanda, or in several Latin American countries, as in Guatemala or El Salvador, they suddenly and with overwhelming force descend upon their victims. With rare exceptions, the perpetrators manage to kill an extraordinarily high percentage of the victims they actually try to apprehend. They succeed similarly with expulsions and eliminationist incarceration campaigns. Few other political programs are so successful and produce such high yields.

All this is organized with varying combinations of centralized control and local initiative. Political leaders, after opting for annihilation programs, almost always orchestrate them from the political center, with standard communication channels transmitting orders to killing institutions and field commanders. As with other aspects of mass murder, how regimes manage and monitor those implementing their eliminationist and exterminationist programs varies. Different killing sites and institutions provide a range of opportunities for perpetrators to take lethal initiative. Regimes can more easily oversee camp guards than perpetrators shepherding death marches or in mobile killing squads, especially when killing in small groups. Most eliminationist assaults have poor command and control structures because they take place in technologically underdeveloped countries, such as Turkey in 1915, Cambodia, or Rwanda, with poorly monitored new institutions and under improvised conditions over vast terrains.

Whatever the formal command pathways, the reality, which leaders understand, is that at the point of attack, perpetrators can themselves decide a great deal about how and whom to kill. Dejan Pavlović, an independent Serbian journalist, explains how it worked in Bosnia: "State

Security sent men to each Bosnian municipality looking for trusted persons who would act as allies. These 'trusted persons' would be told that the area needed to be secured for reasons of convoy security or military strategy, and that as a result, the Muslims needed to be cleared out." Sometimes the local police chief, sometimes the mayor, sometimes the hospital director would be in charge. "You'll never find one method or one chain of command for ethnic cleansing," Pavlović comments about the former Yugoslavia, "because in each area, the person or group responsible for carrying out the ethnic cleansing was different. Each commander used a different method based on the tools he had."[35] The Germans' command and control systems were probably as formal and good as any, yet every German in the east could at a whim choose to murder Jews and other so-called subhumans without fearing punishment. In eliminationist assaults, the perpetrators quickly learn that overzealousness in wiping out the targeted enemy is not penalized. The perpetrators know they may do as they wish. The number of instances in which perpetrators have been reprimanded or punished for overdoing it is, as far as we know, exceedingly small.

Just as eliminationist and annihilationist institutions vary temporally and spatially, so do eliminationist programs as a whole. Temporally, mass murders and eliminations can be (1) focused, a single, time-bounded assault, (2) iterative, a series of focused assaults, or (3) systemic, continual and drawn out.

Focused mass murders and eliminations are common. Where the targeted group or groups' death is pursued as an end in itself, or for some immediate strategic gain, and not as part of some larger transformative project, focused killings result. The Americans' nuclear bombings of the Japanese in Hiroshima and Nagasaki constitute the most fearsome, instantaneous of all mass murders. Each attack lasted a few seconds (although many died later and others continued to suffer from radiation poisoning). If the American attacks on Hiroshima's and Nagasaki's people are seen as the culmination of the annihilative bombing campaign against the Japanese in Tokyo, Kyoto, and elsewhere, then Americans' slaughtering of Japanese from the air lasted somewhat longer. Focused mass killings and eliminations, other than nuclear annihilations, can begin and end quickly, as did Al Qaeda's destruction of the World Trade Center, and Assad's mass murder of Hama's people. They can also last months or even several years, as did the Germans' extermination of the Herero and then of the Nama, Indonesians' slaughter of communists, the Serbs' various eliminationist onslaughts of the 1990s, and Saddam's eliminationist assault against the Marsh people.

Iterative mass murders and eliminations consist of political leaders initiating the slaughter of a group's members, halting it, and then re-launching the slaughter sometimes years later. The Turks mass murdered Armenians on three occasions. Although these slaughters spanned almost two decades, they were of one piece. Since decoloniza-tion, Burundi has seen four substantial murderous forays by Tutsi against Hutu, killing thousands in 1965, more than 100,000 in 1972, perhaps 20,000 in 1988, and 3,000 in 1991. In 1993, reciprocal killings, first of Tutsi by Hutu, and then by the Tutsi army of Hutu, took an estimated 25,000 lives on each side. Neighboring Rwanda saw the first mass slaughter between these two groups, when the Hutu killed perhaps 10,000 Tutsi in December 1963 and January 1964 (which inflamed and heightened the insecurity of the Tutsi in neigh-boring Burundi) and then the colossal bloodbath of 800,000 Tutsi in 1994. The Croats' successive slaughter of Serbs during World War II, and then again their murder and expulsion campaign during Yu-goslavia's breakup, could also be seen as iterative slaughters, as could the Serbs' reciprocal slaughter of Croats in 1991–1992. Iterative mass murdering and elimination may be part of a general eliminationist, even annihilationist strategy, or it may be lethal domination's most brutal form, used to thin out and weaken the targeted people and to intimi-date them with the real threat of renewed annihilative assaults.

Systemic mass annihilation and elimination consist of ongoing acts that are not iterative and episodic, but an integral part of a regime's rule. For this to happen, regimes establish enduring eliminationist in-stitutions, typically a camp system. This occurred in the brutal Belgian and French colonial regimes in Congo and French Equatorial Africa, re-spectively; Germany during the Nazi period; the Soviet Union; mid-century Japan; communist China; the British colonization of Kenya; Cambodia; Baathist Iraq; and North Korea. Other regimes, also some-times using camps, undertake frequent eliminationist and extermina-tionist assaults or campaigns, often repeatedly using the same cadres of killers, who may be special army units. Such regimes existed in

Uganda, Chile, Argentina, Guatemala, Vietnam, and Iraq. Systemic mass murder and elimination occur when political leaders decide to achieve their goals, or deal with opposition or unwanted people, with lethal violence or policies that, whatever the reasons for their design, the leaders know will end in mass death. Even though political leaders' attacks against some discrete groups are sometimes focused, as were the Khmer Rouge's killing of the Cham and the Germans' murderous assault against the Polish elite in 1940, mass murder and elimination become these leaders' normal political practice as they impose their rule on highly resistant populations or ones not conforming to the leaders' transformative visions. It is those leaders seeking to alter their societies in some revolutionary ideology's image who construct vast camp systems, as both sustainable and flexible tools for sequestering and dominating or, over time, killing vast numbers of people.

Some perpetrators' eliminationist campaigns, both focused and iterative, are related to the assaults others perpetrate upon them and other people. Poles, Czechs, and others' expulsions and killings of ethnic Germans after World War II immediately followed the Germans' annihilationist onslaughts in Central and Eastern Europe, though their occupation of Czech lands had been, by the Germans' standards, relatively tame. Croats and Serbs have iteratively slaughtered one another, during World War II and then fifty years later during Yugoslavia's breakup. The Hutu and Tutsi in Burundi and Rwanda have iteratively slaughtered one another and caused hundreds of thousands to flee in seven major exterminationist episodes since the countries gained independence from Belgium in 1962. In these places, a clear dynamic of reciprocity has set in, where mass elimination has become each group's principal tool for neutralizing real and perceived enemies.

Mass murder and elimination's spatial and temporal aspects tend to be intertwined. Focused mass murderers mainly kill their victims around where they find them, whether in the victims' homes, outdoors, or at some nearby designated killing site. When the perpetrators of focused mass slaughters and expulsions remove people from their locales, they often use death marches. Iterative mass murders mimic focused ones spatially. Systemic mass murders and eliminations have longer time horizons and institutional structures that include enduring, fixed installations, so their perpetrators regularly remove the victims from their home environs, especially to camps, even if they also may conduct, as the Germans in particular did, local killing operations.

The Sympathies of Others and the Problem of Resistance

Many people, aside from the perpetrators and victims, know of the ongoing assaults and (unlike the generally helpless victims) have some capacity to influence them. These bystanders may be physically present watching the killings, living in the perpetrators' countries or areas of occupation, or powerful actors, such as presidents and prime ministers, in countries outside the eliminationist zones. In overt or subtle ways, they either help or hinder the perpetrators. The failure of families, friends, and countrymen to disapprove of, or to hinder eliminationist acts, can help the perpetrators, especially when it strengthens their resolve to kill. The moral status of such acts of omission, important to investigate, is a long discussion that I have taken up in A Moral Reckoning.

Similar to perpetrators, bystanders are positioned differently vis-à-vis mass killing and elimination. Some work in state or military institutions, even in eliminationist institutions, without being involved in the eliminationist program. Others, the ones most frequently referred to as bystanders, stand by while the perpetrators drag entire families, often neighbors, from their houses, watch as they shoot or stab their victims or as death marches limp through their towns, or dwell near the camps where victims live in misery and die. Most frequently, these bystanders—sharing the critical identity (national, ethnic, religious, etc.) with the perpetrators—know that the perpetrators believe themselves to be acting in the bystanders' name and for their good. Such bystanders have existed in virtually every mass murder and elimination. Turks, Germans, Indians and Pakistanis, British settlers in Kenya, Hutu, Serbs, and many other peoples have literally and figuratively watched their countrymen butcher or otherwise eliminate their neighbors. Some bystanders, such as the peoples of occupied countries or of nonperpetrator groups, do not share the perpetrators' critical identity. They are under the occupier's boot, subject to violence, and, as a group, might be potential victims. Such bystanders include Poles and others under German occupation, repressed minorities in the Soviet Union, and people in any occupied country or disputed territory where a large but not comprehensive mass murder is being perpetrated. Finally, bystanders exist outside the mass murder or elimination's geographic realm. The most important are state leaders and officials, and sometimes those of transnational organizations, such as the Catholic Church, the Red Cross, or corporations. How they can influence a mass annihilation or elimination is taken up in later chapters.

Domestic bystanders can have a direct or indirect influence on mass murder. In many countries, bystanders help perpetrators by identifying victims or locating where they are hiding. In doing so, they transform themselves into perpetrators. Many other bystanders succor the perpetrators with expressions of approval or encouragement, or solidaristic hatred, or with tangible aid of food, shelter, and goods. Just by not conveying disapproval in overt or subtle ways, bystanders reassure perpetrators that they do not stand alone.

When bystanders disapprove of an eliminationist assault, they can save people's lives. It is nonsense to maintain that it is impossible to aid people targeted for extermination—a notion that so many writers about Nazism and the Holocaust have put forward that exculpates Germans, the peoples of occupied countries, and religious institutions, especially the Catholic Church. Looking to guerrilla insurgencies, we know that if a country's people do not support its government, the insurgents will receive food, shelter, aid, and intelligence. This was true for Polish partisans in Poland, Soviet partisans in the Soviet Union, the French underground in France, to name just a few, during World War II. Similar aid could be given, and sometimes is, to the people targeted in eliminationist assaults. When it is not, it tells us a great deal about a populace's attitude toward the mass killing and elimination. When people give aid, many lives can be preserved. The Danish people saved virtually all the Jews among them, including many non-Danes, by ferrying them to noncombatant Sweden. Although the Bulgarian government handed over Jews from territories it occupied in Greece and Yugoslavia to the Germans who slaughtered them, under much pressure from the Bulgarian public, parliamentarians, and most significant, the Bulgarian Orthodox Church's leadership, it refused to allow the Germans to deport and murder Bulgaria's own Jews. If a large percentage of Germans or Hutu or Serbs had believed the annihilation of Jews, Tutsi, or

Muslims, respectively, to be one of our age's great horrors, then their countrymen certainly would have killed many fewer Jews, Tutsi, or Muslims, perhaps not even a substantial number at all. More locally, the French of Le Chambon-sur-Lignon saved between three thousand and five thousand Jews, even though Germans were all around their region and often in their town. Across Europe, including in many Catholic institutions, individual dissenters saved Jews, totaling in the thousands. In Rwanda, individual Hutu who dissented from the common anti-Tutsi creed managed to save many Tutsi, and Hutu Muslims frequently showed solidarity for and aided their Tutsi coreligionists. Even if the circumstances, institutional infrastructure, and resources inhibit large-scale rescues, disapproving bystanders *can still save many lives,* one by one, or a handful here and a handful there.

Mao Zedong's famous dictum provides an essential question: Who are the fish in the sea of bystanders—the perpetrators or the victims? When it is the perpetrators, which has been the rule, then the victims have nowhere to run or hide. Bystander hostility to victims is ultimately a significant factor contributing directly and contextually to an enormous number of deaths. The bystander problem, as it is typically discussed, is: Why do people stand by idly in the face of horrors? But as we see, this renders the issue falsely by concealing more than a figurative half of the problem, which is the various kinds of support that bystanders freely give to the perpetrators.

Bystanders' support for mass exterminations and eliminations is critical for another important reason: The perpetrators are rarely confronted with widespread, let alone successful, resistance because without bystander support the victims have no reasonable prospect of preventing the executioners from killing or eliminating them. This would hardly be worth mentioning, except that the blame-the-victim cliché has been intoned incessantly when discussing the Jews' conduct—"like sheep to slaughter"—during the Holocaust. For people to resist eliminationist assaults, they must have some possibility of success. Under hopeless conditions, usually only small-scale, symbolic resistance is possible. Rational calculation and people's psychological propensities suppress the urge to fight. The targeted groups understand that resistance guarantees death, and as long as people hold out hope of survival, they are unlikely to fight. This is especially so as men (who generally lead resistance) have endangered families requiring their continuing presence. Not surprisingly, Jews in some ghettos and camps revolted when the annihilation's comprehensiveness had proceeded to a point of absolute hopelessness. These revolts produced, perhaps, symbolic victory but ended in catastrophic defeat.

Many factors must be present for resistance to be more than quixotic or symbolic. The victims must have weapons, organization, time to coordinate, military experience, leadership, and refuge (which requires sympathetic bystanders locally or across reachable international borders). Absent any of these factors, effective resistance is not possible. These factors are almost never all present, and they certainly were not for the Jews facing the Germans' military and annihilationist colossus. The Jews were dragooned by the military machine that had smashed Europe's armies. The Jews had few weapons, no military or paramilitary organization, little military expertise, no time whatsoever to organize themselves before being pulverized, and no refuge, because in many countries, especially in Eastern Europe, the local population generally hated them. Moreover, the Germans quickly starved the Jews of Eastern Europe into weakened and sickened states. The Jews in ghettos and camps were surrounded by overwhelming force, unable even to leave their prisons' confines.

The non-Jews forming major resistance movements against the Germans had enormously more favorable conditions: friendly populations, arms, military know-how and organization, help from the allies, etc., and they were not penned in camps, surrounded by machine guns. Even with such advantages, most, representing a tiny part of their country's populations, were unable to become operational until the Germans had already slaughtered most of the Jews they would kill. How could the Jews have done better? Millions of Soviet POWs, young military men with organization, and leadership, and initial vigor, died passively in German camps. If these men, whose families were not with them, could not muster themselves against the Germans, how could the Jews be expected to have done *more*?

Effective resistance to annihilationist and eliminationist onslaughts has been rare. The overwhelming majority of our age's victims have not raised a hand, armed or otherwise, in self-defense. In China, the Soviet Union, and Japanese-occupied Asia, in Turkey, Burundi, and

Bosnia, in South-West Africa, Cambodia, and Rwanda, in Indonesia, Iraq, and Sudan, and on and on, unendangered perpetrators have slaughtered, expelled, or incarcerated masses of impotent people. The Indonesians' sudden onslaught upon the communist victims so stunned them that they offered little resistance, and in some areas even went to their deaths in an orderly and expectant manner, as in Bali, where communists donned "white ceremonial burial robes and marched calmly with policemen or village officials to their places of execution."[36] A mass murderer in Java relates an episode that to him was emblematic of the victims' pliancy: "There was an instance, where a Communist was kneeling to have his head cut off. The executioner told him, 'Lift up your head a little, so I can cut better.' The man about to die immediately lifted his head to help his executioner."[37] And the Indonesian victims were members of a militant and highly organized political party! People targeted by annihilationist and eliminationist assaults usually have only the most circumscribed agency of choosing to die earlier, and in one way rather than another. Except for the lucky or extraordinary few individual victims, mass murders and eliminations are almost purely a perpetrator-run affair.

Victims have resisted when they are already armed, organized, and not so overwhelmingly outgunned. In Rwanda, as word spread of the Hutu's accelerating mass murdering, few Tutsi initially resisted. The Tutsi's already operational rebel army did launch an offensive campaign that eventually stopped the mass murder, defeating the Hutu and conquering the country. Sometimes targeted people can anticipate a coming attack and flee to safety. German Jews knew that the Germans, who had made them socially dead, were bent upon their violent elimination. In just six years, starting in 1933, almost two-thirds of them fled Germany even though gaining admittance to other countries was very difficult and they had to forfeit most of their wealth. Then the war began making escape impossible. Similarly, Denmark's Jews' stealing away to hospitable Sweden was an escape of the slaughter, though not by suicidal armed resistance. Other Jews managing to elude the Germans had the worse fortune of reaching "neutral" Switzerland, which often forced them to return to Germany, to death.

When an annihilationist campaign begins, particularly in developing countries where governments and armies have but tenuous control, many flee the murderers, producing a second eliminationist result and huge refugee problems. Causing such flight is often an integral part of the eliminationist plan. Short of the victims' leaving preemptively or having armed forces ready to meet the perpetrators on their killing fields, the denouement has already been scripted: Most of the targeted people die. Even in Rwanda, the Tutsi cavalry arrived 800,000 or more lives late.

Perpetrators employ a number of tactics to reduce resistance. They surprise or overwhelm the victims, leaving them no time to flee, let alone to organize effective resistance. The Germans, the Indonesians, the Hutu, the Guatemalans, the Baathists, the Serbs, and the Political Islamic Sudanese, among others, did this. Perpetrators also forestall effective resistance by terrorizing victims so they know that resistance portends catastrophic retribution. The Soviets, Chinese, Khmer Rouge, North Koreans, Baathists in Syria, and Baathists in Iraq, Germans, and others did this. Finally, there is the Khmer Rouge's strategy of such intensive supervision and terror that the victims fear communicating with one another even to the most minimal degree necessary for organizing resistance. The North Koreans, and to some extent the Soviets, appear also to have done this.

Mass murder and elimination are not like war. Their success rate is enormously higher than that of military campaigns. No army opposes the perpetrators as they descend on their victims and expel, kill, or imprison them in camps. Perpetrators' casualties are almost always tiny because the victims often do nothing more than occasionally raising an unarmed hand in self-defense as the machete comes down or as the trigger is pulled. Books about mass murders and endless pages of eyewitness testimonies—from perpetrators, victims, and bystanders—rarely report victims killing perpetrators. The perpetrators know that they face no immediate martial threat from their victims and can proceed virtually unimpeded. They know this even when they attack civilians who actually or putatively support rebels or the opposing side in a civil war. Eliminationist perpetrators often later claim they were acting defensively, yet in any conventional military sense of an imminent threat, the perpetrators know that there is none. In any conventional sense of what constitutes a palpable actual threat—as opposed to a threat the perpetrators, owing to their hatred, prejudices, or political ideology, may believe exists—such claims are transparently false. (The Germans while slaughtering *six million* Jews lost perhaps a few hundred men, most of whom died when Jews in camps and ghettos, seeing that the end was near, revolted.) The British at the time of their eliminationist campaign against the Kikuyu put forward this preposterous claim. They incarcerated approximately 1.5 million Kikuyu in a brutal camp system and killed tens of thousands (estimates range from 50,000 to 300,000), all, according to the British, in response to the putative acute threat and unsurpassable savagery of the Kikuyu liberation movement known as Mau Mau. How many whites did the bestial Mau Mau kill? Thirty-two. Such similarly transparently false claims by perpetrators that they face an imminent physical threat have been made by (or in defense of) Turks, Germans, Harry Truman, Indonesians, Tutsi in Burundi, and Hutu in Rwanda. They have been made on behalf of perpetrators across Latin America, in Chile, Argentina, Guatemala, and El Salvador, where the Right was fending off the Left. And on behalf of the Soviets and the Chinese, namely of communist regimes battling real and imaginary enemies who threatened the chimerical harmonious communist future.

Such false justifications continue to be put forward today in setting after setting by retrospective apologists, who act as guardians of national or group honor. They claim that the perpetrators had the mindset of those at war, or that they genuinely feared their victims as if the fear had been anything but an outgrowth of their prejudice, racism, and hatred. Yet nothing about mass slaughter and elimination, with the exception of pulling the trigger, is like military conflict or an actual emergency situation where the victims threaten the perpetrators or their countrymen's lives. This is self-evidently the case when, as they typically do, the perpetrators slaughter or brutally drive from their homes women and children. As Pancrace Hakizamungili, a Hutu mass murderer, explains, "In a war, you kill someone who fights you or promises you harm. In killings of this kind, you kill the Tutsi woman you used to listen to the radio with, or the kind lady who put medicinal plants on your wound, or your sister who was married to a Tutsi. . . . You slaughter the woman same as the man. That is the difference, which changes everything."[38] A wealth of evidence from perpetrators around the world, especially the Germans during the Nazi period, flatly falsifies the military comparison and the notion that their manifestly helpless victims ever posed a physical or military threat. Instead, the perpetrators know their mass slaughter and elimination are purposive political acts that irrevocably transform their societies and polities.

Transformative Politics, Transformative Results

Eliminationist assaults are strategic political acts embedded in larger political contexts, practices, and goals. Perpetrators therefore do things to their victims that, strictly speaking, go beyond their immediate tasks of annihilating, expelling, or incarcerating them, and their acts have political, social, economic, and cultural consequences beyond the already momentous facts that people lose their homes, families, and lives. What follows is a preparatory sketch about these themes that subsequent chapters elaborate upon.

Politically, the perpetrators with their eliminationist programs remove or at least severely weaken people who would contest their power. In Burundi, Tutsi slaughtered Hutu in a more targeted fashion, and in Rwanda, Hutu slaughtered Tutsi comprehensively, each to forestall a lessening of their power. Liisa Malkki quotes Burundian Hutu survivors describing the Tutsi's systematic decapitation of the Hutu by slaughtering their elite:

> They wanted to kill my clan because my clan was educated. The clans which were educated, cultivated, they were killed. In my clan there were school teachers, medical assistants, agronomists . . . some evangelists—not yet priests—and two who were in the army. . . . All have been exterminated. Among those [kin] who were educated, it is I alone who remain. . . . There are many persons who leave Burundi to-day because one kills every day. The pupils, the students . . . It is because these are intellectuals. . . . One killed *many* Hutu university people.
>
> The government workers . . . They were arrested when they were in their offices working. The others also in their places—for example, an agronomist, when he was walking in the fields where he works, he was arrested. There were medical technicians, professors. . . . Or the artisans

in the garage, or those who worked in printing houses or in the ateliers where furniture is made. They were killed there, on the spot.

Be you a student, this is a cause; be you a rich [person], that is a cause; be you a man who dares to say a valid word to the population, that is a cause. In short, it is a racial hate.[39]

The Indonesian government, with the army and nonmilitary anticommunists, removed its opponents from contesting political power by annihilating the critical mass of a popular communist party, putting many other communists in camps, and forcing still others to convert to either Islam or Christianity. The Pakistanis targeted the Bengalis' political, communal, and intellectual elite, most intensively when the Indians were about to defeat them, which is when they began during a three-day period to systematically slaughter the leadership of the soon-to-be rival country. In many Latin American countries, including Argentina and El Salvador, rightist tyrannies victimized people challenging power from the Left. In Chile the Right's mass murdering and removal of the Left started with its overthrow of a democratically elected Marxist government. In Germany the Nazis killed or incarcerated leading German communists and socialists to consolidate their power in 1933. And after conquering Poland, they slaughtered members of the Polish elite to reduce resistance to the Germans' occupation and transformative plans. Hans Frank, the German governor of Poland, in a planning meeting for the "extraordinary pacification" of Poland, reported that Hitler had told him that (these are Frank's words) "what we have now identified as the leadership elements in Poland is what is to be liquidated."[40] The Germans' assault on the Poles combined the qualities of a nineteenth-century imperial land grab with the purposeful murder of significant elements of the population and brutal suppression and exploitation of those left alive. Similarly in the Soviet Union, the Germans sought out and killed the communist elites. But the Germans did not kill Jews for reasons of power, because Germany's Jews did not contest power and had nothing that the Germans wanted. This is also true of other countries' Jews, who were no more dangerous to Germany than their countrymen. After consolidating their rule, the Soviets, the Chinese communists, and other communist regimes also faced no contestation of power, so it was not an actual factor in their mass eliminations. Removing political rivals or those who might foment resistance increases the perpetrators' security and power and, once eliminationist assaults are decided upon and begun, the perpetrators facilitate their eliminationist and political projects' further execution by initially killing the targeted people's elites. Targeting elites was also part of the eliminationist programs of the Turks, British in Kenya, Indonesians, Guatemalans, Serbs, Hutu, and many more.

Socially and economically, perpetrators expropriate targeted peoples sometimes of territory and always of homes, belongings, and social and economic positions (though individual perpetrators often do not personally benefit). While the victims' personal losses are almost always incidental to mass annihilations and eliminations' larger political goals, their territorial losses have often been integral to them. This was the case for the Germans in South-West Africa, for the Belgians in Congo, for the Turks' slaughter of the Armenians, for the Germans' push into Eastern Europe, where they sought *Lebensraum,* imperial living space, for the Poles' expulsion of ethnic Germans from Poland after World War II, for the British in Kenya, for the Chinese eliminationist campaign in Tibet, for the Serbs' onslaughts in Bosnia and Kosovo, and many others. But it was not the case for the Germans' slaughter of the Jews, Sinti, and Roma, the communists' decades-long slaughters in China proper, or the Khmer Rouge's mass murders. Serbs killed and expelled their Bosnian Muslim neighbors not only to Serbify the territory. Some also took the victims' homes, belongings, and places in the social and economic order. While the Khmer Rouge removed their victims from their homes and belongings, they, unlike the Serbs, had no designs upon such possessions.

Economically, the perpetrators can also exploit the victims' labor— even if they do so irrationally and, according to ordinary standards, unproductively. They put victims to work for prior ideological and expressive reasons, as the Germans did to the Jews or the Khmer Rouge did to Cambodians. They also do so as a practical and almost incidental accoutrement to the fundamental eliminationist enterprise itself.

Eliminationist perpetrators alter their societies' social composition and structure. Their societies' faces are irrevocably changed, and the social structures are mangled and shuffled. The obvious losers are the victims. The winners, those assuming improved places in the social array, are variable. Sometimes the perpetrators themselves gain new positions—victims' homes, valuables, and goods. But it is usually by-standers, or selected groups or individuals among them, who take over the victims' social positions.

Culturally, the perpetrators spread their dominance by annihilating completely or partially (and then suppressing) competing forms and practices. Eliminationist assaults almost always substantially homoge-nize a country, not only politically and socially but also in this way. The perpetrators often destroy and expel people precisely because they bear despised or rival cultural ideas and practices. This is particularly evident when religion is the impetus for one leadership and group to slaughter or eliminate another. Religious leaders' support of mass mur-derers and their eliminationist goals often shocks, though it should not. German Catholic and Protestant clergy supported, often tangibly, the Jews' elimination from German society, and some even justified, pro-moted, or tacitly supported the mass annihilation itself. The Slovakian Catholic Church was itself deeply complicit in the mass murder of the country's Jews, issuing an avowedly antisemitic pastoral letter to be read in every church explaining and justifying the Jews' deportation (to Auschwitz). Catholic bishops and priests supported the Croats' mur-derous onslaught against Jews and Orthodox Serbs during World War II. Orthodox leaders supported the Serbs' eliminationist assaults against Muslims during the 1990s, even opening their churches to the perpetrators for planning and organizing local eliminationist cam-paigns. The Orthodox Bishop Vasilije of Tuzla-Zvornik in Bosnia, an area of intensive killings and other brutalities, was one of Arkan's more impassioned supporters. Several Orthodox bishops from Croatia and Bosnia presided over Arkan's wedding in 1994, two years after he ini-tiated the eliminationist assaults in Bosnia. During the fully mytholo-gized event, celebrating Arkan's exploits symbolically, Arkan clothed himself as a Serbian hero and his bride was the Maiden of Kosovo, a Mary Magdalene figure.[41] In Turkey, Japan, Indonesia, and elsewhere, Islamic, Buddhist, Christian, and other religious leaders have sup-ported, blessed, and sometimes participated in mass murder and elim-inations. In Rwanda, many Catholic clergy tangibly assisted the mass murderers, lending themselves and their authority to organizational meetings, delivering Tutsi to the executioners, ferreting out hiding parishioners, and even participating in the actual killings. A Tutsi woman, a Catholic elementary school teacher, recalls:

> The priest, Nyandwe, came to my house. My husband [who is Hutu] was not there. Nyandwe asked my children, "Where is she?" They said that I was sick. He came into the house, entering even into my bedroom. He said, "come! I will hide you, because there is an attack." . . . He said "I'll take you to the CND [police]." He grabbed me by the arm and took me by force. He dragged me out into the street and we started to go by foot toward the church. But arriving on the path, I saw a huge crowd. There were many people, wearing banana leaves, carrying machetes. I broke free from him and ran. I went to hide in the home of a friend. He wanted to turn me over to the crowd that was preparing to attack the church. It was he who prevented people from leaving the church.[42]

Whether or not the perpetrators understand cultural homogenization to be an important goal, their eliminationist onslaughts increase it substantially. During World War II the Soviets deported and dispersed different national groups Stalin deemed disloyal and thereby, in addition to substantial human losses, destroyed the infrastructure—schools, newspapers, cultural institutions—necessary for maintaining a thriving ethnic culture. Sometimes an eliminationist onslaught is, or includes, a nonmurderous, transformative cultural (and social) initiative, such as when perpetrators compel victims to convert or renounce their religion, as the Khmer Rouge forced the Muslim Cham to do. The result is a transformed public cultural life, in which previously contested or plural cultural ideas or practices, including historical understandings, disappear, initiating the reign of a far more homogenized and diminished field of culture that is more to the perpetrators' liking.

The perpetrators know that destroying the victims' cultural institutions, objects, and artifacts further undermines them. Serbs purposely shelled the major cultural institutions in Bosnia's capital, Sarajevo, as they sought not only to eliminate Bosniaks from Bosnia but also to obliterate their communal and cultural existence's foundation. They first destroyed the Oriental Institute, burning the largest collection of Islamic and Jewish manuscripts in southeastern Europe, then the National

Museum, and finally the National Library, incinerating more than one million books, more than 100,000 manuscripts and rare books, and centuries of the country's historical records. For the artist Aida Mušanović, and certainly for other Sarajevans, seeing their principal cultural repository engulfed in flames and then having the smoke, ash, and wisps of burnt paper hovering over and raining down on their city, "was the most apocalyptic thing I'd ever seen."[43] Indonesians forced 2.5 million communists to adopt religion and thereby renounce godless communist atheism. Communists routinely destroyed or appropriated for other uses churches, temples, and other buildings belonging to different religions. The Germans destroyed or burned more than 250 synagogues in Germany alone on Kristallnacht, the proto-genocidal assault of November 9, 1938, and they destroyed many more across Europe, sometimes, as in Białystok's main synagogue, using them as figurative and ironic funeral pyres to burn hundreds or thousands of Jews alive. Serbs, as a self-conscious attempt to eradicate all vestiges of and the foundations for Muslim life in the hoped-for greater Serbia, systematically destroyed mosques and entire Bosniak and Kosovar villages, as the Germans before them had destroyed hundreds of Polish areas they wished to Germanify. Croats, in their own eliminationist assault on Serbs and Bosniaks, did the same to Orthodox churches and mosques. Perpetrators target not just the victim groups' religious buildings and symbols but also their religious leaders. Of the ten thousand Tibetans the Chinese slaughtered in suppressing a rebellion in the capital of Lhasa in 1959, they killed eight hundred Buddhist monks. A novice monk recalls, "The Chinese began closing down monasteries and arresting the high lamas and abbots. Those abbots who had opposed the Chinese were arrested, subjected to thamzing [a 'struggle session' that often included verbal condemnations and severe beatings] and sent to prison. Many died under torture, others committed suicide." The Chinese used the rebellion as a pretext to stamp out Tibetan Buddhism, destroying most of the country's monasteries by 1961, and killing, sending to labor camps, or compelling most of the monks to leave the few surviving monasteries.[44] In Cambodia, the Khmer Rouge methodically destroyed Buddhist temples and shrines, and slaughtered Buddhist monks, so that only *seventy* of 2,680 monks from eight monasteries were alive when the Khmer Rouge fell after only four years. Extrapolating to the rest of Cambodia, which the evidence suggests is warranted, fewer than two thousand of seventy thousand monks may have survived, a 97 percent extermination rate.[45] The Germans, having thought out and planned the Jews' total eradication with an unparalleled purposefulness, precision, and thoroughness, set about to save Jewish books, artifacts, and photographs so that when there were no Jews or Jewishness on the planet, they would have evidence of the putative demonic race that walked the earth until the Germans had extirpated it.

The perpetrators do butcher the political, social, economic, and cultural spheres of their society or of other countries, yet their most immediate objects of transformation are the individual bodies and psyches of their victims—of those left alive and even often, before striking the lethal blow, those they kill. As in Franz Kafka's penal colony, they seek to inscribe on their victims' bodies and souls their own conceptions of them as degraded, worthless, or hated, to be used, maimed, discarded at the perpetrators' pleasure. Some perpetrators kill their victims, doing little or nothing else to them, and when the perpetrators slaughter or expel their victims by the tens of thousands or hundreds of thousands many victims perish without suffering any additional personal act of cruelty or degradation. Yet those eliminating their real or putative enemies often seek to mark them before snuffing out their lives or banishing them from the land. As one Tibetan explains, "We were forced to see our orderly Buddhist universe collapse into chaos, both in mental and physical terms. The Chinese Communists, full of revolutionary zeal and utterly without any human sentiment, deliberately set out to prove to us that what we pathetically believed in was nothing more than a mirage."[46] The perpetrators make their victims hear their hatred. They taunt and mock them. They torture them in myriad ways. They physically mark and maim them. A specific torture, understood by the perpetrators but rarely by interpreters to be torture, and which needs separate analysis (see Chapter 9), is rape. Perpetrators use their victims as playthings, forcing them to perform painful, self-denigrating, and, for the perpetrators, amusing acts. They laugh at their victims' sufferings. They express their domination and vent their passions and aggression against them, all the while conveying the victims' powerlessness. The murderers and torturers physically and symbolically transcribe the new power and the new social and moral relationships on the victims' bodies and minds. Even though many, in some cases all, of the victims will perish, the perpetrators in varying degrees seek to express their power, have it understood, and thereby legitimize it to themselves as they announce that no political rules, law, or morality apply to the victims save their victimizers' matrix of suffering, degradation, and death.

Mass murders and eliminations ultimately are far-flung transformative political campaigns that—even if not always so conceived—leave a more thoroughgoing mark on societies and set more profound processes of change in motion than virtually any other kind of politics or individual program. For many societies afflicted by such politics, eliminationist and exterminationist programs are the *most* profound of any political program that takes place within their extended time period, rivaling or exceeding even the effects of major economic growth. In many instances, these transformative effects are part of a visionary goal of creating a new society, but even when not linked to calls to transformative arms, they radically transform the societies, often beyond recognition, albeit in a somewhat different manner, anyway.

CHAPTER FIVE

Why the Perpetrators Act

To understand what motivates mass murderers and eliminationists, we must keep in mind *all* the perpetrators do. Until recently, the rare analyses of mass murder that focus on the perpetrators' conduct addressed only the killing itself. Such blinders exclude much, perhaps most, of the perpetrators' conduct needing explanation, specifically the perpetrators' other eliminationist deeds, brutalities, and expressive acts. For instance, the perpetrators' treatment of children is not focused on, let alone appropriately highlighted, even though they immensely brutalize children and kill them, often most gruesomely. This failure, repeated for the perpetrators' other nonlethal acts, effectively excludes or greatly reduces such acts' enormous descriptive significance from the recounting of events, and their analytical centrality from the inquiry into the events' causes and meaning. Such omissions produce faulty depictions, conclusions, and explanations of the perpetrators' actions, and false understandings of the broader events—renderings that bear only a caricatured relationship to the actual horrors and their commission.

Perhaps even more surprising, until a dozen years ago the writings about mass murder paid little attention to the perpetrators and their actions. This oversight probably derived from various factors, the most important being the widespread reflexive assumption among interpreters and the general public that genocidal killers approve of their own deeds. There was no pressing reason to investigate something that seemed so obvious. Still, even since this theme became a topic of investigation, a systematic lack of engagement and therefore clarity about the killers' actions and motives remain. The perpetrators' willing participation

145

in Cambodia, the former Yugoslavia, Rwanda, Darfur, and elsewhere seems so obvious that in treatments of individual mass murders the question "*Why* did they do what they did?" has been mainly a nonissue. Yet in general treatments of genocide, one or another untested postulate that, strangely, often denies this willingness, is simply asserted. Thus critical questions are not explicitly asked: Do the perpetrators think their victims deserving or undeserving of their fate? This question may seem akin to asking whether Japanese soldiers in World War II wanted to win and believed killing American soldiers right, or whether the American soldiers fighting the Japanese similarly supported their cause. The question seems nonsensical, or certainly not worth dwelling upon. As a result, the relevant evidence is not systematically explored. The answers to this and other questions are therefore also not sharply etched.

To be sure, slaughtering unarmed men, women, and children might be met with more varied and complex attitudes than killing enemy soldiers in a war that is deemed just. And in some wars, many soldiers are uncertain about their cause's wisdom and justice. This was so for American soldiers in Vietnam, particularly in the war's latter stages, producing widespread insubordination, including soldiers killing officers so frequently that the term for it, *fragging*, entered the war's lexicon.

The questions about people's willingness to perpetrate violence are anything but nonsensical—for war, mass murder, and eliminations. When leaders give eliminationist orders, why do people implement them? In answering this question we must consider that the motivations of the eliminationist leaders and of their followers committing the brutalities and murders might not be the same. As with other political acts, leaders might not be candid about their motives and aspirations, being more interested in gaining their followers' compliance than ensuring their agreement. The perpetrators on the ground may have reasons to act that, while compatible with the leaders' goals, differ from what moves the leaders. Just as leaders have various reasons for initiating eliminationist programs, including mass murder, and just as virtually every aspect of such programs varies, it may be that, in different mass murders and eliminations, killers kill and eliminate their victims for different reasons, whatever commonalities or patterns also exist.

Why do the killers kill? Why do they slaughter children? Why do they treat their victims in *all* their dehumanizing and violent ways? Analogous questions about bystanders' actions and nonactions should be asked. Why do they do what they do?

Bringing clarity to this nexus of themes about perpetrators' willingness and motivation to kill (and about bystanders) requires that a series of related questions and possibilities be systematically addressed so that some notions can be excluded and others examined in greater depth. The most important and certainly the initial such question is: Does the perpetrator believe the victims deserve to die or, more broadly, to be eliminated? This question is critical and unavoidable, even if it is typically ignored and unmentioned. It is not possible for people *not* to have a view about whether it is right or wrong to slaughter or to drive from their homes and country thousands, tens of thousands, or millions of men, women, and children. A two-by-two matrix, with one dimension being a perpetrator's attitude to the annihilation (or elimination)—does he approve or not approve?—and the second dimension being his actions— does he kill or does he not kill?—specifies in each case the question that must be answered:

Person's Attitude Toward the Annihilation

		Approves	*Disapproves*
	Kills	QUESTION: How does he come to approve?	QUESTION: What induces/compels him to kill?
Person's Action	*Does Not Kill*	QUESTION: Why does he become a supporting bystander?	QUESTION: How does he avoid killing?

If the answer is *yes*, that the perpetrator believes the victims deserve to die, that the eliminationist program, including its lethal component, is right and just, then the next question is: How does he come to believe this? If the answer is *no*, namely that the perpetrator thinks that killing or eliminating the victims is morally wrong, then other questions must be asked to ascertain why he kills or contributes to the elimination program's goals. Does he believe the victims are dangerous, guilty of severe transgressions, unfit to exist within the perpetrators' society, or for whatever reason deserving of elimination, but disapproves of the punishment of death or of other violent eliminationist measures? If this is so, does he disapprove because he deems the punishment too harsh—in other words, unjust because it is disproportionate—or because he considers the punishment itself inherently immoral? If the perpetrator is disapproving for whatever reason, then he is being induced to act against his will. How is this done?

Put differently, do the perpetrators think they are doing their people a great, historic service, or do they think they are morally transgressing and committing a great crime? If the latter, then how, emotionally and psychologically, do they persist?

To answer the questions relevant to understanding why the perpetrators act as they do, we must first establish why the killers kill and why the expellers expel.

Why Do the Killers Kill?

Two fundamentally opposed positions hold that a perpetrator kills because he approves of the act, or that he kills despite his disapproval or lack of approval. Various postulates have been put forward to explain how people are brought to kill even though, as is sometimes claimed, all, or most, of them think the killing to be wrong and criminal or at least do not believe it to be right.

Perhaps the most prevalent notion explicitly or implicitly governing discussions of mass murder is that the perpetrators are coerced. This explanation is put forward, like a mantra, by those wishing to absolve Germans of the Holocaust, not least of all by many Germans themselves, those alive during the Nazi period and those who later came of age. Coercion is also asserted or insinuated by other eliminationist assaults' perpetrators and their apologists (when not denying the events themselves). It is understandable that defeated or deposed perpetrators reflexively try to escape culpability and to that end seek to elicit pity by claiming they were terrorized and coerced into doing terrible things, or without making explicit such claims, focus attention on the mass murdering regime's real or alleged brutality and tyranny. Even independent of such claims' rhetorical power, many people reflexively conclude that many perpetrators must have been forced to kill because, after all, they were serving brutal dictatorships. Moreover, there is a reinforcing tendency to equate power with agency and, therefore, to wrongly deny agency and responsibility to the less powerful followers.

The claim of coercion has been most stridently pressed and most thoroughly, indeed exhaustively, investigated for the German perpetrators. It has been *proven* to be a fiction. It was concocted and eagerly accepted by those wishing to absolve Germans of criminal culpability. During the Holocaust, no German perpetrator was ever killed, sent to a concentration camp, imprisoned, or punished in any serious way for refusing to kill Jews. Many knew they did not have to kill, because their commanders explicitly told them so. Some men accepted their commander's offer and removed themselves from the task of killing. Nothing happened to them; they were given other duties. And their mass-murdering comrades knew this. We know of these *facts* principally because the perpetrators themselves have testified they did not have to kill and because the Federal Republic of Germany's legal authorities have investigated every claim that someone was killed or severely punished for refusing to kill and have demonstrably proven them false.[1] The German mass murderers were not coerced, and of the many who were explicitly offered a way not to kill, almost every one *chose*—that's right, *chose*—to exterminate Jews, including Jewish children. Knowing this suggests that we should think about the issue more generally. When we do, it becomes clear why leaders do not use coercion to get their followers to slaughter others.

All political regimes, all leaders, rely on followers to uphold their existence and rule, and to implement their policies. When a regime's existence depends upon the regular use or manifest threat of violence to suppress substantial parts of populaces at home or abroad, its followers must apply the violence and make the threat credible. If the regime's followers stop supporting a regime that depends upon violence to sustain itself, then the regime itself will not survive. Few regimes and leaders want to risk turning their followers against them. Few regimes have such a hold on society that they would chance alienating their core followers, and alienating them in the most thoroughgoing way, by forcing them to slaughter people they think—if they did actually think it—are innocent or undeserving of their fate. Simply put, except possibly in the rare instances of an utterly terrorized society—and this has not been so in virtually every mass extermination and elimination, including those by the Turks, Indonesians, Pakistanis, Guatemalans, Serbs, Hutu, Sudanese, and even the overwhelming majority of Germans during the Nazi period—it is extraordinarily difficult, verging on impossible, for a regime to terrorize all perpetrators and potential perpetrators. (This is especially so because intensifying terror and totalitarian control to this enormous degree makes productive economic and social life, which depends upon people's generally willing compliance, all but impossible, endangering the regime and its leaders, as well as crippling their capacity to carry out other projects.) Coercing the regime's most loyal followers into committing mass murder is morally and psychologically akin to attacking them—leaving no one to defend the regime and its leaders. And if the leaders' followers themselves do not want to slaughter the intended victims, who would coerce them anyway? Few political leaders would dare, or are in a position, to risk in this way losing the people on whom their power, lives, and goals depend.

The evidence is that, except possibly in a few mass annihilations and eliminations, leaders do not coerce their followers. In mass murder's vast annals, there is little credible evidence of such coercion, and certainly not on a widespread basis. Sometimes a regime's killers coerce local civilians to aid them in killing. The Indonesian perpetrators who slaughtered communists did this in some towns. The Guatemalan mass murderers of Maya did this in some villages. In Rwanda, where popular participation in the mass murder was so enormously widespread, some Hutu were compelled to participate along with the hundreds of thousands who killed willingly. Mectilde Kantarama, a Tutsi survivor, explains: "Ten percent helped; 30 percent were forced to kill; 20 percent killed reluctantly; 40 percent killed enthusiastically."[2] In speaking about the 20 percent who killed "reluctantly," she does not mean they opposed the killing (otherwise, she would have added them with the 30 percent she estimates were "forced to kill"), but merely that they were less enthusiastic than the enthusiastic killers, of which there were so many and whose enthusiasm was so stunningly effervescent that run-of-the-mill willing executioners looked temperate by comparison. By her count, which is but one person's estimate, 60 percent of the enormous number of ordinary Hutu who slaughtered Tutsi did so willingly and 40 percent were "enthusiastic" killers of their neighbors. Such figures are especially amazing given the mass-murdering machete season's brutality and gruesomeness—which should be kept in mind when considering why the 30 percent might not have wanted to wade in blood (notice that Kantarama did not say they *opposed* the extermination). Ample witnesses and perpetrators alike confirm this mass social participation in and assent to the killing. It is no surprise that in these rare circumstances of virtually an entire society falling upon its ethnic minority in machete-wielding butchery—spearheaded by the zealous Hutu Interahamwe paramilitary—the majority dragged some along, forcing them to kill. Even so, the majority, perhaps the vast majority, did so willingly. And as the substantial, candid testimony of the Hutu killers in the commune of Nyamata indicates, except for the first few days when people had to participate, people were not forced to kill, and indeed, the whole atmosphere of killing was rather lax, with all kinds of opportunities for Hutu to adjust how and when, and whether they slaughtered their Tutsi neighbors.

As with this majority of Hutu, the Germans in South-West Africa, the Belgians in Congo, the Turks, the Germans during the Nazi period, the British in Kenya, the Indonesians, the Khmer Rouge, the Pakistanis, the Tutsi in Burundi, the Guatemalans, the Serbs, and the Sudanese, the general absence of coercion has been the rule of eliminationist assaults, and easy to explain: In mass murder after mass murder, leaders have easily found people wanting to kill the targeted victims. Coercion has been unnecessary. Therefore, when select individuals have not wanted to kill, the regime did not need to make them. More than enough people have been willing to do the job.

Authority is a second notion commonly invoked to account for how people who supposedly do not believe the victims deserve to die will nonetheless kill them. Authority is deemed so powerful, it might as well be hypnotizing. The contention is that when authority, particularly state authority, issues an order, it assumes an ineluctable quality of rightness and necessity. People who would otherwise disapprove of the act deem it a duty to perform it anyway. This notion, that state authority elicits its own obedience, is frequently invoked for the Germans killing Jews, and put forward also for other mass murderers, particularly the Hutu. It is an especially convenient trope for those seeking to exonerate the perpetrators.

This *crimes of obedience* postulate actually has two different, if sometimes overlapping, parts. The first is that state authority is seen with reverence and awe, and therefore individuals believe they are *duty bound* to carry out state orders even when they themselves believe the orders are wrong or immoral. The second is that state orders tend to be seen as inherently legitimate, so people find themselves *accepting their rightness* assuming, or with the reasoning, that the country's leaders would never issue fundamentally immoral or criminal orders. Although this argument's second version must be examined, it is not about how people can be brought to kill others they believe undeserving of death, but about how people might come to believe the killing is necessary and right (so it is discussed later). The *crimes of obedience* argument's first version, that state orders are thought to be sacrosanct and therefore lead people to act against their inner beliefs, to willingly commit deeds they believe criminal, is the relevant version here.

The notion is manifestly absurd. People disobey, evade, and ignore state and governmental orders, laws, and regulations all the time. They do so in democracies and in dictatorships, in society's loosely and heavily policed areas. They do so whether the issuing authority is a supposedly divinely ruling monarch, a popular democratic president, a supposedly charismatic leader, or an all-powerful totalitarian ruler. People the world over (not just proverbially in Italy) evade taxes. In all human societies crime of all kinds exists. Policemen in all types of societies fail to enforce certain laws they dislike or think unwise, and they themselves often break the law. Even soldiers, from generals to privates, often disobey or turn on their leaders. The czar's soldiers during the 1917 Russian Revolution would not fire on the revolutionaries. In 1986 Filipino soldiers disobeyed orders to suppress those challenging Ferdinand Marcos' rule. In the Lebanon war of 2006, Israeli soldiers refused orders to advance. American draft dodgers refused to serve in Vietnam, and many American soldiers were insubordinate in Vietnam during the war. Desertion, often on a massive scale, has beset armies throughout history and during our time. But such insubordination and desertion has not been a problem for the legions of perpetrators carrying out eliminationist projects.

Such enormously widespread and varied disobeying, evading, and ignoring of state authority, institutions, and laws and policies disproves the notion that people deem state authority sacrosanct. What's more, virtually every country's people have seen even greater challenges to state authority: rebellions, coup d'états, and revolutions. Germany, home to the people imputed to be slavish executors of state orders par excellence, has had many. The Nazis themselves fought in the streets to overthrow the existing state authority of Weimar. During the Nazi period, Germans disobeyed the state on all manner of matters and the perpetrators themselves often disobeyed and did not implement orders they disliked.[3] It has been no less true around the world, and particularly in countries where governments have initiated mass slaughters and eliminations. In many of those countries—Turkey, Germany, the Soviet Union, China, Indonesia, Uganda, Iraq, Chile, Argentina, Guatemala, Rwanda, Sudan, and many more—the mass-murdering regimes themselves came to power by rebelling and overthrowing the *previously lawful state authority*. Often soldiers, actually generals, the people deemed to be the most reflexively order-following, are the revolutionaries. More generally, most of these countries' peoples had nothing like the culture of hallowed obedience to the state allegedly once characterizing certain stable European monarchies grounding their right to rule in God. Many countries where mass murders and eliminations occur are characterized by widespread, endemic violence; state authority and legitimacy are enormously weak; and the alleged blind reverence for and obedience to the state has simply never existed or even been said to exist, as it has been in the mainly fictitious intellectualized form that was asserted to exist in Prussia and which then somehow instantaneously spread throughout Germany when Germany was formed in 1871 and then throughout Austria when Germany annexed it in 1938.

Authority, including governmental authority, orders, and policies, is contested all the time, at all levels, by societies as a whole, groups within societies, including insurgent groups, and individuals—those who would overthrow the authority or who disagree with specific policies. This notion of blind obedience to authority seemed to have some applicability only when supported by clichés about Germans and the virtually racist, dehumanizing accounts of their putative inability to make moral judgments for themselves that cast them as barely human robots. Despite its obvious flaws, this notion gained further credence when it was undergirded by Stanley Milgram's pseudoscientific social psychological experiments at Yale University in the 1960s, which purported to show that in response to an authority figure's exhortation, human beings will do almost anything. Milgram, to lend credence to his otherwise invalid conclusion, invoked the one seemingly propitious case, that of the putatively robotic Germans and the Holocaust, and asserted that he had the key to it. Had Milgram instead written about paying taxes or voluntary corporate compliance with governmental laws and regulations, let alone crime in general, his notion that people just do what the government says only because of the magical power of its authority would have been treated as a put-on.

As we coolly examine the vast historical record and move beyond the mythical world of clichés, unsupported assertions, and badly understood pseudoscientific laboratory experiments, the evidence actually demonstrates government authority's *weak* power to get people to comply only and merely because the government says something should be done. The postulate's sheer implausibility that people will feel duty bound, namely an absolute moral necessity, to kill their neighbors, to slaughter children, just because a government says to, is in itself stunning. It is difficult to understand—aside from people's political and personal interests in exonerating the perpetrators and rehabilitating Germany—how such a notion about the perpetrators could have ever gained such great currency.[4]

Another commonly adduced postulate to account for why the perpetrators kill is that social psychological pressure moves people to slaughter others. This notion has many variants, though their essence is that particular social circumstances are *in themselves* sufficiently powerful to propel people to kill. This argument is no more sensible than the one about government authority. To begin with, the general social psychological context for the perpetrators varies enormously from one mass murder to the next and even varies greatly for the perpetrators of a given mass murder working in different killing institutions and settings. No *general* argument about social psychological pressure's potency to turn all people into killers even makes sense, because whatever the *specific* social psychological facts a given postulate presumes, these "facts" have not been present for enormous numbers of perpetrators or in many mass murders.

The typical form this social psychological assertion takes is that peer pressure compels people to kill others. Subjected to other people's words, the prospect of their disapproval, or the example of their actions, people's conduct, it is said, inevitably falls into line. Yet in one mass murder after another, no *actual evidence* exists that this has occurred. And no evidence whatsoever exists to show it is a widespread phenomenon. Additionally, this postulate suffers a disqualifying flaw, which its proponents do not address. Even if it correctly describes certain perpetrators' actions, it cannot explain why the *majority* of perpetrators kill. This postulate relies on an *assumption* that makes impossible what its proponents claim to explain: It assumes that most perpetrators actually want to kill, because for there to be such social psychological pressure, the majority, probably the overwhelming majority, must favor the deed. This willing majority supposedly pressures the unwilling minority. Therefore, the social psychological postulate, by definition, cannot apply to *most* of the killers, who according to the postulate already want to kill. If, however, the majority, not to mention the overwhelming majority, does not want to kill, then there would be no peer pressure to kill but precisely the opposite: a common resolve not to kill.

As a *general* explanation, peer pressure implodes on itself. It cannot possibly explain why the perpetrators in general kill their victims. At most it might provide clues about the conduct of disapproving individuals finding themselves surrounded by willing killers who furthermore create intolerance against dissenters. But even so, the postulate is useless in explaining the existence and character of the majority's initial approval and willingness—which is the fundamental fact that must be explained and on which the postulate's existence depends.

Thus, in the best known instance of a peer-pressure argument, the author strained to get out of this problem by advancing a convoluted variation on the theme. Even though precious few of these German mass murderers in the single unit he studied wanted to kill, each one felt obliged not to excuse himself from the killing. Why? Because it was more important for virtually every one of them not to leave the dirty work to his comrades. So virtually every one of them preferred to slaughter men, women, and children whom he believed to be wholly undeserving of dying and thereby to make himself into a mass *murderer*, and to commit the gravest crime, moral transgression, and sin against God (many of them were practicing Christians) rather than to let others dirty their hands. These were the Germans of Police Battalion 101 who murdered tens of thousands of Jews over the course of months, and who had been told by their solicitous and beloved commander, Major Wilhelm "Papa" Trapp, that they did not have to kill.

Aside from this convoluted claim's sheer implausibility, the author, to even advance it, had to ignore or downplay much evidence of the perpetrators' willingness, including that these supposedly reluctant men, unbidden by their superiors, repeatedly brutalized and tortured their victims, so much so that their commander reprimanded them for their rampant cruelty! How, furthermore, could these men persist psychologically in slaughtering so many people, often shooting them at point-blank range, if they had really thought it a crime, murder, and (for the religious among them) a sin, even a mortal sin? But let us imagine against the evidence that this sort of peer pressure—for every man to choose to do what none of them wants to choose to do—had somehow operated on this unit's men merely because, according to this author, they came from the same metropolis of Hamburg, which, despite its being a big, anonymous city, somehow made them feel such overwhelming duty to one another. It still would be all but irrelevant to explaining the perpetrators' conduct. Why? Because this alleged critical fact of a common city or town of origin (which magically produces adamantine solidarity among killers) did not exist for most killers in most killing institutions during the Nazi period, in which strangers from all regions of Germany (including Austria) were often thrown together to kill. It also did not exist for most, probably the overwhelming majority, of our age's mass murders. So, aside from all the other reasons that this peer-pressure postulate is hollow even for the *single unit* for which it was advanced—and not just one unit but one idiosyncratic unit among the German killing institutions and among killing institutions and perpetrators in general—the postulate would in any event have no general relevance for explaining perpetrators' conduct. Even the existence of the underlying fact that makes this argument possible, namely the supposedly psychologically overwhelming solidarity, is highly dubious. In big cities, such as Hamburg, the sense of identity and communal solidarity with strangers is notoriously weak, and in this particular unit many men were relative newcomers, so when they began mass murdering there had been virtually no time to develop strong bonds. Moreover, the extensive records about these men and their deeds contains very little real evidence that such group solidarity existed. Aside from these many disqualifying features that this sort, or any sort, of peer pressure moved these men to slaughter Jewish men, women, and children, not a single man among the more than two hundred in this unit who testified about their mass murdering ever said this sort of peer pressure existed, let alone ever pointed to such pressure to explain why he or his comrades killed.[5]

One of the best-known postulates for why individuals participate in mass murder is the putative bureaucratic mindset. This claim was put forward by Hannah Arendt, who used the phrase "the banality of evil" to characterize Adolf Eichmann and has been picked up by theorists of modernity, exculpators of Germans, and by many who know little of what actually happened during the Holocaust or in mass annihilations more generally. The argument boils down to an *anyone will do it* postulate. It's simple: In the modern world, bureaucracies create a performance-for-performance's-sake mindset, so bureaucrats do what bureaucrats do, a job well done, regardless of the attitude toward the task itself that he might otherwise have. This is different from the obedience-to-authority postulate, which holds that government authority either convinces people that a task is good and necessary or that they have a higher duty to obey government authority than their consciences. The bureaucratic postulate treats the individual as having turned off his conscience and being incapable of exercising judgment in the first place.

The problems with this explanation of Eichmann in particular, who (amazingly) was Arendt's single example justifying her claim, and of the perpetrators in general, are legion and disqualifying. The *real* Eichmann was an intense, proud antisemite. He explicitly described himself as internally motivated by the rightness of his deed, which is what produced his fanaticism:

And so the Jews are actually right. To tell the truth, I was working relentlessly to kindle the fire wherever I thought there was a sign of resistance. Had I been just a recipient of orders, then I would have been a simpleton. I was thinking matters over. I was an idealist. When I reached the conclusion that it was necessary to do to the Jews what we did, I worked with the fanaticism a man can expect from himself. No doubt they considered me the right man in the right place. . . . I always acted 100 per cent, and in the giving of orders I certainly was not lukewarm.

Even more, Eichmann boasted of *his* mass murdering of the Jews. A few months before the war's end he told his deputy: "I [shall] laugh when I jump into the grave, because of the feeling that I have killed five million Jews. That gives me a lot of satisfaction and pleasure."[6] Are these the words of a bureaucrat mindlessly, unreflectively doing his job about which he has no particular view?

Those who worked for Eichmann were also antisemitic true believers in the need to annihilate Jews. Alois Brunner, a "functionary" who was one of Eichmann's chief assistants and oversaw deporting Jews from many countries and regions, wrote in 1943 to a "comrade" a revealing letter from Saloniki, Greece, from where he was soon to deport the area's Jews to Auschwitz:

The weather is growing more and more beautiful and our work proceeds fabulously. On February 25 the yellow stars [the identifying mark the Germans forced Jews to wear visibly on their clothes] began to sparkle here. And the Greek population is so happy with the marking of the Jews and their ghettoization that I said to myself that it is a crime that the appropriate measures had not been taken before. The inflation and the black market would have never assumed its proportions if one had properly watched the Jews. At present, there is no store without a plaque saying "Jewish store" affixed to its exterior. And when we begin to get going with them [deporting the Jews to Auschwitz], Greeks will break out in jubilation.

Hans Safrian, who has studied Brunner and others working with Eichmann, comments: "One cannot speak here of 'misguided fulfillment of duty' and 'bureaucratic corpse-like obedience'—with unmistakable satisfaction and joy Brunner reports about the 'sparkle of the yellow star' and his 'fabulous' 'work.'" Safrian adds that Brunner's letter conveys "an impression of the customary daily tones of the men around Eichmann."[7] If Arendt had presented these and many other facts about Eichmann, which she pointedly did not (Eichmann's boast about laughing while going to his grave knowing he had killed five million Jews appeared in one of *Time* magazine's most famous interviews ever!), then her startling claim would have never seemed even superficially plausible, and this vast, empirically empty edifice of thought about the bureaucracy of killing or bureaucratic killing would have been bereft of its foundation of this solitary example of Eichmann. Arendt's false rendering of Eichmann's greatest irony is that Eichmann, by his own proud account, is the exemplar of the opposite of the thoughtless bureaucratic implementer of any orders. Motivated by his ideals, he was a thinking, self-reflective, dedicated, and fanatical executioner of Jews.

More generally, this bureaucratic view relies on the notion that modern bureaucracy, particularly under so-called totalitarian systems, can blunt people's moral faculties so much that they can be brought to kill. Another version of this bureaucratic view holds that modern bureaucracy so splits up a task that no one believes himself responsible, and therefore that a disapproving person can contentedly make his contribution to it. For mass murder's perpetrators this view is patently absurd. To attain even superficial plausibility, it mischaracterizes and misdescribes the killers, redefining them into something they manifestly are not. Perpetrators of mass murder, particularly at the point of attack, are not bureaucrats. They do not work in bureaucracies. The task they undertake is not split up among many people. Their deeds' real character is not opaque to them. Mass murder's perpetrators know precisely what they do. They slaughter people, slaughter children, often face-to-face, by shooting them at point-blank range, or by hacking or beating them to death, bespattering themselves with their victims' blood, bone, and brain matter. It is wrong for us to pretend that such a perpetrator's position vis-à-vis his deed is akin to a bureaucrat in Ohio, Bavaria, or Lancashire implementing a tax measure from Washington, Berlin, or London he might not fully understand or like. Here are a few examples:

A German businessman in Nanjing relates one after another "hair-raising" personalized Japanese brutality he witnessed or eyewitnesses reported to him: Japanese soldiers, after dispossessing about fifty former Chinese soldiers whom they tricked into stepping forward from a crowd, they "tied [them] up together in groups of five. Then the Japanese built a large bonfire in the courtyard, led the groups out one by one, bayoneted the men and tossed them still alive on the fire."[8] A Bosnian woman, like so many others forced to witness Serbs killing family members, in her case her grandfather, describes what was a fairly typical face-to-face manner of the Serbs' slaughtering: "They cut off his ears, then his throat. They threw him behind the house."[9] A Rwandan Tutsi describes the final mass murderous assault upon him and many other Tutsi holed up in a church, surrounded for eight days by their soon-to-be murderers. It exemplified the Hutu's killing mode and personal intimacy: "At about 11:00 a.m., soldiers and interahamwe, including some women came. Somebody threw something at the door and then there was this cloud which made us cough and choke. Your eyes burned as if on pepper. Then the attackers entered. With nothing to fight with, some young men broke off pieces of the seats and threw them at the attackers. Soldiers shot these young men dead. There was a huge mob of interahamwe, including many of our neighbours. They came in and began to machete. They macheted, macheted and macheted."[10]

Such instances of personal, face-to-face killing and torturing, where the perpetrators (it should go without saying) knew exactly what they were doing, could be multiplied a thousand-, a millionfold, and presented from virtually every mass extermination and elimination of our time. The official Guatemalan historical commission explains that in Guatemala,

> the counterinsurgency strategy not only led to violations of basic human rights [of Maya], but also to the fact that these crimes were committed with particular cruelty, with massacres representing their archetypal form. In the majority of massacres there is evidence of multiple acts of savagery, which preceded, accompanied or occurred after the deaths of the victims. Acts such as the killing of defenseless children, often by beating them against walls or throwing them alive into pits where the corpses of adults were later thrown; the amputation of limbs; the impaling of victims; the killing of persons by cov-

Heaps of dead Chinese in Nanjing

ering them in petrol and burning them alive; the extraction, in the presence of others, of the viscera of victims who were still alive; the confinement of people who had been mortally tortured, in agony for days; the opening of the wombs of pregnant women, and other similarly atrocious acts, were not only actions of extreme cruelty against the victims, but also morally degraded the perpetrators and those who inspired, ordered or tolerated these actions.[11]

Personalized, conscious, and willful killing and brutality has been the norm in the vast majority of mass murders. This includes the Holocaust, for which the bureaucratic postulate (and the other faulty ones analyzed here) was invented. One German perpetrator relates a scene from a search-and-destroy mission to kill hidden Jews: "Today I still remember exactly that we were already right before the bunker when a five-year-old boy came out crawling. He was immediately grabbed by a policeman and led aside. This policeman then set the pistol to his neck and shot him. He was an active policeman who when with us was employed as a medical orderly."[12]

Describing these and our age's mass murderers as bureaucrats is akin to discussing soldiers in a firefight or hand-to-hand combat as if they are sitting safely at home requisitioning equipment. But this is precisely what the bureaucratic postulate's proponents do.* The bureaucratic postulate's second component, that killers have no view as to whether their deeds, including slaughtering children, are right or wrong is not only psychologically implausible but also without empirical foundation, as not even the perpetrators themselves say this.

The problems with the bureaucratic postulate are still more extensive. It is erroneous even for actual bureaucracies. It is based on an account of bureaucrats and bureaucracies that an extensive body of empirical social science has demonstrated to be wrong, and that virtually anyone ever working in a large institution, public or private, knows to be wrong. Bureaucrats and administrators are hardly empty, passive vessels. They often have well-formed views about what is desirable and feasible. They spend their professional lives immersed in areas about which they are especially competent and inevitably form views, often deeply considered and passionate ones. Thus armed, bureaucrats—and this includes members of police forces—often take initiative to formulate policy and to implement it in their own manner—often partially, ineffectually, late, or not at all.[13] Police in all countries frequently fail to effectively enforce laws with which they disagree, or to observe the legal constraints placed on them. Police corruption and criminality is widespread, if highly variable, everywhere and is so acute in some countries that people fear calling on them. Yet the bureaucratic postulate declares that the "bureaucrats" perpetrating mass murder are, alone among those working for state and governmental institutions, incapable of judging the rightness of policies, incapable of taking initiative, incapable of wanting to or actually disobeying orders.

---

*How distancing perpetrators from the effects of their killings might make them more willing to slaughter others, which may have occurred with the firebombing, carpet bombing, and nuclear bombing during World War II, is a different matter. But in the overwhelming majority of eliminationist assaults in our time and before, face-to-face has been mass elimination and slaughter's dominant mode. Had the United States, for example, established the beachhead in Japan hypothesized in this book's opening, Truman likely would not have ordered American officers and soldiers to systematically execute tens of thousands of Japanese men, women, and children or, had he done so, they likely would have refused to do it.

Bureaucrats and others working in hierarchically organized institutions, including police, operate under constraints, but they are not the robots the Arendtian caricature has cast them as, cloaked in the mind-deadening catchphrase *banality of evil*. People working in bureaucracies have no less a view of what is right and wrong when in their offices during the day than at home at night, or than their friends do who are not bureaucrats. We can safely assume, and an overwhelming body of evidence suggests, that such people do have views about whether it is right to slaughter people by the thousands or millions, whether killing a given peoples' children is right.

As virtually everyone knows, furthermore, real-life bureaucrats and bureaucracies, as opposed to Arendt's caricature, are not slavishly devoted to implementing *any* orders, let alone with enormous energy, but are difficult to get to implement a regime's policies they think profoundly wrong. Germans in the Weimar civil service and justice system consistently sabotaged the democratic system, its laws, and its governments. The truth then, and the truth generally, is that it is immensely difficult to move bureaucrats and bureaucracies against their will. People in Western and non-Western societies, in advanced industrial and developing societies alike, see real-life bureaucrats not as Arendtian robotic, superzealous order implementers but as unmotivated, relatively inefficient foot-draggers: "Bureaucrats" and "bureaucracy" are synonyms for *not getting things done*. Bureaucrats are not always that way, but they can be and often are. This makes it that much more curious that in only one area does the image of the bureaucrat deviate from the norm and deviate so much as to become the opposite: those taking part in mass murder, especially, and sometimes only, the Germans who did so. And remember, the vast majority of the perpetrators were *not* bureaucrats and what they were actually doing can only falsely be depicted and conveyed by the word "bureaucrat." Moreover, in many mass murders and eliminationist onslaughts—in Turkey, Uganda, the former Yugoslavia, Rwanda, Sudan, Democratic Republic of the Congo, Darfur, in our era's dozens and dozens against indigenous peoples, and many others—many or most of the killers were not organized in anything resembling a classically well-governed and -regulated bureaucracy animated by Max Weber's idealized modern bureaucratic ethos.

In light of our age's extensive record of face-to-face mass murdering by the most "civilized" Europeans (including Belgians, British, French, Germans, Italians in Ethiopia, and Portuguese in Africa) and also by the peoples of African, Asian, and Latin American countries mainly within their own countries, it is strange that people would ask the pseudo-profound, seemingly paradoxical question, as a *rhetorical* question, of how Germans, Europe's most literate and civilized people, could produce the Holocaust, and then incant one of the even more pseudo-profound answers: "authority" or "bureaucracy" or "modernity" or "peer pressure." A mere four decades prior to the Holocaust in very premodern and unbureaucratic-like circumstances, the "civilized" Germans in South-West Africa had shown that Germans had no trouble hunting down and mercilessly slaughtering, by shooting or bayoneting, men, women, and children they considered subhuman. The French had brutalized and killed with similar ease in French Equatorial Africa, the Belgians in Congo, the British in Kenya, and earlier the Americans during their continental conquest and the elimination of Native Americans. It is amazing that anyone not wishing to exculpate the German perpetrators, or not thinking Europeans are intrinsically morally or culturally superior, or people of color count less than whites, could put forth these preposterous notions, which were developed with tunnel vision fixated on the Germans as a way out of the Holocaust's fictional paradoxes and which our time's many dozens of mass murders and eliminations so belie.

Another claim about what moves the perpetrators to kill holds that they personally benefit from killing, so much so as to lead them to murder, to mass murder, men, women, and children whom they have no reason to think deserve to die. Instances of the perpetrators' booty or added benefits are pointed to or imputed to exist, as supposed and sufficient evidence that material gain is the motive moving the killers. In some mass murders and eliminations—in Turkey, the former Yugoslavia, Rwanda—many perpetrators (as opposed to the regime or bystanders) stole or plundered the victims' belongings. Yet even in these, there is no good reason to think the perpetrators believed the victims undeserving of their fate and self-consciously chose to slaughter, often to butcher, so many people merely to steal some things from a few of them.

This plunder postulate is inadequate for several reasons, starting with the obvious: We would naturally expect and see as hardly remarkable that people slaughtering or expelling others they hate or see as threatening would also dispossess them. After all, the victims' homes and possessions are now for the taking, and *someone* will get them. Who would expect the many perpetrators, especially in poor countries, to, like ascetic monks, turn their backs on the possessions of people they had just killed? In Rwanda, where there was much plundering, the same Hutu mass murderers recounting their fellow Hutu's looting the victims' possessions are also emphatic that they hated and feared the Tutsi, believing they ought to die.[14] Such enrichment is far more likely the *byproduct* of executing people the perpetrators believe deserve of death than an impetus for them to mass *murder* men, women, and children they think innocent. As, the Hutu killer Adalbert Munzigura commented when discussing the killing logistics, as a secondary matter "the lucky ones could look around for chances to loot," of which there was a great deal, as the Hutu perpetrators self-satisfyingly report.[15]

The plunder view of mass murdering has two versions or components: Plundering is the prime motive for initiating mass murder, or is what moves the killers on the ground. Neither, however, can account for the basic facts, including the perpetrators' choices. This view ignores that the perpetrators could just rob the people without killing them. It cannot explain why the perpetrators kill women and children. Or why they did not adopt lesser eliminationist means, such as expulsion, which as Berthe Mwanankabandi, a Tutsi survivor, points out, the perpetrators certainly know they could: "Those who only wanted to steal our land could have simply chased us out, as they did to our parents and grandparents in the North. Why cut us as well?"[16] And the general psychological objection applies here: Would people without animus for the targeted people, believing them wholly undeserving of death, slaughter them by the thousands, kill children sometimes living in their neighborhood, town, or region, just for a few dollars, or whatever booty they might pillage? Would you?

But the still more telling reason to dismiss the postulate that material gain has been the motive for perpetrators to annihilate tens of millions is that in the overwhelming majority of our time's mass killings the perpetrators have not tangibly benefited materially from their deeds. In many mass murders and eliminations the perpetrators operated in military or police institutions, governed by their restrictive rules. No evidence suggests that the majority, not to mention the overwhelming majority of mass murderers, gained non-negligible material benefits, including promotion, for killing, let alone that such putative benefits motivated the perpetrators to kill people they had no other reason to kill. Both German and Soviet perpetrators who enriched themselves could be and sometimes were punished. Anecdotes about personal enrichment, which is all that is typically put forward to make a general case that plunder motivates perpetrators to commit mass murder, does not constitute general evidence.

Finally, a postulate discussed earlier that is partly articulated and partly free-floating holds that when law and sanctions' constraints are lifted and people are allowed to kill, they will. Brutality resides in human nature. Killing is enjoyable. Civilization's patina is thin. The heart of darkness lurks within us, waiting to express its most murderous self. This postulate is advanced either as a general account about human beings or as a specific account of certain peoples. As a general claim, it is wrong. Many people historically could have killed others with impunity and have chosen not to. Most people, by word and deed, indicate they abhor the killing of innocent people. This "human nature" explanation, like other ones, is the refuge of those who want to wish the problem away by asserting, against or without evidence, that killing is in our genes, so people are programmed. Sometimes this argument is not advanced for people in general but only for specific peoples, particularly those from countries or civilizations that are not advanced technologically or considered "civilized," specifically for people in African and Asian countries—whom many Europeans and Americans are ready to believe are barbarians or bloodthirsty primitives who, absent civilization's restraints, go wild to act as they do. While this position is rarely stated openly, at least in the public sphere's polite company, it is easy enough to detect it underlying or informing how people discuss many mass slaughters. Claudine Kayitesi, a Tutsi survivor, has no patience for such talk: "To hear Whites talking, the genocide is supposedly a madness, but this is not true. It is a job meticulously prepared and efficiently carried out."[17] Kayitesi understands that genocide is a political, and purposefully calculated, act.

The postulates about how people said to disapprove, or not approve, of an annihilationist project can be brought to carry it out are falsified by the facts. None has ever been *demonstrated* to be true. Most have had little more substantiation than the power of assertion and a few anecdotes. None has been critically investigated, let alone worked through sufficiently by its proponents, let alone been worked through comparatively against a range of possible explanations. Those supporting such views have also not done what, analytically, is necessary: to demonstrate that the starting point for their reasoning is actually true, that starting point being that the perpetrators *did not approve* or *disapproved* of their own deeds. Instead, this alleged lack of approval is assumed, then presented as an uncontested fact, and then built upon by asserting that the alleged lack of approval or the disapproval was overcome by one of the postulated mechanisms just discussed. Such interpreters focus their and the readers' attention on those mechanisms, without giving a hint that the assumption on which the whole analysis is based is contestable, indeed without the necessary empirical foundation to believe it is true. Most of the postulates also suffer from stunning psychological implausibility.

Merely casting an eye over another aspect of life under some of our time's most mass-murderous regimes further reveals the analytical bankruptcy and the psychological implausibility of such assumptions and the assertions built upon them. The Soviet Union, communist China, North Korea, and other communist countries could not get people to work productively. They could not, even though the regimes had vast coercive and terror capacities, and even though virtually everyone worked for the "authoritative" state, either formally as a bureaucrat or in a state-owned enterprise. Authoritative orders or directives from these states failed to get workers to work hard, to work with zeal and energy, to take initiative to solve problems. Without the internal desire to work, a desire created under capitalism by the incentive of wages and other forms of advancement, under communism no amount of coercion, terror, state authority, peer pressure, bureaucratic structures, or ethos could get people to work hard and work well. Indeed, peer pressure operated just as I suggest it would if units of men told to slaughter men, women, and children believed it violated their deepest values. In the Soviet Union and other communist countries, peer pressure operated to strengthen workers' resolve not to give their all to the regime and its work (and work did not even violate the people's deepest values!). The joke in the Soviet Union was: They pretend to pay us and we pretend to work. Yet these same mechanisms—coercion, obedience to authority, peer pressure, and bureaucratic norms—are supposed to suddenly and magically succeed in getting people to act against their wishes to do something far more radical: to mass slaughter men, women, and children. And in this one realm of the magic's effectiveness, it is still more powerful than merely producing compliance: It super-magically gets people to work extraordinarily well and, what's more, with enormous initiative, energy, and zeal in, what is for killers, an exemplary way.

These postulates, as accounts for the perpetrators' killing other people—or for the perpetrators' other eliminationist policies and actions, which those who advance the postulates rarely, and then barely, address—are riddled with disqualifying conceptual, theoretical, comparative, and empirical problems, and repeatedly fail any real-world test when applied to other circumstances or held up against what we know about people's actual conduct in all kinds of social and political settings. Yet because coercion, the force of authority, peer pressure, and so on can get some people to do some things they would otherwise refuse to do, these postulates, at least at first glance, seem superficially plausible. That they manage even this, however, depends on a second sleight of hand: excluding from view and from analytical consideration the perpetrators' many other actions, which are regularly and integrally part of exterminationist and eliminationist assaults, that could not be the acts of people who do not approve of their deeds.

The Perpetrators' Other Actions

Perpetrators of mass slaughter and elimination do not conduct themselves as clinicians. They do many other things to their victims besides killing or expelling them, and do many other things to bring themselves and their victims to the moment of annihilation or expulsion. In surveying mass slaughters, the great zeal and energy with which perpetrators pursue and kill their victims is most striking. Germans in South-West Africa; Turks; Germans across Europe; Lithuanians, Romanians, and Ukrainians helping the Germans exterminate Jews; the British in Kenya; Indonesians slaughtering communists; the Khmer Rouge; Tutsi in Burundi; Pakistanis in Bangladesh; Guatemalans killing Maya; Serbs; Political Islamists in Sudan; and many more have been the picture of dedication and abandon in seeking out and slaughtering their victims. This was also true of the Hutu in Rwanda:

> Because of the situation, some [Tutsi] went out running and Interahamwe ran after them until they killed them. Some hid in bushes, sorghum fields, in ditches, in caves. Those ones were hunted down and they even used dogs to flush them out and then killed them. In addition, those who were caught were asked names of other people who hid with them while beating them because they had lists of those who were not yet killed. It was a very hard time. . . . Sometimes they cut down bushes, sorghum and banana trees hunting down Tutsi who were apparently hiding there.[18]

Alphonse Hitiyaremye, a Hutu killer, recalls that when reinforcements came, they could take "advantage of having these attackers along to bring off more profitable hunting expeditions."[19] Prefiguring the Hutu's "hunting expeditions" were the Germans' search-and-destroy missions, for which the perpetrators regularly volunteered and had a special, approving name: "Jew hunts." Henry Orenstein, a survivor, describes the Germans' zeal to ensure they killed every last Jew after having already slaughtered the bulk of one town's Jews. It was then that

> the hunt for those who had gone into hiding [began]. It was a hunt the likes of which mankind had never seen. Whole families would hide out in skrytkas [hideouts] as we had in Włodzimierz, and they would be hunted down inexorably, relentlessly. Street by street, house by house, inch by inch, from attic to cellar. The Germans became expert at finding these hiding places. When they searched a house, they went tapping the walls, listening for the hollow sound that indicated a double wall. They punched holes in ceilings or floors. . . .

These were no longer limited "actions"; this was total annihilation. Teams of SS men roamed the streets, searching ditches, outhouses, bushes, barns, stables, pigsties. And they caught and killed Jews by the thousands; then by the hundreds; then by tens, and finally one by one.[20]

No explanation that holds the perpetrators to have disapproved of their deeds can explain the source of the zeal and enormous energy, the "enthusiasm," that routinely characterizes mass slaughter and elimination's perpetrators.

This initiative is properly conceived of not as a bureaucrat's mindless or simply job-doing act, but as the action of human beings, human agents who, informed by their values and beliefs, choose to act as they do. In one mass murder and elimination after another, perpetrators take initiatives to ensure that they manage to apprehend and then kill, incarcerate, or deport as many of their victims as possible. They improvise when searching for victims; they undertake killings that they are not, strictly speaking, ordered to. They overcome emerging logistical difficulties on their own. They problem-solve. It is precisely because the perpetrators often operate in fluid institutions, which accord them substantial freedom—and not in highly regimented and rule-governed institutions (such as classic bureaucracies) where specific procedures spell out their actions—that, in annihilationist and eliminationist assaults, the perpetrators' conduct overwhelmingly accords with the image of self-initiating and self-motivating human beings, human agents, informed by their beliefs and values, and not that of robotic bureaucrats.

In bringing the victims to the point of annihilation, the perpetrators act with energy, zeal, and initiative—not foot dragging, lethargy, and obstructionism. Yet these acts and displays are only a figurative half of what, aside from the killing itself, the perpetrators do that demands analysis and explanation. The other half consists of the other ways the perpetrators treat their victims. They routinely talk to them, taunt them, conveying to them their belief in their deeds' rightness and justice, and their joy in performing them. Rarely in mass murder and elimination's annals (some Serbs in Bosnia and Hutu in Rwanda did) do we learn of perpetrators contemporaneously telling victims, or by-

standers or friends, that they regret their actions. Esperance Nyirarugira, Concessa Kayiraba, and Veronique Mukasinafi, who with others
form a small, informal community of rape and genocide survivors,
whose family members their neighbors and other Hutu from their community butchered, came into contact with many perpetrators and other
Hutu during the exterminationist assault. Asked whether any Hutu expressed sympathy for them or came to their aid, Mukasinafi replied for
them all: "No."[21]

After the fact, when the perpetrators face punishment, or even after
their sentencing, confronted by a condemning world, they protest their
innocence or say whatever might exculpate them. In this sense they resemble all criminals. Men convicted in the United States of possessing
or distributing child pornography reveal how much perpetrators of
heinous crimes hide, and how little their denials can be believed. At
sentencing, 26 percent of the 155 offenders studied were known to have
committed "hands-on" offenses against children, in other words sexually abusing them. Yet, when the same offenders in an eighteen-month
prison treatment program filled out anonymous sexual histories, 85
percent admitted they had molested children. *At least 59 percent of
them had—when it mattered—lied*, concealing their crimes, to present
themselves to the legal authorities and the disapproving world as innocent of the heinous acts they actually committed. In the anonymous
sexual histories, each one provided a "victims list," which revealed that
regarding the number of victims these perpetrators had concealed from
the legal authorities, the extent of the self-protective lying was even
more stunning. At sentencing, the authorities knew of seventy-five children these 155 men had, in sum, victimized. In the anonymous sexual
histories, the same exact men named 1,777 children they had molested.
This group of perpetrators had hidden and, after conviction, continued to hide from the legal authorities (at least) *96 percent of all their
crimes and crime victims!*[22]

Perpetrators of mass murder and elimination, after the fact, are no
different. Srebrenica massacre survivor Sabaheta Fejzíc, whose sixteen-
year-old son Serbian mass murderers dragged away and killed (while
kicking and beating her and calling her a derogatory epithet for Muslims), explains: "Thirteen years later many of the perpetrators are still
walking freely around Srebrenica and the Pedrinje region, while most of

them are safe in Serbia. . . . Not one of them ever admitted they had committed any crime. They denied but we all saw them. I personally saw my neighbors, my former friends, and they can only tell lies. But the truth is there, the real truth."[23] Emmanuel Gatali, a Tutsi survivor, lost many family members and friends killed by their neighbors: "Before we knew it, Interahamwe and all villagers, the whole community rushed down to us, they used whatever weapon they had: machetes, arrows, big sticks, all sorts of traditional weapons, they whacked people, grounded them, slashed parts of their bodies." Gatali, himself having seen people he knew kill with unmistakable passion and zeal, scoffs at ordinary Hutu's self-exonerations that they were forced to kill and were not willing killers. "Even those Hutu that are confessing [to killing] are not sorry, they just want to be free," Gatali explains, referring to Hutu who before the Gacaca courts confess as a condition of receiving much shorter sentences and being sent to a minimum-security work camp instead of harsh prison. Gatali is emphatic: "It was their will to kill and it's in their nature."[24] Similarly, Hutu of Mukasinafi's community cut her husband and children to pieces. She and the other rape and genocide survivors from her village knew many perpetrators well and heard many things directly from them. She explains, "The country was in their hands. They just wanted to exterminate their enemy. Because a Tutsi was an enemy to them . . . They did it willingly and happily. They did it with a lot of passion saying that they are doing it for [President] Habyarimana because he was killed by Tutsi. . . . They loved doing it. They were actually happy doing it. But they all say in Gacaca [courts] that they were ordered by the government."[25] Attempting to explain the perpetrators' actions, indeed just writing a history of any mass elimination, by relying on their self-exonerating testimony would be akin to writing a history of criminality in America by relying on criminals' self-exonerating statements to police, prosecutors, and the courts, or in public opinion's court, the media.[26] Unless criminals are arrested, almost none volunteers that he committed the crimes he willfully committed. Most criminals who are arrested assert that they have been wrongly accused. If they cannot plausibly deny their material culpability, they attribute responsibility for the crimes to others. They ordinarily profess, with seeming conviction and great passion, to abhor the crimes that, their protestations notwithstanding, they freely committed. When facing the authorities, as well as the general society, criminals lie about their actions and motivations. Even after conviction, criminals habitually proclaim, indeed insist upon, their innocence. Admitting the truth of their crimes will elicit still more intensive social condemnation. And, as with these sexual predators, how many criminals publicize to the police, before the court, while in prison, or after release, to anyone and everyone, the crimes they have committed of which people are not aware? Why, then, should we think that the people complicit in human history's largest murders and worst horrors should be more honest, more self-incriminating, more eager to volunteer the full and self-condemning truths about what they have done?[27]

The perpetrators of mass murder, expulsions, incarcerations, and other brutalities, of all forms of eliminationist politics, lie to the world. They say whatever might exculpate themselves, from falsely claiming they were not at the killing or elimination scene, to, if it can be proven they had been there, that they killed or brutalized no one, to, if it can be proven they did, that they were coerced. They also regularly tell tales of having saved people. The reality according to Alphonse, a Hutu killer, was that "we killed everything we tracked down in the papyrus. We had no reason to choose, to expect or fear anyone in particular. We were cutters of acquaintances, cutters of neighbors, just plain cutters." Yet the stories told since the Hutu's defeat differ. Their self-exoneration tactics are well worked out. According to Alphonse, "Today some name acquaintances they supposedly spared, because they know these are no longer living to contradict them. They tell the tales to attract the favor of suffering families, they invent rescues to ease their return [to their villages]. We joke about those fake stratagems." Léopord Twagirayezu, another Hutu killer, explains the other main strategy: "He keeps saying [that] he remembers nothing or only piddling things—that he wasn't there and suchlike nonsense." According to Léopord,* "there are many such liars." Why do they do it? "He bows down to lies in the hope of evading retribution and reproach."[28]

Such self-protective and exonerating lying is a known commonplace among the Hutu killers—I have heard them myself—and among many

---

*Jean Hatzfeld's book of Hutu perpetrators' testimony identifies them throughout by their first name, so I follow his practice here.

others, especially among the Holocaust's perpetrators. German after German who served in killing institutions would so routinely deny that he himself killed anyone that, if we were to believe each one's testimony, then we would have to conclude that units that we know slaughtered on a given day hundreds or thousands of Jews (even by the perpetrators' admission) actually killed very few, if any. Why? Because only a few, if any, of the units' members admit to having themselves fired the shots. And in the Federal Republic of Germany's own trials, thousands of perpetrators were proven guilty of *willfully* murdering Jews *despite* their vehement denials of culpability. Otto Ohlendorf, the commander of an Einsatzgruppe that slaughtered ninety thousand Jews in the Soviet Union, asserted emphatically at his trial at Nuremberg (ending in his conviction and hanging) that he was duty bound to follow orders and that is why he commanded his men to kill. That is what he told the world. Yet in a contemporaneous letter to his wife smuggled from prison, he revealed that his public protestations were nothing but a self-exonerating fabrication. In reality he was a convinced antisemite and a believing dedicated executioner. Jewry, even after the war, Ohlendorf confided to his wife, "has continued to sow hate; and it reaps hate again. . . . How else would one see it as anything but the work of demons who wage their battle against us?"[29] Like the German perpetrators, eliminationist perpetrators in general present false, self-protective, and exonerating fronts to the world. But the truth is different. Asked whether the Hutu in prison are more sorry they killed Tutsi or that they did not exterminate them all, Marcel Munyabugingo, himself a killer, is clear about what they say when talking among themselves: "They still feel bad they did not succeed in killing everyone."[30] Élie Mizinge, one of the forthcoming Hutu perpetrators, elaborates. The killers "who keep saying that they weren't there during the fatal moments, that they don't remember a thing, that they lost their machetes and tripe like that, they are bowing down with the hope of evading punishment— while waiting to start all over again." But what do the killers really think? What do they say among themselves? Élie explains: "Most of the killers are sorry they didn't finish the job. They accuse themselves of negligence rather than wickedness."[31]

In contrast to the transparently demonstrably false denials of culpability that perpetrators make *after* being defeated, when facing criminal prosecution, or when warding off social sanctions and condemnation, while committing their murderous and eliminationist acts they tell a different story:

IN SOUTH-WEST AFRICA

Jan Cloete, a Cape Baster, working as a guide for the Germans: "A German soldier found a little Herero baby boy about nine months old lying in the bush. The child was crying. He brought it into the camp where I was. The soldiers formed a ring and started throwing the child to one another and catching it as if it were a ball. The child was terrified and hurt and was crying very much. After a time they got tired of this and one of the soldiers fixed his bayonet on his rifle and said he would catch the baby. The child was tossed into the air towards him and as it fell he caught it and transfixed the body with the bayonet. The child died in a few minutes and the incident was greeted with roars of laughter by the Germans, who seemed to think it was a great joke." [32]

Leslie Bartlet, an Englishman living in the German colony, testified that the German soldiers "seemed to take a pride in wrecking vengeance on those unfortunate women. When the railway from Luderitzbucht to Keetmanshoop was started, gangs of prisoners, mostly women, scarcely able to walk from weakness and starvation were employed as labourers. They were brutally treated. I personally saw a gang of these prisoners, all women, carrying a heavy double line of rails with iron sleepers attached on their shoulders, and unable to bear the weight they fell. One woman fell under the rails which broke her leg and held it fast. The Schachtmeister [ganger], without causing the rail to be lifted, dragged the woman from under and threw her on one side, where she died untended. The general treatment was cruel, and many instances were told to me, but that which I have stated I personally saw." [33]

IN TURKEY

E. H. Jones, a British prisoner of war, hearing the candid speech of the guards who had also slaughtered Armenians, reports: "The butchery had taken place in a valley some dozen miles outside the town. . . . Amongst our sentries were men who had slain men, women and children till their arms were too tired to strike. They boasted of it among themselves."[34]

DURING THE HOLOCAUST

German Gestapo man Felix Landau recorded in his diary what transpired in Lviv, Ukraine: "We went to the citadel; there we saw things that few people have ever seen. At the entrance of the citadel there were [German] soldiers standing guard. They were holding clubs as thick as a man's wrist and were lashing out and hitting anyone who crossed their path. The Jews were pouring out of the entrance. There were rows of Jews lying one on top of the other like pigs whimpering horribly. The Jews kept streaming out of the citadel completely covered in blood. We stopped and tried to see who was in charge of the Kommando. 'Nobody.' Someone had let the Jews go. They were just being hit out of rage and hatred.

"Nothing against that—only they should not let the Jews walk about in such a state. . . . Our work is over for today. Camaraderie is still good for the time being."[35]

A German executioner testifies about a killing operation against Jews: "Next to me was the Policeman Koch. . . . He had to shoot a small boy of perhaps twelve years. We had been expressly told that we should hold the gun's barrel eight inches from the head. Koch had apparently not done this, because while leaving the execution site, the other comrades laughed at me, because pieces of the child's brains had spattered onto my sidearm and had stuck there. I first asked, why are you laughing, whereupon Koch, pointing to the brains on my sidearm, said: That's from mine, he has stopped twitching. He said this in an obviously boastful tone. . . . I have experienced more obscenities of this kind."[36]

IN BRITISH-OCCUPIED KENYA

Beatrice Gatonye, a Kikuyu woman forced to fingerprint the decomposing dead, explains: "The job we were told to do was just to torture us." How so? "The flesh would come off in our hands and you couldn't get it off of you. For days you would have this sticky substance attached to your skin, knowing that it was the skin of someone else. We never managed to get many fingerprints. Anyway, those white men in charge would just stand near us with their guns joking and laughing with each other and at us, smoking their cigarettes."[37]

IN INDONESIA

A member of a left-wing youth organization who escaped being caught: "Another body was also thrown in, also headless. I couldn't count how many headless corpses passed by me. Every time, the head was put in the gunny sack. Then I heard a shout from a voice I recognized and froze; it was Pak Mataim, our bicycle repairman who I think was illiterate. He seemed very thin, and he too was dragged along like a banana stalk. He moaned, begging for mercy, for his life to be spared. They laughed, mocking him. He was terrified. The rope around his feet was taken off, leaving his hands still tied. He cried, and because he couldn't keep quiet, they plugged up his mouth with a clump of earth.

"Rejo went into action, and like lightning, his machete cut through the neck of his victim, the one-eyed, powerless, bicycle repairman. His head went into the sack."[38]

IN BANGLADESH

Abdul Halim recounts Pakistani soldiers' search for the parents of the local sheikh in his village: "Then they dragged me up to where the Sheikh's father was sitting and repeated, 'We shall shoot you in 10 minutes.' Pointing to the Sheikh's father I asked: 'What's the point of shooting him? He's an old man and a Government pensioner.' The soldiers replied, 'Because he has produced a devil.'"[39]

IN BURUNDI

A Hutu survivor discusses the Tutsi's views of the moral significance of not using bullets to kill Hutu: "But nothing frightens the Tutsi. They laughed while a man [was] in the process of dying. . . . Many, many manners were used. . . . It was said that the shot from a gun is the best death—the death of a soldier or of a Tutsi. This death, they said, is not designated for the Hutu."[40]

IN CAMBODIA

Sophea Mouth describes a lurid scene he had to witness: "A man was holding a sharp ax rotated backward in his right hand, and with his left, he had a firm grip on another man's shoulder. At the instant, the edge of the ax cut open the man's chest. Blood spurted and I heard a roaring groan, loud enough to startle the animals. I stood there smiling deceitfully in shock because it was the first killing I had seen.

"After the cadre had opened up the man's chest, he took out the liver. One man exclaimed, 'One man's liver is another man's food.' Then a second man quickly placed the liver on an old stump where he sliced it horizontally and fried it in a pan with pig grease above the fire that one of the cadres had built.

"When the liver was cooked, the cadre leader took out two bottles of rice-distilled whiskey, which they drank cheerfully. I was too young and the cadres didn't allow me to participate in their celebration, although I had no desire to taste human liver."[41]

Teap, a Khmer Rouge cadre, describes how the Khmer Rouge killers operated more generally and their candid speech among themselves: "They executed people like we kill fish. . . . They killed at night and didn't have any responsibilities during the day. They just rested and ate well, much better than the people. . . . Their work began near dusk, when the soldiers would begin to sharpen their knives and axes. They'd roll up their pant legs and sleeves, put a scarf on their head and disappear. . . . When they returned, they would sometimes have blood stains on their clothes or even spots of blood on their faces. They went and bathed by [Rom's] house, where I was guarding nearby and could overhear them. Sometimes they would return happy, laughing and shouting things like 'That despicable one jumped well [when he was killed], did you see him?' or 'That despicable one fainted before he even reached the ditch' or 'There was another one who pissed so much that he completely soaked himself and even got you wet!' . . . When they looked at their victims, they didn't think they were killing fellow Khmer, just enemies."[42]

IN GUATEMALA

Tomasa Osorio Chen recounts a scene from the ferocious Rio Negro massacre that included an enormous amount of raping, which she survived: "When the killing began, they tied them [the women] up and hit them to kill them. One of the women asked, 'why are you killing me?' She kicked the PAC [the civil patroller]. That PAC slit her in the stomach with a machete. When he slit her with the machete, the PAC wiped his hand on the machete and sucked on the blood."[43]

IN BOSNIA IN A SERBIAN RAPE CAMP

Kadira, a Bosnian victim from the Doboj rape camp, recalls: "I saw about seven or eight little girls who died after they were raped. I saw how they took them away to be raped and then brought them back unconscious. They [the Serbs] threw them down in front of us, and we weren't allowed to look at them; you had to keep looking at the floor the whole time. And then they'd announce: 'Look, that's what'll happen to you too if you resist and disobey Serbian law.'" Kadira explains that the Serbs "wanted to kill us slowly, torture us to death, they wanted us to suffer, they wanted to show us in every way they could that they were stronger." A second victim, Ifeta, concurs: The Serbs "didn't want sex. They were gloating because they were humiliating Muslim women."[44]

IN RWANDA

Fulgence Bunani, a Hutu killer, recalls his comrades' laughter: "When we saw Tutsi wriggling like snakes in the marshes, it made the guys laugh. Some let them crawl awhile longer for more fun. But that was not the case for everybody. Some didn't care one way or the other and didn't bother with that mockery. If it was easier to catch them crawling, that was better, and that was all."[45]

Patricia Musabyemaria, who had been incarcerated by Hutu in the interahamwe: "They ordered me to take Déo [her two-year-old son] to a pit latrine. When we got there, I saw that it was already full of corpses. I was to kill him myself but I refused. I pleaded with those who would kill him to allow me to go away before they macheted him. After a few minutes, I saw them looking for hoes to put the soil on my son's body. They were boasting that 'The father was the first in the pit. Now, let the son act as the lid.'"[46]

IN DARFUR

Masalit women recall the words of the Janjaweed perpetrators: "Slaves! Nubas! Do you have a god? Break the Ramadan! Even we with pale skins don't observe the Ramadan. You, ugly black pretend . . . We are your god! Your god is Omar al-Bashir [Sudan's Political Islamic president]" and "You blacks, you have spoilt the country! We are here to burn you. . . . We will kill your husbands and sons and we will sleep with you! You will be our wives!"[47]

The perpetrators' speech and emotional displays convey their attitudes toward the ignominies, cruelties, and lethal blows they inflict on their victims. The perpetrators express their hatred for the victims. The perpetrators impart their conceptions of the victims as beings that deserve their fates. The perpetrators' exclaim words of joy about their deeds. They gloat. They boast. They take pride in their deeds. They mock the victims and celebrate their deaths. And the perpetrators laugh, again and again we hear their laughter, at the victims' suffering, at what they themselves are doing to them. As the reports from perpetrators themselves, bystanders, and surviving victims from one eliminationist assault to the next make clear, the perpetrators' speech and emotional displays *at the time* they were handling, brutalizing, and killing their victims constitute overwhelming evidence that they were assenting and willing executioners.

Erwin Grafmann, a member of a unit of five hundred ordinary Germans (not SS men) that killed and deported to their deaths tens of thousands of Jews, reports that, after their commander, Papa Trapp, told them they did not have to kill, "I did not witness that a single one of my comrades said that he did not want to participate." The rightness of killing Jews was so self-evident to them that "at the time, we did not give it any second thoughts at all." Why? One of Grafmann's comrades explains that to Jews, whom they deemed equivalent to bandits, "the cate-

Jesús Tecú Osorio, Rabinal, Guatemala, June 2008

gory of human being was not applicable."[48] In South-West Africa four decades earlier, German soldiers took the initiative to confine twenty-five half-starved Herero "men, women and children and little girls" in a small enclosure of thorn bushes, surrounded and covered them with logs and branches, sprinkled the fuel with lamp oil, and burnt the Herero "to a cinder." "I saw this personally," says Hendrik Fraser, a Baster. "The Germans said 'We should burn all these dogs and baboons in this fashion.'"[49] "It became clear to us very quickly," reports a Kikuyu survivor about the Kikuyu's shared conclusions of the British generally, "that the British wanted to kill us, and those that were not killed were going to suffer. That was what those times were like. They just thought we were animals."[50] Jesús Tecú Osorio, who lost his parents and many family members during the Rio Negro massacre in Guatemala and is now one of the country's best-known human rights advocates, says about the obvious willingness of the perpetrators: "When they committed the acts, almost all acted with their own will. Perhaps they weren't obligated, but during the massacres they could do whatever they wanted. They could rape the women. So at the massacre of Rio Negro, perhaps it was not their first experience. They could've had other experiences. So that day they acted very willingly. That is how I saw it that day."[51] Similarly, Cambodian survivors regularly describe the Khmer Rouge as wholly willing and impassioned mass murderers, declaiming the necessity of their deeds, including exterminating people for the sake of "Angkar," a shorthand for the transformed and purified Cambodian society they sought to create. Rithy Uong endured four years under the Khmer Rouge in a mobile labor unit, so he encountered an enormous number of Khmer Rouge. He recounts the perpetrators telling the victims many things indicating they believed what they were doing to the victims right, even explicitly that "they enjoy it." How does he know this? His speech quickens and becomes emphatic: "Oh yes. They say they enjoy it. They just said you are, what we call . . . the wealthy people. You know, you believe in imperialism." When being asked how many perpetrators said such things, Uong replies with animation and conviction, "All the Khmer. All the soldiers. All the people that watch us, they say that."[52] In Bosnia, Alisa Muratčauš, herself a rape victim and rape camp survivor, speaks authoritatively not only from her own experience but also on behalf of the six thousand members of the Association of Concentration Camp Torture Survivors in Sarajevo, of which she is president. They collectively have firsthand, intimate experience with an enormous number of Serbian perpetrators. Muratčauš describes the perpetrators as wholly willing and eager executioners and vocal about their approval, expressing their hatred and their desire to utterly rid Bosnia of Bosnians. "Definitely, definitely," she says, referring to the perpetrators' willingness, hatred for the victims, and use of rape as a political weapon. It was an "expression of hatred, definitely, all of these, all of these."[53] Anne, a Tutsi survivor captured hiding in the bush as Hutu used dogs to ferret out every last Tutsi, first had to watch as the Hutu "killed all my children in front of me and they slashed my right arm." Then "while they were raping me, they were saying that they wanted to kill all Tutsi so that in the future all that would be left would be drawings to show that there were once a people called the Tutsi."[54] And why did the Hutu want to obliterate the Tutsi? Elie Ngarambe, a Hutu killer, explains that the killers "did not know that the [Tutsi] were human beings, because if they had thought about that they wouldn't have killed them. Let me also include myself as someone who accepted it: I wouldn't have accepted that they [the Tutsi] are human beings." Ngarambe is emphatic about this being the common view and common knowledge: "As I was hearing it, I had the same perception as others at that time," adding, as

Elie Ngarambe, Kigali, Rwanda, May 2008

this was such a fact of Hutu society, that no Hutu "could swear and lie to you that he did not know that." The effect of this, he explains: "It is a cloud that came into people's hearts and covered them, and everything became dark, because to see someone standing in front of you without any energy and you hold your machete high or a club and hit him . . . it is something difficult that was done with a lot of anger and rage, I mean this genocide."[55]

The facts of the perpetrators' bodily actions offer voluminous evidence that seamlessly complements the evidence of the perpetrators' words, showing that they approve of the eliminationist assaults and goals to which they contribute. As these and legions of other instances demonstrate, eliminationist perpetrators routinely degrade and torture their victims physically. They degrade them by using them as playthings, bending them to their will, using them to display their dominance, showing them in so many, often diabolical, ways that they are masters and the victims are without rights, respect, or the basic human protections. The perpetrators imprint on their victims' bodies, and thereby their psyches, their conception of them as worthless or vile beings who deserve their hopeless fate. Breaking the victims' bodies and spirit is often integral to the eliminationist project. For those victims for whom such cruelty is a prelude to death, they suffer the expressive venting of the perpetrators' hatred. For those victims left alive,

Shortly before deporting the Jews of Łuków, Poland, to Treblinka's gas chambers in November 1942, Germans of Police Battalion 101 take time out to force Jews to pose for photographic mementos.

the crippling, defining memories of suffering are also meant to warn them of their fate should they resist or seek to turn the tables. The perpetrators' organized raping, such as the Serbs' institutionalized raping of Bosniak and Kosovar women, is a textbook instance.

Such perpetrators' actions and expressions are mass extermination and elimination's commonplaces, familiar to those even passably acquainted with such operations. They cannot possibly be accounted for by any postulate holding the perpetrators to disapprove or not approve of their deeds. If you are told to kill or guard a person, you do not have to degrade, mock, and torture that person. You do not have to pursue her death with zeal, passion, and energy, and take initiative to execute the deed. You do not have to memorialize the deed by taking trophy photographs of your quarry or handiwork, of the kind contained in the photo album of a Japanese soldier in Manchuria, titled "Bandit Suppression Operation Commemorative Picture," which captured soldiers going into action. The album contained several photos of scenes in which the soldier himself had participated: "One showed three severed heads, one with eyes still staring, balanced on a fence; another, a soldier

Auschwitz personnel gather for drinks at a hunting lodge, Solahütte retreat near Auschwitz, Poland, 1944.

holding a precisely severed head by its hair, the face turned toward the camera; yet another of a Chinese, his arms bound tightly, is captured in [the soldier's own] hand, 'his life hangs by a thread.'"[56]

A fact ignored by all those denying the German perpetrators' willingness and approval is the reason archives filled with photographs of the Holocaust exist: The perpetrators took them. They did so, obviously, not to create evidence to indict themselves but to memorialize and celebrate their deeds. In emblematic scenes from the Holocaust, German personnel at Auschwitz, where the Germans gassed more than a million Jews, let themselves be photographed in festive, merry poses, preserved in a photo album of Karl Höcker, the adjutant to the camp commander. Similarly, Kurt Franz, the commander of Treblinka, where the Germans gassed more than 700,000 Jews, kept a photographic scrapbook celebrating his time there, as his handwritten words on one page tells us, as "The Good Old Days."

The Germans regularly photographed the Jews in agony or dead (often in piles), or themselves in joyous poses mocking them, frequently forcing them to pose in genre scenes. The Germans were brazen and proud about their photographs. They passed them around, sent them

Dead Polish Jews, spring 1942

home to loved ones, enshrined them in photo albums. German perpetrators treated the memorializing photographs of their extermination operations of Jews, including of "Jew hunts," as their common property. One unit of ordinary German perpetrators hung their photographs in their headquarters, so that the unit's members could order copies.[57] Of these men who sent copies to their families, we do not know what they wrote. But we do know what Ferdinand Welz, an artillery man, wrote in May 1942, when he sent his parents several photographs. The batch included the extraordinarily gruesome, almost surrealistic bird's-eye-view photograph (reproduced above) of naked and partly clothed corpses of Polish Jews piled on top of one another in a ditch, with arms and legs and heads and torsos intertwined. Few people could look at such a shocking scene—of the sort many have probably never beheld—without recoiling in horror. Referring to these photographs, Welz wrote: "I am enclosing for you several photographs, which I hope will not make you feel ill. Yes, they're Jews. For them, the dream of Germany's annihilation is over."[58] He tells his parents that he no longer has the negatives; could they please preserve the photos for him?

Certainly, if you are told to kill a person, you do not have to celebrate and feast afterward. In Rwanda such festivities began almost immediately with Major Bernard Ntuyahaga, initially in charge of mass murdering Tutsi in Kigali's central residential area, celebrating the success afterward "in noisy parties at his home."[59] In the Nyamata commune, where ordinary Hutu hacked to death fifty thousand of the fifty-nine thousand Tutsi living among them, the celebrations began after the first day of killing and continued on a nightly basis, as different Hutu killers report. "The evening atmosphere was festive," says one. Another concurs: "In the evening, families listened to music. . . . The men sang, everyone drank, the women changed dresses three times in an evening. It was noisier than weddings, it was drunken reveling every day."[60]

The Germans also frequently marked their killings with symbolic displays. Particularly after large killing operations, or when milestones had been reached in exterminating the Jews of a particular area, they held "death banquets," "victory celebrations," or as the Chelmno extermination camp's staff did, upon the camp's closing after annihilating more than 145,000 Jews, a self-satisfied farewell party.[61] Serbs similarly festively marked their deeds in Bosnia, with no less than communal celebrations blessed by their church leaders, who conducted formal rituals celebrating town "cleansings" of all non-Serbs.[62]

If you disapproved of mass killings, you would not do these things. If you believed that you had to kill someone or the person telling you to do so would kill you, or were somehow pressured or somehow felt duty bound to kill someone you held to be an innocent victim, you would not choose to torture the person first, or increase his suffering, let alone do so with evident glee. You would do the opposite. Yet the evidence suggests that few actual perpetrators ever did. Had the perpetrators disapproved of mass murder and elimination, they would have created a substantial record, a vast record, of such disapproval—in contemporaneous utterances, letters to family and friends, and diaries, in their actions in so many ways, by foot dragging, sabotage, doing the job badly, and by acting and speaking kindly to the victims, which survivors would have surely eagerly reported in gratitude. All that has come to light from all our age's mass murders and eliminations amounts to virtually nothing, to no credible record of such disapproval and dissent. This absence is all the more striking because people living under the most coercive regimes—including people living under the very regimes that practiced eliminationist politics—have left vast records of disapproval, dissent, and resistance against the regimes and against their measures that the people actually disliked.

The postulates that the perpetrators disapprove or do not approve of their deeds are falsified by the facts of just the eliminationist politics' signature act, for which they were put forward: the killing itself. When such claims are held up to the perpetrators' other actions—which the claims studiously and not surprisingly ignore—they do not even make sense. These widespread acts of cruelty and celebration, the perpetrators' approving words when dealing with, brutalizing, and killing their victims, reveal themselves to be integral to the eliminationist projects' execution. They flatly contradict the notion that those implementing them see the projects as wrong.

Had the perpetrators the world over never killed a single person but still done all the other things they actually did do to their victims, then I think two things would have happened. The perpetrators' many and various nonlethal acts toward their victims would not have been lost, let alone been almost entirely obscured, in the shadow cast by the killing and its horror, and lost—as they are in study after study—from our analytical view. And, in light of the then overwhelming and manifest evidence that makes the idea that perpetrators disapproved of all their own cruelties, brutalities, and degradations of the victims, and disapproved of their expressions of hatred and mockery and of approval and merriment, utterly absurd, no one would have seriously put forward postulates depending on the notion that the perpetrators saw their own eliminationist acts as wrong.[63]

These postulates have been most systematically and thoroughly assessed for the mass murder for which many were first advanced, and have been most frequently and forcefully asserted: the Germans' annihilation of the Jews. In *Hitler's Willing Executioners* I demonstrated that they are conceptually untenable and belied by overwhelming evidence, including the voluminous testimony of the survivors (each one having often observed over the years, many, frequently hundreds of German perpetrators) and the testimony of those killers who speak candidly. As one ordinary German perpetrator explains, in giving testimony about all those he knew during the annihilation: "I must admit that we felt a certain joy when we would seize a Jew whom one could kill. I cannot remember an instance when a policeman had to be ordered to an execution. The shootings were, to my knowledge, always carried out on a voluntary basis; one could have gained the impression that various policemen got a big kick out of it."[64] Oscar Pinkus, a Jewish survivor, drawing on his own experience and other Jewish victims' observations, does not blame the Germans for implementing their orders, because "we never expected individual Germans to disobey orders." Instead, the Germans' "record is fatal because, above and beyond the orders, they individually and voluntarily, actively and tacitly, endorsed, enjoyed and enlarged the official program [of extermination]."[65] Pinkus could have been speaking for the survivors of one mass murder and elimination after the next. In their vast testimony, survivors of eliminationist assaults, when they address the issues, say almost in a single voice that the perpetrators hated and *wanted* to kill them. They give no reason to think the perpetrators were disapproving, reluctant, or unwilling, and every reason to believe that perpetrators endorsed, enjoyed, and enlarged the eliminationist program.

There is simply no plausible account that does not make up or ignore the basic facts that can tell us why, absent massive coercion, so many people *against their will* would slaughter other people. And there is no plausible account of any kind for why disapproving people, indeed so many disapproving people across cultures and time, would torture the victims and celebrate in their deaths and expulsions. If we wish to understand and explain why the killers kill, why the eliminationist warriors physically and symbolically assault their victims, we must first recognize the sobering truth that perpetrators, exceptions notwithstanding, approve of what they do. Fulgence, an ordinary Hutu who willingly slaughtered Tutsi, epigrammatically and emblematically conveys what has been true of perpetrators: "I thought wrong. I went wrong. I did wrong."[66] Recognizing this then leads to the question, and the investigation, of *how* the perpetrators came to this approval, came to the point where they "thought wrong," and *why* they see the annihilation, expulsion, and incarceration of other peoples and groups as right, necessary, and laudable.

Before exploring this, another aspect of mass slaughters must be fully confronted and analyzed: the gruesomeness. Treatments of the Holocaust, because of their omission of the perpetrators and their analytically misleading emphasis on the faceless gas chambers, which established a sanitized paradigm of inquiry and understanding for mass murders in general, have effectively obscured the horror of the *act* of killing—not for the victims, which we all know—but for the perpetrators. In the overwhelming majority of our time's mass murders, the perpetrators killed their victims face-to-face, typically individual killer to individual victim. In very many, the killers slaughtered people with handheld implements. For so many perpetrators it is literally true, and for so many more it would be metaphorically correct, to say that they—Germans, British in Kenya, Indonesians, Khmer Rouge, Guatemalans, Tutsi in Burundi, Hutu in Rwanda, Serbs, Sudanese, and many more—*butchered* their victims. Elie Ngarambe, a Hutu killer, now mild mannered, is by his own account utterly transformed because he and other demythologized killers no longer believe as they once did that Tutsi are not human beings but snakes and cockroaches seeking to enslave the Hutu. He looks back on the events with understanding but also with a degree of incredulity, at how he and all the others could cut up people: "I cannot find a way to explain that, but the only answer I can get is that it was like a cloud, something like darkness. I can call it ignorance." Then he corrects himself, for even though the poisonous things they held Tutsi to be were a kind of ignorance, "but [it] is not ignorance. It is cruelty that we worked with, with my fellow criminals in Rwanda." What they did, their cruelty, Ngarambe demonstrated for me with chopping hand motions of great precision, showing me how Hutu "cut" their victims "into pieces": "You see, you would hold a machete like this. Then you would run after a person and hack him like this. Slash him, and after that you would ground him, and cut him into pieces. But the most common

Individual victims of the Khmer Rouge in Tuol Sleng prison, Phnom Penh, Cambodia, August 1989

[weapon] was a club. You would hit, and ground the head. With a machete, it was like how you cut a banana tree. The only difference is that flesh is soft but the tree is hard. A person you cut once and the second time he is in pieces."[67] Blood everywhere. Screams of agony. Victims pleading for their lives, or alternately to be killed more quickly to end their pain. How would the perpetrators, uncoerced, summon the psychological and emotional wherewithal to do this if they did not believe their actions were right, good, and necessary? How would they do it time after time?

Think of the difficulty you may have, and that so many people do have, in reading this book's descriptions of perpetrators torturing or killing innocent men, women, or children. Think of people, perhaps including you, wincing when reading such accounts or seeing such scenes in documentaries. Think of how much harder—ten, a hundred, a thousand, an infinite number of times harder—it would be for *you* to be killing, slaughtering, butchering a man with a machete. Or a woman. Or a child. You cut him. Then cut him again. They cut him again and again. Think of listening to the person you are about to murder begging, crying for mercy, for her life. Think of hearing your victim's screams, as you hack at or "cut" her and then cut her again, and again and again, or the screams of a boy as you hack at his eight-year-old body. Yet the perpetrators do it, and hear it. And they do it with zeal, alacrity, and self-satisfaction, even enjoyment. *They* do it again and again and again. Ngarambe explains that the people pleaded, saying, "'Please forgive me; I am going to give you money.' Or a woman would say, 'Please forgive me. Or take me and take care of me. See I am a beautiful woman.' And you say, 'No, I am going to kill you instead.'"[68] Then the perpetrator would cut or club his victim, and cut or club her or him again, in the manner Ngarambe demonstrated and described in blow-by-blow detail.

Not surprisingly, some zealous executioners, including some Hutu, found it sometimes difficult to kill people they knew. This was met with a mixture of understanding and mild rebuke or a fine for the perpetrator but no mercy for the victim. Élie explains that "someone who avoided the fatal gesture before a good acquaintance did it out of kindness to himself, not to his acquaintance, because he knew it brought no mercy to the other person, who'd be struck down anyhow. Quite the contrary, the victim might wind up cut more cruelly, for having slowed up the job for a moment."[69] Not surprisingly, some others find the actual butchery's blood and guts distasteful, just as not all meat eaters want to work the slaughterhouse, and some killers need to acclimate themselves to the gore. One testifying German mass murderer makes it clear that he approved of the Jews' extermination. Yet his first time killing he felt discomfort. After he had already shot "between about ten to twenty" Jews, "I requested to be relieved particularly because my neighbor shot so ineptly. Apparently, he always held the barrel of the rifle too high because horrible wounds were inflicted on the victims. In some cases, the entire rear skull of a victim was so shattered that brain matter spattered about. I simply could not look at it any longer."[70] Not moral opposition but disgust led him to ask for relief, a request his understanding superiors almost naturally granted. Just as it is wrong to gullibly accept the perpetrators' routine denials of their involvement, agency, and culpability, it is wrong, as some eagerly do, to point to a perpetrator shying away from killing an acquaintance or having such a visceral reaction, especially the first time he kills, as proof that he thinks his victims innocent and do not deserve to die. Testimony from the Indonesians' slaughter of communists, by a man referring to himself (conforming to Indonesian politeness rules, in the third person) as Kartawidjaja's Son No. 2, speaks to this and other important themes.

> Usually, those Communists whom people had managed to round up were turned over to an executioner, so that he could dispatch their souls to another world. Not everyone is capable of killing (though there are some exceptions). According to what a number of executioners themselves claimed (for Kartawidjaja's Son No. 2 had many friends among them), killing isn't easy. After dispatching the first victim, one's body usually feels feverish and one can't sleep. But once one has sent off a lot of souls to another world, one gets used to killing. "It's just like butchering a goat," they'd claim. And the fact is that Kartawidjaja's Son No. 2 often stole out of the house, either to help guard the [local] PNI [Indonesian National Party] headquarters located in the home of Pak Salim (the driver of the school bus in the area around Ngadirejo) or to watch the d[i]spatch of human souls. This too made sleeping difficult. Remembering the moans of the victims as they begged for mercy, the sound of the blood bursting from the victims' bodies, or the spouting of fresh blood when a victim was beheaded. All of this pretty much made one's hair stand on end. To say nothing of the screams of a Gerwani leader as her vagina was pierced with a sharpened bamboo pole. Many of the corpses lay sprawled like chickens after decapitation.

How could the perpetrators bear doing this? More, since they obviously approved of their deeds, as their symbolic degradation of the Gerwani leader indisputably shows, why did they relish it? Kartawidjaja's Son No. 2, because he draws on his friends' contemporaneous confidences to him, knows. He explains in his very next sentence that the executioners' finding the blood and the gore unsettling had nothing to do with principled disapproval of the deed. Far from it: "But even though such events were pretty horrifying, the participants felt thankful to have been given the chance to join in destroying infidels."[71]

The Perpetrators' Beliefs and
How They Come to Hold Them

The questions, "Do the killers believe the victims deserve what they are getting?" and "Do the killers think their deeds are right and necessary?" are not the most significant ones. The answer is all but invariably *yes*. The crucial question is why and how eliminationist perpetrators come to view their victims, and their slaughtering of their victims, in this way. This question has more complex and variable answers. Only by tackling it directly can we gain certain necessary insights into mass murder and elimination's genesis and course. This requires exploring the perpetrators' motives and the political, social, cultural, and situational contexts in which their motives come into being.

How perpetrators *conceive* of the targeted people is the critical factor in their willingness to participate in mass murder and elimination in the first place, in their willingness to visit nonlethal atrocities upon the victims, and in the character and scope of their assault. Kartawidjaja's Son No. 2's acquaintances, and the Indonesian mass murderers generally, saw the communists as enormously threatening infidels, whose souls had to be dispatched to another world. So when a throng of perpetrators from Nahdatul Ulama (NU), the main Muslim political party, converged upon a Communist Party office, Kartawidjaja's Son No. 2 reports that "as usual, before carrying out their task, the NU masses roared 'Allahu Akbar [Allah is great!]'" They then brutally beat a man they found in front of the office and burned the building down.[72] This is a textbook illustration of the intimate relationship between belief, motive, and action.

Structures—such as living under a particular regime, or being a guard in a camp—could not possibly explain the perpetrators' actions, because structural explanations deny that such a relationship exists, let alone that it has the central place it in reality occupies. Structural explanations hold that what is in a person's head is essentially unimportant for generating his actions. Instead, the political or social structures of institutions or circumstances themselves produce people's conduct, and do so invariably. Aside from the multiple conceptual and empirical reasons to reject the conventional explanations that have been shown here to be hopelessly faulty, coercion, authority, social psychological pressure, and bureaucratic membership are different kinds of structures. So they, like structural forces in general, also cannot explain the variations in what they must explain. And they cannot, because a *constant* force or influence cannot be the cause of *inconstant* or *variable* actions or outcomes. So the structure itself, which is invariable, cannot explain eliminationist assaults' many variations, some of which were strikingly in evidence in Germany and Rwanda.

The Germans had differential success in finding willing helpers and general social support in the different countries they occupied, and within each country there was variation in people's support for the Germans' eliminationist assault on the Jews in the first place. These variations did not derive from variations in the German occupation's severity but had everything to do with local antisemitism's extent and character. Danes, by and large, did not help the Germans. Lithuanians, Poles, Slovaks, and Ukrainians much more frequently did. Indeed in Lithuania, Ukraine, and elsewhere, upon the Germans' defeat of the Soviets, local peoples having received the green light from the Germans, voluntarily and with enormous brutality slaughtered the Jews among them. Italians helped the Germans only infrequently. French did so more but with enormous variability. The Germans could not turn just anyone into a willing mass murderer. Many helped willingly and many other people, in different countries, resisted.[73] And just as they knew their own people, the German leaders knew that the antisemitic peoples of many other countries would help them, while some would not, correctly anticipating at the Wannsee Conference genocidal planning meeting that they would have difficulty getting Danes and others in Scandinavia to go along with the deportation and mass murder of the Jews: "Under State Secretary [Martin] Luther comments that if this problem is dealt with thoroughly then difficulties will arise in some countries, for example in the nordic countries, and it would therefore be advisable to exclude these countries for the time being."[74] Even the clergy of different Christian churches in different countries took strikingly different stances toward the Jews' persecution and mass murder. The stances generally accorded with their own particular churches' religious and cultural attitudes toward Jews, which were embedded in their countries' particular national cultures. Among Protestant churches, the German Protestant churches supported the eliminationist assault the most. The Catholic Church overall and individual national Catholic Churches were openly behind the general eliminationist program (much more than their conational Protestant churches were), and sometimes vigorously supported its different aspects, in some countries even publicly encouraging or supporting the extermination itself.[75]

Rwanda provides the rare eliminationist instance of a government's unleashing and empowering one entire people, the Hutu, to slaughter a second entire people, the Tutsi, who everywhere were the first group's coworkers, classmates, and neighbors. Any Hutu could join the slaughtering right in his own town, village, or neighborhood. Many Hutu were encouraged to; some were compelled. While Tutsi survivors' extensive testimony, corroborated by Hutu perpetrators, recounts a staggering number of ordinary Hutu with evident willingness and zeal killing Tutsi, there is also credible testimony that in certain villages and communes some Hutu resisted killing their Tutsi neighbors. Some but not all of them then faced the unbearable choice of kill or be killed. But the overwhelming majority of the Hutu who killed did not. They fell upon the Tutsi, strangers or neighbors, with approval and many even with alacrity. Hutu Christian clergy aided and joined in.

Many other variations in the perpetrators' actions cannot be explained by the political or institutional structures. In camps, *all* victims are powerless and all perpetrators are unconstrained and all-powerful. Yet the perpetrators systematically treat different victim categories differently. In some eliminationist onslaughts, as in the Holocaust and Rwanda, the fates of victim men, women, and children were largely undifferentiated. In others, as in the Turkish, Indonesian, and Serbian onslaughts, the perpetrators treated them markedly dissimilarly.

In light of these and other variations (discussed in depth below), three sets of themes need to be investigated: (1) How, when, and over what period are the perpetrators' beliefs generated? (2) Are all mass murderous or eliminationist beliefs roughly equivalent and, if not, then how do they vary, and how do these variations matter? (3) How do other factors, such as fellow killers' enthusiasm, intersect with and perhaps reinforce the perpetrators' beliefs about the target groups, to influence the perpetrators to act as they do?

Much writing about mass murder erroneously assumes it is a unitary phenomenon and that an explanation of how the desire to slaughter people is generated in one instance must be true in all instances. Mass murders have certain common features, but they also have others, including motives and the processes that produce the motives, that vary. Not surprisingly, how people come to think that other people ought to die occurs in different ways.

Our analysis begins with a well-grounded view already present in this discussion: Peoples of most countries and cultures live with an ethic that holds human beings to have a basic human value, which means that killing a person is a morally significant act of some kind or, as a shorthand, a moral act (usually deemed immoral), in the way that cutting the grass or inadvertently stepping on an ant is not. The view that killing a person *is* a moral act leads to the question: How do people develop the contrary belief that certain specific groups do *not* possess that human value, so that killing them is not immoral? How is the moral position developed that the members of those groups must die?

There are four basic ways this willingness to kill comes about. The first has a different starting point from the others. There have been societies and cultures—probably the majority of them prior to the Enlightenment and then the dissemination of its ideas—that have *not* recognized human beings' universality and moral equality. Instead human value was seen to be possessed only by a minority, often only a given society's or culture's members. The ancient Greeks, those romanticized civilizers, while sometimes democrats among themselves (really only among certain classes of men), held slaves, who according to no one less than Aristotle lacked reason. Greeks believed non-Greeks, deemed barbarians, lacked full human qualities. In such cases throughout history a dominant group's instrumental treatment of people, to be used or eliminated according to the dominant group's needs and capabilities, has been the norm. The dehumanized status and treatment of many peoples historically is particularly well known for one common condition, slavery. Most human societies historically have enslaved others, who were also subject to being killed, except when a slaveholding society's laws forbade it to protect the polity's interests and norms. European colonizers treated people of color the world over as beings of a different kind, often as barely human, to be dispensed with, including as slaves, or production factors, or corpses, according to convenience and practicality.

We must consider that also during our time certain societies and cultures have not accorded basic human value to all or most human beings long prior to its members' committing mass murder, and that killing people has therefore not depended upon stripping this value from them. It may be that in some societies and cultures (or subcultures) there has been a generalized disregard for human life, save perhaps people's own reference group, so killing people has not been the existentially monumental and morally significant act that, during our age, it otherwise has been. Because societies and cultures can nurture people with such an ethnocentric ethic, we must acknowledge the possibility that in our era certain perpetrators have easily come to see slaughtering their victims as desirable because it has been seen as necessary, and they could come to view mass killing, what we would call mass *murder*, this way because they never saw their victims as having fundamental human value and therefore certain basic rights in the first place. Nothing moral had to be removed, no great transformation had to occur, for them to be incapable of feeling genuine sympathy with the target groups. Such killers' language of justification is amoral utilitarianism.

In the first centuries of their colonialism, Europeans treated the technologically inferior African, Asian, and Native American peoples they conquered generally with amoral utilitarianism, to be employed or disposed of according to the Europeans' needs. Also the "natives," by their resistance to the so-called civilizing process or merely to the self-styled superior Europeans' goals, gave proof of their putative inherent inferiority and unfitness. How long this attitude continued to prevail varied from country to country and people to people, though it certainly moved the European perpetrators in their eliminationist assaults on African peoples during our time. In Asia, the Chinese's colossal mass murders before and after the communist takeover, which occurred under several political contexts and regimes, raise the question of whether this amoral utilitarianism has at least partly existed there, at least until midway through the twentieth century. The extremely culturally ethnocentric imperial Japan preyed on Asian peoples in this manner, hearkening back to European colonialists, though drawing on indigenous Japanese cultural sources for these attitudes and practices.[76] It may also be that such attitudes existed amidst the Democratic Republic of the Congo's violent anarchy during the past several years. Yet in the story of our time, these instances, as important as they are, are the exceptions.

Our age's mass murders and eliminations have overwhelmingly been perpetrated by people nurtured in societies and cultures that assigned fundamental human value to people in general. In such societies, this protective attribute had to be stripped away for the perpetrators to see other people as deserving death or elimination. This has occurred in three basic ways.

1. People who had no particular prejudice or animus for another group can have hatred forged in the heat of real (usually military) conflicts that lead them to believe that the enemy people must be defeated at any cost (permanently) and deserve the worst.
2. People can become beholden to political ideologies that call for destroying or eliminating others. If such ideological regimes are in power long enough to socialize new generations, they can educate a reservoir of like-minded followers who will willingly act upon the regime's and their own eliminationist beliefs.
3. People can have preexisting powerful prejudices against specific groups, which then get activated for lethal and other eliminationist aims by leaders bent on eliminationist politics.

More than one of these pathways can be operating, sometimes on different perpetrators, sometimes regarding different victim groups. Nevertheless, whatever the complexity, one of them is usually dominant and its lineaments are easily discernable.

Real conflicts, when unusually brutal or posing an existential threat, have occasionally forged mass-murderous responses. These are essentially reactions to suffering at the hands of an actual antagonist. Even if the reactions are immoral and unjust, they have an air of retributive justice and sometimes the veneer of military or existential necessity, which is how the perpetrators justify and rationalize them.

The most obvious context that engendered eliminationist assaults, including mass murder, were Germany's and Japan's imperial, predatory, and annihilationist invasions and occupations of various countries and peoples. The Germans' and Japanese's barbarities during their respective attacks and occupations produced in their victims an intense hatred far exceeding what had existed before and (in many cases there was no particular prejudice at all) that in some instances got translated into eliminationist and mass-murderous revenge assaults upon the Germans and Japanese.

To most Americans, little-known Japan, halfway across the globe, had been virtually absent from their mental world. Even if many, certainly on the West Coast, were prejudiced against East Asians in general, including the Japanese, they felt no *enmity* for Japanese. Yet, owing to several features of the war, Americans developed a dehumanized image and hatred of Japanese that led them to conclude that just about any action was permissible against this heinous enemy. Japan's surprise attack on Pearl Harbor was a far more threatening assault upon the United States, and a greater shock to Americans, than Al Qaeda's 9/11 attacks. Overnight, it plunged the United States into a world war that consumed and disrupted the country for years, took almost 300,000 American lives, wounded an additional 700,000, and risked millions more. This produced the axiomatic view that the Japanese violated civilized society's most basic rules, a view that transformed them into a nation of outlaws. This view was inflamed by how the Japanese fought in battle and treated conquered peoples and prisoners of war. Already before Pearl Harbor, the Japanese's mass murder of perhaps 200,000 Chinese in the notorious Rape of Nanking (Nanjing) had become well known to Americans, a moniker for what could be expected from the Japanese during war. The Japanese's subsequent killings and abuse of conquered peoples amplified this image. Their fanaticism in fighting to the death, including their kamikaze and other suicide attacks, construed them as an enemy that would rather die in order to kill Americans than succumb. Their treatment of allied POWs, especially the infamous Bataan death march, during which they killed twenty thousand (mainly) Filipino and American prisoners, reinforced the image of the Japanese as uncivilized, treacherous, and uncompromisingly dangerous.

Born of the manner in which the Japanese fought and treated civilian populations, a racially grounded demonizing of the Japanese developed among Americans, placing the Japanese beyond the pale of humanity, which suggested that no measure should remain unused when trying to defeat them. Americans routinely referred to Japanese as monkeys, baboons, dogs, rats, vipers, cockroaches, or vermin. Leading American civilian and military leaders developed and articulated eliminationist, even explicitly genocidal views about what should be done to the Japanese. President Franklin Roosevelt's son and confidante, Elliott, told Vice President Henry Wallace in May 1945, shortly after Germany's capitulation, that the United States should bomb Japan "until we have destroyed about half the Japanese civilian population." Such views were echoed in popular opinion. In December 1944, in response to the public opinion survey question "What do you think we should do with Japan as a country after the war?" 13 percent of Americans chose "kill all Japanese."[77] So it is no surprise that Americans perpetrated and supported mass slaughters—Tokyo's firebombing and then nuclear incinerations—in the name of saving American lives, and of giving the Japanese what they richly deserved.

So Harry Truman became a mass murderer. And 85 percent of Americans at the time approved of Truman's actions—23 percent admitted that they wished that "many more of them [atomic bombs] had been used before Japan had a chance to surrender." Today a large majority of Americans still approve of the nuclear bombing, as they widely believe the fiction of its military necessity. This fiction continues to be propagated by American apologists and guardians of national honor, even though it was known *not to be true* at the time. Truman and his advisers were well aware that, facing an already militarily defeated Japan in a virtual stranglehold, they could have likely imminently ended the war without invading Japan or using nuclear weapons.[78] Sharing Eisenhower's belief that "Japan was, at that very moment, seeking some way to surrender with a minimum loss of 'face,'" Admiral William Leahy, Truman's chief of staff, maintained that "the use of this barbarous weapon at Hiroshima and Nagasaki was of no material assistance in our war against Japan. The Japanese were already defeated and ready to surrender."[79]

They started it is an emotionally and rhetorically powerful rationale and retort, used by children on the playground and men—Truman "repaid [them] many fold"—deciding who should live or die. It is especially powerful when *they* really did start it, and continue to shoot at you, insisting that they not stop short of victory that will bring incalculable

Firebombed Tokyo

destruction and death to your country and countrymen. Whatever the military purposes also were, *they started it* was and continues to be the rationale for the American and British bombings of Japanese and German cities in those instances when the actual principal purpose was to kill civilians and destroy their infrastructure of existence, thereby weakening civilian support for the war effort. The Americans firebombed Tokyo, killing more than eighty thousand. The British and Americans bombed Dresden, purposely destroying most of the city and killing between eighteen thousand and twenty-five thousand Germans. That the Germans had previously, with bombing, virtually destroyed Guernica in 1937 and Rotterdam's inner city in May 1940, and in the 1940–1941 blitz on London killed twenty thousand people and destroyed or damaged a good part of the city—crucial facts, particularly the slaughter of Londoners, conveniently forgotten or skirted in today's political attempts to reconstruct Germans as victims—and would have done much worse, only further reinforced the Allies' resolve to let the Germans reap what they sowed. The Japanese in May 1939 similarly started such bombing in the Asian theater, with incendiary bombing of Chongqing, the Nationalist Chinese capital, killing perhaps more than five thousand.

The retributive anti-German reaction after World War II by Poles, Czechs, and others to the Germans' conquest and, in many areas, their murderous and brutal overlordship can be seen as an on-the-ground partial parallel to the murderous Allied wartime air campaign (that did have a military strategic component). The animus the Japanese and Germans engendered among their surviving victims led to counter-slaughters and counterexpulsions justified by military or national political necessity or expedience. In Europe, they also produced a broad-based counterassault upon Germans and ethnic Germans, owing to, as a British review of the Czech press concluded about Czechoslovakia, "a universal and burning hatred of the Germans . . . and a demand that they should go, and go quickly," both to achieve national homogenization and as revenge or justice. Poland's provisional governor of Silesia explained, "We will deal with the German population inhabiting these lands, which have been Polish since before the beginning of time, just as the Germans taught us." The Germans—not just SS men but ordinary Germans—had conducted themselves monstrously in these countries, where the image of them was as monsters. This image was not Americans' fanciful caricatures about the distant, analogously brutal Japanese, but one etched by direct experience, and enhanced and extended by human beings' penchant to generalize. The Polish military command articulated the region's understandable and commonsense, if factually and morally indefensible, view that the "entire German people" were responsible for the "criminal" war.[80]

The eliminationist campaigns against ethnic Germans, while drawing on long-standing anti-German prejudices, at least among some Poles, Czechs, and others, were vehement reactions to these peoples' own suffering and derived from a self-protective logic (Germans should never again have cause to invade in order to "protect" ethnic Germans) even among people who would have earlier deplored such measures. Poles, mainly from the Polish annexed parts of eastern Germany, and Czechs conducted a thoroughgoing and sometimes murderous expulsion of Germans on the order of ten million people, set up temporary camps for hundreds of thousands, and killed tens of thousands. The burning animus against ethnic Germans led to the rare instance of a democratic regime, in Czechoslovakia, practicing large-scale and lethal domestic eliminationist politics, with the support—as in Poland—of people of all political parties and aspirations. The first, most brutal and lethal phase of what became known as "wild expulsions" took place in the aftermath of liberation from the Germans, as the Poles and Czechs together with their leaders descended upon local Germans in a fury. Poles and Czechs expelled the vast majority of the ethnic Germans later in an organized and orderly fashion and with the consent of the victorious Allies, who, seeing the Poles' and Czechs' determination, approved it at the postwar Potsdam Conference.

In addition to the other justifications, the perpetrators' actions were wrapped up in the simple belief that this was payback: "We proceed with the Germans," according to the Second Polish Army command, "as they did with us."[81] A sign at one Czech camp's entrance declared "An Eye for an Eye—A Tooth for a Tooth."[82] This moral and prudential justificatory logic and language was so strikingly prevalent, and still is, that to this day the countries involved have produced little self-doubt and criticism. Although such thinking, emotions, and acts might be psychologically understandable, it should be unambiguously understood that the eliminationist acts are criminal.

The instances of brutal *war* engendering motives for actual retributive or reactive eliminationist onslaughts have been surprisingly few. As we saw earlier, in the overwhelming majority of instances, war in itself does not generate an eliminationist orientation and mass murder. Even in the Central and Eastern Europeans' massive eliminationist campaign against ethnic Germans, it was not the war fighting itself, but the Germans' subsequent murderous and predatory occupation, including their brutal and racist attempts to expunge other nations' and peoples' existence, that generated the beliefs and attendant rage motivating the counterexpulsions and killings.

A second, more frequent and more deadly path has led people to see others as deserving death or elimination. The sway of ideologies has bloodied our time. People governed by communist regimes on the left and by dictatorships on the right have come to see large groups of enemies standing in their way or threatening their existence, and concluded that exterminating and eliminating them is necessary and just.

All ideologies answer three questions: What is the problem, who is the enemy, what is the solution? Ideologies, as opposed to prejudices, specify enemies based on a *political* worldview about society's proper organization. The understanding of the problems and the solutions (utopian, dystopian, or otherwise) suggests or logically intimates that certain categories of people, often including individuals opposing the ideologues and their ambitions, need to be eliminated somehow— suppressed, reeducated, expelled from their homes, confined in camps, or killed. In such instances, an eliminationist assault's initial impetus is not prejudice against particular ethnic or religious groups, but the execution of a political blueprint. The perpetrators choose targets not because of a long-standing antipathy or a cultural aversion or animus toward them, and (certainly initially) not because of the people's as-criptive identity. They choose targets because of a political conception of the world that defines certain people into enemies.

The ideologizing of a society, or a good portion of it, has two stages. The political movement's cadres taking power, usually through revolution or coup, become literally empowered, becoming the regime's shock troops willing, even eager, to carry out its defensive or transformative projects. They also set about educating the young in their creed, and try their best (typically with uneven results) to reeducate the adult population. After several years they succeed in rearing their first cohorts of young adults who share their worldview, with its designated problems, enemies, and solutions. In the countries where eliminationist regimes maintain their power, an ever-growing reservoir of people subscribe to the beliefs that will make them willing to eliminate enemies, including by lethal means.

Such eliminationist ideologies' content varies greatly. The political Right's murderous ideologies tend to speak in the nation's name, some-times in a racist manner, have a militarized conception of politics and society, and construe the regime's enemies or opponents, or just those expressing ordinary political dissent and calling for economic and social change or justice, as equivalent to being the people's enemies. Whatever their many and substantial differences, this has been true of Nazism, Croatia's Ustasha, the rightist regimes in Latin America, including in Argentina, Chile, Guatemala, and El Salvador. Often a national-security mentality prevails, construing those expressing political dissent as as-saulting the state's or the nation's security or stability.

The political Left's murderous ideologies, communisms of various hues, seek to reorganize society according to a totalizing political and social vision, glorify that vision and the class or segment of society that is declared to be its bearer, and declare as enemies all individuals and groups that consider themselves or that are "objectively" defined to be opposed to that vision. This vision admits little possibility of coexistence with doubters and dissenters, let alone actual enemies. Communist regimes and their followers have a strong proclivity for eliminating the communist vision's opponents. Because Marxism promises and requires a homogenous, dissent-free paradise, and because it posits sizable groups as being, by definition, "socially dangerous elements," powerful roadblocks to that world's creation, communists see the need to remove them as acute, so the restraints on how it may be done crumble.

Mass-murdering communist regimes have most notably, after initially drawing on poor and resentful proletarians and peasants, reared generations of true believers, by inculcating the young, who then readily lend themselves to eliminationist programs. Especially using their control of schools, the Soviets, communist Chinese, and communist North Koreans instilled in many of their subjects the fanatical belief in their political systems' rightness, in the existence of systematic enmity among many people inside and outside the country, and the systematic need to do just about anything to eliminate those enemies. The Soviets erected the gulag, produced mass famine death, and deported putatively disloyal peoples. In some Soviet satellite countries, communist regimes killed (especially in Yugoslavia) and imprisoned in labor camps (as in Romania) real and imagined enemies. The communist Chinese slaughtered more people than the Soviets, including mass numbers in their Laogai labor camp gulag. North Korea's true believers have turned the entire country into a quasi-gulag, with a landscape peppered by the camps of the regime's formal gulag, the Kwanliso, or Special Control Institutions. Each communist system's most loyal supporters were continuously replenished by new communist-raised generations. (This would have almost certainly been true of a longer-lasting Khmer Rouge.) Their zealous devotion to "purifying" their societies of class, ethnic, or religious enemies drove them, to a degree reminiscent of the Christian Crusaders' analogous fanaticism, to slaughter Jews and Muslims in Christianity's name and cause. Yet these latter-day communist crusaders, using a modern state, could better organize and systematize their murderousness, making it much deadlier.

In the name of creating a fantasized society of plenty, harmony, and total equality, despotic communist parties instituted dictatorships of extreme, homogenizing control over society, economy, culture, and thought, which deadened society, created a dysfunctional economy, desiccated culture, and stultified thought. The communists' gross inhumanity and manifestly false claims about the world prevented them from turning all their subjects into supporters. Nevertheless, communist regimes did find and socialized many acolytes, and created a huge reservoir of willing perpetrators upon which they drew when staffing their eliminationist institutions, though many communist regimes never perpetrated horrors on the scale of the most notorious ones. The phenomenon of parents fearing their children might wittingly or unwittingly send them to the gulag by betraying the parents' dissent from the regime expressed these regimes' powerful socializing capacity.

Marxism's universal principles recognize no differences of national or ethnic origin, but real-world communism typically attaches its Marxism to a national or ethnic chauvinism. In some instances, such as in China and in Cambodia, communist leaders grafted communism onto peasants' resentment and hatred of landlords or urban dwellers, deemed class or national enemies. One Chinese peasant explained forthrightly in an interview why he killed and cut open the chest of a former landlord's son, a boy: "The person I killed is an enemy. . . . Ha, ha! I make revolution, and my heart is red! Didn't Chairman Mao say: It's either we kill them or they kill us? You die and I live. This is class struggle!"[83] This has all been clearest, though by no means singular, with the xenophobic Khmer Rouge, which celebrated the Khmer (Cambodia's majority ethnic group) as the one authentic people capable of building true communism. The Khmer Rouge inculcated poorly educated peasant teenagers and boys with a bristling hatred for all things and all people supposedly standing in the way of Angkar, the romanticized pure Khmer civilization that they sought to re-create. These fully ideologized teenagers and young men came to believe that those not serving Angkar had to be destroyed. A full analysis of any given communist leadership and its followers' murderousness would require that other factors, including long existing prejudices, be considered, yet there can be no doubt that communists' exterminationist and eliminationist campaigns have been overwhelmingly ideologically motivated and driven.

The mass murderers of 9/11, all members of Al Qaeda, were classic ideological zealots, and yet they are unusual in our time because their fanaticism's foundation, or at least its disinhibiting mechanism, was religion. These shock troops of a transnational and, at the time, a quasi-state political entity based in Afghanistan, were animated by a political ideology of extreme intolerance calling for the destruction of the civilization, Western civilization, which they believed had held back Islam and which stood for the liberation of people from many kinds of oppression. The West is especially noxious to the perpetrators because it opposes religious domination and gender domination, which the perpetrators wanted to maintain and intensify where they exist in Islamic form, and to further spread them beyond, ultimately all over the world. Their religiously grounded dreams and justifications of murdering millions, including four million Americans, according to Al Qaeda,[84] exceed anything that other major political movements and governments have ever dared broadcast to the world, let alone with such explicit and clear mass-murderous formulations. Moreover, Al Qaeda is part of a larger transnational, though loosely organized (and sometimes internecine), mass-murderous political movement (discussed in depth in Chapter 10), best called Political Islam, that preaches and acts upon a lethal eliminationist political creed grounded in Political Islamists' understanding of Allah's commands and promises. Vast differences notwithstanding, Political Islam resembles Nazism in its murderousness. In addition to Al Qaeda, this movement exists in many countries and terror groups, holding power in Iran, Sudan, the Palestinian Authority especially in Hamas, and Hezbollah in Lebanon.

The third and probably most common path to producing our time's eliminationist mindsets is forged in powerful prejudices.

The Germans in South-West Africa were old-fashioned racists, believing Africans were subhumans who could, in a utilitarian manner, be cleared from the land that had been their homes long before the Germans arrived. One missionary explains: "The average German looks down upon the natives as being about on the same level as the higher primates ('baboon' being their favorite term for the natives) and treats them like animals. The settler holds that the native has a right to exist only in so far as he is useful to the white man. It follows that the whites value horses and even their oxen more than they value the natives."[85] When these putative subhumans became too resistant, the Germans systematically slaughtered them. General Lothar von Trotha explained to German Chief of Staff General Alfred von Schlieffen his thinking, which, in light of the Herero's rebellion, prevailed: "The ideas of the governor and the other old African hands and my ideas are diametrically opposed. For a long time they have wanted to negotiate and have insisted that the Herero are a necessary raw material for the future of the land. I totally oppose this view. I believe that the nation as such must be annihilated."[86] An ideology of German expansionism, later part of the foundation of the destructive mid-twentieth-century empire in Eastern Europe, was at work here. But it was a mere adjunct to German settlers' deep racism that denied Africans the most basic moral respect and human rights. The Germans deemed Africans a "raw material"—even those Germans holding the comparatively benign view of them—that, in the Herero's case, eventually became too costly and dangerous to work with. So they were junked.

The Turks' various murderous assaults upon the Armenians over the course of more than two decades were animated by a long-existing, intensive prejudice and hatred, which the Armenians' desires for greater self-governance and autonomy further fed. The largest annihilative onslaught, of 1915–1916, occurred during World War I, but, as the Turkish leaders' own words and documents tell us, they saw the war as an opportunity to implement their long-standing wish to solve their geopolitical Armenian problem. The Turkish leaders were, whatever their prejudices, moved by cold eliminationist calculations of power and opportunity. Their followers were animated by bigotry's more primal beliefs and emotions, leading them to believe in the necessity of eliminating the non-Turkic and non-Islamic Armenians, a putatively foreign, corrosive people, with alien, infidel, and polluting religion and practices. A Turkish killer, Captain Shükrü, admitted to Krikoris Balakian, an Armenian priest, that in annihilating the Armenians they were conducting a "holy war." Afterward, in accord with the Muslim notion of jihad, Shükrü said he "would say a prayer and his soul would be absolved."[87] American Ambassador Henry Morgenthau knew about the calls to jihad, which was part of Turkey's declaration of war, followed by the Sheik-ul-Islam's call to Turks "to arise and massacre their Christian oppressors." (This was directed specifically at Russia, England, and France as part of a general call to arms.) Commenting on such exhortations to commit jihad (particularly an incendiary pamphlet the Germans wrote and distributed throughout Turkey and other Muslim countries), Morgenthau explains: "It aroused in the Mohammedan soul all that intense animosity toward the Christian which is the fundamental fact in his strange emotional nature, and thus started passions aflame that afterward spent themselves in the massacres of the Armenians and other subject peoples."[88]

The Turks' assaults exemplify a phenomenon found in many other eliminationist programs, a disjunction between leaders' and followers' motives. The Turkish leaders, aware of this disjunction, cynically exploited it, as indicated in their "Ten Commandments," which codified their easily executable plan to "excite Moslem opinion," because "the Armenians have already won the hatred of the Moslems." Leaders, to serve their more coolly calculated policies (which also are often ultimately grounded in prejudice), happily mobilize the visceral prejudices and hatred among their followers—in the case of the Turkish leadership when discussing the "Moslems," whom they so clearly see as being different from themselves, to "provoke organized massacres."[89] Charlotte Kechejian, an Armenian survivor, answers the question of why the Turks slaughtered Armenians, by repeatedly stating, "They hate the Christians. They hate Christians and they were Muslims."[90] Turks' widespread animus against Armenians was long-standing, though it remained relatively quiescent until cynical leaders repeatedly ignited it to produce murderous conflagration. This is one of many classic instances (others are explored below) of prejudice's lurking power and of leaders' strategically mobilizing existing eliminationist sentiment at a chosen time for lethal outcomes.

The territories of Yugoslavia have been the locus of deeply rooted prejudices and hatred and, during our time, of various mass-murderous and eliminationist eruptions. Several small and contested political regions have housed imperfectly the different ethnic groups, including Serbs, Croats, Albanians, Bosniaks, Montenegrins, and Slovenians, which were further divided by powerful religious affiliations to Catholicism, Orthodoxy, and Islam. These groups have periodically mobilized around nationalist politics for independence, for the subjugation of one or another of the others, with and against powerful eschatological or militaristic ideologies of communism and fascism, and often in the name of exclusivist religious salvation. The region has been prone to eliminationist hatred, fantasies, and initiatives that have always been grounded in generations-old prejudices and mutual hatred between Croats and Serbs, between Orthodox and Catholics, between Christians and Muslims, and more. When during our era this region has had its two major bouts of mass murder and elimination, political leaderships easily mobilized many people to eliminate their enemies and rivals. During the 1940s the Germans' conquest and creation of a new German-allied Croatia under the leadership of the murderous Ustasha movement produced the conditions that allowed the fascist Catholic Croats finally to act upon their preexisting desires to rid themselves of the Orthodox Serbs. After the war, Yugoslavia's Josip Tito's communist state, preaching interethnic harmony, suppressed these ethnic hatreds. Yet, despite the communist regime's genuine efforts to eradicate them, they continued to simmer beneath the surface. During the 1990s, with communist Yugoslavia's breakup the now-dominant Serbs acted upon their long-existing and, owing to the Serbs' genuine suffering in the 1940s, greatly inflamed hatred of Croats to undertake an eliminationist onslaught against them as part of their attempt to secure a greater Serbia in the face of the Croats' drive for an independent state. The Croats returned the favor in kind. And both, especially the Serbs, sought to eliminate their hated Islamic co-territorialists, in Bosnia. Finally, and most colossally (though less explicitly murderously), the Serbs did the same in Kosovo. Although the mutual and serial "ethnic cleansings" in the 1990s served to forge new ethnic and religious enmities among these groups, the foundations of these various ethnic perpetrators' willingness to expel and kill their victims were laid long ago, with the prejudices and hatred of decades and centuries, and with the mass-murderous violence during World War II, mainly by Croats against Serbs but also by Serb partisans against Croats and others. Milorad Ekmečić, a Bosnian Serb founder of an ultra-Serbian nationalist party, asserts that Croats killed seventy-eight members of his family in one village in 1941. "Over the years," he recounts, "when I came to visit [the village] for weddings and funerals the stories they told were about the massacres during the war. They were possessed by the memories of 1941–45. Probably it was the same with the Muslims and the Croats."[91] But under communism's extreme repression, neither Serbs nor Croats could act upon their mutual hatred. As one Bosnian Croat explains, "We lived in peace and harmony because every hundred meters we had a policeman to make sure we loved each other very much."[92] He might have added that once communism's policemen were gone, political leaders pushed, the simmering hatred and murderous desires became activated, and all hell broke loose.

In South Asia, Muslim-Hindu and Pakistani-Bengali prejudices and hatred have structured much of the region's politics and have been inflamed into periodic conflagrations. During the partition of India and Pakistan, the prejudices and intense emotions on all sides led ordinary Muslims and Hindus, mainly in paramilitaries, though often in mobs the paramilitaries directed, to slaughter one another. Local leaders, under the direction or with the go-ahead of their respective main political leaders or military and police forces, organized most of them to commit systematic, though not comprehensive, murderous assaults all over the region, including by attacking trains transporting people from one side of the partition line to the other. The partition itself was predicated on the notion that the principally religious-based mutual prejudices and enmities made coexistence extremely difficult. Where geographic separation—including massive population transfer— was feasible, it had to be done, especially given the intensifying conflicts. As Mohandas Gandhi declared in 1946, "We are not yet in the midst of a civil war. But we are nearing it." This, among complex reasons of nationalist ideology and aspirations, as well as considerations of personal interest, meant, as Jawaharlal Nehru, India's political father, explained years later, that "the plan for partition offered a way out and we took it."[93]

Sorting out these antagonistic populations, however necessary it may have been to reduce the likelihood of civil war, proved disastrous for millions and further intensified the prejudices. It also produced one of the most artificial countries ever, Pakistan, composed of two territories, West Pakistan and East Pakistan, divided by more than six hundred miles of India. The discrimination of the dominant non-Bengali

West Pakistanis against the Bengali East Pakistanis itself eventually led to the 1971 civil war, during which the West Pakistanis murdered between one million and three million Bengalis in East Pakistan, and then an Indian invasion of East Pakistan that resulted in the new country Bangladesh.

The scores of slaughters of indigenous peoples during our time, in Asia, Africa, and Latin America—the Germans' annihilation of the Herero and the Nama included—by many societies' dominant groups, led or green-lighted by their governing political regimes, have had as their foundation prejudices that include a thorough deprecation of the targeted people's moral worth. For generations, prejudices have demeaned indigenous peoples as "subhumans," "baboons," "savages," "vermin," or "nuisances." Those holding these prejudices have been prone to reacting to conflict with their eventual victims over territory or resources with a dismissive, exterminatory impulse and follow-through. In country after country where indigenous peoples have been the objects of exterminationist and other eliminationist assaults, the common justification of their putative backwardness, noxious qualities, or diminished human and moral worth have disinhibited, indeed spurred, the perpetrators to solve their "problem" in violent and murderous ways. As one Mayan human rights activist and anthropologist says, "indigenous people are killed simply for who they are."[94]

During their colonial rule over central Africa, the Belgians nurtured if not set in motion the Tutsi and Hutu's mutual demonizing and dehumanizing. The Belgians had earlier pursued the most brutal politics of domination, exploitation, and mass murder in neighboring Congo, slaughtering three million, five million, ten million people (no one really knows), starting in the nineteenth century and ending in 1908. In Burundi and Rwanda, the Belgians practiced a politics of extensive ethnic stratification, a divide-and-rule tactic that produced ethnic antipathy onto which was grafted a racist prejudice that in postcolonial times, if not before, reached almost Nazi-like proportions. As each country's politics became organized around these heightened, ethnically grounded suspicions and antagonisms, extreme conflict and eliminationist politics between Hutu and Tutsi in both Burundi and Rwanda produced a temporal web of reciprocal—which does not mean exactly equivalent—prejudice and hatred, which was fed by real and imagined experience, resulting in mass murder. The mutual prejudice and hatred have been so intensive that when the political leaders of either group decided to solve their "problems" lethally, they easily unleashed their ethnic constituents, often organized in killing institutions. Also, neighbors readily fell upon neighbors in Burundi, where Tutsi have been the principal perpetrators, and in Rwanda, where Hutu have been the mass murderers.

In Sudan's various immense eliminationist assaults, with the one in Darfur ongoing, the perpetrators have been animated by deep-seated prejudice that has two sources, racism and a highly aggressive political Islamic religious hostility, that were mutually reinforcing in the attack on the black animist southern Sudanese. According to the Sudanese regime, a religious and fundamentalist Islamic politics under continuing minority Arab domination must govern all Sudan. The non-Islamic peoples of the south and blacks in all parts of the country naturally resisted this. Hence the regime's thoroughgoing and enduring annihilationist and eliminationist politics. There is a good reason for seeing the Arab political Islamist regime in Khartoum as much of Sudan's imperial occupier, convinced of its own god-given right to convert, rule, and displace non-Muslims and blacks, whom the perpetrators repeatedly refer to as slaves. Combining the mindset of imperial conquerors intent on subjugating a vast, far-flung population with the fire of Political Islamic conviction of acting in Allah's name against infidels and Allah's enemies, the Political Islamic leaders and followers have practiced eliminationist politics over a longer period (now in the third decade) and with more catastrophic consequences (more than two million killed and millions more expelled) than only a few of our age's most murderous regimes.

The Germans' eliminationist campaigns during the Nazi period, because they were so various in scope and targets, compose the most complicated case (which is treated in depth in Part III). The Germans' murderousness *overall* is an instance of mixed motives and mechanisms. Our era's most unambiguous case of activating long-standing, intensive prejudice for the mass murder of a discrete group is the Germans' annihilation of the Jews, the source of which one ordinary German mass murderer who killed Jews in Poland's Lublin region explains, speaking for the German mass murderers and most Germans as well:

"The Jew was not acknowledged by us to be a human being."[95] The Germans' apocalyptic onslaught in the Soviet Union and elsewhere against Bolshevism and its willing adherents and unwilling subjects was an instance of ideologically driven killing undertaken as an end in itself and to create a German empire. The Germans' killing and population transfers of Slavic peoples such as Poles emerged out of a mixture of prejudice, ideological fantasy, and the brutal utilitarian calculus of a disinhibited occupying power and its troops. The Nazis were also set upon imbuing Germans with a racist worldview—broadly resonating with widespread existing prejudices in Germany—that denied a common humanity's existence. By 1940 the Nazis had succeeded in educating a generation of young adults who, on top of their society's profound prejudices and hatred, generally disregarded human life that was not of the privileged "Aryan" or Germanic variety. Proof of this was a German high school class' project in the 1980s to investigate their school's curriculum and pedagogy during the Nazi period. After studying curricula, textbooks, and lesson plans, and interviewing former teachers and students, they published their findings in a book titled *Schools in the Third Reich: Education for Death*.[96] This worldview made these Nazi-era young Germans their country's most relentless and promiscuous mass murderers.

Just as Germans in general and not only German men, and just as Turks in general and not only Turkish men, and in the former Yugoslavia, Serbs and not only Serbian men, and in Rwanda, Hutu and not only Hutu men came to see exterminating and eliminating the targeted peoples as necessary, so too have women and not only men acted upon these socially shared beliefs to willingly lend themselves, including as perpetrators, to exterminationist and eliminationist assaults. When we look to the populations in whose name eliminationist politics are perpetrated, women are no less supportive than men, and are no less desirous of the broader political and social transformations undergirding such politics than the men are. In those mass murders and eliminations where substantial evidence exists—among colonialists everywhere, including the British in Kenya, Germans during the Nazi period, Serbs, and Hutu, the eliminationist conceptions of the victims and the stances taken toward the exterminationist and eliminationist assaults were shared by men and women alike. This is not surprising.

Prejudices, hatred, and eliminationist beliefs are nongendered. The mechanisms, whichever they are, generating them for a society's or group's men and boys, generate them also for its women and girls. Everything we know about human cognition, and more specifically about belief systems and prejudices, indicates that when eliminationist views broadly exist in a society, they become the property of men and women equally, and so they are equally potential participants in mass murder, even if their actual rates of participation, because of social and political norms, differ markedly.

From Beliefs to Action

Ideologies, ideas and values, beliefs about other people and the world, prejudices and hatreds, these are the things, mechanisms—call them what you will—that have moved the perpetrators of these and many other mass murders and eliminations. The people slaughtering, eliminating, and inflicting immense suffering on other people, upon millions of children, have been motivated by their beliefs about the victims and about the treatment or punishments they justly deserve. Mass murder begins not in abstract structures or inchoate psychological pressures, but in the minds and hearts of men and women.

When leaders are ready for elimination and the kill, they activate people's otherwise inert eliminationist beliefs by announcing themselves or through surrogates, publicly or only within eliminationist institutions, that the onslaught is necessary and about to begin. Depending on how much people have contemplated what to actually do to the targeted groups, different reactions greet the eliminationist announcement or notification.

To those believing in the necessity of dealing somehow with the acute problem the victims putatively pose, yet who themselves have not dwelled on solutions, especially the most radical ones, learning of an eliminationist campaign comes as an epiphany or relief. Upon their leader's or government's decision to expel or kill the despised and feared group, or upon witnessing the onslaught itself, many react with satisfaction and approval. They finally apprehend what was always within them about how they must proceed. Just as, in the words of the critic Roger Fry, an artist with a great artwork can teach people something new about themselves, so too can the leader who offers a new way of looking at and solving a commonly agreed-upon problem: "We feel that he has expressed something which was latent in us all the time, but which we never realized, that he has revealed us to ourselves in revealing himself."[97] A heady sense of righteousness and mission can also accompany this epiphany, which coalesces into a person's determination to contribute to the heroic enterprise. Kristallnacht, the proto-genocidal nationwide assault in 1938 upon Germany's Jews, their synagogues and communal institutions, their businesses and homes, initially shook Melita Maschmann, a teenager fully subscribing to the demonological image of Jews in Germany. Then belief's logic took hold:

> For a space of a second I was clearly aware that something terrible had happened there. Something frighteningly brutal. But almost at once I switched over to accepting what had happened as over and done with and avoiding critical reflection. I said to myself: the Jews are the enemies of the new Germany. Last night they had a taste of what this means. Let us hope that World Jewry, which has resolved to hinder Germany's "new steps towards greatness," will take the events of last night as a warning. If the Jews sow hatred against us all over the world, they must learn that we have hostages for them in our hands.[98]

Another class of people is not surprised because they have had foresight or a self-articulated desire for a concrete eliminationist solution. Upon learning of the actual eliminationist program, they react more matter-of-factly, which does not mean without jubilation, but without experiencing an epiphany. For them, it's about time. Let's get on with it. Finally. A Hutu executioner, Pancrace Hakizamungili, explains: "The first day, a messenger from the municipal judge went house to house summoning us to a meeting right away. There the judge announced that the reason for the meeting was the killing of every Tutsi without exception. It was simply said, and it was simple to understand." Fulgence, a comrade, concurs: "The judge told everyone that from then on we were to do nothing but kill Tutsi. Well, we understood: that was a final plan. The atmosphere had changed."[99]

Arkan (Željko Ražnatović) with his Tigers

Others chomping at the bit have been waiting to act upon long-standing wishes. When the enabling orders come, they can finally have a go at the enemies, give the hated people what they deserve and more. Such reactions are found among the shock troops of murderous leaderships, such as the SA and SS in Germany, the students of China's Cultural Revolution, the Khmer Rouge's cadres, Iraq's Republican Guards, the Serbs' Arkan Tigers, the Hutu's Interahamwe, and others. Like eager, impassioned soldiers primed for battle, these people understand that their leaders have been pointing them, sometimes explicitly, toward eliminating their enemies, want it to happen, and, when it does, finally let loose their pent-up hatred. Many such people are already in institutions that mobilize for killing. Others are among the larger pool of potential perpetrators, in other words, the general populace governed by eliminationist prejudices.

That is why some popular assaults, sometimes called pogroms or riots, are initially so wild and frenzied. Often, they are analyzed misleadingly as "mob psychology" or "crowd behavior." If we see such assaults not as the mob's licentiousness somehow magically taking over people, but as sudden activating, unleashing, and channeling of people's preexisting, pent-up animosities and desires toward their targets, then we can *understand* such explosions and their frenzied quality. Mob or crowd psychology's clichéd account is inapplicable to eliminationist assaults, or, if applicable, then at most to an insignificant part of them. People's prior beliefs and hatreds' activation and validation, their satisfaction of acting upon them, and their immediate social reinforcement from their collective participation in a common valued project characterize these initial popular responses to the announcement of exterminationist and eliminationist assaults. Mob psychology cannot be what is driving them to act, because in so many cases, the people continue, after the initial spasm of violence, to brutalize and kill the targeted group, or to support those who do. The person in the "crowd" thinks or says *I did something I never imagined myself doing*, but he does not say *I suddenly had my views of the people I assaulted utterly and forever changed, and for the first time saw them to be so pernicious as to deserve what they got.*

Among those believing that the people targeted for elimination in principle deserve their fate are those nevertheless disapproving of a given punishment, particularly mass annihilation, because they deem it immoral. This attitude—belief in a person's guilt, belief in the need for severe punishment, but opposition to killing—characterizes in many societies people opposing the death penalty, even for criminals committing the most heinous acts. Thus, some people animated by great prejudice against a group balk at the most final eliminationist solutions. This moral inhibition may come from a person's individual moral sense or be culturally derived from various sources, especially religion. Religious leaders sharing in their society's or group's prejudices and hatreds often support eliminationist onslaughts, even lethal ones. But others resist acting upon their beliefs' logic because of the values informing their understanding of the human and divine order. Many Catholic clergy, while agreeing with Germans and many other Europeans regarding the Jews' supposed pernicious nature and guilt, and the need to eliminate them and their influence from European society, balked at mass murder. The Vatican's authoritative journal *Civiltà cattolica* in 1937, before the systematic mass murder began, explicitly expressed this when contemplating what ought to be done with the Jews. It was "an obvious fact that the Jews are a disruptive element because of their dominating spirit and their revolutionary tendency. Judaism is . . . a foreign body that irritates and provokes the reactions of the organism it has contaminated." The journal discussed solutions to the "Jewish Problem" ambivalently and explicitly considered various forms of, in its own formulation, "elimination" *as functional equivalents.* *Civiltà cattolica* thereby indicated that the different solutions were, in principle, compatible with its assessment of the Jews' evil and their supposed threat to Christian society. In addition to "segregation" (not categorized as "elimination"), it discussed undertaking the Jews' "expulsion." The Vatican's authoritative journal also proposed a still more extreme solution to the putative problem of the Jews, which it called the "clearly hostile manner" of "destruction."[100]

The need to eliminate the Jews was self-evident to and stated as a matter of course by the Catholic Church's leaders. After all, it was a long-standing doctrinal position and robust discourse grounded in it. The Church's prominent intellectual leaders publishing *Civiltà cattolica* articulated to its readership, the Church's leadership, almost matter-of-factly, that mass slaughter was in principle a logically thinkable solution to the Jewish problem as they conceived it, though in this article they rejected wholesale killing as un-Christian. Not surprisingly, the Church's leadership across Europe welcomed eliminationist policies against the Jews short of mass murder, because such policies concorded with their eliminationist beliefs without violating their ethical views.

Those explicitly approving in principle of a policy of mass annihilation or elimination's justness or deservedness might think it impractical or unwise, as von Schlieffen did, regarding the Herero. He wrote to Chancellor Bernard von Bülow, "One can agree with [von Trotha's] plan of annihilating the whole people or driving them from the land. . . . The intention of General von Trotha can therefore be approved. The only problem is that he does not have the power to carry it out." So von Schlieffen recommended to von Bülow, who viewed the annihilation as un-Christian, economically injurious, and harmful to

Germans' reputation among Europeans, that von Trotha's annihilation order be rescinded. Kaiser Wilhelm II, who himself had declared Christian principles invalid for dealing with heathens and savages, after weeks of foot dragging, finally did so. The eliminationist means changed from total annihilation, but not in favor of expulsion (the Herero, according to von Schlieffen, "would present a constant threat"). Instead, they settled for another of the interchangeable eliminationist options: chaining and turning those surrendering into slaves, including by branding each one's body with a *GH* for *gefangene Herero*, "captured Herero."[101] The Germans' formal halt of mass killing, because it was born of practicality, was only partial. They continued their annihilationist practices against the rebellious Nama, slaughtering an estimated 75 percent of them and depositing most of the rest in camps as forced laborers.

Such initial disquietude with eliminationist assaults occurs mainly when the policies are new, or newly publicized. Once mass extermination and elimination becomes a country's common practice and a political norm, such reactions likely further diminish except perhaps among children upon becoming conscious of the destruction. Particularly in societies with working camp systems or with eliminationist assaults under way, as in Rwanda or the former Yugoslavia, such initial reactions give way to the new common-sense political reality: killing just is. It is, like other central features, part of these societies' taken-for-granted, natural order.

Because perpetrators typically believe they are performing a historic, difficult, and extraordinary, albeit radical, act by slaughtering, expelling, or incarcerating their people's enemies, and that they act in the name of their nation or ethnic or religious group, their need for approval from people of their society or group, the bystanders, is important for their sense of self-justification. The principal exception to this has been communist regimes' perpetrators, who conceive of their peoples as not mature enough to understand the communist future's necessity. Their educational dictatorships must force, often with violence, their people to build and join the communist promised land. But perpetrators not beholden to such a self-inoculating ideology are situated differently socially. If their own people actually condemned the eliminationist program, it would powerfully undercut their rationale for acting and their confidence in their views' rightness. Being seen as a mass murderer and heinous criminal by one's people and community is not an inviting prospect. Most exterminationist and eliminationist perpetrators know that this fate does not await them. It did not happen in Turkey, Japan, Germany, Burundi, or Rwanda (among Hutu), Serbia, and elsewhere.

Our investigation of the perpetrators suggests that we must be similarly skeptical of received views and must ask the same kinds of probing questions about bystanders' critical role. Instead of closing down the investigation before it has begun, accepting the hollow cliché of bystanders' impotence, we must similarly ascertain the bystanders' stances to an eliminationist onslaught. The first and most critical issue is whether and how much bystanders identify with the perpetrators' actions. If bystanders support them, if they believe that the annihilation is just, good, and necessary, then, even without further tangible aid, they already provide the social lubricant easing the wheels of slaughter by affirming to the perpetrators that they serve a necessary, even noble purpose and will be welcomed, perhaps feted, upon returning to their communities. If bystanders support perpetrators' eliminationist goals, then questions about the putative or real coercion or terror that supposedly stops them from aiding victims are rendered moot, exposed as diversionary exculpatory discourses, parallel to the ones for the perpetrators. A Hutu who hid eleven Tutsi, when asked if he knew of others who hid Tutsi, said no. When further asked why others had not been like him, he did not intone the exculpatory clichés about coercion or fear or peer pressure. Instead this former policeman knowingly replied: "People don't have the same mind."[102] They did not apprehend the Tutsi extermination as he did. Only when bystanders actually condemn, as this exceptional Hutu did, the ongoing mass annihilation, expulsion, or incarceration do questions become relevant about the opportunities and risks of acting on the victims' behalf.[103]

Most bystanders during many eliminationist onslaughts so evidently identify intensely with the perpetrators that the victims (and others) hold them responsible or guilty together with the actual perpetrators. After all, people watching their countrymen corral, brutalize, and slaughter or drive from their homes other people whom they despise often demonstrate their approval, even by jeering or lording it over the victims—that is, when not taking initiative to lend a hand themselves. The victims' accumulated experience of the bystanders' general identification with the perpetrators' eliminationist projects was true for Armenians of Turks, for Jews of Germans (and Poles, Lithuanians, and others), for other victim peoples (Poles, Czechs, French, Dutch, and others) of the German occupiers and ethnic Germans among them, for Bosnian Muslims of Serbs, and for Tutsi of Hutu that it became a kind of common sense for these (and other) mass murders and eliminations. A similar such identification of bystanders with perpetrators is absent among many communist regimes' victims, because these victims knew that large portions of their societies were the regimes' targets or potential targets.

When victims closely identify bystanders with perpetrators, they regularly make the accusation of "collective guilt" (meaning that the perpetrators' nation, people, or group are criminally guilty). This charge has a powerful experiential foundation in the overwhelming support the victims see the broader populace giving to the eliminationist enterprise, so that those opposing it appear to be rare exceptions. The gross error of the collective-guilt charge is typically not in its experiential basis, but, as I argue in *Hitler's Willing Executioners* and then at great length in *A Moral Reckoning*, in the victims' conceptual elaboration of that experience. Victims and other contemporaries *know* that bystanding compatriots or ethnic or racial clansmen by and large support the mass murders and eliminations. That is correct. But moving from this fact to charging collective guilt is based upon some combination of three errors: that *all* members of the perpetrators' group are implicated (instead of only those, perhaps very many, who committed actual transgressions); are implicated merely owing to their *membership* in that group (instead of each person's individual acts); and are *legally* implicated in the eliminationist acts themselves and therefore *guilty*, instead of being only morally blameworthy for the eliminationist acts they themselves did not commit but merely supported, which is a different culpability from *legal guilt*. People can be deemed guilty only as individuals for their individual acts (guilt cannot be inherited by subsequent generations) and, guilty in a legal sense, only when those acts are crimes. It has been the case, certainly, that many Turkish, German, Serbian, and Hutu perpetrators were *collectively* guilty in that as perpetrators they brutalized, expelled, and murdered in concert, but this is different from saying *all* Turks, Germans, Serbs, or Hutu are guilty because they are members of peoples that broadly supported the perpetrators of eliminations. Individual Turks, Germans, Serbs, and Hutu should be held *legally* culpable for their *individual* criminal deeds (which can include membership in criminal organizations) but deemed *morally blameworthy* for their individual moral positions.[104]

To be sure, some bystanders, like some perpetrators, materially benefit from their neighbors' destruction or expulsion. People who hate other people and see them as a mortal danger are often happy to improve their own material or professional lives when their self-conceived enemies are eliminated. Yet there is little evidence that personal benefit has been a widespread or determinative motive leading bystanders to support mass murder and elimination or that absent such material benefits, they would oppose them. (If such an acquisitive motive were operative, it would mean that these same bystanders would approve of the extermination or expulsion of *any* group, *any* neighbors, including men, women, and children, merely to gain a few material possessions, a position that is, on its face, untenable, just as it is about the perpetrators' willingness to commit their deeds.) In all mass murders, expulsions, and incarcerations, only a certain (often small) percentage of the people stand to enrich themselves. Support for the perpetrators appears to be equally widespread among bystanders who gain nothing and those who benefit materially, because the perpetrators are their people's, or large portions of their people's, representatives in that they share a common conception and hatred of the victims and common goals.

While the perpetrators implement the leaders' will and the bystanders support the deeds out of conviction, they, as we see, develop their varying views about the deed's justice and desirability in different ways. Perpetrators also react differently (as do bystanders) when learning of the eliminationist campaigns that are consonant with the logic of their prejudices and hatreds. Whether because of the general disregard for the lives of noncommunal members, because of hatreds forged in the heat of conflict, because of ideologically derived eliminationist visions, or because of long-standing eliminationist bigotry that is activated, the perpetrators (and, as a rule, bystanders from among their own group) come in some way to approve of the deed. Whether surprised, relieved, or enthused when learning of the intended acts, the bearers of eliminationist sentiments' various reactions are nevertheless predicated upon their shared approval for those acts. Differences in how the approval is generated help us understand the eliminationist assaults, but only in part. The *actual beliefs*, as distinct from the mechanisms producing them, need also to be analyzed, because they vary significantly and their variations are critically important for explaining why the perpetrators in different eliminationist onslaughts conduct themselves differently. These many themes are taken up in Part II.

From this discussion several conclusions follow.

The Holocaust was singular in certain dimensions (as are other eliminationist assaults), but not in the general congruence of leaders' and perpetrators' beliefs, or in its perpetrators' moral approval. Both are common, constituent features of mass murder and elimination. Hence, the relationship between leaders and followers needs to be rethought no less than other faulty received notions (about bureaucracies, authority, etc.) that have been put forward without regard and in firm contradiction to what we know about politics and social life. For mass murders, the relationship between leaders and perpetrators is usually analyzed as one of psychological dependence, authority, or compulsion. The leaders are usually presented as all-powerful agents and the followers as people with no or little capacity to adopt their own positions, and then to have those positions matter by affecting their own conduct, influencing leaders' estimations of what is possible or desirable, or having an effect in any way over what happens. But this is, of course, not at all how politics works or how we, in every sphere of politics except eliminationist politics—which is commonly reduced to the mind-numbing word *genocide*—think of the relationship between leaders and followers, whether the politics are democratic or nondemocratic. In no other area of politics do we assume or assert as a matter of faith that followers do not reflect upon the rightness of their leaders' politics and policies, reflexively accept or follow their leaders' wishes, or are passive vessels to be infused with and moved by whatever leaders want. Dissent from, suspicion of, and resistance to political leaders' wishes, programs, and policies is the norm throughout the world under *all kinds* of regimes—including during war—in general and particularly when people disagree with those policies, especially when those policies violate people's deepest moral values—as a policy to slaughter other human beings, to slaughter children would, if indeed people thought it wrong. What is missing from the theorized and nontheoretical discussion of eliminationist politics is commonplace in the understanding and theorizing of other kinds of politics: the fundamental recognition of people's agency, and of the complex relationship that that agency necessarily creates between them and their leaders, and between them, the circumstances of their actions, and what they actually do.

Working through these relationships, both theoretically and in concrete cases, necessitates among others two things: first, a reintegration of the cognitive and moral dimensions of the followers' stances toward their leaders in general and, at least as critically, toward particular policies, initiatives, and goals that their leaders adopt or seek to pursue. Followers' views about people designated as targets, and their understanding of acceptable and appropriate moral action, are critical for how they will respond psychologically, how they will perceive the legitimacy of authority, including so-called charismatic authority, and whether compulsion would be necessary, might be tried, or would succeed. Second, we need to recognize that the eliminationist situation is inherently fluid, with leaders calling on preexisting beliefs, helping sometimes to intensify and further shape them or to overcome lingering moral inhibitions, able to do so often only under the prior constraints those existing beliefs and values create. Our analysis of this complex and fluid relationship, and the conduct that emerges from it, must necessarily also be fluid. It is true that predispositions among followers to eliminate potential target groups must often be cultivated and must all but invariably be called upon by leaders, if the followers are not to remain relatively quiescent. It is also the case that, absent some catastrophic assault upon a people, leaders cannot, certainly not in a few weeks or even a few years, create a large, willing, let alone eager followership for vast exterminationist and eliminationist policies—for children's mass annihilation—if those followers do not already accept the fundamentals of the leaders' worldview about the victims and about the aspects of society and politics relevant for determining what ought to be done with the victims. Leaders can get followers to go willingly only where the followers are already in some sense prepared to go. This was true for Mehmet Talât and Turks, for Hitler and Germans during the Nazi period, for Slobodan Milošević and Serbs, and for the Hutu leaders and Hutu. It has been true across our time's exterminationist and eliminationist assaults.

We must jettison the rigid, typically dichotomous thinking that in three related respects characterize discussion of mass murder (and eliminations more broadly, though eliminations are left out of such discussions). First, and touched on earlier, mass murder's interpreters attribute agency and efficacy to leaders or to followers, but not to *both*, and certainly fail to treat both as capable agents acting in a fluid relationship of mutual influence as movement occurs toward eliminationist measures. This dichotomous thinking has been almost uniform among writers about the Holocaust as well as in the faulty paradigmatic thinking about perpetrators its interpreters have generated.

Second, the sometimes explicit though mainly implicit model that dominates discussions about mass murder maintains, dichotomously, that perpetrators must have *always* wanted to kill the victims or, if not, then prior beliefs about the victims must be irrelevant, and the perpetrators must have undergone a coercive transformation, not necessarily in belief, but in conduct—either through brainwashing, blind obedience, or some kind of psychological or threatening pressure. The strange reasoning underlying this position is that if the perpetrators, or more broadly a people, had had exterminationist-compatible beliefs about others, then they would have annihilated them long before they finally did. Or in the rhetorical question that is so often used to make this point, "Then why didn't it happen earlier?" Because the perpetrators did not kill earlier, then the exterminationist beliefs—so the thinking continues—could not have been there, and therefore, when the perpetrators do actually kill, they cannot be willing killers in any meaningful sense of *willing*. The flip side of this mode of thinking—common to society-centered explanations of eliminationist assaults' initiation—is that if murderous beliefs were always present, the leadership is but the conveyor belt of popular sentiment and intentions.

If instead we understand first that prior beliefs predisposing people to adopt an eliminationist solution can exist while lying dormant, or that such beliefs might not have yet coalesced around a particular solution, or that their bearers might need a moral example and push, and second that leaders activate, shape (intellectually, with policy, and organizationally), and sanction dormant beliefs and moral views, then we can understand the complex of beliefs, policy, and actions at the heart of the process that leads from initiation to implementation.

The third misleading rigid manner of thinking (which is implicated in the second) holds that beliefs and action have a one-to-one relationship. Beliefs about despised people and the actions desired by their bearers are treated by commentators as so intertwined that they are collapsed into each other, as if they are the same thing. This means that if someone supported or implemented one eliminationist solution, say forced emigration, then—so goes the faulty conclusion—he must have opposed more radical eliminationist solutions, such as annihilation. But, as we know, eliminationist beliefs are compatible with various policy solutions, including various eliminationist ones. Beliefs' multiple potential for action is obvious in our own social experience and in politics. When thinking about people's or politicians' stances, say, toward crime, no one adopts the stilted unrealistic paradigm that characterizes mass murder's discussions. People can be willing to accept a wide range of laws and punishments as good or as merely adequate (if the alternative is to do nothing). It is astonishing that the same flexible relationship between people's beliefs and the range of policies they would willingly support is explicitly or implicitly denied for the *political* issues of how people might treat despised and feared groups. Why and how different eliminationist solutions and mixes are decided upon in one instance and not another and then, in any given instance, different ones during the evolution of policy must be explored.

Recognizing the critical quality of ordinary people's beliefs and values is the first important step. Recognizing the complexity of the relationship between beliefs and desired action is another. Refashioning our understanding of the relationships of beliefs and values, and desired actions, to other factors, which are also complex and changing, is necessary and predicated upon adopting a more fluid view of each component and its relationships to the others.

As most people know from their own experience, we sometimes begin to look at a thing in certain ways only when relevant courses of action become possible. Newfound options can induce us to focus on an old matter with new intensity, from new angles, and with new reasoning. Suddenly, our previous thinking about the matter appears inadequate, a new solution is necessary, a newly offered one desirable. None of this is inevitable. At other times, when new courses of action present themselves, sometimes nothing changes. And sometimes new options, socially or politically, have the opposite effect. As people realize the conduct that logically follows on their views is unpalatable, they might conclude that the views themselves are mistaken and need revision. This occurred for many deeply antisemitic Christian churches after the Holocaust, as their leaders and members came to see the perniciousness, indeed, in their terminology, the evil of antisemitic beliefs that had wrought such human destruction. However, if new ways of acting are compatible with our established views, we so often see the desirability of adopting them. This has been at the heart of eliminationist and exterminationist politics.

The relationships among people's beliefs, the solutions they are willing to consider to perceived problems, and the actions they deem appropriate are complicated and fluid. The issue is not, as so many postulate, that eliminationist beliefs are suddenly created out of nowhere by structures, orders, or pressures. Rather—as Fulgence so pithily captured it when he explained that "the atmosphere had changed"—newly emerging, favorable circumstances provide contexts for existing eliminationist beliefs to be massaged, channeled, and activated in varying forms and directions, resulting in their bearers' willingness to act, even to kill.

While this can happen in several ways that have been discussed here, we need to appreciate the frequent component of epiphany. The sudden realization that unimagined or unexpected actual possibilities exist, that novel solutions could improve one's life or the lives of one's loved ones or community, can galvanize people in unexpected ways and even, precisely because of the sense of newness and good fortune, produce the euphoric zeal so often seen among the perpetrators. Such instances are human history's commonplaces. One occurred in 1989 when Romanian dictator President Nicolae Ceausescu's mass rally went awry with millions of Romanians watching on television:

> The young people started to boo. They jeered the President, who still appeared unaware that trouble was mounting, rattled along denouncing anti-communist forces. The booing grew louder and was

briefly heard by the television audience before technicians took over and voiced-over a sound track of canned applause.

It was a moment that made Rumanians realize that their all-powerful leader was, in fact, vulnerable. It unleashed an afternoon of demonstrations in the capital and a second night of bloodshed.[105]

These youths did not trick or transform their countrymen, but unleashed the repressed passions, and mobilized the latent beliefs, among Romanians that would eventually bring down a so-called charismatic leader. And so, the people acted. Similarly, it is not political leaders' alleged charisma that magically dupes thousands, tens of thousands, hundreds of thousands, even millions of people to support eliminationist ideals and programs that would otherwise violate their deepest beliefs and values. Aside from the simple fact that even the most supposedly charismatic leaders, including the allegedly most charismatic of all, Hitler, regularly meet resistance when they move against such cherished beliefs and values, no such so-called charismatic leaders exist in many mass murders and eliminations. Sometimes the leader's identity or character is barely known. So-called charismatic leadership was absent in German South-West Africa, in Turkey, in British Kenya, in Indonesia, in many Latin American countries, in Burundi, in Rwanda, and in so many other eliminations.

When leaders, whether putatively charismatic or not, offer people a heretofore unimagined or seemingly implausible opportunity to act violently and lethally that accords with—in fact, fulfills—their deepest existing values and beliefs, people suddenly realize they can solve a previously unsolvable though grave problem. The Hutu mass murderer Pancrace explains along these lines how we should understand the critical mobilizing place of "the president's death and a fear of falling under the rule of the *inkotanyi* [cockroaches]" in the Hutu's complex of prior dormant beliefs and subsequent impassioned action:

> The Hutu always suspects that some plans are cooking deep in the Tutsi character, nourished in secret since the passing of the ancien régime. He sees a threat lurking in even the feeblest or kindest Tutsi. But it is suspicion, not hatred. The hatred came over us suddenly after our president's plane crashed. The intimidators shouted, "Just

look at these cockroaches—we told you so!" And we yelled, "Right, let's go hunting!" We weren't that angry; more than anything else, we were *relieved* (my emphasis).[106]

We should accept the fluidity (which does not mean total malleability) of this complex of beliefs, solutions, opportunity, calls to action, and conduct because it accounts best for the facts. It helps us make sense of the indeterminacy of beliefs and values, while according them their essential place in the eliminationist equation. It allows us to explore the complicated relationship between eliminationist beliefs and eliminationist action (in Part II), which is at once the core of the eliminationist stance and deed, and very hard to know.

When, as the perpetrators almost always have, people believe that other groups, other people, are of a character that makes eliminating them, including with lethal violence, right and necessary, then once unleashed, these people become the most self-motivated, zealous, and effective implementers of political policy the world has known. Hence, the paradox that confounds so many: Without political leadership, the overwhelming majority of the perpetrators would not lift a finger in harm, but once set in motion, typically but with a few encouraging and enabling words, they, both the eliminationist regimes' shock troops and their societies' ordinary members—be they ordinary Turks, ordinary Germans, ordinary Indonesians, ordinary Tutsi, ordinary Serbs, or ordinary Hutu—give themselves, body and soul, to death. They do so easily, effortlessly, and to them, logically. "I think the possibility of genocide fell out as it did because it was lying in wait—for time's signal, like the plane crash, to nudge it at the last moment," explains the Hutu perpetrator Ignace Rukiramacumu. "There was never any need to talk about it among ourselves. The thoughtfulness of the authorities ripened it naturally, and then it was proposed to us. As it was their only proposal and it promised to be final, we seized the opportunity. We knew full well what had to be done, and we set to doing it without flinching because it seemed like the perfect solution."[107]

CHAPTER SIX

Why They End

ALL ELIMINATIONIST ONSLAUGHTS END sooner or later, but not for the same reason. Why they end is an important question. Why they do not end earlier is perhaps an even more important question. Answering these questions requires us to broaden our view, to examine not only the perpetrators and their states and societies, but also their relations with other peoples and states

The effects of mass murder and elimination are well known. The perpetrators are roundly condemned and repudiated abroad, except by self-interested apologists. Less well known, discussed, and analyzed are the broader contexts in which mass murders transpire, which include the reactions of neighboring countries and the world. This is not because the topic is insignificant. The international environment critically influences political leaders' decision-making about people's fundamental rights within their own countries and abroad, and how, as a practical matter, they must govern and treat different people and groups. Witness the prominent and often dominant emphasis on human rights in international relations. During the past two decades, various countries, regional entities such as the European Union, and transnational and international institutions have encouraged countries to move toward democratic politics and free markets, positively influencing many countries' societies and politics.

We must reinsert our thinking about eliminationist and exterminationist politics into an understanding of *international* politics. Eliminationist politics is part of a world system of countries that, by acting or not acting, affect one another economically, politically, socially, and culturally, and over life and death. The formal position and claim that countries do not intervene in other countries' affairs has governed the international state system for generations and is enshrined as binding international law in the UN Charter. Nevertheless, (1) countries' political intervention, singly and in concert, into other countries' affairs has actually been normal, and (2) countries, by varied means, regularly signal other countries about possible interventions.

States have always tried to influence the character of other states, societies, and peoples. Conquest and colonization have been staples of human civilization, including during our age. Countries successfully repulsing aggressors have continued beyond their own borders until the attacking countries sue for peace, often relinquishing territory, or are conquered, the offending regimes replaced, or critical features of state or society are altered. A central goal of international institutions and alliances and of individual countries' foreign policies has been to support and create abroad favorable political regimes and economic systems, and to undermine or prevent unfavorable regimes. During the cold war, much of the world was divided into two camps led by the two superpowers, with each side seeking to sustain its members' political and economic systems, undermine those of the opposing camp, and influence nonaligned countries' domestic politics and economics to make them friendlier. Today many countries interfere in other countries' domestic politics by promoting democracy and free markets, among many more specific features of state and society. Such attempts employ the full range of political means available, from implementing military intervention or its threat; to imposing economic sanctions or their threat; to setting down political, economic, and social conditions and human rights standards countries must meet in order to make treaties, join international federations, participate in international organizations and commercial relations; to diplomatic initiatives; to public praise or denunciation. Regardless of whether such acts accord with international law and treaties, states have always tried to shape other countries' domestic politics and practices, and they have often succeeded.

The notion that states must not intervene in other countries' domestic affairs and that sovereignty is inviolable is, in practice, ignored all the time. Intervention today is typically done in the name of freedom and other higher, universal values, and the rule of law, though this is often cynical cover for motives of political or economic power or advantage. Either way, intervention has been and is a common practice, and noble principles are put forward and often accepted as legitimizing justifications.

States have been able to influence other countries' leaders who contemplate and then begin to carry out eliminationist assaults. Yet, in contrast to all the other ways that states have claimed to be legitimately influencing the domestic practices of other states, societies, and peoples, political leaders have rarely defended the innocent abroad by seriously trying to forestall or stop mass murder, let alone mass elimination.

The Genocide Convention

Until after the Holocaust, mass murder was not even broadly perceived as a problem, much less one that must be addressed politically, including in international law and treaties. The various Geneva conventions (the first one signed in 1864) and other conventions for rights of prisoners of war long predated international conventions on the rights of citizens. This was not an accident. Soldiers needed protection because they fought to uphold states and their governments. But states saw no reason to protect the rights of noncombatants during war, or of ordinary people in general, not to be wantonly murdered because the states' own prerogatives to act as they wished would thereby be compromised. Political leaders wanted impunity to slaughter or to violently repress their own people as necessary, and to slaughter, expel, coerce, even enslave other peoples abroad. A world dominated by imperialist powers is almost guaranteed not to create laws, institutions, or norms for the prevention of eliminationist, including exterminationist, politics and practices, because imperialism depends upon the violent domination of conquered peoples and has a strong, almost ineluctable tendency to become eliminationist in intent and practice for many reasons, not least because of subjugated and colonized people's inevitable and ongoing resistance. This blinkered view of the necessity to safeguard certain small classes of people (such as prisoners of war) but not humankind's overwhelming majority is not at all surprising in a predemocratic era that denied the rights of all peoples to be self-governing. Until the second half of the twentieth century, few rulers saw their people as *citizens*

with rights. Instead they treated them as *subjects* to be subordinated to
the rulers' economic and political interests. The great powers practiced
imperialism. So there was no powerful constituency for prohibiting
eliminationist politics or even its mass-murder variant. Only with the
powerful impetus provided by the Germans' mass murdering all over
Europe, and especially the Holocaust's existential and real horror, did
statutes against mass murder enter international law. In December
1948, the UN General Assembly passed its Convention on the Prevention and Punishment of the Crime of Genocide, consisting of nineteen
articles, with the critical Article II stating:

> In the present Convention, genocide means any of the following acts
> committed with intent to destroy, in whole or in part, a national, eth-
> nical, racial or religious group, as such:
>   (a) Killing members of the group;
>   (b) Causing serious bodily or mental harm to members of the
> group;
>   (c) Deliberately inflicting on the group conditions of life calculated
> to bring about its physical destruction in whole or in part;
>   (d) Imposing measures intended to prevent births within the group;
>   (e) Forcibly transferring children of the group to another group.

The government of any signatory country can bring a charge of genocide to the Security Council, which, if it first issues a finding that genocide is being committed, may then "take such action under the Charter
of the United Nations as they consider appropriate for the prevention
and suppression of acts of genocide or any of the other acts enumer-
ated in Article III," such as the "attempt to commit genocide," and
the like.[1]

In its bare bones, the genocide convention seems to (1) outlaw genocide and (2) call for intervention when it occurs. But its drafters crafted
specific provisions to so eviscerate these two elements that the convention effectively does neither, and is meaningless as a working body of
law and as a basis for action against genocide. This should not have
been surprising, if for no other reason than that one of the all-time most
egregiously mass-murdering regimes, the Soviet Union, had veto power
over the convention's content.

Most severe and ridiculous are the definitional problems. The convention does not cover groups slaughtered for *political* reasons or as *economic* targets. It prohibits the mass murder of only "national, ethnical, racial or religious" groups. The Soviet Union insisted upon this exclusion because, even as it was negotiating the convention's terms, its gulag was still fully operational. The consequence of this definitional omission has been even more catastrophic than it first appears. It allows any mass-murdering regime to claim it is engaged in a political struggle. The UN members wanting cover for their inaction can similarly pretend that mass murder's victims are not national, ethnic, religious, or racial groups but political ones.

Even more problematic is the genocide convention's failure to define genocide, let alone include objective criteria (such as a threshold number of people killed) that allow the international community to readily identify genocide while it is happening. This permits the world's countries to pretend that genocide is not being perpetrated when by any reasonable definition it is. In genocide after genocide, the countries that should have invoked the genocide convention circumvented compliance with its provisions by refusing to utter the word "genocide." The United States did this in Rwanda, explicitly refusing, in full awareness of the actual events, to call the Hutu's all-out slaughter of the Tutsi genocide. The United Nations has yet to declare the Sudanese regime's ongoing genocide in Darfur "genocide." Only long after any reasonable threshold of genocide had been crossed did the American government, in September 2004, finally use the word "genocide"—and yet the Americans nevertheless failed to urge forceful, effective intervention, and even worked to ensure that the United Nations would not adopt language suggesting that intervention is necessary and obligatory.[2]

As much as all this robs the genocide convention of meaning and force, there is an even more crippling aspect of the definition of the phenomenon it purports to outlaw. The convention is clearly meant and has been taken to mean only enormous mass slaughters of hundreds of thousands, or millions of people. So a regime may slaughter twenty thousand to forty thousand people—as Hafez al-Assad's Baathist regime did in Syria—without the principal convention that purports to combat the enormous world problem of mass murder outlawing it. Indeed, the Syrian regime essentially had international immunity for leveling a good part of Hama and wantonly slaughtering its inhabitants. Or a regime that, over decades, murders a few hundred thousand people—as Saddam Hussein's Baathist regime did in Iraq—is not considered to violate this convention or trigger its provisions. Most mass murders do not, according to the convention's definition of genocide, qualify for international intervention. The de facto consequence of the convention, the United Nations' constitution and inaction, and international law has been to sanction a political leadership murdering five thousand or even fifty thousand of its country's people (particularly if done not too ostentatiously). The international community or some of its members may say that such political leaders are very, very bad people and eventually seek to put some of them on trial. But military intervention to stop the mass murdering would be without a legal foundation and therefore criminal.

Another grave problem plaguing the genocide convention is its failure to treat genocide—more properly mass murder—as part of a continuum of eliminationist politics. Hence, "ethnic cleansing"—expelling huge populations while murdering "only" a small percentage totaling many thousands—does not fall under the genocide convention. Intervention is not triggered. NATO's interventions in the former Yugoslavia, first in Bosnia and then in Kosovo, came much too late, after the perpetrators had victimized millions. When NATO finally did act, owing to mounting domestic pressure in Western countries and the desire to make sure the situation did not spin utterly out of control, NATO was *without* UN authorization and *without* the genocide convention's having been invoked. Indeed, international legal experts deemed NATO's belated intervention illegal because it lacked a basis in international law for outsiders to stop the Serbs from brutalizing, torturing, and expelling Bosnians and Kosovars from their homes and country, and murdering them. If you, as a political leader, want to attack people for whatever reason (they oppose you, you consider them evil, you want to transform the country), then the international community, represented by the United Nations and its powerful countries, tells you that as long as you drive most of them from their homes, even if you kill thousands, for legal and political reasons you will not lawfully face international intervention.

As if all this is not debilitating enough for establishing an intervention regime that might work against mass murder *and* eliminations, the convention's Article II defines genocide as the "*intent* to destroy, in whole or in part, a national, ethnical, racial or religious group" (my emphasis). The convention's crafters included the word "intent" as an artful and catastrophic dodge of the problem. A regime slaughtering hundreds of thousands can allege that it is an anti-insurgency campaign's collateral damage, or famine's unfortunate consequence, even if the regime willfully causes or fails to alleviate the famine. It can maintain it has never *intended* to destroy one of the designated kinds of groups. According to the convention, such acts are not genocide. (As I was composing this section, the United Nations issued its disgraceful report that the Sudanese government's colossal eliminationist and murderous assault in Darfur is not genocide and therefore does not qualify, under the genocide convention, for intervention.) A regime fighting an insurgency that withholds food from a famine-ridden region can claim that the insurgency itself is preventing the food delivery and thus avoid international intervention because no *intent* to kill through starvation can be proven. Without a mass-murdering regime's secret records, it is *almost always impossible to meet a legal threshold of proving intent.* This makes it all but impossible for the United Nations to establish a legal finding of genocide while mass murder is under way, while acting against the murderers and saving lives is possible.

The genocide convention's second colossal problem complements its foundational definitional problem, to produce a political and legal climate of neglect, inaction, and all but total cynicism: It contains no effective enforcement mechanism. The convention must be invoked by the very states that typically have no desire to intervene to stop mass murders, and by some that want the killing to proceed. It contains no trigger mechanism, such as a threshold number of slaughtered people. It relies on no authoritative body, aside from the self-interested noninterveners, such as the Soviets for their own mass murders and those of other communist regimes, the Americans for the Indonesians' slaughter of communists (which the Americans green-lighted), the British in Kenya, the French in Rwanda, the Chinese in Tibet, the Russians in Chechnya. Even if the convention were deemed applicable to a given onslaught, it contains nothing but hortatory words to produce intervention: The member states may take action that they "consider appropriate for the prevention and suppression of acts of genocide."

Acting upon the genocide convention's provision to actually do something effective is essentially *at will*.

The genocide convention has utterly failed to serve as a practical impediment to regimes slaughtering or expelling their peoples. In its sixty years, it has never been triggered or used for intervention, despite the many tens of millions of people that mass murderers (and the practitioners of eliminationism) have victimized around the world. It was not invoked for the Soviets' gulag, the communists' gargantuan slaughters in China, the Indonesians' slaughter of communists, the Pakistanis' annihilationist and eliminationist onslaught against the Bangladeshis, not for the Khmer Rouge's annihilation of Cambodians, for the mass murders in Burundi and in Rwanda, the Ethiopians' killing of the people of the north, the rightists' mass murdering in Latin America, including the Guatemalans' against the Maya, not for the mass slaughters and expulsions in the former Yugoslavia, Saddam's various mass murders in Iraq, the eliminationist and genocidal onslaught by Political Islamists in Sudan first against the country's southern non-Muslims, and then against the peoples of Darfur. For establishing law adequate to what it purportedly wants to outlaw, and for mobilizing the world against exterminationist and eliminationist politics, the genocide convention might as well be in invisible ink.

Its immense failure notwithstanding, the genocide convention was immensely important. It took the ad hoc law made at the Nuremberg Trials of the German leadership and turned it into general international law and formal norms. It is the only human rights convention that empowers UN members to intervene militarily in other countries to stop eliminationist assaults. It bolstered the foundation for the development of the international law of retributive justice, by authorizing an "international penal tribunal" to try those charged with genocide, and mandated (at least on paper) that perpetrators be tried.[3] These provisions have led to the ad hoc criminal tribunals for Yugoslavia, Rwanda, and Sierra Leone, and recently the permanent International Criminal Court in The Hague—an important development examined in Chapter 11. The genocide convention has also critically contributed, at least rhetorically and vaguely normatively, to creating a place for mass murder's proscription in the world's politics, both internationally and sometimes domestically, a break with thousands of years of practice.

The International Political Environment's Crucial Context

With this in mind, we see immediately that our age has had various international political environments regarding mass murder. Understanding them depends upon delineating and analyzing, albeit briefly, the international political environments' four relevant dimensions. The first is legal: Is mass murder legally proscribed? The second is rhetorical: Is mass murder publicly discussed and brought to the attention of the world community? Is it loudly condemned, especially in the media and by governments? The third is action: Are outside actors, states and international organizations, permissive toward mass murdering? Or do they intervene to stop it? The fourth dimension, related to and independent of the third, is hortatory: Do outside actors, by their public or behind-the-scenes stances, actually encourage certain leaders to commit mass murder, or support them when they do?

There has been substantial variation on each dimension and in the overall international political environments these dimensions—legal, rhetorical, political action, and political exhortation—together compose. Regarding mass murder, four basic international political environments have characterized our time.

Until after World War II, with the Nuremberg Trials and Tokyo Trials, and then the passing of the genocide convention in 1948, the international environment was all but wholly permissive of mass murder. No law proscribed it. Mass murder barely registered on the radar screens of governments, media, and public. Hardly a word was uttered against it. Little if any rhetorical pressure was brought against those implementing eliminationist policies. This was partly due to primitive technological and news-gathering capabilities, and the virtual absence of truly independent media, which left events in many parts of the world unknown in other parts. But even when knowledge came to those who might have raised a cry, they said little, suggesting that better information-gathering capacities would not have changed things. A partial exception was the condemnation of the mass murders that the two major international aggressors, Germany and Japan, committed. The Japanese Rape of Nanking (Nanjing) in 1937 did cause an enormous international outcry, partly because of the West's racism against the Japanese but also because of the butchery's sheer brutality, licentiousness, and shamelessness done in plain view of Western diplomats and newsmen. The Germans' mass murdering of Jews and others initially gained little notice around the world. The Germans' crimes and the upcoming reckoning was little discussed in the Allies' propaganda or in American, British, and other governmental organs' public pronouncements. After the war, though, it became a central theme of international discussion. During this period, the international environment, though nearly totally permissive toward mass murderers, generally did not actively encourage it. Murderous regimes were left to do as they pleased, though others did not spur them onward. The principal exceptions were the Germans, urging their satellites and collaborators to join the slaughter of Jews and others, and the Catholic Church, which around Europe supported the Jews' eliminationist persecution (though only certain portions of the Church in some countries actively supported the mass murder itself).[4]

From 1948 until the late 1970s the international environment saw one positive change. One critical kind of eliminationist politics had become illegal, as the genocide convention formally outlawed mass murders classifiable as genocides. That aside, the rhetorical and practical permissiveness toward mass murder and elimination remained roughly as it had for centuries. A new development, seen in earlier eras in the transnational actor (and at times sovereign country) of the Catholic Church, was outside actors' active or tacit encouragement of mass murder. This included Western intellectuals' legitimation of the Soviets' and other communists' eliminationist politics, about which they could no longer deny (as they might have in the 1930s) they knew. Playwright Berthold Brecht, philosopher Jean-Paul Sartre, and other equal and lesser luminaries supportive of this notorious eliminationist regime became known as "fellow travelers." Still, whatever caché these individuals lent, the two principal culprits in tolerating or welcoming eliminationist politics were the Soviet Union and the United States, within their respective spheres of influence. Each superpower helped engineer certain eliminationist assaults. The Soviets did this (before the Sino-Soviet split) in China and in its European client states' initial years. The United States did it in many rightist Latin American regimes, Chile, Argentina, and Guatemala included, and elsewhere, most disastrously in Indonesia. *Time* magazine, in a 1965 article called "Vengeance with a Smile" that reflected and further reinforced this view that prevailed in

the United States, dubbed the Indonesians' exterminationist and eliminationist assault on the Communist Party's members "the West's best
news for years in Asia."[5]

The third period stretched from roughly the late 1970s until the early
1990s. The international legal stance toward eliminationism did not
improve. Only mass murders that qualified as genocides were illegal.
The rhetorical condemnation of mass murder did, however, increase.
This was partly owing to American President Jimmy Carter's emphasis
on human rights, and partly to the effects of détente and the Soviet
Union's manifest decline, which meant that in the West more people
were willing to openly question the American government's neglect,
not to mention encouragement, of client or supportive states' mass
murders. Nevertheless, permissiveness prevailed, and no government,
alliance, or group of countries, whether under UN auspices or not, seriously considered intervening in Burundi, Guatemala, Cambodia,
Syria, Iraq, and other countries that slaughtered their own people. And
despite more rhetorical condemnation, the superpowers continued to
encourage or permit client states to murder real or putative threats to
their power. The United States did this in Guatemala and El Salvador,
the Chinese in Cambodia, and earlier the Soviets in China. One of the
most bizarre and undeniably craven international stances of our time
was, under Presidents Carter and Ronald Reagan, the United States'
continued recognition of the eliminationist Khmer Rouge regime and its
possession of Cambodia's UN seat, even after the regime's 1979 defeat. These presidents had no affection for these mass-murdering communists, but they were the enemies of the United States' even more
detested enemy, the Vietnamese, who had installed the successor Cambodian regime.

The contemporary period began in the early 1990s, after the disintegration of the Soviet Union and most of the communist world. The
legal status of eliminationist onslaughts remained as before with only
those few massive *annihilationist* assaults that legally qualify as genocide being proscribed. The internationalized media, ever more able to
quickly report events around the world, helped develop a greater self-
and public awareness of mass murder and eliminationist politics. The
former Yugoslavia's protracted horrors on Western Europe's back
porch hastened this by thrusting eliminationism under the Western

spotlight and fixing the euphemistic "ethnic cleansing" in the global lexicon. General permissiveness continues for extensive killing in the developing world; witness Saddam's Iraq, Sudan, and Democratic Republic of the Congo, particularly when the eliminationist campaign is more grinding and gradual—a few thousand here, a few thousand there. Nevertheless, today there is greater public and political pressure for interventions, and there have been some, such as the counterproductive UN insertion of "peacekeepers" in Bosnia that enabled the Serbs' mass murdering in Srebrenica and elsewhere, NATO's subsequent, more effective interventions in Bosnia and Kosovo, and the international community's forceful diplomatic intervention in Kenya to halt the postelection eliminationist assault on Kikuyu in 2008 that took 1,500 lives and expelled hundreds of thousands, and that could have escalated into a much larger bloodbath. The critical change is the drying up of outside encouragement for regimes to practice eliminationist politics. With the cold war's dissolution, the global geostrategic rationale for the superpowers to encourage clients to commit mass murder ended. What remains are local and often stunningly petty reasons, such as the French political leadership's desire to promote Francophone peoples and therefore its active support for the Hutu's butchery in Rwanda.

Exceptions to these general characterizations of the four international environments regarding mass murder and elimination notwithstanding, we have seen over the course of our time some progress, in fits and starts, regarding mass murder, though barely any at all, regarding other eliminationist assaults. Yet the progress is meager, if we use the reasonable standard that (1) *all* eliminationist assaults (or even just mass murder) are illegal; (2) the United Nations, member states, the international media, and attentive publics immediately and universally condemn them; (3) mechanisms exist for powerful international intervention, including a legal basis for individual states to intervene to halt mass murder and eliminations within other countries; and (4) forceful intervention occurs as soon as eliminationist politics begin.

Instead, we live in the continuing, deadly hypocrisies that have characterized our era, a world governed by cynical leaders giving lip service to morality. We have let thousands, hundreds of thousands, millions of people die, without raising a hand, or even seriously consider doing so. American President Bill Clinton apologized in March 1998, long after the fact, for having let Hutu murder so many Tutsi, saying that he and others had not realized the extent of the mass murder. (Was Clinton saying that had the Hutu been killing—what?—a mere 10,000 or 100,000 Tutsi, then his inaction would have been justified?) Clinton's apology was cynical posturing for political consumption, and for enhancing his reputation. While Clinton was letting Hutu butcher hundreds of thousands, he and his administration knew the facts for which he would later apologize. So why had Clinton enabled the mass murder? He was not willing to expend domestic political capital, especially after the loss of American lives in the short-lived intervention in Mogadishu, Somalia, the previous year, to save the lives of hundreds of thousands of Africans—men, women, and children. In Rwanda, Clinton made a calculated decision, not a "mistake," which he actually articulated during the Hutu's slaughter, while covering his tracks by falsely portraying the all-out genocide as an "ethnic conflict" and, what's more, but one among so many other ethnic conflicts. In the commencement address at the U.S. Naval Academy on May 25, 1994, Clinton declared, "We cannot solve every such outburst of civil strife. . . . Whether we get involved in any of the world's ethnic conflicts in the end must depend on the cumulative weight of the American interests at stake."[6] Morality did not enter the decision-making, even as 1 percent. Clinton and his administration were so little concerned about the Hutu's mass butchery of Tutsi that, as he admitted in September 2006, "We never even had a staff meeting on it."[7] Not until 1998, almost four years after the genocide, did Clinton see the necessity of trying to position himself as a moral man (gaining plaudits for his willingness to apologize!) without ever owning up to his actual transgression.

Perpetrators perpetrate with a sense of impunity from intervention or punishment. Such impunity is not much reduced from what has existed throughout our age and before. The creation of several ad hoc criminal tribunals, including ones for Yugoslavia and Rwanda, and recently the International Criminal Court, constitute in themselves little change overall, or even in eliminationist politics' overall legal status. It took the UN Security Council until March 31, 2005—two years, more than 750 days, after Sudan's exterminationist and eliminationist onslaught in Darfur began—to take the minimal step of referring the "situation" to the International Criminal Court (though not as an instance of genocide but as "a threat to international peace and security" and owing to "violations of international humanitarian law and human rights law"). The International Criminal Court so far has been agonizingly slow in issuing warrants for only a small number of perpetrators, finally indicting the genocide's mastermind, Omar al-Bashir, in March 2009, though not for genocide. Yet the Sudanese government and its militias have killed perhaps 400,000 people and driven from their homes more than 2.5 million more. (And the United Nations' and the court's deplorably tardy and minimal reaction is for a political Islamic regime that previously committed an even more colossal exterminationist and eliminationist assault against southern Sudanese, for which the United Nations did *nothing*.) Such small steps, and such considerable inaction, hardly inspire confidence in those who look to the international community to act effectively to stop mass murder and elimination. Nevertheless, the International Criminal Court's establishment offers some promise of progress.

Understanding the international environment and its evolution, and how it has provided a somewhat changing though fundamentally continuous context for mass-murdering leaders, helps us understand why outside actors have not systematically stopped mass murders and eliminations, once begun. Understanding the nature of outside actors, with their different capacities, is also important for comprehending what has happened, and for thinking about how to craft more effective anti-eliminationist politics.

Outsiders' capacity to intervene against mass murders and eliminations has increased substantially during our time. Modernity's enormous growth in state power generally, including technological, organizational, and monitoring capacities, has also applied to the power of states to work against eliminationist politics. Earlier, mass slaughters, such as the Germans' in South-West Africa or the Belgians' in Congo, could go on for months or years before their existence or magnitude was, if ever, known to the outside world. Discerning the extent and effects of eliminationist assaults in faraway lands was often beyond the ordinary capacities of outside actors with few resources and little access in the region. Publics had little if any knowledge of areas of the world beyond their immediate geostrategic environments, and even in those it was often poor. If information gathering was one critical problem, then acting on it, even if the will to do so existed, was often extremely difficult and required substantial lead time. States' capacities to stop mass murders in distant regions were highly attenuated. Nonmilitary means for pressuring other states were few and weak. Projecting power, especially far away, was extremely difficult. Starting a military campaign to stop annihilations would have taken a long time at great relative cost to states that had few financial resources. That is not to say interventions would not have been effective, especially in Congo, where the Belgians committed their vast mass murder over two decades.

States today, whether neighboring states or those able to project power beyond their immediate environs, have enormously greater capacities to learn of mass slaughters and eliminations and to intervene promptly and, in many cases, decisively. (The United States and its allies routed the political Islamic Taliban state and Al Qaeda in Afghanistan in a few weeks, even if a powerful insurgency has since developed.) Since World War II, the emergence of many international institutions and regional associations also establishes, at least in theory, an infrastructure that facilitates far greater international coordination to stop *all* kinds of eliminations. Today there are many more potential actors. When European imperialist powers, which themselves often used eliminationist violence to suppress colonized peoples, controlled large portions of the world, mass-murdering regimes had fewer neighboring states on their borders. As the past century wore on, with progressive decolonization, mass murderers had to potentially contend with both neighboring states and more distant powers which in principle could intervene.

We have seen a growth in the availability of verifiable information about what is occurring, in states' capacities to intervene, and in potential interveners against eliminationist campaigns. We have also witnessed the establishment of international institutions, the United Nations, the European Union, NATO, and other regional organizations and international trade organizations, which in principle can act effectively against mass murder and elimination. International institutions have increased the world's capacity for intervention, because of their power and their ability to facilitate states' acting together. Yet we have seen almost no increase in intervention and only small though positive changes in the international environment for eliminationist politics.

Why? Because without a substantial change in the laws, norms, and pressures upon political leaders to change their calculus, business as usual has prevailed. Powerful considerations, often also put forward as justifications, for states not to act to halt exterminationist and elim- inationist onslaughts have prevailed.

At the height of the Hutu's mass butchery, U.S. UN Ambassador Madeleine Albright washed her and everyone's hands of the genocide (which the United States was denying was a genocide), saying that though the United Nations might eventually do something to help, "ul- timately, the future of Rwanda is in Rwandan hands." She infamously declared that "without a sound plan of operations" intervention would be "folly."[8] Aside from the transparent cynicism of her attempt to short-circuit a serious discussion of effective outside intervention by de- claring it outside reason's bounds—even though the genocide had been under way *for more than a month* and hundreds of thousands had been allowed to be butchered—Albright's statement was deemed plausibly correct and adequate by elites and publics alike, as the mute reaction to it confirms. What assumptions made her assertion of "folly" plausible?

Beyond holding up the fig leaf of the need for operational planning, Albright was vague about the reasons for the folly. She thus allowed people to activate the range of reasons that has for decades undergirded the widespread consensus opposing American (and not just American) foreign intervention against mass murder (and elimination, which in any case barely registers). I list them in no particular order and without maintaining they are equally widespread, central, or openly articulated.

- It is not in the United States' "national interest" to enter conflicts not tangibly and substantially affecting the United States or its close allies.
- It is *their* conflict; let them settle it.
- The local situation is too complicated.
- There are killing and atrocities on both sides, as there often are in war.
- American boys should not die to save another country's people.
- They are just a bunch of barbarians killing each other.
- We cannot solve the problem anyway.
- Why should we pay for their actions?

- It is not our right to intervene.
- Let the international community or nearby countries do it.
- We have too many important priorities at home.

These excuses for allowing hundreds of thousands to be slaughtered abroad would never be tolerated by Americans, Britons, Germans, Spanish, Italians, or Japanese if applied to the similar slaughter of, say, only one hundred people in any of their own countries (or even of a close Western ally). For peoples in faraway or seemingly enormously different countries, these powerfully effective excuses are grounded in three factors that produce policy detachment: an overriding doctrine of national interest, racism, and a failure to morally engage the issues.

To start with the last, I have yet to see anyone address two related questions: How many African or Asian lives is one American life worth? Why is the American life deemed so much more valuable? Put differently, why do we value the life of an American (or in Germany a German, in the United Kingdom a Briton, in Italy an Italian, in Japan a Japanese) so much more highly than African or Asian lives in the thousands, tens of thousands, or hundreds of thousands? How can this be justified morally, or even politically? Putting the question this way dissolves many of the thoughtlessly uttered justifications for *allowing*, which is in effect *enabling*, the killing of thousands, tens of thousands, hundreds of thousands, or millions, and the habitual assent those justifications find.

The racism of people in the West is palpable, if usually unarticulated, when it comes to mass murders and eliminations among peoples of color. Racism underlies the *they are just barbarians* mentality and the *these people are governed by uncontrollable primordial hatreds* explanation, which offer the speaker and his listeners implicit justification for inaction. This dismissive reasoning ignores first that these putative barbarians' political and military leaders are, with few exceptions, university graduates, sophisticated, and well-spoken, and often thoroughly westernized; second, in all exterminationist and other eliminationist assaults, political leaders for ideological and political reasons coolly practice their destructive politics; and third, perpetrators *everywhere* are moved by various overlapping or kindred notions, prejudices, and hatreds that lead them to think the killing is right. This was true of "civilized" Germans (and their many collaborators in many other "civilized" European countries) during the Nazi period no less than "uncivilized" Hutu in Rwanda, Serbs in Bosnia or Kosovo, or Muslim "tribesmen" in Sudan today.

Finally, the doctrine of *national interest*, much criticized in the scholarly international relations literature, has gained such currency in the United States and other countries, such as France (even conceptions of national interest vary substantively from country to country), as to squelch serious questioning of its conventional wisdom. That Secretary of State Warren Christopher would unashamedly declare in July 1993 that the United States was following its "national interest" in Bosnia, as a definitive justification for why it should stand idly by and let the Serbs continue mass murdering and eliminating Muslims, conveys the power of the national-interest doctrine.[9] The most basic question, why so-called national interest should be the governing concept for acting internationally, is hardly asked. In the United States in particular, even those wanting to intervene against annihilationist assaults appear to think themselves obliged to assert that such intervention is in the American national interest. They support this assertion by arguing that American values are part of the country's interests, and the United States' moral standing in the world and therefore American interests will be detrimentally affected if the United States does not intervene, or by offering some other unconvincing attempt to employ the lowest-moral-denominator language to an end for which it is palpably unsuited.

Political leaders and other elites would object to aspects of this analysis, such as racism. Yet, they would accept the power of the national interest as a source of their inaction but not see it as revealing failures or as an indictment, but as a justifiable, even laudatory principle for their do-nothing stances. There is, however, another class of reasons for political leaders' inaction, which few today would justify openly.

Some political leaders (and their followers) choose to overlook eliminationist assaults as they transpire because they care more about countervailing geopolitical or economic considerations. States and their leaders often give tacit support, remain silent, or make quiet pro forma objections when allies or other important countries commit mass murders or eliminations. Aside from a few tepid and oblique objections, this has characterized virtually every state's stance toward the Russians' mass murdering and vast destruction in Chechnya. Among world leaders the Chinese's decades-long eliminationist campaign in Tibet to Sinofy the region barely meets a whispered criticism, unless open conflict erupts, as it did in spring 2008 during the lead-up to that summer's Olympic Games in Beijing. The more powerful the country perpetrating mass murder and elimination, the more states and political leaders would pay materially or diplomatically for speaking out. So unless a powerful motive impels them to object, or to take symbolic or more effective action, they usually keep quiet.

Some political leaders, elites, and peoples ignore mass slaughters and eliminationist campaigns because they identify or sympathize with the perpetrators. The most obvious ones are those of Arab and other Islamic countries who have consistently refused to condemn mass murders of tens of thousands or hundreds of thousands committed by Arab states—Assad in Syria, Saddam in Iraq, al-Bashir first in southern Sudan and then in Darfur—while vociferously condemning Israelis for every Palestinian they kill. Their total or near total silence is mirrored by their counterparts in Europe and around the world supporting Palestinian nationalism or so hostile to the United States and Israel that they are loath to criticize the enemies of those they hate.

Although not mass murder or elimination, the Americans' crimes in Abu Ghraib prison and elsewhere in Iraq should be mentioned in this context. Many American commentators' unwillingness to speak plainly and forcefully (though, of course, many others have done so) about the extent of Americans' systematic torturing of imprisoned Iraqis and the responsibility for them that went up the chain of command is not in essence different (even if the deeds are markedly different) from Arab political and media elites' refusal to speak plainly and forcefully about Arab and Islamic states' mass murdering and eliminations. The unwillingness to criticize here, as elsewhere, reflected the general political allegiance many American commentators had for the United States' toppling of Saddam or for the Bush administration generally. They failed to differentiate between the justness of the war itself and its strategic goals—in which they believe—and the justness of aspects of how Americans fought the war—which many of them certainly privately abhor and should condemn.

We see then that another factor is necessary for eliminationist and exterminationist politics to be practiced, which though obvious is overlooked perhaps because it is not seen as a constituent factor actively promoting and therefore helping to *produce* eliminationist assaults. That factor is: a permissive outside world unwilling to use its great power to prevent most any regime or perpetrators from consummating their destructive ambitions. The genocide convention and the United Nations do more to provide cover for mass murderers than to stop them, and in only a few instances has there been effective intervention to prevent the further annihilation and expulsion of more victims. The price paid by those practicing eliminationist politics owing to actions taken by the international community has, in historical terms, been miniscule. The current international political system, in which eliminationist politics is embedded, is, whatever its self-presentations, amenable to mass murder, expulsions, and eliminationist politics. As I discuss in Chapter 11, this can be altered.

How Eliminationist Assaults End

The discussion of the international environment regarding eliminationist politics, and the essential immorality of those acting within it, provides the necessary context for investigating why individual mass murders and eliminations have ended, and why they did so when they did, and not earlier. Understanding political leaders' failure to intervene to stop the world's greatest horrors explains why eliminationist assaults have ended: not because of world outrage, not because of mobilization against mass murder, but because of internal developments among the perpetrators or external happenstance.

The Germans' annihilation of the Herero proceeded apace without external pressure or serious internal condemnation, ending only when the Germans had killed enough, about 80 percent, to solve their "Herero problem." It was then that German Chancellor von Bülow pressured the kaiser, for presumptive reputational reasons, to stop the wanton mass murder. The Germans had more or less finished the job and in any case, after the mass murder's formal cessation, continued to assault the Herero with other brutal, though mainly nonlethal, eliminationist means. The Belgians stopped their gargantuan annihilation of Congo's people in 1908 on their own accord. The Turks' annihilation of the Armenians similarly did not falter until they had depopulated Anatolia of Armenians and accomplished their eliminationist goal. With the Russian czar's overthrow, the Turks seized the opportunity to restart their annihilationist assault in 1918 to slaughter Armenians who had fled Turkey to Transcaucasia, known as Russian Armenia, as well as Armenians already living there. The Indonesians stopped slaughtering communists because they decided the job was finished. The Pakistanis ceased killing Bengalis only upon being militarily defeated by the Indians, who fought the Pakistanis for their own geostrategic reasons. Assad stopped slaughtering Hama's people when the destruction was sufficiently horrific to deter other Syrians from challenging his dictatorship. Pol Pot and the Khmer Rouge had to be defeated by the Vietnamese, who fought the war not as anti-eliminationists (they, after all, had their own gulag), but because the Khmer Rouge attacked Vietnam. And the many mass murderers of indigenous peoples around the world, all but ignored by the international community, have killed and expelled these internationally invisible peoples and then stopped, according to their own rhythms and self-conceived needs.

Annihilationist and eliminationist regimes targeting several groups often end the various assaults in their own ways. The Soviets' eliminationist policies went through different phases, which individually came to an end when Joseph Stalin deemed the job completed or when it seemed prudent to desist, such as during the war with Germany. After the war, Stalin resumed purges, although on a smaller scale, which ceased only with the regime's change upon his death in 1953. The Communist Party continued to rule the Soviet Union. Yet its new leaders decided to break with Stalin's eliminationist politics, so only days after he died, they began to end the regime's terror and close down the gulag. Similarly, Saddam stopped the murderous assault upon the Kurds, the Marsh people, and the rebellious Shia when he was satisfied the job was well enough done. Yet his general murderousness ended only when the Americans and British deposed him for geostrategic reasons having nothing to do with his domestic slaughters and eliminations.

An accounting of the cessation of the Germans' mass murdering of the Jews, and then of other targeted groups and peoples, differs by country and group. For the Jews, the Germans' and their collaborators' mass murdering in a country or region, such as in Lithuania, ended— except for the hunting down of those in hiding—when they succeeded in annihilating the country's Jews or deporting them for extermination elsewhere. For other targeted groups, such as the Polish elite, whose members the Germans partly targeted in 1939 and 1940, the Germans stopped their concerted campaign upon achieving their temporary goal. But their general mass murdering ended in a country or region, and then completely, only with military rollback and then defeat by the Allies, who themselves were fighting not because of the Germans' eliminationist assaults per se, but because they needed to destroy the regime waging an apocalyptic war of continental conquest. Had the Germans not been defeated, they might never have stopped, because their blueprint for the world, mandating the master race's subjugation and exploitation of all "lesser" races, would have required an unprecedented scale of destruction and ongoing use of all eliminationist means—repression, expulsion, transformation, prevention of reproduction, and extermination—to keep the "lesser" races dragooned and sufficiently diminished as to be controllable. The Germans' allies in mass murder, in Vichy France and Yugoslavia, in Slovakia, stopped their eliminationist programs as the job was reaching completion or the Germans' fortunes waned and occupation ended. The end of the Japanese mass murdering resembled the Germans', with the crescendo having been Americans' militarily unnecessary twin counterslaughters in Hiroshima and Nagasaki.

Our age's other gargantuan mass-murder regime, in communist China, also had ebbs and flows in its eliminationist policies and targets, which Mao, ideologically driven, turned on and off according to the intersection of his political goals and his read of changing conditions. He stopped the colossally murderous Great Leap Forward, for example, almost overnight in 1961. As with the Soviets, the general exterminationist policies ended through internal regime change, finally stopped for good, at least on an epic scale, by Mao's death in 1976. Yet the Chinese continue their imperialist eliminationist program in Tibet.

No matter where on the globe, or when in our time, one looks, the basic findings do not change. With few exceptions, eliminationist and exterminationist programs have ended because (1) the perpetrators reached their goals, (2) there was internal change owing to a leader's death, the perpetrating regime took a new direction, or it was overthrown, or (3) the states lost wars that were waged against them *not* to stop mass murders and eliminations but for other reasons. Outside intervention with the explicit intent to stop mass murder or eliminations—such as NATO's late interventions in Bosnia and Kosovo and the United Nations' insertion of peacekeepers in East Timor in 1999—has almost never happened. Even serious and effective sanctions expressly targeted to stop mass-murdering regimes from slaughtering more people have almost never been imposed. And those regimes that stopped their mass killing for their own reasons, not because of military defeat, often continue to assault the same groups and peoples, using other eliminationist means, including camps. As much as political leaders have learned they can slaughter with impunity, they know even better that lesser eliminationist measures, including expulsion, incarceration in camps, and the destruction of towns and homes, are in themselves that much less likely to produce a concerted international effort to thwart them.

Could these and other mass murders and eliminations have been stopped earlier? In so many instances the answer is obviously yes, or the international community or powerful countries could have at least made serious attempts offering a reasonable probability of success.

In Burundi, the Tutsi's wanton butchery of Hutu, targeting the Hutu elite and middle class, lasted from May to July 1972. The personalized killing, face to face with machetes, was an inverted precursor to the Rwandan mass murder two and a half decades later. The world's political leaders knew of the Burundian killing, on a scale that at least resembled genocide, while it was under way. Only the Belgians, the region's former colonials, made even token noises to stop the killing. The secretary general of the Organization of African Unity (OAU), then African countries' major international political organization, visited Burundi's capital during the height of the slaughter and formally declared: "The OAU, being essentially an organization based on solidarity, my presence here signifies the total solidarity of the Secretariat with the President of Burundi, with the government and the fraternal people of Burundi." UN Secretary General Kurt Waldheim was only slightly less craven in his public enabling of the mass murder. He conveyed his "fervent hopes that peace, harmony and stability can be brought about successfully and speedily, that Burundi will thereby achieve the goals of social progress, better standards of living and other ideals and principles set forth in the UN Charter." *This was the United Nations' official response* to a frenzy of killing that led the U.S. embassy's chief of mission to cable the State Department: "No respite, no letup. What apparently is a genocide continues. Arrests going on around the clock."[10] Yet American President Richard Nixon did nothing. The U.S. Congress never discussed the matter. No economic pressure, which would have been virtually cost-free to the United States, was put on this desperately poor country. Intervention to save Africans' lives in an all but militarily defenseless country did not take place. The possibility seems never to have occurred to anyone. The four other instances of Tutsi perpetrating substantial slaughters of Hutu in Burundi elicited effectively no response from the international community.

Similarly, in Chile, Argentina, El Salvador, and elsewhere in Latin America where U.S. influence with their rightist governments was vast, the Americans had enormous power and could have halted the mass murders and eliminations at little cost. In some instances, it may have taken but a few words. But as we know, in some instances the United States actively or tacitly encouraged the slaughters. As Clinton has now conceded about the Guatemalan regime's murder of 200,000 people in its eliminationist campaign, mainly aimed at Maya: "It is important that I state clearly that [American] support for military forces or intelligence units which engaged in violent and widespread repression of the kind described in the report was wrong." Indeed, it was not just "support" for such forces and it was not just "violent and widespread repression," as bad as that would be. It was much worse. The United States set the contours of the national security policy that informed the Guatemalan (and other) regimes, and helped train the Guatemalan security forces in the counterinsurgency tactics they would use against Maya communities. The violent repression included widespread mass slaughter and expulsion. The Guatemalans' exterminationist and eliminationist assault against the Maya came to an end when the Guatemalan leadership that deposed Ríos Montt decided the eliminationist task had been sufficiently completed as to render their self-conceived Mayan problem solved.

In the aftermath of the first Gulf War, President George H. W. Bush's American administration first encouraged southern Iraq's Marsh people to rebel against Saddam and then forsook them. Although the Americans had just pulverized the now defenseless Saddam's military capacity, he and his armed forces proceeded to wage a lethal eliminationist campaign against the Marsh people, systematically exterminating them and laying waste to their villages and region, killing perhaps forty thousand, and driving hundreds of thousands from their homes forever. During the 1992 assault, British Member of Parliament Emma Nicholson reported:

> Saddam has stepped up his onslaught in the marshes themselves. . . . I traveled through marshes smoking from ground-launched bombardments . . . reed-built villages have been razed, their small rice plots burned. . . . I reached the heart of the marshes, one mile from Saddam's front line. There I found people starving, desperate people, drinking filthy water and eating contaminated fish. They had fled villages under assault by Saddam's forces. . . . Many refugees like these have made the dash across the border into Iran. But to make the crossing, they must brave mined waters and a line of Saddam's soldiers.[11]

Nicholson knew about it. The British government knew about it. The Americans knew about it. Everyone knew about it, including the coalition of more than thirty countries whose troops had just defeated the Iraqi army and ended Saddam's imperial conquest of Kuwait. Yet they did nothing because geopolitical considerations—wanting to maintain Iraq as a countervailing force against Iran, not wanting to alienate the Americans' Arab coalition allies by invading an Arab country—took precedence. If ever an instance existed for the absolute necessity of American intervention to stop mass murder and elimination, this was it: The Americans had *encouraged* the rebellion that catalyzed Saddam's murderous eliminationist campaign; the mass murderer had just provoked a war with the United States, which soundly defeated him; and overpowering American military force was at hand. Nevertheless, Bush let the slaughter proceed unimpeded.

The eliminationist assaults in the former Yugoslavia by Serbs, first against Bosnians and Croats, then Kosovars, and by Croats against Serbs are more instances of how little political leaders are willing to do to stop mass murder, even at their doorstep. European nations, their political and media elites alike, often present themselves as paragons of moral conscience in contrast to the avaricious American colossus. Yet European governments individually and collectively stood by and watched systematic mass murder return, after less than a half century's absence, to their continent. Some European voices urged intervention, but these were relatively weak and ineffectual. The major and minor countries' political leaders and political classes did all they could to look the other way, explain away the problem as not being genocidal or as being intractable, fail to act forcefully, and drag their feet. In some instances, such as the Germans' premature recognition of Slovenian independence in violation of European Union policy, they actually helped precipitate the various stages of the crisis. All in all, the Europeans did nothing discernable to brake the killings and expulsions. Neither did the United States under Bush and during the Clinton administration's first three years, even though the first Bush administration knew about the Serbs' mass-murderous and eliminationist designs on Bosnia before the assault began, and immediately understood the assault for what it was once it did begin. Had Bush or Clinton decided to meet Slobodan Milošević with a credible threat of the actual force Clinton eventually did effectively apply—just serious bombing—the Serbs would not have slaughtered tens of thousands of Muslims, brutally expelled hundreds of thousands, or raped enormous numbers of women, and a more just cultural and political settlement would have emerged from Yugoslavia's breakup. Only when Clinton, much too late, used American airpower in Kosovo in what was formally, as it had also been in Bosnia, a NATO intervention was Milošević's eliminationist rampage in the West Europeans' backyard finally halted.

The story in Rwanda is even more sordid. The French, serving as the Francophone Hutu's guardians, and UN leaders possessed explicit advance knowledge that the Hutu leadership intended to embark upon a colossal mass murder of the Tutsi. The French had even armed and trained the eventual murderers. Did French President François Mitterrand or the head of the UN peacekeeping force, Kofi Annan (later rewarded with a promotion to UN secretary-general!), warn the Tutsi or the world? No. Did they tell the Hutu political leadership that the international community would intervene to stop them and would treat them as criminals if they proceeded with the mass murder? No. Did they seek to mobilize troops to intervene, or even just to make a credible threat that might give the regime pause? No. What did they do? First, when General Romeo Dallaire, the military commander of the UN peacekeeping force in Rwanda, informed Annan of the Hutu's plan to exterminate Tutsi leaders and Belgian peacekeepers to get the United Nations to withdraw its peacekeepers, Annan forbade Dallaire from intervening to protect the Tutsi, an order Annan never rescinded. Annan and Mitterrand kept quiet about the plans, providing cover for the mass murderers. Once the killing began, the United Nations withdrew its troops, abandoning the Tutsi and giving the Hutu the green light to slaughter them. The French did eventually send soldiers, which they have had no compunction to do in Africa to serve their interests, though here it was not to stop but effectively facilitate the butchery by protecting the Hutu regime. The rest of the world mobilized very late in the killing process to send some troops, in order to create a few safe havens but not to stop the mass murdering more generally—although halting the poorly armed and -trained perpetrators would have been easy. The killing continued until a Tutsi army, invading Rwanda from Uganda, defeated the Hutu militarily.

The French political leaders were at the helm of a democratic country that, like other democracies, is generally supportive of human rights. Why then did they collaborate in a mass murder that was of an intensity (number killed per month) that exceeded the Germans' slaughter of European Jews? Because the Hutu are Francophones and the Tutsi from Uganda who threatened the Hutu's tyrannical rule are not. The French, engaged in a virtually magical realist struggle to maintain their waning cultural importance around the world, decided that their self-image trumped the lives of 800,000 men, women, and children. Why did Annan permit the mass annihilation to proceed unimpeded? Anyone might assume that someone authorizing such intervention and going against the international community's status quo hands-off policies would make a mortal enemy of France, a UN Security Council permanent member with veto power over who becomes secretary-general.

In Rwanda, the world failed to work to stop the colossal slaughter taking place in full view, which it easily could have done at any of several stages, including before its inception. Some of its leading members also made the bloodbath possible, or at least far more likely and more deadly.

The far more formidable Taliban ruling Afghanistan, home to the genocidal bin Laden and Al Qaeda, was toppled easily by a mainly American campaign aided by an international expeditionary force. It took the American and allied forces only two weeks after inserting troops (following bombing) to rout the regime. (Subsequent strategic and tactical blunders have allowed a powerful insurgency to grow.) Unusual for a Western power, the United States was highly motivated to act against this mass-murdering regime for the obvious reason that it was the haven and staging ground for Al Qaeda, which had destroyed the Twin Towers of the World Trade Center on 9/11, damaged the Pentagon, killed three thousand people, and stunned and mobilized the American people. Would the motivation have been there had the Taliban or bin Laden slaughtered three thousand Afghanis? Or ten thousand? Or even 100,000? Of course not. Each of the many other instances of large domestic killing repeatedly answers this question for the United States and the powerful countries in the negative. Dislodging the Hutu genocidal regime in geographically small Rwanda, one of the world's poorest countries, would have been easy and not very costly. But 800,000 Tutsi's lives are evidently less valuable than 3,000 American lives.

These instances show how little the world, the United Nations, the major powers, the political decision-makers have done even when it would have been relatively easy to stop mass murder. The world's political heavyweights do not act to save innocent lives, because the nation-state is egoistic and its leaders are self-interested, and because the lives of people who are deemed to be unlike those living in the powerful countries are devalued. As Dallaire in 2004 said about the Hutu's slaughter of the Tutsi, "I still believe that if an organization decided to wipe out the 320 mountain gorillas there would be still more of a reaction by the international community to curtail or to stop that than there would be still today in attempting to protect thousands of human beings being slaughtered in the same country."[12]

Once the mechanisms that have stopped mass murder and eliminations are known, the question as to why eliminations do not end *earlier* than they do mainly answers itself. In almost all of our time's mass slaughters and eliminations, the leaders of the powerful international institutions and states, the effective agents capable of stopping a dedicated eliminationist regime, have not acted at all. So, obviously, they were never going to intervene early, to stop, let alone prevent, the catastrophes, while tens of thousands or hundreds of thousands of lives could be saved.

Intervention can take place. The horrible record of countries and their leaders need not be reproduced forever. To bring about effective change, we need to consider how we can transform the international environment regarding eliminationist politics, including the incentive structure that potential mass murderers and eliminationists confront, and how to promote right and necessary action among the world's powerful political actors.

PART II

MODERN ELIMINATIONIST POLITICS

CHAPTER SEVEN

Sources and Patterns

MASS MURDER IS A *political* act. It is not a frenzied outburst of crazed individuals. It is not the lashing out of a psychically or materially wounded collectivity. It is not a suprahuman or historically determined occurrence caused by prior acts of people long dead or continents away. It is not the mere expression of modernity's conditions or bureaucracies, or the explosive result of social psychological pressures. It is not driven by the darker, barbaric self supposedly within us all. And it is not the mere expression of one single man's or a small group of men's will, any more than other major political initiatives and policies are.

Because mass murders and eliminations are political acts, to understand and account for them, we must reinsert them into our understanding of politics *and* fundamentally change or expand our conception of politics to include them. I do not mean merely that we need to say that such assaults are "political," which is at once not recognized by many and treated as a truism requiring little elaboration or exploration by others. Instead, we must explore eliminationist programs' political complexities and integrate our understanding of them into a robust understanding of modern politics—domestic, international, and the intersection of the two. Thus, it is both true *and* not enough to say that an exterminationist or eliminationist assault is the result of a leader or leaders' decision for political ends. We need to further recognize and explore the other factors influencing leaders and the considerations they take into account in making their political decisions to mass murder or eliminate others—explorations that should produce analyses as full and true to the project's enormity as those we give to political leaders' decisions about other major policies, every-thing from national economic initiatives and social programs to going to war: How do the eliminationist assault's political goals advance the leaders' still larger political aspirations and initiatives? Will slaughter-ing or eliminating the targeted groups be popular with their supporters? Do they have the requisite resources, personnel, and organizations? Is the time ripe for the initiative? What are the potential costs, and the probabilities they will occur? How do the cost-benefit probabilities of initiating an eliminationist program compare to those of doing nothing, or of taking an entirely different approach to the perceived problems?

Leaders contemplating mass murder and elimination are not all ra-tional actors, using sophisticated algorithms to calculate a complex ma-trix of variables' costs and benefits before arriving at their decisions to expel or kill targeted groups, or to repress or tolerate them. Politics does not operate so neatly, and neither does the politics of mass elimination. Moreover, however rationally more conventionally conceived politics seems to be practiced—particularly when the well-understood norms of power, wealth, or moral responsibility are dominant—eliminationist politics are often governed at root by eschatological or millennial ori-entations, fantastical beliefs, or intense emotions that render talk of ra-tionality, or even instrumental calculation, misplaced. As we do with political leaders making other momentous decisions, including about war, we must neither treat eliminationist leaders as purely rational actors nor neglect the rational calculations such leaders regularly make.

War is a political act. Whatever their significant differences, so too are mass murder and elimination. War is part of political leaders' repertoire. So are eliminationist and exterminationist politics. It would seem foolish to explain the outbreak of a specific war or wars in gen-eral by reducing them to ancient prejudices, supposedly transhistorical qualities such as the supposed barbarian within us all, the social psy-chology of small-group life, or some invariable outcome of social struc-tures, such as capitalism or globalization. We understand that the decision to start a war is a choice by political leaders—a calculated choice taking into account many factors, including their often erro-neous, prejudice-laden worldviews. We understand it is a choice that could be made differently and, in practice, has been made differently again and again, with leaders opting for nonmilitary solutions to problems, effectively saying *no* to war. All this is true for mass murder and elimination.

All attempts to explain, as ironclad cause and effect, why wars break out have failed. The contingency of the political, the irreducibility of leaders' decision-making, the intelligence, passions, and wisdom of particular leaders doom the quest for scientific-like causal explanations. They also suggest how misplaced and misguided the quest is. The high-stakes confrontation of the Cuban Missile Crisis in 1961 demonstrates the foolishness of the notion that decisions to initiate a war or an eliminationist assault are foreordained by social structures or other "forces." (The tapes of the meetings in which American President John Kennedy and his advisers flail about while groping for a course of action should disabuse anyone of such an illusion.[1]) Most notably, Kennedy was under enormous pressure from American military leaders to strike Cuba, killing a projected ten thousand to twenty thousand people and risking a nuclear exchange with the Soviet Union. Kennedy said *no*.

Beyond the contingency of political developments and processes, and of individual leaders' personal imprints on events, leaders are embedded in such different political worlds in different historical periods and contexts that factors that might tend to lead them to opt for war in one period or place do not in another. Moreover, individual wars' timing and character also cannot be explained in a generalized way. Neither can the outcomes, except perhaps in the most prosaic, though hardly trivial, sense of who wins.

Take war's most catastrophic instance. World War II's major elements and features are not explainable without foregrounding the person, personality, intelligence, and pathologies of Adolf Hitler.* In 1928, it was not inevitable that Germany would bring Hitler to power or in a decade seek to conquer Europe and eventually the world. Had someone assassinated Hitler, or had any of many contingent historical

---

*Similarly, the Bolshevik Revolution and all that followed, including Joseph Stalin's rise to power, likely never would have occurred had Lenin not returned to Russia from Switzerland—even Leon Trotsky, an avowed Marxist, conceded this—which itself occurred only because of the cunning, strategically brilliant decision by the Germans to transport Lenin in 1917 from exile back to Russia so he could foment revolution and hasten Germany's defeat of Russia in World War I.

developments turned out differently, then there would have been no war, certainly no apocalyptic war (and mass elimination) that produced tens of millions of deaths. Even in 1933, when Hitler, as the leader of parliament's strongest political party, became Germany's chancellor, war, let alone its timing, scope, course, and destructiveness, was anything but inevitable. The same can be said for 1938, when Germany was still weak, though by then, short of a military coup deposing Hitler, some military conflict was likely. Had the Allies not caved in to Hitler's demands at Munich or had Stalin not made the disastrous calculations that led him in August 1939 to sign a nonaggression treaty with Hitler and thereby give Hitler the green light for a general war, European and world history would have unfolded substantially differently. His armies then still relatively weak, Hitler might not have started a two-front war, the avoidance of which he had always understood to be the sine qua non of expansionist military success. Even if he had wanted to start such a war against the most powerful countries to the west and east, would he have judged his military leadership willing to follow? Would they have been? Or would they have balked at a seemingly disastrous course? If Hitler had nevertheless initiated a two-front war, would he have been able in the spring of 1940 to conquer France and knock Britain off the continent? If, alternately, Hitler, in the face of an antagonistic Stalin, had waited, with the Allies rearming, his relative military strength might only have deteriorated. How events would have unfolded is anyone's guess. The political and military developments of the late 1930s and 1940s were hugely contingent. Perhaps Germany would have been contained, and Hitler deposed. Perhaps Germany would have been defeated in a more geographically limited war, sparing millions of lives.

The only relatively certain major military development about World War II in Europe is that the United States' entry meant Germany was likely to lose (unless Germany developed nuclear weapons first). And without Germany's initiation of a general war, it is also likely Japan, standing alone against the American colossus, a powerful Britain, and an unengaged, antagonistic Soviet Union, would not have attacked the United States and initiated a general Pacific war.

Without Hitler, the visionary apocalyptic warrior, the world would have been substantially different and in so many critical ways unpredictably so. Two all but certain things are that there would have been no Holocaust, and no world war at any time remotely close to when it occurred, if ever. Other things are less certain. A powerful Germany, which likely would not have been democratic, would have continued to occupy the heart of Europe. An imperial Japan might have continued to uneasily coexist with East Asia, Britain, and the United States. The Soviet empire in Eastern Europe would never have been established. The rapid postwar decolonization, owing in part to the war's mortal blows to the British and French empires, likely would have unfolded considerably later and more slowly. But how all this and much more would have played out is impossible to say.

Hitler was a rational calculator, an astute, adept politician, *and* an obsessive governed by a hallucinatory image of humanity and the world and of his megalomaniacal role in it, and a person operating under domestic and international political circumstances that constrained and enabled him. Yet nothing about Hitler's rise to power and decisions that led Germany and Germans, and then much of the world, hurtling to disaster, can be understood without accounting for Hitler's cunning mind and calculations. Nothing about it can be understood without privileging his irrational elements, his personal pathologies, and his political beliefs, prejudices, and hatreds. And nothing about it can be understood without embedding it all in an understanding of politics—Germany's politics, in which ordinary Germans resonating with Hitler's own beliefs and prejudices played a substantial role, and international politics, including the domestic politics moving the major international actors.

Just as leaders' decisions for or against war take into account a range of factors, including the prospect of winning and of being able to fight—whether they will receive compliance and support from those who must fight and from the broader population—so does the decision to practice eliminationist politics. In fact, leaders opting for mass elimination, especially extermination, depend significantly more on followers' having supportive beliefs and values, for two related reasons: the cognitive, emotional, and moral threshold for killing unarmed men, women, and children ordinarily greatly exceeds killing enemy soldiers. And for waging war there is a well-established, politically legitimate, existing institution, the military, that as a socially accepted practice prepares its members for fighting and for overcoming inhibitions (if any) in killing enemy soldiers. For eliminationist onslaughts, similar institutions and preparation are typically initially absent, so the intended perpetrators, and the general populace, have less formal preparation for overcoming the ordinarily greater inhibitions against slaughtering unarmed noncombatants, in other words massacring civilian adults and children. Because the decision to pursue eliminationist politics, especially mass extermination, depends on the ready willingness of those in whose name the politics would be pursued, the decision in itself is obviously not sufficient to explain the perpetrators' participation. The "great man" view of genocide—best known for being applied to the so-called charismatic leader Hitler and as an exculpatory argument to spare the perpetrators' character and responsibility from being probed—is obviously only partially correct. Political leaders are critical for determining whether eliminationist onslaughts take place at all, but they cannot do it or, as seems often to be believed, *will* it alone. To understand the translation of their will into social and political action on the part of thousands we need to move from analyzing the leader's and his circle's individual beliefs, values, and psychology to considering broadly dispersed political and social beliefs and values.

The same complex and multifaceted analyses that exist of major political policies, including war, must characterize investigations and understandings of eliminationist politics. The literatures on either world war are examples. Take World War I. A vast body of scholarship (and popular writing) dissects and tries to make sense of why the war happened, examining all aspects that may have contributed to its outbreak, including political, social, economic, imperial, and individual psychological dimensions. Vast literatures examine the war itself in its every detail, the soldiers' lives, understanding, and motives, and the mobilizing of domestic support, the war's domestic consequences, and its aftermath. Standard political questions of leadership and followership, of the mobilization of resources, of institutional design and performance, of motivating the soldiers and the broader population for participation and sacrifices are not assumed away. They are asked, by and large, without their answers being presumed or asserted with some agenda of inculpation or exculpation. The same could be said for World War II, the Vietnam War, the Iraq War, and a host of others.

Compared to this, our treatment and understanding of eliminationist politics is analytically thin and one-dimensional. The same telling comparison could be made by looking at the complexity and multidimensionality of how other, more hum-drum aspects of American politics are investigated, whether it is the New Deal, the civil rights movement, the "Reagan Revolution," or the politics of health care during the administration of President Bill Clinton.

We must stop detaching mass elimination and its mass-murder variant from our understanding of politics. We must stop thinking it is sufficient for historians to describe the events themselves and then posit some (reductionist) "explanation." Or for social psychologists to reduce it to social psychology. Or for diversionists to attribute structural causality and responsibility to abstract institutions or to systems far removed—either in time, such as long-gone colonizers, or in space, such as global capitalism—from the agents of violence and death and the countries of their destructive deeds. *Eliminationist politics, like the politics of war, is a politics of purposive acts to achieve political outcomes, often of ultimate ends and often of desired power redistribution.* Only when we recognize this can we begin to understand the varied phenomena that compose eliminationist politics and respond better to them politically.

This suggests that there is no single explanation for mass murder or more generally mass elimination. Eliminationist politics has many diverse aspects. Some resist general or systematic explanation. Others do not. Some lend themselves to probabilistic statements. Some fall into patterns that can be analytically usefully categorized. Our task is to make sense of eliminationist politics' various aspects, or at least as much sense as each allows.

We have seen that eliminationist politics are an extension of politics by other means. But are they really an *extension*? The history of our time suggests that eliminationism is actually *integral* to politics, as its diverse forms and policy options have often been used and are readily available. Interstate war has become exceptional. Yet violent domestic conflict (including civil wars), domination, and repression are commonly practiced around the world, and eliminationist politics, including mass murder, is conceptually and as a matter of practice on a continuum with other violent domestic forms of control and suppression. The number of those

Eliminationist Politics in the Ten Most Populous Countries and the European Union

	Country	Population in Millions (2009)	Selected Eliminationist Assaults
1	China	1,339	Communist Chinese slaughter of tens of millions
2	India	1,166	Partition mass murders and expulsions
3	European Union	492	Germans' mass murdering across continent
4	United States	307	Incinerating Japanese cities, and home to numerous survivor communities
5	Indonesia	240	Slaughter of communists and of East Timorese
6	Brazil	199	Killing and elimination of indigenous peoples
7	Pakistan	176	Partition, and mass murder in Bangladesh
8	Bangladesh	156	Partition, and mass murder by Pakistanis
9	Nigeria	149	Slaughters during civil war
10	Russia	140	Victims of German, Soviet mass murders
11	Japan	127	Mass murders in Asia, and victims of nuclear weapons

Estimated population figures from July 2009, *CIA World Factbook*, https://www.cia.gov/library/publications/the-world-factbook/rankorder/2119rank.html. In choosing to treat the European Union as the third most populous political entity at 492 million people, let us not forget that Germany's mass-murderous predations were a primary, if not the primary, impetus for establishing a European federation that would eventually evolve and expand into the European Union.

dying because of eliminationist politics is vast. The number of instances of such politics being practiced is too numerous to easily count. The number of moments that eliminationist politics have *not* been practiced during our era is zero, and the instances where its most violent and lethal forms of mass expulsion, incarceration, enslavement, and killing have not been practiced also number zero. The number of countries and groups having either practiced eliminationist politics or had such violence practiced upon them is enormous. Without a thorough reckoning of eliminationist politics' character and effects, our time's history dating from the twentieth century's beginning, many of its major geopolitical developments, and states' and societies' constellation today cannot be understood properly. Eliminationist politics have shaped Europe's and Asia's maps, and the histories, social compositions, and politics of the world's most populous countries and so many smaller ones.

Each of the ten most populous countries and the European Union (which with regard to mass murder during World War II has shared experience and relatively common consciousness) has perpetrated or been the victim of large-scale, nationally traumatic murderous eliminationist politics.* In recent history mass murder has deeply scarred countries home to 4.4 billion people, two-thirds of the world's population.

Imagine mass murderers had targeted you, that somehow you had managed to escape, or they had "merely" driven you from your home or imprisoned you in a camp and brutalized you, or you had lived for years fearing they might kill you. Or imagine eliminationist executioners had targeted and "merely" brutalized or actually killed your family, ethnic group, community, or coreligionists. Or imagine that you lived in a community where such executioners had so targeted, brutalized, or killed people of other ethnicities or religions. How would any of these circumstances of your life, how would these horrors that engulfed you and/or those around you, scar or mar you? If imagining rampaging mass murderers seems far-fetched, imagine hooligans had broken into the house next door and brutally beaten and murdered your neighbor, and his son had seen it happen. Think of how it would indelibly transform the boy's life. Think of how it would affect yours, knowing what had befallen your neighbor and how that boy, whom you see daily, had to bear the daily burden of being fatherless and having witnessed such brutality perpetrated on his father, and thereby on him. These are the eliminationist politics and acts that have worsened and coarsened the existence of billions of people alive today. Such politics have been mainly the province of nondemocratic regimes. Even so, democratic regimes succeeding them must pick up the pieces, process (including by suppressing knowledge of) what has happened, and live with exterminationist and eliminationist assaults' society-deforming and personally devastating consequences.

If we understand eliminationist politics as a constituent feature of politics and of leaders' available political repertoire, and realize that eliminationist beliefs and hatreds have existed broadly among many

---

*Brazil may be the exception insofar as Brazilians' destruction of the country's indigenous peoples may not have imprinted Brazilians' consciousnesses as profoundly as the other eliminationist assaults have other peoples'.

countries' leaders and peoples, then the attacks' high incidence and victims' staggering number are not so startling.

Modernity and Eliminationist Politics

Just as our time's politics have differed from those of previous ages, so
too have the eliminationist politics. Although a complex interactive relationship exists between a specific country's politics and society, we
can identify several political factors that crucially contribute to the initiation and character of our time's mass murders and eliminations:

1. Features of modernity itself and of the modern state
2. Structural relationships that exist domestically within countries
3. International contexts (or environments)
4. Beliefs about certain groups and understandings of politics and
   society that lead leaders and followers to think eliminating those
   groups desirable
5. Proximate factors that produce the opportunity and the will to take
   the political step of turning eliminationist desires into actuality

In discussing these political factors we can explore eliminationist politics' broader outcomes, some of which are by now familiar: What has
been the character of our era's mass-murder and eliminationist politics, and why has it differed from that of other periods? Why have our
time's attacks occurred? What do eliminationist programs have in common? How do they vary? Why do perpetrators treat different victim
groups differently during a given eliminationist program? Examining
eliminationist politics through these wide-angle and narrowly focusing
lenses reveals similarities and identifiable patterns in mass murder and
elimination's causes and mechanisms, and various differences in the results, some patterned, others not.

Modernity, a defining aspect of which is the modern nation-state,
has features promoting and informing our time's eliminationist and exterminationist politics. Among the modern state's distinctive qualities is
its enormous and unprecedented power to transform the physical and
social world—dwarfing anything states could do even in the nineteenth

century. This is owing to the modern world's gargantuan growth technologically and industrially, and also to its equally prodigious, though much less recognized, growth in organizational sophistication and means of control, and knowledge about society and how to shape it. A concomitant distinctive feature of our time is the transformative visions and related transformative ideologies that political leaders and their followers develop. Eighteenth- and nineteenth-century states—American, German, Japanese, Russian—were essentially caretaker entities that pacified their territories, governed them lightly—if often brutally—and had as a principal activity raising taxes to finance small bureaucracies and militaries, safeguard the privileged classes, and facilitate industrialization to various degrees. Much of the nineteenth-century globe, conquered and subjugated by European imperial powers, lacked indigenous states or substantial political capacities. Our era's states, ever increasingly, are comparative institutional behemoths, with the resources, staff, communications, and organization to do, figuratively, a million times more for or against society and its members.

The capacity to transform the world, to think not just about ruling over the territory in which people live but also about shaping and governing the people themselves, in every aspect of their lives, produces an orientation that can give rise to powerful transformative politics. Modern leaders can, in a practical sense, consider governing hundreds of millions, even billions of people, and not just loosely being sovereign over territory, but of controlling social, economic, and cultural life, even down to the family unit. They can in a practical sense think of slaughtering millions across large geographic areas. They have the power to change the social and economic order in radical ways, and relatively quickly. They can create a blueprint to fundamentally refashion societies socially and culturally, which they can—confident of substantial success—decide to implement. Many transformative projects (communist, Nazi, nationalist, ethnic, religious, and others) face real or imagined human impediments, groups of people putatively standing in the way, or who, as a matter of definition, must be eliminated. This modern political mindset includes a particularly modern political aesthetic of design and control. The mindset's fundamentals characterize democratic and nonmurderous regimes no less than nondemocratic and murderous ones. But when wedded to other ideas, which happens especially frequently among nondemocratic regimes' rulers and supporters, this modern political aesthetic can lead to plans for recrafting society, a wish for purity, as it is conceived, and intolerance of perceived imperfection or deviation.

The most striking example of this eliminationist and exterminationist dreaming, planning, and implementation is, as with much else under discussion here, the Nazis. In January 1942, months after the Germans had already moved into the systematic extermination phase of their eliminationist assault against the Jews, Reinhard Heydrich, who was in charge of the program, convened a meeting of leading officials from the relevant state and governmental ministries to discuss their participation. Heydrich itemized country by country, including ones not yet conquered, such as England, Ireland, Switzerland, and Turkey, the number of Jews they would slaughter. Mass murderers often make lists of people they intend to kill, but they are usually lists of individuals, or members of a political opposition or a targeted people's elite. In the vast annals of eliminationist politics, there has never been, except in this one instance, a formal document itemizing country by country, across a continent, the millions of people slated for extermination. The German leadership had embarked on a program to slaughter more than eleven million Jews.[2]

Modernity has bestowed upon the nation-state an increased communicative and learning capacity. Particularly starting with the second part of the twentieth century, and continuously accelerating, political leaders learn quickly of others' policies and measures, and their successes or failures. These include policies and techniques of control, repression, and elimination. Our era has produced among political leaders (and even, if unconceptualized, among publics) around the world a much greater consciousness about eliminationist politics' normalcy and practical efficacy, from erecting camps (both the Soviets and Nazis were inspired by the British "concentration camps" for the Boers) to mass murder. Many mass murderers or would-be mass murderers have explicitly referred to previous genocidal killers' models, starting perhaps with Hitler himself invoking the slaughter of the Armenians, and continuing to Political Islamists today who, when contemplating their hoped-for annihilation of Israel's Jews, regularly refer admiringly to the Germans' exterminationist assault on the Jews, often lamenting

L a n d	Zahl
A. Altreich	131.800
Ostmark	43.700
Ostgebiete	420.000
Generalgouvernement	2.284.000
Bialystok	400.000
Protektorat Böhmen und Mähren	74.200
Estland – judenfrei –	
Lettland	3.500
Litauen	34.000
Belgien	43.000
Dänemark	5.600
Frankreich / Besetztes Gebiet	165.000
Unbesetztes Gebiet	700.000
Griechenland	69.600
Niederlande	160.800
Norwegen	1.300
B. Bulgarien	48.000
England	330.000
Finnland	2.300
Irland	4.000
Italien einschl. Sardinien	58.000
Albanien	200
Kroatien	40.000
Portugal	3.000
Rumänien einschl. Bessarabien	342.000
Schweden	8.000
Schweiz	18.000
Serbien	10.000
Slowakei	88.000
Spanien	6.000
Türkei (europ. Teil)	55.500
Ungarn	742.800
UdSSR	5.000.000
Ukraine 2.994.684	
Weißrußland aus- schl. Bialystok 446.484	
Zusammen: über	11.000.000

From the minutes of the Wannsee Conference, January 1942

that the Germans did not finish the job. The Holocaust, commonly referred to by the Nazis' favorite euphemism, the "final solution," is by
far the model most frequently invoked by would-be mass murderers.
This is so probably for many reasons: the Holocaust's notoriety, its unequivocal annihilationist character, and the Jews' continued status as
targets for Arab leaders, media, and thinkers and for Political Islamists

more generally, which only further increases the renown of Hitler, the Nazis, and the Holocaust among those contemplating killing others.

While the nation-state's real power has made imagining, planning for, and then undertaking eliminationist politics a frequent and often practical activity, these conditions of greater power and greater transformative and destructive vision have themselves not produced our time's mass slaughters and eliminations. A second structural political condition of modernity has turned standard antipathies and antagonisms into the basis for eliminationist politics.

Prior to the advent of modernity, and particularly the twentieth century, humanity was mainly in a prepolitical state. Most people were not part of politics: They were cowed or quiescent subjects of emperors, kings, and nobles, not citizens or even potential citizens of countries. There was no real sense that people could govern themselves or participate meaningfully in their lives' political governance, so they demanded few goods or services from their rulers (who had little capacity to supply them). This was so not because people were individually incapable of self-governance, but because the political and social structures did not allow for it. It was a predemocratic time. There could always be rebellions from within or invasion from without. Yet authoritarian governance's fundamental legitimacy was, almost everywhere, not an issue. Indeed, authoritarian rule over a country's or region's depoliticized population was often sacralized by the so-called divine right of kings or churches. It was the unquestioned, perceived natural order.

In our time, every person is a citizen or a potential citizen, every person is mobilized or potentially mobilized into politics. Political leaders face much more dissent and potential dissent than the rulers of predemocratic times did. In the modern world, if leaders are unwilling to accommodate the populace's demands, including those of its different groups, then the leaders must be prepared to quell the dissent. Governing leaders, and the groups that support them, who oppose democracy or a necessary degree of universalist pluralism *inevitably* will have their rule and their regimes contested by people resolutely seeking democracy, self-determination, or pluralism, and a minimally fair portion of society's economic product and social benefits. Leaders of nondemocratic regimes know this. Such political leaders also know that those pressing for fundamental political and economic change, including possibly self-determination and territorial secession, will not easily cease, and repression's costs will likely grow.

In the modern world, leaders of dictatorships of all kinds are therefore prone to using increasing repression and violence, which, being on a continuum with elimination's other forms, tend to make leaders want to solve their self-conceived or self-created problems in a definitive and final manner by eliminating putatively problematic people. Modern dictatorship, requiring increasing repression and violence, produces a totalitarian logic and drive. Political leaders and their regime perceive the need to penetrate society ever more pervasively, to control as much of social life as possible. As repression and control increase, the stakes for the power holders and their followers grow, and the enmity of the repressed similarly deepens. The totalitarian impulse thus exacerbates modern dictatorship's already inherent tendency to resort to eliminationist politics because it leads those in power and those benefiting from existing politics to perceive more and more social or political conduct as threatening, and to fear the consequences of a political reversal of fortune ever more intensely.

Within the modern nation-state, systematic political and social tensions exist, making for high-stakes conflicts conducive to eliminationist politics and practice. In all countries economic development and people's mobilization into politics create enormous strains. Rapid population growth in many countries further leads to intensive competition over scarce resources, including farmland in developing countries. These strains often produce a zero-sum politics, where one group's benefits come at the expense of another's. This in itself makes consensual and democratic politics a more difficult art to practice and sustain, and therefore tends to produce a politics of domination and repression, which inherently include an eliminationist impulse.

Nation-building and its attendant challenges and problems have produced a second set of widespread strains. Nation-building requires political leaders to create a common sense of national belonging sufficient for a modern polity to function without state-rending conflict. Most acutely, problems of nation-building have existed in the countries that emerged after decolonization. Many of them were artificial in the sense of suddenly being composed of ethnic and religious groups thrown together with little in common, except sometimes their competition if not enmity for one another. These countries were torn not only by internal social and political conflicts and also cross-border conflicts with neighboring countries into which the same ethnic or religious groups had been split off, but also by their people's generally poor preparation for managing a state in the modern world, a world of politically mobilized peoples, and of transforming eighteenth-century economies into twentieth-century ones. Nowhere has this problem been more visible and deadly than in the central African region containing Rwanda, Burundi, and Democratic Republic of the Congo, where different ethnic groups, most notably the bitter enemies Hutu and Tutsi, have cohabited in desperately poor countries and also split up among them, leading to repeated, serial, and sometimes colossal instances of mass slaughter. This region, like almost no other, can be characterized as being in a semipermanent state of eliminationist politics. In such states, civil war, or even smaller-scale internal conflict, tends to produce eliminationist inclinations because the enemy, even when vanquished, will still regularly contest power, and therefore be threatening.

The challenges of nation-building or any kind of structural conflict, including those caused by economic development and modern inclusive politics, do not in themselves produce eliminationist responses, or eliminationist responses of any particular kind. That is dependent on other factors (discussed below). Nevertheless, these challenges and conflicts have given powerful impetus to one group or another, one set of rulers or another, to opt first for repressive politics and then for a politics of mass elimination. This has particularly been the case because such conflicts tend to produce eliminationist ideologies that then organize political thinking, strategies, and action.

In our era, when norms of universal rights, self-determination, and democracy prevail and economic and social change is a constant, nondemocratic politics and regimes are qualitatively different from previous eras. Today, they have a built-in propensity—a real one, and not just a hypothetical one—to adopt eliminationist politics, including their lethal variant. This propensity is so embedded in the structure of contemporary nondemocratic rule and tyranny that we must conceive of nondemocratic and tyrannical regimes as inherently proto-eliminationist, even exterminationist, and respond to them politically (as discussed in Chapter 11) in a manner reflecting this.

As the previous chapter's discussion shows, the international political environment critically influences the incidence of eliminationist assaults. When we consider that during our time, the international context has generally been, as it was in previous ages, permissive toward such politics, we see more clearly why our age has been so mass-murderously combustible. The international context's contribution to enabling eliminationist politics has been still worse during our time. The international environment's earlier permissive baseline toward eliminationist politics was due to states' and international institutions' hands-off approach to other states' eliminationist politics. Our time has probably seen more deviation from this baseline in *encouraging* mass murder and eliminations than in discouraging them. Modernity's international system has provided yet another distinctive impetus to make our time's eliminationist politics unusually deadly.

Modernity creates a transformative capacity and mindset that includes an eliminationist component. The structural conditions of modern nondemocracies and tyrannies inherently produce intensive political conflicts—often resulting from the dislocation of nation-building and of economic development. These conflicts create a propensity on the part of such systems' inherently insecure power holders, drawing on their great capacities and inspired by their eliminationist notions, to adopt eliminationist solutions to eradicate political challenges and social unrest. But these structural conditions are only a portion of the eliminationist equation. Some proximate conditions, when present, tend to make leaders more likely to consider practicing, and then adopting, eliminationist politics and, when absent, tend to militate against such politics. Note the word *tend*. These paths are not determined. Precisely because they are not, we must return to the topic of why leaders *decide* to initiate mass murders and eliminations. The decision to eliminate people cannot be reduced to factors beyond the beliefs, personality, psychology, and moral character of the decision-makers. Nevertheless, some factors render this decision more or less possible and probable.

Most leaders deciding to eliminate groups of people are fervent in their desire. Many are fanatical. But they are not crazy in the sense of being incapable of assessing the practicality of implementing their wishes. These men have managed to rise to power, a feat all but impossible to accomplish for any but a pragmatic practitioner of the possible. Hitler is a quintessential example. Having succeeded in a few years in turning a political party of two dozen into a mass movement, becoming Germany's chancellor through the ballot box, and consolidating power into an immensely popular dictatorship, he then set out to fulfill his ideological program by exterminating and eliminating millions of people. Even then he carefully waited for the right time and opportunities to implement his murderous plans step by step. Whatever their differences, our time's other mass murdering political leaders, Mehmet Talât and Ismail Enver, Stalin, Father Josef Tiso, Anton Pavelić, Mao Zedong, Haji Muhammad Suharto, Idi Amin, Pol Pot, Augusto Pinochet, the junta leaders in Argentina, Mengistu Haile Mariam, Ríos Montt, Hafez al-Assad, Slobodan Milošević, Saddam Hussein, Théoneste Bagosora and the other Rwandan Hutu leaders, Omar al-Bashir in Sudan, and many more, were similar human amalgams of cunning and evil, adept Machiavellians, and hate-filled destroyers of targeted portions of humanity, against which they conducted a one-sided war.

Because annihilationist and eliminationist assaults against large population groups are not trivial or routine undertakings, leaders must have a profound reason to pursue policies that could damn them among humanity's worst criminals. Some vision of a fundamentally transformed society provides them with the idea and the drive to eliminate groups of people, instead of responding to real (or even imagined) conflicts with negotiation, accommodation, and compromise, or even— if deemed necessary—with lesser repressive measures. Whatever the particular rationale for mass elimination, whatever the particular conception of the intended victims, almost always there is at the root a complex of thinking that amalgamates three related, though by no means congruent, notions: the need for absolute control, the desire for purity, and the imperative to prevent the apocalypse. This radical antipluralist mindset seeks to forge a society of extreme, even total obedience—to regulate social and personal life; to purge domestic (and sometimes international) society of social and human impurities; and to fend off the catastrophe that putatively dissenting or impure people will bring about, hence a frequent apocalyptic mentality and commensurate action. Some variant of this mindset has been integral to most of our time's eliminationist campaigns. The specific beliefs' nature, from Nazi to communist to nationalist to racist to religious, that governs leaders bent upon eliminating, typically lethally, unwanted groups varies greatly—and the differences matter enormously for their eliminationist programs—but they share, without being reducible to, this radical intolerance complex.

Still, some are more intolerant than others. Certain movements and regimes, Nazism, various communist regimes, and, today, Political Islam (discussed in Chapter 10), distinguish themselves among those which wanted and want to remold society, as eliminationist intolerance's champions. These movements share three critical characteristics. First, they require conformity from people that many are unable to or would never want to fulfill. For the Nazis, most of humanity's putatively immutable racial inferiority disqualifies them; for the communists, different social classes and groups were not ready or able to march in lockstep with history; and for the Political Islamists, the powerful, corrupt infidels will never acquiesce to Political Islam's stultifying political-religious creed and practices. Second, these movements' visions for society's transformation require its utter purification. For the Nazis, in different ways, different racially disparaged groups posed various severe threats; for communists, until they realized the communist utopia, recalcitrant social groups always threatened counterrevolution; and for the Political Islamists, God's will demands that all people serve him and live according to his Political Islamic law. Third, these movements conceive of their visionary transformations as necessary in their own societies *and* transnationally, ultimately for all humanity, because only then—for each movement differently—would harmony follow.

These visions lead to the need to bring the world in line and extirpate all that is deemed recalcitrant, what the Nazis called *Gleichschaltung;* to create total unanimity of thought, meaning total conformity, what the Soviets called *yedinomyshlenie;* or to compel everyone to live according to strict laws allowing little room for personal freedom or deviation, what the Political Islamists call *sharia*. In each case, they reverse democratic pluralist societies' basic creed, as all nondemocratic and tyrannical regimes do to varying degrees. The democratic creed is: *He who is not against me is for me.* Those not actively attacking their government or fellow citizens, breaking or seeking to tear down society's laws, no matter how they otherwise choose to live their lives, are respected and allowed to exercise their political and civil rights, and follow their own notions of personal freedom of thought, conscience, and conduct. The creed of such visionary and radically intolerant dispensations as Nazism, various communisms, and Political Islam is: *He who is not for me is against me.* Anyone unable to or refusing to fall in line behind the prescribed transformative vision is an objective enemy who cannot be tolerated but must have the recalcitrant part of himself—or if that is not possible, then the person as a whole—eliminated. Each movement has conceived of much though not all of humanity as Immanuel Kant's "crooked timber," out of which he declared "no straight thing was ever made." Each, in its own way, cannot abide unstraightened human timber, and thus seeks to break and recast humanity—casting much into history's garbage heap—and reshape and refasten the remaining portion according to each movement's respective procrustean notions. Thus, their thoroughgoing eliminationist desires and assaults: Nazism's Herculean destructiveness, Soviet, Chinese, North Korean, and Khmer Rouge communism's "permanent purge," and Political Islamists' calls to kill millions, which some have already begun to execute. The Khmer Rouge's maxim applies to them all: "What is too long must be shortened and made the right length," with the added fact that for each, much of society and the world is "too long."[3]

When any leader, politician, or person speaks the language of absolute control, purity, or earthly or otherworldly apocalypse, he reveals a potentially eliminationist and exterminationist mindset. Still, this drive to eliminate targeted groups in itself is not sufficient for a program to be enacted. Leaders must believe that they can act with a high probability of success before they will risk initiating mass murder or elimination. Otherwise, their policy would be self-defeating. Leaders must believe that three conditions for success appear likely. They must have access to the targeted people. (This is usually not a problem when, as most are, the victims are a minority in that country.) They must judge that they can act with impunity domestically. They must also believe they act with impunity internationally, so their eliminationist program will not be self-defeating, triggering powerful outside intervention. This in particular is why war often serves as the best context for undertaking preexisting eliminationist desires. As Talât and Enver explained in a memorandum to German officials in which they discussed the Armenians' elimination, "The work that is to be done must be done *now;* after the war it will be too late."[4] During war, other states have difficulty knowing what is happening within combatant countries and can more easily maintain or feign ignorance about the mass murdering, which reduces domestic and international pressure on them to intervene. War itself, whether interstate or civil, or counterinsurgent, usually places a country's leaders at maximum risk, so the added danger to them of implementing an eliminationist campaign is small. Thus war and domestic military conflicts frequently alter the cost-benefit calculus, finally tipping the scales in favor of eliminating the hated groups, or become the domestic and international pretext for leaders to set in motion their willing followers, who are still easier to mobilize with even more plausible accounts for why, during war, the country must eliminate its enemies.

Mass murder and eliminations are, as those contemplating them understand, both high-risk strategies, because the danger for the political leaders undertaking them is enormous, and low-risk strategies with high payoffs, because political leaders undertake such campaigns when they expect success. When circumstances, such as war or domestic civil conflict, can be engineered to decrease the additional risk of moving against hated groups, then the time has come for the would-be perpetrators to act, and to act in accordance with their and their followers' preexisting eliminationist beliefs, and with concrete strategic and often detailed tactical plans. This includes creating new eliminationist institutions, or designating existing ones for eliminationist operations, mapping out, as in a military campaign, operational zones and attack plans, and drawing up categories (often prioritized) of people to be slaughtered or expelled, and specific lists of people, including enemy elites, to be especially targeted.

Such politically conscious and *preexisting*, concrete exterminationist and eliminationist measures guided the Turks' murderous assault on the Armenians, the Germans' eliminationist assaults on Jews and many others, the Indonesians' slaughter of the communists among them, the Pakistanis' butchery of Bangladeshis, the Serbs' various eliminationist onslaughts of the 1990s, and many other mass slaughters and eliminations up to and including the Political Islamic Sudanese's assault on Darfurians. In Rwanda, in December 1993, four months before the Hutu leaders' plans to annihilate the Tutsi were put into effect, the Rwandan journal *Le Flambeau* published inside information about the training

and planning given to the paramilitary Interahamwe, which in its out-
lines proved to be accurate:

> We learn today, with the greatest stupefaction that these Rwandese
> "tontons macoutes" [the brutal henchmen of the murderous Duvalier
> regime in Haiti] will implement a plot which the plotters will pass
> off as a civil war. The day of 20 December 1993, other sources talk
> of 23 December 1993, will be the fatal day of the "final solution."
>
> Let us recall that the Nazi Germans and their chief Hitler baptised
> the operation to exterminate those they considered as the enemy of the
> blossoming of the Aryan race, notably the Jews, [the] final solution.
>
> Rwandese fascists and their chief have decided to apply "the final
> solution" to their fellow citizens judged enemies of the regime. This
> refers to their political adversaries, defenceless populations but also
> and above all those who have seen the hand of the regime in the lat-
> est massacres of the population.[5]

The plan, several years in preparation, took a few months longer before
the Hutu's leaders found the propitious moment to implement it. During its preparation's final phase, the Interahamwe rank and file received
a crash course in weaponry so they could aid the mass killing. According to Jacques, who says he killed "about ten,"

> We were taught by corporals from the gendarmes. They gave us
> three days [of training]. . . . They only taught us how to use grenades
> and guns. Rifle training started in the city. But for the grenades it was
> elsewhere. Two days after the President died, thousands were trained
> at once.
>
> Three days after the President was killed, the military began to or-
> ganize the interahamwe so that they could maintain the roadblocks.
> And youths from each neighbourhood went to get training to fight.[6]

Eliminationist ideals and intent are almost never forged in the heat of
battle. They are usually long in existence as desires, with their progen-
itors and bearers waiting for the right time to turn them into concrete,
operational plans, and then still later, for the right opportunity to im-

plement them. In February 1994, on the eve of the mass-murderous assault when the time seemed ripe and opportunity seemed around the corner, talk of slaughtering the Tutsi was already common in Kigali. A magazine published an article with the headline, "By the way, the Tutsi race could be extinguished." The previous month the prominent Hutu newspaper *Kangura* (Wake Others Up) wrote revealingly and prophetically, "Who will survive the March War? [. . .] The masses will rise with the help of the army and the blood will flow freely."[7]

Political leaders, even tyrants, can sometimes have inhibitions against the radical measures of eliminationist assaults. But nothing more effectively disinhibits leaders and followers alike than a rationale for not having inhibitions in the first place, which eliminationist beliefs of many kinds supply. Less frequent, though in many instances critically important, has been the sight of one's enemy slaughtering or expelling members of one's own people or of other peoples, who is therefore said to have proven himself by his own hand to be a threatening barbarian deserving no mercy. The German occupation forces in the Soviet Union found dead (non-German) political prisoners the retreating Soviets had killed and left behind. This further reinforced their demonological views about a construct of their own fantasies, "Jewish-Bolshevism," and their desire to eradicate the Jews, to whom they falsely imputed the murders (that many of the executed prisoners were Jewish mattered not at all to the Germans). One real or manufactured act of brutality by a member of a hated group can be enough to become a powerful symbol of malevolence and threat that becomes a battle cry or ideological sustenance for an eliminationist purge. For the British settlers in Kenya, this process of turning a few instances of violence into powerful symbols undergirding an eliminationist ideology against the Mau Mau, and more broadly against the Kikuyu people, has been well documented. During Mau Mau leader Johnstone "Jomo" Kenyatta's trial, which began in December 1952, the British settlers in Kenya were up in arms, with many calling for the extermination of the Kikuyu. At a protest rally of more than 1,500 settlers (out of a total settler population of only 50,000) in January 1953 in Nairobi, calling for the elimination of the Mau Mau and the summary conviction of Kenyatta

and his five codefendants, one British settler addressed Kenyan Leg-
islative Council member Michael Blundell, who was trying to quell the
crowd: "Michael, you'll never cure this problem, you'll never cure it.
You put the troops into the [Kikuyu] villages and you shoot 50,000 of
them, men, women and children."[8]

Tales, real or invented, of people killing or brutalizing members of
another group when the thinking about that people is already grounded
in deep prejudice and hatred has provided the impetus in many countries, and circumstances for those ready to join an eliminationist assault, to give themselves to their leaders' initiatives to expel or slaughter
the enemy people. This happened in the most concentrated fashion in
Rwanda, where the assassination of Hutu President Juvénal Habyarimana (likely perpetrated by Hutu members of his own movement) was
the spectacular event blamed on the Tutsi, and the pretext for the exterminationist leadership of the governing National Republican Movement for Democracy to put into action plans long germinating for the
"final solution" to their Tutsi problem. Pancrace Hakizamungili, a
Hutu mass murderer, who told us of how Hutu always "sees a threat
lurking in even the feeblest or kindest Tutsi," explains more of this dynamic: "The radios were yammering at us since 1992 to kill all the
Tutsi; there was anger after the president's death and a fear of falling
under the rule of the *inkotanyi*." And so with the hatred welling up in
them, they yelled "let's go hunting!"

As in Rwanda, hearing reports of the enemy's real or alleged atrocities can render this enemy, and the people in whose name they apparently act, dangerous in a qualitatively different way from ordinary
enemies. In Rwanda and elsewhere, Hutu were continuously warned—
it was an integral part of the Hutu's cultural discourse even before Habyarimana's assassination—that the struggle with the Tutsi was one of
"kill or be killed." Such alleged or real individual acts of violence by the
hated group, often accompanied by readily believed accusations that
such violence is a harbinger of a generalized assault, creates the rationale for treating this enemy, including noncombatants, with lethal final-
ity. Such an enemy's own putative conduct further easily engenders the
thought that such people have already placed themselves outside any
law and forfeited all rights and protections, and that by killing them

as payback, one is only giving them what they deserve, a kind of rough justice. These cognitive and emotional mechanisms operated powerfully in the aftermath of World War II in Central and Eastern Europe, as the peoples of many of those countries drove millions of ethnic Germans from their homes, killing many tens of thousands during the course of their self-understood revenge.

Four Kinds of Eliminationist Assaults

The critical nature of such beliefs, and the fact—it is a fact—that structural conditions and opportunity alone do not in themselves produce mass murders and eliminations, can be seen by examining eliminationist onslaughts along two fundamental dimensions. Almost all mass-murder and eliminationist politics are rooted in conflict over the scarce resources of territory and power, often grounded in the uncertainties of, and group demands made during, economic and political transformations. Who will control territory and who will have the power to define society's nature and rhythms prominently play into how people conceive of the others' putative threat and what, including economic advantage, is actually fought over. Yet because controlling territory is itself a form of power, a critical distinction exists between those instances where power alone is sought (to dominate and create a society of the perpetrators' image), and where territory is also at stake. The other relevant dimension for mapping eliminationist onslaughts is whether the eliminationist politics are practiced domestically or outside the perpetrators' country. All instances of eliminationist politics can be arrayed along these two dimensions of whether territory is contested and, when it is, whether it is contested within a country's borders or abroad.

Category 3 eliminationist assaults, *imperialism at home,* consists mainly of a state often representing society's dominant group attacking a group or groups to take or secure their territory. The targeted group usually predominates in a particular area and is a perceived threat to secede or to overthrow the state and/or the groups it represents. The Turks' slaughter of the Armenians, the Ibos' slaughter of Hausa, the

Eliminationist Assaults

Location of Contest

		Internal	External
Nature of Contest	Not Over Territory	*(1) Domestic Domination and Transformation* Germans: communists, gay men, mentally ill Croats: Jews Slovaks: Jews Soviets: most victims Poles: Germans Communist Chinese: most victims Indonesians: communists Syrian Baathists: Hama Iraqi Baathists: enemies of regime Chilean rightists: leftists Argentinean rightists: leftists El Salvador rightists: leftists Guatemalans: leftists and Maya Khmer Rouge: Khmer Burundian Tutsi: Hutu Rwandan Hutu: Tutsi North Korean communists: Koreans Al Qaeda: Americans	*(2) Madness Abroad* Germans: Jews Germans: Sinti and Roma
	Over Territory	*(3) Imperialism at Home* Americans: Native Americans Turks: Armenians Germans: enemy "hostages" Soviets: non-Russian minorities Croats: Serbs Partition of India: both sides Ibo: Hausa Pakistanis: Bangladeshis El Salvadorans: Indians Serbs: Croats, Bosniaks, Kosovars Congo: most victims Sudan: black Africans Russia: Chechens	*(4) Imperialism Abroad* Belgians: Congolese French: Africans in French Equatorial Africa Germans: Herero and Nama Japanese: most victims Germans: Slavs Communist Chinese: Tibetans British: Kikuyu Portuguese: Angolans French: Algerian Muslims Indonesians: East Timorese

slaughters during Yugoslavia's breakup, the Russians' slaughter of Chechens, and the Sudanese Political Islamists' slaughter of Darfurians today are such eliminationist assaults.

Category 1 assaults are primarily aimed at *domestic domination and transformation,* not territory. They seek more to purify a country of a perceived ideological threat or to transform its polity and society to accord with the state's and often the dominant group's vision. Typically this includes the desire to secure the dominant or insurgent groups' position and power. Such mass murdering and elimination include most communist slaughters, the lethal campaigns against leftists in Latin America, Saddam's mass murdering, and the reciprocal killings in Rwanda and Burundi of Hutu and Tutsi. The strange case is Al Qaeda. Because Osama bin Laden and other Al Qaeda leaders perceived the United States as the principal impediment to their totalitarian aims of dominating and transforming Islamic countries into Political Islamic theocracies, they struck the American homeland making it also madness abroad. But their aspirations were always overwhelmingly domestic.

Category 4 assaults, *imperialism abroad,* consist of a state and its people seeking to subdue a foreign territory, to colonize or exploit it. Usually, the national group killing, expelling, incarcerating, or brutally subjugating the foreign territory's people is within that territory a minority, often a tiny minority compared to the victim group. This was so of the Belgians in Congo, the Japanese in Asia, the Germans in Poland, Ukraine, and Russia, the British in Kenya, the Indonesians in East Timor, and the Chinese in Tibet.

Category 2 assaults, *madness abroad,* are the least numerous. They are slaughters abroad having nothing to do with territorial domination or with domestic conflicts that have a foreign component. The only such eliminationist assaults, all of them mass murders, are the Germans' extermination of the Jews, Sinti, and Roma.

Mapping eliminationist onslaughts along these two dimensions helps clarify several differing features. If we were to compare this breakdown to one for the eighteenth and nineteenth centuries, the earlier eliminationist assaults would be weighted to category 4, imperialism abroad, when European colonizing powers sought to gain or secure territories on other continents. By the second half of the twentieth century, the age of imperialism was winding down, making for fewer contested territories abroad.

This makes apparent a fundamental fact that is crucial for crafting institutions and policies to reduce eliminationist politics' incidence: Almost all such politics in the recent past and today are domestic rather than international.* At least for the foreseeable future, the world is unlikely to see large-scale imperialist conquest. It is more likely to continue to suffer murderous domestic power struggles for group domination or a country's integrity being contested from within.

This matrix also highlights the realistic nature of the conflicts that are the contexts for eliminationist politics and mass murder. When people kill or expel others, power, control, or territory is almost always acutely at issue—even though their hatred or demonology wildly exceeds the real or perceived threat, and the murderous reaction is evil and irrational. Understanding most such assaults' realistic basis further explains not only why the eliminationist politics of category 4, *imperialism abroad,* has mainly disappeared, but also why we are unlikely to see many such foreign imperialist and eliminationist forays as long as the international state system and international institutions maintain something resembling their current configurations (these issues are discussed further in Chapter 11).

The realistic basis of eliminationist politics also highlights the oddness that category 2, *madness abroad,* is not empty. It is understandable that one country's people might try to kill or eliminate the people of the territory or country they conquer and wish to control, exploit for resources, or colonize. But why the Germans would undertake a global assault on the Jews, seeking to annihilate a people abroad posing no threat to them, having no enmity for them, controlling no territory or critical resources that they wanted is simply not, by any rational standard, comprehensible. Only a rare and powerful ideological pathology

---

*This is that much truer if we (as I do) conceive of the eliminationist politics that follow the breakup of empires and of countries, or attempted secessions, as domestic. In the former Soviet Union and the former Yugoslavia, different governments and ethnic groups fought over whether territories would remain a part of the countries or emerge as independent successor states. Essentially, secessionist movements contested territories formerly dominated by central governments and the ethnic groups they represented.

could produce such bizarre politics—with a manifestly self-injurious cost-benefit calculus historically at odds with other mass eliminations. If the Germans had not slaughtered the Jews (and Sinti and Roma), most people, I expect, would have said that the mass murder of an utterly figmental enemy outside one's country would never take place, and category 2 should be empty. It was *madness* abroad. That it has happened highlights the almost singular place of Jews (and Sinti and Roma) as victims in eliminationism's annals.

But this type of annihilationist assault is now more possible. As never before, technology empowers the weak to strike anywhere, making it thinkable for quasi-hallucinatory regimes and groups to lash out abroad genocidally, as Al Qaeda did at the United States and its people. With an unrivaled global power guaranteeing the world's basic international political and economic order, suicidal attacks upon the United States can seem to make sense to the ideologized mind. Interestingly, the perpetrators of *madness abroad*'s two principal mass murders conceived of the assaults as defensive and liberationist against two targets, the Jews and the United States, deemed to be global powers and principally responsible for the world's evil. This was totally fictional regarding Jews, making the madness complete. This was not fictional at least about the United States' power, its actual and immensely powerful antagonism against Political Islam, making the attack grounded in reality *and* a militarily self-defeating, suicidal act of madness.

For general explanatory purposes such exceptional and strange cases are far less important than the norm: realistic conflict over power, territory, or the desire to create a new political and social order. Such real conflicts are or could be almost everywhere. The danger of the most catastrophic forms of eliminationist politics is enormously widespread.

Noneliminationist Outcomes

Political leaders and followers have frequently practiced eliminationist politics. Yet compared to the enormously greater incidence of conflicts over power and territory and the desire to craft a new political and social order, such politics has been *relatively* infrequent. Why then do such conflicts and transformative desires *sometimes* produce eliminationist politics but *mostly* not? The answer cannot be the conflict's kind or the structural conditions alone, including stressors or economic and political development, because many societies with such conflicts and structural relationships have *not* erupted in mass murder or elimination. The matrix below illustrates similar kinds of conflicts and structural relationships that have *not* produced eliminationist outcomes.

Noneliminationist Outcomes

		Location of Contest	
		Internal	External
Nature of Contest	Not Over Territory	*(1) Domestic Domination and Transformation* Nazis with German communists United States with Nazis Cambodia with Khmer Rouge Former communist countries with former communists Black-dominated South Africa with whites Egypt with Political Islamists	*(2) Madness Abroad* Innumerable instances
	Over Territory	*(3) Imperialism at Home* Britain: Northern Ireland Catholics Czechs and Slovaks Gorbachev's Soviet Union with Ukraine, etc. Former Yugoslavia: Slovenes	*(4) Imperialism Abroad* Germany: France Soviet Union: uprisings in Hungary, Poland, East Germany Gorbachev's Soviet Union with Soviet Empire United States: Iraq

This matrix's cases had similar causal factors of conflict, territory, context, etc. But those political leaders and regimes did not murder or eliminate their enemies. Why? Among the various reasons, two have been critical: their different, noneliminationist conceptions of the potential victims, and their adherence to a noneliminationist social and moral theory about right action. The idea that the potential targets are beings of a type that deserve to be eliminated is *not* one that animates the potential perpetrators. In those instances where such eliminationist notions might have existed, the regimes have been led by people embedded in unpropitious politics (including democratic politics) or simply unwilling to act politically in such a manner. Even if they have been, then they would have had to contend with societies unlikely to follow them.

South Africa is a critical and revealing example. The conditions for a murderous onslaught by whites against blacks and then blacks against whites were there. The conventional wisdom about what produces genocides, focusing on structural conditions, conflict-ridden societies, enormous suffering, enormous hatred, or a previously suppressed and newly empowered majority's thirst for revenge, suggests a bloodbath or perhaps two reciprocal bloodbaths. At the time, this was a widely articulated conventional wisdom about blacks' coming to power. Whites did use political and legal measures and violence to control and exploit blacks in an elaborate and brutal system of segregation and disabilities, called apartheid, which itself was a complex form of eliminationist politics. However, the whites never expelled or slaughtered large numbers of blacks and never, as far as we know, considered it. Had the apartheid leaders not feared the highly attentive West's reactions, they likely would have utterly eliminated the anti-apartheid black political leadership.

The more predicted mass-murderous and eliminationist violence was expected to come from blacks against whites, led by the insurgent African National Congress, which for decades had been resisting and fighting the whites' apartheid regime. The extreme oppression, exploitation, and violence blacks had suffered had lasted generations. Blacks lived in impoverished, barren reservations, known as Bantustans, while whites lived in relative luxury, even at European levels. Hatred of the whites, particularly of Afrikaners, for keeping blacks poor, denying them basic rights and freedoms, and using violence against them, was widespread. Why then, after decades of this unjust and dehumanizing system, was there no substantial revenge, no eliminationist onslaught?

Many factors came into play, including the drawn-out negotiation process that created an understanding among white and black leaders; the peaceful transfer of power with interim confidence-building arrangements; the lessons African National Congress leaders undoubtedly drew from other African countries, such as Mozambique, where white minorities fled or were hounded out after black majorities wrested power from them, wrecking the national economy. But still, why did the structural conditions of a bitter conflict, lasting years and soaked in blood and suffering, with deep racial, linguistic, economic, and political fissures, resulting in the once subjugated, desperately needy majority turning the tables on a relatively small dominant minority, not lead to a slaughter or expulsion or some other form of violent domination and expropriation? The answer is as obvious as theories of structural causes are wrong: political leadership, and specifically the character, disposition, and foresight of the African National Congress' most critical leader, Nelson Mandela, who had no desire to undertake an eliminationist program. Had black South Africans had a non-Mandelan leadership animated by an ideology of revenge, black nationalism, Marxist revolution, or self-enrichment, then it would have been easy to unleash the African National Congress and its followers in a violent eliminationist and expropriationist campaign against whites. With different political leaders operating under similar circumstances against a similar foe, the spark would have come to ignite hatred and retribution's parched dry timber. A violent catastrophe would have ensued.

Why could Mandela and the other African National Congress leaders see their way to a peaceful new South Africa? They knew the whites were neither demons nor subhumans (the transition process helped further humanize white leaders); they came to understand that the future would be better with whites as part of the nation, governed by democracy, rather than forced out or dispossessed to varying degrees; and no ideological vision of some purified, totalitarian, or millennial South African society guided them. The black leadership therefore created the humanizing Truth and Reconciliation process, where perpetrators, through public admissions of sins and crimes, remade themselves and reentered the ranks of beings fit for human cohabitation.

The course of South African politics utterly falsifies structural theories of mass murder. It highlights political leaders' critical part in deciding whether an eliminationist course will be chosen, and, if so, what kind. Finally, and perhaps most important, it offers lessons—including about political leaders' capacity to *learn* that eliminationist politics may not pay and to choose to act accordingly against such politics—that are critical for designing policy measures to forestall future eliminationist politics.

Ultimately, each case contained in the matrix of noneliminationist outcomes must be investigated individually and in-depth. Nevertheless, the fundamental factors that did not lead *these* contexts to erupt in murderous and eliminationist assaults were the political leaders' differing conceptions of the victims and/or their adherence to a political vision that rendered elimination unthinkable or, in balance, not advisable.

The Crucial Character of Perpetrators' Beliefs

These two matrices help us understand the critical role of the perpetrators' beliefs about hated and disparaged groups in generating their desire and willingness to kill those groups, and then to act upon the desire. Why? Because they reveal the perpetrators' beliefs about the targeted people to be the factor that engenders the motive and the motivation to kill or eliminate the targeted groups. Even with existing conflict, slaughtering or expelling hated or enemy groups is always a choice. Neither poverty nor war, nor multiethnic societies, nor acute ethnic conflict invariably, or even usually, produce mass murder or elimination. They also do not determine what kind and how much there will be.

That the politics that produces mass death and elimination is discretionary can be seen in another related, indeed overlapping, realm, that of famines. Famines are not only or even principally caused by acts of nature. This has been long established, though it is little known. In our time, the modern state's greatly expanded monitoring powers (it knows where food is needed), resource acquisition capacity (it can acquire food), and infrastructure (it can deliver the food) have long overcome nonhuman causes of famines. Whether state leaders decide not to alleviate famine situations or through their own policies to actually cause them, or armed killers physically prevent states and nonstate actors from providing food to famine regions and peoples, the cause and result are the same: willful political choices that predictably result in mass death, sometimes millions, with the means of death being willful starvation.

That famine is a matter of politics and political leaders' choices has been generally shown, though it can be most strikingly seen in the Indian subcontinent's history alone, and then by comparing it with other regions. The subcontinent is a large, historically famine-plagued region containing developing countries of colossal populations. Until Indian independence in 1947, the British colonialists ignored vulnerable and even starving Indians' well-being, so famines were common. Once the country was independent and democratic, Indian political authorities responded to regional and local shortages by bringing food into those regions (sometimes with international aid) and by giving the most destitute the economic means to acquire food for themselves. India ceased to be visited by starvation. This in itself is telling. Comparing India to China further highlights the critical role of politics and of human choice. China, facing similar problems of overpopulation, underdevelopment, and local food shortages, continued to suffer famines, including massive ones. The Great Famine, undoubtedly human history's most deadly famine, occurred in 1959, lasting two years while taking twenty million to forty million lives. It resulted from willful governmental policies.

In the 1970s, two regions suffered from severe drought and a food crisis: India's Maharashtra state and Africa's Sahel region, which includes Ethiopia, Somalia, and Sudan. Maharashtra's crisis, from 1972 to 1974, included a precipitous drop in average per capita food consumption, yet the Indian government intervened and famine was averted. The Sahel drought during the 1970s produced a severe famine that devastated the lives of millions, killing perhaps one million. But their deaths did not result from a natural catastrophe greater than that of Maharashtra. The Sahel countries actually had considerably more food available per capita—two to three times as much—during their famines than Maharashtra had during the dry years, and the Sahel's per capita food availability was roughly equal to that of India as a whole. In the Sahel, political leaders chose not to distribute food to the needy. Finally, in 1974 in Bangladesh, India's neighbor, perhaps one million people died in a famine. Yet in that year more food was available in Bangladesh than in previous or subsequent years, when there was no famine.[10]

The people producing, or not alleviating, famines have various motives. Some famines are a tool in regimes' mass eliminationist repertoire; others are the consequence of political leaders' malign neglect. China's Great Famine resulted from Mao's murderous policies that willfully sacrificed millions in pursuit of his communist goals. The Sahel famine's roots were not classically grounded in mass murder and elimination politics. But even with economic causes of people's vulnerability to famine—insufficient work or wages—governments and political leaders decide whether to right the situation, in the immediate term principally by choosing whether to provide food or income transfers to the endangered people.

Regimes willfully withholding food from people has been one of the recurring features of our time's eliminationist and annihilationist assaults, often employed as an adjunct to other eliminationist measures. This makes analyzing famine politics, and its place in eliminationist politics, somewhat more complex but only when it is hard to decide whether a given instance of general or local food shortages is due to malign neglect, purposeful action, or both. We have already come across any number of instances of purposeful starvation to kill targeted peoples. The Germans fed the Jews in ghettos and camps starvation rations, leading to enormous death rates. The Germans willfully starved most of the millions of Soviet POWs they killed. On death marches regimes and their followers routinely deny adequate food to their victims, or as the Germans did to the Herero and the Turks did to the Armenians, drive them into inhospitable places so they will starve to death. The British, in their multipronged eliminationist program to neutralize the Kikuyu's threat, underfed them, pruning their numbers and pressuring them to capitulate and renounce Mau Mau. Despite the many other horrors the British visited on the Kikuyu (discussed at greater length below), what many Kikuyu remember most about the eliminationist assault is the hunger. It was so bad and so obviously manufactured that many Kikuyu concluded that the British sought to starve them to death or into submission. As Wandia Muriithi explains:

Hunger was the worst problem, that's what was killing most of the people. They were starving us on purpose, hoping we would give in. The little time we were allowed to go to the *shamba* was too short to allow for any meaningful food gathering. Also, the area we were allowed to use was too small, because the largest areas had been declared Special Areas and were off-limits. So the allowed areas had been over-harvested, but that was what we had.

The barbed-wire villages' death tolls were enormous, with the most vulnerable falling prey to disease, as the vulnerable do when starving. One missionary recounts that it "was terribly pitiful how many of the children and the older Kikuyu were dying. They were so emaciated and so very susceptible to any kind of disease that came along."[11] Most of the 50,000 to 300,000 Kikuyu dead resulted from British starvation politics.

Mass elimination is *always* preventable and *always* results from conscious political choice. Therefore, the perpetrators' or potential perpetrators' conception of potential target groups is the critical factor for leaders and followers alike to want to practice mass eliminationist and exterminationist politics and then to be willing to carry out its programs. This suggests several further inquiries. We must investigate more how such eliminationist conceptions about different groups are disseminated, which means also investigating the discourses that are structured by, contain, and spread such notions. We must consider how language is mass murder and elimination's medium. And we must make sense of how such discourses and beliefs vary to produce various kinds of assaults.

When the peculiarly modern mass-eliminationist leadership's mindset finds propitious political circumstances for acting, it draws on, makes central, and sometimes helps solidify and amplify preexisting beliefs or a discourse about elimination, inflaming people's smoldering wishes into burning desires. Discourses deprecating and disparaging targeted groups, leading people to hate and feel threatened by them, prepare the way before a mass elimination program is initiated. These discourses vary greatly. Some are more obviously eliminationist, even explicitly murderous, than others. Sometimes, as in Turkey regarding

Armenians, Germany regarding Jews, Rwanda regarding Tutsi, and Serbia regarding Croats and Muslims, the discourse is long-standing, its underlying beliefs about the intended victims, which it reinforces and further spreads, are themselves deeply rooted in the cultures and widely (though not universally) shared. Other discourses are chronologically proximate to the elimination program's onset while still resonating within the populace and being deeply felt by those sharing its fundamentals. This has often been the case under communist regimes, most notably the Soviets, the Chinese, and the Khmer Rouge. These and other communist leaderships, with newly won power, sought to prepare their followers and society more broadly for eliminationist initiatives, by convincing them that producing the future utopia necessitated the sacrifice of many people, specifically malignant class enemies and other groups deemed inimical to the revolution, the nation, or the future communist paradise. Such new discourses existed in Germany during the Nazi period regarding "life unworthy of living" and "useless eaters," in many Latin American countries regarding leftists, and in the United States regarding Japanese. Because these discourses are less long-standing and are sometimes manufactured mainly from above (sometimes clashing with common deeply held values and beliefs), they often find less societal consensus and are more easily dispensed with when the regime or their proximate cause ends. Antisemitism, an age-old and deep-rooted discourse, continued to be powerful in Germany and many European countries after the war, and continues to this day, while the far less deep-rooted and widespread notion that "life unworthy of living" and "useless eaters" (including the mentally ill) should be killed, itself died with the Nazi regime.

The preparatory Turkish discourse for slaughtering Armenians in 1915 was unmistakable, containing three facets: the need for a Turkic Turkey, an Islamic Turkey, and an internally pure Turkey so it could reestablish its greatness and glory. Under Turkish Ottoman rule, Turks conceived of the Armenians as an alien group to be tolerated as long as they remained loyal. With the Ottomans' decline in the latter part of the nineteenth century and loss of territories to other countries and non-Turkish minorities in the twentieth century's first part, Turks somewhat redefined the ever more nationalist Armenians through the lens of an ever more strident Turkish nationalism: as an alien, hostile, and threatening group. Annihilationist onslaughts from 1894 to 1896 that were essentially a massive crackdown on Armenian demands for more independence, and again after the Young Turk revolution in April 1909, helped form, shape, and intensify the discourse of disloyalty and the need for a purer, more Turkified Turkey. If your countrymen have already justly slaughtered people because of their ethnicity or forced them to convert from a religion deemed noxious and alien, eliminating this people further, including by deadly means, will likely seem justified. Those killed deserved it, being of a character or having committed offenses that made eliminating them necessary and right. Such self-legitimizing, tautological reasoning is powerful. Mass elimination, including the mass murder of children, remains, after the fact, self-justifying to the perpetrating group unless it is explicitly and forcefully delegitimized (as in post–World War II Germany). Mass expulsions and slaughters sow the seeds for future eliminationist assaults. The logic that led to one eliminationist assault provides the rationale for new and future ones, if circumstances and political leaders suggest it. The Turks' massive eliminationist assault upon the Armenians from 1894 to 1896 would rightly be called the Armenian Genocide—had an even more massive mass murder and elimination not followed twenty years later. From 1894 to 1896 the Turks slaughtered 150,000 to 300,000 Armenians, forced another 150,000 to convert to Islam, and expelled an additional 100,000 from the country. The Turks, as perpetrators repeatedly have, employed different eliminationist means as functional equivalents. They also availed themselves of a relatively rare eliminationist option as an acceptable partial "solution" to their "Armenian problem": The character of their religiously infused demonology about the Armenians meant they could convert Armenians to Islam and thereby render them harmless and fit for cohabitation with Turks. By 1915, Turkey was animated by a nationalism much more oriented toward creating a Turkic nation, so the Turks, opting for a still more comprehensive eliminationist assault against the Armenians, began using a more final mix of means, to produce an enormously higher ratio of death and expulsion (close to two million) to forced conversions (of 100,000 to 200,000 women and young children). The German vice-consul in Erzurum, Max

Erwin von Scheubner-Richter, based on his conversations with Turkish officials, reported their thinking in 1916: "The empire must be rebuilt on a Muslim and Pan-Turkist foundation. . . . Non-Muslim communities have to be Islamicized by force or, failing that, eliminated."[12] This more comprehensive murderousness partly resulted from a consciousness that eliminating Armenians must be more final because the Turks' very actions would guarantee the Armenians' enduring enmity. As Talât told American Ambassador Henry Morgenthau, "We have been reproached for making no distinction between the innocent Armenians and the guilty; but that was utterly impossible, in view of the fact that those who were innocent today might be guilty tomorrow."[13] Eliminationist assaults' logic—engendering enmity that might lead to revenge—produces among the perpetrators ever more insecurity and therefore ever more thought to continue or escalate such politics. What a man close to Pol Pot conveyed about the Cambodian mass murderer could be said, if somewhat less breathlessly, about many eliminationist leaders. Pol Pot "saw enemies as rotten flesh, as swollen flesh. Enemies surrounding. Enemies in front, enemies behind, enemies to the north, enemies to the south, enemies to the west, enemies to the east, enemies in all eight directions, enemies coming from all nine directions, closing in, leaving no space for breath. And he continually had us fortify our spirit, fortify our stance, fortify over and over, including measures to kill our own ranks."[14]

In Rwanda a different, more explicitly demonizing and eliminationist discourse governed the country starting before the country's independence from Belgium in 1962. The same can be said about Burundi, its intimate neighbor and sometimes mirror opposite. Each one's eliminationist politics is hard to understand without referring to the other's. In each country, with one group dominating the other, reciprocal racist ideologies of Hutu and Tutsi demonizing each other created ideational powder kegs that political leaders could explode at any moment. Each country's coups, attempted coups, repressions, and violence of one group against the other, including mass slaughters and expulsions, greatly affected the other country's political ideologies and politics. Published tracts codified each one's eliminationist ideology. In 1990 in Rwanda, the politically dominant Hutu published in the authoritative newspaper *Kangura*, the religiously clothed "Ten Commandments of the Hutu." In Burundi, the dominant Tutsi published their analog, "Seventeen Rules of Tutsi Conduct." The Hutu's Ten Commandments presumes and calls for an insuperable social, political, moral, and racial gulf between Hutu and Tutsi, with several of its commandments warning Hutu men of Tutsi women's purely subversive nature, deeming any Hutu man marrying or having sexual relations with a Tutsi woman a "traitor." They deem every Tutsi in business "dishonest," declaring that the Tutsi's "only aim is to enhance the supremacy of his ethnic group." Any Hutu engaging in business with Tutsi is a "traitor." Based in this conception of the Tutsi, the Hutu Ten Commandments logically calls for total Hutu political, educational, and military domination. The Hutu's discourse about Tutsi depicted them as racially unalterable, demonic foes who had been suppressing and injuring the Hutu for hundreds of years.

The Tutsi's reciprocal discourse was at least as racist, dehumanizing, and demonizing. In 1993 the "Seventeen Rules of Tutsi Conduct" codified in published form the long-established eliminationist stance toward the Hutu that had already erupted in several mass slaughters.

> Do not trust a Hutu or anyone supposed to be one. . . . Try to locate Hutu residences so that you will know, when the time comes, whom to save and whom to liquidate. . . . Stay armed so as not to be caught by surprise. . . . Some Hutu women look like Tutsi, and their job is to spy on us. . . . There are subtle ways to exterminate Hutu people; you can isolate them in the bush, and make them disappear one after the other . . . you can send them pretty girls or Rwandese prostitutes; you can put TB in their food or drinks. . . . Hutu kids are spoiled and insouciant: just get hold of the kid who lost his way, then ask his father, elder, brother or mother to come and fetch him, and then kill them all.[15]

The Hutu's and Tutsi's dueling eliminationist discourses partly parallel (while being more explicitly and graphically murderous) the German eliminationist antisemitism about the Jews and the "Jewish problem." What is remarkable about the Hutu's and Tutsi's eliminationist conflict is that it was reciprocal and historically a relatively recent construction, unlike the Germans' one-sided eliminationist antisemitism that had roots and a continuous existence lasting centuries. Cynical Belgian colonialists bred the Hutu's and Tutsi's mutual enmity to more easily and effectively rule their colonial possession. Once the Hutu and Tutsi's divide hardened, producing parallel demonizing discourses, both sides' political and religious leaders and ideologues intensified and further racialized it. This shows that while the origins of an eliminationist discourse and its generational transmission must be explored to fully understand an eliminationist assault's genesis, the discourse's prior longevity is not a critical factor. Its existence at the moment political leaders decide to kill is what counts. Although a Nazi-like discourse about another people as evil cannot be created anywhere, the Tutsi's and Hutu's conflict also shows that under propitious circumstances, such as existed in central Africa (a divided society, with deep inequality and acute conflict over resources, one group's domination of the other—originally Tutsi of Hutu—and determinedly malevolent politicians and propagandists), such views can be produced in a generation, hardened, passed on, and then reinforced as the ensuing violence seems to confirm the eliminationist discourse's underpinnings and claims.

Among our time's many eliminationist assaults, whether against small or large groups, whether over territory or not, whether at home or abroad, only the Germans' slaughter of the Jews needed to be total, because the Germans considered them cosmic biological evil. The ground for mass murder was prepared in other European countries—in Croatia, France, Lithuania, Poland, Romania, Ukraine, and others—by the widespread if varying pan-European Christian antisemitism, especially of the Catholic Church, nationalist and sometimes racist demonological assaults on the Jews, and nonlethal eliminationist policies of the 1930s. The Germans' drive to kill all Jews, especially all Jewish children, has no parallel in mass murder or eliminationist politics' annals. Many mass murderers slaughter children, but the Germans' obsessiveness and ferocity in exterminating Jewish children, conceived of as evil's biological seeds, distinguishes the German executioners from all others. In the camps called ghettos, they killed Jewish women who became pregnant. The biological thinking of German political leaders, the perpetrators, and many other Germans about the Jews' alleged perniciousness resembled the rest of humanity's or at least the public health authorities' thinking about smallpox. To protect the world from smallpox's scourge, *all* smallpox, namely the virus' every instance, needed to be eradicated. One festering smallpox case could infect others, resuming its plague on humanity. On January 1, 1967, the World Health Organization launched its intensified Smallpox Eradication Program against a disease as old as known human history that still threatened 60 percent of the world's population, and that infected at the time ten million to fifteen million people annually, killing between two million and four million, and leaving most of the rest disfigured or blind. The program took almost exactly a decade to produce a smallpox-free world.[16]

The German political leaders and perpetrators considered the Jews such a powerful biological force (like smallpox) for evil, afflicting humanity almost from the beginning of recorded time (like smallpox), that they embarked on a comparable total eradication plan that, coincidentally, moved toward its final goal at a pace—had their conquests continued—similar to the World Health Organization's smallpox eradication campaign. Why would their plan differ given their beliefs, which Hitler summarized in the exterminatory campaign's midst? "The discovery of the Jewish virus is one of the greatest revolutions that have taken place in the world. The battle in which we are engaged to-day is of the same sort as the battle waged, during the last century, by [Louis] Pasteur and [Robert] Koch. How many diseases have their origin in the Jewish virus! Japan would have been contaminated, too, if it had stayed open to the Jews. We shall regain our health only by *eliminating* the Jew. Everything has a cause, nothing comes by chance" (my emphasis).[17] In working through the extermination program's codification, the Wannsee Conference participants discussed the need for every Jew's utter, total, and complete extermination in biological terms. The Germans believed the Jews surviving the brutal work-to-death regimen, to which some would be put, would be the most robust. They would therefore have to kill these especially dangerous foes outright. "For, if released," the Wannsee Protocol tells us, these Jews "would, as a natural selection of the fittest, form a germ cell from which the Jewish race could regenerate itself."[18]

The Nazi leadership and Germans more generally had very different discourses about other groups the regime and its helpers set out to kill or eliminate. Slavic peoples, the mentally ill, Bolsheviks, gays were the victims of prejudicial views rendering them lesser beings of one kind or another, but not the irredeemable, powerful, evil Germans broadly considered Jews to be, the ideological discovery of which Hitler and those sharing his views could speak in world historical terms as one of humankind's "greatest revolutions." Also, these other groups' ideological construction, making it either necessary or permissible to kill them, had lesser degrees of acceptance in Germany. The country's political leaders did not undertake these other groups' total extermination, met far more resistance from Germans to their eliminationist programs against them, and pursued their ultimately partial (though still catastrophic) elimination with considerably less drive and determination.

Analogously, country- or culture-specific powerful eliminationist discourses, grounded in models of the targeted group or groups as permissible or necessary to eliminate, existed for the Germans in South-West Africa, in Japan, for the British in Kenya, in Cambodia, in the Indian subcontinent, in Latin American countries, for other communist regimes, in the former Yugoslavia, for the Hutu, and for Political Islamists, among many others.

Radical intolerance is at the core of the eliminationist mindset. Even when a group—whether ethnic, religious, economic, or political—makes challenging demands on a country's political leaders or dominant group, a more inclusive view of society and the state rather than an eliminationist response can get adopted. Political leaders and the groups they represent can make political compromises and sacrifices, even material ones, to resolve real or imagined conflicts without expulsion or murderous violence. This has often been done, especially but not only in countries that became or are democratic.

It needs to be emphasized that such deprecatory discourses about groups and peoples are not always explicitly eliminationist or murderous. More typically, they portray the people who will eventually be killed as worthless subhumans, evil, or a general threat, so that those participating in and exposed to such discourses become predisposed to accepting an eliminationist program or "solution." The populaces may be aware of this disposition, as in Germany, in Burundi, among Serbs, and in Rwanda, or may not focus on policy options, particularly eliminationist ones, so they do not explicitly tell themselves or others that eliminating, let alone exterminating, the hated or feared group is their goal. Either way, when their political leaders decide to opt for an eliminationist solution, those sharing the discourse's fundamentals and logical predispositions are ready for these beliefs to be activated into political action and to lend themselves in spirit or body to the eliminationist enterprise.

CHAPTER EIGHT

Thinking and Acting

IMAGINE THAT YOU LEARNED your government is about to start annihilating all people with red hair. Or all people in a certain city. Or all people with skin either lighter or darker than a certain shade. Or all people who profess one common religion or another. Would you be incredulous? Could you even make sense of such news? The people of many (though not all) countries would simply not believe it. But imagine you became convinced it is true. You would still be incredulous. *Why would they do it?* you might ask. Why would your government seek to slaughter ten thousand, a hundred thousand, a million, or six million people? Why butcher children by the thousands? For what reason? None of the rationales makes sense, because they violate what you know about your political system and its leaders, your society, and your fellow citizens.

A notable feature of eliminationist onslaughts is how easily the perpetrators, and the wider population from which they come, understand what is being done and why. In exterminationist and eliminationist assaults' voluminous history, we find few instances of perpetrators, or members of their social and political groups, greeting the news of an impending or actual annihilation or elimination with incredulity, either born of a failure to comprehend its rationale or a belief in the deeds' unequivocal monstrousness. This absence of incomprehension is striking, and undoubtedly to many readers startling, given the countries they live in. That perpetrators, and their groups and societies, immediately comprehend the eliminationist and annihilationist program as reasonable is explicable if the people are already prepared to find these eliminationist measures comprehensible, even desirable. In virtually all cases this has been so, as powerful discourses have readied the societies and people to consider the targeted groups noxious and dangerous. (A partial exception was the Soviet Union during the terror that, resulting from Joseph Stalin's paranoia, was often arbitrary—Stalin turned on his party, loyal followers, and military's officer corps.) Such socially shared beliefs remain just that—socially shared beliefs that are, whether partly submerged or publicly prominent, not accompanied by physical attacks—until the right moment arrives. Then, quickly, people understand that action previously deemed unimaginable, improbable, or impractical is now a permissible option. This occurs with many kinds of political opportunities, including when eliminating another sort of enemy, a hated and repressive political regime, suddenly becomes possible. Czechoslovakia's President Václav Havel, during his 1990 New Year's Day address not long after the Velvet Revolution brought down communism, asked, "How is it possible that so many people understood what to do and that none of them needed any advice or instructions?"[1] His rhetorical question applies equally to the perpetrators and social groups that implement and support one eliminationist onslaught after another.

In the former Yugoslavia's various eliminationist assaults, rival ethnic communities, including the potential perpetrators among them, discussed and understood the putative demonic pasts of targeted groups and the necessity of eliminating them. Serbs referred to Bosnian Muslims as *Turks,* Christian Europe's Muslim invaders and the Serbs' centuries-long enemies. Serbs called Croats *Ustashe,* the fascists during the Nazi period who slaughtered Serbs. And Croats faced off against Serbian *Chetniks,* Serb paramilitaries during World War II. Not in the former Yugoslavia and almost never elsewhere do we find evidence that the perpetrators or the broader population were surprised by their leaders' radical and lethal policies, or that they failed to understand the underlying motive grounded in an eliminationist conception of the victims. Some among the populations from which the perpetrators come may dissent from the majority's view of the victims, morally oppose the measures, or deplore the eliminationist methods, particularly an annihilative onslaught's licentiousness. But an overwhelmingly shared understanding of, and agreement with, the eliminationist program's fundamentals has predated the actual assaults.

How does this come about? Not through peer pressure, not through blind obedience to authority, not because modernity has transformed people into bureaucrats, and not due to any other reductionist notion that has been posited in defiance of the historical record. It comes about through language and visual images as the bearers of cultural notions, including how to understand humanity and, in particular, other disparaged peoples and groups.

Of the five factors crucially contributing to our era's exterminationist and eliminationist projects' initiation and character, three—the modern state's enormous transformative power, structural conflicts existing within states, and permissive international contexts—are structural factors that have systematically given impetus to political leaders to conceive of and act upon eliminationist aspirations. A fourth factor, the opportunity or immediate political context that makes it practical for political leaders to act on eliminationist desires, is contingent. The fifth feature, the beliefs that lead people to think it necessary to eliminate others, is, though common, not a systemic property of our time. Because the presence and content of such beliefs are highly variable, exploring them and the means for their widespread dissemination is critically important.

Discourse and the Dissemination of Eliminationist Beliefs

Language is the principal medium for preparing people to support or perpetrate mass murder and elimination, because it is the vehicle for conceptualizing, conveying, and making persuasive the necessary prejudices and ideas. Visual images, such as caricature, often reinforce the prejudices and ideas and powerfully, sometimes more powerfully than language itself, encapsulate them in indelibly memorable forms. Personal experience is not what leads people to believe that those they target are noxious or dangerous, subhuman or demonic. How could it? The targeted people are *overwhelmingly strangers,* numbering in the tens of thousands or millions.

Language's elaborated notions, dire constructs, labeling, caricature, and reductionist and fear-inspiring stories teach people prejudices about *entire* groups of disparaged, despised, or feared people, and the necessity

Cover of December 1993 issue of *Kangura*

or logic of eliminationist solutions. The December 1993 issue of *Kangura* is ironically titled "Tutsi, Race of God" with the vertical words revealing what the Tutsi really are and their threat's severity: "What weapons will we use to win over the inyenzi (cockroaches) for good?" The eliminationist answer, immanent in the discourse's logic, can be seen in the image to the left, a machete, which, together with the anti-Tutsi leader of Rwanda in 1959, tell Hutu all they need to know about what should be and is in the offing. Elie Ngarambe recounts the common things Hutu believed about Tutsi—which made this newspaper cover both unremarkable and immediately comprehensible—as he discusses what they called Tutsi while they raped and killed Tutsi women: "First 'Tutsi are snakes, Tutsi are an enemy, Tutsi are cruel,' to disrespect them. Or 'Inkotanyi they have tails,' so many things to make them lose their true colors. They are 'anti-Rwanda,' 'against the country,' 'anti-survivor,' 'cockroach,' 'snakes.' A snake is very bad, and it means something . . . even the Bible says that snake means something bad, evil. It was to humiliate them. They had no value."[2] So the Hutu killed them.

Language and visual images—conveyed in talk and discussion, newspapers, magazines, and books, and radio, television, and today the Internet—give life to and spread notions that *entire* groups of people are vermin, are inherently treacherous, have the appetites, moral sense, or intellectual capacity of lower primates, pose danger, covet your house, wife, or land, seek your and your kind's destruction, and willfully and obstinately block human or divine prosperity or progress. Herero are baboons and swine. Jews are bacilli or rats, or Bolsheviks or devils. Poles are subhumans. Kikuyu are vermin, animals, and barbarians. Bangladeshis are devils. Putatively impure Khmer are "diseased elements." Maya are animals, pigs, and dogs. Tutsi are cockroaches, dogs, snakes, or zeros. Indonesian communists are infidels, as are Americans and many others. Darfurians are slaves. Metaphors of disease, infestations, predatory or dangerous animals, criminality, subhumanity, and malevolent supernatural beings abound. Such notions are first propagated linguistically and visually, then similarly conveyed to others, taught to new generations, further spread or intensified by political leaders and regimes. Although identifiable sociological or political factors (and occasionally cynical political leaders) may generate such notions, once they consolidate into socially shared prejudice, particularly when reinforced in political practice, they are strongly self-validating and reproducing, becoming the common-sense wisdom of their societies, groups, or cultures (or subcultures), circulating socially among ordinary people, and from parent to child, and then among the children themselves. Any study of mass murder and elimination that fails to give primacy to language and imagery as their generative medium and to the specific beliefs that people, through language, relate to one another and thereby reinforce, denies the fundamental reality of how people, whether leaders or followers, become cognitively, (to a large extent) psychologically, and emotionally prepared to give themselves to the violent elimination of others, and how people become mobilized to attack, dragoon, expel, or kill others.

Language demeaning, expressing hate, or inspiring fear about others often coalesces into a stable, patterned set of beliefs, tropes, symbols, and charges often called a discourse but more properly called—because it conveys its social reality—a conversation. Different societies, ethnic groups, political parties, and political leaders and their followers have explicit, symbol-laden, and encoded conversations about other people or groups they deem noxious or perceive as threatening. These conversations can resemble acquaintances' ongoing, years-long, multistranded discussions, sometimes impassioned and sometimes casual, that pick up where they left off and take off in new directions, repeating and returning to well-known themes even as they incorporate new notions and develop new arguments with unfolding events, resonating powerfully to those familiar with them as they listen attentively or as background music to the familiar tropes, while perhaps sounding striking to newcomers seeking to understand and assimilate their terms. In Rwanda, a powerful Hutu eliminationist discussion of the Tutsi was already long established when the quasi-governmental radio station Radio Télévision Libre des Mille Collines (RTLM) became its new focal point in August 1993. Vianney Higiro, the director of the government's official station, Radio Rwanda, explains in these notable terms: "These broadcasts were like a conversation among Rwandans who knew each other well and were relaxing over some banana beer or a bottle of Primus [the local beer] in a bar. It was a conversation without a moderator and without any requirements as to the truth of what was said. The people who were there recounted what they had seen or heard during the day. The exchanges covered everything: rumors circulating on the hills, news from the national radio, conflicts among local political bosses. . . . It was all in fun. Some people left the bar, others came in, the conversation went on or stopped if it got too late, and the next day it took up again after work."[3] Leading up to the government's initiation of the mass murder, radio stations and other media reinforced Hutu's prejudicial views and deep suspicions of Tutsi, and further prepared them for the coming assault. During the exterminationist assault, radio became the principal source of Hutu's understanding of unfolding events, forcefully exhorting ordinary Hutu to annihilate the Tutsi enemy. Augustin Bazimaziki, one of the Hutu killers, explains that the killing began with the "radio broadcast[ing] some news such as, 'We need to kill all the Tutsi,'" and then, as they were mercilessly hunting them down, "the radio broadcasted the information such that we need to kill Tutsi seven days a week."[4]

Joseph-Désiré Bitero, one of the Nyamata region's and Rwanda's leading perpetrators, suggests how such a discourse can powerfully imbue people with an eliminationist mindset, even while they live side-by-side with those they will eventually attack:

> I was born surrounded by Tutsi in Kanazi. I always had Tutsi acquaintances and thought nothing of it. Still, I did grow up listening to history lessons and radio programs that were always talking about major problems between Hutu and Tutsi—though I lived among Tutsi who posed no problem. The situation was going to pieces due to the impossible gap between the worrisome news about the mess on the country's borders and the peaceful people who lived next door. The situation was bound to come apart and go into either savagery or neighborliness.

Hence the paradox, found in many societies that mass murderously erupt, of an edifice of relatively good local relations among neighbors from different groups existing upon a rotting, tottering foundation of prejudices, hatred, and suspicion that, when activated politically, engulfs all members of the other group, including those neighbors. Even if not literally correct for all mass murders and eliminations, when Bitero says, "You will never see the source of a genocide," he expresses an essential truth about the difficulty of discerning the volcanic destructiveness embedded in something as seemingly innocuous as words, and to see the cause-and-effect relationship between the two, which is why so many who write about genocide do not see (or are unwilling to believe) "the source of a genocide." Bitero explains: "It is buried too deep in grudges, under an accumulation of misunderstandings that we were the last to inherit. We came of age at the worst moment in Rwanda's history: we were taught to obey absolutely, raised in hatred, stuffed with slogans."[5] We must understand more about these socially shared grudges, accumulated misunderstandings, hatreds, and slogans, and about the eliminationist conversations they and other elements compose, including the explicit beliefs and images, and the underlying cultural models about the targeted group they construct, the logic for action they contain, and the relationship of different conversational stages to taking action against human targets.

Such discourses often individually deserve substantial, even book-length treatment to be adequately represented and fully analyzed. Nevertheless, a common core of issues tells us a great deal about these discourses' essence, and allows us to analyze them comparatively and to understand them as springboards to action. How these discourses present potential or intended victims offers insight into mass elimination's patterns and features. Eliminationist discourses have relatively stable constructions or descriptions of the targeted groups, which include explicit, easily graspable accounts of the groups' putative noxiousness, including coherent charges, manifest or implied, about their threat and at least implications of how to meet it. All prejudicial and eliminationist discourses contain a widespread, underlying cognitive model of the disparaged people that provides a foundation and general structure to the discourses' more elaborated narratives, accounts, and characterizations of them.

Three dimensions structure the models underlying such discourses. Groups (and individuals) with antipathies, antagonisms, or animus toward another group have a notion of how *pernicious* and therefore dangerous the group is or can be. They have some understanding of the *source* of that group's perniciousness, whether their biology, their culture (including religion), or changeable environmental conditions, such as education, social opportunities, and discrimination. These two dimensions—putative perniciousness and its source—together provide an understanding of the disparaged group's supposed threat, what might contain, forefend, or diffuse it, and that group's transformability, in the short or long term. The third dimension of *latent-to-manifest* tells us how central these notions are at a given moment to those holding them, and clarifies how prejudices, hatreds, desires for vengeance, and other beliefs and emotions that suggest eliminationist action can simmer beneath the surface relatively harmlessly and then be quickly activated into violent, destructive, murderous action.

An index of imputed group perniciousness and danger could be constructed for any and every group believed to harbor noxious qualities. As intergroup prejudice is commonplace and varies enormously, we would find a wide array of perniciousness scores, including low ones between northern and southern Italians, Prussians and Bavarians, Flemish and Walloons, Americans and Canadians, among Germans, French, Italians, and British for one another, among Danes, Swedes, and Norwegians for one another, and so on, or between German Catholics and Protestants, or Social Democrats and Christian Democrats or their counterparts in one European country after another. Many members of these national, regional, ethnic, religious, and political groups have antipathies or antagonisms for the other domestic or foreign groups, conceiving them to have unpleasant, noxious, or pernicious qualities (which may be moral, dispositional, or aspirational) and therefore to pose a challenge to the first group's well-being or aspirations. Analyzing mild prejudices and antipathies—and real group differences and conflicts—in this way helps us understand that all such group differences can be scored for imputed perniciousness and danger. The noxious qualities imputed by British to French, German Social Democrats to Christian Democrats, Flemish to Walloons, or Swedes and Danes to one another do not remotely suggest to their bearers that an eliminationist solution is necessary. These low-level prejudices do not come close to suggesting the degree of perniciousness eliminationist and exterminationist thinking requires as a foundation.

The enormous *variation* in different prejudices' perniciousness reveals how misguided is the commonplace discussion (in the literatures on genocide and many other themes) of people's construction of groups as an "other." Hundreds, thousands, millions, and billions of *others* exist depending on whether we are discussing nationalities, coalesced groups, genders, or individuals (every person is an *other* for every other person). Whoever identifies himself particularistically with one or more groups, as everyone does, or with those sharing some aspect of his or her identity, always defines those groups and people not falling into that particularistic universe as an *other*. Constructing *others* and having them constructed for you is inherent to human existence. Thus, the *other* is hardly a master category for illuminating eliminationist assaults, and the construction of *others* is effectively irrelevant for understanding or explaining such assaults (or just about anything else in social and political life). The issue is, rather, the kinds of *others* constructed by or for you as a member of a political movement, society, or culture or subculture, and how you conceive of them, including here especially their putative noxious qualities. It is not the undifferentiated notion of the ubiquitous *other*, but the hostile and prejudicial beliefs and emotions one group's members have for another group that must be explored. And these beliefs can, as we see, be analyzed according to their sources and degrees of perniciousness.

If we take an instance of more intense prejudice, in the United States among whites against blacks, it varies from nonexistent, to garden-variety prejudices and antipathies, to more substantial conceptions of blacks' perniciousness. Whatever prejudice's current levels (they have been declining for half a century), an eliminationist initiative against blacks would not even occur to whites. That is, except among white supremacists with a quasi-Nazi-like racist worldview accusing (even prior to Barack Obama's becoming president) blacks, Jews, and others of capturing the American government and of working to subjugate and destroy Aryans or whites (Jews are not considered white). *The Turner Diaries,* a fictional diary of a white supremacist depicting a race war, and perhaps the white supremacist movement's most widely read book, tells of blacks exerting "an increasingly degenerative influence on the culture and life styles of the inhabitants of North America." Because white supremacists' prejudices and political ideology are Nazi-like—their accounts and hatred of Jews sometimes come straight from Nazi writings—they fantasize about, discuss, and plan for an eliminationist assault against those they believe are destroying whiteness, Christianity, and goodness. *The Turner Diaries* explicitly discusses the danger to the white race as so extreme that to quell it, even innocents must perish: "But there is no way we can destroy the System without hurting many thousands of innocent people—no way. It is a cancer too deeply rooted in our flesh. And if we don't destroy the System before it destroys us—if we don't cut this cancer out of our living flesh—our whole race will die."[6] Timothy McVeigh, the mass murderer who in bombing the Oklahoma City federal building in April 1995 killed 168 people (with the injured, the casualties totaled more than one thousand), was a devotee of *The Turner Diaries,* in which such a bombing occurs. A few days before his attack, he sent excerpts from it to his sister. He brought a copy on the trip to Oklahoma City to perpetrate his atrocity against the alleged Zionist Occupation Government of the United States' outpost there.

We can distinguish, as we see for the degrees of perniciousness that American whites attribute to blacks, two fundamentally different conceptions of groups. One is of sufficient perniciousness to include an eliminationist logic suggesting or implying an eliminationist solution. The other is of far less perniciousness, not suggesting eliminationist thinking or acting. Some conceptions of groups occupy the border zone between the two, and because beliefs are somewhat fluid with changing contexts and circumstances, they may move from one side to the other. Most prejudices and hatreds, however, fall clearly on one side or the other of the eliminationist-noneliminationist line.

We can leave behind the enormous number of people's conceptions of groups that are *not* eliminationist to plumb the character and differences of those that have led to exterminationist and eliminationist assaults. Keeping in mind these discourses contain conceptions of the source of groups' perniciousness, we need to think further about the two principal ways they construct an understanding of the hated or feared group: dehumanization and demonization. Whether and how perpetrators dehumanize or demonize people matters enormously because it, together with the perpetrators' broader social and moral theories, informs their eliminationist treatment of them.

Dehumanization and Demonization

The term *dehumanization* is rightly a commonplace of discussions of mass murder. It is used as a master category that describes the attitudes of killers, would-be killers, and larger groups toward actual or intended victims. But, as used, it serves to homogenize different kinds of beliefs, preventing further in-depth and comparative analysis, and most critically to variously elide or conceal two separate conceptual dimensions. A belief (really an assemblage of beliefs) exists that can properly be said to constitute the *dehumanizing* of others. It is that other people inherently lack qualities fundamental to being fully human in the sense of deserving moral respect, rights, and protection. Such beings are said to lack human capacities or powers and, as a definitional matter, do not need to be treated as humans. European colonizers believed this about the peoples of Africa, Asia, and the Americas. A second belief (also complex and various) is the *demonization* of others. This belief is about other people's moral quality, including their moral intentions. It holds the people to be, literally or figuratively, demonic, morally evil. This view can be grounded in a religious or quasi-religious sense that the devil or other malevolent supernatural beings inhabit or control, or are such people. Classic instances of demonization are medieval and early modern Europe's and New England's witch crazes, during which tens of thousands of people, mostly women, were accused of being possessed and demonic. Nevertheless, such beliefs usually have nothing to do with religion or the supernatural but are grounded in the view that people are of such evil nature and intentions they might as well be devils or possessed by one. Though many hated and disparaged groups are neither dehumanized nor demonized, those that are can be so in different ways and to varying degrees, so each dimension is a continuum with a range of values. The dimension of dehumanization is mainly about biological (cognitive, physical, etc.) capacity, held to be impaired. The dimension of demonization is mainly about moral character, held to be depraved, or so debased the people might as well be depraved.

Dehumanization and demonization do not necessarily go hand in hand. The dehumanized are not also always demonized. Whites enslaving blacks in the American South, and later repressing them with Jim Crow, dehumanized them, deeming them subhumans of diminished intellectual (and moral) capabilities, akin to domesticated semi-wild animals that, when kept in check, were useful but if loose could be dangerous. Whites did not construe their slaves, or freed blacks, as malevolent demons bent upon harming them. Imperialist Europeans held similar attitudes toward Asian, African, and American peoples. The Nazis and many Germans dehumanized the mentally ill and developmentally disabled. Karl Binding, the former president of Germany's supreme court, together with psychiatry professor Alfred Hoche, in a 1920 book that created a sensation, *Permission for the Destruction of Worthless Life, Its Extent and Form,* asked rhetorically, giving an affirmative answer: "Are there humans who have lost their human characteristics to such an extent that their continued existence has lost all value both for themselves and for society?" These people, including those described as "incurable lunatics," were not evil, but in not possessing "human characteristics" were "completely worthless."[7] Similarly, Japanese, at least until World War II's end, dehumanized other Asians without demonizing them. Takeuchi Yoshimi, an eminent Japanese scholar and translator of Chinese literature, explained in 1978 that before the war, "when we studied Chinese history and geography we never studied the fact that there were humans there."[8] The Japanese's racist belief in other Asians' lesser human status allowed the Japanese to enslave and kill them at will. But they did not conceive of their victims as demonic in their moral values and intentions. Inferior, yes. Enemies, yes. Dangerous, yes. It was part of the natural order of human enmity and threat, of the logic of power and "conquer or be conquered."

Similarly, not all those demonized are also dehumanized. When asked, Rithy Uong, having spent four years under the Khmer Rouge and coming into contact with an enormous number of them, affirmed that they saw the *new people* as human beings, "but also they saw us as an enemy also. They wouldn't trust us. They just see us as different kind of person . . . new people, they believe that brought nothing except trouble to them."[9] Many mass-murdering communists demonized their enemies without dehumanizing them, holding them as bearers of antagonistic class interests or agents of malevolent capitalism, to be in the grip of interests or ideologies making them dangerous. But they did not deem them to lack fundamental human attributes. Communist leaders—while killing millions—chose not to kill a much greater number opposing them, because, informed by Marxism, they believed people are corrigible and set out to reform them, including sometimes in gulags, from which they eventually released many. Some communist leaders, especially in Central Europe, secure in power because of Soviet backing (and sometimes, as in Poland and Czechoslovakia, because they were not pursuing grand social transformation), did not mass murder their own peoples. During the cold war, neither the Soviet leaders nor the rank and file believed Americans or Western Europeans were less than human, but they did demonize the West's so-called ruling classes as morally corrupt, venal, and seeking to exploit humanity. Conversely, some people, most catastrophically Indonesians, demonized the communists among them, believing that to parry their diabolical challenge they had to eliminate them as a political entity, killing many and compelling so many more to de-demonize themselves by imbibing the prescribed antidote, religious conversion. In general, when facing radical or revolutionary challenges to the socioeconomic and political order, establishments tend to demonize such challengers, sometimes reacting in murderous fury. In many Latin American countries during the 1970s and 1980s, those in power on the political Right killed many more in their counterinsurgency campaigns than the rebellious Left ever killed. Today, Al Qaeda and other Political Islamists demonize infidels, especially those they deem their enemies, but they do not dehumanize them, because all infidels must do to be redeemed is accept Allah, and their danger passes.

The imputed capacity of rehabilitation or redemption is the critical issue for analyzing whether people are dehumanizing demeaned, hated, or feared others. Do they believe the others, at least in principle, can be reformed? The dehumanized, putatively bereft of fundamental human attributes owing to their biology, cannot be reformed, reeducated, civilized, transformed through any process into *full* human beings. In many instances, the source of their dehumanized condition is conceived of in racist terms, deriving from their ethnicity, blood, or race (or genes), biological givens and therefore unchangeable. Their children, by dint of their biology, inherit their putatively debased nature, so they too are automatically dehumanized. To be sure, some dehumanized peoples are thought of in seemingly contradictory ways, as less than human and capable as individuals of becoming civilized and as a collectivity of being reformed, but usually only over the long run. Such was the attitude of (some) British colonizers in India, though by no means everywhere else. This kind of dehumanization, having as its source a cultural theory of the group's nature, is comparatively rare. (Cultural theories, unless they also demonize, do not dehumanize people as much because the condition is not seen as permanent and gradations of human capacities are recognized.)

A simple matrix containing groups that our age's most omnivorous killers, the Nazis, murdered illustrates the separate dimensions of dehumanization and demonization, and also how the same perpetrators conceive of victim groups differently along these dimensions.

	Non-Demonized	*Demonized*
Non-Dehumanized	Enemy "hostages"	German communists, gay men
Dehumanized	Slavs, mentally ill, Sinti and Roma	Jews

The Nazis codified their racist understanding of humanity in a formal pseudoscientific race theory, which they made the German educational system's foundational and unifying theme. This theory defined races according to cranium type, facial features, coloring, height, and other physical features, which also divided the peoples conventionally called "white" or of European descent into various qualitatively distinct races. The Nazis saw different nationalities and ethnic groups as biologically distinct races arrayed on a continuum of human mental capacity and commensurate moral worth. Nordic or Aryan peoples stood at the pinnacle. Slavic peoples stooped below as subhumans, black Africans still further below, hunched down on the cusp between humanity and other primates. A pamphlet titled "The Subhuman," of which the Germans published almost four million copies in German and translated into fourteen other languages, spells out the historically common though rarely so clearly articulated view of dehumanized people:

> The subhuman, that biologically seemingly complete similar creation of nature with hands, feet and a kind of brain, with eyes and a mouth, is nevertheless a completely different, dreadful creature. He is only a rough copy of a human being, with human-like facial traits but nonetheless morally and mentally lower than any animal. Within this creature there is a fearful chaos of wild, uninhibited passions, nameless destructiveness, the most primitive desires, the nakedest vulgarity. Subhuman, otherwise nothing. For all that bear a human face are not equal. Woe to him who forgets it.[10]

For Nazis, the Slavic peoples were not more evil or demonic than a gorilla but, like gorillas, were inherently amoral and dangerous and thus to be kept in check. Slavs were lower beings, fit to be beasts of burden, used as slaves or killed depending on the Germans' needs. Because the Germans viewed the Slavic peoples as numerous beyond the German empire's needs, Germans readily killed millions and would have eliminated and killed tens of millions more had they won the war. Similarly, people who were mentally ill, developmentally disabled, or with congenital diseases were dehumanized as individuals, deemed bereft of fundamental human attributes, "lives unworthy of life" in the Nazi argot, useless eaters, a drag on Germany's economic and biological stock. So they could be and were killed. Many Germans responded to this aspect of their government's mass murderousness with horror—the regime was killing Germans' own relatives and community members—and protested with some effect. Yet those Germans who had most internalized the regnant biological determinism—and this included the physicians and nurses murdering these people—considered killing them a praiseworthy act serving the German people's national health and well-being.

In contrast to these dehumanized groups and individuals, the Nazis *demonized* political opponents, particularly communists. In the Nazi worldview, the virus of communism (an allegedly Jewish invention) had infected these people, despite their good racial stock, transforming them into demonic enemies, bent upon wreaking havoc in Germany, weakening and decimating the German people, and delivering Germany to Bolshevik Russia. Within Germany, the Nazis incarcerated and killed the communist (and socialist) leadership but they allowed the rank-and-file communists, seen as (relatively easily) deprogrammable, to continue living in German society. Because the source of the communists' threat was not biological, the Nazis did not need a biological solution. Communist people were not subhuman, so once German communists abandoned their communist practices, the Nazis treated them as good Germans. Ex-communist Roland Freisler rose to be chief of the regime's People's Court, presiding over the country's show trials of those who resisted the regime.

The Nazis had other enemies, including the French, whom they neither dehumanized nor demonized, but saw as old-fashioned enemies to be defeated and controlled brutally. Applying the logic of morally unrestrained warfare, they murdered French by the hundreds after suffering sabotage or other attacks, as retribution and deterrent.

The Nazis' fantastical ideological view of the Jews construed them as Germany's most dangerous enemy. The Jews' unusual place even among the Nazis' long list of enemy and hated groups was such that the Nazis, and Germans in general, considered Jews to be a breed apart, less than human, indeed not even human, *and* demonic, powerfully malevolent to the core.

Kurt Möbius, serving in the Chelmno death camp, explained his thinking, the norm among Germans, about the orders to annihilate the Jews: "It did not at all occur to me that these orders could be unjust." It made sense to him. He, like his countrymen, had been prepared for the exterminationist assault by German society's powerful elimina-

An octopus with a Star of David over its head has its tentacles encompassing a globe, circa 1938.

tionist discourse: "I was then of the conviction that the Jews were not innocent but guilty. I believed the propaganda that all Jews were criminals and subhumans and that they were the cause of Germany's decline after the First World War. The thought that one should disobey or evade the order to participate in the extermination of the Jews did not therefore enter my mind at all."[11] In addition to this man's clear explanation of how he was prepared to exterminate all Jews because of what he already believed about them, long before he received the killing order, he also succinctly captures and conveys both the dehumanized *and* demonized view of the Jews that was then Germans' common sense: *All* Jews were "criminals," in other words demonized, and *all* Jews were "subhumans," in other words dehumanized.

According to the Nazis and ordinary Germans alike, Jews were racially (genetically) programmed to undermine, enslave, even destroy humanity, especially its most exalted people, the Germans. They were, in a common formulation Heinrich Himmler employed at a 1938 conference of SS generals, the "primordial matter of everything negative."[12] Adolf Hitler attributed to them unparalleled cosmic malevolence and apocalyptic power, warning all Germans in *Mein Kampf,* his candid guide to his worldview and political thinking, of the consequences of a victorious Jewry: "And as, in this greatest of all recognizable organisms, the result of an application of such a law could only be chaos, on earth it could only be destruction for the inhabitants of this planet. If, with the help of his Marxist creed, the Jew is victorious over the other peoples of the world, his crown will be the funeral wreath of humanity and this planet will, as it did millions of years ago, move through the ether devoid of men."[13] Nowhere else in prejudice's annals (certainly in modern times) except against Jews, have people, let alone political leaders, conceived of groups in such cosmologically evil terms. For Germans (and other similar European racist antisemites), the continuum of *human* races did not include the Jews, conceived of as an anti-race, the Antichrist's human equivalent, to be not of diminished intellectual and moral capacity (as subhumans almost always are conceived), but highly capable and depraved, dangerous, and determined, a threat that would never end.

Before expanding the discussion of dehumanization and demonization beyond Germany during the Nazi period, we need to recognize that not every demeaned, hated, or feared group can be so easily classified. As with most belief systems, a diversity of views often exists among the people who despise others. Also, whether people initially dehumanize or demonize others, their prejudicial conception sometimes leads them to respond to new developments by grafting the other prejudicial conception onto it. Thus, those dehumanizing others sometimes begin to believe that the putative subhumans are vulnerable to demonic powers or ideologies, such as communism. Similarly, those demonizing an *ethnic* group can tend to dehumanize it as well, to see the demonic qualities as residing in the group's biology. Aside from such complexity, the prejudiced and haters are not scholars concerned with category boundaries and expressive clarity, so discerning their views' real basis can be challenging. Finally, the two dimensions do not capture everything relevant to categorizing prejudice and hatred, which are each internally complex. Two kinds of examples bring out this general complexity.

The first is the British conception of the Kikuyu supporting the Mau Mau rebellion against colonial rule in Kenya starting in the mid-1950s. The British colonial administration and settlers, numbering fifty thousand, conceived of the Kikuyu in dehumanized terms. Comporting with Europeans' general racism toward Africans, the British believed Kikuyu to be of diminished human capacity—as Paul Mahehu, a survivor who had served with the British for years, first in Burma during World War II and then afterward in Africa, attests, the British thought them to be more like monkeys than human beings.[14] Befitting their putative nature, the Kikuyu were fit to be ruled and exploited. John Nottingham, a former British district officer in Kenya during the Mau Mau period, while agreeing with this animalistic analogy, also articulated this fundamental racism in other terms: "The general view was that they [Africans and Kenyans] were limited in the responsibilities that could be given to them. That they were limited in their education abilities, that they were people who were in some ways children even though grown up in most other ways. So there was a general attitude of paternalism, patronizing, and a lack of belief in their total honesty."[15] The British believed that this putatively diminished capacity made the Kikuyu prone to accepting poisonous ideas endangering the British (and other Africans). Those Kikuyu taking the Mau Mau *oath* of allegiance turned themselves, in the British colonialists' minds, into demonic creatures who had to be eliminated. The British grafted a profound demonization of the members of an African liberation movement on top of a classically racist European conception of the colonized Africans.

Britons' deeply rooted dehumanization of the Kikuyu as subhumans had begun decades earlier. Their demonization of them, though of recent vintage, was easily incorporated by the British into their conception of the dehumanized masses, whom the British now saw as inherently unstable, "mad," and prey to becoming possessed by the Mau Mau devil. A Briton, Ronald Sherbrooke-Walker, visiting friends in Kenya in early 1953, toward the beginning of Mau Mau, reported:

What do the settlers say? They know the primitive East African mentality and that "black brother" is a thousand years behind the

European in outlook, and the "Kuke" [Kikuyu], who are causing the present trouble, are much inferior to the other Kenya tribes in moral qualities. If Europeans were to abandon the country voluntarily, or be squeezed out politically, without the Pax Britannica it would revert to blood-thirsty barbarism.[16]

Classifying and analyzing the various attitudes toward the targeted Kikuyu is further complicated in that many Kikuyu loyalists, organized into the Home Guard, helped the British fight the Mau Mau rebellion and conduct their eliminationist assault against actual or suspected Mau Mau supporters. We know little of Kikuyu loyalists' views. Some might have imbibed the British hierarchical view of humanity and of the white man's racial superiority, but they could hardly have deemed rebellious Kikuyu subhuman in racist terms because it also would have applied to them. Their demonization of Mau Mau supporters as "scum," "filthy pigs," and "savage animals" to be wiped out resembles the classical demonization of people beholden to threatening ideologies, such as communism, though here cast in the British eliminationist idiom. For the Kikuyu loyalists and their British overlords, the Mau Mau oath, namely their ideology, was the principal problem. They saw Mau Mau as a contagious "mind-destroying disease." Even according to Thomas Askwith, the colonial administrator most hoping to "rehabilitate" (as opposed to destroying) the Mau Mau, the "oath represented everything evil in Mau Mau." Caroline Elkins, having plumbed the British eliminationist assault on the Kikuyu's real character, explains: "It was the distinctive quality of Mau Mau oathing rituals, and methods of killing, that transformed the virulent racism that had been the cornerstone of settler racial attitudes for over half a decade into something even more lethal. Settlers and colonial officials alike were repelled by the Kikuyu oaths, which used powerful symbols like goats' blood and eyeballs, and ram intestines and scrotums."[17] Believing this putatively demonic oath had led the Kikuyu astray, the British and their Kikuyu supporters, following on this logic, considered Kikuyu who took an anti–Mau Mau oath, repudiating the Mau Mau ideology and movement, as de-demonized and rehabilitated. Getting Kikuyu to take an anti–Mau Mau oath became a principal British policy goal, even though strong sentiment, put into much practice, always existed that the British would probably have to violently eliminate the Kikuyu.

Nottingham conveys British settlers and colonial administrators' reigning view: "All we heard was how savage Mau Mau was, shoot to kill. You can't imagine how often I heard, 'The only good Kuke is a dead Kuke.' There was this idea that Mau Mau was savage, just completely atavistic, and somehow had to be gotten rid of, regardless of how it was done. This idea was everywhere."[18] These beliefs, according to Nottingham, were so axiomatic among the British that even other district officers who had been at Oxford with him, even those who were to the left politically, believed they were justified and just in treating the Kikuyu brutally and murderously. Nottingham lays out the various elements of the cause and effect of the Britons' beliefs and actions. First the racism: "The Kikuyu were considered as animals. Even wild animals." Then the demonization grafted on top of it: "If you took the oath the British thought that this meant you were now throwing aside all things European. You were going back to what the Europeans mostly thought was the savage existence that you had before the Europeans came." Then how this dehumanized and demonized amalgam shaped the Britons' thinking about what they may and ought to do: "I think the Europeans thought that someone who took the oath was no longer acceptable as a human being. . . . and therefore they were beginning to act more and more as if they were faced with animals and not human beings. . . . I think that actually is what many of them really did think in the way that they talked." This thinking led to the Britons' murderous conduct and, because of its content, kept their consciences clear: "They [the Kikuyu] were therefore treated in the way that you would shoot a wild animal. And you wouldn't think, 'No, this has gone wrong. Sorry.' . . . All they were shooting was a wild animal. Not a human being. Or if they were beating in a camp a wild animal, then they were just beating a wild animal and not a human being."[19]

A second example of such complexity is the Nazis' and, more generally, Germans' conception of Sinti and Roma, commonly called Gypsies. They dehumanized them in the extreme. Drawing on long-standing Europe-wide prejudice, the Germans deemed them worthless racial mishmash, asocial people, a disruptive excrescence on society. Yet they did not exactly demonize the Sinti and the Roma. Germans did not consider them to be, as they did Jews, secular incarnations of the devil, with conscious malevolence governing their every move, and therefore to seriously or existentially threaten Germans. While Germans coming into contact or under the influence of Jews could become, in the Germans' hallucinatory conception, "verjudet" or "Jewified," Germans had no notion that Sinti or Roma could spiritually or even physically contaminate them or, for that matter, that any other putative subhumans could (and neither do other eliminationist assaults' perpetrators think this of their victims). Nevertheless, Germans deemed Sinti and Roma to be personally morally depraved and asocial, a kind of racial pollution that inevitably enormously harmed society. So they hunted down the Sinti and the Roma, exterminating between a quarter million and half a million of them around Europe. Yet these victims, whom the Germans mainly conceived of as one people, were never central to the Germans' worldview, mindset, or eliminationist programs and policies, and, unlike with the Jews, the Germans did not expressly devote themselves to killing every last one.

Dealing with Demons

With these caveats in mind, analysis of eliminationist assaults' can be greatly furthered by categorizing victims according to the perpetrators' conception of them, using these two dimensions. This produces four victim categories: existential enemies, heretics, subhumans, and demons. Language and images dehumanizing or demonizing others communicate to those listening and sharing the discussion's assumptions that an eliminationist drive against the disparaged and despised people makes sense. If a being is like a disease, or a bug, or a wild animal, or a barbarian, incapable of being reasoned with; if a being willfully threatens all that is good, the Volk, God, a world of justice and plenty for all; if a being is evil incarnate, then it follows that one must eradicate the disease, squash the bug, kill the wild animal, expel or slay the barbarian, destroy the threat, or extirpate the evil. Not to do so would be negligent folly, like leaving your young child in a bear- or devil-infested forest. The language of existential or national threat itself, or of the necessity to usher in the millennium, also often takes on

Patterns of Dehumanization and Demonization of Eliminationist Victims

	Non-Demonized	Demonized
Non-Dehumanized	*(1) Existential Enemies* Turks: Armenians Germans: enemy "hostages" Soviets: Kulaks Americans: Japanese-Americans Poles: ethnic Germans Ibos: Hausa Pakistanis: Bangladeshis Syrian Baathists: Hama Iraqi Baathists: Kurds, Shia, and enemies of regime Serbs: Croats, Bosniaks, Kosovars Croats: Serbs Congo: most victims North Korea: Koreans Russia: Chechens	*(2) Heretics* Germans: communists, gay men Soviets: many victims Communist Chinese: many victims Hindus and Muslims during 1947 partition Indonesians: communists Chile: leftists Argentina: leftists El Salvador: leftists Guatemala: leftists Political Islamists: infidels/Americans Khmer Rouge: most victims
Dehumanized	*(3) Subhumans* Americans: Native Americans Belgians: Congolese Germans: Herero, Nama Turks: Armenians Germans: Slavs, mentally ill, Sinti, and Roma Japanese: most victims Britons: Kikuyu El Salvador: Indians Guatemalans: Maya Political Islamic Sudanese: black Africans Indonesians: East Timorese	*(4) Demons* Germans: Jews Croats: Jews Slovaks: Jews Burundian Tutsi: Hutu Rwandan Hutu: Tutsi Political Islamists: Jews

dehumanizing and demonizing tones toward the putatively problematic groups, providing a similar, powerful justification for eliminationist assaults.

Analyzing potential perpetrators' views of potential victims along these two dimensions provides critical distinctions for understanding their conception of the victims, and eliminationist politics' internal logic, including what perpetrators do (or potential perpetrators might do) to deal with disparaged and despised groups. Category 1, *existential enemies,* contains people who are not dehumanized or demonized. They are targeted as enemies because they compete for resources or political power and, in the natural and unalterable struggle for domination and existence, must be vanquished before they vanquish you. In category 3, *subhumans,* are groups of dehumanized but not demonized people. They are seen as potentially but not necessarily dangerous barbarians or brutes or animals, unworthy of moral consideration. In category 2, *heretics,* are capable, demonized but not dehumanized human beings. Conceived of as not biologically different from other people, they, for some articulated reason—usually in the grip of a pernicious religious or secular ideology—willfully dissent from the hallowed creed and seek to harm you or prevent humanity's salvation. And category 4, *demons,* are demonized *and* dehumanized beings. They are deemed inhuman creatures, willfully malevolent, a Christian secular incarnation of the devil or his minions.

Perhaps surprisingly, these two imputed qualities of dehumanization and demonization not only are distinct from one another, but only infrequently appear together and rarely simultaneously in full force. Plumbing their relationship's complexity and each notion's generation would take us far afield. Two aspects need to be highlighted. Dehumanization, which almost inherently includes placing a diminished moral value on the dehumanized, is an attributed status principally informing how *you* treat such beings. Demonization, which is about others' moral depravity and willful threat, is principally an attribute of how you think *such beings* treat or would treat you. These two qualities are not logically or empirically conjoined. Second, demonized beings tend to be thought of as too dangerous to live among you, which militates against people demonizing slaves or serfs or people too numerous (or in some ways too useful) to get rid of. Beasts of burden need not also be demons. Demonization, however, is often attached to people of the same nationality, ethnicity, even religion adhering to threatening political ideologies or political movements, so dehumanizing them (a biologically based inferiority) makes no sense, as you would explicitly or implicitly be dehumanizing yourself.

Discourses dehumanizing and demonizing ethnic, social, political, or other groups typically enjoy popular participation and assent. Such discourses' purpose, when not already taken for granted in a political culture, is to persuade others. When political regimes are also animated by such views, they can further intensify and spread the already powerful prejudices using governmental offices, the news media, and the educational system, and now the Internet. This creates a hothouse effect, turning such discourses into much of society's common sense, percolating both downward and upward from civil society's informal conversations, with people already harboring such views finding their views intensifying and becoming more central to their outlook. In almost all eliminationist discourses presaging eliminationist assaults, such broad popular participation and assent exists.

The categories emerging from the dimensions of dehumanization and demonization suggest certain patterns of outcomes and explanations, but they do not provide a full account of exterminationist and eliminationist assaults, because other critical factors also influence the actors' thinking and opportunities to act. Two other critical elements need to be examined, ultimately on a case-by-case basis. The perpetrators embed their understanding of the targeted group in broader social theories about politics, society, and humanity, and moral theories about goodness and right conduct. Some important general things can be said about this. Second, partly derived from this are perpetrators' conceptions of the perniciousness of their targets, the source of the perniciousness, and the danger's imminence.[20]

People, both leaders and followers, consciously or not, adopt social and moral theories that guide them in deciding how to deal with people seemingly posing an extreme threat to their lives or well-being, or to cherished goals. Whether we call these stances theories, mindsets, or simply ways of thinking about disposing of such people, different approaches are discernible that form patterns: Certain ways of categorizing targeted peoples go hand-in-hand with certain kinds of programs. Logically and empirically, a different type of moral and social thinking tends to inform considerations of how to deal with each of the different kinds of targets, *existential enemies, subhumans, heretics,* and *demons.*

Those facing *existential enemies* typically adopt a realpolitik approach and moral theory to their victims, which historically has governed group conflicts, and even in our time, probably more than any other. The world consists of power and domination, and intergroup life is inherently conflictual, with little possibility of peaceable and mutually beneficial solutions. In this world of zero-sum conflicts, you renounce violence and brutality at your peril. For eliminationist politics governed by such thinking, survival or prosperity mandates that you deal with your enemies—even though they are human beings like you and not demonic—according to dog-eat-dog realism. This, together with sufficient prejudice or group conflict, justifies eliminating your enemies. Slaughters and eliminationist assaults against *subhumans,* not necessarily total or gargantuan, follow as such thinking is applied to national or cultural groups contesting (or potentially contesting) power or territory.

Those conceiving of enemies as *heretics* are themselves typically acting in the name of religious movements, whether classical religions such as Christianity or Islam, or secular religions such as communism (grounded in Marxism), or alternately in the battle against such movements. Their social and moral theory is concerned with bringing about the end of days, or a new order ushering in the terrestrial millennium, or at least preventing others from imposing on society a seemingly dystopian vision or apocalypse. Their need and justification is the call of God or history or a utopian end to conflict and facilitation of harmony and plenty. This thinking renders human beings puny abstractions, robbing them of moral standing or protection that is overridden by the moral call to bring about utopia. A stock Khmer Rouge phrase about those refusing to reform themselves and serve the revolution, repeated often during their murderous reign, encapsulates this thinking: "Keeping [urban dwellers] is no benefit; losing them is no loss."[21] Teeda Butt Mam, a survivor, heard it herself, as she explains: "They told us we were *void.* We were less than a grain of rice in a large pile. The Khmer Rouge said that the Communist revolution could be successful with only two people. Our lives had no significance to their great Communist nation, and they told us, 'To keep you is no benefit, to destroy you is no loss.'"[22] The eliminationist politics following from such thinking, often found in onslaughts against *heretics*—said to embody the demonic principles or ideas they bear—can easily escalate to gargantuan slaughters, because these religious and political-religious movements' and regimes' adherents can see their enemies to be legion, as they consist not only of active ideological opponents but those who merely adhere to the old order or rival religious or political views.

The utilitarian social and moral theory strongly characterizing eliminationist onslaughts against *subhumans* sees these dehumanized people in purely instrumental terms, to be killed, kept alive, or enslaved according to the perpetrators' interests and needs. If subhumans are too numerous, then you kill the unnecessary or troublesome ones. If you need labor to produce your food or goods, then you enslave them. This mindset differs from that of realpolitik because the utilitarian calculus leads its bearers to dispose of people utterly callously, according to an economic calculus similar to using or disposing of animals or other resources. Edmond Picard, a Belgian senator, captures this mindset's effects in his description of a caravan of dehumanized Africans, enslaved as porters carrying massive loads around rapids, whom he encountered in 1896 in the Belgian Congo:

> Unceasingly we meet these porters . . . black, miserable, with only a horribly filthy loin-cloth for clothing, frizzy and bare head supporting the load—box, bale, ivory tusk . . . barrel-chested; most of them sickly, drooping under a burden increased by tiredness and insufficient food— a handful of rice and some stinking dried fish; pitiful walking caryatids, beasts of burden with thin monkey legs, with drawn features, eyes fixed and round from preoccupation with keeping their balance and from the daze of exhaustion. They come and go like this by the thousands . . . requisitioned by the State armed with its powerful militia, handed over by chiefs whose slaves they are and who make off with their salaries, trotting with bent knees, belly forward, an arm raised to steady the load, the other leaning on a long walking-stick, dusty and sweaty, insects spreading out across the mountains and valleys their many files and their task of Sisyphus, dying along the road or, the journey over, heading off to die from overwork in their villages.[23]

Picard's description of the effects of the Belgians' brutal utilitarianism was, if in different form, articulated fifty years later by Himmler as a normative principle in a 1943 speech in Posen to the assembled leadership corps of the SS:

> For the SS Man, one principle must apply absolutely: we must be honest, decent, loyal, and comradely to members of our own blood,

and to no one else. What happens to the Russians, the Czechs, is totally indifferent to me. Whatever is available to us in good blood of
our type, we will take for ourselves, that is, we will steal their children and bring them up with us, if necessary. Whether other races
live well or die of hunger is only of interest to me insofar as we need
them as slaves for our culture; otherwise that doesn't interest me.
Whether 10,000 Russian women fall down from exhaustion in building a tank ditch is of interest to me only insofar as the tank ditches
are finished for Germany.[24]

Other than abducting those Slavic children who, according to the
Germans' pseudo-biologistic racism, were of good racial stock, the Germans were to use the Slavic peoples mercilessly as production factors—
which, it is worth noting, differed from Himmler and Germans'
conception of Jews as demons to be exterminated.

When perpetrators want nothing from their *subhuman* targets but
their land, they dispose of them one way or another, as required. When
perpetrators are imperial colonialists not wishing to fully settle the territory and displace the putative subhumans, then their killing, though
sometimes massive—as was the Belgians' in Congo and the Germans' in
Poland and the Soviet Union—is usually more selective. When perpetrators see the putative subhumans as supportive (or potentially supportive) of resistance against them, they dispose of them murderously.

A striking feature of perpetrators' stance toward subhumans standing in their way—by just being there or being seen as potentially resisting or prone to adopting demonized ideologies—is how prone they
are to using eliminationist violence, how rarely they seek other solutions, how little are the hesitations, how quick is the trigger reflex, and
how low the standard is for them to conclude the putative subhumans
are or will become a threat. This common propensity among such perpetrators existed in Guatemala, as a secret CIA cable from Guatemala
to Washington in February 1982 describes. Even though, the CIA reported, "the army has yet to encounter any major guerrilla force in the
area," it conducted an extensive eliminationist campaign against the
Maya, following its instructions to "destroy all towns and villages
which are cooperating with the Guerrilla Army of the Poor (EGP) and
eliminate all sources or resistance." What did this mean in an area

where the guerrillas were not present? The CIA report explains: "The well documented belief by the army that the entire Ixil [Maya] population is pro-EGP has created a situation in which the army can be expected to give no quarter to combatants and non-combatants alike." Because of the perpetrators' beliefs about the putative subhumans, they need little real evidence to conclude that a given village, people and buildings, must be destroyed. The CIA cable further explains: "When an army patrol meets resistance and takes fire from a town or a village it is assumed that the entire town is hostile and it is subsequently destroyed. The army has found that most of the villages have been abandoned before the military forces arrive. An empty village is assumed to have been supporting the EGP, and it is destroyed."[25] The CIA rightly said the Maya's hostility—not welcoming this murderous army with open arms—"is assumed." Just as one would preemptively clear away brush to prevent brush fires, the Guatemalan regime and its followers cut down the subhuman Mayan brush before the guerrillas (here not even present) could set them off. Starting soon thereafter, the Guatemalan perpetrators executed a detailed, coordinated plan to sweep through Mayan areas, slaughtering the men, women, and children they found, because they defined the putatively subhuman Maya, likened to animals, as supporters or potential supporters of the still small, barely potent insurgency.

Perpetrators treat *demons* according to a perverted or inverted categorical imperative. The perpetrators act not out of a belief in zero-sum realpolitik or an eschatological mindset (though that might also be present), or some utilitarian calculus (unless the calculus always produces the same result), but according to their social and moral theory that they *must* destroy demons because doing so is in itself right, a warped categorical imperative. A German perpetrator from Vienna, who helped slaughter more than two thousand Jews in Mogilev in the Soviet Union, explained to his wife how his conception of the Jews helped calm his visceral discomfort at acting on this imperative: "My hand was shaking a bit with the first cars," he wrote. "By the tenth car, I was aiming calmly and shooting dependably at the many women, children and babies. Bearing in mind that I have two babies at home, I knew that they would suffer exactly the same treatment, if not ten times as bad, at the hands of these hordes."[26] Perpetrators easily imagine beings they consider born demons committing the most heinous acts, as this man did, fantasizing as he shoots babies that the Jewish "hordes" might do "ten times as bad"!—whatever that could possibly mean. The perpetrators see themselves duty bound to eliminate such born demons, ideally to destroy them, even if they might control and temporarily use them before the final reckoning. They also, as the German serving at the Chelmno death camp conveyed in saying the Jews are born subhuman criminals, see killing such beings as natural. Himmler, in his Posen speech, made clear that annihilating the putative Jewish demons had become common sense: "I am thinking now of the evacuation of the Jews, the extirpation of the Jewish people. It is one of those things that's easy to say: *'The Jewish people will be extirpated,'* says every Party comrade, *'that's quite clear, it's in our program: elimination of the Jews, extirpation; that's what we're doing.'*" Because Himmler and the German perpetrators believed it necessary and just to extirpate such demons, Himmler could with genuineness offer his listeners a paean to their initial and enduring purity: "We can say that we have carried out this most difficult task out of love for our own people. And we have suffered no harm to our inner self, our soul, our character in so doing."[27]

These mindsets can escalate to mass murder, even colossal ones. Whether they do, as we see, depends on many factors, including opportunity and contingent developments, such as political leaders attaining power wishing to act upon them. When they do act, such eliminationist conceptions can and do lead to different policies precisely because these beliefs and mindsets are compatible with multiple eliminationist practices. The people considering eliminating dehumanized or demonized people typically focus more on the need to eliminate the victims *somehow* using the functionally equivalent and compatible eliminationist means, rather than on specific policy proposals.

Leaders and followers alike generally do not publicly discuss (it is unnecessary) their eliminationist conceptions' various practical potentialities—which depend upon contingent developments—until or shortly before the attack. This poses few if any problems for mobilizing the perpetrators and broader support, because widespread eliminationist beliefs preparing the way suggest the kinds of things that are sensible and that eventually will be done. If you know a wildfire, hurricane, or flood is coming your way, you need not hear of the necessity of protective measures, and when you learn of logical options or the ones the authorities adopt, you understand immediately the reasons for them and are likely to implement or support them to protect yourself and your family, property, and community. Putative human threats differ from natural disasters, but when severe—you believe another people wishes to enslave or kill all your people—the logic of understood response and necessary action are no different or less pressing. Hence the ease of activating and mobilizing previously latent or dormant beliefs for eliminationist assaults. What differs from a looming natural catastrophe is precisely the human (actually subhuman or demonic) element of the threat, often engendering a personalized fury in would-be and actual perpetrators, and, second, unlike natural catastrophes from which one can flee or just protect oneself, one can strike down the human threats, seeking to eliminate them altogether. Although perpetrators might not ideally choose the most radical and final eliminationist solution, if other eliminationist options appear insufficient, then extermination becomes more expedient. In some societies perpetrators merely wait for an opportunity to act. Opportunity becomes the limiting or enabling condition rather than the motive.

As we see, several factors influence when and what people will do to ensure their subjective sense of security and well-being. Still, certain patterns emerge.

Mass murders and eliminationist onslaughts against *existential enemies*—the Serbs' serial assaults on Croats, Bosniaks, and Kosovars, and Saddam Hussein's assaults on Kurds, Shias, and others—usually result from the brutal logic of war without moral restraints, including the one-sided war tyrants wage to sustain their conquest of their own countries' populations, even when the victims are considered neither demons nor subhumans. This occurs in the struggle for territory or for extremely scarce or valuable resources, but also develops when perpetrators consider an enemy to have waged illegitimately savage war. Such assaults are often undertaken by tyrannical leaders seeking power and advantage at all costs, using terror and mass murder as a means of securing their suzerainty. How regimes deal with existential enemies is most difficult to explain in the sense of its being the least obvious. As realpolitik governs its amoral thinking, it can produce subjugation and selective killing, or more thoroughgoing slaughters. If territory is to be cleared, then the killing and elimination can be vast. If the eliminationist thrust is principally for domination, less killing ensues, because terror can work with much smaller killings. The social and moral theory underlying the perpetrators' conceptions of the victims, group and political life, and acceptable conduct inform the perpetrators' choices. After all, most vanquished enemies in most wars are neither dehumanized nor demonized (and therefore qualify in eliminationist terms as *existential enemies*), and the winners, the potential perpetrators, choose not to eliminate them, lethally or otherwise.

The eliminations and slaughters of *heretics* include many of our time's most massive ones. They are typically ideological assaults, whether politically or religiously based. The perpetrators deem the targets so inimical to their vision of the world as to be currently incorrigible, and therefore necessary to eliminate. The perpetrators' visions of bringing about the political or religious millennium often render individual human beings into building blocks or inconsequential obstacles that must sometimes, if with a heavy heart, be discarded. Because such annihilations and eliminations are ideological and wedded to such unachievable goals, they often engender a drive to kill that is firmly rooted in the fundamentals of the perpetrators' worldview: Hence frequently their long duration and numerous victims. Potential perpetrators, lacking a positive reason to kill or permanently eliminate them, such as seeing them as an uncontrollable threat, often opt to de-demonize them by repressing and reeducating them, essentially a form of forced conversion, whether to a conventional religion or a secular one, such as communism. Whatever the chosen means, perpetrators tend to subject peoples construed as dangerous heretics to semipermanent eliminationism, because they see the enemies of the regime (religious or secular) to be vast and needing constant weeding; hence the establishment of totalitarian-like control, including camp systems that institutionalize eliminationist measures as politics' and society's constituent feature. There are two types of such political regimes. World systems are explicitly totalitarian in aspiration because they seek to reorder the world according to a fixed blueprint. Yet the world will not conform to the unworkable vision, so such regimes create more permanent institutions of domination, institutionalize their elimination programs, and make them their systems' permanent or semipermanent part, lasting longer than other eliminationist forays. Non-world systems, non-totalitarian in aspiration, usually of the political Right, are more focused and less destructively omnivorous. The ideology animating the perpetrators' and the designated enemies' identities critically influences which type of eliminationist regime emerges.

People have a proclivity to eliminate *subhumans*. How they do, with what utilitarian positions, depends critically on their particular social theory about the putative subhumans, including their potential threat, and the perpetrators' moral theory about themselves. The eliminationist options are principally a mixture of repression, enslavement, and killing. Shortly after General Lothar von Trotha's annihilation edict for the Herero, German Chief of Staff General Alfred von Schlieffen explained the situation to Chancellor Bernard von Bülow: "One can agree with his plan of annihilating the whole people or driving them from the land. The possibility of whites living peacefully together with blacks after what has happened is very slight unless at first the blacks are reduced to forced labor, that is, a sort of slavery. An enflamed racial war can be ended only through the annihilation or complete subjugation of one of the parties." For some perpetrators, locked in a territorial struggle, annihilation becomes a perceived necessity. For others there is a drive to eliminate the putative subhumans as they stand in the way of other goals, which for Germans during the Nazi period was world conquest in the context of ceaseless Darwinian struggle among races. Generally, the larger the dehumanized groups (if subjugation seems necessary), the larger (and more brutal) are the slaughters and eliminations. The other strategy for dealing with large groups of putative subhumans is decapitating their elites and killing a number sufficient to keep them in check.

Eliminationist attacks against *demons,* beings deemed an incorrigible extreme threat, also becomes permanent politics by total mass murder, or mass murder as social control. Because elimination, including extirpation of the putative demons, is an end in itself, the perpetrators generally wait for the opportunity to solve their so-called problem once and for all and then embark on systematic projects of total annihilation.

From Discourse to Action

Language, talk, conversation, discourses, and imagery are the medium of mass elimination, more properly the media that prepare people to countenance or perpetrate mass murder and elimination. They become more eliminationist in potential when their eliminationist fundamentals constitute a substantial part of a society's or group's culture or subculture. And the manner in which a group's conversations deprecate other people critically informs its members' manner of treating those people once an eliminationist campaign has been decided upon.

We need to think more about several critical things we know too little about in general: language as the soil containing the seeds of action, in this case mass murder and eliminationist politics more generally; the mechanisms transforming language and belief into action; and state-societal relations and the place of eliminationist language and discourse in them.

One of eliminationist politics' most crucial and least understood aspects is how people, including potential perpetrators, make the transition from an initial language state and stage, composed of prejudice and hatred or the desire to purge and transform society, to a second one of talk of an actual elimination campaign, and then to the third in which the language of action is accompanied by its implementation. For eliminationist leaders, these transitions are generally straightforward and obvious. From prejudice and hatred, or the coolly calculated understanding of power, political leaders develop first the *ideals* of a partly or fully purged society, then the *intention* to turn the ideal into action should propitious circumstances materialize, and then, when the conditions for action are actually in place, they develop, promulgate, and begin to implement an actual *policy* of elimination. Ideals, in this case, are normative notions about a society's and polity's constitution, and the hated or feared group's disposition. Intentions are the resolve to find a way to bring about that vision of a reconstituted society and polity. Policy is the actual implementation of plans reflecting the intentions.

The distinctiveness empirically and logically of each of these stages is clear. It is analogous to the process of first wanting to build a house of your dreams (the ideal), deciding that the time has arrived, so you begin thinking about finding a property and engaging an architect (the intention), and then after setting sights on the land and getting everything else in place, you acquire the property, commission a design, and build the house (the policy). Analyses of mass murder and eliminations typically fail to make these necessary distinctions, collapsing the three stages into an overwhelming focus on actual policy.

To understand more than policy implementation's nuts and bolts, including identifying and making sense of imminently eliminationist political constellations, we need to explore in each eliminationist onslaught and future actual and potential one, all three aspects: ideals, intentions, and policy.

Mehmet Talât, Hitler, Mao Zedong, Pol Pot, Saddam Hussein, Slobodan Milošević, and Radovan Karadžić in Yugoslavia, and leader after leader went through these stages.* For Hitler, the ideal of a world without Jews dates from his political career's beginning, which he articulated in one of his first political speeches in 1920 as "the removal of the Jews from our *Volk*," which he specified during another speech that year as being so necessary that "we are animated with an inexorable resolve to seize the Evil [the Jews] by the roots and to exterminate it root and branch." Yet Hitler—then a beer-hall rabble-rouser—was aware his ideals would remain idle until he had the capacity and opportunity to act, so he prophesied that an organization must arise "which one day will proceed with the deed." Two years later journalist Josef Hell asked Hitler what he would do if ever he had a free hand with the Jews. Hitler, according to Hell, fell into a kind of reverie, "was seized by a sort of paroxysm," raised his voice, and eventually shouted:

> Once I really am in power, my first and foremost task will be the annihilation of the Jews. As soon as I have the power to do so, I will have gallows built in rows—at the Marienplatz in Munich for example—as many as traffic allows. Then the Jews will be hanged indiscriminately, and they will remain hanging until they stink; they will hang there as long as the principles of hygiene permit. As soon as they have

---

*This is, however, not true of Lenin and initially probably Stalin, the revolutionary vanguard of Marxist revolutions, supported at first by only 100,000 communists, and unexpectedly governing a vast, mainly peasant, and resistant society. They improvised a great deal, though in keeping with their Marxist understanding of how, under the urgent pressure of "history," to forge the future utopia.

been untied, the next batch will be strung up, and so on down the line, until the last Jew in Munich has been exterminated. Other cities will follow suit precisely in this fashion, until all Germany has been completely cleansed of Jews.[28]

Hitler knew that for his ideals to be acted upon, he needed power. Once in power, more than a decade later, Hitler, the prudent politician, knew he must bide his time before erecting the gallows. Still, his elimination-ist ideals did become firm intentions, which he began to act upon in the 1930s first with generally nonlethal means. Then with the attack on the Soviet Union in 1941, when a comprehensive lethal program against the Jews finally became practical, Hitler acted on his by then firm in-tention, initiating the genocidal assault. That Hitler's long-standing, ar-ticulated murderous ideals preceded his formulated intentions or plans, which preceded implemented policy is, as his own public and private words repeatedly conveyed, irrefutable.[29]

For Mao and the Chinese communist leaders, the *ideal* of a trans-formed and purified communist society derived from Marxism. The knowledge that they must use violence to achieve it derived from the experience of their mentors, the Soviets. Therefore, the *intention* to practice thoroughgoing eliminationist politics took shape much earlier than it had with the Soviets, crystallizing in mass-murderous thinking as the communists' victory over the nationalists and assumption of power neared. In 1948, Mao in "agrarian reform" study materials con-veyed to the party membership that his schemes for restructuring over-populated China required that "one-tenth of the peasants would have to be destroyed." One tenth of half a billion is fifty million. In 1948, Jen Pi-shih of the Communist Party's Central Committee declared in a speech to the party cadres that "30,000,000 landlords and rich peas-ants would have to be destroyed."[30] The communist leadership's *in-tention* already well formulated (and communicated to their ideologically like-minded followers), they began, upon taking power, to implement their eliminationist *policies* in programs of population movement, mass executions, and mass incarcerations of landlords, rich peasants, and other class enemies in the vast camp system they created. The communists exterminated Chinese on the order of magnitude that Mao and Jen had foretold well before they had begun.

The Serbian leadership had long harbored the ideal of eliminating non-Serbs and non-Orthodox from their dreamed-of greater Serbia, which as part of Yugoslavia was peopled by other ethnic groups. Among the many striking aspects of the Serbs' mass-murderous and eliminationist assault on Croats, Bosniaks, and Kosovars are the many Serbian intellectuals involved, having also prepared the killing fields by enunciating and broadly disseminating eliminationist *ideals* among ordinary Serbs. The most widely read and influential Serbian literary work among Serbs was *The Mountain Wreath,* an epic poem published in 1847 by Vladika Petar Petrović Njegoš, who was the Montenegrin Orthodox Church's head, Montenegro's ruler, and modern Montenegrin and Serbian literature's founder. *The Mountain Wreath* explicitly glorifies and calls for mass extermination. This archbishop's poem, recognizing different eliminationist means' functional equivalence and that the heretical enemies are, as heretics in principle are, redeemable, adopts a broader eliminationist tone, offering Muslims the eliminationist choice: convert or die:

> *The blasphemers of Christ's name*
> *we will baptize with water or with blood!*
> *We'll drive the plague out of the pen!*
> *Let the song of horror ring forth,*
> *A true altar on a blood-stained rock.*[31]

Grounded in this blood-stained, horror-exalting poem and vibrant corpus of literature, art, folk songs, symbols, and mythology, especially the Kosovo myth calling for vengeance against the Turks (a synonym for Muslims) and the Serbian empire's reestablishment, Serbs developed a cultural orientation portraying themselves as a Christlike, victim people, needing to turn the sword on their enemies to re-create Christian Serbian virtue's lost kingdom. In an infamous *Serbian Memorandum* published in 1986, sixteen members of the Serbian Academy of Arts and Sciences called for Serbs to prevent the further strangulation, indeed a grinding cultural and actual genocide of their people, and thereby provided the intellectual ideals and foundation for Milošević to act when the opportunity soon presented itself. Two hundred Serbian intellectuals submitted the memorandum as a petition to the Yugoslavian and Serbian national assemblies. It declared: "In less than fifty years, during two successive generations [the Serbian people was] twice exposed to physical annihilation, forced assimilation, conversion, cultural genocide, ideological indoctrination, devaluation and rejection of its own tradition under an imposed guilt complex, [and] intellectually and politically disarmed." All Serbs had to be brought together into one nation-state for self-defense and to vanquish their enemies in their midst.[32] Such was the Serbian social discourse structured around an *ideal* enunciated in poetry, myth, and "scientific" pronouncements, long before a firm *intent* could crystallize, and long before political organization came into being and opportunity materialized to make these Serbian intellectuals, poets, and leaders' ideals the basis for a practical program and an executable policy.

More than in any of our time's other eliminationist assaults, the Serbian leaders had imbibed and themselves helped to construct a discourse composed of a set of *articulated* eliminationist ideals, glorified in hortatory literary works, including poetry. When opportunity appeared, a striking number of such literary mass murderers forged the sword from the pen. Radovan Karadžić, a practicing psychiatrist and published poet, powerfully embodies how ideals precede intention and then their realization in policy. In 1971, he published the poem "Sarajevo," which like many of his poems courses with the images of annihilation it foretold:

> *I can hear the disaster actually marching*
> *transformed into a bug—when the moment arrives:*
> *it will crush the bug as a worn-out singer*
> *is crushed by the silence and transformed into a voice.*
>
> *The city is burning like a lump of incense,*
> *our conscience is twisting in the smoke, too.*
> *Empty clothes glide through the city. The stone,*
> *built into houses, is dying red. The plague!*[33]

Karadžić would become the Bosnian Serbs' leader and the orchestrator of the Serbs' mass murder and elimination in Bosnia. This included their almost four-year siege of multiethnic and therefore detested Sarajevo, destroying much of the city, systematically shelling its cultural institutions housing Bosnian Muslim history and culture, killing thousands, and driving away many more. Finally, Karadžić was able to fulfill his once idle ideal—twenty years later—so he did.

Vuk Drašković was even more explicit about his early mass-murderous ideals. Perhaps the leading figure among the Serbian writers' cultural surge in the 1980s, he produced a spate of novels spreading anti-Croatian and anti-Muslim eliminationist ideals. Drašković, picking up on the deeply entrenched Serbian literary tradition of demonizing Muslims, penned a personal dedication in one of Vojislav Lubarda's own novels, *The Prayer*, which he sent to Lubarda, thanking him for his inspirational novels conjuring hatred and calling for revenge against Bosnian Muslims, glorifying violence, and revering the knife. Drašković, adopting this theme in his own novel *The Knife*, wrote Lubarda: "While I was writing *The Knife* and both *Prayers*, and even *The Judge*, I could not shake off myself, out of myself, the excitement, the desperation and the desire, a horrible and immense desire to transform my pen into a sword . . . an excitement that has haunted me since the day when I read [your] *Proud Stumbling*. I thank you for it." Drašković's ideal, his desire, lay dormant. Then opportunity came. So this immensely popular and influential Serbian novelist, weaver of eliminationist ideals, founded and led a major Serbian nationalist political party and established the paramilitary Serbian Guard that committed mass murder and eliminations against Croats and Bosnians. The Serbian Guard's military commander explained that Drašković's words, his ideals, had moved him to action already in the 1980s, before Yugoslavia's breakup: "I beat up many Muslims and Croatians on vacation in Cavtat [Croatia] because of his *Nož* [*The Knife*]. Reading that book, I would see red, I would get up, select the biggest fellow on the beach, and smash his teeth."[34]

For political leaders' followers and like-minded populaces, the various stages of ideals, intentions, and action, and the transitions through them, are less clear and more variable. Generally, followers move through a phase of discourse, a societal conversation (the regime might take a prominent, even preeminent, role) about the putatively problematic people that is typically heavy in deprecation, imprecation, and hatred, and light and vague in proposals; then, around the time of the leadership's decision to attack, to considering programmatic solutions to the problem; and then finally to a conversation about action and the willingness to act, and, for those participating, the action itself. We saw Adolf Eichmann describing the three stages he went through: "I was an idealist. When I reached the conclusion that it was necessary to do to the Jews what we did, I worked with the fanaticism a man can expect from himself." First his ideals, then his conclusion about the right policy, then his willing and devoted action.[35] The populace usually skips the intention stage—after all, ordinary people do not formulate policy—which is when the wish for a policy exists yet leaders must wait for the right time to enact it. For the populace, the three stages of variable length are imbibing and spreading notions about the putatively problematic people's noxiousness, including often only some vague solutions; then either being signaled or learning of an impending solution; and finally resolving to support it (or not), including those called upon to willingly take part in the eliminationist assault.

In Kenya, the British settlers easily moved from having initial beliefs dehumanizing the Kikuyu to, when facing a powerful Kikuyu liberation movement and a few attacks, believing in radical action to meet the Kikuyu's threat, to finally accepting or, as many did, even agitating that the radical measures must be eliminationist, even lethal. When dehumanized people appear to be no longer manageable or useful to those dehumanizing them, it seems so sensible as to feel natural to move rapidly from a utilitarian stance of domination and exploitation to being willing, even eager, to kill them or exploit them more brutally. Such a stance predominated among the British colonialists from when they colonized Kenya in the first part of the twentieth century. Francis Hall, who fought the Kikuyu, explains: "There is only one way of improving the Wakikuyu [and] that is wipe them out; I should be only too delighted to do so, but we have to depend on them for food supplies."[36] When the British came to see Kikuyu as undependable and, worse, an active threat, they altered their practical thinking. For some British the transition was immediate, for others—holdout liberals—it lasted a year. The British moved from the half-century-long classical colonial domination, land expropriation, and labor exploitation stance, to seeking near total elimination, with differences only about the appropriate mix of killing, expulsion, and incarceration, and, for some, rehabilitation. Frank Lloyd, a Briton later knighted for his service to the British Empire, worked in the colonial administration throughout the eliminationist assault. Mau Mau, he explained, was "bestial," an "evil movement." He left no doubt about his and others' conclusions: "Mau Mau had to be eliminated at all costs." And by any means, as "something had to be done to remove these people from society."[37]

Again and again one group's members make an easy transition from an initial state of holding dehumanizing and/or demonizing beliefs about other groups' or people's perniciousness, which in their daily lives are tertiary, simmering with only latent potential beneath the surface, to a second state of these same beliefs becoming utterly central to their bearers' consciousness and stance toward society and politics. All people can think of notions, beliefs, emotions they have about one thing or another that exist in relative states of latency, often for long periods, and then when circumstances change suddenly become far more central and urgent in their lives, thinking, and acting. This happens commonly with religious beliefs. During her life, a person's belief in God may move between a relatively latent state of keeping God at bay, to times, perhaps during a personal crisis, a family death, or developing a relationship with a more religious person, when God becomes more central, perhaps only to recede again, and then continuing to wax and wane, become more and less present, more and less of an accepted guide to practice, including church attendance, and self-governance. The bedrock belief in God may never change. How important or central it is, in the complex of that person's beliefs about the world, and in his or her complicated personal and social life, with all its personal, professional, and communal demands, how that person understands God's place in his or her inventory of conduct, and many other aspects of that person's life, can vary enormously, from being relatively latent to relatively manifest.

Less exalted beliefs, including eliminationist ones, move along this latent/manifest dimension. Bedrock beliefs demonizing or dehumanizing others that include hatred, prejudices, and fantastical notions, suggest in their logic that those people should have their pernicious qualities neutralized. Yet such beliefs might also find—depending on personal, social, and most critically political conditions, circumstances, and opportunities—lesser and greater expression and be a lesser or greater guide to action.

One Yugoslavian diplomat, a non-nationalist ethnic Croat, who knew from his own experience that only the communist dictatorship's force had made the intense hatreds latent, used to love traveling in Bosnia's "lovely countryside" and "entrancing" cities and towns. Yet he knew "there was a darker shadow to it all, not yet premonitory for us, but causing unease . . . we also sensed something was amiss." What was it?

> To be sure, the visible evidence of an undisturbed, ethnically mixed life was real. But something seemed to smolder beneath, a kind of second reality. Undercurrents of intolerance and suspicion could be spotted in unguarded, chance remarks of hateful envy or in snide comments about "those Croats," or "Serbs," or "Muslims," "always sticking together"; in occasional displays of rage over real or alleged pork-barrel monies "always benefiting them"; and in furtive glances at Muslims going to the mosque in a largely Christian village, or at Catholics or Orthodox going to their churches in predominantly Muslim towns. Sotto voce one was told of widespread mutual mistrust, more in the countryside than in Sarajevo, but in some Sarajevo suburbs too. But this particular darker shadow was nothing uniquely Bosnian. It is equally descriptive of the conditions in the 1970s and particularly in the 1980s in many regions and localities all over Yugoslavia.[38]

Superficially, Serbs and Croats got along with each other, and with Muslims, without their prejudices, suspicions, or hatreds being extinguished. Their simmering antipathies persisted despite the communist leadership's genuine endeavors to expel them from the minds and hearts of Yugoslavia's various ethnic groups who, clinging also to their ethnic identities, never became "Yugoslavs." The communist leadership's multiethnic composition—Josip Tito was a Croat; the other leaders were Serbs, Slovenes, and Muslims—and the Marxist teaching of socialist harmony enforced by state power produced a thin veneer concealing the latent hatred. In Yugoslavia, as elsewhere, this time servicing an anti-eliminationist ideal, the government was ineffectual in teaching people views that went against their deepest beliefs and values.

During the 1970s, the time of greatest Potemkin harmony, one elderly Serb confessed about Croats, in the words of the American diplomat to whom he spoke, that "sometimes when he looked into their eyes, he could not help recalling the blood that stained the hands of those responsible for the slaughter of Serbs during the Second World War."[39]

"He could not help recalling" this but he recalled it only "sometimes" under the Tito years' politically imposed and harshly enforced long truce and cohabitation. One can easily see such thinking quickly moving from this relatively latent state to being manifest, central to this man's views about, and bearing toward, the Croats in his sphere, when socialist harmony's patina dissipated in a historical instant and expressing ethnic identities, prejudices, hatreds was unshackled, allowing ethnicity to resume as the main organizing principle of the country's social and political life. So this man smiled disingenuously when such smiling was life's condition, conscious of his real animus toward Croats—perhaps a mixture of hatred and anger, and of questions about what the Croats would again do with opportunity. Would he have smiled the same once life's conditions, once his country's and region's politics, no longer demanded it but instead allowed for the opposite, and more? The same Serb harboring the same beliefs about Croats could, as so many did, become utterly transformed in his outward stance as his beliefs migrated from relative latency to a manifest state calling for urgent action. Hence the reams of testimony, especially from Bosnian Muslims, about their once-friendly neighbors falling upon them, revealing themselves to harbor the worst views, and expressing them physically, by beating, raping, torturing, driving from their homes, and killing those with whom they, as this Serb had, once lived and worked side-by-side smiling.

Tutsi survivors and Hutu mass murderers alike recount how the Hutu's hatred for Tutsi and discrimination against them was the underlying context for neighborly coexistence—which contrary to how some portray it, particularly foreigners who did not live it, was often not so neighborly—and also the context for the Hutu's rapidly turning on them. I spoke about the issue with Esperance Nyirarugira, a rape victim, whose parents, six brothers, and other relatives Hutu neighbors all "cut into pieces with a machete."

Esperance Nyirarugira, Concessa Kayiraba, and Veronique Mukasinafi,
Rwamagana District, Eastern Province, Rwanda, April 2008

Q: Were these just local people who lived near here?

A: Yes, they were living here; they were not only neighbors but also
our friends.

Q: Why would they do that to your family and to others?

A: I really don't know. That one who killed my father was a good
friend of his, very close friend. My dad had given him a cow. I
really don't understand.

Q: Did anybody force them to do it?

A: No. They killed us saying that we were Tutsi.

Q: Did you hear them say other things that would tell us anything
about what they thought of Tutsi or why they were doing it?

A: They were saying that Tutsi are dangerous, that they are snakes,
they should be all killed, they should be exterminated.

Q: And did many people say this?

A: Yes, very many people were saying that.

Q: How is it that they were one day living together and friends and
then how did it change?

A: I really don't know. They changed like animals, we were living
together, marrying each other, and people had kids together.

Her friend, also a rape victim, Concessa Kayiraba agrees that the government "sensitized them [the Hutu] but they wouldn't have done it if they [hadn't] wanted to. They would have said that this person has shared everything with us; water, they have given us food and so on. . . . People you had given cows are the one who came and killed you. People who had married in both families killed their grandchildren. There are so many Hutu women in this area who took their children to hide them at their parents' and they were killed by their brothers. . . . During the genocide people had changed. They had become like animals. They did not have any mercy for anyone." Nyirarugira is clear about the reason for this: "Based on what I saw, Hutu thought of Tutsi as animals. They did not have the value of a human being." Where did it come from?

Q: Before the genocide, did you hear any anti-Tutsi propaganda?
A: Yes, people were saying it.
Q: But what kinds of things were being said?
A: You could pass some people and they shout at you saying, "look at that cockroach," "look at that snake." All those kind of names. And during that time no Tutsi kid would pass in school.

Kayiraba elaborates: "Hutu thought of Tutsi as animals because they were even calling them snakes. They were saying that when you want to kill snakes you hit them on the head. They said a lot of things. But they thought of us like animals . . . dangerous ones. They called us snakes most of the times because a snake is a very dangerous animal and poisonous." According to their friend Veronique Mukasinafi, who with the others are part of a community of rape and genocide survivors, the Hutu used the very same language, images, and motivations from thirty years earlier when Hutu, then persecuting and killing Tutsi, apprehended her father "because they wanted to kill him. They took him and they were going to kill Tutsi, saying that they were cockroaches. They were calling their children snakes. Even in schools they were calling upon Tutsi to stand so that they can see them and Hutu to stay seated. Children were growing up knowing that they were either Tutsi or Hutu."[40]

A powerful, long-standing social discourse in the family, in the schools, by the government, with many signal moments, including the

1959 Hutu assault on Tutsi, conveyed the essential prejudicial notions and fanned that hatred. The Hutu killer Elie Ngarambe conveys the essence of this deeply rooted discourse of multiple strands:

> I am thirty-eight years old, I went to school even though I did not attend primary, and go to secondary. . . . But at school in 1983–1984, I was studying in fifth grade and sixth grade. We used to be taught history. As soon as we entered the classrooms, they were asking your identity. They were asking, who were Hutu. You, this one is a Hutu, son of this one, who was born there, or this one who is a Tutsi was born in that place or there, so we grew up hearing those things. But we were also hearing the same things from our great-grandfather. We were hearing it also from our grandfather. When the war began in 1959 people [Tutsi] managed to flee, they went to the church and they did not . . . they managed to survive, others went to the neighboring provinces and they survived, but you think about it people were united that time. As the time went by . . . the cruelty also increased, the authority became tougher, the authority took tough measures, the enemy became Tutsi. In 1959 Tutsi felt discriminated and they fled away. After the Tutsi had fled Habyarimana took over the power in 1973 and that is when things became worse. It was impossible for Tutsi to get places in schools, and they couldn't get jobs. . . . That is when they started the ideology of discriminating by region and race. It started to be chaos slowly, slowly and it was time for multiple political parties. Things became worse. Even the kid that learned that in school put it in practice based on what the teacher taught him. And that is how the killings started.[41]

Hutu executioners describe how, while growing up around and playing soccer with Tutsi, they thought the worst things about them and said, as the mass murderer Pio Mutungirehe reports, that "we did not want them anywhere around us anymore." Yet without the circumstances to act on these beliefs, they nevertheless lived with them relatively untroubled side-by-side. Another Hutu killer, Léopord Twagirayezu, captures this dissonant situation's social and psychological complexity:

It is awkward to talk about hatred between Hutu and Tutsi, because words changed meaning after the killings. Before, we [Hutu] could fool around among ourselves and say we were going to kill them all, and the next moment we would join them to share some work or a bottle. Jokes and threats were mixed together. We no longer paid heed to what we said. We could toss around awful words without awful thoughts. The Tutsi did not even get very upset. I mean, they didn't draw apart because of those unfortunate discussions. Since then we have seen: those words brought on grave consequences.

As Pio observes, believing and saying the things the Hutu did about the Tutsi, including drawing the logical conclusions about how they should solve their Tutsi problem, "it's already sharpening the machete."[42] And when the Hutu leaders activated the latent beliefs, ordinary Hutu took out their already sharpened machetes and used them. Simmering, smoldering hatreds conveyed in everyday talk are powerful, with a violent potential ready to be tapped. Ngarambe says it well that in the immediate period before the genocide, as the anti-Tutsi public discourse intensified, "the hatred grew, grew, grew, and things became worse when they said that the [president's] plane crashed, because of what they [the Hutu] were taught, they thought 'the enemy has come, he is going to kill you, they are fighting to come and take over the power, so let's kill them [the Tutsi] and finish them all and we keep the country to ourselves."[43]

The Indonesians' mass slaughter of communists surprised nearly all Western observers. Yet when the military engineered one eliminationist context, falsely blaming a failed coup on the lawful and peaceful Indonesian Communist Party, the passionately anticommunist military and religious political parties, with American encouragement, easily decided to initiate the annihilation of the communists. Once deciding upon this eliminationist solution to the electorally ascendant Communist Party's political and social challenge, they easily mobilized anticommunist supporters across Indonesia, many being deeply religious, usually Islamic, of religious parties' and orders' followers, who butchered the atheistic communists among them, usually with bayonets or machetes, often leaving their bodies in rivers or caves, a potent warning to other would-be communists.

The same has happened in so many mass slaughters and eliminations, from Turkey to the Holocaust to Guatemala to Rwanda, in eruptions that sometimes seem to come from nowhere—especially to outsiders knowing little more than that the perpetrators and victims were living intermingled relatively violence-free. Yet upon closer examination, these withering assaults have been shown to enjoy widespread social approval and participation because of hibernating, simmering, or only partly expressed beliefs by the peoples or groups whose members have risen to slaughter or eliminate the people they have always in their heart of hearts wanted to be rid of one way or another. Often members of the perpetrators' group attack in unorganized or impromptu assaults, riots, or pogroms the members of the group the politically centrally initiated eliminationist program eventually victimizes. This in itself indicates eliminationist beliefs' *prior* presence and their easy inflammation into violence. During the 1930s this occurred throughout Germany's towns and villages once the Nazis governed Germany, and in Austria after Germany annexed it. Germans and Austrians previously living peacefully with Jews suddenly turned on them, sometimes at the behest of the regime's officials or paramilitary storm troopers, persecuting them socially and assaulting them physically. In Germany, even before Kristallnacht, the orchestrated nationwide proto-genocidal assault on the Jews in November 1938, Germans had made most of its rural areas and small towns Judenrein, "cleansed" of Jews, the Jews fleeing to the big cities' relative anonymity. When in March 1938 the Germans marched in, ordinary Austrians spontaneously and ferociously assaulted and degraded the Jews among them, surprising even the Germans. Scenes of fur-bedecked Viennese women gleefully watching Jews compelled to wash streets with toothbrushes were emblematic. Then when the German government moved the eliminationist assault to its mass-murdering phase, many of these and other ordinary Germans and Austrians willingly lent themselves to it body and soul.

A particularly significant moment when latent eliminationist beliefs became suddenly activated occurred across Eastern Europe, including in many locales in Lithuania, Ukraine, and Romania, in the immediate wake of the Germans' attack on the Soviet Union at the end of June 1941. With the Germans' emerging exterminationist assault upon the

Jews giving the green light to the local peoples to vent their hatreds in violence, they sometimes in security forces, sometimes in paramilitaries, sometimes in impromptu groups, fell upon the Jews who for generations had lived among them, slaughtering them mercilessly, torturing them gleefully, sparing the Germans from doing the job themselves. In Eastern Galicia, Ukrainians rose up to slaughter Jews in village after village. Yeoshua Gertner, a survivor, reports from Eastern Galicia's Kossiv region:

We received reports from villages in the high mountains that initially struck us as hard to believe. The Hutsuls in the village of Jablonica, part of a mountain-dwelling Ukrainian group that had always lived in peace and harmony with the Jews, had seized the Jews in the village, locked them in a cellar on the pretext that the Romanians were coming to exterminate them, and herded them into the torrential Cheremosh River, where they all drowned. The man who had instigated this crime was reportedly the village priest. Only one Jewish woman survived; she fled to Kosov after the culprits had gone away. The next day the Hutsuls entered the neighboring village. To assure that no one would escape, they bound the Jews in barbed wire, in groups of three, before they tossed them into the rushing waters. There were seventy-four victims. The murderers looted everything they had left behind.

Having completed their slaughter in the neighboring village, they went on to nearby Hriniowa. The Hutsuls who lived there, however, would not let them enter the village, maintaining that the killing of Jews was a matter for those native to the village, not for outsiders. In Hriniowa, no Jews were murdered; the local Hutsuls merely drove them from the village to Zabie and then looted their possessions.

In Kosov, Hutsuls recounted what their priest had said about this in his sermon: those from Jablonica were much liked in the eyes of God, because they had both dispossessed *and* drowned the Jews; they would certainly be rewarded with Paradise. But the Hutsuls from Hriniowa, the priest intoned, would not enter the Garden of Eden. Yes, they had totally dispossessed the Jews but, for having been so neglectful as to spare their lives, would surely go to hell.[44]

This uncoordinated but similar array of exterminationist forays, led by local elites, including sometimes priests who consecrated the exterminationist assaults, expressed the dual pathology of the powerful antisemitism coursing through the local cultures and peoples. The first pathology was the antisemitism itself, which, though differing from the racist-based form predominating among Germans, nevertheless was a fearsome religious-based antisemitism thoroughly demonizing the Jews as Christ killers, spoilers, and exploiters. The second pathology was this first one's outgrowth, namely the antisemitically induced identification of the local Jews with the godless Bolsheviks, who had since 1939 occupied these regions, owing to the Hitler-Stalin Pact that had temporarily carved up Poland and other parts of Eastern Europe between the two mass murderers. Because the local peoples, as a matter of antisemitic hallucination, conceived of the Jews collectively as Bolsheviks, working with the Bolsheviks and committing or supporting the Bolsheviks' crimes, when the Soviets retreated before the Germans' military onslaught, they rose to rid themselves finally of the putative alien and pernicious Jewish presence, and did so with vengeance's ferocious motivational fury in the most telling and cruel ways, by the hundreds and thousands in community after community. These mass murders are particularly significant because they, like so many of our time's eliminationist assaults, demonstrate latent eliminationist beliefs rapidly channeling toward mass murder, and for two other reasons: Across regions and countries, from the north of Eastern Europe toward the south, the same latent hatred, without coordination, issued in kindred murderous results. Second, the local peoples committing the mass murder served not their own governments but an alien occupying force that had no legitimate authority over them whatsoever. The local peoples turned perpetrators were in no sense acting under state compulsion, or being obedient to authority, or being subjected to peer pressure by those serving in state units, or carrying out bureaucratic assignments. The local peoples turned willful perpetrators, finally able to act with impunity, were plainly and simply having a go at, and taking subjective revenge on, the hated and demonized Jews.

If we think clearly about what we know about individual and social life in general, instead of allowing exterminationist and eliminationist assaults' enormity to turn our heads inside-out, and to be explained away with mind-numbing clichés as out-of-this-world phenomena, then we can immediately grasp the normalcy of simmering, latent beliefs suddenly becoming manifest, potent, and deadly, and politically, which means as part of politics, how this works. How many individuals know others they believe (correctly or incorrectly) have wronged, injured, or treated them grossly unfairly, and, if allowed, would be happy, even eager, to beat up, "teach a lesson to," "pay back," perhaps kill them—and to do so with gusto? Some people feel this way about neighbors, coworkers, members of their social circle, not to mention competitors, outright antagonists, and those having vanquished them. Yet, with exceptions, these same people do not express their anger and hatreds, their conception of their tormentors' due—in action or usually even verbally in public. Perhaps they do not think about it much, certainly not in these terms, because vengeance's sine qua non—the opportunity to act with impunity—will never present itself. Yet if opportunity ever materialized, so the angry, resentful, and hating person could act with guaranteed impunity, even with social approval, then he likely would take his vengeance. If we think beyond one individual, to many people with such simmering hatreds born of the belief that another's willful hands had unjustly and gravely harmed each of them, would we not expect many to eagerly exact revenge when socially sanctioned opportunity and impunity appeared?

Why is it so hard to accept the same about the subterranean phenomenon of dehumanized and demonized conceptions of other people and other groups, of beliefs deeming them pernicious, dangerous, a source of great injury or a potential threat? They too burst out when political leaders offer bearers of such views the opportunity to vent them in word and particularly in deed. This is the real beast within unleashed. It is not some Conradian brute indiscriminately assaulting any targets just for fun, or some will-less automaton killing anyone just because someone tells him he should, or some fictitious bureaucratic mentality supposedly controlling the minds of modern man and woman. The beast is the latent prejudices, hatreds, and beliefs in others' guilt or danger, which, when widely socially shared, quickly become manifest, and can be politically mobilized to produce eliminationist conflagrations.

Nothing could be more ordinary.

CHAPTER NINE

Actual Minds, Actual Worlds

PERHAPS THE MOST STUNNING fact about eliminationist and extermi-nationist politics is that the perpetrators almost always get their vic-tims. In few social and political endeavors of comparable scale are the goals so regularly and fully achieved. Indeed, large eliminationist on-slaughts, as we now know, usually begin only when the perpetrators are confident of success, owing to the overwhelmingly superior force they can unleash against defenseless people. More easily than the German army swept away the archaic Polish army in September 1939, the per-petrators, steamrolling stunned civilian populations, kill and eliminate a strikingly high percentage of their intended victims—often approaching 100 percent. We know this because indications of failure—substantial armed resistance, perpetrator casualties, mass escapes (that are not ef-fectively expulsions)—rarely exist.

Thus, unlike with other state policies, what produces an elimina-tionist policy's *successful* implementation is not the issue. Instead, it is: What do the perpetrators *want* to do, and why? Perpetrators' wants and their ensuing acts are themselves embedded in a larger transfor-mative agenda of recasting and refashioning their world. What kinds of worlds do the perpetrators seek to create? What worlds do they make?

Eliminationist politics is a politics of radical refashioning. Those pur-suing it seek to transform societies and politics, by eradicating popula-tions, recasting power relations, and homogenizing culture, values, and practices. The perpetrators thoroughly alter their domain—locally, na-tionally, regionally, or globally—leaders *and* followers swaggering godlike to transform their world as folk myths have gods do. Nikita Khrushchev, Joseph Stalin's successor, recounts Stalin's words upon deciding to move against Yugoslavia: "All I have to do is wiggle my finger and there will be no more Tito." Khrushchev adds: "He didn't succeed in the case of Tito. But inside our country he butchered and annihilated millions of people."[1] German planners in the Ministry for the Occupied Eastern Territories, animated by their politics' untrammeled eliminationist spirit, drew up blueprints to deport to (not yet conquered) Siberia thirty-one million of the forty-five million inhabitants of large swaths of Eastern Europe, including Poland, Ukraine, and the Baltics, noting almost in passing the extermination of the region's five million to six million Jews. The Hutu became euphoric at refashioning their world. Elie Ngarambe, in the thick of it, explains: "Everyone who was a Hutu at that time during that regime, he thought of himself as strong, he thought he was on the top, he even thought that nothing would touch him, he even thought that the death was . . . death would not come down on him and kill him. He was hearing people [Tutsi] dying on the hill, cries of agony, noises. People. . . . and he was thinking he was powerful. I think he thought that there were no consequences. He thought he was successful. He thought that nothing would happen to him. He thought there was nothing. . . . nothing would happen to him or nothing would touch him. So, he thought only that one is supposed to die, and that the death would never approach him."[2]

Many ancient myths are Manichean tales of good and evil, creation and destruction, joy and suffering, and the world's shaping and reshaping. Such myths resonate with many perpetrators' self-conceptions, vaulting aspirations, and omnipotent powers to obliterate hated peoples— as Turks thought about Armenians, Germans about Jews, and Hutu about Tutsi. They resonate with why and what the perpetrators do to alter the world. They resonate with the perpetrators' dual sense of acting in goodness's cause *and* without restraint. Human conduct's ordinary rules do not apply. Volcanic violence and the eradication of peoples ensues. What could be more godlike?

Seeing the perpetrators as godlike and world refashioners is still more apt for those self-consciously acting in a deity's name, often a secular god, in order to serve their people, purify them, hasten the end of days, prevent the apocalypse. While perpetrators are focused on the enemy before them—the individual Herero, Armenian, Jew, Pole, Korean, Kulak, Chinese, Kikuyu, communist, Bangladeshi imperialist, Maya, Kurd, Bosnian, Tutsi, Hutu, or infidel—they concentrate on the immediate task. Yet they also know that their eliminationist politics refashions their world. They discuss it. They see it. They understand how they do it.

From top to bottom eliminationist perpetrators refashion the world, yet the transformations do not all have the same effects or origins. Understanding the actual refashionings requires us to look to the perpetrators' actual mindsets, to their conceptions of what they want, including crucially their conceptions of the victims whom the perpetrators (wrongly) understand as the causes of their actions.*

I examine here four of the central refashionings of eliminationist perpetrators. I start with their most general reshaping of the world, their overall treatment, and variation in treatment, of different victim groups, including relative mortality rates. *Actual minds do create different eliminationist worlds.* I then move to a critical, underinvestigated theme, how *actual minds create different communal worlds*, namely the perpetrators' communities. The perpetrators have a ready-made new social world, their eliminationist institutions. Beyond them, the perpetrators are embedded in a series of broader communities, including national communities, each a world of relations, sometimes overlapping, sometimes discrete, which the perpetrators alter to varying degrees. One such communal world, the camp world, bears special attention, as perpetrators are its founders. *Actual minds create different camp worlds*, for the perpetrators a new societal system, and for the victims a new immiserating world. Why do they create this new world, and how do different camp systems function? Finally, at the most personal, elemental level, *actual minds create different personal worlds*. The perpetrators refashion their own and their victims' individual worlds, with their personalized treatment of every individual, especially with their mind- and body-destroying cruelty.

Perpetrators' *different actual minds* producing different eliminationist politics *create different actual worlds*.

---

*Although perpetrators' intentions are not relevant for *defining* mass murders and eliminations, they are critical for the different task of explaining eliminationism's various outcomes.

Eliminationist Worlds

When political leaders activate eliminationist beliefs and their bearers are ready to act on their logic, two things conjoin to greatly influence what happens: the perpetrators' and especially the leaders' conception of the victims (dehumanized or demonized, and the nature of their threat) and their political goals, including for social and political transformation. The perpetrators' *thinking* about the world in itself produces substantial variation in their reshaping of it, in their treatment of victims and potential victims. *Different* eliminationist regimes' perpetrators differently dispose of victim groups. And a *single* eliminationist regime's perpetrators also often treat different victim groups dissimilarly.

We can further examine these variations by looking at certain regimes, conventionally called totalitarian, that, in seeking to refashion society or the multitude of societies, have initiated vast domestic and international eliminationist programs to exert total control, purify, fend off the apocalypse, bring about the promised paradisial future.

Within the Germans' empire, the differential treatment of the peoples of different "races," biologies, and allegiances varied on so many dimensions that just a few examples must suffice. Beginning with the most obvious but wholly overlooked issue, never accorded its critical analytical significance, are the peoples Germans marked or did not mark for eliminationist treatment. Neither the German leadership nor those implementing policies treated all conquered peoples similarly.

Against the French, Germany's greatest and most dangerous enemy, the Germans did *not* undertake a mass eliminationist assault. In seventy years, the Germans and French had fought three major wars. In World War I, Germany suffered a devastating and humiliating military defeat, followed by the Versailles Treaty's ignominious postwar settlement, which Germans principally blamed on the French. Germany had to cede substantial regions to various countries, including Alsace-Lorraine to France and the Saar to a fifteen-year League of Nations mandate, which meant French occupation until 1935. Germany had to pay economically crippling reparations to France, and, owing to conflicts over reparations in 1923, France occupied and pillaged Germany's industrial heartland, the Ruhr, producing Germany's most ruinous economic disaster ever, hyperinflation: One trillion marks equaled one dollar. During World War II, the German occupation of France was severe, but Germany did not even initially occupy all of France, granting its southern part formal independence with its own (albeit puppet) government in Vichy. The Germans did not systematically exterminate the French, save French Jews. French life, society, and culture continued.

Flanking Germany to the east as France did to the west was militarily anemic Poland. Poles had not caused Germany and Germans a hundredth of the conflict, loss of life, and suffering the French had. For decades, France loomed largest in Germany's geostrategic and military thinking, as a concern and an actual martial antagonist. Poland and Poles were a comparative afterthought, having not even existed as an independent country for a hundred years. The Versailles Treaty resurrected it, ceded it German territories, thus giving Germany one realistic antagonism against Poland paralleling France. Yet unlike the Germans' conventional, if exploitive and brutal, occupation of France, the Germans articulated and practiced thoroughgoing eliminationist politics against the Polish people and were turning Poland into a giant concentration camp. They slaughtered segments of the Polish elite and many other Poles (in addition to the nearly completed extermination of Poland's three million Jews) and were reducing those Poles they would not kill or expel into helots, beings toiling in abject servitude and slavery. Martin Bormann, Adolf Hitler's chief of staff, in "Eight Principles for the Government of the Eastern Territories," summarized Hitler's views on the Poles' and other Slavic peoples' futures the Germans were creating:

> The Slavs are to work for us. Insofar as we don't need them, they may die. Therefore compulsory vaccination and German health services are superfluous. The fertility of the Slavs is undesirable. They may use contraceptives and practice abortion, the more the better. Education is dangerous. It is sufficient if they can count up to a hundred. At best an education is admissible which produces useful servants for us. Every educated person is a future enemy. Religion we leave to them as a means of diversion. As to food, they are not to get more than necessary. We are the masters, we come first.[3]

The Germans' vastly different treatment of the French and the Poles had nothing to do with war, nothing to do with each peoples' respective enmity for Germans or suffering they had caused Germans, nothing to do with the intensity of the ethnic conflicts, nothing to do with Germans' psychological reaction to fortune, whether good or bad, and nothing to do with their expectations or the realities of either people's resistance. The Germans' different treatment of the French and Poles had nothing to do with these or the other structural explanations denying the perpetrators' agency and the critical, almost all-defining element: the Germans' racial-biological conception of each national group. Indeed, structural explanations suggest that had the Germans subjected one of the peoples to an eliminationist assault, they would have targeted the French. But the Germans did the opposite. Why? From Hitler on down, Germans considered the French (though enemies) part of the human family, but the Poles a subhuman race, rightless beings for the master race to use or eliminate as necessary. Even more acutely, the related question poses itself: Why did the Germans slate the defenseless Jews for total extermination? Many Jews were themselves devoted and loyal Germans. Non-German Jews, many germanophiles, loved German culture, teaching their children German. Unlike the French, they harbored no enmity for and had never harmed Germany.

Surveying Europe, the Germans' treatment of conquered peoples, in overall policy and by the ordinary Germans on the ground, accorded with the Germans' notions of different "races" and peoples, and about individual and group biology, which, bizarrely, came down to stature, physiognomy, coloration, and notions about "blood." They privileged tall, blond and blue-eyed, thin-faced people. They valued peoples or "races" in particular, and then individuals within different races, mainly according to the people's proximity to or distance from this racist ideal. The Germans treated the Nordic peoples, such as Danes, the best, Western Europeans the next best, southern Europeans worse but still much better than Slavic peoples, whom they treated most brutally and murderously, except for peoples Germans deemed racially or biologically polluted or dangerous, mentally ill and developmentally disabled people, Sintis, Romas, and the Jews.

Any theory or explanation of mass murder or elimination must account for the Jews' singular position among eliminationism's victims, during our time *and* throughout history. Jews have been eliminationist politics' most frequent and varied victims—victimized longer, by the most diverse groups of perpetrators, and in the most countries. Speaking this obvious truth about the Jews' singularity as victims does not make their mass murder or eliminationist persecutions factually or morally worse.[4] It merely establishes factual differences, and that any general account must prominently deal with the singularity. Furthermore, because so many states, regimes, and peoples have practiced eliminationism toward Jews in so many forms, the Jews' fate provides particular insight into eliminationist politics and assaults. Just as the Nazis were our time's most omnivorous and versatile mass murderers and eliminators, their principal, most passionately pursued victims, the Jews, are unparalleled among eliminationist onslaughts' victims. More specifically:

1. The Holocaust is our time's only mass murder where the perpetrators consciously sought (even declaring as much) the *total* extermination of the targeted group, without exception, everywhere (even if their immediate operational plans were mainly restricted to the *entire* European continent). Heinrich Himmler, the head of the SS, in a self-congratulatory speech in 1943 to the assembled governmental and Nazi Party leaders, at once echoed their common beliefs and articulated the imperative guiding their ongoing campaign: "This people must disappear from the face of the earth."[5]

2. The Holocaust (together with the parallel killing of the Sinti and Roma) is the only mass murder that perpetrators carried out outside their country *not* aimed at territorial aggrandizement or consolidation.

3. Aside from a few other groups the Nazis targeted, the Holocaust is the only mass murder without any foundation in realistic conflict.

4. The Holocaust is the only mass murder assented and contributed to by significant portions of many different national, ethnic, and religious groups (some themselves being attacked by the Germans), and in which coalitions of governments participated in an *international genocidal alliance*.

5. The Jews are the only group against whom there has been and continues to be (among Political Islamists and many Arabs) an

ongoing eliminationist politics (including exterminationist moments) across centuries, even millennia, perpetrated by enormously varied regimes, political movements, and peoples. These eliminationist politics have also spanned three continents and found grounding in two major religions, Christianity and Islam, and the world's principal secular religion, Marxism.

6. The Jews are the only people attacked for being wealthy and being poor, for being stateless and having a state, for remaining separate from countries' majority groups and assimilating into them, for being religious and being secular.

7. The profound anti-Jewish prejudice, known as antisemitism, whatever its sometimes substantial variations, is the only discourse, ideology, hatred that was and is truly transnational and woven into modern (as well as premodern) civilization's very fabric.[6] Hence the eliminationist assault upon Jews' transnationality and endurance.

The distinctiveness of the Germans' total annihilationist assault upon the Jews in itself shows that the Germans' conception of peoples and groups (also shaping the Germans' political, including imperial, designs) explains not only whom they targeted (Jews and Poles) and did not target (Danes and French) for eliminationist politics. It also explains the Germans' differing eliminationist means and treatment of the various peoples they did choose to target in eliminationist onslaughts. Sociologist Anna Pawełczyńska, a Polish survivor of Auschwitz, explains:

A prisoner's nationality and citizenship . . . became a differentiating criterion with far-reaching consequences for his or her chances of surviving. Replacing national distinctions, pseudo-scientific theories of race began to take drastic effect by ranking the different nationalities of prisoners, thus spelling out for them their turns to die. That ranking decidedly foredoomed their chances of survival. First place in this sequence of dying was assigned to prisoners of Jewish descent and Gypsies . . . and the proof was their mass murder through the use of assembly-line techniques.

Slavs (especially Poles and Soviet citizens) were put in second place; the expressions of this were the various methods of murder used against them at different times and the (unrealized) program of general sterilization.

Third came the other nations of Europe for whom (as the documents show) the program of extermination or exploitation had not been precisely established. Only prisoners of German nationality were excluded from this plan; for this and various other reasons the odds for their survival were considerably greater than those of other prisoners.[7]

The Germans' conception of various peoples and groups is the *only* adequate explanation for which peoples the Germans exterminated totally or partially, and if partially, to what degree, for which peoples the Germans were helotizing, and how they prioritized their eliminationist assaults. It is the only adequate explanation for the relative death rates of different peoples in structurally similar situations (as the Mauthausen camp figures, cited in Chapter 4, show), and, as I discuss shortly, the Germans' treatment of different peoples' children and relative cruelty toward different victim peoples. It is the only adequate explanation for the Germans' use of nonexterminationist means when dealing with other putatively lesser beings or lesser threats, and that while all other eliminationist perpetrators also employ various eliminationist means and partial assaults on their victims, the Germans always deemed nonlethal measures against the Jews inadequate unless as a stepping stone (which is how the Germans usually conceived of them) to utter extermination. Friedrich Übelhör, the top civil administrator in the Łódź District of Poland, articulated this when discussing the eventually highly productive Łódź Ghetto's establishment: "The creation of the ghetto is, of course, only a transition measure. I shall determine at what time and with what means the ghetto—and thereby also the city of Łódź—will be cleansed of Jews. The final goal, at any rate, must be that we burn out this bubonic plague utterly."[8] The final goal. Bubonic plague. Burn it out. Utterly. He might have added for the history of eliminationist assaults: only *by* the Germans and only *for* the Jews.

Finally, and also analytically ignored, the Nazis failed to treat their real and dangerous domestic enemies as every structural theory and every theory of totalitarian politics mandates. The German political Left, especially communists, were the Nazis' bitter enemies, having fought them in the Weimar Republic's streets, and after World War I taken power temporarily with a revolutionary insurgency in Bavaria. The German Left had a million-fold large, disciplined, and martial followership. Yet the Nazis did not proceed as communist totalitarian regimes did, to systematically eliminate their real enemies—the Soviets established their initial "Terror" and gulag for their czarist and other enemies. The Nazis killed comparatively few among these real domestic enemies, even among their leadership, and left their millions of followers all but unscathed—relatively unmolested, unmonitored, unthreatened. Yet in the Soviet Union's western regions, the Germans did the opposite, extirpating the bearers of Soviet communism, which they conceived of as "Jewish-Bolshevism," a Jewish-created and -controlled ideological disease and threat.

Why the difference? Why yet another instance of an eliminationist assault's absence, especially given the Nazis' unequaled readiness to practice eliminationist politics? The Nazis' racism deemed German communists and socialists members of the master race, meaning that when cured of the putative poisonous influence of the Jews and of their communist ideological leaders, they would embrace Nazism and help build the Nazi-Germanic empire and future. As in almost every critical respect, here the Nazi leaders knew their people well, correctly expecting that legions of the political Left's rank and file, sharing their racist views, would forsake their Marxism and willingly contribute to the Jews' elimination and Europe's conquest and subjugation.

The communist Khmer Rouge resembled the Germans in much of Europe by turning Cambodia into a gargantuan camp, though the Khmer Rouge exerted a thorough totalitarian penetration of social life that other regimes seeking total control only dream of, and to which the Nazis never aspired or came close to achieving. (For non-Jewish, non-gay, non-Gypsy Germans, the Nazis allowed a surprising degree of freedom.) The Khmer Rouge, like the Nazis, designated a range of ideological enemies, considered, to various degrees, polluted racially and by foreign acculturation, and also differentially dangerous to the Khmer Rouge and the putatively pure Khmer (Cambodian) people. Even though the Khmer Rouge controlled all Cambodians equally, their eliminationist orientation, like that of the Germans, played itself out markedly differently with different groups.

The Khmer Rouge wanted to utterly purify the Khmer people according to their antimodern, racist, Marxist ideological amalgam, calling for primitive socialist equality and conformity. This accounts for their hatred of urban life and their intention that only racially pure Khmer live within Cambodia. The Khmer Rouge sought to reduce or destroy the country's putative polluted essence by eliminating all people of non-Khmer races, religions, locales, and allegiance. Theirs was to be the most thoroughgoing and rapid eliminationist transformation yet. In September 1975, the Khmer Rouge leaders told Cambodia's former ruler Prince Norodom Sihanouk they wanted to outdo their role models, the communist Chinese: "We want to have our name in history as the ones who can reach total communism with one leap forward. So we have to be more extremist than Madame Mao Tse-tung and the Cultural Revolution leadership in China. We want to be known as the only communist party to communize a country without a step-by-stop policy, without going through socialism."[9] In 1976 the Khmer Rouge expressed similar aspirations and self-praise in their government's newspaper, criticizing the Vietnamese communists as "too slow": "The Khmer method has no need of numerous personnel. We've overturned the basket, and with it all the fruit it contained. From now on we will choose only the fruit that suit us perfectly. The Vietnamese have removed only the rotten fruit and this causes them to lose time." On the radio, the Khmer Rouge broadcasted their guiding ideological maxims, including: "What is infected must be cut out," and "What is too long must be shortened and made the right length."[10] As the Khmer Rouge wanted only people suiting them "perfectly," the range and number of those infected or too long, needing to be cut out or shortened, was expansive.

The Khmer Rouge's ideology held modern and urban life to be inauthentically Khmer. In their first act to overturn the entire fruit basket, within days of taking power, they began to eliminate people from cities, driving millions on death marches to inhospitable rural destinations. The Khmer Rouge, the modern world's most extreme levelers, then subjected Cambodians to an ideologically driven brutal regimen expressing the radical eliminationist orientation that made Cambodia our time's most murderous small country. Arn Yan, a survivor, explains, the Khmer Rouge's "doctrine gave us no human rights, no sympathy, and no freedom to do anything." The Khmer Rouge treated any failure to conform, however inadvertent or unavoidable, as a willful assault upon the regime. That is why, as Yan recalls, "sometimes we would make only a small mistake but they pointed us out to the killers and we would be killed."[11] Nevertheless, the Khmer Rouge's lethality varied greatly for different Cambodian groups, flowing, as it did, from the leaders' and their followers' differing conceptions of those groups. This included their fundamentally differentiated conception and treatment of *base people*, also known as *old people*, those under the Khmer Rouge's territorial control prior to their final military conquest of all Cambodia, whom the Khmer Rouge therefore favored, and of *new people*, those falling into the Khmer Rouge's hands with the final victory, and therefore, only due to this small temporal difference, not an ethnic difference, deemed far less reliable. Under the Khmer Rouge, approximate death tolls and mortality figures were:[12]

Approximate Death Tolls Under the Khmer Rouge, 1975–1979

Social Group	1975 Population	Number Who Perished	Percentage
"New People"			
urban Khmer	2,000,000	500,000	25
rural Khmer	600,000	150,000	25
Chinese (all urban)	430,000	215,000	50
Vietnamese (urban)	10,000	10,000	100
Lao (rural)	10,000	4,000	40
Total new people	3,050,000	879,000	29
"Base People"			
rural Khmer	4,500,000	675,000	15
[Khmer Krom]	[5,000]	[2,000]	[40]
Cham (all rural)	250,000	90,000	36
Vietnamese (rural)	10,000	10,000	100
Thai (rural)	20,000	8,000	40
upland minorities	60,000	9,000	15
Total base people	4,840,000	792,000	16
Total Cambodia	7,890,000	1,671,000	21

This regime's murderousness, like the Nazis', was clearly differentiated and targeted according to its conception of the victims. Chhun Von explains that "the old people, they have more rights, they have more freedom, they have enough food to eat. They have a good doctor to treat them when they get sick, but the new people never. They treat the new people like animals."[13] The Khmer Rouge killed *base* (or *old*) *people* and *new people* at very different rates. The mortality rate among the new people was 80 percent greater. For the rural Khmer alone, the most privileged social category, the Khmer Rouge killed those deemed new at a two-thirds greater rate than those deemed old. And much testimony from survivors verifies that these differential numbers also reflected the Khmer Rouge perpetrators' much greater harshness and brutality and outright murderousness toward the new people. Teeda Butt Mam, a survivor, conveys the Khmer Rouge's mindset:

> The people on the Khmer Rouge death list were the group called the city people. They were the "new" people. These were any Cambodian men, women, girls, boys, and babies who did not live in their "liberated zones" before they won the war in 1975. Their crime was that they lived in the enemy's zone, helping and supporting the enemy.
>
> The city people were the enemy, and the list was long. Former soldiers, the police, the CIA and the KGB. Their crime was fighting in the civil war. The merchants, the capitalists, and the businessmen. Their crime was exploiting the poor. The rich farmers and the landlords. Their crime was exploiting the peasants. The intellectuals, the doctors, the lawyers, the monks, the teachers, and the civil servants. These people thought, and their memories were tainted by the evil Westerners. Students were getting education to exploit the poor. Former celebrities, the poets. These people carried bad memories of the old, corrupted Cambodia.
>
> The list goes on and on. The rebellious, the kind-hearted, the brave, the clever, the individualists, the people who wore glasses, the literate, the popular, the complainers, the lazy, those with talent, those with trouble getting along with others, and those with soft hands. These people were corrupted and lived off the blood and sweat of the farmers and the poor.
>
> Very few of us escaped these categories.[14]

No data capture the mortality rate of people the Khmer Rouge considered particularly westernized—the highly educated and professionals—especially ideologically polluted and dangerous. Yet much testimony indicates the perpetrators were particularly brutal and murderous toward them, targeting them initially for extermination.

The Khmer Rouge's racism, wedded to its apocalyptic vision of Cambodia's current situation and future, inspired them to adopt a near total eliminationist policy against non-Khmer races and people putatively bearing non-Khmer cultural sources. This was presaged in the regime's ideological declaration that ethnic minorities, more than 15 percent of Cambodia, composed only 1 percent of the population—an error likely reflecting the Khmer Rouge's racist and cultural eliminationist politics' intent, rather than a wildly poor demographic estimate. Conceiving of people with skin lighter than the dark putative pure Khmer as corrupted, the Khmer Rouge sought to eliminate them. Moly Ly recalls that one day, "About fifty families were transferred to another district. . . . A few days later it was revealed by the local soldiers that these families had Vietnamese blood and for that reason were put to death. I lost quite a few friends, most of them were Chinese Cambodians. The complexion of their skin was only a little lighter than mine."[15] This was one small moment in the Khmer Rouge's campaign to eradicate ethnic Vietnamese Cambodians. Upon taking power they expelled 85 percent of them and then annihilated *all* remaining twenty thousand. By 1979 no ethnic Vietnamese remained alive in the country.

The Khmer Rouge's eliminationist campaign included exterminating the Chams, an indigenous people, deemed doubly suspect due to their distinct ethnicity and Islamic faith. They expelled the Chams from their 113 villages, murdering 100,000 and sprinkling the remaining 150,000 in small groups around the country. They slaughtered the Chams' leaders and elites, banned their "foreign language," and prohibited Islam. One Cham peasant explains, "Some Cham villages completely disappeared; only two or three people remained. We were persecuted much more than Khmers."[16] They killed about 40 percent of other ethnic minorities, Chinese, Laotians, and Thais. They appear to have entirely obliterated one people, the Kola, numbering perhaps two thousand. They considered Buddhist monks the bearers of an alien religious encrustation upon Cambodians. It may be that only 3 percent of seventy thousand monks survived.

The Khmer Rouge's murderousness and brutality varied regionally. On the ground, local perpetrators greatly affect targeted peoples' fate.

The Khmer Rouge leadership's infighting for power and position also led to differential murderousness and some internal purges. Nevertheless, the overall and highly differentiated eliminationist assaults upon the different discrete groups is unmistakable, driven by the Khmer Rouge's conception of humanity and of existing and desired Cambodian politics and society. They wanted to eliminate the categories of urban dwellers and urban life; indeed they seemed to want to eradicate urban life's very notion, so they emptied the cities, towns, and even villages. They beheld the Vietnamese as the Khmers' ancient foe to be totally eradicated, so they expelled most and slaughtered the rest. They especially targeted elites, including Khmers, for extermination. They exterminated non-Khmer religious bearers, both Buddhist and Islamic, almost completely.

The relationship between intent and action here is ironclad and unmistakable. Eerily reminiscent of the German leadership's discussion at the Wannsee Conference of their already operational plans to exterminate European Jewry, Pol Pot, shortly after taking power, laid down the general contours of the Khmer Rouge's eliminationist program at their five-day leadership meeting. Monks "had to be wiped out." The Chams, as a putatively foreign and an Islamic people, had to be utterly eliminated as a people, with a large percentage slaughtered and the rest expelled, scattered, and repressed. The remaining Khmer, differentiated in Khmer Rouge thinking, needed their ranks radically thinned, albeit at a much lower rate, which amounted to this backward-looking Marxist-racist regime and its adherents murdering a still stunning 15 percent to 25 percent in less than five years. Had the hundred thousand or so Vietnamese the Khmer Rouge chose to eliminate through expulsion resisted and tried to stay in their homes, the Khmer Rouge certainly would have slaughtered every last one—just as they killed all the remaining Vietnamese—in which case they would have murdered not 20,000 but 120,000. This is, among our time's many other instances, an unambiguous example of eliminationist means' interchangeability, the perpetrators deeming expulsion and killing equivalent substitutes and solutions to the same problem. This again underscores that examining mass killing in isolation of other eliminationist acts fundamentally fails to specify the real political and social phenomenon, and inherently produces erroneous analyses and conclusions. Because the

Khmer Rouge differentiated Cambodia's people according to ascriptive and racist categories, they generally did not distinguish among men and women, or adults and children. To them, each person's nature was principally determined not by his or her deeds or threats or by individual acculturation or stances but by the perpetrators' social and political mapping of each person's group membership. The Khmer Rouge conceived of westernized people, the racially impure, and others as "carriers of germs." Their imputed corruption was infectious, an incurable, dangerous virus threatening everyone. Thus the Khmer Rouge leaders urged their followers to "cut down" and "uproot" not only those whose putative nature or actions earned them this fate, but also their children.[17]

Just as the peoples and groups a given eliminationist system's perpetrators choose to target vary, and just as the perpetrators' relative lethality toward different target groups varies, death rates also vary enormously from one eliminationist system to the next. Because mass annihilation and elimination are purposeful and discretionary political acts, such systems' variable overall destructiveness needs to be explained rather than ignored, taken for granted as such systems' natural feature, or treated as structural features of such systems, regimes, the international order, etc. Take five major eliminationist political systems oriented toward refashioning their domestic or regional worlds with a sustained eliminationist orientation and programs: communist China, Soviet Union, Nazi Germany, imperial Japan, and Khmer Rouge. Although establishing a firm numerical basis for comparison is hard, because death tolls are imprecise and the adequate metric, owing to the vastly differently sized (and in some cases rapidly changing) populations under each regime's control, is difficult to establish, some instructive conclusions can be drawn. Even if a higher estimate is correct that the Soviets killed on the order of 20 million people during their thirty-five years of mass murdering, the yearly average would be close to 600,000 people. If the lower 8.5 million estimate is correct, the yearly average would be 250,000. The communist Chinese killed on the order of 50 million during their twenty-six years of systematic mass murdering that coincided with Mao's reign, so approximately 2 million a year. (This excludes the Chinese's longer and annually less deadly eliminationist campaign in Tibet, which, if included, would substantially reduce the yearly average.) The Japanese annihilated on the order of 6 million people during their eight years of mass murdering, a yearly toll of 750,000 (a higher estimate of 10 million makes the yearly average 1.25 million). The Khmer Rouge killed by far the highest percentage of their (small) dominion's people, roughly 20 percent, though the yearly total was less than these other regimes, about 400,000. The Germans killed on the order of 20 million people during their four years of systematic mass murdering, making them by far the most intensive mass murderers, at almost 5 million annually. Even if we date their systematic mass murdering from the war's beginning in 1939, rather than the implementation of their coincident decision in 1941 to systematically slaughter the Jews and attack the Soviet Union, this still yields the highest yearly mass-murder rate at 3.3 million. The Germans' extermination of the Jews, at 1.5 million per year, makes just this aspect of their mass murdering more *annually* annihilationist than the other regimes' total mass murdering, except for that of the communist Chinese. The Germans' murderousness of the Jews was so intensive, even before they had moved to their eliminationist assault's explicit total exterminationist phase, that had the communist totalitarian regimes adopted that killing rate (the percentage of total inhabitants killed per year), they would have reached their actual victim totals much sooner. At the Germans' killing rate (mainly through starvation) in the Warsaw Ghetto camp, which shortly after its establishment with about a half million Jews was about 1 percent per month, or more than 10 percent per year, the Soviets would have killed all their victims (depending on the estimate) in about half a year to one year, instead of thirty-five. The communist Chinese would have needed a little more than a half year, not a quarter century. Even the thoroughly murderous Khmer Rouge would have murdered all their victims in less than half the actual time.

Why did the Germans' annual mass-murder rate exceed, indeed dwarf, the others' already colossal rates?* Unlike that of the various communist murderers and the Japanese, the Germans' creed was *explicitly annihilationist*. As a core matter of ideology and policy it called for the elimination, with a lethal reflexiveness, of tens of millions (eventually

---

*Accounting for population size, the Germans' rate compared to that of the second largest per-year killers, the communist Chinese, becomes enormously greater. The Chinese dominion contained more than 700 million people, two to five times that of the Germans (fluctuating with the war's course) during their most intensive mass murdering.

probably hundreds of millions) of people. Unlike the communists, the Germans did not want to rehabilitate people they incorporated through conquest, because they grounded most of their victims' undesirability in their imputed racial and biologically based inferiority and perniciousness. The Germans' proactive plans to annihilate an itemized list of more than eleven million Jews, their official programs to slaughter those they deemed mentally ill and developmentally disabled, their general exterminationist drive against Sinti and Roma, their wanton murder of millions in Poland and the Soviet Union fundamentally differentiated them in two respects from the communists. First, when the Nazis and all those Germans following them surveyed the map of Europe and beyond, they saw peoples to be destroyed, violently subjugated, enslaved, or somehow eliminated. When the communists gazed upon their relevant maps, they did not particularly covet others' territory or think it must be cleared of human impediments. They did not see peoples in all directions to be destroyed. But they did see people they had to transform, to fit their mold, which meant possibly sacrificing a substantial number for the greater good. Indeed, their Marxist social theory, whatever its substantial pathologies and inhumanity, sought positive social transformation through economic restructuring and change. They (except the Khmer Rouge) did not, as the Nazis did, study these maps with general murder in their eyes. The second difference followed from the first: killing's motive and consequent manner. The communists—though not the Japanese—killed human beings in their understanding of humanity's cause, envisioning a beneficent communist future for *all* humanity—thriving, having plenty, and living in freedom and harmony. This vision of humanity was an ideologically driven fantasia and therefore foundationally unreal and unrealizable, requiring inhumane means, with inhumane, indeed catastrophically inhumane results. But this is a far cry from the Germans' annihilationist ethos and practice seeking to place one race above all others, to refashion all human society according to a racial biological, draconian cast and slave system, and to kill vast numbers practically for its own sake. Hence, the Germans' far greater murderousness, its different quality.

Slaughtering people on a scale unparalleled in human history came to the Germans during the Nazi period as easily and reflexively as swatting flies. The Germans actively killed most of their victims as part of an explicit exterminationist policy, by shooting, gassing, and purposely starving them to death. The communists killed most or even the vast majority of their victims with catastrophic, ideologically induced, and cockeyed economic policies, using humans as production factors, or sacrificing human beings for humanity's good or history's march. The Soviets executed perhaps around 10 percent of their more than eight million killed. Had Mao not hatched his murderous Great Leap Forward economic scheme, then millions, indeed perhaps twenty million more Chinese, would not have died. None of this makes these regimes' murderousness any less murderous than the murderousness of others, or their victims' deaths any less morally condemnable, significant, or meaningful. But unlike those of the other colossally mass elimination-ist and murderous regimes, the Nazis' drive to slaughter people was or-ganic to their ideology with its racist-biological conception of humanity and human worth and its concomitant drive for racial purity, expan-sion, and dominance. It was an ideology of destruction.

Had the Germans won the war, they would have slaughtered the five million additional Jews documented at Wannsee and, if able to, Jews beyond Europe, especially in the United States. They would have slaughtered everywhere mentally ill and developmentally disabled peo-ple; all people they called Gypsies; and Poles, Ukrainians, Russians, and other peoples to their east in the tens of millions, as they refashioned the Eurasian continent and humanity. They would have slaughtered, or prevented the birth of, children, as the biological seeds of peoples they wanted to destroy or numerically control, or considered superfluous. As they moved into Africa and Asia, they would have slaughtered or let perish untold millions of various *subhumans*, Asians being deemed racial cripples and blacks semi-apes. Had the Germans prevailed, they would have destroyed civilization and humanity as we know it.

If the communists were a heresy on Western civilization, accepting many of its fundamental values and tenets if in a perverted way, the Nazis were an apostasy, seeking its destruction and replacement by a German racial dominion, a world of masters and, of those permitted to live, mainly slaves. After seventy years of communist rule, Russia, Ukraine, the Baltics, and elsewhere, countries and peoples resumed con-trol of their futures. After almost half a century of Soviet domination in Central Europe, in Poland, Hungary, Czechoslovakia, and elsewhere, the countries' peoples emerged intact and educated, and able to pick up, much the poorer in many ways, where they had been nationally and culturally. Had the Nazis ruled these same lands for half or three quarters of a century, no Ukraine or Ukrainian people, no Poland or Polish people, no Russia or Russian people would have been left to resuscitate. The Germans would have repopulated their lands with colonists, slaughtered and enslaved their peoples, obliterated their religions and churches, their cultures and communities. The Germans developed plans to begin this vast systematic destruction, most notably the General Plan for the East, and had in almost no time already started to implement their desires. After half a century or more under a victorious Nazi Germany, European, Western, even pre-Nazi German civilization, would have been destroyed, unrecognizable, incapable of resurrection. Such was Nazism's caesura with Western civilization. Such was its unparalleled destructiveness.

No general structural view of mass murder or elimination can account for each individual system's perpetrators' enormously variable treatment of their *potential* victims and then, once an eliminationist campaign begins, of the different groups they *actually* victimize. Such structural accounts—precisely because they deem irrelevant the perpetrators' conception of the victims—imply, instead of such variation, a structurally, authority-based, or psychologically or social-psychologically induced uniformity in treatment. Different potential target groups' different objective political challenges or threats also cannot explain the perpetrators' varied treatment of potential and actual victims, because most victims posed no threat. After the eliminationist regimes quickly consolidated control, they faced almost no organized domestic political opposition (especially the extremely popular Nazis, widely seen as legitimate in Germany). Each country's people were in varying combinations supportive or prostrate.

Aside from political leaders' strategic decisions about timing and scope, eliminationist programs' local and regional implementation varies for two principal reasons. Highly centrally organized mass slaughters and eliminations tend to produce more consistency. In those with greater depth and breadth of the target groups' dehumanization and/or demonization, the perpetrators and the supporting population tend to treat the victims more uniformly. Thus, less centrally controlled eliminationist assaults can produce substantial regional and local variation, depending on local leaders' decisions and variable local beliefs about the targets. This occurred in Cambodia because the Khmer Rouge's regional cadres were somewhat differently oriented toward the eliminationist project; in Rwanda because, depending on local leaders and local Hutu-Tutsi relations, some communes' and villages' Hutu were easier to unleash into mass-murderous assaults while in others more Hutu dissented and resisted; and in Indonesia, because the centrally initiated and directed murderous assault depended greatly on local leaders and self-organizing groups of executioners, producing substantial regional variation owing to the nature of the hatreds and pre-existing communal conflicts. A better and more differentiated understanding of the relationship between eliminationist assaults' centralized initiation and organization, and their local organization and implementation, requires far more knowledge about most individual eliminationist programs than we have.

Similarly, far too little is known about the percentage of dissenters and resisters among perpetrators and among the peoples in whose names the perpetrators act. In many eliminationist assaults, as we now know, little evidence exists of widespread, principled disapproval of the general eliminationist project itself or the specific killings, expulsions, and incarcerations, either among the perpetrators or broader populaces, which reflects their dehumanized and/or demonized conception of the victims' considerable depth and breadth. Nevertheless, any eliminationist politics has dissenters and resisters, some of whom succeed. Knowing more, substantially more, about their numbers and nature (we know so little probably because usually they were small minorities) would considerably deepen our understanding of individual eliminationist assaults and the occasional variation in their implementation's success.

Communal Worlds

Although significant, dissenters, both individuals and small groups, receive disproportionate attention compared to an overwhelmingly important but neglected theme: the perpetrators' communities. In *Hitler's Willing Executioners*, I wrote about the Holocaust's perpetrators in a

manner that restored their humanity. I treated them fully as human beings having views about their deeds and making decisions about how to
act, not as abstractions wrested from their lives' real social contexts
but, as they actually were, embedded in their social relations. Such an
approach was at the time absent, even stridently opposed. The German
perpetrators of the Holocaust *and* of eliminationist and exterminationist assaults on Poles, Russians, Sinti, Roma, and other targeted peoples operated within broader communities. They undertook their deeds
often over long periods, always with considerable time on their hands
to reflect. They had social lives. Wives and girlfriends accompanied
many of them (many of whom also became perpetrators). The perpetrators went to church, played sports, even organized athletic competi-
tions. They attended cultural events, went to movies, and had parties.
They wrote revealing letters to loved ones and went home on furlough.
Most of all they talked—while on duty, while off duty, while eating
meals and driving places, among themselves and others, discussing the
days' events, their historic deeds, and more. Those many German perpetrators carrying out their brutal eliminationist tasks in Germany itself, especially in the camps densely blanketing the country, often lived
at home. After a day of mistreating and brutalizing, and even killing
victims, they returned to their families, had dinner, played with their
children. They spent time with friends, also went to church, and did all
the social and communal things, including talking about work, that
people do. What is true about the German perpetrators' rich social and
communal lives is also obviously true, a commonplace, about other
mass eliminations' perpetrators.

Yet if you pretend people killing, expelling, or brutalizing others are
atomized individuals, are under authority's hammer or intense social
psychological pressure with no capacity to think, or are bureaucratic
abstractions instead of real human beings; if you toss around mind-
deadening phrases such as "banality of evil" or "obedience to authority" or "group pressure," or treat mass murder as if an artificial social
psychological environment, such as the Zimbardo Experiment of a tiny
number of people (twenty-four) for a short time (six days) with no ex-
perimental controls to speak of, so it was not really an "experiment" in
a scientific or social scientific sense, is a guide to its perpetrators' reality and existences as people with families, friends, and communal lives;

or if you postulate these fictive and dehumanizing reductions of the perpetrators as a tautological account of their actions and, more broadly, as a way of conceiving and discussing them, then there is no reason, as we have seen, to investigate how they come to hold their views about the world and their victims (or even what those views are). There is also no reason to examine the perpetrators in their multiple communal contexts while committing their eliminationist acts or to examine their social relations, ways of living, and activities. The hardheaded questions we ask to ascertain the perpetrators' motives and their sources, and the bystanders' attitudes and their sources, also provide answers that can be built upon to explore the perpetrators' relationship to the bystanders helping to form the communal contexts of the perpetrators' eliminationist actions and lives.

The analytically unfortunate fact is that we know little about eliminationist perpetrators' communal lives. Some perpetrators, in the Soviet gulag's frozen reaches, were removed from conventional social life. Yet many other eliminationist perpetrators are like the Germans, going home to dinner and out with friends, partaking in cultural events, attending church, talking about their deeds with others and among themselves—comparing notes, swapping stories, and discussing their deeds' historic significance—and carrying on with their lives. This was so for the Japanese in Asia, the British in Kenya, the Indonesians slaughtering communists, the communist Chinese, the Tutsi in Burundi, the Serbs in Bosnia, the Hutu in Rwanda, the Political Islamists in Sudan, and so many more, certainly of most perpetrators killing people within their own country. As do other Hutu executioners, Léopord Twagirayezu conveys the easy conversational and convivial nature of the perpetrators' talk and social lives: "In the evening, we told about Tutsi who had been obstinate, those who had gotten themselves caught, those who had gotten away. Some of us had contests. Others made predictions or bets to win an extra Primus [beer]. The bragging amused us—even if you lost, you put on a smile."[18]

The evidence strongly suggests that perpetrators live in a milieu overwhelmingly supporting and affirming their treatment of the victims in the name of and *for* their people. As with eliminationist assaults' many other aspects, if broad principled opposition or dissent had existed, then there would be abundant credible contemporaneous evidence about it. It does not. Nothing suggests that family and friends, or community members generally, saw or treated the perpetrators with disapproval, let alone the withering condemnation that would be directed at those considered among humanity's worst criminals. Nothing suggests that family, friends, and community members treated the killing and other eliminationist acts as anything more distasteful than an unpleasant part of a necessary eliminationist time and project. Nothing suggests that the perpetrators' community and social and recreational lives were normalcy's salve to guilty consciences. And nothing suggests that their communities were saying to them: You are a good man *despite* what you do. Rather the communal verdict was: You are a good man *because of* what you do. Nothing suggests that during eliminationist onslaughts the perpetrators' existences are psychically and social-relationally fragmented. Rather, they consisted of integrated selves, with integrated minds, in integrated communities with their self-conceived heroic, violent acts on behalf of their country, their people, their God, or humanity harmonizing with their communal existences and with family, friends, and acquaintances. In Indonesia, throughout Bali, "whole villages, including children, took part in an island-wide witch-hunt for Communists, who were slashed and clubbed and chopped to death by communal consent."[19] In Bosnia, the ethnic Serbian community was so supportive of the eliminationist assault, and so deeply complicit and involved, that the extremely knowledgeable Alisa Muratčauš, president of the Association of Concentration Camp Torture Survivors in Sarajevo, maintains that "a lot of people from Republika Srpska [Bosnian Serbs] were involved in the crimes, and I think that actually maybe 70 or 80 percent of Republika Srpska's population should be actually punished in prison, in jail." Adamant that she does not mean they merely "supported" the crimes of raping, torturing, expelling, and killing people, destroying their houses, and more, she explains that they "actually committed crimes. People who returned to their original community meet very often their perpetrators, [who say] 'Oh, hi, hello.'"[20] In Rwanda, an in-depth study about one community of killers shows how the perpetrators slaughtered their victims with incredible cruelty *and* lived their lives with family, friends, and community in a thoroughly integrated and symbiotic way. Jean Hatzfeld, its author, writes: "In 1994, between eleven in the morning on Monday April 11 and two in the afternoon on Saturday May 14, about fifty thousand Tutsi, out of a population of around fifty-

Clothing of the victims, Nyamata Genocide Memorial, Bugesera District, Rwanda, April 2008

nine thousand, were massacred by machete, murdered every day of the week, from nine-thirty in the morning until four in the afternoon, by Hutu neighbors and militiamen, on the hills of the commune of Nyamata, in Rwanda." This, he adds, "is the point of departure of this book."[21]

Although we need more evidence to draw firmly grounded general conclusions for certain eliminationist assaults, the substantial existing evidence suggests that, overwhelmingly, ordinary people, moved by their hatreds and prejudices, by their beliefs in victims' evil or noxiousness, by their conviction that they and others ought to eliminate the victims, support their countrymen, ethnic group members, or village or communal members' killing, expelling, or brutalizing others—as Germans did during the Nazi period, as Poles of Jedwabne did, as the peoples of Central and Eastern Europe did regarding ethnic Germans, as British settlers in Kenya did, as Bosnian Serbs did, and as Hutu across Rwanda did. The killers, and those near them in their cities, towns, and villages, and especially those emotionally dear to them, constitute mutually supportive eliminationist communities. Alphonse Hitiyaremye, a Hutu mass murderer, conveys how the Nyamata commune's ordinary Hutu had this unmistakably affirmed, starting with the killing's first day, a machete butchering orgy of five thousand Tutsi holed up in the local church and then in the Sainte-Marthe Maternity Hospital:

> The first evening, coming home from the massacre in the church, our welcome was very well put together by the organizers. We all met up back on the soccer field. Guns were shooting in the air, whistles and suchlike musical instruments were sounding.
>
> The children pushed into the center all the cows rounded up during the day. Burgomaster [the mayor] Bernard offered the forty fattest ones to the *interahamwe*, to thank them, and the other cows to the people, to encourage them. We spent the evening slaughtering the cattle, singing, and chatting about the new days on the way. It was the most terrific celebration.[22]

The perpetrators of mass annihilation and elimination know they exist in supportive eliminationist milieus; they themselves witness the open communal expressions of support. The eliminationist campaign against the Jews was immensely popular among Germans not only during the pre-exterminationist phase of the 1930s, as *everyone* in Germany knew—the regime and ordinary Germans alike openly celebrated it with fanfare—but also during the mass-murderous phase starting in 1941.

To see how this knowledge of the Germans' broad base of support for the Jews' elimination was acted upon by the regime, shared by German bystanders, and communicated by the perpetrators to their loved ones, we need merely to look to Europe's largest concentration of Jews, the Warsaw Ghetto camp in the heart of Poland's capital. Did the German leadership try to hide half a million Jews' inhuman conditions? Not at all. In the midst of the Germans' all-out extermination of the Jews, the German Labor Front's recreational organization for German workers, called Strength Through Joy, organized coach tours of the ghetto where the Germans were starving the Jews to death on fewer than four hundred calories a day.

The Polish government in exile reported in May 1942:

> Every day large coaches come to the ghetto; they take soldiers through as if it was a zoo. It is the thing to do to provoke the wild animals. Often soldiers strike out at passers-by with long whips as they

Pedestrians in the Warsaw Ghetto walk past corpses lying on the pavement on Rynkowa Street, near the ghetto wall, Warsaw, Poland, 1940–1941.

drive through. They go to the cemetery where they take pictures. They compel the families of the dead and the rabbis to interrupt the funeral and to pose in front of their lenses. They set up genre pictures (old Jew above the corpse of a young girl).

The brutality—whips!—the photographing, the mocking, the joyfulness and obvious approval (already seen and further discussed below), these recurring features of eliminationist assaults were apparent (1) in the tourism itself (common among German bystanders where perpetrators brutalized or slaughtered Jews), (2) in the acts of these coachloads of ordinary Germans, and, of course, (3) for all the perpetrators in Warsaw and other places hosting such tourists to see. The regime, knowledgeable of Germans' broad solidarity with their eliminationist project, also made films of the ghetto, showing them in Germany. Members of the German press, so that they, the eyes of the people, could be fully knowledgeable of what the regime was doing, toured ghettos. One, named Roßberg, wrote in a manner capturing Germans' common knowledge of this eliminationist assault's character, great support for it, and transmutation of ordinary emotional responses into their opposite upon beholding Jews:

> I had the opportunity to get to know the ghetto in Lublin and the one in Warsaw. The sights are so appalling and probably also so well-known to the editorial staffs that a description is presumably superfluous. If there are any people left who still somehow have sympathy with the Jews then they ought to be recommended to have a look at such a ghetto. Seeing this race en masse, which is decaying, decomposing, and rotten to the core will banish any sentimental humanitarianism.[23]

Germans seeing people in a state ordinarily evoking compassion and pity are expected, when the people are "this race," to behold them as a physical embodiment of their true, hateful nature. We have no reason to believe they did otherwise. After the Germans had methodically deported to Treblinka's gas chambers the Warsaw Ghetto's inhabitants they had not already starved to death, the surviving Jews decided to go down fighting, rebelling in April 1943, until after a month the overwhelmingly militarily superior Germans crushed them. Many Germans celebrated the ghetto's utter destruction. Air force sergeant Herbert Habermalz, wanting to make his comrades similarly joyful, wrote his former place of employment, a farm equipment manufacturer, a letter that, as letter writers knew, was likely to circulate among the workers: "We flew several circles above the city. And with great satisfaction we could recognize the complete extermination of the Jewish Ghetto. There our folks did really a fantastic job. There is no house which has not been totally destroyed." That Habermalz wrote, without thinking he needed to explain to them anything about the "complete extermination" of a Jewish ghetto once containing nearly half a million Jews, merely confirms what a vast array of sources definitively show: The Jews' systematic annihilation was well known and well supported among Germans, so much so that Habermalz unabashedly termed the job done "fantastic."[24]

To develop a systematic and comparative understanding of the perpetrators' social existences and communal lives, and how their social embeddedness affects or reflects treatment of their victims, we need to examine the perpetrators' various communities and social relations. We must replace the fictitious general image of the frightened, atomized, isolated killer (said to exist under a regime's draconian authority, or under group pressure), with a realistic account of the perpetrators' social, psychological, and moral communal existences. These vary substantially across eliminationist assaults, and even within given eliminationist assaults when a particular eliminationist program covers large territories or long periods.

The framework for the needed extensive empirical inquiry into the perpetrators' communal lives in individual eliminations and then comparatively distinguishes five principal kinds of communities that form the social context for the perpetrators' actions. First, the community of the perpetrators themselves, including but not restricted to men serving in the same camp, mobile killing squad, death march, and other eliminationist institutions. Second, the broader nonperpetrator communities in which they are embedded while eliminating their victims. These consist of local cities and towns where the perpetrators are stationed, whether at home or abroad, and the social communities and lives their governments and institutions at times create for them. Third, their home communities, to which most of them will return, of family, friends, neighbors, acquaintances, and fellow members of their local national, ethnic, or communal groups. Fourth, related to the third, the more abstract—though given the power of nationalism and ethnic or religious group membership to move people, hardly trivial—larger national, ethnic, religious, or political communities. Fifth, far more distant and less relevant for most perpetrators, the international community, the rest of humanity.

The perpetrators live in all or most of these communities while they kill and eliminate their victims. Their physical and social existences are continuous in some, episodic in others, and nonexistent or almost so in others. But in them all, though obviously varying substantially, the perpetrators are situated socially, psychologically, or morally, and even in those they do not physically inhabit while acting as perpetrators, they know they eventually *will* have some relationship of moral

The perpetrators' community: SS female auxiliaries and Karl Höcker, the adjutant to Auschwitz's camp commander, eat bowls of blueberries to accordion music, Solahütte retreat near Auschwitz, Poland, 1944.

accountability, psychological influence, or social or political consequence. This knowledge is relevant, can be powerful, and should not continue to be discounted. Still, whatever is generally true about the perpetrators' various communities, including their general supportiveness, more can be said about each of them, and their interconnectedness.

Working in eliminationist institutions can be utterly normal (or at least can become utterly normal after a perpetrator's initial participation in an eliminationist operation) when the need to carry out the eliminationist assault seems unquestionable. Even among perpetrators viewing the victims as sufficiently noxious or threatening to warrant or necessitate their elimination, including lethally, some may doubt such actions' wisdom or morality. In such circumstances, a perpetrator's comrades' validation of the violence, or the knowledge that he operates under the state's aegis, or as the nation's or the perpetrators' ethnic or religious group's representative and guardian, can help quell a perpetrator's lingering doubts. The eliminationist regime's character, and the specific eliminationist institution's character, can affect the perpetrators' understanding of their deeds and their lives' quality while killing, expelling, torturing, and immiserating their victims. Some regimes and killing institutions, such as the Germans', were organized and hierarchical, *and* relatively lax and understanding toward the perpetrators. They were also characterized by considerable off-duty comradeship and conviviality.

Some, also organized and hierarchical, are harsher, as the Guatemalan mobile killing squads could be. Others have more variable, fluid, and intermittent qualities, such as that of the far less formally organized and hierarchical Hutu. The Hutu's killing operations' character depended on whether the villagers were left on their own for a given day's killing expeditions—villagers not feeling up to joining that day's hunt staying behind—or they were under the supervision of the Interahamwe, which sometimes forbade a day off. But for the reasons already established and more addressed below, the various eliminationist institutions' other features—from their hierarchical structures, the actual or implied coercion that might exist, the normative world of support for killing and elimination—have not been the perpetrators' prime movers, and could not have been given their actual conduct. Sometimes when killers speak frankly, they, in a jumble, adduce a host of factors and circumstances that composed the mass-murderous complex of their actions. But when doing so, there is an assumption, explicit or clearly implicit, of underlying consent to the deed, born of their shared conception of the targeted peoples as noxious or threatening, of deserving their fate. Some Rwandan perpetrators speak in such a logically incoherent but psychologically plausible muddle. At one moment they discuss how they got drunk on their greed for looting. At another moment they mention that the Interahamwe—dedicated executioners—would not permit them to take a day off or would reproach them for not killing an acquaintance, or would fine them for not going into the bush to kill (hardly a plausible burden as it was easily paid from their looting's proceeds), or would threaten them with death for not killing. At yet another moment the same perpetrators openly state that they and their comrades and all Hutu hated the Tutsi, thought the Tutsi were not human beings but snakes, cockroaches, and vermin who wanted to enslave all Hutu, so they believed it imperative to free their country of the Tutsi scourge, so they "cut them." Elie Ngarambe, in a work camp prison when I interviewed him, also speaks in such a vein, asserting among other things that he was coerced, as were other Hutu, but then, when trying to convey to me the character of the genocide and the various facets of what really happened, says and indicates in many ways that he and ordinary Hutu, perpetrators and bystanders alike, hated the Tutsi, thought them not to be human beings, wanted to destroy them, and pursued or supported these goals with amazing and cruel vigor. When asked, "Were most Hutu happy to get rid of the Tutsi in one way or another, even if they themselves didn't want to do the killing?" he replies, "They felt like they should be eliminated and wiped out," explaining that Hutu shared the government's "bad ideology," which told them to "start from a small child, continue with a pregnant woman, kill her with her husband, her in-laws, and all her families, eliminate them all, eat their things, after you finish everything take their land, take their cars. Think of how long they have been fighting against us." Ngarambe is emphatic. "They [the Hutu] wanted to eliminate all of them [the Tutsi]. They did not want to see anyone surviving." Ngarambe has confessed to participating in the killing of only two people, but similarly in the course of his own testimony (some quoted here) betrays himself, repeatedly making it clear that he was daily in the thick of the mass murder, participating in the butchery of many more.*25

The complex interactive effects of various influences upon some perpetrators, and yet their willingness and conviction in the rightness of the *principle of eliminating* the targeted people and of the killing itself that *are* the foundation of the perpetrators' deeds and the members of their enormously supportive societies or groups' views about what ought to be done, are captured also by others. Pancrace Hakizamungili discourses in a jumble about having no choice, having hesitations including those born of what will happen should they *fail* (which a "good organizer" can quell), and about his and the other Hutu's hatred for the Tutsi, their enthusiasm in going on the hunt, and their relief at finally ridding themselves of the Tutsi. And so, from Pancrace's mouth come words that

---

*Another example: "We peasants, we were using our traditional weapons. It is for that reason that when you were hacking you were supposed to cut [the Tutsi] into two pieces. There was times where you would hack him and not cut him into two pieces and you hurt him only and think that he was dead. . . . Let's say that we are going in the squad that is going to kill and loot, we meet someone and we are almost five of us, one of us says, 'Let's see who is going to be the first to hack him.' The one who hacks the first runs, and the second one also hacks and runs."

The local community: A group of German soldiers and civilians looks on as a Jewish man is forced to cut the beard of another in Tomaszow Mazowiecki, Poland, September–October 1939.

could serve as a motto for our age's willing executioners, whether ordinary Germans, ordinary Serbs, or ordinary Hutu, "you obey freely."[26]

The second kind of community, the communities physically encompassing or abutting the perpetrators while at their eliminationist tasks, forms the perpetrators' immediate social context. These communities vary enormously. If the perpetrators are killing in their own country but not near home, they live as visitors or temporary residents. If in a conquered or colonial area, their government or they and their compatriots construct a local perpetrator community (the nearby victim peoples usually being communally irrelevant). These can vary from settler communities, as the British had in Kenya, the Japanese founded in Korea, the Germans created in Poland, and the Chinese established in Tibet, to imperial garrison communities with impromptu human and institutional infrastructural support, as the Japanese and the Germans had in some of their conquered areas. Everyone in such communities knows about the perpetrators' deeds. They see them. They mingle with the perpetrators. They work with them. They often revel in the perpetrators' deeds. They service and supply them, and collaborate with them in noneliminationist activities. Such people are not formally perpetrators (some do cross the line), yet they implicate themselves in the deeds, or they so intimately rub shoulders with the perpetrators that they belong to the perpetrator community. Everything suggests they are consensual communities.

The third community, consisting of the perpetrators' families, neighborhoods, and towns, powerfully exists for all mass annihilations and eliminations' perpetrators, though differently depending on where the perpetrators work their violence. Perpetrators, usually sooner than later, visit or return to their families and home communities, to loved ones, friends, and others, who often, probably usually, know at least the basics of the perpetrators' deeds. The perpetrators must inevitably consider how these people will judge their deeds. In many mass eliminations perpetrators operate in their home environs. As they brutalize, expel, and kill people, they, embedded in those communities day and night, do not have to wonder what their families and communities will someday say. This was true of those in Turkey attacking Armenian death marches as they trudged by impromptu perpetrators' towns, of the enormous number of Germans guarding or servicing camps in their own cities, towns, and neighborhoods, of Indonesians slaughtering communists, of Serbs in Bosnia, Tutsi in Burundi, Hutu in Rwanda, and more.

Beyond their local communities is the larger reference group of the nation, the people, the political movement, the tribe, or the religious group, in whose name perpetrators act. Perpetrators kill, expel, and incarcerate their victims to secure the future for themselves and their families by reconstituting society. As we repeatedly see, they also understand themselves to be acting for their larger communities. What will be their personal legacies to their people? How do they expect their people to see and judge them, to thank and celebrate or to shun and punish them? Such considerations unquestioningly affect many perpetrators, potentially all of them.

Finally, there is the international community or humanity—the real human beings, not the abstraction of humanity moving many communists, or the Germans' and the Japanese's restricted racist conceptions of humanity, consigning peoples to subhumanity. Perpetrators facing their victims likely do not think much about the international community. Yet, as much testimony indicates, the perpetrators are aware of a larger world, which they usually understand will condemn their actual and prospective eliminationist violence. In the past several decades, the

The national community: Austrian Nazis and local residents look on as Jews are forced on hands and knees to scrub the pavement, Vienna, Austria, March–April 1938.

spread of telecommunications has made perpetrators increasingly aware their acts will receive international scrutiny. Nevertheless, most perpetrators appear but tenuously connected psychologically to these distant and rather abstract community considerations. After all, when perpetrators face the "work of demons who wage their battle against us" or other putatively threatening or problematic subhumans, people across an ocean, or over a border or two, must seem irrelevant. Political leaders initiating and overseeing eliminationist assaults, however, are acutely conscious (if often ultimately dismissive) of the international community. The critical issue, taken up in Chapter 11, is how to vastly increase the international community's psychological and moral centrality, and relative weight among the perpetrators' various more immediate communities, for actual or prospective perpetrators—from the man on the ground, gun or machete in his hand, to his immediate commanders, to those running eliminationist institutions, and especially to the political leaders unleashing and orchestrating the eliminationist assaults.

Few, if any, perpetrators likely self-consciously disaggregate their embeddedness in various communities, or regularly assess how each community and its many members (even leaving aside the distant international community) judge or will judge their deeds and ultimately them. For many, especially those working at home, no difference exists among some of their communities. For some, such as the Indonesians slaughtering communists and, even more so, Serbs in Bosnia and Hutu in Rwanda, the communities of killers, of immediate locale, of home, and even of the nation collapse into an integrated mass-murderous and eliminationist consensual community. In addition to these instances, the judgment of communities, except the international one, is obviously generally a nonissue for killers, expellers, and guards. The perpetrators move in overlapping or intersecting communities approving their deeds, so acute moral doubt and existential discomfort do not arise.

In addition to the expressed approval and acceptance various relevant communities give them, the perpetrators know that those belonging to their country, people, ethnic group, political movement, or religion, having been party to their society's conversation about the dehumanized or demonized victims, widely share their views. The perpetrators know they similarly believe the perpetrators' deeds are right and necessary, support them, are even thankful the perpetrators are eliminating the people they commonly hate or fear. Because the eliminationist *logic* of the perpetrators' beliefs applies equally to the many others sharing those beliefs who have not been asked to act upon them, it is abundantly clear that many other people in the perpetrators' communities and societies would also have brutalized, incarcerated, expelled, and killed the victim groups had they been asked or put in the position to do so. This, that the vast majority of ordinary Germans would have also been *Hitler's willing executioners*, I demonstrated for Germans during the Nazi period.[27] Though for other eliminationist assaults the data do not lend themselves to the same methodologically inescapable, surefire generalization to the perpetrators' societies and communities (exceptions notwithstanding), we can still say, for various reasons, that so many others from those communities would have willingly acted as the perpetrators did. The perpetrators know this very well. The perpetrators do not necessarily ponder how the members of their various communities work through the logic of their beliefs and what they therefore think about the perpetrators' deeds, or what they would do if mobilized for the eliminationist assault. Neither do soldiers in war. Absent demonstrable opposition at home, soldiers do not wonder about their countrymen's support or readiness to join them. They naturally assume both. So too the eliminationist perpetrators, conceiving of themselves, like soldiers, to be conducting a war against their people's dangerous enemies. The public discourse—more intensified, explicit, and public immediately preceding and during eliminationist assaults—about the need to exterminate-the-brute or to eliminate-the-plague, merely confirms to the perpetrators what the same discourse had already prepared them and their communities for. When governmental organs, civil leaders, media, intellectuals, and religious leaders repeatedly publicly proclaim—as they have so often done—people's noxiousness and threat, and even call for their elimination, they further affirm what the perpetrators already know, having watched family, friends, and others nod in agreement or approvingly repeat what is in the air. "The Jews are our misfortune" was one of the German public sphere's most oft-repeated phrases in the 1930s and 1940s. British colonial officials and ordinary settlers alike casually and reflexively spoke of the putatively savage, bloodthirsty, murderous Mau Mau. Ladino Guatemalans called Maya "animals." Serbs as a matter of course referred to Bosnian Muslims as "Turks," constructing them as the Serbs' historic and eternal enemy, and as Bosnia's rightless alien invaders. The Rwandan airwaves coursed with, and Hutu newspapers and popular publications printed, hate-filled accounts of the Tutsi "cockroaches" and calls to exterminate them. These and other commonplaces solidify the sense of a community of like-minded thought, values, hatreds, and actions among the perpetrators and those around them. As Pancrace, echoing so many others, explained: "The radios were yammering at us since 1992 to kill all the Tutsi," which found echoes in an activated and intensified Hutu conversation, as Christine reports: "In the cabarets, men had begun talking about massacres in 1992" with the president of their commune visiting their houses "to see that the tools behind sacks of beans were well sharpened."[28]

A striking feature of prejudices and hatreds, of the dehumanizing and demonizing conceptions one group's members have for another's, is their intellectual and social leveling—within communities and, whatever the specific beliefs' differences, across societies and civilizations.

In given eliminationist communities, university professors and high school–educated janitors share common murderous views about targeted people. The same talk animates the lecture hall and the beer hall, the principal difference being the little separating highfalutin nonsense from plain nonsense. The "people of poets and thinkers," as the Germans, Europe's most highly educated people, liked to call themselves, were no different from illiterate Hutu farmers (Rwanda's adult literacy rate, at around 50 percent, was among the world's lowest). Intellectuals, lawyers, teachers, doctors, and clergy—the opinion leaders and in some cases, especially the clergy, moral leaders—validate the eliminationist beliefs and acts of their societies' ordinary members and prospectively further sustain the perpetrators' confidence in their people's solidarity. We have already explored how Serbian writers and intellectuals, including the country's most influential body of thinkers, the Serbian Academy of Arts and Sciences, laid down the common ideational foundation and even provided the political leadership for the Serbs' eliminationist assaults. German intellectuals, doctors, jurists, teachers, clergy critically contributed to spreading eliminationist antisemitism and other racist and dehumanizing views in Germany before and during the Nazi period. Shelves of books, including some of the very early scholarly works on Nazism and the Holocaust, bear such titles as *Hitler's Professors*, *The Third Reich and Its Thinkers*, *The Nazi Doctors*, *Hitler's Justice*, *Revolutionary Antisemitism in Germany from Kant to Wagner*.[29] Such socially and culturally crucial people analogously prepared the ground for our time's other mass slaughters and eliminations, including those done in the name of Marx and the promised land he and his intellectual epigones promised. Vladimir Lenin, Leon Trotsky, and others, who laid the foundation for and initiated the communists' long-term eliminationist assault on many portions of Soviet society, were extremely intelligent men and authors of learned Marxist works. Pol Pot and other Khmer Rouge leaders were also relatively highly educated, having imbibed their foundational Marxism in Paris. In Rwanda, intellectuals prepared Hutu for what was to come, as Innocent Rwililiza, a Tutsi survivor, explains: "Genocide is not really a matter of poverty or lack of education. . . . In 1959 the Hutu relentlessly robbed, killed, and drove away Tutsi, but they never for a single day imagined exterminating them. It is the intellectuals who emancipated them, by planting the idea of genocide in their heads and sweeping away their hesitations."[30] After the fact, some perpetrators, finally seeing their deeds through the outside world's condemning eyes, reflect on how their intellectuals, elites, and clergy led them astray.

Intellectuals, doctors, teachers, lawyers, and clergy are also part of their societies. They too participate in the hateful discourses, in which they are no less, and often more, embedded than the communities' other members who also create and sustain them. They too act or support the acts that follow on their logic. No significant part of the German elites thought the Jews *wholly innocent* and therefore dissented from the fundamentals of the eliminationist project against the Jews (though some would have preferred a nonlethal eliminationist solution). Even the leading German resistance groups to Hitler were profoundly antisemitic, which informed their future plans for Jews. One of the resistance's central documents, prepared by leading Protestant theologians and university professors, contained an appendix called "Proposals for a Solution to the Jewish Problem in Germany," which, referring to Jews, stated that a post-Nazi Germany would be justified in taking steps "to ward off the calamitous influence of one race on the national community." Yet thanks to the highly effective exterminationist program, they could perhaps tolerate Jews in Germany, because "the number of Jews surviving and returning to Germany will not be so large that they could still be regarded as a danger to the German nation."[31] German elites were active, willing, and leading participants in the annihilationist assault on the Jews and in the Germans' other eliminationist projects. Einsatzgruppen leaders slaughtering Jews in the Soviet Union were academically trained, as did the principal author and others working on the murderous and eliminationist anti-Slav General Plan for the East. Church leaders and clergy the world over, from Turkey, to Germany, to Croatia, to Indonesia, to Serbia, to Rwanda, and to the Political Islamic religious leaders and clerics in different countries, have actively and tacitly blessed mass murder. (Where, we should ask, have religious leaders opposed their countrymen's or clansmen's eliminationist assaults? If they had, such as the Bulgarian Orthodox Church leaders who were instrumental in preventing the Bulgarian Jews' deportation, or Pastor André Trocmé, who led an effort in Le Chambon-sur-Lignon in France that saved five thousand Jews, we would know and they would have prevented countless deaths. Yet we know of so few.) Local dignitaries often organized and led the Bosnian Serbs' paramilitary or local killing institutions. In Rwanda, the local intellectuals were in the thick of the mass murder. Jean-Baptiste Munyankore, a Tutsi teacher and survivor, explains: "The principal and the inspector of schools in my district participated in the killings with nail-studded clubs. . . . A priest, the burgomaster, the subprefect, a doctor—they all killed with their own hands. . . . These well educated people were calm, and they rolled up their sleeves to get a good grip on their machetes."[32] Well-educated people, leading professionals of one society after the next, together with those looking up to them, have closed ranks in a community of murderous consent.

After eliminationist assaults, after the massive death toll and the vast suffering the perpetrators have inflicted become clear, in country after country, in town after town, the perpetrators return to their people, whose names they have blackened in the world's eyes, but evidently not in their own. In every mass murder and elimination's aftermath, the broader community in whose name the perpetrators acted has not socially or politically rejected, let alone punished, the perpetrators. (Punishment has occasionally been meted out by those defeating perpetrators or those replacing the perpetrating regime.) The perpetrators have not been turned into outcasts, not shunned, not treated in any way as a community would ordinarily treat murderers, let alone mass murderers in their midst. It did not happen in Turkey, in Germany, in Indonesia, in Serbia or among Serbs in Bosnia—who after the eliminationist assault continued to celebrate the Bosnian Serbian eliminationist architects Radovan Karadžić and Ratko Mladić as heroes—in Burundi, in Rwanda among the Hutu themselves. Communities welcome the perpetrators back and, when necessary and feasible, have passionately risen to *defend* them. The social and communal solidarity the perpetrators find in the posteliminationist era merely continues the solidarity they experienced while assaulting their victims.

We do not know the percentage of each community's people who have supported the exterminationist and eliminationist politics perpetrators practiced in their name. Everywhere—among Turks, among Serbs, among Hutu—there has been some communal dissent. Even in Germany, where the evidence of broad and deep popular support for the eliminationist assault against the Jews is overwhelming, some dissent existed. (The ready knowledge we have of it and, often by the dissenters' own admission, of their exceptional nature and isolation, further confirms Germans' overwhelming support for the elimination.) Nevertheless, in our time's lethal and nonlethal eliminationist assaults, we find among the broader relevant national or ethnic communities little credible evidence of widespread dissent from the eliminationist conceptions of the victims and the thinking underlying such politics, or of actual opposition to the eliminationist onslaughts themselves. But we have abundant evidence of active communal support and encouragement for the perpetrators, of the perpetrators' comfort within their various communities and among their countrymen, and of the perpetrators' smooth reintegration into their accepting communities when the mass killings, expulsions, and incarcerations end.

Camp Worlds

One kind of community deserves special attention, as it is prominent among the things making our age politically distinctive: camps—usually called concentration camps—or more precisely, camp systems. They are typically worlds unto themselves. The camp system, distinct from yet intermeshing with society's other systems, is a novel feature of eliminationist politics (differing from, though related to, earlier slave camps used to extract labor), and its creation critically demarcates one type of eliminationist onslaught from all others. Spatially fixed and temporally durable, a camp system usually marks mass murder and elimination as integral to a country's social and political system. Its creation derives more from its leaders' general conception of politics and the society they wish to govern or forge than from the specific conception of the victims (aside from the foundational belief that the victims must be violently eliminated).

Blame for inventing modern camp systems belongs to the Spaniards, who emptied a good portion of Cuba for "concentration" into camps in 1896 to defeat rebellion. The Spaniards kept the camps in deplorable conditions so that perhaps 200,000 people, mainly women and children, perished. In South Africa in the twentieth century's first years,

Entrance to the gulag camp Vorkuta, Soviet Union

the British, likely inspired by the Spaniards, incarcerated more than 100,000 Boer women and children, and blacks rebelling against them, in a camp system, taking more than 40,000 people's lives, with each group's minimum toll at 20,000. The British, wishing to secure their colonial rule against insurgencies, used camps elsewhere. In Malaysia, they sought to quash the communist and nationalist insurgency with a declared emergency in 1948 lasting years and a detention camp system incarcerating thirty thousand people, from which they expelled more than half to China. This turned out to be a strategic pilot program the British implemented full force in the 1950s in Kenya. After losing India, the empire's "crown jewel," in 1947, they were desperate to hold on to Kenya when, in 1952, the Mau Mau liberation movement challenged their draconian rule. Given that Mau Mau enjoyed the allegiance of most Kikuyu, whom the fifty thousand British settlers had been systematically dispossessing of their land, the British, in order to secure their colonial position, decided to eliminate Mau Mau and its bearers, which meant eliminating the Kikuyu population as effective claimants to their own land and to self-determination. They created an extensive and murderous camp system—so murderous that the common view was that their purpose was to kill Kikuyu, as they starved them, refused to let them farm their lands, and denied them medical treatment.[33] This system was internally differentiated with several categories of camps, the British assigning individual Kikuyu to camps of varying severity designed to incarcerate, break, warehouse, or kill them. The British incarcerated perhaps 1.5 million Kikuyu, a good portion of the people, and killed tens of thousands (estimates range from 50,000 to 300,000).

The British demonized the Kikuyu as Mau Mau cannibals (a wholly invented charge). This was layered upon a profound racism that held black Africans to be mentally and morally inferior, mixed with fear of Mau Mau insurgents who attacked and killed, initially, a few British settlers. Soon after the Mau Mau's attacks began, the British, with both colonial administrators and settlers often forming the shock troops of the grinding onslaught, quickly created the "pipeline," an array of more than one hundred formal camps, meant to be a system of holding pens and reeducative institutions (further augmented by scores of unofficial private settler camps and other camps) into which they drove perhaps a half million Kikuyu. The British then restricted most Kikuyu, more than one million deemed less threatening, to thoroughly inadequate tribal reserves, which, consisting literally of barbed-wire villages, were camps, or in John Nottingham's formulation, "concentration camp villages," except in name.[34] As the British changed individual victims' status, they imprisoned and shuttled them around the gulag of increasingly harsh concentration camps. The "pipeline" itself quickly worsened, as "reeducative" camps do, because of the inherent contradictions of such camps, which whatever their formal purpose incarcerate people the perpetrators believe must be eliminated. Josiah Mwangi Kariuki, a long-time British camp inmate, explains that as the British had set for themselves the impossible eliminationist task of eradicating the Mau Mau from the Kikuyu by getting Kikuyu to confess and recant, the camps devolved into something more horrible: "The 'pipeline' system in its original conception did not involve beating or hitting in any way. But because it was basically unsound it began to go slower and slower and it was at this stage that the Government officers employed the violence that in the end destroyed the use of confession as the foundation of the 'pipeline.' Few people anywhere feel bound by words uttered under torture."[35] Beyond this feature of the "pipeline," the British colonial officials and settlers subjected the Kikuyu herded into camps to severe undernourishment, brutality, torture, and murder. Fueled by racism, a hallucinatory image of the Kikuyu as bloodthirsty savages, and the seemingly limitlessly justifying emotion of revenge, British perpetrators conducted themselves with cruelty reminiscent of the Germans' treatment of Jews and others. Paul Mahehu, a Kikuyu survivor, explains that as he was watching a film about the Germans' treatment of Jews in camps, he was thinking that that was what the British had done to his people.[36]

The politics engendering camp systems are typically long-term imperial domination or the visionary transformation of a country's social and political structure and fabric. For the Germans, the two went hand-in-hand. Such projects necessitate the violent domination or elimination of targeted, unwanted, or putatively recalcitrant groups, sometimes numbering tens of millions. The Germans, Soviets, Chinese communists, Khmer Rouge, and North Korean communists sought to transform society into subjectively ideal realms, purified by purging all they deemed inimical and unwholesome—albeit according to enormously different visions—which necessitated the elimination of millions or tens of millions of people, for whom they erected camps as the permanent instrument of a combination of domination, exploitation, and annihilation. The Japanese, like the British in Kenya, followed no such eschatological transformative vision. They erected their vast camp system for merciless domination and exploitation. Such political goals, which visionary transformative regimes often share, are incompatible with the quick and final kill, leading political leaders to create camp systems and their followers to staff them sympathetically. The Japanese sought to occupy East Asia as a gigantic empire to serve their master race, enslaving tens of millions as disposable minions to be worked brutally, including to death, to extract the natural resources and produce the materials necessary for Japan to expand and maintain its Orwellian-named "co-prosperity" sphere. The Germans sought to transform the European land mass, particularly in Germany and to the east, into a vast racialized latifundium that German overlords would settle, and enslaved putative subhumans would work to sustain while being pruned and kept in check through reproduction prevention and steady killing.

Already in the fall of 1940, Hans Frank, the German governor of Poland, clearly outlined this vision of Europe while speaking specifically of Poland. "We think here in imperial terms, in the most grandiose style of all times. The imperialism that we develop is incomparable with those miserable attempts that previous weak German governments have undertaken in Africa." Frank reported to his audience that "the Führer has further said explicitly" that Poland is (in Frank's paraphrase) "destined" to be a "gigantic work camp, where everything that means power and independence is in the hands of the Germans." No Pole would receive higher education, and "none may rise to a rank higher than foreman." In Hitler and Frank's view, the Polish state would never be restored. The Poles would be permanently "subjugated" to the master race. Frank's elaboration upon this vision of the concentration camp as the model for Poland was not secret but expressed in two speeches to his administration's department heads as the governing ethos to the people governing Poland. Hitler's and his political blueprint is what the Germans were actually implementing in Poland and elsewhere east of Germany. As Himmler, the principal operational architect of the Germans' eliminationist policies and practices, is reported to have communicated to one of the SS and police forces' leaders in charge of an occupied area of the Soviet Union, "The Ukrainians should become a people of Helots that work only for us."[37]

As tools in their eliminationist politics, the Germans erected twenty thousand camps, mainly in Germany and conquered eastern territories, the formal extermination camps for Jews being the most infamous. (Some Germans' allied and puppet regimes set up parallel camps, most notably the Croats' camps, where they victimized and slaughtered Serbs, Jews, Sinti, and Roma.) The Germans established camps in 1933, and once established, particularly with the military conquests after 1939, the system expanded easily and, according to the Nazis' logic, naturally. It became a permanent system of German society and of the Germans' empire of suffering and exploitation they were creating in Europe. It was the theoretical and de facto model for much of Europe, not just Poland, that the Germans were creating.[38] A demythologized Waffen-SS man, Otto-Ernst Duscheleit, who saw firsthand his countrymen's transformation in the East, when asked what the world would have looked like had they won the war, explains: "It would have been terrible. I am not capable of imagining how bad this would have been. Hitler wanted not only Germany, he wanted to defeat the whole world, and everything would have been transformed into a huge concentration camp."[39]

The Germans' camp world contained many gradations depending on the principal incarcerated groups' racial, political, and sexual definition, the camps' formal functions, and their staffs. In all cases, the camps were integrated into their regions' politics, society, and economy. In Eastern Europe, they were the foundation of Germans' politics. In Germany itself, camps, fully integrated into the German economy and society, were an unavoidable part of the urban and rural landscape. In them, the Germans incarcerated an ever-growing slave population, mainly of Slavic peoples. In the small state of Hesse, at least 606 camps—one for every five-by-seven-mile area—apocalyptically shaped the physical and social landscape. Berlin, the country's capital and showpiece, housed 645 camps just for slave laborers. It would be interesting to ascertain how small the mean physical distance was between Germans and a camp, how many camps each German on average encountered during a week, and how little removed the most distant spot in Germany was from a camp.[40]

The Soviets' gulag was a sprawling camp world of more than 470 individual camp systems, each having hundreds or thousands of individual camps. The Soviets used this vast eliminationist infrastructure to help govern their empire of domination and communist fantasy and transformation, consuming millions of real, designated, and fantasized enemies. Like the German camp system, the gulag was a multifunctional lethal, exploitative, and penal system where the Soviets warehoused, enslaved, and killed their designated enemies. Kolyma, the most infamous Soviet camp complex, in the Arctic's frozen tundra, rivaled the most lethal German camps in overall murderousness (though not in annual death toll), consuming from 1937 to 1953 hundreds of thousands of lives. Like the Germans' camp world, the Soviets' camps, starting small and easily expanding into the vast gulag archipelago, were employed to house and coordinate a slave population, with perhaps eighteen million people passing through them, which the Soviets, as in Kolyma, often used as production factors, often working them quickly or slowly to death.

Galician Kalinnikovich, imprisoned for fifteen years in the gulag, began working in the Kalamar mines early in his imprisonment in Oc-

Gulag prisoners at work

tober 1938, when the gulag was at its worst. He describes how the prisoners worked and died in the arctic Siberian wasteland, from the "inhuman conditions . . . from hunger, from hunger. It was 70 degrees below. They worked twelve hours [a day]. The barracks were freezing cold. And people perished in these conditions. Sometimes you'd walk to work and on the way, people would freeze to death there who couldn't make it to camp. That's the kind of conditions they had. It was before the war. By 1941 it got a little better. And in 1941, the war started, the workday became sixteen hours. Imagine, working sixteen hours in the freezing cold, rain, snow, no matter, we worked." Of 1,500 in his group, 450, about one-third, died within the first three months, which Kalinnikovich says was a "quite usual" death rate for the various Kalamar camps.[41]

Whatever the Soviet gulag's formal and sometimes substantive similarities to the Germans' camp world, the differences were profound and fundamental, so much so that equating them is a mistake. Ukhnalev Ilyich, when wanting to convey the character of work in the arctic Vorkuta camps during his imprisonment starting in 1948, spontaneously, without any prompting, brought up the German camps. "You see," he explains, "it wasn't the same kind of camps as the German concentration camps. . . . People who had been arrested and

brought there [to the gulag] were there in order to work and not for
extermination. In other words, the goal to annihilate wasn't there."[42]
The sprawling gulag was an enormously variable system, which the
German camps were not for Jews, and were much less so even for
other prisoner groups. The gulag's camps had widely varying death
rates, and conditions and treatment of its prisoners, which depended
on the camps' locations, their work, and the orientation of individual
camps' commanders and staffs. Although camp staff often treated political prisoners and criminals differently (regularly pitting the two
groups against each other), a hierarchy of treatment and cruelty toward different victim groups akin to the Germans' (discussed below)
did not exist. The gulag's character also changed enormously over
time, including in the treatment of prisoners, in a manner the German
camp world did not once it expanded into its mature form. (The German camps existed more briefly but because they used them to execute well-articulated and long-term eliminationist plans, mainly to
destroy or eliminate people considered demons or subhumans, it is
hard to see how that camp world would have been tempered significantly.) The gulag was its most brutal and lethal in the late 1930s, and
by the late 1940s, owing to various causes, including a relaxation from
the top, had become, though still an abominable if not hellish place,
far less deadly and punitive toward its denizens. Kalinnikovich freely
describes the gulag's inhumanity and enormous death rates during its
worst years, including especially in the Arctic Kolyma camp Berlag.
"The situation there was one thousand times worse than usually in a
camp. First of all, they were taken to work shackled. That's one. Second, once they finish their work, they'd be locked up and [the guards]
put a bucket there. And can you imagine. You say . . . why people
died? People got emaciated very quickly." Kalinnikovich also conveys
the gulag's changes and how it differed fundamentally from the German camps:

> There were parcels. They were allowed. Letters were allowed. But
> everything was checked, so . . . Well, I, of course, sent [letters] via
> "the free people" [those in Kolyma who were not prisoners]. I had
> friends among the free people and I would send my wife money and
> prior to being released, I had already an outfit. . . . the clothes my

wife had sent me. I had everything in Kolyma. That was doable. I
have to say that towards the end, in the years beginning after the war,
the regime softened. There was less tyranny. . . . Before, we were the
prisoner swine and besides we were the enemy of the people. That
put a certain imprint on us as well as the way "the free people dealt
with us." But during this whole time, during the war time, the free
people understood what kind of enemy of the people we were. And
that's why . . . during my stay in Kolyma, fifteen years, the view was
turned upside-down.[43]

The gulag, unlike the Nazi camps, allowed cultural lives for the prisoners, including orchestras in some. There was a "cultural educational
division," Ilyich explains, "there were actors there, musicians, and
among them the camp artists."[44] The camp had workshops for the
prisoners to make things to use, sell, and barter. It had medical facilities with doctors or nurses. Prisoners were allowed contact with the
outside world by mail. Many prisoners received monthly packages
from their families containing food and tobacco. And many prisoners
were released, when their sentences were served, back into Soviet society. Because the Soviet leadership and the camps' personnel (and even
some prisoners!) conceived of the gulag as necessary to bring about
the communist paradise, the guards often had a paradoxical attitude
toward the prisoners. Vladimir Bukovsky, the Soviet dissident and
prisoner, explains: "In our camps, you were expected not only to be a
slave laborer, but to sing and smile while you worked as well. They
didn't just want to oppress us: they wanted us to thank them for it."[45]
And, as time went on, they, like the gulag itself, often softened up. All
this was unthinkable for the German camps, which for most of its inhabitants were utterly and only places of damnation, torture, and
death, which was exactly the Germans' intention. In many ways, the
gulag was a highly exacerbated eliminationist version or extension of
Soviet society itself, with all its pathologies. That is why people could
enter the gulag and then be released and why free people could live
nearby and have humane relations with the prisoners. The Germans,
by contrast, created a camp world unto itself, inhabited by putative
subhumans and demons, which was nothing like the life of the self-
conceived master race.

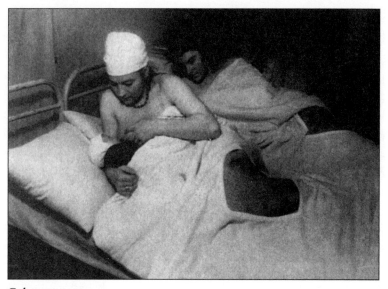

Gulag camp nursery

As in the Soviet Union, the communist Chinese had a range of institutions that functionally were camps, starting with their formal camp system, the Laogai, which they constructed upon taking power, and in which they incarcerated and put to work real and imagined enemies. As the Soviets had, the Chinese communists eliminated tens of millions by placing them in forced-labor camps, so that at any given moment for at least two decades, each communist system housed in their camps more than ten million people, who also suffered enormous mortality rates.[46] From 1949 to 1953, when the Chinese communists were consolidating power and laying the groundwork for their vast country's social and economic transformation to communism, the regime killed on the order of ten million people, mainly in their camps.

The communists' transformative programs' intensity reached two additional peaks: during the Great Leap Forward, from 1958 to 1961, and the Cultural Revolution, from 1966 to 1976. The Great Leap Forward was intended to hasten the creation of the ideal economic order and powerhouse promised by Marxist theory. The Cultural Revolution was to bring about the ideological purity the communist transformative project required, by purging society, especially the Communist Party itself, of those deemed impediments either ideologically or by deed. As is typical of vast camp systems, the regime and its perpetrators turned the prisoners into slaves, using them brutally for economic production, although, typical for such systems, highly irrationally from an economic point of view.

Once camp systems are created, perpetrators tend to expand and use them increasingly liberally as they do with mass murder. Eliminationist institutions' existence, including camps, forecloses or makes other kinds of politics—from accommodation and compromise to conventional, if brutal, repression—less used, less practiced, less available, and less normative. Camps' existence alters the perpetrators' cost-benefit calculus, rendering the camp system's use and expansion ever more instrumentally rational compared to alternatives for perpetrators to act upon their hatreds, solve the perceived human, social, and political problems, and consolidate and further their power.

Still, these systems are not mindless omnivores. Anthropomorphizing accounts holding camp systems or the systems creating them as some sort of autonomous, hungry, and insatiable consumers of lives are not grounded in reality. Camp systems are measured tools of eliminationist political regimes bent upon refashioning or purifying societies according to thoroughgoing transformative visions—the Nazi German, the imperial Japanese, the communisms of the Soviets, Chinese, North Koreans, and Khmer Rouge. The more we learn about camp systems, the clearer they systematically express their regimes' and staffs' ideological underpinnings. The perpetrators treat these systems' victims, those perishing and those suffering other horrible fates, according to their conceptions of the threats they and their country or ethnic group face, which is grounded in the particular character of their prejudices and hatreds (discussed below). Camp systems afford perpetrators the constant opportunity to include new, real, or imagined enemies in their eliminationist project, which changes as its implementation unfolds. It is striking how camp systems' expansions vary enormously from one eliminationist system to the next, in the range of victims, their functions, and their transformation's pace and size.

The Nazis started with a few so-called wild camps, improvised detention places serving principally as chambers to torture their political enemies. Later, with public announcement and fanfare, they institutionalized these wild camps into a formal camp system, which quickly grew so that many tens of thousands passed through, although the regime released most of them. By 1939 the camp system had been reduced to twenty-five thousand inmates. The Germans began expanding the camp population explosively only upon acquiring their empire and the opportunity to begin implementing their preconceived eliminationist and exterminationist projects. The Soviets established the gulag's rudiments early on, systematically expanding it along with their destructive grip on Soviet society, mainly for putative domestic enemies. In the first phase, they incarcerated mainly the regime's real enemies, who had fought them or resisted their assumption and consolidation of power. In the 1930s, the camps became depositories for those seen as impediments to the Soviets' transformation of their country's agricultural and industrial systems. In the 1940s and 1950s, the camps gobbled up the victims of Stalin's growing paranoia. The Chinese communists created a colossal and fully mature camp system soon after taking power. The Americans' camp system for the Japanese, the most rationally organized and least brutal, had a specific warehousing purpose. It did not expand, and was closed down when that purpose—ill-conceived and criminal as it was—became unnecessary, upon Japan's defeat. The British camp system in Kenya grew in stages, in a manner unplanned and unforeseen, as their assault's intensity on the Kikuyu increased. That the Khmer Rouge sent most Cambodians on their way into camps within a few days of seizing power precluded the need to expand the system dramatically.

Whatever particular camp systems' trajectories, regimes establishing such systems are usually engaged in long processes of murderous domination or eschatological transformation, processes that the camp systems' existence and availability further strengthen.

The Soviets were trying to bring about the impossible, a modern industrialized society based on a social theory, Marxism, denying a functioning modernity's certain fundamentals: free markets and free labor. When the millennial zeal died along with the paranoid tyrant Stalin, Khrushchev and those around him dismantled the camp system. The Germans, by contrast, were trying to bring about the possible: a European and eventually a world empire that, as Himmler and Frank indicated with their policy statements and instructions and as ordinary German perpetrators understood, was to be a huge concentration camp, organized according to racial-biological domination, exploitation, and extermination principles. The Japanese were intent upon something similar in Asia. The Khmer Rouge succeeded in bringing about their idiosyncratic version of Marxist transformation because they sought not a modern but a primitive totalitarian society wedded to a backward-looking nationalist agenda. Theirs was a workable, easily constructable model predicated on unfreedom, both economic and human. Seeking only to purify the Khmer people and enforce their ideological dictates, they made their camps into places of total atomization and premodern primitivism. Given the more limited aspirations of the Americans to warehouse Japanese-Americans and the British to eliminate the Kikuyu's threat to their colonial rule, the Americans succeeded partly because their aspirations were temporary and the British succeeded only temporarily because, short of still vaster mass murder, their colonial racial domination, historically passé, was doomed.

Understanding camp systems' overall purpose, character, and trajectory is only the larger part of their place as integral tools of eliminationist politics. The other part is their actual functioning. Except for the rare instances of single-purpose killing installations, such as the Germans' camps of Chelmno, Treblinka, and Sobibór, on the one hand, and temporary warehousing, such as the Americans' camps for Japanese-Americans, on the other, camps and camp systems are internally complex institutions riven by contradictory purposes.

They kill and create deadly conditions producing high, often massmurderous mortality rates, yet they pursue ideological dictates, including punishment and some reeducation, requiring victims to remain alive. They make varying attempts to be economically productive, yet according to any rational understanding of economic organization, they are thoroughly irrational—they intrinsically produce harsh, debilitating conditions for the inmates, because they are, as a rule, underfunded and undersupplied in every respect, especially food. (Because they are economically unviable, an additional economic calculus victimizes their inmates—why should scarce economic resources be allocated to these economic black holes?—leading to an even greater undersupply of food and other things.) Within camps themselves, regimes and their followers treat different prisoners differently: They immediately slaughter some, incarcerate others indefinitely, warehouse others temporarily.

Camps are run by low-quality staff, often by people who before coming to the camps already dehumanized or demonized victims. Day to day, camps and their personnel often operate relatively autonomously from the regime, aside from its broad ideological dictates, governed less by rules and more by personalistic and arbitrary whim. The perpetrators staffing camps exercise virtually unrestrained power over victims, inherently producing great abuses. In light of these features, it is no wonder that camp worlds, while coherent as general places of elimination, domination, and destruction, are incoherent in their actual running, including the multiple ways that camps' various aspects systematically conflict.

The most obvious and acute contradictions are camps' destructive and productive uses. Perpetrators employ many camp systems or individual camps as vehicles of death, often through massive expected or calculated attrition owing to the inhuman conditions and treatment. Almost all camp systems also compel their victims to work, seeking to produce some economic value. Yet, at most, victims' work defrays a (usually small) portion of the huge economic loss of wresting productive workers from the normal economy (which also is not always governed by rational economic principles). Putting the victims to work is but a natural corollary of the eliminationist project and what every eliminationist project is at heart: a massive, economically destructive initiative. American Ambassador Henry Morgenthau appealed to economic rationality to deter Mehmet Talât from completing his exterminationist program against the Armenians: "If you are not influenced by humane considerations," Morgenthau reasoned, "think of the material loss. These people are your business men. They control many of your industries. They are very large tax-payers. What would become of you commercially without them?" Talât replied that they had already calculated all this and that it did not matter: "We care nothing about the commercial loss." Without disputing Morgenthau's warning that in killing the Armenians they were "ruining the country economically"—or in the words of American Consul Leslie Davis, "by one stroke, the country was to be set back a century"—Ismail Enver reiterated this point, definitively declaring that "economic considerations are of no importance at this time."[47]

The Germans similarly did not care that by destroying the Jews they enormously damaged their economy, and even their chances of winning the war. So economically irrational was their ideologically driven treatment of the Jews that, in the face of a massive labor shortage of more than 2.5 million workers, according to their own report about the part of occupied Poland called the Generalgouvernement, they employed full time only 450,000 out of 1.4 million Jewish workers. The rest, totaling almost one million, "were employed for a short period."[48] Of course, under their total annihilation program, the Germans killed almost all these Jewish workers in the next months anyway. This accorded exactly with the German leadership's understanding of their exterminationist priorities' colossal economic destructiveness. Reinhard Heydrich explained at the Wannsee Conference, "The Jews will be conscripted for labor . . . and undoubtedly a large number of them will drop out through natural wastage." The rest they would kill.[49] Such was the relationship between annihilation and work, the annihilation's primacy, and how an eliminationist program is the sine qua non for the creation of the derivative phenomenon of camps.

The Soviet gulag is the camp system most clearly intended for something approximating rational economic exploitation, with production goals assigned to the camps and, by individual camp administrations, to the individual inmates. Moreover, the gulag's administration and the Soviet regime devoted considerable energy to using the camps economically and more productively. Yet the gulag could not overcome its many contradictions inhibiting production, including its fundamental noneconomic eliminationist reason for being. This made it utterly irrational economically, unprofitable, and far less productive than free labor—as the Soviet regime's members themselves knew from the beginning. The regime's own records demonstrate this, as early as July 1919 and in the 1920s. In 1938, in response to the camps' massive production shortfalls, the Communist Party leaders responsible for the gulag held candid meetings about their ongoing economic catastrophe. "Chaos and disorder," "our camps are organized unsystematically," a "particularly difficult situation with food supplies," which led to "an enormous percentage of weak workers, an enormous percentage of prisoners who couldn't work at all, and a high death rate and illness rate" were among their many withering economic criticisms. This continued throughout. Fifteen years later, in 1953, an inspection the Communist Party's Central Committee ordered determined that camps were enormously unprofitable, costing more to maintain than their laborers produced.[50] Not only did camp labor not produce *more* than the general economy's labor, but it was negatively productive, running a *deficit*, soaking up badly needed capital from genuine economic enterprises in a capital-starved economy.

The official Guatemalan Commission for Historical Clarification, established with the mandate to investigate and report on the Guatemalan government's eliminationist assault upon leftists and Maya, calculated that in the ten-year period from 1980 to 1989 alone "the total direct quantifiable costs were equivalent to zero production in Guatemala for almost 15 months, equal to 121% of the 1990 Gross Domestic Product (GDP)." That is an astonishing amount of economic loss. Moreover, the total losses were considerably greater, because the eliminationist onslaught and destruction lasted many more years and this calculation included only five of the seven most destructive years (1978–1985). The report further detailed the losses:

> The majority of the costs, equivalent to 90% of the 1990 GDP, resulted from the loss of production potential due to the death, disappearance or forced displacement of individuals who had to abandon their daily activities, or from recruitment into the PAC, the Army or the guerrillas. The destruction of physical assets, including private and community property, and the loss of infrastructure, such as bridges and electrical towers, also represented considerable losses, over 6% of the 1990 GDP. These material losses frequently involved the total destruction of family capital, especially among Mayan families, particularly in the west and north-west of Guatemala.[51]

Exterminationist and eliminationist assaults are economically utterly irrational. The Guatemalan assault highlights the critical issue: The economic loss owing to just the *lost productivity* of the victims was 90 percent of the overall economic loss, which was equivalent to shutting down the country's entire economy for *a year and a quarter*. Had the Guatemalan perpetrators, instead of slaughtering and driving Maya from the country, deposited them in camps, grossly underfed them, subjected them to most camp systems' brutal work and living conditions, producing extremely high mortality rates, and then worked them as slaves in irrationally organized and outfitted sites, the lost economic productivity, perhaps somewhat less, would still have been catastrophic. It is simply bizarre to think that such standard camp conditions are a recipe for greater economic output than what the Guatemalan economy lost owing to the regime's elimination of Maya, or for that matter than what any other economy lost with its eliminationist program. Soviet camp commanders particularly interested in economic production recognized this and therefore chose to undermine the gulag's ordinary regimen. One commander, according to former prisoner Aleksi Pryadilov, "ran the camp like an economic organization, and behaved toward prisoners not as if they were criminals or enemies, whom it was necessary to 're-educate,' but as though they were workers." Why? "He was convinced that there was no point in trying to get good work out of hungry people."[52]

None of this is surprising, as perpetrators do not create camp systems for economic purposes. The notion that they do is ideological nonsense, serving the perpetrators' wish to conceal their real motives and purposes, as well as their many interpreters' and apologists' desires to justify the perpetrators' actions, deflect attention from the truth, or ideologically indict a political-economic dispensation. Economic rationality was manifestly not the core conception of regimes—the Germans in South-West Africa, Soviets, Nazis, Croatians, Chinese, Americans, North Koreans, the British in Kenya, Indonesians, Ethiopians, Khmer Rouge, Serbs, and many others—in creating camps to eliminate real or imagined enemies. This aside, only camps' ideologized supporters or people sympathetic to the camps' irrational underpinnings can believe that plunging people into inhuman, debilitating conditions and turning productive workers with differentiated skills into weakened and sick slaves laboring at unfamiliar tasks often below their skill levels is a program for rational economic organization and high productivity.

Any idea that a regime's economic need brings people into camps, even in camp systems' most rationally organized part, misconstrues the causal relationship. The perpetrators' ideological worldview brings camps into being, sustains them, and engenders the image of humanity and society that first *creates* victims and then mobilizes them as irrationally used workers. The Khmer Rouge turned a country self-sufficient in foodstuffs (rice being the agricultural staple) into an agricultural and economic disaster, so naturally they worked people in the communes growing rice. Ratha Duong (a pen name), then a child, conveys this, as well as her clear understanding that she was, and was to be, a victim of one of the Khmer Rouge's many interchangeable eliminationist means, of which enslavement was one: "In November and early December 1976 there was no food to eat. I was sick. I asked myself when I was going to die. Would I die by starvation or by torture? I thought that if I died, I would no longer have to work like an animal. I asked my group leader for permission to rest one day. She said no. So I worked in the field planting rice. My legs were weak from standing in the mud. The rain fell hard and my body shook with chills. My eyes couldn't see. I felt dizzy and then I collapsed into the mud. I heard the group leader tell girls to carry me out under the tree. I was unconscious."[53] Virtually everything the Khmer Rouge had people do and how they had them live, including how they prepared the young for adult life, violated any notion of economic rationality. One eleven-year-old boy describes how the Khmer Rouge reared him and other teenage boys, having, as they had with most children in Cambodia, separated them from their families. The boys were "not taught to read or write or to sing any songs; we were never shown any radios, books or magazines." Instead they were compelled to build a road that was supposed to cross hundreds of kilometers of uninhabited forest. How did these "workers" do it? "We all worked at the rate of two or three metres of road per day, using locally-made buckets to shift the earth; some boys threw up the soil while others packed it down into a road surface. By the time I left this site five months later, no vehicles had yet been seen on the road."[54] At that rate, these young boys would have taken a year to complete just one kilometer. The Khmer Rouge's worldview, producing Cambodia's total economic catastrophe, was but the extreme variant of our age's economically irrational and self-destructive ideologies creating camps and governing their work.

Camps' simple logic is that the people consigned to them are putative subhumans or demons, dangerous or criminal, certainly enemies of the regime, the future, and goodness, so an eliminationist regime might as well benefit from the victims before killing or otherwise disposing of them. The gulag's murderous nature and conditions were so great already in 1926, long before the gulag became its most deadly in the late

1930s, that S. A. Malsagoff, in a camp on an island in the Arctic Sea, reported: "I gathered from the candid statements of the Tchekists that the Gpu has now no need to make a regular practice of mass shootings, because more humane measures—slow murder from starvation, work beyond the prisoners' strength, and 'medical help'—are perfectly adequate substitutes."[55] If you are going to kill those people designated as enemies, as subhumans or demons, why not get them to work in the meantime? Mao revealed this logic to be explicitly guiding him in an order from May 1951. The victims, according to Mao, had "committed crimes that deserve to be punished by death," but if they were immediately executed, "we would lose a large labour force."[56] So Mao sent them to a system of labor camps designed to house them under hellish conditions to temporarily produce some surplus.

The perpetrators' knowledge that the camps' victims enjoy a momentary reprieve before execution, or their belief that the inmates are socially dead and can or must be eliminated, allows them to temporarily use the victims brutally and irrationally as workers. The Khmer Rouge, having caught Moly Ly leaving his slave labor village, where they had already reduced him to "a worn-out, skeletal figure craving food," sent him to a worse facility.

> Once there, I was stunned to see only four women and a man. Without observing the clothes they wore, it was difficult to tell the difference between the man and the women. They had extremely fragile figures. Bones were popping out from everywhere in their bodies. At night our feet were cuffed with a special kind of wood to prevent us from escaping. At dawn we were dragged to work near the jail, plucking the soil.
>
> The next day, one of the women died in her sleep. Her ankles had been cuffed. I now realized that this was a death camp to cruelly torture people by starving and overworking them. Sometimes they threw food scraps at our faces and laughed. Other times we were beaten for being so exhausted from the hard work. I could no longer function like a human being. I knew in my heart that my spirit was going to die.[57]

If the people slated for elimination end up producing something useful, all the better. Mey Komphot conveys the thoughts he had about

Cambodians' situation around the time the Khmer Rouge had been in power for a month. He was in one of the hellish cooperatives with a pound of rice per day, the ration for an adult—no other food whatsoever—so five hundred calories a day, minimal protein, virtually no vitamins and minerals. Children received nothing. The new Cambodian reality dawned on him: "I realized we were expendable. All the analyses we had done during the war, all of our ideas about what Cambodia would be like, were so wrong I had no room in my imagination for what was happening. I finally understood what it meant to be called [by the Khmer Rouge cadres] to 'study'—those people were murdered. Those of us who were spared were to become work animals. We were barely surviving."[58] Even if in some camp systems attempts are made to enhance camps' productivity, many perpetrators' prevailing attitude has been that the prisoners should work for working's sake, the economic outcome be damned.

Given camps' multiple economic irrationalities, it is no surprise that regimes putting people to work in camp systems rarely conceive of the work in any conventional sense and force people to work for various reasons having nothing to do with rational economics. The most obvious reason is by now clear: The perpetrators readily and variously exploit people they want to eliminate, including for labor. For many regimes, compelling the hated enemies to work also satisfies ideological dictates and is emotionally satisfying. Germans, beholden to antisemitic lore (deeply grounded in Christian accounts about Jews, including centrally in Martin Luther's writings), which held that Jews do not labor honestly, conceived of the simple act of labor to be punishment for Jews. Throughout their camp system, the Germans worked Jews just for the sake of working them. The harder the better. This can be seen both in the work's abysmal organization and productivity, and in the Germans' frequent resort to productiveless labor, such as compelling Jews to run with big rocks or full sacks from one place to a second and then back to the first, under the Germans' hail of blows, taunts, and laughter. According to one non-Jewish survivor from Buchenwald, "Some of the work in camp was useful but some of it was utterly senseless, intended only as a form of torture, a diversion engaged in by the SS 'for fun.' The Jews especially, often had to build walls, only to tear them down the next day, rebuild them again, and so on."[59] Communist regimes deemed the bourgeoisie and, in the case of Asian communisms, urban dwellers to be class enemies—parasites living off workers' or peasants' sweat. In the Soviet Union's early years it was dangerous to have uncallused hands, which indicated that a person had not labored honestly and so was a member of the bourgeoisie. As an act of retribution and justice, communist regimes put these "enemies" to work.

This is what Hendrik Fraser, a Baster accompanying the Germans in South-West Africa, reported on the work they compelled captured Herero to perform:

> There must have been about 600 men, women and children prisoners. They were in an enclosure on the beach, fenced in with barbed wire. The women were made to do hard labor just like the men. The sand is very deep and heavy there. The women had to load and unload carts and trolleys, and also to draw Scotch-cart loads of goods to Nonidas (9–10 kilos. away) where there was a depot. The women were put in spans of eight to each Scotch-cart and were made to pull like draught animals. Many were half-starved and weak, and died of sheer exhaustion. Those who did not work well were brutally flogged with sjamboks [heavy rhinoceros-hide whips]. I even saw women knocked down with pick handles. The German soldiers did this. I personally saw six women (Herero girls) murdered by German soldiers. They were ripped open with bayonets. I saw the bodies. I was there six months, and the Hereros died daily in large numbers as a result of exhaustion, ill-treatment and exposure.[60]

This, too, qualifies as "work." The prisoners produced some economic output, yet it was a small, incidental detour on the Germans' path to exterminating them. This was also true of the "labor battalions" Turks formed with Armenians soldiers in the Turkish army. An American hospital doctor reported on the Turks' treatment of these workers: "It was mid-summer, they, the soldiers were allowed no water and no rest, and were driven with clubs and gunstocks by the gendarmes. . . . They stayed thus in this building without water for three days and even soaked the urine from the ground with handkerchiefs and drank it."[61] What Beatrice Gatonye, a Kikuyu incarcerated in a British camp, said about the task the British made her and other Kikuyu women do, of fingerprinting decomposing bodies whose skin would just come off on them, is true of so much of victims' work under eliminationist regimes: "The job we were told to do was just to torture us."[62] Of course, not all camp work and not all treatment of the ostensible workers has so shockingly little to do with economic productivity's norms and procedures as did the Germans', Turks', and Britons' practices. But a stunning percentage of it does.

The perpetrators' relative emphasis on killing and immiseration, or on work, varies from camp system to system, and within a given system over time. On its face, the two are in inherent tension (assuming the perpetrators really aim for productive labor). Economic productivity requires everything camps often are not: using people's skills appropriately, husbanding human capital, having rational institutions and plants for work. None of these is typically present in any conventionally rational degree. Thus camp systems tend to be economically irrational at their core. To the extent that perpetrators use camps to slaughter people rather than to keep them fit, they undermine the camp's economic purposes. To the extent that such a dehumanizing world prevents regimes and societies from maintaining minimal nutrition and health, productive labor is undermined across the board. But to the ideologized perpetrators these contradictions matter not. Rithy Uong explains: "The food wasn't the issue. All those Khmer [Rouge] people had plenty of food to eat. But they would not give it to us. They wanted us to work hard *and* starve to death" [my emphasis].[63]

Camp systems' broad goals make them irrational labor institutions. Work's economic rationality is further undermined even while the victims are doing work because of the perpetrators' treatment of them. Just as many regimes conceive of work in ideological terms, so too do the perpetrators in camps. Communist regimes, drawing on Marxist theory, conceive of work as reeducative, even redemptive. (GULAG is a Russian acronym for Main Administration of Corrective Labor Camps, and the Chinese called their camps Labor Reform Camps.) Working the regime's enemies—many of whom are seen as having shunned productive labor—is ideologically necessary, containing educative and punitive dimensions that Bukovsky conveys when discussing the oxymoronic roles the perpetrators assigned prisoners as thankful slaves. The Germans' view of work as exquisite punishment for the putatively parasitical Jews governed the Germans' use of Jews' work more than conventional economic considerations. In the "work" camp Majdanek, the prisoners had morning roll call.

> Then we went to "work." In our wooden shoes we were chased by blows from rods into a corner of the field and had to fill sometimes our caps, at other times our jackets, with stones, wet sand or mud, and, holding them with both hands and running under a hail of blows, bring them to the opposite corner of the field, empty the stuff, refill it and bring it back to the opposite corner, and so on. A gauntlet of screaming SS men and privileged prisoners, armed with rods and whips, let loose on us a hail of blows. It was hell.[64]

The Germans' manner of employing Jews in camps was so utterly irrational and self-destructive that Joseph Schupack, the memoirist describing such work above, put "work" in quotation marks. Thinking of work as ideologically necessary, whether for reeducating victims or making them suffer, is bound to undermine labor's rational allocation and use, as it has in camp worlds across the globe.

Getting prisoners to work (something socially useful) expresses and confirms the perpetrators' and their broader communities' subjectively just control of their victims. That prisoners, however coerced, appear to slavishly serve perpetrators gratifies them and seems to further validate their rule's justness. Thus camps resemble slave institutions more than prisons, the inmates often functioning as slaves. However, unlike slaves, who often receive minimal legal protections, move among the enslaving society's general population, and can have relationships with a measure of subjective affection from their masters, the camp worlds' inmates are beyond the law, (with exceptions) ordinary social intercourse's realm, or affective ties with their "masters."

Beyond punishment, work serves as fulfillment or redemption. In the modern world, work is seen as not only economically valuable but a mark of a person's willingness to contribute to a community. Therefore, getting people to work is its own end. This is true for prisoners eventually going free, making work a perverse reeducational school, or dying, making work an expiatory act. This most clearly existed in the German camps' early years, when many prisoners, the regime's political opponents, would eventually return to society, and under communist

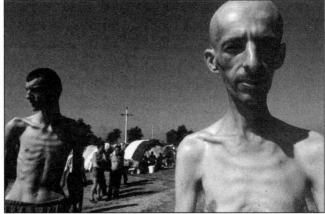

Serbian camp
victims in
Trnopolje, Bosnia
and Herzegovina,
August 1992

regimes, including the Chinese and Vietnamese, with their so-called
reeducation camps. For the Khmer Rouge this was axiomatic. Uong
explains that the Khmer Rouge "said they want to clean the imperialism ideas from you." So "they told us. Here are your hoes. Here is the
rice field. This is your school. Do it. Okay, you learn from the rice field,
and exactly what they say, they preach to us every single day. And every
single day after work we had to sit down for a meeting and we had to
criticize ourselves, what had we done, done wrong."[65] In the warped
worldviews of many eliminationist assaults' perpetrators, an honest
day's labor helps make an honest man, or at least the shell of one.

A principal operational purpose of camp systems is degrading the
victims, to make them understand their subjugated, demeaned, and
rightless state. The men and women shaping or carrying out eliminationist projects are rarely policy's cool, detached, neutral executors.
How could they be? The killers often wade in the victims' blood, spat-
tering themselves with flesh and blood, bone and brain matter, after
hearing their victim's mercy pleas and suffering cries, only to turn to the
next victim, the next, and the next. Men doing this are not, in one
writer's conceptually, descriptively, and morally obtuse language, mere
"shooters" of victims—technical operators, trigger fingers, in a non-
moral, technical enterprise. Guards in camps, even those not slaughtering victims, brutalize them, watch them starve to death, work them
to the bone and beyond, let fester debilitating illnesses and conditions.

The perpetrators want the victims to know who the master is. They
want to refashion the victims according to their images of them. The

Germans infamously reshaped their victims in camps, particularly Jews, Sintis, Roma, and Russians, quickly transforming them through malnutrition, privation, and neglect into beings physically resembling the subhumans of the Germans' fantasies, the worst off becoming mere skeletal human shadows verging on death, called *Muselmänner* (Muslims). The Soviets in their brutal camps, without this kind of ideological intent, but no less deadly, created the *dokhodyaga* ("goner"), the "men who have been reduced to such a low level mentally and physically that even as workers they are of very limited value."[66] The Khmer Rouge turned their communes' denizens into the atomized, robot-like or animal-like, asocial beings they wanted for their dystopian fantasy future. "During the day," recalls Savuth Penn, who was then a child, "I would hunt for food like snakes and rats or anything that moved. This was allowed only during a short break after the long labor-intensive work. My body was so thin and weak from lack of adequate nutrition. The other young boys were in the same condition as me. We looked liked grandpas to one another. We rarely played or had long conversations because we lacked energy and tried to conserve it for the next day's work quota."[67] In all cases, eliminationist perpetrators violently pry from their victims basic qualities marking people as full human beings. They deny the victims' fundamental human bonds, ripping families apart, including parents from children as they might divide different-sized stones into piles. They shear the victims' hair and deny them marks of individuality, including in clothing. They rob their names, renaming them or reducing them to nameless tattooed numbers, as the Germans did in Auschwitz. They forbid them many basic human qualities of sociability, including, as the British did in Kenya, communicating with each other all day (except when in their barracks), including during backbreaking work. If the victims dare act as human beings, instead of as their masters' pliant nonhuman objects? For conversing, the Kikuyu prisoners could be punished and beaten individually or collectively. Karue Kibicho, a Kikuyu victim, once impermissibly spoke to another prisoner: "The guard on the watchtower blew his whistle, and the *askaris*, who we called *rioti* [riot squad], were set upon us all. They were using their hoe-handle clubs, clubbing us indiscriminately. Some of the detainees died from the beatings before we were all told to come out of our compound naked, holding our clothing and blankets in our hands. This was not done peacefully, because the *askaris* were inside the compound beating us, and as we hurried out there were others waiting for us, beating us some more. . . . It was total mayhem, and the white man in charge just stood there screaming, '*Piga, piga sana*' [hit them, hit them more]."[68]

Even regimes and perpetrators without such explicit ideological conceptions of their victims related to work tend to force their putatively demonic or subhuman enemies to work in camps to their limit and beyond. Furthermore, for some perpetrators, work becomes a convenient means of inflicting suffering without conceiving of themselves as torturers. Perpetrators can think that if the victims were not such miscreants they would labor harder (no matter how objectively false this is). And they see even excruciatingly hard labor as a socializing means, getting the victims to at least act as contributors to the commonweal.

Camp victims actually producing substantial economic output are often used as brute production factors. The perpetrators destroy their bodies, not to mention their souls, to get their relatively paltry returns. Mao formulated, already in 1933, the ideologically inspired notion of working people to death as production factors, by having them "do limitless forced labor."[69] No rational economy would be run according to the camp worlds' principles, which often lead to annual workforce mortality rates of 10 percent. Zhao Yushu, the head of Fengyang country, epitomized the Chinese communists' utter disregard for economic rationality in camps and in general, when he said during the Great Leap Forward, "Even if ninety-nine percent die, we still have to hold high the red flag."[70] Only a deeply ideologized and nonproductively oriented regime and people (apparently as in North Korea) would conceive of constructing an economy along the lines of camps, whether German, Soviet, Chinese, British, or Khmer Rouge. The Khmer Rouge, having destroyed practically Cambodia's entire physical plant, and, shunning modern machinery, shutting down the urban economy and all but ruining the agricultural one, compelled Cambodia's people to work growing rice and to fulfill the ideological need to work for working's sake, even in the most irrational ways. Tens of thousands of Cambodians died digging irrigation canals with the most primitive implements, including their bare hands, all to restore the Angkor Wat Empire's twelfth-century glories, which rested partly on agricultural canals. Excavating massive quantities of dirt and rock in this way has been a common feature of the German, Soviet, British, and Chinese camp worlds. One Chinese survivor of Mao's Great Leap Forward conveys the utter irrationality of labor use during this ideologically produced economic and human catastrophe, when the communists dumped expellees in Manchuria's wilderness with no shelter, which they had to make using wheat stems in temperatures as low as –36 degrees Fahrenheit (–38 Celsius). With a fire, their huts warmed up to "a dozen or so degrees below zero [Celsius or 10 degrees Fahrenheit]," yet "the grass and beaten earth huts we lived in had wind coming in from all sides . . . there were hardly any vegetables or meat. . . . We got up . . . just after 4 at dawn, and did not stop until 7 or 8 in the evening. . . . In these 15–16 hours . . . we basically worked non-stop . . . in summer. . . . We had to get up at 2 am. . . . We had at most three hours' sleep."[71] Although the landscape was different, Navy Dy describes the analogous irrationality of the creation and character of Cambodia's ostensible work camps. Those who survived the death march to the village of Moung arrived with almost nothing.

> When I got to that village I saw only a few small houses, rice fields, and small irrigation ditches. We had to build our own camp under a mango tree with the other ten families by using every scrap of our old clothes and plastic. Later, my father built a small barn for us. Moung was supposed to be very poor land. There was no river water, but a small pit with very dirty water; no orchids or fruit trees or even soil, but an empty desert with a few mango trees.
>
> About 300 families moved to this place, but three-quarters of them died from disease, starvation, and harsh, bloody torture.[72]

Only an ideologue—then or now—can see economic concerns or rationality governing the camp world and "work." Put differently, economic purposes can be seen to have been at work only if one accepts these regimes and their camp world's eliminationist foundations, and the perpetrators' dehumanizing or demonizing assumptions. This was explicit and striking in Kenya, where these features coalesced in an official policy. The British, desperate to hold on to Kenya, expelled most Kikuyu from their homes and regions, placing them in the unsustainable, deadly barbed-wire villages. They declared the eliminationist "exile" permanent, as the colony's governor, Evelyn Baring, publicly explained, "There is no

question whatsoever of irreconcilables being allowed to return to areas
where loyal Kikuyu live." They then undertook a massive "development
plan" for the Kikuyu, now forced to inhabit formerly uncultivated and
inhospitable land. How did the British do it? With brute labor, slave
labor, people used as production factors, including by compelling shackled Kikuyu victims to dig an eleven-mile canal by hand. "This was the
most miserable experience of my life," explains Charles Karumi. "Many
men died from diseases, I think because we were so weak from the labor
and beatings. The white man in charge kept yelling at us to keep working, and ordered the *askaris* to set on us with their clubs if we moved
too slowly."[73] Only because the British had decided to eliminate the
Kikuyu from their homes and deposit them in the middle of nowhere did
"developing" this area of Kenya become seemingly necessary, as did
working slaves brutally and economically irrationally, resulting in an
enormous death toll of the putatively subhuman "workers." Only in the
context and assumptions of an eliminationist regime and program, such
as that of the British, does "working" people so unproductively for "development" make sense.

Once established, functioning camps cannot escape their inherent
pathologies and contradictions: the desire to punish the prisoners, make
them suffer, and make them understand their degraded and subhuman
or dehumanized status; the subversion of economic potential by starving the camps of necessary factors and conditions of production; and
the perpetrators' tendencies within the camp to abuse their absolute
power for personal satisfaction.

Camp systems' enormous significance, as we see, is multifaceted.
Whatever their many variations in size, victims and the perpetrators'
conceptions of them, duration, mix of eliminationist means, and overall destructiveness, camp systems institutionalize eliminationist policies as a core, if not the core, political thrust of regime and society. They
integrate eliminationist politics and practices deeply into the broader
societies and involve ever more people, often in vast numbers, from the
state and civil society to run, maintain, and service them. In so doing,
they steadily warp (or further warp) society's economic, social, and cultural spheres, in addition to its politics, not only by enmeshing ever
more people in their assault on humanity but also by creating perverse
incentives and corrupting practices at all levels. While the camp world,

like many institutions, tends to be self-reinforcing and self-reproducing, and even expanding, the regimes building and maintaining camps also *purposefully* employ them throughout for political domination and destruction.

Camp systems are significant for another reason. As systems of society, they encapsulate or contain the different worlds the perpetrators create. They are in themselves eliminationist worlds. They are communal worlds and are embedded in still broader communities. And they are sites where the perpetrators create personal worlds, especially through cruelty. In camps and elsewhere, perpetrators personally, face-to-face, inflict cruelty on victims, as to make cruelty many mass murders and eliminations' constituent feature. They are cruel to the victims in general. They are cruel to women in specific ways. They are differentially murderous and cruel to children.

Personal Worlds

Cruelty refashions worlds.

For a victim, intense physical and psychological pain concentrates the mind exclusively on the pain itself, becoming his world. Acute pain alters the nexus of space and time as nothing else does. It compresses space so all one can apprehend is located on the (often tiny) afflicted body part. It changes the experience of time, elongating every second, every minute, every hour, every day. Each seems to stretch and drag on beyond what time's actual unit can contain and the sufferer can bear. Think of pain's instant effect on you: slicing your hand, hitting your finger with a hammer, or twisting your ankle. Think how your world shrinks in that elongated moment, which compared to eliminationist cruelty's victims' suffering is a droplet of intensity and duration. Multiply the pain, your world's shrinking and time's elongation, by a hundred, a thousand, a million, by some indeterminably large number, and imaginatively enter the physical world of cruelty and suffering the perpetrators create for the victims. Then add the commensurate psychological and emotional suffering. The perpetrators' cruelty for the victims can, perhaps, now somewhat come into focus. For as long as the perpetrators' domination lasts, such cruelty refashions the victims' world, because even if a respite occurs, they know the perpetrators can and likely will resume. If the victims survive, such cruelty refashions their world *forever*. The victims never forget their pain, torment, and suffering. The horror will always cast a pall over their lives. It will likely become a life-defining experience, perhaps *the* defining one, to be re-lived and relived, whether they want to remember it or, much more likely, though they wish to forget it forever.

For the perpetrator, cruelty also concentrates the mind. It is an unusual social moment most perpetrators have never had: rendering human beings into playthings. Some practitioners of cruelty turn the humanistic Kantian maxim—not to use people as means but to treat them as ends—on its head, toying with and hurting the victims for amusement, pleasure, and gratification. Other practitioners of cruelty expand the Kantian maxim into the definitive instance of using people as means *and* ends. They use the victims as playthings and inflict their cruelty for another purpose: to teach the victims—in the perpetrator's eyes, finally and properly—how abject they are. For the perpetrator, cruelty brings enormous satisfaction. He enjoys it. He revels in it. It invigorates and sustains him. He creates an out-of-this-world world for himself in the concentrated moment of flogging, battering, or dismembering his victims, and an out-of-this-world world for communities of cruelty as perpetrators share their joys collectively. The question is: What forms of cruelty do perpetrators inflict on the victims and why?

Cruelty is a common feature of eliminationist assaults. Cruelty is also an enormously significant aspect of them. It is significant foremost because the victims endure violence and suffering at their tormentors' hands. It is also significant because its perpetration tells us much about the perpetrators. Yet such cruelty remains little analyzed and poorly understood.

Without taking up the fine conceptual and psychological aspects of defining cruelty and torture, we can say the perpetrators know their victims suffer, and while they, at least in principle, might not wish their victims to suffer excessively beyond the already enormous suffering their eliminationist assault and act itself require for their execution, they minimally are at least willing (almost always gladly and rarely with lament) to inflict that high baseline of suffering. In an expansive notion of torture and cruelty's meaning and universe, eliminationist policies and their acts themselves might rightly be seen as cruelty if not torture. Many countries' legal systems and people consider the death penalty cruel and inhumane punishment. Treating exterminationist acts as inherently cruel is an easily sustainable position. The same could be said for other elim-inationist acts, such as driving people from their homes or incarcerating them in camps. Death marches are almost always a particularly cruel way to kill people, as the perpetrators themselves recognize. When mis-sionaries asked a Turkish perpetrator why the Turks did not kill women and children on the spot and chose instead to make them so "wretched" by sending them on a death march, he explained that in addition to being a good way to prevent corpses from stinking up their villages, "It is right so, they must become wretched."[74]

Nevertheless, for analytical purposes, I leave the eliminationist acts themselves aside and consider only perpetrators' acts of cruelty or tor-ture going *beyond* what is strictly required of them in eliminating the victims. When a person's task is to kill someone, he need not gratu-itously beat, torture, or degrade that person first. He need not take ini-tiative to augment her suffering. Yet perpetrators routinely do, so much so that just in the killing act itself in one of the eliminationist assaults where it is most frequently said the perpetrators were conscripted and had no choice, the perpetrators subjected an amazingly high percentage of the victims to enormous gratuitous cruelty and suffering. When asked what "overkill" means, Fredy Peccerelli, head of the Guatemalan Forensic Anthropology Foundation processing victims' remains uncov-ered in mass graves, explains: "Well, see, overkill would be associated, like I said, to many different strikes or many different impacts when they're not necessary to cause a person's death. And they're more geared to brutality and to this part of human nature that I don't fully understand, when things get out of hand and it becomes a matter of just making this person pay for something or making a point of the killing." Asked to estimate the percentage of victims on whom the Guatemalan perpetrators inflicted overkill, Peccerelli replies, "I would say maybe between 15 to 20 percent."[75] This incredibly high number comes just from the moment of the kill, just from assessing the small percentage of all the perpetrators' cruelties cutting all the way to, and incising marks into, the victims' bones (the skeletal remains being all the forensic pathologists can investigate decades after the fact), and just from the bones uncovered for each victim, many skeletons being far from complete, leaving many additional instances of even to-the-bone overkill undetected.

By no means are the perpetrators cruel toward their victims and torturing them only when killing them, but far more often when they are guarding, herding, or just passing by them. In Kenya, Major wa Wanjiru, a notorious killer, and his men regularly tortured Kikuyu before killing them. Esther Muchiri describes an episode where the perpetrators stripped her and several dozen men and women naked:

> We were beaten the whole day until evening, when we were separated from the men, who were ordered to sit a distance away with their hands cuffed together. Then the interrogators started to squeeze their private parts with a pair of pliers. There was only a short distance between where they were and ourselves. I even saw one of them being hit on his face, a blow that sent him sprawling down unconscious. A whole bucket of water had to be poured on his body to revive him. The same evening, the men were loaded onto a vehicle and driven away. We were to learn the following morning that all of them had been executed.[76]

Such cruelty that is unnecessary for carrying out the eliminationist act itself—whether or not during the act of killing or elimination—constitutes *excess cruelty*. In eliminationist and exterminationist assaults, excess cruelty *is* a commonplace, *and* it varies widely from one eliminationist assault to the next. Both these aspects, and their sources, are significant and need to be explored if we are to understand our time's mass murders and eliminations.

There are different kinds of excess cruelty. A two-dimensional matrix, with one dimension being whether the cruelty is ordered from above and the other being whether it is individually or collectively performed, specifies four kinds of excess cruelty.

	Ordered from Above	*Not Ordered*
Collective	Organized and structured	Group performance
Individual	Supervised	Individual initiative

In the annals of eliminationist assaults, individually supervised cruelty is rarely ordered from above. A second kind of cruelty ordered or governed from above, which is collective and not performed by individuals, is exterminationist and eliminationist programs' constitutive feature. This organized and structured cruelty is embedded in the fabric of the world the perpetrators create for the victims. It includes the pain and suffering in how they house them, undernourish them, systematically punish them, transport them, and generally mistreat them, including by tearing families apart. Camps are such cruelty's quintessential sites. Perpetrators create them in a manner guaranteeing the victims will suffer such cruelty—regularly, daily and nightly, often in virtually every moment and aspect of life. "Work," a central feature of camp life, often as the perpetrators' explicit intention and almost always effectively, is classic structured cruelty. Having just explored camps and their multifarious structured (and often unstructured) cruelties (and their variations), the discussion here concentrates on the cruelties not ordered from above, on individual excesses and group performances, although the analysis often pertains also to structured cruelty, especially in camps.

Killing in a manner inflicting maximal suffering—systematic torturing of individuals, beating, brutalizing, maiming, sexually abusing, ritually degrading, mocking, using victims as playthings, and more—is the hallmark of eliminationist politics and onslaughts. Clémentine, a Hutu from Nyamata, describes how the killers sometimes returned from a search-and-destroy mission with a victim, whom they brought to the marketplace:

> These doomed victims were usually acquaintances who had tried to cheat—to pass for Hutu, for example. Or people who had been rich and important before. Or acquaintances disliked because of old quarrels.
>
> The killers would call everyone to watch. All the women and children would gather to see the show. There were people still carrying drinks, or nurslings on their backs. The killers would cut off the victims' limbs, they would crush their bones with a club, but without killing them. They wanted them to last. They wanted the audience to learn from these torments. Shouts would rise up from all sides. These were raucous village jamborees, quite rare and quite popular.[77]

This account's elements are instructive. For these ceremonial torture performances, the perpetrators usually chose a known person, one particularly incensing them. There was an element of score-settling. Yet the score could be for an act not injuring the perpetrators individually but transgressing against the Hutu collectively—something as impersonal as a Tutsi trying to pass for a Hutu. It may be that personal acquaintanceship was also important because it provided the perpetrators and the onlooking community the joint opportunity to teach the victim more meaningfully what happens to Tutsi trying to cheat or cross the Hutu. The more personal it is, the more the victim understands his abject state as his life dissipates in agony. The perpetrators did not seek to hide their deeds. They were not ashamed of their butchery. The opposite: They celebrated their deeds. More, they expected, correctly, that their community would joyfully share in their celebration. All the women willingly came to watch. They brought their children. Perhaps most significant, aside from the victims' unspeakable suffering and the perpetrators' unspeakable cruelty, which were the bases of collective enjoyment that become the whole community's festive, "raucous" affairs, was the perpetrators' elongating the misery because they "wanted the audience to learn from these torments." To learn what? Obviously not torture's techniques, but the right way to treat a Tutsi. That is why the perpetrators made especially sure the children attended these episodic educational sessions. These jamborees were popular affairs. They reflected the popular will and further helped to cement it with the celebratory dismemberings that produced this Durkheimian collective effervescence or euphoria. The community was saying to itself Tutsi should—even must—be treated in this manner.

Dwelling even briefly on eliminationist assaults' personalized violence and cruelty is enough to sicken anyone possessing a shred of fellow feeling. To sit before and listen to victims around the world recount the cruelties they suffered, as I have, is all but unbearable. Yet to the perpetrators, as individuals and often as a class, and even to the broader societies from which they come, this fellow feeling has been blunted for contemplating the targeted groups and even when watching them suffer collectively and individually. More revolting, this fellow feeling has been corrupted and inverted so that, for perpetrators and their approving bystanders, the most horrifying acts become self-righteous justice's satisfying, even aesthetically pleasurable, expressive displays.

The prejudice, hatred, and enmity moving perpetrators to kill, expel, or otherwise eliminate the victims of their mental and emotional animosity also predispose them to want to take other retribution (as they understand it) upon them. After all, they are killing, forcing from their homes and country, or incarcerating in hellish camps people they deem less than fully human or demonic, or consider to have already greatly harmed or to be threatening to harm them and their loved ones. It would be unusual if the perpetrators did not treat the victims extremely brutally, with excess cruelty. Given how easily human aggression is switched on, especially in situations of actual or potential face-to-face physical conflict (which any personalized eliminationist moment is), and how satisfying aggression's venting can feel, it is no surprise that excess cruelty is virtually the constituent feature of eliminationist programs. Nevertheless, enormous differences exist. Sometimes cruelty is institutionalized, namely ordered from above or embedded into the rules, practices, and patterns of given eliminationist situations or institutions, such as camps. Sometimes groups collectively perform cruelty in patterned ways. Sometimes individuals take their own initiative to make their victims suffer excessively. It needs to be emphasized that, just as illuminating similarities and differences among different eliminationist and exterminationist assaults does not value any victims' lives more or less, or make a person's death in one onslaught any less or more meaningful or tragic than another's death, neither does comparing cruelty, brutality, and torture make one eliminationist assault morally worse or more meaningful than another.[78]

As we know, camps are places of extreme, deadly privation, the American camps, however inadequate and horrible, interning more than 100,000 Japanese Americans being the exception. Perpetrators, those creating the camps' overall conditions and those manning its daily operations, normally systematically, extremely, and callously disregard the prisoners' well-being. Yet some camps and camp systems direct far more organized or more personal cruelty at the victims. Comparing the full character and extent of such excess cruelty from camp system to camp system, not to mention from one eliminationist onslaught to the next, requires far more knowledge than we have or are likely to acquire of many systems, given their vastness, the highly incomplete to nonexistent records (in no small measure owing to the witnesses' deaths), and the certain variability from camp to camp, from killing locale to killing locale, within each vast camp system and larger eliminationist program. Nonetheless, concerted research projects into every camp system's and eliminationist program's cruelty would considerably enhance our understanding of cruelty's commonalities, patterns, and variations, and therefore of eliminationist programs themselves.

The eliminationist assaults we know the most about, the Germans' various programs against the Jews, mentally ill, Sinti, Roma, Poles, Russians, and others, and an eliminationist camp system we have recently learned much more about, that of the British in Kenya, illustrate (by themselves and when compared to other eliminationist assaults) several critical distinctions among types of cruelty that help us better understand cruelty's sources and nature.

To begin with, the evidence is overwhelming that the Germans' cruelty toward Jews was virtually unsurpassable, not in the sense that other perpetrators did not commit unspeakable brutalities against their victims, because, as the sickening evidence presented here from so many eliminationist assaults unequivocally demonstrates, they did. Unlike other eliminationist perpetrators whose cruelties consisted mainly of time-limited torturing and literally butchering their victims to death, or episodic cruelties over longer periods, the Germans were cruel to their Jewish victims steadily over extensive periods, daily and hourly, with an incessantness and drive that is singular and gave the appearance of people acting on a compulsion. A work camp the Germans set up just for Jews they were keeping alive to "work," the Lipowa Camp near Lublin, Poland, is illustrative. Virtually all of Lipowa's personnel carried whips or some functional equivalent, and the survivors' testimony makes clear almost all used the whips frequently, energetically, and willfully without being under any supervision, striking the Jews often arbitrarily and without any apparent cause, even by the Germans' liberal notions of causality. In addition to such quotidian use of whips, the Germans' routine cruelty took particular forms including:

- Brutal beatings with whips into which small iron balls had been wrought

- Incarceration in a bunker for indeterminate time
- Beatings in a bunker on a special "whipping table" one of the Germans had invented specifically for such occasions
- Forcing the Jews to run the gauntlet
- Torturing Jews with electric shocks
- Compelling Jews to stand for hours barefoot in the snow, after waking them with blows
- Public hangings, which terrorized the Jews still more than unseen executions

Of the forty-six members discussed during the postwar legal investigation of the camp's personnel, survivors indicate only three who departed from these cruel practices, one beating them *only* when under supervision, which shows that the others, able to do the same, chose not to. Day after day, time after time, they *chose* to be cruel and torture the Jews.[79] When German perpetrators testify that beating Jews was, in their common phrase, their "daily bread," they convey how regularly and reflexively they beat them. In another sense, beating Jews was, like bread for their bodies, daily nourishment for their psyches, sating their seeming persistent need to make the Jews suffer. If a person innocently surveyed the Germans' treatment of Jews in camps, their constant physical and symbolic degradation and cruelty toward utterly helpless and defenseless people whom they had, by starving them, turned into barely alive, skeletal, and sore-infested creatures, he might have concluded, if judging just by the evidence of his senses, that the Germans kept the Jews alive to gratify a desire to make them suffer or, since their conduct appeared to have no other rational purpose, to satisfy some unknown cosmological principle requiring Jews' suffering akin to the Aztecs' belief that daily human sacrifice was necessary to make the sun rise.

The Germans' cruelty toward Jews was more frequent and intensive than their also brutal—often extremely brutal—treatment of other victim peoples. The Germans' cruelty is so significant analytically because it demonstrates definitively that the perpetrators' varying conceptions of the different victim groups systematically and commensurately govern their relative *brutality* and cruelty toward victims. From camp to camp, outside camps across different settings and different units, the same uncoordinated pattern of hierarchical brutality toward different victim groups emerged during the Germans' continent-wide predations. Paralleling different groups' differing mortality rates in camps, the Germans' general treatment of and cruelty toward the Jews, the putative antihuman demons, was the worst; toward the Russians, those putative Bolshevik-bearing subhumans the next worst; other putatively subhuman Slavic peoples the next worst; Western Europeans better; Nordic Northern Europeans the best. So where the same structural conditions existed, in a given camp and then in camp after camp, of the German perpetrators as absolute lords equally over all the defenseless incarcerated peoples, the Germans treated the different victims markedly differently, the Jews receiving such manifestly worse treatment that even non-Jewish prisoners comment on it.

While the Germans demonstrate that the structural conditions of complete freedom and domination do not produce eliminationist onslaughts' differing brutality and cruelty, they also show that such conditions do not instigate the brutality. There are two parts to this point: First, wildly different structural conditions are compatible with enormous brutality. As we know, the German perpetrators, the overwhelming majority being not SS or Nazi Party members, came from all social backgrounds and constituted a representative cross-section of German society, making them ordinary Germans of their time. They also traveled widely varying institutional paths to becoming mass murderers. They served in the most varied range of killing and eliminationist institutions and settings, in camps, ghettos, mobile units of various kinds, search-and-destroy missions, death marches, and more. They did so in geographically and politically disparate locations, in Germany itself, in occupied countries, as part of, in proximity to, and isolated from neighboring communities' peoples. Despite all these different factors, the perpetrators treated Jews in the various institutions of killing nearly uniformly cruelly, always or nearly always with immense surplus physical brutality, symbolic degradation, and mockery. As the other factors vary, only their common demonological conception of the Jews can explain the Germans' relatively uniform conduct. Second, similar structural conditions, such as of guards having absolute power over victims in camps, have not produced similarly widespread and intensive cruelty everywhere. As brutal, harsh, and deadly as the gulag's living, sanitation, and nutritional conditions were, incessant cruelty paralleling the

Germans' cruelty toward the Jews, and to a lesser extent putative sub-humans, was absent. The Germans manning camps, as in Majdanek, Lipowa, and many others, literally walked around with whips in hand, using them liberally. This was unthinkable for the gulag's guards. A far more brutal and, for the guards, behaviorally permissive ideational regime governed the Germans' camps, but the gulag personnel's comparative restraint toward the prisoners did not artificially result from imposed regulations holding back hate-filled guards chomping at the bit. The perpetrators' variable treatment of victims in the same structural conditions, their fundamental capacity to govern their own cruelty, and the ideational sources of both cruelty and its variability could be seen repeatedly in the gulag, as former prisoners attest: The guards "were, like everyone, all different," explains Galina Smirnova. "There were sick sadists, and there were completely normal, good people," reports Anna Andreeva. The gulag's guards who were brutal to the prisoners were so because of what they believed the prisoners to be and to deserve. Not being so ideologized as the Germans were toward Jews, the gulag's personnel were able, more quickly or slowly, to see reality: The prisoners were not as the regime's ideology portrayed. Even the worst guards, at first acting "like beasts," grew to treat the prisoners better, as Irena Arginskaya, a former prisoner, explains, because "after a time they began to understand—not all of them, but a large part— and they often changed."[80] Once altering their own conception of the victims, they, governing their own conduct and cruelty, concomitantly diminished their treatment's severity. More generally, though the gulag's guards were very hard on the prisoners, as befit their status, they did not make gratuitous torture a constituent part of the prisoners' daily world. Ilyich conveys how little he and the others feared such cruelty, explaining that the guards, not even carrying weapons in the camp, left the prisoners alone when not at work. Those accompanying them to work "could be cruel, and they often were." But for actual infractions— not gratuitously: "If there weren't any violations about which they had warned, then everything was pretty calm."[81] The same can be said of the otherwise brutal and highly lethal Chinese Laogai, whose guards are "rarely described as intentionally cruel."[82]

In the same eliminationist assault, the baseline cruelty and brutality varies somewhat according to settings, the eliminationist institutions' character, and local perpetrator cultures. The baseline cruelty also varies owing to individual perpetrators' personalities, taste for violence and suffering, and relationship to the victims, including the variations in their individual conceptions of them. Such onslaughts obviously open the door for sadists to express their sadism, for those hating the victims that much more to inscribe their wrath in the victims' bodies and souls, and for those seeing overt enthusiasm in their common destructive enterprise as an avenue for promotion to mix business with pleasure. The Hutu's butchery of Tutsi was attended by perpetrators' cruelty that was Nazi-like, and in the frequency of wanton, literal butchery, exceeded what the Germans did to Jews. Yet, the existing record reveals that, as with the Germans toward the Jews and as with the overwhelming majority of perpetrators of mass slaughters, the Hutu's individual cruelty was almost always voluntary. Élie Mizinge, a Hutu killer, explains: "Making someone suffer was up to each person, as long as he did his job. The intimidators gave no particular order to encourage or discourage it. They repeated, 'Just kill, that is the main thing.' We didn't care. If a colleague had to play around with a victim, we kept going."[83] Every exterminationist and eliminationist assault has its own particular baseline level of excess cruelty, its own "taste for barbarity," its own, so aptly put by Élie, "play[ing] around" with victims, with the cruelty perpetrated in a given individual killing institution and by individual perpetrators varying, sometimes enormously, from that baseline.

Surveying the vast world of perpetrators' excess cruelty suggests five central kinds, which can be called Conradian, Zimbardoian, condign, vengeful, and Machiavellian.

Conradian cruelty, after Joseph Conrad's antihero Kurtz in *Heart of Darkness*, is the cruelty of the beast within humans unleashed. Remove civilization's restraints, so goes the thinking, and man (or woman) lets loose upon his victims his basest, primordial passions. This sort of cruelty, it seems, has unreflectively been assumed to be at work in all exterminationist and eliminationist assaults in a more or less expected and undifferentiated way, so much so that the need to investigate excess cruelty's nature and incidence has all but escaped our analytic view. But this assumption cannot hold. As we know, not all people harbor such beasts, or are all equally beastly—in particular there is variation in beastliness across cultures and subcultures. Nor do all people visit their base impulses upon all victims equally. That is one reason excess cruelty varies enormously from one eliminationist assault to the next and also across a given eliminationist program's terrain. Nevertheless, Conrad correctly identified some people's behavioral metamorphosis when civilization's restraints are unloosed, especially against people considered subhumans.

A second type of cruelty is Zimbardoian, after the prison experiments Philip Zimbardo conducted at Stanford University showing that when college students were assigned roles as prison guards and prisoners, the guards, in order to control the noncompliant prisoners, instituted a strict and brutal regime. Structural conditions within camps, or even of rounding up victims and deporting them, can produce excessive cruelty serving operational domination. And although Zimbardo's experiment was too artificial, brief (six days), and limited in number (twenty-four) and type of participants (Stanford University undergraduates) to know much about its general validity or what it actually reveals, the structural situation it sought to capture can clearly produce conduct in some people having no prior animus toward the victims.

For several reasons, Zimbardoian cruelty is probably a less frequent kind during eliminationist assaults, and it could not possibly be (as is commonly postulated) *the* general source of perpetrators' brutality. In many eliminationist assaults, including Indonesia, Burundi, and Rwanda, the perpetrators' task is to kill their victims immediately. This requires no Zimbardoian control mechanisms. Yet, they torture, beat, degrade, and taunt their victims anyway. In fact, in killing their victims, which by definition has nothing to do with establishing dominance for present and future control, the perpetrators of these and other mass murders often butchered them in maximally painful ways, deriving pleasure from their suffering. Eliminationist programs' most nonexplicitly murderous aspects—in Turkey, German-dominated Europe, Japanese-dominated Asia, the Soviet Union, China, Cambodia, Guatemala, Sudan, and elsewhere, whether they are employing camps, death marches, or other mechanisms—usually have perpetrators controlling or herding a weakened, overwhelmed, unthreatening, and pliant population (including children). The actual or psychological need to respond to victims' challenges or even to preemptively dragoon them is simply nonexistent. So a mechanism predicated on such a need's existence could not produce the perpetrators' actual vast and gleeful cruelty. In many eliminationist settings, even in camps (ironically, the institutions most approximating the "prison" Zimbardo constructed), the utterly powerless and defenseless prisoners—unlike Zimbardo's actively rebellious Stanford University student "prisoners," soon to return to their privileged existences on their country-club campus—are as a rule cowed and compliant. Finally, if a Zimbardoian mechanism (or some other social-psychological mechanism or setting) generally generates the perpetrators' cruelty, then each individual eliminationist assault and the variety of eliminationist assaults should generate substantial variation in cruelty, according to the Zimbardoian character of the setting of each small group of perpetrators. Even a cursory knowledge of eliminationist assaults shows this is false.

The third kind of cruelty, condign, emerges from the perpetrators' belief that the beings they confront and are eliminating deserve to suffer. In this case, excess cruelty in all forms—beatings, systematic torture, inventive, even playful, painful use of the victims, actual and symbolic degradation, verbal taunting and mocking—are not the individual expression of human nature exposed, as in Conradian cruelty, or of human nature awry, as in individual psychopathology. Condign cruelty is begotten of the normative view that treating the victims in this manner is right and fitting, and desisting from inflicting pain on them would violate what the victims' inherent nature requires. Flowing from the perpetrators' conception of the victims, this kind of cruelty could also be called ideological cruelty. But it is a specific kind of ideological cruelty with a strong normative core suggesting to the perpetrator that he fulfills a *moral* imperative to make the victims suffer.

Vengeful cruelty merges passion with self-righteousness. A striking feature of eliminationist assaults is that the perpetrators and the social groups they come from, represent, and in whose name they act regularly conceive of themselves as *reacting* rather then *acting*. Believing that the victims have already perpetrated or intend to perpetrate great injury upon them, they understand their assault as essentially defensive, necessary to forestall further harm, rather than as offensive against an unthreatening party. Perpetrators' and their supporters' ease in convincing themselves they are justly giving the victims what the victims had inflicted or would inflict upon them, when it is overwhelmingly evident that this is wrong, demonstrates human beings' great vulnerability to prejudices and ideologies positing that a disparaged, hated, or alien group poses a dire threat. This sense of victimhood, the rage it induces, and the perpetrators' self-righteousness in administering hard justice combine to produce an appetite for vengeance and pleasure in meting it out: vengeful cruelty. Analyzing the Khmer Rouge perpetrators, Von reports that "ninety-nine percent of them were cruel."[84] Why? "They just want[ed] to revenge [themselves] on the new people." By ideological definition, the new people were rich, imperialist exploiters of the true Khmer. Thus, as Uong explains, the Khmer Rouge took "revenge against them. . . . [They] just enjoyed torturing those rich people that live the easy life. You know, the imperialist . . . people."[85] Soviet-front newspapers urged soldiers to record in a "book of revenge" their and their families' suffering to ready themselves to treat the Germans as they supposedly deserved. The Supreme Soviet military commander Marshall Georgy Zhukov's orders to his armies before a major offensive in January 1945 echoed this theme: "Woe to the land of the murderers," the orders told the men. "We will get our terrible revenge for everything." In an archetypical way, Soviet road signs in eastern Germany encouraged the already willing soldiers to exact their personal tolls on the Germans whose country and army (but not the individual women whom the Soviets raped in enormous numbers) had made the Soviet peoples suffer: "Soldier: you are in Germany, take revenge on the Hitlerites."[86] With a cruel teacher's relish to a recalcitrant and transgressive student, perpetrators whip their victims, shouting, "*You will learn.*" What will the victims learn? What it means to suffer as they supposedly made others suffer. What it means to be subjected to the wrath of their betters, their masters. What truth and justice, in the perpetrators' eyes, means.

Eliminationist perpetrators frequently practice vengeful cruelty, though, as with cruelty's other forms, variably. While excess cruelty's other forms seem to contain rage at the victims for not bending to the perpetrators' will or for (owing to the victims' own putative misconduct) obliging the perpetrators to act in an ordinarily antisocial and punishable way, vengeful cruelty contains this rageful element constitutively. There appears to be a basis grounded in the nature of experience and in neurology for this excessive rage (even according to what the perpetrators claim to have suffered) and its excessive application, which context and other emotions amplify.[87] Suffering, real or imagined, to the perpetrator himself, or through identification with that of his family, social circle, or wider community, becomes amplified because it is *his* suffering, always more intensely felt, more real in effect and more powerful in impact, than other people's suffering. Even if the perpetrator seeks to mete out mere rough justice, exactly proportionate to his own suffering, he will subject his victim to considerably more pain because experientially only an added hefty dose seems to equal his own. But, as we know, the perpetrators do not choose to practice strict proportionality, but to make their victims suffer according to their own liberally cruel intellectual, psychological, and emotional needs. Even so, owing to this and other cognitive and psychological mechanisms, the perpetrators underestimate their victims' suffering. Thus, to achieve the retributive satisfaction they crave, they brutalize their victims still more. And the more the victim comprehends he deserves this suffering and the more intense it is, the more satisfying its infliction is.

Finally, there is Machiavellian cruelty, which, true to Niccolò Machiavelli's clear-eyed, heartless advice to rulers in *The Prince*, is politically calculated brutality to advance cogent strategic or tactical goals. Perpetrators use such cruelty to terrorize targeted peoples, to bend them to the perpetrators' eliminationist will, or to systematically scar the victims physically and emotionally so as to diminish them and their putative danger. Classic instances are torturing a person to extract information, flogging camp inmates before the assembled prisoners, to convey the price of resistance or disobedience, and publicly torturing members of targeted communities so others know what awaits them if they do not heel or, as in eliminationist expulsions, cooperate and flee.

Each kind of excess cruelty has a different source and is grounded in a different aspect of personal or social life. Conradian cruelty originates in aspects of *human nature*—humanity's capacities and dispositions developed through evolution—which presumably are relatively constant across humanity, and in the psychological and social-psychological dispositions common to a society's or culture's members, which vary enormously. There does appear to be some fundamental and widely distributed human capacity to be cruel, to vent the passions civilization normally constrains, perhaps even more intensively because they ordinarily do not find outlets. But this general capacity and propensity (whatever it is) to express itself does not explain why cruelty comes out in different eliminationist assaults and in different settings by different perpetrators toward different victims to differing degrees. Different cultures socialize people with different emotional stances toward others' suffering, different tastes for violence and brutality, and with different practices toward outgroups, not to mention toward enemies. When restraints are lifted, when people are licensed to do as they please with others, what people of different societies and cultures will happily do varies enormously. Human nature must be a powerful source of eliminationist onslaughts' cruelty, but it hardly explains cruelty's character, quantity, and distribution across such political practice. Even adding perpetrators' social and cultural differences would explain only part of the variation.

Zimbardoian cruelty emerges from the *structure of relations*, namely the dynamic of the conflict between guards for domination and prisoners to resist or free themselves. It is the structure—the guards' objective and then psychologically grafted need to keep the prisoners cowed—that leads them to adopt brutal practices.

Condign cruelty is grounded in *norms* of right conduct, which, though perverted or inverted according to our moral compass, guide the executioners, administrators of subjectively just and necessary sentences of suffering, as other moral norms have guided religious crusaders of various kinds. Across cultures criminals would be punished even if they no longer posed a threat and punishing them had no deterrent value, merely because people believe those committing crimes deserve punishment. In some societies and cultures, historically and today, the further moral belief has broadly existed that criminals' punishment should be hard and they should suffer to a greater or lesser degree. So too the practitioner of condign cruelty is animated to make the putative criminals before him suffer.

Vengeful cruelty is grounded in *experience*, the experience of one's own people's suffering at the hands of one's victims. The experience may be real (the Soviet peoples did actually suffer at the Germans' hands), but it is usually figmental, derived from the perpetrators' prior prejudices about their victims. Even if real, the perpetrators typically

magnify the suffering wildly and apply responsibility for it so indiscriminately to the target group according to the blanket, unforgiving,
and even paranoid thinking of the perpetrators' prejudices, racism, and
hatreds, that the kernel of truth that may seed the perpetrators' vast
fury is barely relevant for understanding the perpetrators' brutality.
"Experience" in this context does not mean the individual perpetrator's experience but almost always his knowledge (faulty though it may
be) acquired from others about the victims' putative harming of him,
his people, or his ethnic group, society, or country. The perpetrator
comes to experience these supposed injuries *as if they had been done to
him or a loved one*, or as if they are in the offing, producing in him the
rage of people being physically or otherwise attacked or threatened.
This sense of injury or danger can well up inside the perpetrator whenever he confronts or thinks of confronting his victims.

Machiavellian or purposeful cruelty is grounded in *eliminationist
aims* beyond the immediate gratification of passions, self-expression,
or the structuring of relations between the perpetrator and his victims. It is a consciously calculated choice and strategy to achieve a well-
defined goal.

These five kinds of excess cruelty are grounded in five sources: Conradian in human nature, Zimbardoian in social relations, condign in
moral norms, vengeful in collective experience, and Machiavellian in
political aims. Each source and thus each kind of cruelty is sociological,
having nothing to do with the individual perpetrator's personality or
psychology. They are patterned forms of excess cruelty within the cognitively and politically unleashed eliminationist project, the prerequisite
of which is the perpetrators' conceiving of the targets as people deserving elimination. Two of them, Zimbardoian and Machiavellian, can
further be called *instrumental cruelty* in that they have some conventionally understood purpose other than, or often in addition to, the victims' suffering itself or the satisfaction of teaching the victims a lesson.
Rouen Sam recounts an instance when the instrumental purpose of the
Khmer Rouge's cruelty supplemented the perpetrators' satisfaction derived from their treatment of a Khmer who enraged his tormentors
when, instead of gratifying them by providing a show "confession" in
front of assembled children prisoners, he, protesting his innocence, accused the Khmer Rouge of injustice:

Suddenly one of them hit him from the back, pushing him, and he fell face to the ground. It was raining. We sat in the rain, and then the rain became blood. He was hit with a shovel and then he went unconscious and began to have a seizure. Then Angka [the Khmer Rouge] took out a sharp knife and cut the man from his breastbone all the way down to his stomach. They took out his organs.

When I saw this I felt so shocked, like I was blind. It felt like they were hitting me just as they hit the prisoner. The person cut him open and took a sharp piece of wire and stuck it in what I think was the liver and the bowels. They tied the organs with wire on the handlebars of a bicycle and biked away, leaving a bloody trail.

Angka calmly told us over the microphone, "All girls and boys, you have seen with your own eyes. If someone feels compassion or sympathy for the enemy that has just died, then you will be punished just like him."[88]

Zimbardoian cruelty arises out of the perpetrators' need to control insubordination, which here, with utterly cowed children, was not at issue. Perpetrators use Machiavellian cruelty for strategic political ends, such as terrorizing the victims, here to further dam up the children's compassion. These two forms of instrumental cruelty are by far the least frequent kinds of cruelty in eliminationist assaults, and as in this instance's Machiavellian display, they almost always combine with or are grafted onto other forms of cruelty. The other three far more common kinds of cruelty, all noninstrumental, are ends in themselves, providing moral and psychic satisfaction to the perpetrators. The Tutsi survivor Rwililiza, his sociological and psychological knowledge rooted in vast bitter experience, speaks to the Hutu butchers' voluntarism and its utterly noninstrumental sources:

So why did they chop people up instead of killing them straightaway? I do not think it was to punish them for having tried to escape. Nor to discourage the living from running, from fleeing from the assassins all day long, saving themselves any way they could. Or perhaps they did so for a tiny percentage only. Whatever the case, these villains thought they would end it for us.

They chopped us out of a taste for barbarity, nothing more.[89]

Each exterminationist and eliminationist assault's brutality *is* patterned. Within the context of the character of an individual eliminationist program's general cruelty, perpetrators express their shared and individual emotional and psychological, even psychopathological, propensities, intensifying or ameliorating that onslaught's baseline brutality in general or its particular settings. Rwililiza explains: "Amongst them there were normal Hutu who killed normally, wicked Hutu who killed wickedly—most often *interahamwe*; and finally there were extremists in wickedness who killed with extreme wickedness."[90] Sometimes, as among the Jews, Kikuyu, and Tutsi, when survivors describe a particularly cruel perpetrator, they take their tormentors' enormous baseline cruelty so much for granted that they remark upon the perpetrators' routine cruelty in passing, as an ordinary expectation. One Jewish victim, a woman, reports that in her camp "Wagner was a sadist. He would not only beat the women; that was done by all the SS men." She explains further: "He was active not with a gun, but with a whip, and he frequently beat women so terribly that they died of the effects. . . . In his sadism towards women, Wagner appeared to us to be absolutely abnormal; the other SS men, who held total power over us, were of course also very cruel, but were not sadistic in the same way as Wagner."[91]

In principle, we could construct a better understanding, singly and comparatively, of perpetrators' cruelty by systematically collecting and analyzing all relevant data in light of cruelty's five types and sources.* Even with our current knowledge we can understand a great deal about the perpetrators' excess cruelty merely by finally focusing on it and analyzing it according to its variable nature and sources.

Substantial correspondence exists between the social theory governing perpetrators' treatment of targeted groups—deriving from their conception of them—and their excessive cruelty's character. Perpetrators almost always see *existential enemies* as having inflicted great in-

---

*In most settings, given current empirical knowledge (and even under better informational conditions), it is difficult to disentangle the mix of cruelty's different types and sources, and to confidently analyze their distribution in a given eliminationist assault or even in a single camp. We know little about this crucial aspect of the perpetrators' conduct and inner lives—most about the Germans and increasingly more about the Hutu—because cruelty's precise nature and sources are difficult to fathom, and for the different eliminationist assaults in general, we either have few or no such investigations.

jury upon them and their society, and (by definition) of wanting to continue. The perpetrators are in a rage. In their eyes the eliminationist assaults are almost by definition retributive. The social theory that tends to inform the perpetrators' treatment of existential enemies is realpolitik, which complements their aggression, and desire to wreak vengeance, with a sense that they must be brutal to their victims—not necessarily in a calculated way but almost as a constituent aspect of their relations with them, to keep them down and in check.

Perpetrators approach putative *subhumans* with a utilitarian social theory akin to using implements, animals, and things, with one critical difference. Because the putative subhumans have understanding, speak, and display (sub)human emotions, the perpetrators can take pleasure in mistreating them, in being cruel to them, as they cannot for things or implements, or even animals. Because they conceive the victims to lack some fundamental human quality, their eliminationist assaults tend to produce the purist Conradian brutality, allowing the perpetrators, absent civilization's restraints, to repeatedly express and sate their most violent urges. Their cruelty toward subhumans has two additional aspects: The perpetrators, because their conception of humanity dehumanizes others, are already enmeshed in a brutalizing worldview that inhibits fellow feeling and promotes licentiousness and their taking out of their otherwise bottled-up aggression and urges on the subhuman victims and playthings. Someone unable to kick his boss might kick his dog, or anger quickly at his children, or punch a wall, or rip something up. Such a dynamic affected the Japanese perpetrators in Nanjing and across their Asian empire, especially soldiers. As masters of colonial subhumans, they acted upon the pent-up resentment and rage at their own culture's and institutions' brutal treatment of them. They butchered their victims with abandon and glee.[92] John Rabe, the German businessman documenting in his diary the Japanese's predations in Nanjing, recorded that the "same reports are coming in from all sides [in the region] about rapes, murder, and mayhem," leading him to observe that "one might be led to think that the entire criminal population of Japan is in uniform here."[93]

The perpetrators of eliminationist violence against putative subhumans, including the Japanese perpetrators, come from societies and cultures that do not recognize human beings' universal and intrinsic moral equality. In their eyes the victims have rendered themselves fit and necessary to be eliminated not by contingent beliefs or actions but intrinsically by the danger of their diminished human, in other words subhuman, essence. In such contexts, though anything is permissible, cruelty is not necessary. The perpetrators' have nothing more complex to teach the subhumans about their place than they would a pack of dogs.

Perpetrators assaulting demonized victims, whether *heretics* (who are demonized) or *demons* (who are demonized and dehumanized), tend to express condign cruelty, wanting to treat their victims according to, in the case of heretics, their eschatological moral theory, or in the case of demons, their inverted Kantian morality. The brutality is often justified according to a well-articulated ideology and moral theory about treating or instructing the miscreants about the one true path they unconscionably oppose: Demons and heretics must suffer at the hands of their betters, goodness' guardians. Only then will they come to know their way's error, apostasy, inhumanity. The members of the perpetrators' communities are welcome to know and to watch all this, so they too can feel righteous and even, as in the Rwandan village's torture jamborees, "learn from these torments." The particular social and moral theories governing the perpetrators can produce widely differing expressions of brutality, from the Soviets' comparatively low incidence of excess cruelty to the Germans' and the Hutu's virtually boundless cruelty toward, respectively, the putatively irredeemable Jews and Tutsi.

Whatever the central tendencies of perpetrators' cruelty during each kind of eliminationist assault, perpetrators frequently convince themselves that, whatever else they do, they also avenge or prophylactically prevent heinous crimes against themselves and their societies. Thus, vengeful cruelty, rooted in this imagined experience, exists across eliminationist assaults.

If Conradian cruelty has central tendencies, though also a potential near ubiquity, if Zimbardoian cruelty appears only in selected circumstances, if condign cruelty is an attribute of the slayers and eliminators of demons and heretics, and if vengeful cruelty also has its central tendencies and ubiquity, Machiavellian cruelty of political aims is least patterned. As all eliminationist assaults are political, Machiavellian cruelty could inherently be produced in any of them. Yet such cruelty ap-

pears only when the leaders and their followers choose to conceptual-
ize excess cruelty as a political instrument, which, like eliminationist
slaughters themselves, is unpredictable and happens less frequently than
might be supposed.

Whenever a perpetrator strikes a victim with the instrumental purpose of affecting, including by terrorizing, other victims or of weakening the victim group, it is politically motivated excess cruelty. This kind
of cruelty, like other widespread cruelties having such consequences,
might—as its explicit purpose is eliminationist—also be conceptualized
as an eliminationist means in its own right, and not just an eliminationist assault's complement or byproduct. But however we conceive
it, politically inspired cruelty often appears in conjunction with cruelty's other forms, meaning cruelty's infliction has mixed sources, motives, and types, which complicates the isolation and identification of
Machiavellian cruelty's presence.

Aside from these general kinds of cruelty, perpetrators reserve certain
cruelties for certain specific members of targeted people or groups. If
far too little attention is devoted to collecting information on, publicizing, and analyzing perpetrators' cruelty in general, still less attention
goes to perpetrators' cruelty toward specific subgroups of victims. Perpetrators often target two such kinds of victims, women and children,
with specific horrors—though their deeds are little recognized, and not
conceptualized and analyzed as specific instances of cruelty. This failure
reflects the general lack of attentive analysis given to the perpetrators'
acts in general—almost all studies focus on killing, but not the perpetrators' *manner* of killing, *general* treatment of the victims, and other
acts. Yet it also reflects women's and children's general invisibility as
distinct victim groups. Women's and children's *particularity* cannot
rightly be ignored by subsuming them under the general category of
victims, or by treating them as no different from men. The perpetrators' particular treatment of and cruelty toward women and children,
perhaps even more than general cruelty, has not been focused upon
probably for another reason: Doing so reveals the hollowness of so
much existing analysis.

Perpetrators' sexual cruelty toward women of targeted groups,
though vast, is generally poorly documented and significantly under-
analyzed. For decades, really throughout the past, such cruelty has been

treated—if deemed noteworthy at all—as an otherwise nonsignificant byproduct of war and other assaults and of men's nature. With the feminist revolution in the 1960s and 1970s, and the concomitant discovery of women and gender as historical and political subjects, the intellectual space opened up for devoting proper attention to eliminationist assaults' sexual cruelty, the most common kind being rape. Nevertheless, in retrospect it took longer than might have been expected, especially as the Pakistanis' vast sexual cruelty against Bangladeshi women in 1971 was contemporaneously recognized. Only in the twentieth century's last decade did people begin to understand such cruelty as often being politically inspired—Machiavellian in the term's fullest, most dastardly, and cruelest sense.

Such politically inspired cruelty's classical instance—it was here the phenomenon was first "discovered" and became an investigative theme—was the Serbs' sexual cruelty against Bosniak women and later against Kosovar women. Serbs, during their eliminationist assault in Bosnia, killed many military-age men and expelled others from their villages and regions. They also decided to systematically rape Muslim women as another means of undermining the Bosniak people. They physically and/or emotionally maimed a huge number of individual women, their families, who, in this shame culture, had to absorb the shame, and Bosniak society itself, which treated raped women as polluted and untouchable. Knowing this, Serbs calculated that the more women they raped, the more the number of reproductive Bosniak women and future Bosniak generations would decline. The rapes' political purposefulness and central organization is clear. Melika Kreitmayer, the doctor leading a gynecological team that examined twenty-five victims, reports that the rapes were meant "to humiliate Muslim women, to insult them, to destroy their persons and to cause shock. . . . These women were raped not because it was the male instinct. They were raped because it was the goal of the war." She adds, "My impression is that someone had an order to rape the girls," an impression the victims corroborate, recounting their rapists explicitly telling them they were on a mission.[94] To achieve their political ends, the Serbs set up rape camps where soldiers, paramilitary troops, and others could regularly rape the women. Serb rape gangs roamed Bosnia. The Serbian leadership essentially green-lighted any Serb to rape any

Muslim woman anywhere. After impregnating Muslim women, which was also this cruelty's explicit political purpose, the Serbs often incarcerated them until they could no longer safely terminate the pregnancy, forcing them to bear children of Serbian men whom they (and apparently many Bosniaks) believed would weaken and dilute the Bosniak people. "We're bringing you to a concentration camp," one Bosniak woman reports being told. "The next time we meet, you'll have one of our kids in your belly." A Serb she knew prior to the eliminationist campaign raped her, saying "[I] was the hundredth one to be raped anyway [in that camp], and I certainly wouldn't be the last."[95] In this political campaign of sexual cruelty, Serbs raped between twenty thousand and fifty thousand women, many of them dozens of times.[96]

The Serbs' systematic raping of Bosniak women returns us to the issue of whether certain kinds of excess cruelty, particularly Machiavellian, in themselves constitute an eliminationist means (beyond the International Criminal Court's codifying it as a *crime against humanity*). Even more than general politically inspired cruelty, intended to weaken or subjugate victim peoples, the Serbs raped Bosnian women as an explicit strategy: eliminationism by preventing a people's reproduction. They sought—effectively—to create a form of social sterilization that was cheaper, easier, and far more emotionally and psychically gratifying to administer than surgical sterilization. Thus, the Serbs' eliminationist means, used as interchangeable or complementary instruments against Bosniaks, included killing, expulsion, *and* rape, to prevent reproduction and terrorize the Bosniaks into fleeing forever.

The Serbs repeated this political sexual cruelty strategy, this sexual eliminationist strategy, in Kosovo. It utterly terrorized the Kosovars, who already knew of the Serbs' raping in Bosnia. One woman conveyed the terror's magnitude in unmistakable comparative terms: "I wasn't afraid of the killing. I was afraid of the raping."[97] According to a Kosovar doctor in Pristina, "Rape was our greatest fear. Our main goal was to get our daughters—aged twenty-five, twenty-one, fourteen, and ten—out of the country."[98]

Even before raping as a constitutive feature of some eliminationist assaults became broadly known to the world, Pakistanis employed the same strategy in their mass-murderous and eliminationist attack in 1971 against Bangladesh, raping perhaps 200,000 Bangladeshi women.

Pakistanis regularly raped them in front of family members and established rape camps for their soldiers. One Indian liberator testified to two such places in Vurungamari:

> After breaking down the door of the room [of the Circle Officer's office], where the women were kept, we were dumbfounded. We found four naked young women, who had been physically tortured, raped, and battered by the Pakistani soldiers. . . . We tried to talk to them, but all of them were still in shock. One of them was six to seven months pregnant. One was a college student from Mymensingh. . . . We found sixteen other women locked up in a room at Vurungamari High School. These women were brought in for the Pakistani soldiers from nearby villages. We found evidence in the rooms of the Circle Officers office which showed that these women were tied to the windowbars and were repeatedly raped by the Pakistani soldiers. The whole floor was covered with blood, torn pieces of clothing, and strands of long hair.[99]

The vast scale and systematic character of the Pakistanis' raping led Mulk Raj Anand, an Indian novelist, to conclude it must have been a policy "planned by the West Pakistanis in a deliberate effort to create a new race," or at least an enormous number of outcasts, to weaken Bangladeshi society. The Pakistanis understood well their sexual violence's political efficacy. A month after Pakistanis had gang-raped one young woman, then a bride, she was in a shelter for rape victims in Dhaka. Her husband had cast her out, her father was "ashamed," and the people of her village "did not want me."[100]

Throughout history, raping the enemy has often been seen as a war spoil. No doubt the intersection of war's violence and licentiousness and (young) men's sexual urges, together with hatred of the enemy, has formed a combustible context for Conradian sexual cruelty and vengeful sexual cruelty. Such cruelty's emblem is perhaps the Japanese assault on Nanjing in 1937. In the first month the Japanese raped and murdered perhaps twenty thousand Chinese women so openly and blatantly that the entire mass murder and eliminationist subjugation became known as the Rape of Nanking (Nanjing).[101] Not just eliminationist assaults but, barring extremely tight monitoring and severe sanctions, large-scale military conflicts usually include considerable sexual cruelty. Soldiers often feel rage toward the people of the country or the group they fight for, having endangered their lives, having plunged them into war's barbarous and discomfiting conditions, having injured, killed, or otherwise harmed their comrades, loved ones, and people. They can and often do take out this rage in retributive sprees upon the easy and fulfilling targets of conquered women. Victorious Soviet soldiers, whose country suffered immensely at the hands of the German army and occupiers, were repeatedly urged to wreak vengeance on the Germans. They did so on a vast scale against German women.

Most eliminationist assaults, as we know, are nothing like war, as the perpetrators themselves do not face armies. They are politically inspired and politically understood programs designed to achieve transformative goals. In Bosnia and then Kosovo, and earlier in Bangladesh, the perpetrators institutionalized sexual cruelty as a critical eliminationist political strategy. As with eliminationist assaults in general, the perpetrators' conception of their victims prepared them to use sexual cruelty instrumentally. Members of strongly patriarchal cultures often depict rival, hated, or enemy groups' women in a symbolically potent manner, wresting all virtue from them, including by contrasting them unfavorably to their own culture's women, deemed (at least comparatively) wholesome. They also see the demeaned women (standing in for the whole group) as a source of disorder and others' corruption. Long before the Serbs' eliminationist assault began in full force against the Kosovars, the Serbs had degraded Kosovar women so viciously as to border on dehumanization. Serbian society's discourse, including crucially on state-run media, presented Kosovar women as baby factories and their many children as "biological bombs" that obviously had to be defused.[102] According to one Kosovar woman, "During the late 1980s there was tremendous propaganda against [Kosovar] Albanian women—we were portrayed as open-legged, stupid, uneducated women ready to have sex."[103] When the eliminationist assault began, the Serbs, reviving their Bosnian strategy, carried out their ideologically driven mission of sexual cruelty, raping the women they construed as asking for it.

In Darfur, the Political Islamic regime's perpetrators, many of whom are part of the government-sponsored and -aided Janjaweed militia,

have also been using rape as a political weapon to terrorize the Darfurians, get them to flee, and undermine their collective strength. The
extensive testimonies Amnesty International collected "point to rape
and other forms of sexual violence being used as a weapon of war in
Darfur, in order to humiliate, punish, control, inflict fear and displace
women and their communities. Rape and other forms of sexual violence
in Darfur are not just a consequence of the conflict or the result of the
conduct of undisciplined troops."[104] The voluminous reports of the perpetrators' raping have understated its actual incidence, because—as
always—many women shy away from reporting rape, and additionally,
as one victim explains, "in our culture it is a shame, and women will
hide this in their hearts so that the men do not hear about it." If the
men do, the consequences in this patriarchal and puritanical society are
often terrible. One sixteen-year-old explained in 2005 what happened
when, after being gang-raped the year before, she told her family: "They
threw me out of home and I had to build my own hut away from them.
I was engaged to a man and I was so much looking forward to getting
married. After I got raped, he did not want to marry me and broke off
the engagement because he said that I was now disgraced and spoilt. It
is the worst thing for me." When she was eight months pregnant the
police arrested her at gunpoint. "I told them that I had been raped. They
told me that as I was not married, I will deliver this baby illegally. They
beat me with a whip on the chest and back and put me in jail," where,
housed in deplorable conditions with other similarly situated women,
she stayed for ten days.[105] The perpetrators know well how the women
they rape will be treated in their communities, and the long-term harm
they do the women, as well as their families and society.

The Political Islamists laying waste to Darfur have integrated rape
into their eliminationist repertoire of descending on villages, burning
homes, killing many people, expelling many more, and raping as they
please. Like the Serbs in Bosnia, they have set up rape camps, where
they enslave Darfurian women. One victim, Asha, describes the rape
camp of her imprisonment as systematically run. "There were 35
women taken and they split us up, one for each group of Janjaweed."
This is common procedure. "If women are few, they divide us five or
six Janjaweed per woman. If there are enough women after their daily
collections then it's one to one."[106]

This points to another of the Holocaust's unusual features. Germans rarely raped Jewish women. Why, given the Germans' total demonization and dehumanization of Jews, their unsurpassable thirst for vengeance, their ready and steady infliction of virtually every kind of horror upon them, did they desist in this one cruel practice that is eliminationist assaults' virtual hallmark, which perpetrators appear to need little more than Conradian opportunity to widely practice? The Germans' sexual restraint vis-à-vis Jews is still more noteworthy as it differed from their ready sexual use and abuse of non-Jewish victims, including the dehumanized (but not demonized) Russians and others.

The Germans did not rape Jewish women for powerful and mutually reinforcing reasons. The German regime outlawed sexual relations with Jews, severely punishing offenders, sometimes by death. While this may seem to demonstrate regimes' power to prevent excess cruelty, in many, perhaps most, settings, individual or small groups of Germans could do whatever they wanted with Jewish women with de facto impunity, as the German authorities deemed a Jew's testimony, as a matter of definition, mendacious and without value, especially against a German's word. And, according to the Germans' security service's own report in 1942, similar German army attempts "to ban any kind of sexual intercourse with Russian women and girls have up to now been without any noteworthy effect."[107] This included widespread rape. So probably a second reason far more powerfully inhibited Germans from raping Jewish women. Germans genuinely feared that these enemies, deemed biologically potent and demonic, would pollute them. They wanted to expose themselves to this danger no more than to intimate contact with a leper or, more precisely, a demonic leper. The Germans genuinely held that sexual relations with Jewish women would racially (i.e., biologically) endanger the German race. The act evoked such horror it had a German name, *Rassenschande*, meaning race defilement, which was also the punishable legal offense's name.

The Germans' reserve toward Jewish women aside, exterminationist and eliminationist perpetrators, as with excess cruelty's other major forms, frequently practiced rape. The Guatemalan Commission for Historical Clarification's "investigation has demonstrated that the rape of women, during torture or before being murdered, was a common practice aimed at destroying one of the most intimate and vulnerable aspects of the individual's dignity. The majority of rape victims were Mayan women. Those who survived the crime still suffer profound trauma as a result of this aggression, and the communities themselves were deeply offended by this practice. The presence of sexual violence in the social memory of the communities has become a source of collective shame."[108]

Yet raping varies from one eliminationist onslaught to the next, depending on a host of familiar factors, including perpetrators' conception of the victims, commanders' restraints, if any, on their men, each eliminationist onslaught's character, creating differing settings and opportunities, and the perpetrators' political understanding of chastity, defilement, even ethnically mixed progeny, and the aims to which they may be put. For the British in Kenya, raping the putatively subhuman Kikuyu women seems hardly to have been a socially significant act. Milka Muriuki explains: "The white officers had no shame. They would rape women in full view of everyone. They would take whomever they wanted at one corner and just do it right there." The British, seeing the Kikuyu women as utilitarian playthings, raped them regularly. While respecting the colonialist pecking order, either themselves raping their victims first and then letting the British Home Guards, their Kikuyu loyalists, take their turns, or dividing them up with the British taking the choicest victims, usually adolescents, whom they called "un-plucked chickens," for themselves.[109] The scene described earlier of Major wa Wanjiru and his men torturing Kikuyu men and women, culminating with them carting the men away and killing them, continued in a different manner of cruelty for the women. Esther Muchiri explains: "That night all of the women including myself were divided amongst the Home Guards and raped. Even this lady who was eight months pregnant was not spared. We were raped throughout the night."[110] Whatever a given eliminationist assault's baseline sexual cruelty, it varies, as with other forms of excess cruelty, in its implementation according to individual perpetrators' personalities and pathologies.

Rape is a familiar but little-focused-upon and theorized aspect of mass murders, expulsions, and eliminationist politics. Eliminationist rape has produced an institution that until the Serbs' assault on Bosnians was not known or recognized for what it is, a new kind of camp in the universe of camps, the rape camp. This failure occurred even though one formal rape camp system, although not conceptualized as such and not leading to further study and theorizing, has been well known: the Japanese's so-called Comfort Stations populating their vast domination, elimination, and exploitation empire. In them, they imprisoned perhaps 200,000 sex slaves, euphemistically called "comfort women." Yasuji Kaneko, a Japanese soldier, raped countless women in such camps and also in villages in China with, whatever other emotions, a blunt callousness: "They cried out, but it didn't matter to us whether the women lived or died." The Japanese master race, especially its warriors, conceived of these women, as subhumans to be used, like all Chinese, Koreans, and others, in a utilitarian manner, as objects to be exploited or discarded. "We were the emperor's soldiers. Whether in military brothels or in the villages, we raped without reluctance."[111]

Eliminationist rape remains out of focus and untheorized as a political and eliminationist act and strategy even though it appears to be as widespread as such assaults' other aspects. Johannes Kruger, a prominent Baster serving with the Germans through their annihilationist campaign against the Herero, conveys the slaughter's extended butchery, and that for Germans raping and killing, usually with bayonets, went hand-in-hand. Kruger says he and the other Africans "refused to kill Herero women and children, but the Germans spared none. They killed thousands and thousands. I saw this bloody work for days and days and every day. Often, and especially at Waterberg, the young Herero women and girls were violated by the German soldiers before being killed. Two of my Hottentots . . . were invited by the German soldiers to join them in violating Herero girls. The two Hottentots refused to do so."[112] Many Armenian survivors testify to their own and others' rapes. One woman relates that on her death march, "all the old women and the weak who were unable to walk were killed. There were about one hundred Kurdish guards over us, and our lives depended on their pleasure. It was a very common thing for them to rape our girls in our presence. Very often they violated eight- or ten-year-old girls, and as a consequence many would be unable to walk and were shot." When their forlorn, bedraggled column passed a village and "a Kurd fancied a girl, nothing would prevent him from taking her."[113] Reciting this practice's sickening horrors alone could fill an entire book. In scenes perpetrators acted out seemingly endlessly in Bosnia and other eliminationist onslaughts, two Bosnian women in Foca recount Serbs bringing them and two other women to an apartment and repeatedly raping them while their children watched. Their sexual torturers continually conveyed to them their motivation's eliminationist dimension. One woman explains: "The four of them raped me, one after the other. They told us we were going to give birth to Serbian children and they would do everything they could so we wouldn't even dare think of coming back again." The second woman recalls the rapists becoming enraged when she stood up without permission even though they had ordered her to do the dishes, "Fuck your Turkish mother" and "Death to all Turkish sperm."[114] These women's and much other testimony demonstrates that the perpetrators conceive of politically inspired and organized rape as constituting a particular form of eliminationist violence. As one Serb explained to his victim, the Serbs wanted to "plant the seeds of Serbs in Bosnia," and as another Bosnian rape victim recounts, her tormenters "said they wanted to drive us out, that there shouldn't be any more Muslims in Europe."[115] The Political Islamic Janjaweed perpetrators in Darfur are just as explicit. Many rape victims and witnesses report that the Janjaweed, or the women accompanying them, have sought to humiliate them with abusive language and songs. One victim relates, "When we tried to escape they shot more children. They raped women; I saw many cases of Janjaweed raping women and girls. They are happy when they rape. They sing when they rape and they tell that we are just slaves and that they can do with us how they wish."[116] Another woman testifies that "I was sleeping when the attack on Disa started. I was taken away by the attackers, they were all in uniforms. They took dozens of other girls and made us walk for three hours. During the day we were beaten and they were telling us: 'You, the black women, we will exterminate you, you have no god.' At night we were raped several times."[117]

Eliminationist rape and other sexual violence constitute excess cruelty directed at women. They differ from eliminationist politics, violence, and cruelty's other forms, which perpetrators, in principle and usually in practice, inflict against all the victim groups' available members, men or women, young or old. The perpetrators' particular and politically purposeful victimization of women in this singular way, especially when sanctioned, creates a daily impetus, indeed libidinal drive, to make the victims suffer, producing excess violence and suffering that are more frequent, systematic, and widespread than the perpetrators' other cruelties. Lest anyone think the raping, especially when organized and institutionalized, is just boys being boys, or something other than intricately interwoven into eliminationist or exterminationist assaults' other purposely cruel aspects, everyone should ponder certain indicative rapes from Rwanda.

Discussing the Hutu's "massive, massive indiscriminate raping of women, old, young, children," Rwandan Minister of Justice Tharcisse Karugarama in one brilliant answer to the question *What motivated the perpetrators to rape?* lays out eliminationist rape's critical elements. First he explains rape's purpose: "Rape was used as an instrument of genocide. To humiliate the people, to humiliate the victims." Then he explains its particular source grounded in the perpetrators' conception of the victims, which produced in the Hutu the desire for vengeance: "Because there was this feeling that these guys [the Tutsi] despise you. Their women think you are not worth their sex. So violate them." Then Karugarama adduces what can be seen as eliminationist rape's emblematic and most analytically significant instance: "We have a woman in Arusha who was standing, encouraging her sons to rape, as a sign of victory, as a sign of self-important and self-aggrandizement. As a sign of being raised to another level, of having raped a Tutsi woman." He continues: "We have instances where women encouraged their husbands to rape, as a sign that these women have now conquered the Tutsi woman. They are now more superior because the Tutsi woman is down and beaten." This is not boys being boys. It is *mothers and wives being boys.* Yet mothers and wives were driving their sons and husbands to rape for reasons that had nothing to do with sexual pleasure but for *eliminationist* ends, for some combination of *cruelty's* multiple purposes and satisfactions. Karugarama concludes his analysis: "So you can imagine under normal circumstances their wife would never encourage their husband to do rape."[118] Exactly. Eliminationist circumstances, cruelty's vengeance and satisfactions, here gave women the spur to become rapists, and to reveal the raping's real nature.

In another way, Constance's and Denise's stories do as well. Constance, along with other Tutsi women, was a rape camp prisoner:

"Over time, all the women became weaker and weaker because we had not been given any food. The Interahamwe told us that they would kill us before we died of hunger, but that they wanted to make us suffer more." The repeated and institutionalized raping was an integral part of the Hutu's larger eliminationist agenda. The perpetrators starved the women, told them they would kill them, and let them know they intended to keep them alive as long as possible, while starving them, so the women would suffer maximally. This rape camp interlude of this cruelty and torture's multiple and intertwined forms came immediately after these same perpetrators had slaughtered the women's husbands and children, and immediately before they fulfilled their promise to kill all the women, whom they eventually marched away and macheted to the last one. Constance too: "I was cut on the head with a machete and left because they thought I was dead. I was put into a mass grave that night and when I regained consciousness, I got out of the grave and ran in the bushes," only, before eventually fleeing to safety, to be raped again by four young Hutu, one as young as twelve, at a roadblock where older Hutu "watched and encouraged" them.[119]

When the Hutu attacked Denise's community, her husband jumped out of their house's window and fled. Some neighbors were among the six or so Hutu barging into her house with machetes and torches. When Denise refused to reveal her husband's whereabouts, "they began to beat me on the legs with sticks. Then one of them raped me. He said, 'you are lucky. Your god is still with you because we don't want to kill you. Now the Hutu have won. You Tutsi, we are going to exterminate you. You won't own anything.'" Then after lording it over her that the Hutu were vanquishing and exterminating all the Tutsi except her, he demonstrated his sickening sarcasm in saying that she, unlike all other Tutsi slated for death, was "lucky" in being spared.

> When he finished he took me inside and put me on a bed. He held one leg of mine open and another one held the other leg. He called everyone who was outside and said, "you come and see how Tutsikazi are on the inside." Then he said, "You Tutsikazi, you think you are the only beautiful women in the world." Then he cut out the inside of my vagina. He took the flesh outside, took a small stick and put what he had cut on the top. He stuck the stick in the ground outside the

door and was shouting, "Everyone who comes past her will see how Tutsikazi look." Then he came back inside and beat me again.[120]

Here, and often across Rwanda, the perpetrators' raping was accompanied by gruesome genital mutilation and torture. The Hutu were exacting sexual revenge against Tutsi women, whom they said, mantra-like, thought themselves better and more beautiful than Hutu. Additionally, perpetrators often performed this sexual revenge for demonstration purposes and, in this instance, to create a singularly grotesque display they fully expected onlooking Hutu to enjoy.

The shamelessness, indeed the moral order's inversion—public demonstration of cruelty and otherwise unimaginable suffering as righting the world—is eliminationist assaults' common feature. The gruesome cruelty, so revolting yet so common and so eagerly inflicted, and then publicly consumed and appreciated among Rwanda's Hutu, and by other eliminationist assaults' perpetrators and supporting community members, is enormously lurid and disturbing merely as print on the page. I considered not including here even the words of Denise, this last victim, which as mere words do not and cannot convey one one-thousandth of her pain and suffering's horror. I nevertheless decided to present her testimony because we must behold, as best we can, the perpetrators' *actual*, not sanitized, deeds, if we want to understand why they do what they do, which is not to robotically and clinically and dispassionately "execute" their victims (and do nothing else to them), but, among the many other nonrobotic, nonclinical, non-foot-dragging, nonreluctant, noncoerced, and horrifying acts the perpetrators regularly perpetrate, is to do *that*.

A Human Rights Watch study of Hutu's raping during the annihilationist onslaught, based on extensive interviews with victims, concludes:

> Often the rape of women was accompanied or followed by mutilation of the sexual organs or of features held to be characteristic of the Tutsi ethnic group. Sexual mutilations included the pouring of boiling water into the vagina; the opening of the womb to cut out an unborn child before killing the mother; cutting off breasts; slashing the pelvis area; and the mutilation of vaginas. . . . Assailants mutilated features considered "Tutsi," including thin noses and long fingers.[121]

Concessa Kayiraba, part of a community of rape victims, victimized by the Hutu of their own village, including their own neighbors, explains: "They used their sex as a killing weapon. After that they would insert objects in the vagina like sticks and add in chili pepper. So I think their plan was to kill. They were evil."[122] Ngarambe, speaking for the perpetrators, who he says boasted about raping Tutsi women, confirms the Hutu rapists' eliminationist motivation: "There was nothing else they wanted them [the Tutsi they raped] for, except to humiliate them, to throw away their humanness, and to make them lose their Rwandan image they had before."[123]

The annals of eliminationist rape, in Rwanda, in Bosnia and elsewhere, and now, especially with Rwandan exile Hutu militias in Democratic Republic of the Congo, and Political Islamists in Darfur, contain legions of such sexual mutilation, which, together with the perpetrators' boastful statements, show that the perpetrators' pleasure in raping is principally the pleasure of making the hated victims suffer, of displaying the perpetrators' utter domination, of appropriating the victims' women, of, in the perpetrators' minds, multiple layers of irony, mocking and cruelty, enjoyment, physically and symbolically turning the tables on, and permanently marking the victims, done all in the name of what the perpetrators believe the victims deserve.

Alisa Muratčauš, in addition to being president of the Association of Concentration Camp Torture Survivors in Sarajevo, to which a thousand women belong, many of whom were raped and held in rape camps, was herself a rape victim and rape camp survivor. She could not be clearer that for the perpetrators rape was a politically motivated eliminationist weapon, emanating from hatred, hatred born of their conception of Muslims as pernicious alien invaders who had to be eradicated. She knows it because the Serbs repeatedly told it to her, to her sister, and the other victims (including five thousand men) for whom she speaks—as she in so many ways conveyed to me during a long interview in Sarajevo:

A lot of women, especially Bosniak women and Catholic [Croatian] women, we are brutally raped and suffered the grossest kind of physical and psychological torture at the hands of the enemies. Rape was systemically used as a weapon of biological genocide to separate

Alisa Muratčauš, Sarajevo, Bosnia and Herzegovina, July 2008

women from their communities, to separate women from families, to criminally humiliate the family of raped women. Women of different ages were raped. Some were only eleven or twelve years old, and some of these young children often died because of the extreme assault. . . .

Some soldiers raped my sister. Told [her] "you will have a baby. You will bring new life. It will be Serbian. Serbian. Just Serbian people. We will destroy you, all of you. We will destroy, definitely. Bosnia is and Herzegovina is a Serbian land, and there will be no Croatian people, Bosnian people, just Serbian people."

The Serbs explained to her and others the source of their hatred: "They told us, you are Turkish. You are Balia [a derogatory term]. We will kill you. We will rape you, kill you, hard." Asked whether the Serbs explained why they wanted to kill her, she chuckled as if the question were naïve and absurd, the answer being so obvious: "Yes, [laughing] they just needed to know that we are Bosniak. It's enough for them. 'Okay, we will kill you. We will expel you. This is Serbian land, and just Serbian people will live here. Not you.'" The Serbs raped the Bosniak women in anything but a matter-of-fact way, of having a job to do. The rapists lorded their eliminationist deeds over them, "cut[ting them] with their knives," carving into their breasts an "Orthodox cross." Why? "They hated us a lot. This is really a special hate." The Serbs boasted to their victims: "They were yelling at us, 'ha-ha-ha, you will have Serbian babies, Serbian children,'" and mockingly offered to bring their victims an "Orthodox priest if you want" to hasten their Serbification. Asked whether the Serbs ever showed sympathy toward the victims, Muratčauš was emphatic: "No. Actually, sexually they enjoy it to [make you] suffer, to torture you. . . . They enjoyed to torture you, to show they are . . . very brave. That they are very strong." Muratčauš told me that the raping was unequivocally "political": "Definitely, it was, yes. Not sexual expression. Just the expression of the—actually they hated us. Just to cause fear in us. To expel us. To speed up ethnic cleansing. Definitely."[124]

Women's particular vulnerability to this particular cruelty and torture and the predictable and special fear it engenders, when perpetrators practice it widely, render women's plight under eliminationist politics' threat, or as its intended victims, in this significant aspect and probably overall, qualitatively different from and often worse than men's. While analysis of and policy response to eliminationist politics must focus on its core, this sui generis feature requires special attention. This ought to include the fundamental recognition that rape, as excess cruelty and preventive reproduction, is in many eliminationist assaults a principal eliminationist means, complementing and functionally equivalent to mass murder and expulsion. A Masaleit woman from West Darfur, raped by ten soldiers in the presence of her baby and daughter, and left bleeding and unable to walk, explains that the perpetrators themselves, who burnt down her undefended and rebel-free village, portray rape, just as the Serbs in Bosnia did, in this way: "They were saying the government from Khartoum sent [them] and we [were to be] killed and raped and cleaned [from] the land."[125]

Just as eliminationist perpetrators target women in particular ways, they do children as well. Obviously, children are innocent of committing any transgression. Yet race, kinship, group membership, or some other perpetrator principle leads most eliminationist perpetrators to think children ought to roughly share their parents and people's fate. The perpetrators' conception of their victims as existential enemies, heretics, subhumans, or demons usually, though far from invariably, encompasses the victims' children as well and, powerfully informing emotions, manages to efface the tenderness and protectiveness many feel, seemingly naturally, for children. Even worse, the brutality eliminationist politics' perpetrators inflict upon children is often ferocious.

As with excess cruelty, we need to account for the perpetrators' violence against children, even small children, and then its variations. That perpetrators willfully, even eagerly, slaughter or expel children, and furthermore, often subject them to excess cruelty, is comprehensible, once it is understood that perpetrators willingly target groups and peoples for elimination because they believe them to be (frequently dehumanized or demonized) beings substantially endangering the perpetrators, their families, or their transformative vision. In short, according to perpetrators' conception of the victim group, the children, if not already noxious, will grow into the putatively hateful and dangerous beings their parents are. They pose an inherent potential future threat, which perpetrators expect will further intensify, as will the children's desire to revenge themselves on the people behind their parents' suffering and elimination. So the children, like their parents, must, in one way or another, go. While this line of reasoning's particulars vary depending on perpetrators' conception of victims as existential enemies, heretics, subhumans, or demons, its essential easy-to-follow thread helps explain why the perpetrators and their supporters, often parents themselves, shut down the solicitude ordinarily reserved for children, feeling little or no compunction in eliminating them. Once children are caught in eliminationist violence's maelstrom that, in any case, tends to become indiscriminate at the point of attack, the perpetrators treat them horribly. Because children, especially infants and small children, are especially vulnerable, they suffer and die disproportionately more just by receiving equal treatment.

Nevertheless, children's fates vary widely during eliminationist onslaughts. When eliminationist assaults are wholly or primarily mass murderous, the perpetrators' treatment of children takes three basic forms, each deriving mainly from the perpetrators' conception of the victims and their threat.

In some eliminationist assaults, the perpetrators treat children utterly differently from their parents by choosing not to target them. This was true for communist regimes, which, unlike the Nazis, did not target children. The Soviets, who, in consigning the vast majority of their victims to the gulag, did not include their victims' children (though when they expelled entire minority groups or kulaks from their homes and regions, the children suffered and died along with their parents). The Soviets knew the children were themselves not a manifest threat and could always be reared, in the ideological school that Soviet society was, as good communists. In other eliminationist programs against *heretics*, the perpetrators have similarly often spared children, at least when targeting people for real or alleged political beliefs and actions. This appears to have happened frequently during the Indonesians' slaughter of communists. The perpetrators have not seen heretics' children as guilty (they are prepolitical) and could therefore safely live with their surviving relatives (the Indonesian often also spared women) or be raised by others and imbued with the dominant group's worldview.

Eliminationist perpetrators' second mode of treating children is to subject them to a less severe eliminationist fate than that of their parents. This occurs frequently when perpetrators employ various means, including but not only annihilation, or when the assault is selective, focusing on weakening the enemy with strategic killing (the number can still be enormous) of part of a targeted people. The Serbs, in their eliminationist onslaughts both against the Bosniaks and the Kosovars, restricted their targeted killing mainly to men and teenage boys. They did not systematically target younger children for death, instead expelling them together with their families' and communities' remnants. Perpetrators eliminating many peoples, even when targeting children, often are less consistent in killing them, because, whatever they believe about the victim peoples, the children are, after all, just children and manifestly not threatening. For them perpetrators often choose lesser eliminationist means such as expulsion.

Finally, in the third modal treatments, perpetrators dispose of children as they do adults. When a political community conducts an all-out, unrestrained, eliminationist assault on a minority, the perpetrators tend to victimize children as if they were mere smaller adults. Nottingham, the former British district officer in Kenya, explains how the British, who certainly recognized that Kikuyu children had committed no transgression, could nevertheless treat children cruelly and murderously: "By the time that I'm talking of, the fact that a child was a child was almost irrelevant. The point was he was a Kikuyu."[126] This has been true for perpetrators assaulting targets deemed subhumans, existential enemies, or heretics—the German annihilators of the Herero and Nama, the Japanese in Nanjing and elsewhere, the Germans' treatment of Poles, Russians, Sintis, Roma, and others, Britons' mass incarceration of Kikuyu, the Khmer Rouge's eliminationist slaughter or imprisonment of virtually all of Cambodian society, the Syrian slaughterers of Hama's people, Saddam's assault upon southern Iraq's Marsh people and northern Iraq's Kurds, the Sudanese killers in Darfur. In Guatemala, where the perpetrators' cruelty toward children was, in general, widespread and acute, they particularly targeted boys, like men, according to the perpetrators themselves, to prevent Mayan society's regeneration and future retribution against them:

> Well, they told my sister—since among the soldiers there was one who spoke our language—and he told my sister that they had to finish off all the men and all the male children in order to eliminate the guerrillas. "And why?" she asked, "and why are you killing the children?" "Because those wretches are going to come some day and screw us over." That was their intention when they killed the little ones too.

Another Maya explains further: "The army's plan was to get rid of the seeds. Even if it was a little one- or two-year-old child, they are all bad seeds, so they say. This was the army's plan. This is what I have seen."[127] The brutal realpolitik behind the perpetrators' treatment of existential enemies, and the utilitarian calculus perpetrators use for handling subhumans, together with the general disinhibition of internal restraints both mindsets produce, lead perpetrators to dispose of their victims' children as they do their parents, often to ensure the "seeds" will never sprout, that their putative problems never regenerate. Neither social theory, realpolitik or brutal utilitarianism, gives the perpetrators any general reason to privilege children. The Guatemalan perpetrators generally did not (except for those they kidnapped and enslaved). Guatemala's foremost forensic expert, Peccerelli, explains the perpetrators' regular mode of killing children: "Yeah, basically swung [children] into rocks, trees, anything big and stable that you can smash a kid up against. The little older kids, the little heavier, harder to handle, they would just shoot and then the older ones a combination of everything, a combination of gunshot wounds and sharp force trauma."[128]

These three modal ways in which perpetrators treat targeted groups' children—exempting them, going "easy" on them with lesser eliminationist means, and treating them no differently from their parents—are instantly comprehensible, covering a normal range of options. There are two additional, less frequent, perpetrator means of treating children.

With the first, perpetrators hold children to be actually or potentially different, and better, than their parents' fate. In some instances, owing to the perpetrators' social theory, they treat children of groups targeted because of ethnicity or nationality radically differently from their parents. The Turks, conceiving of their existential enemies the Armenians not entirely coherently, an unstable agglomeration of a national/ethnic/religious-based hatred, nevertheless had a decidedly nonracist view of them. This permitted the Turks to think of young Armenian children as redeemable because they had not been, in a sense, Armenianized by being inculcated with an unalterable Armenian identity, cultural practices, or characteristics. In principle, the Turks could spare young Armenian children, allowing Turkish families to take them in, convert them to Islam, and raise them as Turks, which they did by the tens of thousands. The Turkish leadership enunciated this principle as policy when planning the exterminationist and eliminationist program. The fifth of their "Ten Commandments" for conducting the eliminationist assault: "Apply measures to exterminate all males under 50, priests and teachers, leave girls and children to be Islamized."[129] Although the Turks killed most Armenian girls and children—often cruelly and gleefully, such as by swinging them and smashing their heads—and although kidnapping children is barbaric, the Turks' choice to spare such children's lives reveals their social theory's power to get them to substantially depart from their otherwise utter eliminationist brutality, and that the flow of fellow feeling and human pity was not indiscriminately dammed up in them. Allowing some Armenian children to live likely provided balm for some Turkish perpetrators' consciences—they could tell themselves they were exterminating only those leaving them no choice. But without the social theory guiding them, at odds with the social theories informing many other eliminationist assaults' perpetrators, they would not have allowed the Armenian children to live, albeit as Turks.

In this respect, and in forcing an enormous number of Armenian women to convert or to enter slavery, the Turks, exceptional among the perpetrators of our time's mass murders and eliminations, resembled premodern times' eliminationist warriors, who also incorporated the vanquished people's children (and women) into their communities. In other instances, usually when eliminating heretics, perpetrators do not target children, as the Soviets did not for most of their victims, and the perpetrators of some of Latin Americans' dirty wars against leftists did not. In these instances, the perpetrators could be seen as conceiving of the children as the Turks did of the Armenians. But instead, these are episodes of perpetrators being wrathful against particular adults because of their real or alleged *individual* beliefs or actions (and not because of ascriptive characteristics, such as ethnicity or nationality), which means that the perpetrators harbored no direct eliminationist animus toward their targets' relatives, including their children.

The Germans, governed by their idiosyncratic racial-biological view of humanity, also stole children from the vanquished. But not from all the groups they were slaughtering or eliminating. The Nazis' race theory held, bizarrely, that a person's individual physiognomy governed his racial destiny, meaning that a Nordic-looking child born to Slavic parents, be they Poles, Ukrainians, or others, was of sound, indeed exalted biology, and should, indeed must, be incorporated into the master race's community as one of its own. As Himmler confirmed in his 1943 speech to the SS leadership, "Whatever is available to us in good blood of our type, we will take for ourselves, that is, we will steal their children and bring them up with us, if necessary."[130] The Germans created an extensive, formal program to identify these individually putatively physiognomically privileged children, kidnap them, and deliver them to German families for adoption, and supposed master-race acculturation. They conducted modern times' most extensive child kidnapping program to incorporate into the German racial body unknown thousands of such children.

Jewish children's fate at the Germans' hands was the opposite, constituting the other principal exception to the three modal ways perpetrators treat children. The German perpetrators did not subject Jewish children merely to their parents' brutal and lethal fate, but often treated them worse. The added callousness, if not enjoyment, that perpetrators express just by subjecting children's helpless and extra-vulnerable beings to the same privations as their parents was fully evident among the Germans. They inflicted enormous suffering on Jewish children by starving them, often to death (the Warsaw Ghetto camp's official daily ration was 350 calories), forcing them into the ghettos' hellish living conditions (the Warsaw Ghetto's population density was, according to German statistics, initially six to seven people *per room*), deporting them, like their parents, packed like sardines in nearly airless, locked freight cars for days on end. They killed them mercilessly. But in several ways, the Germans' ferocity and cruelty toward children exceeded even their treatment of Jewish adults.

The Germans often slaughtered Jewish children before their parents, leaving the adults alive for days, weeks, months, resulting in many Jews surviving the war without their children. In Auschwitz and other camps, they reflexively killed arriving Jewish children. When the Germans learned a Jewish woman was pregnant, they killed her immediately, often in a brutally cruel manner. This was officially conveyed in the infamous Jäger Report, an itemized accounting of the Germans' and their local helpers' slaughtering of 137,346 Jews in the comprehensive extermination program's first months in Lithuania, which starts off: "Today I can confirm that our objective, to solve the Jewish problem for Lithuania, has been achieved." They left alive only those Jews needed as temporary workers. Karl Jäger, as if to allay possible concerns about the long-term consequences for the exterminationist project of temporarily enslaving these Jews, discusses in his report one of the Germans' complementary eliminationist means: "I am of the view that the sterilization program of the male worker Jews should be started immediately so that reproduction is prevented. If despite sterilization a Jewess becomes pregnant she will be liquidated."[131]

The German perpetrators reacted with fury upon encountering a pregnant Jewish woman, putatively harboring the biological seed of the Germans' undoing—their view of the gestating child. The sight of a pregnant Jew, carrying a future life, did not warm the Germans' hearts but incited a heightened consciousness of danger threatening to multiply before their eyes. This also occurred when they came upon Jewish infants and young children during roundups and deportations. The Germans often killed them in the most gruesome manner, shooting them at point-blank range in their mothers' arms or, after snatching them, swinging them by their heels to smash their heads against a tree or a building wall. This was the purest rage, having no purposeful domination or demonstration purpose. It was their hatred's expression at coming across the symbol of their putative enemies' future and hope, a threat born of the Germans' hallucinatory sense of endangerment. An adult brutally killing another adult face-to-face involves an element of domination, establishing in the final second a clear, unalterable master and victim hierarchy that each recognizes before or even as the perpetrator strikes the final blow. But a young child, an infant, cannot comprehend this and therefore provide the psychic satisfaction perpetrators the world over take in looking into their victims' eyes, reflecting back the perpetrators' physical mastery and desired emotional and moral mastery. The Germans' unsurpassed drive to destroy Jewish children— they slated *every* Jewish child for death—their extra ferocity and brutality toward them, and their obvious special, cruel satisfaction in inflicting cruelty on them, set them apart yet again. No exterminationist program has come close to matching the Germans' systematic and obsessive killing of children, so much so that they devoted considerable resources to ferret out hidden Jewish children. This distinguishes the Germans even in the long history of annihilative and eliminationist assaults upon Jews, whose perpetrators' fury rarely targeted children or systematically hunted and slaughtered them.

The Tutsi's brutality toward Hutu children in Burundi and then, on a still broader scale, the Hutu's brutality toward Tutsi children in Rwanda appear to have been kindred, exceeding even the baseline brutality and murderousness they showed adults. Similar to the Germans' conception of Jews, Hutu and Tutsi each saw the other group's children as the biological spawn of evil. The licentiousness and ritualized manner of each group's slaughtering the other's children bespoke an unusual viciousness exceeding even conventional eliminationist baselines used for adults. A Hutu survivor from Burundi recalls how girls, who would otherwise grow up to be fertile women, were, with unmistakable symbolism, killed—and by whom: "The [Tutsi] girls in secondary school, they killed each other. The Tutsi girls were given bamboos. They were made to kill by pushing the bamboo from below [from the vagina] to the mouth." Another survivor recounts a second transparently symbolic manner of destruction: "There was a manner of cutting the stomach [of pregnant women]. Everything that was found in the interior was lifted out without cutting the cord. The cadaver of the mama, the cadaver of the baby, of the future, they rotted on the road. Not even a burial." Formulated with tragic poetic insight, the "cadaver . . . of the future . . . rotted on the road."[132] A doctor who fled his hospital in Rwanda after Hutu slaughtered its 150 to 170 patients, including wounded children, explained why the Hutu killed a Tutsi nurse, seven months pregnant. Her crime, according to the murderers, was "she was carrying a Tutsi baby."[133] He did not need to add that for the Hutu the not-yet-born baby was guilty of only one thing: being Tutsi. The Hutu's utter pitilessness and brutality toward Tutsi children did not mean they always treated the youngest with the excess cruelty they did adults. Precisely because babies have no understanding, these condign and vengeful torturers benefitted little from torturing them as they did adults. Babies, according to the perpetrator Alphonse, "were whacked against walls and trees or they were cut right away. But they were killed more quickly, because of their small size and because their suffering was of no use. They say that at the church in Nyamata they burned children with gasoline. Maybe it's true, but that was just a few in the first-day turmoil. Afterward that did not last. In any case I noticed nothing more. The babies could not understand the way of the suffering, it was not worth lingering over them."[134]

Setting out to annihilate or otherwise eliminate people considered to be *demons* can lead perpetrators to intensely focus their wrath on the children, representing the future race of demons, an unending threat.

Mass murder and elimination's perpetrators' comparative treatment of children is significant in multiple ways, beyond the most obvious fact, easily overlooked, that the dearth of systematic knowledge about the fate of children reminds us again that little analytical attention has been paid to exterminationist and eliminationist assaults, and that much knowledge has died with the victims.

First, and most significant, is the perpetrators' disposition of the children themselves. Not that eliminationist perpetrators ever act well toward children or treat them with humanity, but some horrible fates are more horrible than others. Again, the Germans' various eliminationist assaults during the Nazi period offer the greatest insight. Germans adopted most methods for treating children. They did not target German communists and other heretics' children. They generally consigned Poles, Russians, and other putative subhumans' children to their parents' fates. They slaughtered and brutalized with particular thoroughness and relish the putative Jewish demons' demonic children. They stole and reared as Germans victim peoples' children, conforming in their personal physiognomy to the ideal of the master race according to the Germans' crackpot racial-biological ideological and political accounting system.

Second, just as with eliminationist programs' other central aspects, this aspect of the perpetrators' conduct provides insight into their mindsets and motives. Not all cruelties are compatible with all mindsets and motives. The perpetrators' excess cruelty, common in eliminationist and exterminationist onslaughts and so frequent in some as to be a constituent feature, glaringly falsifies all postulates denying the perpetrators' approval of their deeds. This all but ignored analytical point is even much more evident regarding the perpetrators' treatment of and cruelty toward children. All those said to be killing or expelling the victims against their will, or merely out of obedience or because of peer pressure to help their comrades, would not possibly descend on victims' children with the perpetrators' fury, willful excess brutality, and glee.

Third, the perpetrators' enormously widespread cruelty toward children tells us some further specific things about perpetrators' cruelty in general. It is obviously not Zimbardoian, not grounded in the social relations (guards facing recalcitrant prisoners) said to produce Zimbardoian cruelty. The children, posing no threat of resistance whatsoever, cannot possibly induce in the perpetrators the sense they must brutalize prisoners to control them. The perpetrators' cruelty toward children is also Machiavellian, if at all, only rarely. The circumstances and character of the perpetrators' cruelty toward children—perhaps only slightly less true of their cruelty toward adults—clarify their cruelty as an end in itself, for their satisfaction, without instrumental purpose. To the (considerable) extent that the perpetrators' cruelty toward children is vengeful, this merely further demonstrates, or rather unambiguously demonstrates, the perpetrators' thinking about the victims' hallucinatory quality. Children cannot possibly have done anything tangibly bad to the perpetrators, their families, or their groups or nations. Only to mindsets, such as those of the German perpetrators, holding the victim's putative evil spirit to be coursing through *all* the victims' veins, would it make sense for perpetrators to feel such vengeful fury at the targeted group's children.

Finally, the perpetrators' slaughter of and cruelty toward children thoroughly belie their hollow self-exculpatory claims that they merely carry out a necessary task, or did not know they were acting wrongly or criminally, or had no choice, or any of the other postulates that they acted despite their lack of approval of the deed. Of course, their cruelty toward adults also belies their self-exculpatory claims, that they did not want to kill or expel or otherwise brutalize the victim peoples.

Returning to the perpetrators' general practice of cruelty returns us to the discussion's starting point: Whatever the differences in their cruelty's sources and practices, the two most fundamental facts are constant: The perpetrators know the victims suffer excruciating physical and emotional pain and often substantial wounds and injuries, and that they themselves, operating in their leaders' eliminationist programs, cause this suffering. No one can reasonably deny these two facts. The analysis here has focused on *excess* cruelty, for which the perpetrators are, by definition, that much more responsible. Their physical, verbal, and symbolic violence is gratuitous, unnecessary for the simple eliminationist act. They inflict it on their own initiative and at their pleasure. The perpetrators' knowledge of the victims' pain and suffering, and of their role in causing it, is true for excess cruelty's other forms, those embedded in camps' and other eliminationist institutions' structures, in modes of "work," and in the perpetrators' collective displays. All such cruelty appears natural and normative to the perpetrators because they think of those they hate or see as a threat—whether or not they dehumanize or demonize them—as beings they must violently eliminate, having themselves, by their own nature or deeds, earned this deserved fate. This was no less true among the British perpetrators in Kenya than elsewhere, as Nottingham, the former colonial administrator, attests, saying that "the general approach was that they [the Kikuyu] were at fault for what they'd done. Tried to rise up and so . . . okay, it didn't really matter very much how many died. . . . They were just getting what they deserved."[135] The cruelty appears natural also to the victims, a constituent feature of a world—their new world—the universe of eliminationist politics. The victims recognize that the perpetrators' conduct is utterly pathological according to conventional civilization's standards, or rather of noneliminationist civilization. But the perpetrators' quotidian cruelties quickly resocialize the victims to bear and see the pathological as integral to their new social and personal worlds. This cruelty, flowing so naturally from people's eliminationist conceptions, becoming a natural and seemingly normative part of the programs based on such conceptions, is the perpetrators' self-justifying and satisfying self-expression. It is also the perpetrators' means of communicating with the victims—about their nature, their abject state, their hopelessness, the ultimate fate awaiting them at the masters' hands. Just as the perpetrators know they impart messages—often they make doubly sure by articulating them, with overlordship, derision, and laughter—the victims receive the messages unmistakably. Liisa Malkki, after recounting Burundian Tutsi's unbearably gruesome tortures and killings of pregnant Hutu women and others, explains how well the survivors living in the Tanzanian refugee camp she studied understood the messages:

> The disemboweling of pregnant Hutu was interpreted as an effort to destroy the procreative capability, the "new life," of the Hutu people. In several accounts, the unborn child or embryo was referred to, simply, as "the future." The penetration of the head through the anus, as well as other means of crushing the head, were seen as a decapitation of the intellect, and, on a more general level, as an effort to render the Hutu people powerless, politically impotent. (Reference was never made to any mutilation of the penis.) In particular, it was said that the intention was to squash the Hutu's efforts to gain higher education.[136]

The message the Tutsi delivered was the same as the Hutu received, as was true with analogous messages from Germans to Herero, from Turks to Armenians, from Germans to Jews, from Serbs to Bosnians, from Tutsi to Hutu in Rwanda, from Political Islamists to Darfurians, and from many more perpetrators to their victims. In Burundi, the Tutsi combined various eliminationist means to forestall a Hutu challenge to their power. They killed, prevented reproduction, and decapitated the Hutu collectively and individually. The Tutsi conveyed their message with sickening violence and sickening degradation, such as penetrating heads through anuses, in other words, with cruelty's unsurpassable and horrifying clarity.

Actual Worlds

In most eliminationist assaults, the spirit of overall policy, the institutions chosen to implement it, the communities of consent, and the individual actors' treatment of their individual victims spring, by and large, from the perpetrators' shared mindset. The political leaders and perpetrators in the field act with little if any opposition from their own people or from victims. Thus, in each eliminationist assault an unusual consonance typically exists in how the perpetrators reshape the world in their overall treatment of the targeted groups, the nature and functioning of institutions the perpetrators form and of the communities in which they exist and which sustain them, and the perpetrators' personalized actions. These individual eliminationist worlds, communal worlds, institutional worlds, and personal worlds add up everywhere—as perpetrators and their communities know and celebrate—to new or radically altered worlds, or, in Alphonse's words, to "new days on the way."

Nevertheless, differences exist in the worlds practitioners of eliminationist politics seek to create, and in how they choose to excise the malignant social and political tumors they see the targeted groups to be. Differences exist often within individual eliminationist assaults, and certainly across all such assaults, in the perpetrators' comprehensiveness in targeting different categories of victims, from total or near total, to partial, to selective or demonstration killings. Differences exist within individual eliminationist assaults, and across all such assaults, in how the perpetrators combine or selectively employ eliminationist means for their targets—whether the targets are different groups, political, ethnic, religious, and others, or different sexes or ages. The mixtures of transformation, repression (incarceration), expulsion, prevention of reproduction, and extermination vary enormously. The perpetrators' killing and treatment of women and children varies across eliminationist onslaughts, varies even at the same perpetrators' hands. The Nazis slaughtered Jewish, Sinti, and Roma families in toto but did not target their German communist or socialist victims' families, among many others. Differences exist in the perpetrators' sequencing of their attacks, including when they kill people of different categories. Sometimes they target the entire universe of their victims simultaneously, sometimes the men first, sometimes the weak, leaving the strong for temporary labor exploitation. Some perpetrators create a camp system, with its far-reaching consequences for the regimes and societies. Others do not. Differences exist, also substantial, in the extent and kind of perpetrators' cruelty, which, like much else that perpetrators do and do not do, can be theorized and linked to the perpetrators' underlying conception of their victims.

Differences exist, sometimes within individual eliminationist assaults and always across eliminationist assaults, on the level of overall eliminationist strategy, policy, and implementation, on the level of institutional design and functioning, and on the level of individual perpetrators' manner of treating targeted groups and individuals. Differences exist in the antiseptic halls of power, in the preparatory and hortatory airwaves, communities, and other means and locations of disseminating the views about hated and demeaned groups eventually targeted, and in the bloody, orderly, and wild killing fields and camps where the perpetrators, anything but antiseptically, face, use, misuse, and cut down their victims. Some differences and variations can be accounted for only with in-depth treatment of each individual eliminationist assault, focusing on the perpetrators' conceptions of given targeted groups' natures and perniciousness, each country's and regime's politics, especially the political leaders' political thinking and aspirations, each regime's leaders' personal involvement and character, and their opportunities and constraints.

Many eliminationist acts' compatibility with different conceptions of disparaged and despised groups, of perceived enemies, combined with uncertainties about opportunities for implementing different eliminationist measures and their likely efficacy, make it impossible to explain with certitude or to predict the eliminationist strategy, *if any*, leaders will embark upon, and then with what effect. Variations in opportunity, in leaders' calculations, and in the eliminationist desires'

unpredictable expansion once perpetrators begin killing makes pre-
dicting or even retrospectively explaining the outcomes still harder.
About each eliminationist onslaught a story can be told—a simple story
and a multilayered, complex, and detailed narrative—which is true and
which accounts for the kind of world the perpetrators create for themselves and their communities and the place within it, if any, for the targeted peoples. Such a story would account for the initiation of the
slaughter and eliminationist forays, the perpetrators' willingness to kill,
their particular identities and forms of recruitment, the institutions used
or devised, the victims' selection, the mass murder's scope and other
outcomes, the perpetrators' consensual communities' nature, and the
mass murder and elimination's eventual end. But while each individual account is apt and explanatory, still, in sum they coalesce into the
sometimes looser and sometimes firmer patterns seen here about which
we can say and explain a great deal but which often still defy general,
causal explanations. Whatever the other reasons, this, it should be re-
membered, is established as all but inevitable, given the idiosyncratic
nature of the eliminationist mission's initiation and very definition,
which depends so much on a few men's personalities, psychologies, hatreds, and calculations, and then on changing expectations, aspirations,
and strategic goals and tactical possibilities once the always evolving
onslaught begins and unfolds.

How the perpetrators' notions evolve of how many and by what mixture of means they wish to eliminate the targeted group deserves more
attention, as does their success in fulfilling their evolving notions at their
different stages. Notice the term "evolve." In eliminationist politics, the
perpetrators more frequently evolve their notions—from ideals, to intentions, to policy, each one itself sometimes changing with developing
political contexts and events. Sometimes the perpetrators embark on a
focused assault, a coup de grâce, to eliminate once and for all a finite (if
sometimes large) targeted group. In so many such assaults, however, the
intended number of victims and eliminationist means changes along
with facts on the ground, particularly if perpetrators construct a camp
system as their civilization's constituent feature.

Nevertheless, we should never lose sight of eliminationist politics
and assaults' most critical fact influencing virtually every aspect, from
the creation of ideals, to intentions, to plans, to the decision to initiate

them as policy, to the plethora of ways perpetrators on the ground implement them: people's conceptions of the "others." Whether or not the perpetrators demonize or dehumanize them, and how they understand the impediment, danger, or threat they see those "others" to be is fundamental for how they intend to treat the "others," how they actually treat them, and how they would be willing to treat them. The keen memoirist Oscar Pinkus captures this critical and unavoidable eliminationist factor brilliantly in his description of a paradigmatic occurrence in the Germans' eliminationist assault on European Jewry, an account that could have similarly occurred in Bosnia, Rwanda, and so many eliminationist assaults around the world.

In 1940 young German soldiers, western front veterans, arrived in Łosice, a town of eight thousand in Poland's Lublin region. They initially acted courteously. Then they learned the town's denizens were mainly Jews and "immediately they were transformed." Pinkus explains: "Their *Sie* turned to *du*; they made us polish their boots and clubbed us for not tipping our hats promptly."[137] Nothing had changed. The Germans beheld people looking and acting exactly as before. Yet everything had changed. The Germans had gained knowledge that the people's identity was their hated and putatively demonic foes whom they for the first time could attack. Like their countrymen across Central and Eastern Europe, they immediately became—in Pinkus' apt formulation—"transformed," using the demeaning *"du"* form of address, instead of the normal, respectful *"Sie,"* exacting symbolic obeisance, and beating the people not because of anything the people did, and not because of sudden new orders, but for only one reason: the Germans' prior prejudices about and hatreds of Jews.

Actual minds create actual worlds.

PART III

CHANGING THE FUTURE

CHAPTER TEN

Prologue to the Future

ASS MURDER BEGINS in the minds of men. Dreams of eradicating the enemy in one's midst or next door, of living in a purified society free of social, cultural, and political human pollutants, of radically refashioning society according to a promissory blueprint come easily to certain kinds of political leaders and even many ordinary people. But for people to apprehend such goals as a real option, as a legitimate and practical political option, eliminationist possibilities must be part of politics' repertoire, which requires a real-world political context that permits and makes practical the act, and permits and makes practical the thinking. Except for the most wild and vicious dreamers, without such a political context, those exercising power and ordinary citizens alike will rarely even start down the mental pathway of considering how eliminating groups of people might actually be done.

As one political and human catastrophe after another has shown, mass-murderous and eliminationist politics have been on the minds, flowed from the lips, and moved the hands of our age's leaders and followers alike. This past hundred years, humanity's most mass exterminationist and eliminationist period, has seen mass murder, mass expulsions, vast camp systems, and mass rape entering for the first time the consciousness of the entire world, especially that of political leaders. These practices have become an available and potent implement in politics' toolkit, readily and often successfully employed, and, in many political leaders' and people's eyes, deserving hardheaded consideration—in part because such assaults are not seriously attended to by outside countries, let alone met with opposing and decisive force. With all humanity's mobilization into politics, and the growing insecurity of political tyrants and their followers repressing their own societies' members—in addition to the modern world's other specific features promoting eliminationist thinking—eliminationism has been ever more tempting, and practiced on a hitherto unthinkable scale.

This has produced two distinctive forms of mass-murderous and eliminationist politics, in addition to the common focused (or even iterative) eliminationist assault. Some political leaders employ eliminationism—as the extreme violent end of the continuum for dealing with political challenges or socially troublesome, unwanted, or disparaged groups—in a still more politically foundational and sustained manner. They transform their countries into permanent or at least semipermanent eliminationist entities, dependent upon a level of violence, often institutionalized in extensive killing campaigns and camp worlds, far exceeding the conventional repressive measures used to control discontented populations. Often tied to broad and thoroughgoing transformative visions, these eliminationist civilizations—Nazi Germany, the Soviet Union, communist China, imperial Japan, Khmer Rouge Cambodia, and North Korea—include mass murder, expulsion, massive incarceration, and enslavement of peoples, as a constituent feature, sometimes *the* constituent feature, of their politics and societies.

In addition to our time's imperial eliminations, from the Belgians in Congo and the Germans in South-West Africa to the Chinese in Tibet and the Indonesians in Timor, a fearsome kind of *eliminationism as politics,* including in the Balkans and central Africa, has developed. In both areas, reciprocal mass murdering and expulsions, and ongoing eliminationist danger, came to define the region's politics. The Balkans' politics, principally though not exclusively among Serbs, Croats, and Muslims, and central African politics, in Rwanda and Burundi and now Democratic Republic of the Congo, came to be characterized less by regime type, which ordinarily principally defines a country's politics, than by a politics of iterative and reciprocal mass murder and elimination in the thousands, sometimes hundreds of thousands, and in the Democratic Republic of the Congo in the millions. Peace in certain times and regions has been but an interlude between wars. In these two regions, more conventional (if brutal dictatorial and repressive) politics have been but an interlude between mass murders and eliminations. A third instance, abruptly halted, occurred in Central and Eastern Europe. The Germans' continent-wide exterminationist and multidimensional eliminationist assault was followed by the nonapocalyptic counterelimination, primarily expulsive, against ethnic Germans mainly by peoples the Germans had victimized, some of whom could reasonably expect that radical measures were necessary to forestall future German assaults. Germany's long postwar occupation and political division and, in the west, its gradual transformation into a pluralist democracy were part of this radical political solution. In light of the many expelled, brutalized, and murdered ethnic German men, women, and children's enormous suffering, it was by far the better part.

All modern tyrannies—which include nondemocratic regimes and formally democratic countries substantially restricting or violating political rights and civil liberties—have a substantial eliminationist potential. This potential often lurks just beneath the surface of the less destructive (if still destructive) forms of political repression such regimes, by definition, practice. Nevertheless, important developments over several decades and the contemporary political context have removed several major sources of eliminationist politics.

Imperial eliminationism is by and large over, unlikely to return in a world resembling our own. Local and small-scale imperial conquests and slaughters will likely occur. Yet the major powers that once practiced such assaults on a grand scale have tempered and transformed themselves. Nuclear weapons make the return of tyranny's grand imperial aspirations along the lines of midcentury Germany or Japan or the postwar Soviet Union all but unthinkable. Only the United States and China are positioned to act in this manner anytime soon. For all its necessary and discretionary entanglements around the world, the United States is extraordinarily unlikely to embark on eliminationist imperialism abroad. China, in the throes of capitalist transformation, is somewhat of a wild card (and continues to demonstrate parochial eliminationism in Tibet), but its geostrategic territorial aspirations have always been local. China's accelerating development, while retaining extremely troubling features, is on the whole positive.

Grand communist eliminationism is over. Communism as a potent political ideology and force is spent. Its economic model is discredited as an irredeemable failure. Communism is extraordinarily unlikely to return in a world evolving in any manner resembling ours. The anticommunist

Current Political Situation (Relevant to Eliminationist Potential) in the Ten
Most Populous Countries and the European Union

	Country	Population in Millions (2009)	Current Political Situation Relevant to Eliminationist Potential
1	China	1,339	Liberalizing and integrating into world economy
2	India	1,166	Integrating into world economy, regional tensions down
3	European Union	492	Nazism and fascism dead, fully democratic and politically integrated
4	United States	307	Fully democratic
5	Indonesia	240	Imperialist past likely over, no cold-war context
6	Brazil	199	No territorial aspirations, more attentive to indigenous people
7	Pakistan	176	Largest territorial disputes over (except Kashmir, Punjab), though facing a powerful Political Islamic insurgency
8	Bangladesh	156	Territorial disputes over
9	Nigeria	149	Reduced though continuing conflicts
10	Russia	140	Soviet communism dead, though not fully democratic, local territorial disputes
11	Japan	127	Fully democratic with no imperial aspirations

counter- or preemptive slaughters, and the mindsets and politics producing them, have therefore also dissipated. A new democratic Germany
ensconced in a new democratic and politically integrated Europe has replaced the great destructive force in the middle of Europe, Nazi Germany. The bulk of the continent has no realistic prospect of returning to
the mass-murderous or eliminationist past.

More generally, the countries most capable of pursuing substantial
regional eliminationist politics are far less likely to, owing to changes in
the world and the countries' greater mutually beneficial integration
with each other and their regions. Globalization, its problems notwithstanding, promotes interdependent economies, increased cultural learning and shared outlooks, values, and norms, and democratizing and
noninternationally belligerent politics that greatly contribute to this less
threatening domestic and international environment. Looking at the
ten most populous countries and the European Union, all having per-

petrated or suffered eliminationist, including exterminationist, politics, we see that the number of those likely to again commit or suffer mass murder or elimination has dropped dramatically. Compared to almost all of their situations sixty, forty, or twenty years ago, the overall probability of such human catastrophes looks more remote.

These considerable positive developments are a prologue to a more promising future—and yet, mass murder and elimination's reality and threat do continue. Some of the regimes, assaults, and dangers are familiar. Others are new. They portend possible disaster for millions upon millions of people, and the world at large. Their constellation provides a prologue to another kind of future.

Mass murder and eliminationist politics—as I have emphasized, even on a "small" scale of tens of thousands, let alone hundreds of thousands—are being practiced, and remain nontrivial or even likely possibilities in many regions. Sub-Saharan African countries, characterized by tensions and conflicts among domestic groups and peoples partly born of immense poverty, and mostly governed by tyrannical regimes, are still potentially rife for eliminationist onslaughts. The postcolonial reactions that produced the contexts for so many of our time's slaughters have partly worked themselves out, yet the process is hardly complete, and the conflicts are far from fully resolved in many places. Similarly, many unstable and tyrannical regimes rule Asian countries, including some post-Soviet states.

The problem with contemporary dictatorships and tyrannical regimes is threefold. As we see, and as I further discuss in Chapter 11, they are themselves proto-eliminationist entities domestically. They also more frequently covet neighbors' territory, and therefore create the impetus for war, and also for practicing eliminationist politics abroad. Because they do not allow for the development of civil society and the social and political resources for people and groups to learn how to accommodate themselves to each other, regulate conflicts, and find noneliminationist solutions to problems, when the tyrannies finally end, they often leave behind eliminationist powder kegs. That happened in the former Yugoslavia, and this is what many fear for Iraq if the American and British presence becomes a short-lived interlude between Saddam Hussein's mass-murderous regime and another eliminationist context. Even with their presence, there have been low-level, somewhat under the radar, mutual eliminationist expulsions and steady murderousness by Sunni of Shia in Sunni majority areas and by Shia of Sunni in Shia majority areas, which each group's political leaders orchestrated and their various sectarian militias' eliminationist cadres carried out. One or several eliminationist assaults and bloodbaths could yet occur.

In addition to the long-existing worrisome areas and regime types, two new systemic threats, for now greatly overlapping, must be confronted directly: Political Islam and eliminationist nonstate actors, often referred to as terrorist groups.

The New Threats

Political Islam is a powerful transnational movement, with its adherents governing countries and vying for power in others, and with enormous political influence throughout the Middle East and the Islamic world. Several of its regimes have practiced mass murder and eliminationist politics more generally, and many of its regimes, national movements, and leaders openly threaten to do so. Political Islam is today's most dangerous eliminationist political movement. It has eliminationist civilizations' hallmark features: tyrannical regimes, eliminationist-oriented leaders, transformative eschatological visions, populaces brimming with eliminationist beliefs and passions, a sense of impunity, and eliminationism at the center of its normal political repertoire and existing practice.

Political Islam is avowedly totalitarian. Its leaders and followers erase the distinction between politics and religion, wanting to merge politics with and subordinate it to Islam in a domestic, regional, or ultimately global rule of fundamentalist, intolerant versions of Islam (which differ from more tolerant, pluralistic forms that are practiced, including by most Muslim-Americans). Hamas, one such Political Islamic movement, officially called the Islamic Resistance Movement, established its totalitarian grip on Gaza in 2006. Shortly after gaining power, Musa Abu Marzook, Hamas' deputy chief leader-in-exile, said on Israeli radio, one of the principles the group will never compromise is "government according to the laws of the *sharia*," the Quran's fundamentalist, antidemocratic, and antipluralist laws, which after a period of prudential consolidation Hamas began to implement legislatively in December 2008.[1]

Political Islam's common ideological foundation and overarching concerns give it a shared purpose for which its leaders and followers can singly and in concert work (even if prudence dictates some comprise, to compel people already in Islamic countries to live according to Political Islam's dictates, pursue eliminationist strategies against non-Muslims, spread eliminationist hatred, and call openly for mass violence, jihad, and even mass murder. Bin Laden, nakedly revealing Political Islam's core eliminationist foundation, and how its mass murdering is but an interchangeable eliminationist means for nonbelievers, demands Americans' conversion to Islam as a non-negotiable condition for Political Islamists to stop "fight[ing]," meaning killing Americans.[2]

Political Islam has become the governing regime of countries, including Iran, Afghanistan, Sudan, Somalia, and others, quasi-states such as Hezbollah and Hamas, and the Taliban (after being dislodged from ruling Afghanistan), and nonstate entities including Al Qaeda. In many other countries, it is a powerful social and political movement. It already has as followers a good portion of the more than 1.2 billion Muslims in the world (though many Muslims find such politics anathema). Political Islam includes all those in power or vying for power (including secular leaders) using intolerant versions of Islam as a political ideology to mobilize Muslims at home or abroad for aggressive political action. Such politics are typically directed at those defying the Political Islamic line, especially abroad against non-Muslims, derogatorily called "infidels." Political Islamists deem it lawful, even normative—their fatwas say this explicitly—to act against infidels in ways that would be criminal if done to Muslims.

Political Islam's leaders and adherents have committed mass murder and practiced eliminationist politics, or explicitly threaten to do so in Iran, Sudan, and the Palestinian Authority (Hamas), by the Political Islamic quasi-state and terrorist entities of Hezbollah in Lebanon and Al Qaeda. Political Islam is currently the one expressly, publicly, and unabashedly genocidal major political movement.

Because this movement is not Islam itself but a *political* Islamic movement with a coherent and distinctive political ideology and goals, Political Islam is a term preferable to Islamo-fascism, militant Islam, radical Islam, Islamic fundamentalism, etc. Identifying Political Islam for what it is does not implicate Islam itself or all Muslims. Calling it *Political* Islam, and not one of the other terms in use, clarifies that politics, and not religion per se, is the issue. The phenomenon includes only Islamic-grounded *political* regimes, organizations, and initiatives that share (whatever their other, sometimes internecine, differences, Shia versus Sunni, Arab versus Persian, etc.) a common ideological foundation about Islam's *political* primacy or its need to systematically and politically roll back the West—a conviction that the fundamentally corrupt modern world must be refashioned, including by annihilating others. Therein Political Islam resembles the international communist movement in its heyday. Whatever its internal divisions and differences, and antagonisms, it nonetheless sought to overcome putatively corrupt capitalism and reshape with violence the world according to its political ideology. Political Islam in its cohesion differs from the international communist movement, which relied on the Soviet Union's authority and leadership, and political and economic support, for its organization and discipline. Political Islam, whatever the Iranian monetary support flowing to some groups, is, without a coordinating structure, internationally cohering almost exclusively through powerful religiously grounded political ideology.

Political Islam is many things: totalitarian, aggressive, conquering, cocksure about its superiority and destiny to rule, intolerant, bristling with resentment, only tenuously in touch with aspects of reality. These are the hallmark features of past and present eliminationist regimes. Even without additional attributes that promote exterminationist and eliminationist politics, these features alone, especially their totalitarian, aggressive, and fantastical worldview, make Political Islamists, like our age's other such regimes, persistent threats to practice eliminationist politics. Yet Political Islam's threat is still greater because, at its core, Political Islam has three additional features exacerbating these common eliminationist tendencies: (1) the religious consecration of its tenets, emotions, and goals, putatively grounded in God's—that is, Allah's—will and to which slavish devotion is due; (2) the reflexive, insistent public demonization of opponents; and (3) a culture of death. By creating powerful eliminationist views and a powerful eliminationist discourse now central to Political Islamic politics, societies, and cultures, these three features have led Political Islamists to see mass murder and eliminationist assaults as necessary and desirable politics.

Political Islamists, as a matter of oratorical definition, invoke Allah and Islam's sacred text, the Quran, as inspiration, an eliminationist teaching tool, and to legitimize their political tyranny and eliminationist ideology and programs. This is not to say the Quran necessarily says what Political Islamists claim for its individual passages or as a whole, or that it cannot be interpreted or reinterpreted to support nontyrannical and noneliminationist orientations. Like other ancient sacred texts and religions, the Quran and Islam can be tempered or renovated to be more compatible with pluralism, modernity's constituent political and civil feature. This has happened in various forms of Islam and Muslim communities in different countries. But it has not taken place in still many more countries, including by Islam's leading forms in most of the Middle East where Political Islam reigns or is a powerful insurgency against existing regimes, such as the Muslim Brotherhood (of which Hamas is a branch), which seeks to take power in Egypt, and the Taliban and their allies threatening Afghanistan and Pakistan.

Political Islam's second critical aspect is its demonizing of opponents. Its ideology, more than intolerant of other political and social practices, demonizes those not accepting Political Islam's suzerainty and ways, those not converting to the prescribed form of Islam that a given Political Islamist regime, movement, or group practices. Political Islam holds its self-declared enemies, often nothing other than holdouts, to be demonic in their apostasy or, especially, their active resistance or opposition. Fueled and consecrated by their religious interpretations, Political Islamists demonize real and imagined foes seemingly reflexively, because they deem those resisting Political Islamists' dictates as violating Islam, holiness, and Allah. Political Islam therefore provides a ready-made conception of other people and groups that, in God's name, actively calls for their elimination, one way or another. Political Islamists especially consecrate, in their reading of Quranic texts, using lethal violence to bring about their enemies' elimination.

Political Islam's third critical component promoting eliminationism is its culture, even cult, of death, which itself has several central features. Its foundation is the willingness to die (or at least to let Political Islam's duped minions die) for Political Islam's greater earthly and heavenly glory, and a place in paradise for the political-religious martyr. It is astonishing how many people, many educated and middle class, gladly blow themselves up to commit mass murder and spread mass terror demonstrating to the target people's every member that he or she can be slaughtered at any time—all in Political Islam's service.

This culture of death originates and is grounded in the account of the decisive, legendary Battle of Qadisiyya in 636 leading to Islam's conquest of Persia. The commander of the Muslim army and the Prophet Muhammad's warrior, Khalid ibn Al-Walid, sent a message to Khosru, the Persian commander before the battle: "You should convert to Islam, and then you will be safe, for if you don't, you should know that I have come to you with an army of men that love death, as you love life."[3] This willingness to die, and to encourage others to martyr themselves for Allah, is a regular glorified feature of Islamic societies and political movements, of media, sermons, and textbooks, and of Political Islamists' slaughter of their enemies or mobilizing others to do so. It is rhetorically and behaviorally manifest throughout the movement, including in the well-known glorification of suicide bombers' deaths in their and their families' videotapes, public ceremonies, and its most prominent and powerful political leaders' speeches. Hamas' supreme leader Khaled Mashal's broadcast to the world in the wake of Hamas' election victory: "Today, you are fighting the army of Allah. You are fighting against peoples for whom death for the sake of Allah, and for the sake of honor and glory, is preferable to life." Mashal and other major Political Islamic leaders glorify death, disseminate its culture, and deepen its powerful and near ubiquitous eliminationist discourse to its followers—in speeches and sermons, before adoring crowds and in television broadcasts and over the Internet, in interviews with reporters and educational material for children. In 9/11's aftermath, Osama bin Laden explained to a reporter: "We love death. The U.S. loves life. That is the big difference between us."[4] Hassan Nasrallah, Hezbollah's leader, the architect in 2006 of the self-destructive war with Israel in Lebanon and, at least for a time, the Arab world's most admired leader, similarly explained why Political Islamists will triumph over the Jews: "We are going to win, because they love life and we love death."[5] According to Nasrallah, this Political Islamic superiority can be explained by their Islamic faith. Nasrallah broadcast this in a televised speech explaining the joy of dying for Allah, the joy of killing Jews, and the connection between the two:

> How can death become joyous? How can death become happiness? When Al-Hussein asked his nephew Al-Qassem, when he had not yet reached puberty: "How do you like the taste of death, son?" He answered that it was sweeter than honey. How can the foul taste of death become sweeter than honey? Only through conviction, ideology, and faith, through belief, and devotion.
>
> We do not want to live merely in order to eat, drink, and enjoy life's pleasures, and leave our homeland to Israel so it will slaughter it upon the altar of its aspirations, desires, hate, and historic vendettas. Therefore, we are not interested in our own personal security. On the contrary, each of us lives his days and nights hoping more than anything to be killed for the sake of Allah.
>
> The most honorable death is to be killed, as the Leader Imam Al-Khamenei said when Abbas [Musawi] was martyred. He said: "Congratulations to 'Abbas,' congratulations to 'Abbas.'" The most honorable death is death by killing, and the most honorable killing and the most glorious martyrdom is when a man is killed for the sake of Allah, by the enemies of Allah, the murderers of the prophets [i.e., the Jews].[6]

Political Islam's most powerful and revered leaders, Bin Laden, Ayatollah Ruholla Khomeini, Iran's President Mahmoud Ahmadinejad (voice of the ruling mullahs led since 1989 by the country's Supreme Leader Ayatollah Ali Khamenei), Nasrallah, and Mashal, and, more broadly, sheiks, intellectuals, and suicide bombers, and, most fundamentally, the many who read and understand the Quran in this way, profess to love death and convince their followers, especially the children, to want to die and even more to slaughter those designated as Islam's enemies. Little is more chilling, and more indicative of this death culture's power and reach, than Political Islamists' broadcasts and podcasts of music videos directed at children, depicting children happily explaining that they want to die for Allah by killing Islam's enemies.[7]

Another aspect of Political Islamists' culture of death is the willingness to annihilate entire categories of opponents, and the openness to declaim this willingness, together with the drive to attain the requisite operational capability and weaponry. The euphemistic *suicide bombing* should really be called what it is: proto-genocide bombing, or more simply, as Canada's former Justice Minister Irwin Cotler has said, *genocide bombing*. Genocide bombers targeting civilians are saying that any people in a given country, or adhering to a particular non-Islamic creed, are fit to be slaughtered. Each genocide bombing, beyond the actual murders it perpetrates, symbolically mass murders everyone else it could have targeted, and is an installment in an ongoing assault of, if the perpetrators had their way, a stream, perhaps an unending torrent of genocide bombings. Political Islamists have avowed and sometimes centered their political programs around eliminating, even killing, entire categories or enormous numbers of people—sometimes in the millions— among the groups or peoples they designate as enemies. When genocide bombers slaughter such a targeted group's members, the bombing's meaning and intent becomes that much more unmistakable.

Political Islamists responding to something as seemingly trivial in the world of politics as the Danish cartoons of Islam's Prophet Muhammad, published in 2005, with a wave of violent attacks on Western institutions, burnings of buildings, and killings, as well as calls from many, leaders and followers alike, for the mass murder of those who, in their view, insulted or defamed the Prophet. Calls to slaughter Islam's putative enemies, such as "Death to Denmark" in Pakistan, were the protests' commonplace. More specific death threats against publishers and cartoonists alike, including a $1 million bounty for the murder of the Danish cartoonist, seek to silence those whom Political Islamists declare as enemies and to intimidate others into silence.

A complementary event occurred shortly thereafter, with an august protagonist ordinarily treated with reverence or at least utmost respect. In a university lecture in Germany in 2006, Pope Benedict XVI made an inept attempt at comparative religious enlightenment, in which he quoted a fourteenth-century Byzantine emperor's deprecating statement about Islam, in order to claim Christianity as the religion of reason. Leading Political Islamists in different countries greeted this with calls to kill or imprison the pope. Sheikh Abubukar Hassan Malin of the Supreme Islamic Courts Union, the Political Islamic party that was ruling most of Somalia, declared at Friday evening prayers: "We urge you Muslims wherever you are to hunt down the Pope for his barbaric statements as you have pursued Salman Rushdie, the enemy of Allah who offended our religion." Proceeding according to Political Islam's logic, Malin told the Muslim faithful that this applied not only to the pope: "Whoever offends our Prophet Mohammed should be killed on the spot by the nearest Muslim."[8] The Mujahideen Shura Council, an umbrella organization for the Political Islamic insurgency in Iraq, led by Al Qaeda, issued a statement threatening the pope and, because of him, all Christians: "We tell the worshipper of the cross (the Pope) that you and the West will be defeated, as is the case in Iraq, Afghanistan, Chechnya." What's more, "we shall break the cross and spill the wine. . . . God will (help) Muslims to conquer Rome. . . . (May) God enable us to slit their throats, and make their money and descendants the bounty of the mujahideen."[9]

What do these and other such responses to a few uncomfortable, perhaps objectionable words tell us about this movement's murderousness? Never before in our time have significant religious and political leaders publicly called for the pope to be killed—and to be sure, many Political Islamic leaders, knowing the diplomatic catastrophe it would be to join this murderous chorus, contented themselves to echo, often in strikingly inflammatory terms, the common Political Islamist condemnation for the pope. This was all accompanied by church bombings, some killings, threats against Christians in Iraq and elsewhere in the Political Islamic world, seemingly incessant and absurd invoking of the Crusaders, fingerpointing at Christians' real or alleged past crimes, and more. Mohammed Mahdi Akef, the Political Islamic Muslim Brotherhood's Supreme Leader, said that Benedict's remarks "threaten world peace" and "pour oil on the fire and ignite the wrath of the whole Islamic world to prove the claims of enmity of politicians and religious men in the West to whatever is Islamic." Threaten world peace? Whatever one thinks of the pope's statement, the reaction was so wild, so disproportionate, so rhetorically and physically violent—so quintessentially Political Islamic. Ill-chosen words, provocatively chosen words, an expression of, in the world of polemics and politics, rather mainstream views—inspired Political Islamists to threaten the pope with death.

It is not only some putatively blasphemous cartoons or words that put people in the crosshairs of Political Islamists. They also have standing targets. Hamas, as are other Political Islamic governments, movements, and leaders, is armed with a hallucinatory antisemitic and murderous Political Islamic ideology and practice, formalized in its charter. This hefty manifesto—which Hamas has repeatedly reaffirmed, especially its core annihilative element—explains to Palestinians, other Arabs, and Political Islamists around the world (and Westerners paying attention) Political Islam's orientation toward Israel and the "imperialist" powers supporting Israel. In a Nazi-like antisemitic cascade of accusatory fancy, Hamas' charter casts Israel, Zionism, and Jews (used interchangeably) as seeking "to demolish societies, to destroy values, to wreck answerableness, to totter virtues and to wipe out Islam." Zionism even "stands behind the diffusion of drugs and toxics of all kinds in order to facilitate its control and expansion." Hamas' charter calumnies Jews for a vast catalog of invented crimes against humanity, going to the antisemitic continuum's most outlandish end of maintaining that "there was no war that broke out anywhere without their [the Jews'] fingerprints on it." The charter explains that the Jews plan to subjugate the entire Middle East as a stepping stone to turning on the world. According to the charter, all Palestine, which includes all Israel (and lands beyond), must succumb to Hamas' uncompromising Political Islam. Israel, of course, must be destroyed. As the charter, a call to arms, says in its first paragraph, "Israel will rise and will remain erect until Islam eliminates it as it had eliminated its predecessors." The eliminationist ideology, which echoes countless Political Islamic documents and leaders' statements, could not be more explicit, recalling past successes as a spur to redouble efforts toward its intended future one. They do not seek to destroy just Israel, the country. The Jews' very presence in what Political Islamists deem Muslim land must be reversed. The charter is clear: "Israel, by virtue of its being Jewish and of having a Jewish population, defies Islam and the Muslims."

The genocidal and apocalyptic charter declares: "Hamas has been looking forward to implement Allah's promise whatever time it might take. The prophet, prayer and peace be upon him, said: The time will not come until Muslims will fight the Jews (and kill them); until the Jews hide behind rocks and trees, which will cry: O Muslim! there is a Jew hiding behind me, come on and kill him!"[10] Allah's promise is the Palestinians'—indeed all Muslims'—command. Showing that Allah's promise pertains beyond Israel, governing Political Islam's desired treatment of all non-Muslim peoples, Mahmoud Zahar, Hamas' cofounder and later its foreign minister, declared to Italy's *Il Giornale* in February 2006 in reference to the cartoons, "We should have killed all those who offend the Prophet," a genocidal principle common among Political Islamists, as those calling for killing Pope Benedict also enunciated, that obviously translates into killing anyone *ever* offending the Prophet.*

Destructive fervor is central to the Political Islamists' worldview. It can be seen in Hamas' refusal to tame itself after assuming the responsibility of governing. Hamas, under crippling diplomatic and financial pressure, defiantly and loudly holds dearly to its charter and its Nazi-like antisemitic and eliminationist tenets. Its views of Jews and its desire to annihilate Israel, and by definition a good part of its people, if not Jews more broadly, place Hamas squarely within the Political Islamist mainstream and its regimes and insurgencies. The antisemitism animating Hamas, demonizing Jews to a degree that would comfortably fit within Nazism, overflows the airwaves and print media of Political Islamic countries and groups, existing in similar form across the Political Islamic world, indeed even in much of the Islamic world, among leaders and followers alike. This unmistakable antisemitism cannot be confused with or written off to even the most expansive and liberal notions of antagonism toward Israel's policies. Bin Laden, in his speeches, interviews, and videotapes, repeatedly speaks of Jews and of Jews around the world as Islam's enemies, repeatedly invoking Quranic verses to justify his and his followers' enmity, not for Israel the country, but for Jews the people.[11] The international Political Islamist superstar Hezbollah's Nasrallah has explicitly driven the point home that for him and other Political Islamists, Israel and Israelis are not the issue. They hate Jews. According to Nasrallah, "If we searched the entire world for a person more cowardly, despicable, weak and feeble in psyche, mind, ideology and religion, we would not find anyone like the Jew. Notice, I do not say the Israeli."[12]

---

*Although Political Islamists' mass-murderous and eliminationist orientation has not only Israelis but also Jews squarely in its sights (in December 2006, 37 percent of British Muslims said British Jews are "legitimate targets as part of the struggle for justice in the Middle East"), violent eliminationism is by no means exclusively or even principally directed at Jews or Israel.

Political Islamists construct not just Jews, or even chiefly Jews, as demons to be eliminated. Their principal animus and aggression is directed at the West and its greatest power, the United States. They see Israel mainly as the imperial West's outpost, a Western-backed insurgency against Political Islam, making annihilating Israel the first step in a general eliminationist assault on the West. Bin Laden's and Al Qaeda's overwhelming focus, and the target of their mass-murdering and general eliminationist strategies, has not been Israel, which according to bin Laden, Britain and the United States established "as one of the greatest crimes, and you [the United States] are the leaders of its criminals." That is why "the battle is between Muslims—the people of Islam—and the global Crusaders."[13] Even Hezbollah's Nasrallah, who is single-mindedly focused on his struggle with Jews and Israel and extending his Political Islamic control over all Lebanese, sees the United States as the ultimate enemy, as he broadcast to the world on Hezbollah's Al-Manar television shortly after the one-year anniversary of 9/11: "Let the entire world hear me. Our hostility to the Great Satan [America] is absolute. . . . I conclude my speech with the slogan that will continue to reverberate on all occasions so that nobody will think that we have weakened. Regardless of how the world has changed after 11 September, Death to America will remain our reverberating and powerful slogan: Death to America."[14] No less than the original Political Islamic Iranian leadership after the Iranian Revolution did, the current Iranian leadership under Khamenei sees the United States as Public Enemy #1, even if Ahmadinejad's statements receiving the most play in Western media and achieving the most notoriety have been about annihilating Israel and its people. Like Al Qaeda, Hezbollah, and others, the Iranian regime, as Ahmadinejad tells us, thirsts for revenge against the "arrogant" West:

Unfortunately, in the past 300 years, the Islamic world has been in retreat vis-à-vis the World of Arrogance. . . . During the period of the last 100 years, the [walls of the] world of Islam were destroyed and the World of Arrogance turned the regime occupying Jerusalem into a bridge for its dominance over the Islamic world. . . .

   This occupying country [i.e., Israel] is in fact a front of the World of Arrogance in the heart of the Islamic world. They have in fact built a bastion [Israel] from which they can expand their rule to the entire Islamic world. . . . This means that the current war in Palestine is the front line of the Islamic world against the World of Arrogance, and will determine the fate of Palestine for centuries to come.[15]

It matters not that this account of Israel's founding purpose, its role in the Middle East, and United States' and other Western countries' designs is hallucinatory. Political Islamists fervently believe it. It is a central tenet of their ideology. To Political Islamists, the West has for centuries constricted, humiliated, divided, and dominated the Muslim nations. This must now be reversed. Ahmadinejad is murderously explicit: "Our objective is to annihilate all corrupt powers that dominate our planet today."[16]

If among nonstate actors, bin Laden and Al Qaeda most formidably exemplify contemporary Political Islam, among state actors it is Iran's Khamenei, Ahmadinejad, and the ruling Guardian Council, including in their dogged efforts to fund, arm, and support Political Islamist groups, governments, and insurgencies wherever they can—Hamas, Hezbollah, Shia shock troops in Iraq, and elsewhere. Ahmadinejad's notorious Holocaust denial was no act of a rash militant, but the sober act of a calculating and supremely confident political leader, seeking to undermine the legitimacy of Israel. More than merely profoundly anti-semitic, it is a symbolic political gauntlet, a declaration to the West that he, Iran, and Political Islam seek to overturn what is understood to be truth. It is a declaration to establish whom is owed moral respect, and who will determine acceptable politics' contours. It should have been no surprise that Ahmadinejad's Holocaust denial came as warp to his Hitlerian exhortation's woof—a commonplace among Political Islamists—that Israel should be "eliminated from the pages of history" (it has been more commonly rendered as "wiped off the map")[17] and his confrontation with the West over restarting Iran's nuclear production aimed at building a Political Islamic bomb.

This mass-murderous rhetoric, though shocking to Western publics, is entirely consistent with the genocidal rhetoric and proto-genocidal violence that Political Islam's vanguard, especially Hamas and Iranian-controlled Hezbollah, has long practiced with genocide bombing. The Political Islamic Sudanese regime has slaughtered millions and expelled additional millions over more than two decades. Al Qaeda's mass-murderous intent and deeds need no belaboring. Imagine if, that September morning, Al Qaeda had had a deliverable "Islamic bomb." When contemplating this, we should recall Al Qaeda spokesman Suleiman Abu Gheith's subsequent published explanation: "We have the right to kill 4 million Americans—2 million of them children—and to exile twice as many and wound and cripple hundreds of thousands. Furthermore, it is our right to fight them with chemical and biological weapons, so as to afflict them with the fatal maladies that have afflicted the Muslims because of the [Americans'] chemical and biological weapons [sic]." Sheikh Nasir bin Hamid al-Fahd, a leading Saudi cleric, issued a fatwa in 2003, with careful Quranic justification, religiously sanctioning using nuclear weapons as "permissible," in just retribution to kill up to "ten million" Americans.[18]

Not just Americans and other "infidels" ought to fear Political Islamists' eliminationist designs. And it is not just the elites that take part in the eliminationist discourse, which also is powerfully present in Political Islamic media, in the countries beholden to the creed, and at the grass roots. Maajid Nawaz is a former leader of Hizb ut-Tahrir, a Political Islamist movement banned in many countries. Since leaving the movement, he has been warning of Political Islam's danger. Because of the harm he has done, he is now "duty-bound to redress the phenomenon of politically inspired theological interpretations." Hizb ut-Tahrir formally preaches nonviolence to achieve Political Islamists' goals of destroying Israel, overthrowing non–Political Islamist regimes in the Islamic world, and establishing a transnational Political Islamic caliphate. Yet the movement's literature, Nawaz explains, contains an ideology that inexorably produces violence. He points to one of Hizb ut-Tahrir's basic texts, from its founder, Taqiuddin al-Nabhani, which maintains that all Muslims must wage war to overthrow "every single Muslim government, then forcibly unite them into one military state even if it means killing millions of people."[19]

Three successive Iranian presidents have publicly called for Israel's annihilation and the effective mass murder of hundreds of thousands or millions. Falsely depicting Ahmadinejad in this respect as an Iranian "radical," his call that Israel be "eliminated from the pages of history," together with Iran's drive to develop nuclear weapons, echoes "moderate" former president and continuing Iranian power broker Hashemi Rafsanjani's more elaborate account from December 2001 of the underlying thinking of Iran's Political Islamic leadership. "If one day, the Islamic world is also equipped with weapons like those that Israel possesses now, then the imperialists' strategy will reach a standstill because the use of even one nuclear bomb inside Israel will destroy everything. However, it will only harm the Islamic world. It is not irrational to contemplate such an eventuality." Here Rafsanjani dispassionately considers a genocidal policy's implications. One nuclear bomb dropped on Tel Aviv would effectively destroy geographically tiny Israel. He gladly declares to his nation and the world that the costs—including hundreds of thousands, perhaps millions of Iranians dying from Israel's nuclear retaliation—would be worth it. In the context of the heightened confrontation over Iran's constructing its own nuclear capability, Iranian clerics following Ayatollah Mohammad Taghi Mesbah-Yazdi, Ahmadinejad's spiritual adviser, after years of withholding support, issued a fatwa in 2006 justifying the use of nuclear weapons.[20]

Augmenting the willingness of this death culture's members to die for Allah and their desire to slaughter an enormous number of opponents is its members' unabashed rhetorical ease of trumpeting fantasies of killing real or imagined opponents, which is but the most spectacular manifestation of their robust, transnational eliminationist discourse. Political Islamic protesters threatened the West with mass-murderous language, which has not, as far as I know, been seen in Western European capitals since World War II. Marching in London, they brandished murderous banners, including: "Massacre those who insult Islam," and "Butcher those who mock Islam," and "Britain you will pay, 7/7 on its way" (7/7 was the date of the London Underground genocide bombings that murdered fifty-two people) and "Europe you will pay, your 9/11 is on the way." In Gaza, demonstrators demanded that the hands of cartoonists be cut off, and an imam at the Omari mosque declared to nine thousand faithful, "We will not accept less than severing the heads of those responsible."[21]

Toward Israel and Jews, the Political Islamists' exterminationist and eliminationist discourse is explicit, powerful, and robust, with such lurid images and imaginings as commonplaces. Hamas leader Mashal affirmed after Hamas' election victory leading to their takeover of Gaza that Hamas has an unalterable plan to destroy Israel. Mashal said this in a long, chilling address after the Friday sermon at a Damascus mosque aired throughout the Islamic world on Al-Jazeera television, which lays out Hamas' fanatical Political Islamic vision to conquer and slay its enemies. After his speech moved his audience of religious worshipers to interrupt him with the chant "Death to Israel. Death to Israel. Death to America," Mashal lapsed into blood-curdling reverie: "Before Israel dies, it must be humiliated and degraded. Allah willing, before they die, they will experience humiliation and degradation every day. . . . Allah willing, we will make them lose their eyesight, we will make them lose their brains."[22] And shortly after Hamas' election victory, its official Web site began to carry two Hamas genocide bombers' video testaments, one of which included: "My message to the loathed Jews is that there is no god but Allah, we will chase you everywhere! We are a nation that drinks blood, and we know that there is no blood better than the blood of Jews. We will not leave you alone until we have quenched our thirst with your blood, and our children's thirst with your blood."[23] From the "high" Mashal to the "low" mass-murdering bomber, when speaking among themselves it all sounds the same—and just like Hamas' blueprint, its genocidal charter. More than the members of any other major modern political movement, Political Islamists, including their highest leaders, exhibit an archaic bloodlust, speaking with evident relish and unmatched openness of killing their enemies, decapitating people, ghoulishly toying with blood and body parts, and watching them suffer.

Rafsanjani combined this death culture's three components with his public admission that he would contemplate suffering potentially millions of casualties of his own citizens to destroy Israel for Islam's greater glory. What leader, other than from Political Islam, has openly told such a thing to his people? As shocking as this might sound, it comes as no surprise from a regime that, during Iran's war with Iraq in the 1980s, committed mass murder by sending hundreds of thousands of children to their deaths as human mine sweepers and in unarmed human wave attacks, promising the innocent victims and their families a glorious place in paradise.[24]

In the past hundred years, no major political movement, except Nazism and perhaps imperial Japan, has equaled this culture of death.

Regarding Jews, this should also come as no surprise, for whatever Political Islam's religious and other differences with Nazism, it embraces Nazism's hallucinatory antisemitism and its murderous logic, merging it with a violent, totalitarian, and messianic reading of Islam. Like the Nazis, Political Islamists irrationally pursue their death culture's violent maxims, heedless of their frequent self-destructiveness.

Like other regimes governing according to nondemocratic dispensations, Political Islamic regimes, tyrannical in nature, are inherently proto-eliminationist and actually prone to practicing eliminationist politics. Political Islamist regimes are *more* prone to adopting eliminationist politics than many other tyrannical regimes because of their uncompromising totalitarian desire to govern virtually all spheres of public and private life according to fundamentalist notions of Islam. Two additional features, or constellations of features, one inherent to the movement and the second by now embedded in it, further exacerbate this heightened inherent eliminationist bent. The first is Political Islam's hyperaggressive call not only for the world's *conversion* to its political-religious creed, but also for the world's *subjugation,* including or especially by violence. Sustaining and emboldening Political Islamists in this quest is the most coherent and deadly mass-murderous ideology since Nazism, to which many Political Islamists avowedly look with admiration and for inspiration for conceiving of and treating Jews. Built upon and now undergirding this powerfully violent and murderous orientation is the second constellation, born of the economic and technological backwardness of most countries where Islam predominates, and of their conventional military, diplomatic, and economic weakness. This has produced a volcanic resentment against the West for allegedly keeping down Allah's faithful who, in Political Islamists' minds, should be ascendant. It has also produced a paranoiac sense of Islam under siege. The drive to vanquish, attack, lash out against the putative agents of this world-turned-on-its-head is that much more intensive.

Throughout the Political Islamic world, leaders (and followers), embedded in an eliminationist discourse and animated by views suggesting to them that exterminating or utterly vanquishing their many real or imagined enemies is politically necessary and a sacred duty, see eliminationist and exterminationist practices as a real option, have practiced it, declare their ideals and firm intentions to do it, and devote enormous

energy and resources to bringing about conditions to make acting on
their intentions feasible. All this is most naked when they discuss Israel.
Like the Nazis they so admire, Political Islamists are verbally unrestrained regarding Jews, in part because their eliminationist and hallucinatory antisemitism suggest to them that much of the world sides with
them once people realize the Jews' putatively real predatory nature.

Political Islamists have a strategy for triumphing. In Iran, Political
Islam's greatest power, the leaders' pronouncements lay out its contours with a belligerent and global missionary zeal. A renascent and ascendant Muslim world would first acquire nuclear weapons, attaining
strategic parity with the West. Then, using either conventional means—
especially rockets—to terrorize and demoralize Israel, causing ever
more Israelis to abandon the country, or using its nuclear option, Political Islamists would annihilate Israel. Aided by Islamic forces
throughout the world, already showing strength in Europe, Political Islamists would proceed to assail, weaken, and ultimately subdue the
West. Shortly after the 1979 Iranian Revolution, Khomeini, the founding
father of today's Political Islamic Iran, and Khamenei's, Ahmadinejad's,
and the Iranian leaders' continuing spiritual inspiration, declared, "The
Muslims must rise up in this struggle, which is more a struggle between
unbelievers and Islam than one between Iran and America: between all
unbelievers and the Muslims. The Muslims must rise up and triumph in
this struggle."[25] Ahmadinejad, as the voice of the Iranian regime, sets
forth in his speeches the overarching ambition for Political Islamists'
revenge against the West in unabashedly taunting and insulting terms.
Western nations, he proclaims, have stood against the resurgence of
Islam, but the Muslim nations will give them their just desserts. Ahmadinejad boasts of a "wave of Islamic awakening and a gradual collapse of western hegemony." And in an unabashedly eliminationist
reverie, he foresees a world "without America and without Zionism."[26]

The idea of Iran, together with sundry Islamic regimes, scattered terrorist bands, and an activated Muslim street in Europe, defeating the
West should not be dismissed as a Lilliputian megalomaniacal fantasy.
Obviously, many Muslims, including Iranians, and their countries will
not sign on, and Political Islamists, some of whom face potentially
powerful opposition within their countries, cannot ultimately prevail
against a resolute West. Yet they can do enormous damage. Al Qaeda,

for all the death and destruction it has caused in the United States, Afghanistan, Britain, Iraq, and elsewhere, and for all its openly lethal eliminationist strivings, is an eliminationist threat (unless it acquires nuclear weapons) overshadowed by Iran. As the most powerful Political Islamic state, Iran exports terrorist violence through its proxies and, with diplomacy and petrodollars, supports Political Islamic regimes and insurgencies. And nuclear weapons are the great equalizer. Even without them, Al Qaeda, a relatively weak nonstate actor, colossally damaged the American people and economy. Ahmadinejad, conscious of the skepticism his grandiose visions might meet, recalls that the Soviet Union's collapse had also been unimaginable. Yet that superpower crumbled and disintegrated. And so, he declares, "They say it is not possible to have a world without the United States and Zionism. But you know that this is a possible goal and slogan."[27] Ahmadinejad's brazen pronouncements of the West's impending doom echo Soviet leader Nikita Khrushchev's bullying prophecy: "We will bury you."

Such beliefs and reveries appear common among Political Islam's ranks, leaders and followers alike. Bin Laden preached to his followers: "People used to ask us 'How will you defeat the Soviet Empire?' . . . where now is that strong force that God sent to us and our mujahidin brothers?"[28] The United States will similarly crumble: "America appeared so mighty . . . but it was actually weak and cowardly. Look at Vietnam, look at Lebanon. Whenever soldiers start coming home in body bags, Americans panic and retreat. Such a country needs only to be confronted with two or three sharp blows, then it will flee in panic, as it always has. . . . It cannot stand against warriors of faith who do not fear death."[29] A placard in the London anti-cartoon demonstration proclaimed: "Europe you'll come crawling when Mujahideen come roaring!" Lashkar-e-Taiba (the Army of the Pure), South Asia's most potent Political Islamic movement, which in 2008 launched the coordinated mass-murderous attacks in Mumbai, India, hoping to slaughter five thousand, targeting especially Americans and Britons, calls for jihad to conquer a large part of the globe and humanity:

> Muslims ruled Andalusia (Spain) for 800 years but they were finished to the last man. Christians now rule (Spain) and we must wrest it back from them. All of India, including Kashmir, Hyderabad, Assam, Nepal,

Burma, Bihar and Junagadh were part of the Muslim empire that was
lost because Muslims gave up jihad. Palestine is occupied by the Jews.
The Holy Qibla-e-Awwal (First Center of Prayer) in Jerusalem is under
Jewish control. Several countries such as Bulgaria, Hungary, Cyprus,
Sicily, Ethiopia, Russian Turkistan and Chinese Turkistan . . . were
Muslim lands and it is our duty to get these back from unbelievers.
Even parts of France reaching 90 kilometers outside Paris and some of
the forests and mountains of Switzerland were home to Muslim *mu-jahidin* but are now under the occupation of unbelievers.[30]

Such are Political Islamists' expansive eliminationist desires. Among
the measures the annihilationist Lashkar-e-Taiba explicitly calls for as
part of this far-reaching conquest are to "eliminate evil" and "to avenge
the blood of Muslims killed by unbelievers," which in conquering unwilling billions would mean slaughtering untold numbers. Hamas too
dreams of reconquering Seville and extending Islamic power into Europe. Its leader, Mashal, in his Al-Jazeera-televised sermon, after
commanding Europe to apologize to the Islamic nation, warned, "Tomorrow, our nation will sit on the throne of the world. This is not a fig-
ment of the imagination, but a fact. Tomorrow we will lead the world,
Allah willing."[31]

Some people will see this foreboding picture as overdrawn. They will
say much of the Islamic world does not support, let alone take part in,
these developments. They will say the mass-murderous and eliminationist rhetoric is mere domestic political posturing, or a hyperbolic
verbal culture's harmless product. They will say the Islamic world is
hardly threatening. Islamic countries are militarily and politically weak,
and Muslims in Europe are a discriminated-against minority. They
might add that Islamic countries, many lagging economically and technologically, and in their intellectual and political cultures' development,
lack the vibrancy necessary to challenge let alone subdue others.

However weak Islamic countries may be, such thinking is wrong
about Political Islamists' and their threats' strength and gravity. Much
of the Islamic world is in Political Islam's throes, even if much of it is
not. (It's a big world.) Political Islamists control governments and
threaten others, and non–Political Islamic leaders cynically successfully
deploy their creed in various Islamic countries and societies. Although

all tyrannical regimes are inherently unstable and can be overthrown from within precisely because they exist in a modern world that has— as the recent disputed elections in Iran remind us—enshrined democracy and popular representation as a cardinal principle, the countries that many of them rule suffer under their repressive, often totalitarian, and murderous grip (little recognized are the *countless Muslims* suffering under their tyranny and the countless more threatened). Political Islam has highly motivated and effective terror groups. Coming from diverse centers of Islamic politics, Political Islamists speak a clear, menacing message. Anyone indiscriminately targeting civilians in genocide bombing, or applauding such proto-genocidal killing; anyone calling for cartoonists' and their publishers' murder, or applauding such calls; anyone threatening mass murder, while working to conquer the territory or acquire the weaponry making it possible, or applauding such calls, understands in this age of Al-Jazeera and the Internet that this is all part of a widespread Political Islamic assault on the West. In particular, no politician acts or speaks in such a manner frivolously. (If the apologetic argument really is that political leaders threaten mass murder just for domestic consumption, or that Political Islam's power among its people scares governments into becoming more Political Islamic themselves, then this just proves the point about the murderous aspirations and danger of Political Islam's legions of followers.) Adolf Hitler prophesied the Jews' annihilation, saying in January 1939 that a world war would result in the "annihilation of the Jewish race in Europe." Most treated this as empty bluster. The history of our time's genocide and eliminationist politics shows—from Lothar von Trotha to Hitler to bin Laden—that in the rare instances political leaders publicly threaten to annihilate enemy peoples, they mean it.

In discussions of contemporary political issues, politics overwhelms regard for truth. So stating certain undeniable central facts about Political Islam seems sensible:

- Political Islamic leaders have a mass-murderous and more broadly an eliminationist orientation toward those groups, peoples, and countries they deem their enemies. (As do a startlingly large number of followers, who, departing from ordinary people's past practices, themselves openly dream eliminationist and genocidal dreams.)

- Political Islamists ground these stances in the Quran, imbuing them with a sacred quality, making their fulfillment a divine command and a practice securing their practitioners places in heaven.
- Political Islamic leaders, invoking their creed, have perpetrated several annihilationist and eliminationist assaults, killing millions.
- Political Islamic followers, sharing this creed, have willingly carried out these mass slaughters and eliminations.
- Political Islamists govern several countries, with Iran striving to build nuclear weapons, and threaten to take over others, including nuclear Pakistan.

An eliminationist logic linking up to eliminationist acts is at Political Islam's core. Political Islam, like earlier eliminationist movements and civilizations, contains all the elements that produce actual mass murders and eliminations: a powerful eliminationist discourse; a demonized conception of large groups of enemies making their eradication seem good and necessary, indeed a moral and sacred duty; leaders willing to initiate mass murders and eliminations; legions of eager followers willing to carry out such assaults; and existing and foreseeable future opportunities (which some Political Islamists are determined to create) to undertake such assaults against real or imagined enemies. During our time this classic common eliminationist formula has led regimes and peoples all over the world to annihilate millions upon millions of people.

The issues open for discussion and disagreement about Political Islam are about the factors that produced this powerful new totalitarian and eliminationist political movement, and whether it can be tempered or hemmed in, and if so, to what degree and with what means, measures, and policies. But even if partly tempered or contained, Political Islam, with its eliminationist core, will continue, like other aggressive tyrannies, even more than most, to threaten the people it already rules and the many people it wishes to vanquish in political Allah's name.

Political Islam is the only contemporary political ideology with global or large regional aspirations, and preaching the use of violence to reshape many countries' politics, society, and culture and, for many Political Islamists, ultimately the world. This is the Political Islamists' core project—as their leaders in country after country tell us. In this sense Political Islam resembles our time's now-defunct globally or regionally violent eliminationist civilizations, Nazi Germany, imperial Japan, the Soviet Union, and Maoist China. Yet it differs from Nazi Germany and imperial Japan by formally preaching a universalism, and from the Soviet Union and China, because it has no transformative economic vision. In its aspirations and danger, it most recalls the twentieth century's imperial totalitarian regimes in Germany, Japan, and the Soviet Union, which, according to their ideological blueprints, sought to extend their power over vast regions, used military means for conquest, and were willing, indeed eager, to kill an enormous number of people to secure their power and reshape the societies and ultimately the world. Political Islam melds modernity's eliminationist mindset to an archaic political ideology to make war on modernity itself, or at least many of its central aspects, producing an eliminationist elixir unlike our, or any, time's other major destructive political movements.

The emergence of nonstate terror organizations, until now the most threatening ones being Political Islamist, poses the new danger of political leaderships and fanatical followers committed above all else to mass murder, as the means they, leaders and followers alike, think can best produce terror and achieve their political goals. For Political Islamist terror organizations, the goals are to destroy infidels and weaken their countries, to exact Islam's vengeance for humiliations they blame on the West and Israel, and complete Political Islam's conquest of ever more minds and hearts. Al Qaeda's exterminationist assault on the World Trade Center using large, fuel-laden passenger planes is, if it and kindred eliminationist terror organizations have their way, but a first installment. The ever more destructive technologies that might fall into their hands make nonstate terror organizations, for the first time, a real rival to states as practitioners of mass annihilationist politics.

Nuclear weapons can be the great mass-murderous and eliminationist equalizer. Here is where technology changes the genocidal equation. Until today, the strong perpetrated mass exterminations and eliminations against the weak. With high technology, the weak finally have an opportunity to mass murder the strong. With this real possibility, they dream of it. They plan for it. They seek to bring it about. When in history, certainly in modern times, has a nonstate actor dreamt of taking down the world's superpower? When has a political regime governing a country (Iran) with a GDP less than 3 percent of the West's threatened to destroy it, sought the weapons to give it immunity, defiantly pursued them, continuing to likely nuclear capability, which it would, as an apocalyptic sword of Damocles, hang over its enemies' heads and perhaps use against Israel or others?

More generally, the possible proliferation of nuclear weapons (also potentially chemical and biological weapons) into the hands of eliminationist-oriented tyrannies and, through theft or purchase or as a gift, of nonstate actors, makes the most massive annihilationist assault's likelihood more than a remote hypothetical possibility. Industrially and technologically less advanced countries—including backward and bankrupt North Korea—can now develop nuclear weapons and delivery systems, including missiles. In twenty to thirty years, certainly in fifty, the technology and know-how for developing such weaponry will be widely if not generally available.

In thinking about the future of eliminationist politics, we must therefore consider combating these new major eliminationist threats that we have just begun to discern, understand, and figure out how to counteract. One is archaic, a political messianism of imperial religious tribalism, Political Islam, which has captured many states, threatens many more, and animates the most murderous contemporary nonstate actors. The other is science's most powerful stepchild, nuclear weapons, long feared as the ultimate exterminationist and eliminationist tool, though so far kept in abeyance since its annihilationary birth's twinned moment slaughtering Japanese. Uncompromising political messianism combining with nuclear weapons could yet produce the most fearsome instance of the power to commit mass murder.

Beyond these two new systemic eliminationist threats, the nondemocratic and tyrannical regimes composing more than half the world's governments, are, as I discuss in the next chapter, inherently a real threat to perpetrate mass murder and elimination. The eliminationist politics plaguing our time, issuing in so much death and misery, have not faded into the past. To be sure, our twenty-first-century world, for the reasons discussed—communism is dead or spent, Nazism, imperial Japan, and imperialism in general are also gone—differs significantly from the twentieth century. Nevertheless, tyrannies' or dictatorships' continuing existence means the eliminationist past is still the eliminationist present and potentially a still more lethal future.

As we know, beliefs that might suggest eliminationist treatment is the way to deal with certain groups exist in the minds (and hearts) of many countries' people. How many countries, among what people, and against whom, and the ease of activating and channeling them, is obviously unknown, though we can confidently assume such beliefs are in many places and therefore eliminationist politics' now dormant potential is large. We know all nondemocratic, namely tyrannical, regimes are proto-eliminationist, with leaders figuratively at the eliminationist cannon's trigger. So we continue to need, perhaps ever more, systems and policies to contain eliminationist beliefs' latent potential, and to keep leaders from thinking that eliminationist politics makes good and practical political sense.

We must ask: Can we remove eliminationist practices from politics' *normal* repertoire, just as slavery has been removed from social relations' normal repertoire (even if countries continue practicing it clandestinely)? Can we dramatically reduce mass murder and elimination?

What sort of future will we choose to make?

CHAPTER ELEVEN

What We Can Do

C AN THERE BE any doubt that if the former Yugoslavia or Rwanda had been small countries nestled next to the United States, say immediately south of San Diego, then those countries' leaders would not have embarked upon their eliminationist politics, let alone their exterminationist programs? Would Slobodan Milošević have tried to expel 1.5 million Kosovars into California, let alone slaughter eight thousand men (as he did in Srebrenica) in a city where Tijuana is today? Would he have set up concentration and rape camps and had roaming Serbian killing units within shouting distance of the American border, slaughtering men and raping women systematically in town after town? Would Théoneste Bagosora and the Hutu leadership have begun an attack to hack and club to death hundreds of thousands of people in full view of the American public and polity?

To ask these questions is to answer them: No. Milošević would not have dared. Bagosora and the Hutu leaders would not have dared. And had either done so, swift and massive American intervention would have ended the eliminationist assault, whatever its form. What does this thought experiment teach us? We can find out, if we ask why, proximate to San Diego, no political leaders, no matter the circumstances, would initiate mass expulsions and exterminations. What factors would make such a "solution" to any "problem" unfeasible, or unthinkable, even for political leaders wishing to adopt an eliminationist program and who, in other geographic settings and circumstances, would eagerly implement one? Slaughtering or expelling people by the hundreds of thousands in such a hypothetical North American country would be so unfeasible and unthinkable that we would not consider calling it *prevention* if a political leader, fearing intervention, would choose not to implement an eliminationist ideal. Because it would not be *prevention* in the narrow sense of taking action that forestalls an imminent assault, it is difficult for people to see that, in a broader sense, prevention is precisely what it would be.

The topic of prevention must be rethought. Doing so requires embedding its analysis in a discussion of several other themes that have emerged from this investigation. Just as eliminationist assaults are predicated upon a preparatory eliminationist discourse laying out the conceptions of problems and people putatively causing them, which provides the foundation for thinking that acting against those people is necessary and urgent, preventing such assaults requires an analogous, countervailing anti-eliminationist, or pro-human, discourse. This discourse has several components: an accurate recognition of the problem of exterminationist and eliminationist assaults and politics; an accurate understanding of the domestic and international failures producing our catastrophic state of affairs; and an agreement that we must *urgently* act to stop current and prevent future exterminationist and eliminationist assaults (including smaller ones), to send eliminationist politics on the road to extinction. This anti-eliminationist discourse must be structured around eliminationist politics' most fundamental facts: They have been a politics of impunity with the perpetrators' subjective benefits far outweighing the costs. Hence the frequency.

Such an anti-eliminationist discourse prepares the way for redressing the catastrophic state of affairs. This also has several components. We must recognize that the possibility of effecting change in this large, difficult area, though unacknowledged, is real, practical, and achievable. We must establish it as right to do. We must create the necessary resolve to exercise our power for acting upon our duties. And we must devise the measures and policies that will effectively end eliminationist politics. In sum, we must reverse our time's and human history's prevailing equation by ensuring two things: Eliminationist politics will no longer be a politics of impunity, and when political leaders examine the social and political landscape they will know that initiating an exterminationist or eliminationist onslaught will incur for them enormously more costs than benefits.

The Need for a Powerful Anti-Eliminationist Discourse

Ordinary citizens, and political and media elites alike, must recognize eliminationist politics' extent and character. At any moment, the problem, though grave, can appear local when in truth it is of broad, even global significance. A single snapshot often distorts the more general and systemic nature of political and social phenomena, including this one. From the start of the twentieth century, our era's eliminations have, as we now know, produced death tolls of 127 million and perhaps as many as 175 million (or if China's and the Soviet Union's higher estimates are correct, still many more), far outnumbering war's military casualties.

When we look more broadly to *eliminationist* campaigns, particularly including expulsions, the numbers are more shocking. The Soviets, in addition to killing on the order of ten million people, expelled vast populations from their homes and eliminated through incarceration in the gulag many millions more for long periods. The Indonesians slaughtered perhaps half a million communists and, by the regime's own admission, deposited three times as many, 1.5 million, in camps, often for years. As part of their eliminationist campaign against nonbelieving communists, they compelled nonaffiliated Indonesians to adopt religion. In the wake of the mass slaughter, 2.8 million Indonesians in Java, Timor, and North Sumatra converted to Christianity or Islam. The Khmer Rouge killed 1.5 million and expelled and incarcerated in camps virtually the rest of the country's 8 million people. In Ethiopia, the Mengistu regime eliminated from the country's northern regions six to eight times the 250,000 they killed—upward of 2 million. The Guatemalan rightists slaughtered perhaps 200,000 people, leftists and mainly Maya, and expelled two and half to five times more—a half million to a million Maya. Saddam Hussein, in addition to murdering half a million Kurds, Marsh people, Shia, and others, expelled many hundreds of thousands more from their homes and regions. Seeking to eradicate all non-Arabic characteristics from Iraq's Kirkuk region, Saddam also conducted a forced transformation campaign of unknown size, formally begun in 1997, compelling non-Arabic people, especially Kurds, Turkomans, and Assyrians, to renounce their ethnic identities and adopt an

Arab one. The Serbian eliminationists, and their Croatian opposite numbers, in sum killed many tens of thousands and expelled many times that number, including, by the Serbs, 1.5 million Kosovars. As of 2009, Political Islamists have slaughtered more than 400,000 Darfurians and have expelled perhaps six times that number—2.5 million, after having killed two million and expelled more in Southern Sudan. Even the Germans, who readily annihilated those designated for elimination, expelled millions from their homes and regions. The list goes on and on, including India and Pakistan during the partition, China, North Korea, the Pakistanis in Bangladesh, Burundi, Rwanda, and many more.

The countries and peoples either perpetrating or suffering exterminationist and eliminationist campaigns span the globe and humanity. Billions of people have themselves been potential targets or have had relatives, friends, or members of their communities mass murdered or brutally expelled from their homes. It should not need to be said, but it does: Eliminationist politics, and its most acute exterminationist variant, is an urgent, first-order *global* problem.

If next week perpetrators assaulted one or five people in your neighborhood or community solely because of their identity, brutalizing and expelling them from their homes and neighborhood, or butchering them in the street, you would treat it as a cataclysm. It would receive intensive media coverage, produce a communal and societal uproar, and engender an immediate political response. People and resources would insistently mobilize against this and future occurrences. Why should we respond politically to the same acts differently—when the victim numbers multiply by a thousand or a million—just because the people are, or have been, or will be far from our homes?

The problem of eliminationist politics should not be reduced to bromides. The problem is not human nature. Mass murder and eliminations are not inevitable or unavoidable. Transnational forces beyond human control do not cause them. We need not throw up our hands in hopeless despair. The problem is *straightforward and political*. Although difficult, it can and must be addressed politically, with intellect, energy, institutional design, and resources. We must go beyond conventional thinking and practices.

First we must confront the facts—not romanticized fictions, not politicized and therefore obscured fictions, but the facts. Mass murder and eliminationist politics are humanity's human scourge, more devastating than natural disasters, more murderous and worse than war. They destroy the lives of so many more people, devastate survivors among families, scar communities for generations, immutably alter societies and polities. Yet on the nightly local news mass annihilation receive far less attention—in absolute terms—than house fires. In *relative* terms, according to death toll and human suffering, the media underplay eliminationist slaughters and expulsions and incarcerations by a thousand to a million times. Western people's misplaced values direct more attention to the latest sensational murder case—be it celebrity driven or not—than ongoing mass slaughters and eliminations in several countries. Take, in the United States, the media obsession and manufactured sensation (in 2004, while I was drafting this part of the book) of Scott Peterson's murder of his pregnant wife, Laci Peterson, and destruction of the baby she was carrying. For more than a year, newspapers, magazines, and especially television covered the unfolding events with the diligence and fascination due a presidential election: the crime, the hunt for the killer, the arrest of first-name-familiar Scott, the prosecution's and defense's preparations, and, from gavel to gavel, the trial itself. Measured by the media coverage, one would have thought that, aside from the American war and occupation in Iraq and the presidential election itself between George W. Bush and John Kerry, Scott and Laci's story was by far that year's most important political or legal event.

Horrible as Scott's murder of his pregnant wife and son-to-be was, Political Islamic Sudanese Arabs multiplied its horror hundreds of thousands of times with their contemporaneous mass expulsion and mass murder of Darfur's people. Yet that campaign received a tiny fraction of media coverage, attention, and discussion in absolute terms and in proportion to its significance. Multiply this comparative neglect by the number of other American murder cases turned into media sensations for millions of people's lurid viewing, and the neglect of the eliminationist assaults in Darfur—or those in the Democratic Republic of the Congo or Tibet or Chechnya or North Korea, and others—becomes that much more striking and morally reprehensible.

I commit here the supposed sin of sounding preachy. The media must do more to create and sustain a robust anti-eliminationist discourse. They must convey to the public—including political and policy elites—

the facts about mass murders and eliminations *as they take place,* and about the leaders masterminding them. For all their failures, the American media, much too late, finally did this in Bosnia and thereby created pressure on the Clinton administration to act. Bosnia and Herzegovina's President Haris Silajdžić maintains that the media were critical: "The media, the American media helped a great deal. They helped us in getting this story out."[1] Bosnia shows the media's immense power to spur action, which only highlights their deficiencies in almost every other eliminationist instance. When an eliminationist assault begins (or ideally before), the media must immediately and insistently convey that (1) the world community, as a community, faces urgent crises in one or several of its regions, (2) the world community can save the lives of hundreds, thousands, sometimes millions of people, and (3) not to do so is to be complicit in the carnage. This is the media's duty—no less than they would certainly do all three if a criminal or terrorist band held twenty hostages barricaded in a government building in Washington, London, Berlin, Rome, Madrid, Paris, or Tokyo, or for that matter in rural or small-town America, Britain, Germany, Italy, Spain, France, or Japan.

The media's failure to publicize individual mass murders and eliminations as they occur elsewhere is surpassed by their failure to convey the *general* problem of mass murder and elimination's immensity and character. The basic facts are virtually unknown, even to interested elites. Why?

Broad discussion of mass murder and elimination's high frequency and colossal aggregate damage—and the international community's and political leaders' failure to take the easy measures not taken to prevent or stop them—might shame the world's peoples, or at least some of them. Scholars, media, and politicians alike would face the moral burden of confronting their own unwillingness to do what they ought to and easily could do: help end these murders and assaults that dwarf all others. This media and political failure is not equivalent to the failure to publicize and analyze poverty and disease around the world for the simple reason that no domestic or global consensus exists that all people have a right (certainly an enforceable right) to specified minimal living standards (or what those standards would be) or freedom from easily preventable diseases. (The need for such a consensus is another topic.)[2] Yet an international consensus, enshrined in international law, mandates that all people have the right not to be tortured, eliminated through expulsions, or murdered. Slaughtering children is unanimously held to be an unambiguous and great crime. Indeed, these are among the few universal rights international law and the world's people commonly recognize and say it is a legal duty to stop. This norm not to slaughter people en masse, at least as a norm, is so powerful that even regimes routinely violating it formally recognize it.

Discussing the facts about our time's mass murders and eliminationist politics is also unpopular in many countries because so many of us would have to critically examine ourselves or our forbears. Harry Truman *was* a mass murderer. He should be put in the dock no less than Stalin, Pol Pot, and the others. A barrage of vitriolic and dishonest criticism will likely meet these statements. Powerful constituencies—political, media, academic, and others—in every country having practiced eliminationist politics pounce on those daring to speak politically explosive or discomforting truths. This leads to those positioned to disseminate the facts censoring themselves.

After the publication of *Hitler's Willing Executioners*, one European country's former prime minister told me that even though he and, as he put it, "everyone" in his country knew my book about ordinary Germans' antisemitically grounded willingness during the Nazi period to kill Jews is correct, had prospective publishers of the book prior to publication asked, he would have urged them not to publish it because he would have feared (wrongly, he then conceded) that its truths would harm the image of today's Germany and Germans among his countrymen and worsen relations with Germany. Some prominent Jews told me not to address certain pressing issues in *A Moral Reckoning*, my book on the Catholic Church's need to perform repair after the Holocaust—not because I was wrong, but because speaking the truth about the Church's practices and tenets might encourage the Church to criticize those of Jews.

Attacks on and intimidation of people speaking the truth about eliminationist assaults come mainly from those feeling afflicted by the facts, or from their surrogates. Those wanting truths to remain buried about Germans and the Catholic Church respectively, with German politicians, high Church officials, and their politicized allies in the academy leading the way, dishonestly and vociferously attacked my books and me. In 2005, Orhan Pamuk, the soon-to-be Nobel Prize–winning novelist, was subjected to kindred attacks and even indicted in Turkey (immense international pressure eventually led to the charges being dropped) for acknowledging the Turks' genocide of the Armenians. This was part of the Turkish government's and much of its society's intimidation and disinformation campaign to have the world accept the fiction that it never happened. Similarly, Japanese rightists have unremittingly attacked and threatened violence against the Japanese Nobel Prize–winning novelist Kenzaburo Oe for telling the truth about the Japanese eliminationist assault on Okinawans at the end of World War II. In 2005, a Japanese court allowed a rightist-supported suit seeking to suppress his book *Okinawa Notes* about the forced mass suicides. The Japanese government, under the nationalist Prime Minister Shinzo Abe, a systematic denier of Japanese mass murders and eliminations, used the lawsuit as one of several pretexts to try to rewrite Japanese school textbooks to cover up Japanese lethal coercion against Okinawans. This led to Okinawans' massive protest. Oe spent two and a half years successfully defending the lawsuit.[3]

The formal and often well-organized deniers of discomfiting or inconvenient historical truths, such as Holocaust deniers, exist in virtually all countries whose people have perpetrated eliminationist onslaughts. Governments or powerful institutions and groups usually undertake extensive disinformation campaigns to confuse publics, intimidate those wanting to tell the truth, and forestall necessary measures of prevention, intervention, and repair. Turkey is but the best-known current example of prosecuting or intimidating those speaking such historical truths. (A Turkish diplomat in the United States once said privately that his two main tasks were maintaining the American foreign aid level and keeping the Armenian question off the table.) Turkey's genocide denial has become so contentious that the European Union has made Turkey's admission of the genocide a membership condition. In 2007, when the U.S. House of Representatives' Foreign Relations Committee passed a nonbinding resolution (that was never likely to pass the full House) acknowledging the genocide, Turkey recalled its ambassador and threatened noncooperation in the Iraq war. Many German politicians and groups, though acknowledging most of the Holocaust's basic facts, for years tried to suppress the truth about ordinary Germans' willing role in perpetrating the Holocaust (blaming instead abstract structures or faceless Nazis—to which, in the postwar fairy tales, few Germans belonged).[4] The Catholic Church, and for that matter, many European countries' governments and peoples, have long remained silent about or stridently denied their participation in the Jews' eliminationist and exterminationist persecution, though in the past decade some have tried to correct the historical record.[5] After Stalin's death and the gulag was dismantled, the Soviet Union proscribed speaking the truth about the mass murdering, and in Russia today many in and out of government still oppose it. Croats and Serbs each suppress the truth about their respective mass murders and eliminations against each other (and others) during the post-Yugoslavia recent past and the World War II–era more distant past. In Japan, the government and powerful groups systematically deny the Japanese's mass-murdering and eliminationist practices immediately before and during World War II, including the mass murdering in Nanjing and elsewhere in Asia, and the systematic raping of Korean and other women and their enslavement as prostitutes, still referred to by the time's euphemism of "comfort women." A decade after the Hutu's slaughter of the Tutsi, a movement to deny the genocide has developed, sadly including some French officials seeking to defend France's honor by denying the deeds the French government abetted. It goes without saying, but nevertheless deserves emphasis, that during mass eliminations and while the perpetrators remain in power potentially to kill again, they and their supporters, and those not wanting to bring them to justice or remove them, cover up, disinform, and most of all practice silence. Such an example, likely unpopular to discuss in my usual circles, occurred recently.

Publicizing the facts about eliminationist politics and assaults requires that media and politicians not only discuss them more frequently but also change how they do so. They know that the language they use, and how they frame issues, is powerful and persuasive. So let them use it in the service of the victims and potential victims. They do not hesitate to refer to serial killers, murderers of ten or twenty people, as serial killers or even mass murderers. But for the mass murderers of thousands, hundreds of thousands, or millions of people, the media and politicians avoid similar linguistic accuracy and moral rectitude. They do not call the political leaders initiating, organizing, and overseeing such slaughters, or their followers doing the dirty work, *mass murderers*. Think of how different, at home and abroad, the publics' conception would be of Stalin or Mao, or even of Hitler about whom the truth is regularly told, if we routinely referred to them as the mass murderer Stalin, the mass murderer Mao, and the mass murderer Hitler. Consider how different the view of Indonesian leader Haji Muhammad Suharto, Hafez al-Assad of Syria, Fernando Romeo Lucas Garcia and José Efraín Ríos Montt of Guatemala, Milošević of Serbia, Franjo Tudjman of Croatia, Saddam in Iraq, or Omar Hasan Ahmad al-Bashir in Sudan would have been during their rule had we reflexively called them, instead of President Suharto, the Indonesian mass murderer Suharto; instead of President Assad, the Syrian mass murderer Assad; instead of Presidents Lucas Garcia and Ríos Montt, the Guatemalan mass murderers Luca Garcia and Ríos Montt, instead of President Milošević, the Serbian mass murderer Milošević; instead of President Tudjman, the Croatian mass murderer Tudjman; instead of the Iraqi President Saddam Hussein, the mass murderer Saddam Hussein; instead of President al-Bashir, the Sudanese mass murderer al-Bashir. How much harder it would be for anyone abroad—foreign leaders, media, ordinary citizens—to pretend these butchers were legitimate leaders representing their people's interests, fit to be supported or dealt with as anything but colossal criminals and menaces to humanity. With the information power of the Internet and satellite television, local elites and peoples (who might not otherwise know) would see how the world regards their murderous leaders of yesterday and today (and get a preview for thinking about tomorrow's prospective mass murderers). Some (though certainly not all) leaders and their inner circles may be deterred from acting on their eliminationist ideals if they know that "mass murderer" is all but guaranteed to forever be a prefix to their names. Some leaders of countries, including those of democracies, might be deterred from aiding and abetting other regimes' eliminationist onslaughts (several American presidents have lent such aid) if they too would be forever tagged with "mass-murdering accomplices" or "complicit in mass murder."

A new, more accurate, more powerful anti-eliminationist and pro-human discourse about mass murder and eliminations must develop.

The language we use to describe eliminationist onslaughts should be descriptively accurate. We should avoid euphemisms and obfuscating locutions such as "ethnic cleansing." We should call perpetrators committing mass murder "mass murderers." We should use "genocide," though analytically imprecise and therefore employed here sparingly, regularly and liberally for mass murders: It is codified in international law as *the* term to apply to large-scale mass murder and it, more than any other term, conveys the magnitude of the horror of what perpetrators do to their victims. We should apply the term "genocide" to eliminationist programs that combine mass murder with expulsion, even when the perpetrators expel many more than they kill, as the Serbs did to the Kosovars. Of course, we should always specify as accurately as possible the size and mix of large-scale killing, expulsions, and incarcerations in camps—and the perpetrators' other brutalities—and the targets' identities. When the Hutu began mass murdering the Tutsi, the Clinton administration, European governments, African governments, and the United Nations knew almost instantaneously from their diplomats, the UN peacekeepers on the ground, and news reports what the Hutu were doing. All of them should have immediately and unequivocally told their peoples and the world that the Hutu were committing *genocide*. The genocides in the former Yugoslavia should have at once been denounced for what they were, genocide—and the mass murderer Milošević as a genocidal killer—rather than whitewashed into "ethnic cleansing." The burden of proof should have been shifted immediately to Milošević and the Serbs to demonstrate that they were not perpetrating genocide.

Such dissimulation and failure to speak the truth continues today. The United Nations, the political organization most responsible and best positioned to speak and act authoritatively against genocide, is the most glaring offender. But this comes as no surprise for an organization that was complicit in the Rwandan annihilation and silent and inactive as it watched Saddam's various eliminationist onslaughts unfold. When the United Nations issued its misleading Darfur report in January 2005 denying that the Sudanese government was committing genocide ("genocidal intent appears to be missing")—tepidly deeming it a mere "situation" of "violations of international humanitarian law and human rights law"—governments and media around the world should have immediately denounced the report for what it really was: genocide denial more devastating than Holocaust denial, because it was white-washing, minimizing, denying an ongoing genocide. They should have insisted the Political Islamic Sudanese government's mass annihilation and expulsion of Darfurians be called genocide. Nothing less.

Political leaders and the media analyzing mass murder and elimina-tions should avoid four frequent pitfalls: the languages of equivalence, primordial hatred, human nature, and abstract structures. The language of equivalence—explaining mass violence and killing and expulsions as resulting from "ethnic conflict"—is the frequent practice. It suggests that competition for which two parties are responsible produces these deeds. It also suggests that the putative ethnic conflict at issue has somehow spun out of control (as ethnic conflict is allegedly wont to do), that somehow mass murder just happened as a consequence of an escalating process. This misrepresents how mass murders and elimina-tions begin. The second pitfall, the language of primordial hatred, sug-gests inevitability. This, as we now know, is precisely the opposite of mass eliminations' initiation and execution. If mass murder is presented as the outcome of primordial hatred, then it seems beyond rationality and impervious to rational policy initiatives. The third problem, the unarticulated frame for, or variously finding its way into, reporting of genocides is to write them off to human nature, an adult or juvenile variant of "boys will be boys," or to the lamentable notion that cer-tain countries, regimes, or peoples are primitive and cannot be held to civilized standards. All these and other depictions, such as treating killing and brutalities as war's unfortunate or unavoidable byproduct or the expression of the unbearable distress of poverty, colonial injus-tice, or globalization, make annihilationist assaults seem "natural" and in some sense inevitable, or propelled forward by larger intractable forces, and therefore also unpreventable and unstoppable. These notions—whether explicit or implicit—disserve all political leaders and public alike who want mass murder and elimination to end. The fourth prob-lem, a corollary of the first three, is the failure to discuss the real causes of genocide, in general and in individual instances, and specifically *to name* the people responsible. These pitfalls, to a greater or lesser de-gree, are to be found in U.S. President Bill Clinton's cynical justification for standing by idly as the Serbs continued their systematic eliminationist assault on Bosnians: "Until these folks get tired of killing each other, bad things will continue to happen."[6]

The media, by being specific and accurate, can convey to elites and broader publics alike the genocide's reality, that, before the world community's eyes, with every passing day, week, and month, human beings are choosing to slaughter hundreds, thousands, tens of thousands and to brutalize still many more. The media can provide a realistic account of the horrors' causes, helping people to understand the most critical facts: that we can, as a practical matter, stop eliminationist onslaughts before they start or once they are under way. Even if the media do not explicitly urge governments and peoples to act, which they should, they would implicitly do so by making the moral questions unavoidable merely through straightforward reporting of the facts: Political leaders initiate mass murders and eliminations as rational political calculations to achieve political ends (even when based on fantastical notions about the victims). If the media make this clear, they will also convey to everyone that the issue *is* one of evil and good—not some vague notion of evil but concrete evil embodied in the men setting out with full faculties to willfully destroy other human beings. These men, like Hitler and those serving him, can and therefore must be stopped.

Lay out the facts. Lay out the causes. Lay out the (often low-cost) solutions (detailed below) in language that is precise, vivid, and individuated. The perpetrators and the victims should not be treated as abstractions. We should eschew or not use as stand-alone terms, terms such as "Hutu extremists," earlier in Germany "the SS," in Bosnia "Arkan's Tigers," or in Darfur "tribesmen." In general, we should not use terms such as *"extremists"* and *"radicals"* for the perpetrators because they automatically and usually wrongly suggest that conventional political means cannot persuade or stop the perpetrators. Instead, we should regularly refer to them more descriptively accurately as, for example, Turkish, German, Hutu, Serbian, or Sudanese perpetrators or Turkish, German, Hutu, Serbian, or Sudanese killers, or Turkish, German, Hutu, Serbian, or Sudanese executioners, or even executors of their government's or leaders' genocidal policies. We should personalize victims as much as possible, posing the question to the viewing publics: What would you want done, what would you want your government to do, what would you want the international community to do, if the perpetrators were doing this to the family next door, or to the boys and girls living down the street? If the media simply reported and described exterminationist and eliminationist assaults accurately while they take place, many more people would support and even press their political leaders to stop shirking their duty.

Terms such as mass murder and genocide should be readily used while eliminationist assaults take place. The usual practice of prefixing "alleged" before "mass murder," or "genocide," or the name of political leaders or military men responsible for them, only obfuscates what is clearly happening. We do not say the "alleged" war, or "alleged" war initiator to describe a war or the dictator starting it. We must shift the burden of proof in the court of public opinion, and require the prima facie guilty to demonstrate their innocence. After all, the world's media and publics are engaged not in legal proceedings but in an attempt to shed light on catastrophic eliminationist assaults so they can be stopped. Many in the media say they want the world to learn of such horrors so that governments will act to end them. Let the media alter its reporting to facilitate these goals.

This also means the media should tell publics that international institutions and the world's state system currently are ill-equipped to end mass murders and eliminations, and eliminationist politics more generally. Indeed, the international system's institutions are constituted (in part quite purposely) so they *will not* and *cannot* effectively halt eliminationist politics. Exposing the incompetence, negligence, and complicity of international institutions, especially the United Nations, will wrest people from complacency, from assuming reflexively (as many do) that letting existing international institutions and international law operate according to their normal codes and procedures is best. Not surprisingly, many people look to the United Nations for guidance and to coordinate its member states against mass murder and eliminationist politics. This has been and continues to be hopelessly misguided. As the earlier discussion of the genocide convention shows and as I discuss further below, the United Nations has not been a force against mass murder and elimination but their enabler. It has promoted an effective do-nothing approach to ongoing eliminationist assaults. As the hegemonic international institution of the international system, it also prevents an alternative regime or organization from emerging with the structure, charter, membership, and politics to effectively combat and prevent, or at least greatly reduce the toll of, eliminationist politics. People need to see that only by fundamentally changing international institutions, and by pressing them and governments to act in ways they ordinarily do not, will stopping exterminationist politics be possible.

Beyond descriptive and analytical accuracy, we must adopt the language of moral responsibility and a realistic, defensible notion of judgment based on what actually moves people to kill. Although political leaders and a society's fringe elements are deemed capable of having criminal, mass-murderous intentions, ordinary people lending themselves to exterminationist and eliminationist assaults instead are reflexively seen by many either as duped (or in the Germans' case, coerced), or dismissed as uncivilized, backward barbarians. In fact, as we now know, exceptions notwithstanding, ordinary people become perpetrators or supporters of mass murder and eliminations out of conviction. Their beliefs about the putative noxious or threatening nature of, and hatred for, the victims lead them to think eliminating them to be right. So they brutalize, expel, and kill them willingly. How they come to these beliefs and emotions does not alter the basic facts about their mindset at the moment they kill, or expel, or otherwise eliminate their victims: They hate, or coolly decide that mass murder or another form of elimination is morally correct or politically necessary. They may know that others, especially outside their countries, see it as wrong. Yet they choose to kill and brutalize anyway. The problem of moral responsibility, when a perpetrator believes such destructive politics is justified, remains real (no matter how he comes to hate) so long as he acts willingly.

We have no difficulty judging and condemning political leaders for masterminding and setting into motion eliminationist onslaughts. We can judge and condemn individual perpetrators, such as a Serb on trial before the International Criminal Tribunal for the former Yugoslavia in The Hague, or Timothy McVeigh for blowing up the federal building in Oklahoma City and slaughtering 168 people, including 19 children, and injuring another 850. But people have difficulty coming to the same conclusions for large numbers of ordinary Germans, Serbs, Hutu, and others. The vast number of the perpetrators, or their ordinariness (not having previously been members of "radical" political organizations), blunt judgment's normal processes. Is it because we have difficulty in thinking of the perpetrators as anything but a mass, or have been misled into seeing them in this dehumanizing way? Or is it because it is too disturbing or threatening to think of ordinary people—perhaps otherwise seeming like you or me—willingly perpetrating such horrors? Or is it because the problem of genocide is too daunting, the horror too overwhelming, and so we ignore or redefine it (falsely) to manage it psychologically and emotionally? Or are our moral faculties dulled by the encrusted and misleading ways scholars and media, politicians and jurists have dealt with such problems, focusing on the eliminationist leaders and ignoring or denying ordinary perpetrators' culpability, leading people to unthinkingly accept this false paradigm? People's systematic failure in judgment's exact causes are not clear, being likely variable, multiple, and overlapping. In any case, understanding those underlying causes matters less than acknowledging this systematic error: People, failing to maintain the individual perspective, reflexively opt for collective guilt and stereotypes about nationalities, or, this debased moral coin's flip side, for absolving the perpetrators of responsibility, attributing full blame to leaders or structures or some other abstraction, blunting moral responsibility and further clouding our view. Instead, we must maintain an *individual-level* perspective, recognizing that many ordinary people as individuals can and do act in concert to harm and kill other people on a colossal scale for the same or similar reasons that lead a single ordinary person to choose to harm or kill others.

We must make it clear to publics around the world that almost no international prevention, intervention, or moral responses to the continuing succession of large and larger mass murders and eliminations exists. Internationally, eliminationist politics remains a politics of impunity. The problem is not that powerful countries—the United States, the European countries, and Japan—are too involved in foreign entanglements or adventures trying to save or prevent the ruin of millions of lives (though the Americans' engagements in Iraq and, with NATO, in Afghanistan may seem to suggest too much adventurism). The problem is they are too little involved, and in wrong ways. Just as exterminationist and eliminationist politics are comprehensible and explicable, so are the possibilities for ending such politics. Elites and publics need to know explicitly that they—we—can effectively apply the brakes.

A large number of individual human beings (convicted of participating in the mass murder), working singly and together, extinguished the lives of a large number of individual human beings, dying singly and together, Tig prison camp, Kigali, Rwanda, April 2008, and skulls of victims, Nyamata Genocide Memorial, Bugesera District, Rwanda, April 2008.

Before exploring how to change the calculus of mass murder and eliminationist politics, we need to understand current institutional, legal, and policy affairs—particularly internationally—and how we arrived where we are. The historical developments have created certain structures, laws, and norms that powerfully impede states from acting to prevent or stop eliminationist assaults and to bring about necessary changes to the international environment.

The International Community's Promise and Pathologies

The task of ending eliminationist politics might seem less daunting if people understood the enormous fundamental progress we have made in other, equally challenging areas of domestic and international politics. The importance is twofold. First, hard-won, substantial improvement in some critical spheres suggests that progress is possible in others, including in reducing eliminationist politics' incidence and magnitude. Second, the specific progress made in international politics' other spheres helps explain the difficulty in bringing about the changes necessary to diminish eliminationist assaults. Three crucial, major areas of progress, after long, difficult, and costly struggles, are:

1. To provide, in many countries, institutional and political protections for basic civil and human rights domestically.
2. To delegitimize and mainly end the imperial conquest and rule of foreign territories.
3. To remove, to a considerable extent, war (and its possibility) as a fundamental means for countries relating to one another and solving international disputes.

The first, protection of people's basic domestic civil and political rights, has been won in many countries accomplished through sustained political effort to convince people that their societies and they themselves are better off with social and economic peace, the rule of law and respect of human rights, and democratic institutions, and simultaneously to enshrine these practices in society's and politics' organization and to spread their norms so they become the common ethos.

Many revolutions, wars, and domestically less violent battles had to be fought to create the political space for these developments to take place (in part by destroying nondemocratic regimes) and to underscore the folly of organizing politics and society along other lines.

Several international developments contributed to the second and third achievements of decreasing the incidence and political use of war, conquest, and the rule of foreign peoples. War's costs are now recognized to be astronomical. Wars wreak physical destruction, ruin national finances, injure and take the lives of combatants and noncombatants (also having adverse economic consequences), and, in preparing for and then fighting wars, distort a country's economy, society, and polity. Democracy's spread, especially among the most industrially and militarily powerful countries, has also reduced the appetite for war. Democratic regimes rarely fight each other. Democratic governments seek peaceful solutions to conflicts because their publics, ultimately holding them electorally accountable, do not want their husbands, sons, neighbors, and countrymen dying unless necessary for national defense, usually narrowly construed. For these and other reasons, including its delegitimation owing to conceptions of human rights and people's right to self-determination, colonization has become too costly and is seen as wrong. No longer a path to glory and supposed moral virtue and economic benefit, colonization is now commonly understood to bring the opposite—condemnation as oppression and exploitation. In many countries, especially the most powerful ones, two norms have replaced conquest, extraction, and glory: capitalism's bookkeeping calculus—the desire not to sacrifice one's own citizens for archaic values of adventure, manhood, and glory—and people's right to political self-determination. The industrial democracies' immense international, institutional, and informational power has extended democratic and enlightenment values, meaning domestic rights, around the globe, gaining constituencies in other countries. This in itself has strengthened many countries' peoples favoring basic human rights and made such values a part of virtually all countries' public norms, which in turn is powerfully self-ratifying and self-reinforcing, exerting pressure on governments and political leaders to live up to their publicly professed values.

Democratic and enlightenment norms' precise contribution to these developments can be debated. Yet in altering how people, especially economic and political elites, came to understand what they valued and how to achieve their goals, their understanding of the social and political institutions constituting self-interest moved in these more ethically defensible directions. Many countries' leaders and peoples came to understand that democracy—even if it entails sharing wealth and power often with disparaged groups—best promotes domestic peace, security, and prosperity. Most of the leaders and peoples of the world's wealthy and powerful countries have similarly come to understand that imperialism leads to neither glory nor economic benefit (as was believed for hundreds of years), but the opposite. It is costly, distorts a country's priorities, social compact, and politics, and leads to social strife in addition to and partly because of lives lost. War produces war. Many countries' leaders and peoples (especially in democracies) have come to understand that, win or lose, war is economically self-destructive and corrupts one's own society, not to mention kills off its young men. It therefore should not be undertaken lightly or without regard to its enormous human, material, social, and ultimately likely substantial political cost. Essentially, the institutions and norms that reduced domestic oppression and rights violations, imperialism, and (among the economically and politically advanced and powerful countries) war first emerged out of enlightened self-interest before being institutionalized and turned into powerful norms around the world, even if they have been imperfectly distributed and observed. These at least partly self-regarding norms have further, and crucially, become integral to international organizations, treaties, and norms, and built-in political restraints in democratic polities, constitutions (notably Japan's), and policies.

These developments domestically (in many countries) and internationally are major advances. Right-thinking people around the world form a general consensus especially on the need to prevent war and imperialism, which are core principles of the United Nations, international law, and international institutions. These are world historical advances. Yet they *could not have been foreseen in 1900*. Why should we take for granted that other, analogous advances could not also have taken place, or are now not equally possible, no matter how unlikely they may initially appear?

For stopping domestic eliminationist politics and mass murder, such progress is wanting. Whatever the lip service, and whatever the UN genocide convention's seeming provisions, strict and effective measures combating genocide even in genocide's most narrowly construed meaning, let alone eliminationism's many forms, do not exist in the international arena. Why? Answering that question requires us to examine the United Nations' and international law's failure to work toward stopping eliminationist and exterminationist politics *and* their active hindrance of such efforts—paradoxically, owing to advances in precisely some of the same aforementioned norms, considerations, and calculations we celebrate in other realms.

Existing laws and norms against (aggressive or nondefensive) war and against imperialism conflict with the international community's need to intervene to protect other countries' peoples from their own governments' violent abuse. Such international laws and norms enormously hinder the international community and interested states from working effectively to stop such violations, even exterminationist and eliminationist assaults. The problem is clear. Forestalling impending eliminationist assaults, including mass murder, or arresting those under way, often requires countries to make (what is legally defined as) "aggressive" war and abrogate other countries' sovereignty, including perhaps by invading and occupying them, which looks like imperialism.

Norms against war and imperialism have prevented new norms emerging for effective intervention against mass murder, expulsion, and incarceration. By default and design, the existing norms buttress the international community's *do-nothing* practice regarding eliminationist politics. They complement the virtual global absence of a push for effective intervention with an active anti-interventionist stance grounded in norm, institution, and law.

Countries genuinely disapproving of eliminationist politics do not do what they (and others) have done with war and imperialism and what might be expected, namely work passionately toward effective international measures to prevent states from exterminating people. The countries most engaged in domestic eliminationist politics, nondemocracies and sham democracies, better described as tyrannies, including until recently most UN members, want to maintain such politics' availability, so they do not want to empower the United Nations or other countries to interfere in their domestic politics. They fear, perhaps rightly, that their practices of denying democracy, ruling by violence and intimidation, and abrogating civil and human rights would come under international assault. The United Nations' and international law's insidious hands-off politics creates the circumstances for a still greater systematic danger. As today's political repertoire includes eliminationist measures, and as ruling nondemocratic or tyrannical rulers live by the sword, tyrannies' leaders and supporters know they themselves might one day use eliminationist means, which are part of today's normal political repertoire. Most dictatorships employ murder, terror, or other violent practices at least episodically. Many use such violence systematically. All rely upon their threat. None, in principle, is far removed from circumstances that will move its leaders to escalate and expand their daily ruling methods into mass murder or elimination.

To understand why international protections generally favor nondemocratic, brutal governments and not the people they oppress, we must look to the United Nations' history. The United Nations, whatever else it did, for more than forty years served one of our time's most generally destructive and specifically mass-murderous regimes, the Soviet Union, which could veto all resolutions of the Security Council, the United Nations' effective governing and critical lawmaking body. No major initiative, legal or institutional, could succeed that threatened the Soviet Union's or its many client regimes' freedom to practice eliminationist politics. The UN genocide convention's deformities and problems, as we know, greatly resulted from the Soviets' insistence on eviscerating the convention, so it could not stop its own and its clients' eliminationist practices. The convention's exclusion of the mass murder of politically—as opposed to ethnically—defined groups, its requirement that an explicit *intent* to commit genocide be behind the murderous assault, and its high threshold of comprehensiveness and scope for mass murders to qualify as genocide, produced window-dressing law covering up inaction. That the United Nations would not adopt other measures and laws to effectively combat eliminationist politics was a foregone conclusion, given the Soviets' veto, and starting in 1972, communist China's.

Rogue and lawless Soviet Union and later communist China as veto wielders and central lawmakers alone would have inherently corrupted the United Nations and prevented it from combating eliminationist politics. Still, more lies behind its failures. For virtually all its history, the

UN membership has been overwhelmingly dictatorships. As recently as 1987, 60 percent of the member countries were dictatorships, and only in 1991 did electoral democracies finally hit the 50 percent mark. Dictatorships dominated the General Assembly. Many supported the Soviet Union in the Security Council so it would not be isolated and more obviously branded an outlaw regime. Even since the Soviet Union's fall, the UN membership has never dropped much below 40 percent dictatorships. In 2009, it stood at 38 percent. Throughout its history, the United Nations' culture and bureaucracy has been greatly comprised of representatives of regimes wanting most of all a free hand to maintain their illegitimate rule, including by using eliminationist violence against those challenging or seeking to depose them.

Finally, Western countries, particularly the United States, have conducted themselves deplorably during the United Nations' many decades. They too had little desire for the United Nations to act effectively against eliminationist politics, for the same egoistic reasons that democratic countries have barely lifted a finger to stop mass murders. Worse, in the context of the cold war, the United States and other democratic countries prized a regime's political allegiance more than its domestic practices, so they ignored or supported rightist client regimes even when they slaughtered or eliminated their opponents—communists, democrats, members of ethnic groups challenging their rule, or virtually anyone the regimes declared to be allies of their (particularly leftist) opponents. During the 1970s and 1980s, the number of American client states practicing mass-murderous politics exceeded those of the Soviets.

The communist world's implosion, the cold war's end, and democratic countries' numeric increase, since the 1990s, removed or greatly diminished several of the insuperable structural impediments to transforming the United Nations and the international community into effective agents against eliminationist politics. The continuing obstacles of a tamer China and Russia notwithstanding, the international context for combating eliminationist politics has progressed. The cold war's binary logic so overwhelmed political leaders' meager ethical impulses regarding international affairs that progress in combating (or even not encouraging) mass murder was all but impossible. Two of the rare actions, in Bosnia in 1995 and in Kosovo in 1999, to stop eliminationist onslaughts, which under NATO's auspices the United States, together with France, Germany, the United Kingdom, and other alliance members, undertook, would have been unthinkable during the cold war, for fear of escalation into a shooting war with the Soviet Union. For the past ten years, the number of democratic countries has hovered around 120, about 63 percent of all countries, the most since the United Nations' founding, and almost twice as many as just twenty years ago, on the eve of the communist bloc's disintegration.[7] The overwhelming obstacle tyrannical regimes pose to addressing eliminationist politics has substantially lessened.

Another set of factors related to but not reducible to the first has synergistically shaped the United Nations' and the international community's malign neglect of eliminationist politics. The United Nations was founded after two world wars left tens of millions dead, ravaging Europe and East Asia. With modern warfare's unprecedented destructiveness and the development of nuclear weapons, the United Nations' first and overwhelming priority understandably became preventing war. With many new countries and many new UN members emerging with the imperialist powers (United Kingdom, France, etc.) retreating from their colonies around the globe, anti-imperialism understandably and rightly became the developing world's rallying cry, and consequently the rest of the world accepted it as a bedrock principle. Marked by similar deformities of membership and history, the world's major regional organizations, including the African Union, the Association of Southeast Nations, and the Organization of American States, hold as a cardinal principle member states' nonintervention in other member states. The African Union, which was created in 2002 as the Organization of African Unity's successor, for example, explains: "The main objectives of the OAU [created in 1963] were, inter alia, to rid the continent of the remaining vestiges of colonization and apartheid; to promote unity and solidarity among African States; to coordinate and intensify cooperation for development; to safeguard the sovereignty and territorial integrity of Member States and to promote international cooperation within the framework of the United Nations."[8] Anti-imperialism, emphatically yes. Primacy of the member states' sovereignty, emphatically yes. But *nothing* about intervening against those same states to safeguard people's lives and rights, even when a state perpetrates genocide.

Together, the United Nations' foundational mission to prevent aggressive war and its and most countries' reflexive opposition to one country's occupying another, for whatever reason, impede the world from addressing today's acute problem, exceeding certainly imperialism and arguably also interstate war: eliminationist politics, in its most extreme version, mass murder. Why? Because dealing with eliminationist politics effectively, especially once a mass murder or elimination begins, usually requires an intervening country or alliance to initiate hostilities against a country that has not attacked it, and, to replace an eliminationist regime, an outside power or powers likely must occupy the country. The first looks like aggressive war and the second like imperialism. Furthermore, the countries most capable of intervening, including by violating in other ways the near-sacrosanct principle of state sovereignty, are past imperial powers, which the United States is seen (partly rightly) to include, which triggers the developing world's (and their Western vocal sympathizers') anti-imperialist reflexes even more intensively. Thus, for decades, the United Nations, the international community, and its individual members have been all but completely hamstrung in fashioning any real response to the world's rampant eliminationist politics.

One might have thought that now, after the cold war, with war not a thinkable option between a good part of the world's countries, and with imperialism, except in the margins, a dead letter, the United Nations would be able to seriously address eliminationist politics. New, hopeful initiatives reflect this changed international landscape, most notably around the concept of the *responsibility to protect* peoples their own governments kill or harm, a movement that gained steam with its December 2001 foundational report, *The Responsibility to Protect,* calling for states to intervene in a country—in other words, ignore sovereignty, when a government slaughters civilians.[9] In a 2006 resolution the UN Security Council tepidly and in passing acknowledged the *responsibility to protect.*[10] Yet, like the genocide convention itself, the *responsibility to protect* has little actual force, lacking a clear triggering mechanism or prescribed intervention. So far it has not changed the response of the international system, and especially that of the United Nations, to eliminationist politics. Intervention to forcibly stop the massive Political Islamist exterminationist and eliminationist onslaught in Darfur (or the one in Southern Sudan before it) did not happen before the United Nations recognized the doctrine, and it has not happened since.

The United Nations suffers from its first several decades' profound deformities, and the continuing membership, including veto-wielding membership, of countries wanting to preserve their international impunity to slaughter and eliminate unwanted groups. Even today the United Nations, far from being a force against eliminationist politics and assaults, de facto protects if not legitimizes them, by vociferously defending countries' sovereignty (really the sovereignty of states, or their leaders) and the pseudo-principle of noninterference in other countries' internal affairs, even when states slaughter their own people. The American ambassador to Burundi during the 1972 mass butchery could declare shortly thereafter, "The United States simply should not interfere in any way with the internal affairs of another country." Although both a cynical statement (the American government merely followed its self-conceived interests in doing nothing), and a hypocritical one (the United States intervened routinely to weaken or overthrow regimes), the statement also comported with the overwhelmingly defended international consensus the United Nations grounds and most robustly maintains. According to the American ambassador, "Direct unilateral intervention was out of the question." Why? "It would have been contrary to our policy of nonintervention in the affairs of African states." In his view, the United States rightly left it to the Organization of African Unity and the United Nations "to carry out their responsibilities," which everyone knew they would not do.[11] Whatever the United Nations' small symbolic steps against eliminationist politics and assaults may be in general, and whatever occasional good it does to help victim peoples, the United Nations has effectively legitimized, codified, encouraged, and pursued a hands-off politics providing cover to mass-murdering and eliminationist regimes. The United Nations has consistently done this, not just in Burundi but also in China, the former Yugoslavia, Iraq, Rwanda, Democratic Republic of the Congo, Sudan, and elsewhere. Whatever claims and appearances to the contrary, the United Nations and the international legal system are organized to allow states to pursue eliminationist politics, including mass murder.

The debate about the United States' and Britain's prospective invasion of Iraq in 2003, for all its confusion and false pretenses, highlighted this central problem. To be sure, politics—to put it crudely, those against and for American power's exercise—informed people's positions from the run-up to war to the subsequent occupation. Much argumentation on both sides was insincere rhetoric. Nevertheless, one central issue was almost entirely absent from the discussion: Saddam was one of our time's worst mass murderers, which *in principle* should be cause enough to forcibly remove him and his regime from power. What's more, *in principle,* it should be other states' and the international community's duty to do so. Whether it is a wise or prudent undertaking (taking into account other important principles and the costs, damage, and death the practical measures to remove him might produce) is also a critical issue, which becomes relevant, however, and must be assessed case by case only after the primary principle is recognized: Mass murderers have no right to rule and thereby to slaughter people.

Saddam had already started two murderous, aggressive imperial wars: against Iran in 1980, and Kuwait in 1990. His regime had already conducted three systematic exterminationist campaigns against Iraq's people: the Marsh people, Shia, and earlier, including with chemical weapons, Kurds. To maintain his tyranny, he regularly murdered and brutalized and tortured political opponents and others. Saddam, his regime, and the people serving it murdered perhaps half a million Iraqis—in addition to the million deaths he caused in trying to conquer parts of Iran. There was absolutely no reason to believe that absent an invasion (1) Saddam would be deposed anytime soon, that (2) he would not continue mass murdering tens of thousands, perhaps hundreds of thousands more Iraqis, and (3) that his eventual successor would not be another Baathist tyrant, probably a son, probably the similarly brutal and murderous Uday. This is all aside from the untold nonexplicitly murderous misery Saddam was causing Iraqis, including children's and others' deaths from his continuing ruining and plundering of Iraq's economy to maintain his rule and pursue his megalomaniacal schemes of grandeur. When ten, twenty, thirty years down the road the Baathist regime would end, Iraq would have likely faced all the disintegrating tendencies and conflicts that appeared after the American and British military victory, but without the powerful military presence that greatly dampened such disorder and that has at least (for now) provided some possibility that a democratic and peaceful dispensation might follow.

Victims of Saddam's chemical weapons, Halabja, Iraq, March 1988

Those who favored war to topple Saddam and his regime not only acknowledged but hammered home that Saddam was a killer, a brute, a butcher, an "evildoer" of epochal proportions. But, significantly, the arguments put forward to justify the invasion—that he had or would soon acquire weapons of mass destruction, that he sponsored terror, including that of Al Qaeda, and the sometime and related argument that fighting terror in Arab or Islamic countries depended on democratization—did not include the right, need, or duty to depose mass murderers. Bush administration officials did not advance this argument, but not because it had nothing to do with the intervention. Instead, the Bush administration sought to maintain that attacking Iraq did not violate international law. And international law prohibiting nondefensive warmaking left no room, short of the United Nations' invoking the genocide convention and authorizing intervention, for forcibly removing a mass murderer, even one killing hundreds of thousands. Whatever the argument's moral force that the international community should have the duty, or at least the right, to depose such colossally lethal murderers, the Bush administration did not advance the obvious and incontrovertible case that Saddam and his regime had to go, because it would have hurt its case legally and politically, and probably even in the court of public morality shaped by the laws and norms of the international arena.

In making the case for deposing Saddam, the Bush administration and its supporters at least did state clearly that Saddam was a mass murderer, placing him alongside Hitler, Stalin, Pol Pot, and our time's other most brutal killers. Those opposing the prospective American invasion barely addressed this, except for the few saying in passing, *yes, of course Saddam is a bad guy,* or *I'm not defending Saddam, who is a murderer,* before moving on to their many reasons for opposing a war to depose him. The all but complete failure of the war's opponents to acknowledge let alone openly consider the desirability, the necessity, and in principle the duty of deposing mass murderers, and also to see this duty as integral to assessing the rightness and wisdom of getting rid of Saddam, is shocking. This failure was even more glaring in the human rights community, which, with exceptions, stood almost united in opposition to the war *and* in silence about the principle that removing mass murderers from power ought to be a priority in international politics and law.

The long-standing and ongoing international legal and political systems' perverse failure to consider states' and international institutions' rights and duties to stop eliminationist politics *and* depose its practitioners inhibited a discussion of the principle from entering the public discourse in the run-up to the Iraq war. (In my many discussions with scholars and nonscholars before and during the war, and then during the occupation and continuing fighting, including the sectarian slaughter of many Iraqi civilians, my enunciation of this principle was the first time most had heard it.) In other, less heated instances, such a discussion had taken place, including among those earlier calling for or lauding American or NATO intervention to stop Milošević in Bosnia and then in Kosovo, and those in the human rights community already working on developing a political and legal norm of the *responsibility to protect.*[12] Yet when confronting Saddam, acknowledging, even uttering this principle was, for political reasons, anathema to the war's opponents.

There were reasons, including principled ones, to oppose the American and British attack on Iraq. The Bush administration's wholesale misleading of the U.S. Congress, the American people, and the world about Saddam's weapons capabilities and existing programs, and about his ties to Al Qaeda, in retrospect substantially strengthens the prewar arguments against the invasion. Now that the war against Saddam's Iraq itself is over—though the occupation and its aftermath, with its various sectarian insurgencies, are still being played out, at this moment uncertainly, for a democratic, peaceful, and economically prosperous outcome—a retrospective cost-benefit analysis (including the massive death, destruction, and displacement) can seriously begin. But none of this speaks to the principle discussed here, that the international community ought to depose mass murderers.

Before the war, in the United Nations' and in the broader international legal, political, and journalistic discussions about how to proceed, the international community's sacrosanct principle against nondefensive wars trumped almost every other consideration. (The Bush administration's doctrine of *preventive (defensive) war* was meant to stretch the concept of what constitutes "defensive," thereby grafting it onto the generally accepted, legitimated reason for making war.) The principle against nondefensive wars trumped any positive and systematic consideration of the principles and pragmatic arguments for forcibly removing Saddam. Whatever conclusions people would have drawn after assessing the competing principles and the prospective cost-benefit calculus, such an open and honest assessment did not take place, certainly not in the major public forums, not in the United Nations, not by political leaders, and not in major media in different countries of which I am aware.

The Iraq war shows how little the international community and the United Nations are willing to consider the most acutely needed military interventions—to free people not from foreign occupiers but from homegrown tyrannical rulers and regimes. The fraternal principles of sovereignty and proscription of nondefensive wars govern an international system that, its self-professions notwithstanding, effectively and as a practical matter sanctions mass murder by providing tyrannical regimes insurance policies for repressing, terrorizing, and murdering their peoples with impunity.

The *responsibility to protect* movement to sanction intervention against a state's slaughtering its own country's people, and the UN Security Council's recognition of it, makes the international system's recent stance toward eliminationist politics a little more complicated than this. A discussion, and in some quarters a vigorous one, is now taking place about prevention and intervention. Task forces and groups seek to reform the United Nations. Kofi Annan, with the guilt he bears for the Hutu's extermination of the Tutsi, not to mention his inaction as UN secretary-general toward other mass eliminations during his tenure, in 2004 promulgated an action plan (hollow as it was, witness the United Nations' abject failure in Darfur and Democratic Republic of the Congo). The United States established a seemingly serious high-level commission, led by former Secretary of Defense William Cohen and former Secretary of State Madeleine Albright (who has also made an about-face since her infamous statement that intervening in Rwanda would be "folly"), working to produce a comprehensive and effective approach to preventing mass murder. Proposals urge establishing a UN rapid deployment force, which could be a critical aid should an effective one ever exist. We have an International Criminal Court, which, whatever its founders' good intentions, was also a low-cost way for world leaders to seem to be combating mass murder. But unfortunately the discussions that do occur are riddled domestically in the United States (and to a lesser extent elsewhere) by left-right politics, and internationally with the often paralyzing politics resulting from power's and symbolism's calculations. Bad faith and hypocrisy govern discussion about stopping mass murder and other eliminationist onslaughts. Myriad other political considerations unjustifiably take precedence over any serious confrontation of the problem.

In addition to the failure of the Iraq war's opponents to genuinely confront Saddam's mass murdering, the Bush administration's bad faith must be similarly cited. The war's opponents correctly pointed to the selectivity of U.S. interventionism. The argument that because you do not depose all mass murderers, dictators, and brutes, you should not depose any—similar to an argument no one dares to venture that because you do not punish all your society's murderers, you should punish none—is a logical, moral, and policy embarrassment. Nevertheless, it does highlight that the Bush administration, like other American administrations, was unconscionably selective in compassion for victims, blithely inattentive to eliminationist politics' victims elsewhere, and cynically uninterested in stopping the perpetrators.

The United States' woeful response to the catastrophic mass murdering, population expulsions, and related deaths from starvation and disease in the Democratic Republic of the Congo, Southern Sudan, Darfur, and elsewhere demonstrates its political leadership's continuing disregard for seriously combating mass murder and eliminationist politics. Contemporaneous with the run-up to the Iraq war, the war itself, and the war's tottering and uncertain nation-building aftermath, these other mass murders and eliminations exceeded Saddam's in Iraq and would have cost far less to end militarily. Indeed, speaking candidly in the pre-9/11 world, Bush himself declared his real view. On American national television, invoking the morally bankrupt but rhetorically powerful justification of "national interest" (here called "strategic interest"), he proclaimed that the United States "should not send our troops to stop ethnic cleansing and genocide outside our strategic interest."[13] September 11 did not lead Bush to alter his position that when a government is slaughtering and expelling hundreds of thousands of men, women, and children in a country or context deemed not to affect the U.S. national interest, American soldiers must not be risked. Bush's holy grail of "strategic interest," narrowly construed, echoed Clinton, invoking "the cumulative weight of American interests" in 1994 at the height of the Hutu's slaughter of Tutsi to justify his inaction: Clinton's secretary of state, Warren Christopher, citing the absence of any "national interest," a year earlier during the Serbs' eliminationist assault on Bosnians to rationalize the United States' allowing that mass murdering and expulsion to proceed. Bush merely echoed what has guided every American president during our time, and the views most of the policy elite and probably a large majority of the American people appear to share. Bush and his administration, like those before them, stood by and watched the "ethnic cleansing[s] and genocide[s]" before their eyes. The Europeans are better, only occasionally, in paying lip service to how horrible it all is.

The United States has conservative interventionists and conservative isolationists, and liberal interventionists and liberal isolationists. Yet each group's support or opposition to U.S. intervention depends more on the particular case's implications for American power and their respective conceptions of the "national interest" (American power being one integral component). Again and again, political leaders and elites prove themselves egoistic, with little if any inclination to act morally in the international arena, particularly when it might incur substantial costs for them or their societies. Even political leaders and elites, especially powerful international actors, not trumpeting the "national interest" (narrowly construed), tack to it closely. In other countries, similar considerations about American power and their own national interests guide political and media elites' assessments of the desirability of American intervention abroad, which, whether they like it or not, is necessary for effective international intervention in most every part of the world.

The recent, slight progress in the international community's stance regarding eliminationist assaults remains a distraction from the most fundamental and enduring fact: The international community, as exemplified in law, institutions, and politics, is organized in a manner that makes stopping mass-murdering and eliminationist political leaders enormously difficult. Thus, it almost never happens. States sometimes do act, or consider acting, to stop mass murder and other eliminationist policies, when proximity makes such horrors more real, tangible, emotionally unavoidable, or costly. The three principal kinds of proximity affecting political leaders are geographic (actual or virtual, such as on television), circumstances and events impinging on material or political interests, and fellow feeling, commonly called identity. We need to increase leaders' and ordinary citizens' proximity to other peoples along these dimensions. But this is not easy even if some progress is possible and, in any quantity, potentially lifesaving.

The international system's current, disheartening state notwithstanding, a more precise view of its features, and its somewhat improvement, can help us think through the measures that would reduce the mass-murderous and eliminationist toll in the coming century.

Ordinarily, we focus on the factors causing or generating mass murder and elimination. This helps us understand why the horrors occur. It may also point to ways they can be prevented or halted. Yet a different, neglected perspective is also important to develop: a *braking* model of mass eliminations. By examining the elements that, if properly effected, can stop them from happening, we can think more precisely about what has gone wrong and how to recraft institutions or policies to set them right.

Brakes can be set at various levels and in many ways. Reducing exterminationist and eliminationist politics can occur at the international or domestic system level, or both. Even if these general systems are not properly constituted to impede eliminationist politics, mass murder and elimination's incidence can still be reduced by specifically targeting the two groups indispensable for eliminationist and exterminationist politics: the leaders initiating the onslaught, and the followers implementing it.

These four, the international political environment, the domestic political order, leaders, and followers, interact with each other. Interventionist policies can also be intertwined and coordinated. Still, some of these are more potentially effective than others for reducing the frequency and scope of mass murder and elimination. The international arena is the most important. Only by changing its functioning can we at once and systematically affect *all* potential eliminationist states, leaders, and societies.

International environments crucially affect domestic politics and society. In a bellicose world, with countries prone to making war or armed so they could, a country devotes many more resources to armaments and defense than in a more peaceful international environment. Heightened militarism affects and distorts a country's economy, politics, and culture. In turn, it makes actual or potential antagonists more insecure, subjectively needing to further enhance their own military capacities, taking a toll on their own countries' domestic lives. This reaction, then, rebounds back on the first country, which had armed to increase its security, making it again be and feel less secure. (This international environmental paradox of attempts to increase security producing greater insecurity is known as the "security trap.") In a different international environment, an economic one of increased international trade, especially when international trade organizations devoted to maintaining fair trade rules, import and export opportunities affect companies' and workers' strategies in country after country, and the politics that each, as well as national polities, pursue. In yet another international environment that allows most aspects of domestic political life to be governed at least in part at the international level, with organizations that can promulgate and enforce binding rules, a country's domestic politics, economics, society, and culture change procedurally and substantively. This has been most evident with the European Union, which has profoundly affected its members' domestic politics and societies, and their governments' operations, in no small part because a substantial part of members' national legislation implements European Union laws.

The international environment's powerful and general effect on states' and societies' practices extends also to eliminationist politics. Substantially changing the international environment vis-à-vis exterminationist and eliminationist politics would greatly affect their incidence and practice. A changed international environment in a given realm or policy area alters the structure of incentives for leaders, regimes, and followers everywhere in the world. It addresses, as one must when thinking seriously about broad policy responses to worldwide problems, the rational aspects—purposive, cost-benefit calculations—that contribute to exterminationist and eliminationist assaults. It does so in two ways. It creates tangible responses to eliminationist politics' practice. It also induces political leaders to anticipate those international responses and alter their cost-benefit conclusions, motivating them not to initiate or continue with annihilative and other eliminationist programs.

We can wait for the international system to evolve sufficiently, and perhaps it might. But in the meantime, millions will die. We could have similarly urged patience in 1990—and we'd be where we currently are—or we could have in the meantime saved millions of lives from ruination and extinction.

In Chapter 6 I discussed aspects of the international environment, in two respects, showing first the genocide convention's specific multiple and abject failures, and second the international environment's enormous permissiveness toward eliminationist assaults. I identified four dimensions that constitute the international political environment regarding mass murder and eliminations: A legal dimension: Are mass murder or eliminations legally proscribed? A rhetorical dimension: Are they publicly discussed and condemned? An action dimension: Are states and international organizations permissive toward eliminationist assaults in practice and policy, or do they act to stop them? A hortatory dimension: Do outside actors encourage or support other states and political leaders to undertake exterminationist or eliminationist assaults? The analysis revealed our time's three successive periods: The first, prior to Nuremberg and the genocide convention's establishment in 1948; the second, from 1948 through the early 1990s (with substantial changes starting with the advent of human rights doctrine in the late 1970s); and the third from the early 1990s until today. During each period considerable variation has existed along each dimension and their coalescence into a coherent environment, though in sum there has been little progress according to the reasonable standard that the international community (1) proscribes all *eliminationist* assaults (including small-scale and less lethal ones), (2) immediately and forcefully condemns those that occur, (3) allows for any state or states to intervene to stop such assaults, and (4) such intervention actually takes place quickly and effectively. Picking up on that earlier foundational discussion, here I explore in greater depth the *action* dimension. What have the international legal environment and states' *actions* been to prevent or stop eliminationist assaults?

The anti-eliminationist *action* any international political environment offers to combat domestic eliminationist politics has three principal components: *prevention, intervention,* and *justice.* The individual international regimes that develop around each of these anti-eliminationist actions can be institutionalized in international law, international institutions' and federations' policies, and individual countries' law and policies. If and how this happens crucially affects eliminationist assaults' incidence, scope, and success.

Prevention in its broadest sense means creating general conditions likely to inhibit eliminationist and exterminationist politics. An international political prevention regime—laws, institutions, and practices—would work actively to create conditions that stop leaders from choosing to pursue eliminationist politics. It will even remove the practical basis (opportunities for success and getting followers to follow) for leaders to seriously consider such programs and for followers to be willing to implement them. The second component, *intervention,* has international actors—states acting singly or together, or international institutions spearheading member states—taking measures to stop specific mass murders or eliminations. These measures include diplomatic and economic efforts and sanctions, and military intervention, with clear and appropriate circumstances or events triggering them, individually or in conjunction with one another. The third component, *justice,* includes a wide range of necessary features, including punishing per-petrators and offering measures of repair—political, material, and moral. Repair is critical for justice, yet less so for reducing elimina-tionist politics. Hence the ensuing discussion focuses on justice's puni-tive component, which itself has two critical dimensions: how broadly mass murder and elimination's initiators and implementers are pun-ished, and punishment's certitude.

Bearing these three components in mind, what has the international political environment been for combating eliminationist politics? First, unless we confine ourselves to large-scale mass murder, there would be little to analyze. The international community has responded to non-mass-murderous eliminationist domestic politics with near total per-missiveness, offering no serious legal or institutionalized policy response, except humanitarian aid to people insistently referred to eu-phemistically as displaced persons (as if it just somehow happened) in-stead of the expellees that they are. To lethal eliminationist onslaughts the international community has taken occasional ad hoc responses, such as NATO's intervention to stop the Serbs' eliminationist assaults against Bosniaks and again against Kosovars, but each came only after the Serbs—whose murderous intentions and deeds were long known—had killed, burned homes and villages, and expelled their victims in massive numbers. Louis Gentile, the UN high commission for refugees' head of operations in Banja Luka, Bosnia, in January 1994 wrote in the *Globe & Mail:* "It should be known and recorded for all time, that the so-called leaders of the Western world have known for the past year and a half what is happening here. They receive play-by-play reports. They talk of prosecuting war criminals but do nothing to stop the con-tinuing war crimes. May God forgive them, may God forgive us all."[14] In East Timor, success came after an even longer period of shameful failure. When the United Nations inserted peacekeepers in 1999 to fore-stall still more killing and expulsions, it did so only after more than twenty neglectful years, as the world with a willful blind eye watched the Indonesians perpetrate mass murder, mass expulsions, and mass in-carcerations on that island. These interventions, checkered as they are as successes, are all the international community has effectively done.

Paralleling the past hundred years' overall international environ-ment for eliminationist politics, the specific international regime of laws, institutions, and practices for *action* against mass murder can be divided into three periods. Prior to Nuremberg, the international community's treatment of mass murder mirrored other forms of eliminationist politics. It was practically a nonissue. Given international institutions' paucity, save for a few treaties such as the Geneva Convention, this comes as little surprise. The League of Nations, established in 1919 and a forerunner of the United Nations, was weak and poorly functioning. Institutionalized international or multinational state cooperation was restricted mainly to selected economic matters and issues of war. There were no prevention, intervention, or punishment regimes. The institutions did not exist. Even more, among states shaping international relations, the belief was weak to nonexistent that international antigenocide regimes were needed. This too should not surprise, as few countries were democracies. The powerful countries, democratic or not, were themselves imperial powers, either practicing or potentially practicing eliminationist politics, including mass murder, in their colonies.

The shock of the Holocaust and more broadly the Germans' predations across Europe (and to a lesser degree of the Japanese in Asia) ushered in the second period that can be called the United Nations–Nuremberg regime. The victorious Allies established at Nuremberg an ad hoc International Military Tribunal doing three things. It created the first body of international law codifying aspects of mass murder, under the rubrics of "crimes against humanity" and "war crimes." It proscribed these crimes. And it provided punishment for them. This law became the basis for the UN genocide convention, passed in 1948 and ratified in 1949. The United Nations, formally established in 1945, created the first international forum and institution that, in principle, could effectively combat eliminationist politics, though the United Nations' initial concerns (preventing war) and deformities (e.g., the Soviet Union's Security Council veto, the many tyrannies and eliminationist regimes as members) meant it would actually do little. In fact, the establishment of the United Nations and the specific body of law to address mass murder coincided with the Soviet empire's onset in Central and Eastern Europe and the Soviets' ongoing and potential need to eliminate actual or imagined enemies, rendering Nuremberg's and then the genocide convention's substantial rhetorical and paper progress mainly empty symbols. True, at Nuremberg, at the Trial of the Major War Criminals Before the International Military Tribunal and then the successor trials, the most important ones, including of the leaders of the Einsatzgruppen, the Americans held, the courts brought some leading mass murderers to justice and punishment. This was also true in the parallel war crimes trial of Japanese by the International Military Tribunal for the Far East in Tokyo and by courts in countries where the Japanese committed their crimes. Yet, all in all, the regime against mass murder set up in the 1940s and essentially unchanged for half a century proved extremely weak, almost mocking what was needed.

It contained no prevention regime, which is not surprising, as no serious thought was given to what laws, institutions, and practices might reduce mass murder's incidence, aside from the toothless genocide convention. There was manifestly little genuine care about preventing mass murder, and for that matter, given the international community and its institutions' nature, little ability to act even had the care existed. Effectively, no intervention regime existed at the international level, and none was coming from individual states either. This second period saw an enormous number of mass murders and eliminations across the world, each met with inaction or approval, depending on the identity of the bystander states, the perpetrator state, and the victims. In principle, namely on the books, a punishment regime based on the law created at Nuremberg existed. But its implementation required a court and legal institutions to be created ad hoc for each mass murder. Given the general neglectful international environment—at times, each superpower's active encouragement of mass murder—this policy provision failed. More important, it was always unlikely to happen for the next exterminationist assault, and surely every political leadership contemplating mass murder knew this. Effectively, the punishment regime barely existed either.

Most of all, the cold war's paralyzing and murderous politics governed this period. Each superpower shielded its clients' exterminationist and eliminationist practices, and tread lightly in the other's sphere for fear of local conflicts becoming general and going nuclear.

This second period saw some progress. A body of law and an international institution, the United Nations, emerged that in principle could address or become the forum for addressing mass murder. It also saw certain publics recognize mass murder as a problem needing redress, and by the international community. Countries could not be left to police themselves. So this period's developments, though anemic and self-condemning, created a slender foundation for a better international regime.

The third period commenced during the twentieth century's last decade with the dissolution of the Soviet Union and the cold war, a prerequisite for serious progress in fashioning an international environment inhibiting rather than encouraging exterminationist and eliminationist domestic politics. This was for two related reasons. As long as the Soviet Union existed, international law and international politics (as practiced, among other places, in the United Nations) could not develop an effective legal and political regime against genocide and eliminationist politics. The Soviet Union, the world's leading tyranny, impeded such change, even if Western-aligned states also perpetrated mass murder and practiced eliminationist policies. Any antigenocide regime must include legal bases for the international community and outside states to intervene in actual or potential mass-murdering and eliminationist countries. This was anathema to the Soviet Union because of all its abuses and because, as a tyranny ruling a multiethnic and restless empire, it always potentially needed such destructive policies. Second, the cold war blinded American and other Western political leaders, not to mention Western publics, to moral considerations and political practices' unacceptability that they pursued, supported, or tolerated in the anticommunist global struggle. While nothing could excuse such stances and conduct, it is nevertheless hard to believe that absent the cold war, the United States would have supported or so willfully turned a blind eye to the mass murdering its Latin American and other client states or, for that matter, any anticommunist regime perpetrated during the postwar period, such as the Indonesian regime's slaughter of communists and the Guatemalan regime's murderous and eliminationist anti-insurgency campaign against leftists and mainly Maya. The cold war's end returned the United States and other Western countries to their natural, mainly cynical neglectful state, which, however inexcusable, is far preferable to acceptance, connivance, and encouragement of eliminationist practices. Media and publics could expand their capacities to see more accurately and respond more (if still inadequately) appropriately to the horrors of world's eliminationist politics.

This third period, still taking shape, can be called the United Nations–International Criminal Court regime (which perhaps will become the Responsibility to Protect–International Criminal Court regime). Depending on perspective, its practical differences from the second period can be judged to be substantial or minimal. Media and the public are more aware of mass slaughters and eliminationist violence, which sometimes pressures politicians to act. NATO's intervention to stop the Serbs' expulsion and mass murdering in Bosnia and then again in Kosovo, long after the assaults began—three years in Bosnia and a year in Kosovo—were qualified successes. Halfheartedly carried out with bombing, allowing the Serbs' assault in Kosovo to intensify and continue unabated for three months, the interventions eventually succeeded, the one in Kosovo halting the Serbs' string of eliminationist assaults. (During the second period, this intervention never would have occurred.) The establishment of ad hoc international tribunals, the International Criminal Tribunal for the former Yugoslavia in 1993 and the International Criminal Tribunal for Rwanda in 1994, with broad international support and legitimacy (for all the tribunals' considerable failings) was a highly visible and positive development for punishment. The International Criminal Court's subsequent creation in 2002 is a significant step toward creating a working punishment regime. The court is permanent. It can receive referrals from the UN Security Council or member states and can initiate its own prosecutions. It has quickly established its legitimacy and function, having opened, as of March 2009, investigations in four countries: the Central African Republic, Democratic Republic of the Congo, Sudan, and Uganda. In July 2008 it began to consider issuing an arrest warrant for Sudan's President al-Bashir, which it issued in March 2009. This initiative highlights the court's potential and limitations. Following the much-too-late precedent of the Yugoslavia tribunal, which waited six years before indicting Milošević, the International Criminal Court tries to bring to justice an *ongoing* exterminationist and eliminationist assault's mastermind. If successful, it likely would have some deterrent effect on political leaders considering mass murder. But this arrest warrant is five years too late, after al-Bashir has orchestrated the mass murder of hundreds of thousands and expulsion of more than two million, which itself followed his even larger, more devastating eliminationist assault in Southern Sudan, about which the international community has done *nothing* to punish him. From the time the court's prosecutor opened an investigation in June 2005, *three years* elapsed until he issued an indictment. The court then took the better part of *another year* to issue an arrest warrant. The arrest warrant, moreover, is only for al-Bashir himself and not the many other political and military leaders helping to organize and implement the devastating carnage (perhaps a few such indictments will follow), and does not include the charge of genocide, being for crimes against humanity and war crimes. The UN Security Council can still quash the arrest warrant. Even if the Security Council lets it stand, the court has no enforcement capacity to apprehend al-Bashir. These substantial failings notwithstanding, the court's initiative is a beneficial new development. But for all the fanfare celebrating it, during the *almost four years* the court's creaky machinery took to issue the arrest warrant, and not even for genocide, the Political Islamists have killed, raped, and expelled the Darfurians on a vast scale. And because the court and the international community (which so far has relied almost exclusively on the court for action) have loud barks with no real prevention or intervention bite, al-Bashir's reaction to the arrest warrant has been that of a leader with impunity. He has expelled aidworkers and continues to attack the Darfurians. In the name of anti-imperialist solidarity, Arab and African leaders have flocked to his side and risen in his defense.

This third phase's evident progress over the previous two phases holds out considerable potential for more progress. Nevertheless, it falls far short of what is needed. Even NATO's intervention to stop or mainly reverse the effects of the Serbs' mass expulsion of Kosovars (and forestall probable subsequent Serb assaults in the region) came many years, deaths, lives ruined, and mass eliminations late. The failures of the international community, its institutions, and member states in Burundi, Rwanda, Iraq (prior to the American invasion), East Timor for two decades, Sierra Leone, the Democratic Republic of the Congo, Sudan, and elsewhere have been all but total, as great or greater than the second period. Perpetrators have expelled, tortured, and slaughtered hundreds of thousands and millions of defenseless men, women, and children. The whole world, especially the United Nations, the United States, and the Europeans, has watched and done nothing, and France even abetted the Rwandan slaughter. The genocide convention, all but worthless—indeed counterproductive—remains the world's guiding document, and the United Nations, with all its built-in, disqualifying problems, the leading institution. The United States, fearing indictments of its own soldiers and citizens, has not ratified the International Criminal Court, leaving the world's most powerful actor at odds with the court (though how the United States will de facto aid the court's work is evolving and will likely vary case by case). With all its pathologies, the international state system continues to operate at arm's length from eliminationist politics, much as before.

A practically nonexistent prevention regime prevents little. An institutionally and politically extremely weak intervention regime produces few interventions. A considerably improved punishment regime institutionally is, in practice, cumbersome and partial, and, in its appalling record of a few paltry prosecutions, almost mocks justice. The international community's stance toward mass exterminationist and eliminationist politics has been so limited, weak, and ineffective that it actually permits, tolerates, and encourages eliminationist politics.

If political leaders, based on their own country's domestic political landscape alone, had wanted to opt for eliminationist, including exterminationist, politics, what aspects of the international system in any of these three periods would have deterred them from going forward? What in the international system then or today would prevent them from setting their policies in motion? What in the international system would have stopped, or would today stop, them from carrying them out? What about the international system would have made, or would make, punishment certain, so that it even approximated justice, not the International Criminal Tribunal for the former Yugoslavia's four-year (and unbelievably costly) charade of Milošević's trial (which ended inconclusively with his death)? In each case the answer is, effectively, *nothing.*

Crafting a new international political environment to reduce eliminationist and exterminationist politics' incidence and scope requires that we consider such an environment's various possible features, and the mechanisms to bring them about. Of course, any such changes depend upon states and their leaders in some fashion reforming themselves—admittedly a tall order. But, as we now know, our time has seen unforeseeable progress in other enormously difficult areas, including domestic civil and human rights, war, and imperialism. Such advances show that if the proper policies are designed with a realistic view of the current international community, taking its manifold weaknesses into account, then progress in combating eliminationist politics is also possible.

Stopping Eliminationist Politics

How do we break out of this suffocating, mass murder–abetting cynicism and inertia? In principle, it should not be difficult. The world's non-mass-murdering countries are wealthy and powerful, having prodigious military capabilities (and they can band together). The countries perpetrating mass murder and eliminationist politics, or tempted to do so, are overwhelmingly poor and weak (and each stands alone). Many could easily be stopped with a little military power and probably with other available, easily employable means. The powerful countries seriously applying their resources would radically change potential perpetrators' cost-benefit calculus, heavily tilting the scales toward noneliminationist political options.

What might a world standing against eliminationist and exterminationist politics look like? Of a political and legal response to mass murder and eliminationist politics' three components—prevention, cessation or intervention, and punishment—the international community should focus on prevention. For three reasons: First, ideally eliminationist assaults would never begin (precluding the need for intervention and justice). We also know—or at least can strongly presume—that prevention works. It is manifestly so that our era's mass murders and eliminations do not constitute the full set that would have happened had no deterrents—no domestic or international preventive structures—been in place. The simple fact is that democratic political institutions, in contrast to nondemocratic or tyrannical political institutions, radically reduce eliminationist politics' incidence. This fact alone shows prevention's feasibility and, in principle, easy achievability. Prevention works in many other realms internationally (war—how many countries would attack others if there were no military deterrence?) and domestically (crime) to reduce undesired and proscribed deeds. Second, developing an effective prevention regime, whatever the difficulty, is substantially easier than an interventionist one, which the world's countries and their international institutions have shown no willingness to create—and, with the Americans' (and their allies') difficulty in Iraq and Afghanistan, will be still less likely to want, at least for the foreseeable future. External intervention's recent successful instances, though heartening insofar as any such intervention is better than what came before, are less auspicious than they may seem. East Timor was a rare instance today of *imperialist* eliminationism, so it probably has little relevance for domestic eliminationist assaults and, even there, two decades of inaction preceded the intervention. The former Yugoslavia was the closest to some kind of proximity to Western consciences and interests causing huge refugee problems and destabilizing the region, yet even there only after colossal human tolls did NATO—but not the United Nations—mobilize itself to act. So the status quo continues: Eliminationist politics, with few exceptions, stop either when the perpetrating regime finishes its job or decides for other internal reasons to halt the assault, or when the perpetrating regime is defeated in war for reasons having little if anything to do with the eliminationist politics itself. Finally, establishing a preventive regime is also preferable to relying on a justice regime, which operates *after* the mass extermination and elimination have taken their toll. Furthermore, instituting a preventive regime is easier than developing a regime meting out genuine justice (to all perpetrators and not just a select few), i.e., justice that includes some certainty of timely punishment and that fulfills the extensive requirements of perpetrators' political, material, and moral repair to right the wrongs and to repair the harm as best they can.

In thinking about prevention, we should bear in mind eliminationist campaigns' frequent unpredictability. We need general measures that *by their ordinary functioning* will reduce mass slaughters and eliminations. In certain instances, an eliminationist assault, including mass murder's potential imminence, becomes obvious, as it was in Rwanda and Kosovo. In such cases specific interventionist measures ought to be taken (just as intervention can occur immediately, or any time, after the slaughtering begins). But in general, and this is most relevant for crafting anti-eliminationist policies, we cannot count on foreknowledge or, in instances we acquire it, assume the relevant outside actors will decisively act to forestall the assault.

Thinking seriously about prevention should build upon the analysis of the critical political and nonpolitical factors generally producing mass murder and eliminationist politics: (1) features about modernity itself and the modern state; (2) structural relationships of certain states; (3) the international context (or environment); (4) beliefs about certain groups and understandings of politics and society that lead political leaders and their followers to think eliminating those groups desirable; and (5) proximate factors producing the political opportunity and will to turn eliminationist desires into eliminationist onslaughts.

In principle, prevention can take place and therefore target any or all of these factors. But as a practical matter, all these factors are not equally susceptible to alteration. If altered, not all would be equally efficacious in reducing eliminationist politics' incidence and destructiveness. And not all are as easily or likely to be targeted with the necessary measures. Still, examining each one, at first briefly, can help point the way toward thinking more seriously about crafting effective and adequate policies.

The modern state's enormously greater power and the concomitant awareness it can engage in transformative (including eliminationist) projects will only grow. Reorienting political leaders away from destructive toward positive transformative projects may be possible. Yet if we think more imaginatively about the modern state's capacities, we see the international community has failed to recognize and exploit these capacities properly, and therefore to beneficially employ and further this generally positive aspect of modernity. The modern state's transformative power, ability to monitor its domain, to influence and alter its every corner, and to learn quickly new possibilities, processes, and techniques from others have been almost completely lost on the international community, regarding its members individually and collectively considering their own *international* transformative capacities. The modern international community, like the modern nation-state, has enormously greater capacity to know what transpires anywhere in the world, including by monitoring its member states' actions within their own countries, and to effect change with direct intervention and by teaching lessons to its constituent members. Just as today's state capacity to effect transformative change dwarfs that of earlier states, today's international state system's parallel power dwarfs that of its predecessors. True, the international community's stepwise development lagged the modern state's at home, taking off only after World War II with the advent of modern telecommunications, supersonic transport, and the United States' emergence as a superpower with a presence and ability to project power all over the world. The international community's capacity to monitor events recently substantially advanced even more with satellites blanketing the globe—providing imagery even to private corporations and organizations, and to you (through Google)—with the Internet's worldwide instant audio and visual communications, and with all manner of economic, nongovernmental organizational, media, and other personnel, which together compose the de facto information agents of globalization and allow their ever-increasing penetration of virtually all countries. The international system's members have chosen, by and large, to exercise its modern strengths not on what goes on *within* its members' borders, but overwhelmingly on relations among its members. Despite having these enormous capacities, the international community's leaders have chosen not to reorient their decades-long successful emphasis from stopping violence between countries to addressing violence within countries, which is where eliminationist (and other kinds of) violence has overwhelmingly shifted.

Thinking hard about how to translate the modern international system's vast capacities into commensurate practices that would diminish eliminationist politics can yield enormous benefits. In fact, any major prevention strategy's assumption is that states, acting singly and in concert, including by altering the system's fundamentals, *do* have the power to effect such positive transformative politics. While this seems obvious, it is not articulated or taken seriously as a foundation for stamping out eliminationist politics. And it compels us to ask: If the world's anti-eliminationist political leaders genuinely wanted to use their countries' colossal aggregate power to establish policies to reduce such politics' frequency and destructiveness, what would they do?

The second feature of our age's politics that has structurally transformed social antagonisms into the basis for eliminationist politics is the inclusion of all people into politics, meaning that they make or at least potentially will make political, economic, and social demands that cause tyrants and dominant political groups to feel insecure and therefore to be ready to contemplate using violence to eliminate their problem somehow. As Felix Dzerzhinsky, the founder of the Soviet Cheka, explains: "We are terrorizing the enemies of the Soviet government so as to suppress crime in embryo."[15] Even if the Soviets and other communist regimes took this eliminationist logic (by "crime," Dzerzhinsky meant all real or imaginary opposition to the regime and its policies), the logic operates in all nondemocratic, namely tyrannical, regimes, creating an eliminationist propensity. This eliminationist propensity, and the insecurity underlying it, is exacerbated by the dual transitions many countries face: to capitalism and to an industrial or more advanced economy. And to building a nation, which necessitates all people's inclusion in a generally acceptable political and social compact. Each transition typically causes substantial social strains, political demands, and conflicts. An additional, recent structural development, ever more disruptive to settled domestic arrangements, is globalization, which, with its international economic, cultural, and political influences, opens up and closes off opportunities to certain groups and people, creating winners and losers, whether they are ethnic, geographic, or class-based groups. These conflicts can create or exacerbate tensions, increase insecurity, and alter cost-benefit ratios, resulting in political leaders' considering eliminationist politics.

Although conflicts emerging from such structural conditions in themselves do not produce mass murder or eliminations, reducing such conflicts' frequency, scope, or intensity would diminish the basis for political leaders and elites considering employing eliminationist political means. The problem is that those (erroneously) claiming these structural conditions *cause* mass murder would also like—unrealistically and probably to the detriment of many countries' peoples—to stop or greatly curtail these transitions to capitalism and economic development, to nation-building, people's full political inclusion into their country's politics, and to globalization. Whatever these modernizing and globalizing processes' unevenness and short- and medium-term costs and transitions, whatever the considerable need to better manage them, they are surely necessary for general long-term greater prosperity. Within each country, domestic accommodations can be made to relieve the resulting tensions and conflicts, but that differs from self-defeatingly trying to derail these processes because they can engender conflicts, sometimes providing the basis for political leaders and their supporters to seek certain groups' elimination.

Our age's third contributing factor, the international context, has been differently permissive toward eliminationist politics, creating powerful positive or negative incentives for political leaders considering the advisability and feasibility of slaughtering or eliminating unwanted and hated groups. *This* aspect of the eliminationist equation can be radically and effectively altered to reduce such politics' practice. If, for example, the world's powerful countries created and honored an ironclad guarantee that they would invade any country whose people perpetrated mass murder or elimination, stop it, and capture or kill the political leaders, many fewer eliminationist assaults would occur. The tyrants and their cohorts, typically in poor and weak countries, would know that, even if they did not care for their own lives or power (though most obviously dearly do), their now-quixotic, eliminationist policy would be self-defeating. How the international context can be made less permissive toward and more effective in preventing mass murder and elimination, short of such guaranteed measures, is discussed below.

Whatever a country's existing strains and conflicts, ultimately the fourth factor—political leaders' and their critical followers' understanding of the groups they consider pernicious or obstacles to cherished goals—leads to an eliminationist orientation, or not. Such beliefs are typically grounded in (often long-standing) prejudices and hatreds, or derive from an ideological orientation at the core of the political leaders' and followers' stance toward politics, their country, and its future. So altering these views in the short or medium term, and thereby reducing the cognitive and ideological basis for eliminationist or exterminationist politics, is not feasible. Of course, if a new political context internationally and domestically lowers political conflicts' stakes, how political leaders and their followers view certain groups might also improve. This could be a secondary effect of other changes, yet targeting the potential perpetrators' beliefs and values is unlikely to be an efficacious preventive strategy. The eliminationist ideologies rooted not in classical domestic conflicts over territory, resources, or power, but in dehumanizing or demonizing conceptions of certain groups, would in any case not be susceptible to such changes or attempts. The most obvious, widespread, and dangerous such ideology today is Political Islam.

Finally, proximate factors create political leaders' opportunity to transform eliminationist desires into violent eliminationist assaults. Here the modern international system's power can be applied, and policies can be designed to prevent opportunities necessary for political leaders to initiate mass annihilation or elimination from appearing. Thus, in the intersection of proximate factors with the international system (and the context it provides), success in crafting prevention can occur.

Having worked through the five major factors contributing to eliminationist politics, thinking in a hardheaded manner about prevention should continue by building upon the analysis of the immediate general conditions that produce mass murder and eliminationist politics: Political leaders deciding to opt for such politics are able to do so institutionally, and have followers willing to implement the policies. The leaders moved by a conception of the victims, embedded in their understanding of their polity and society (or the ones they desire) and power's dictates, opt at a seemingly propitious time to eliminate the victims or their putative threat. Institutionally, they must be able to put through policies domestically, and not face an international environment determined to make eliminationist politics suicidal. They must believe themselves to be powerful, effective, and immune. Followers must possess a conception of the victims, and a sense of impunity and necessity, that leads them to believe slaughtering or eliminating their neighbors and countrymen, women, and children, is right and desirable, and possible. A prevention regime cannot effectively address all of these elements. Eliminationist politics' sine qua non—for political leaders only slightly less than their followers—is the conception of the victims, typically deep prejudice and hatred, leading the perpetrators to mark targeted groups as fundamentally different and dangerous and therefore in need of elimination. This, though powerfully driving eliminationist politics of all kinds, is, unfortunately, strongly resistant to an *international* prevention regime. Why? Combating prejudice and hatreds is notoriously difficult and can succeed only with enormous effort from *within* the prejudiced society itself, which is extraordinarily unlikely to be pursued in countries such notions and emotions plague. Education, the hoped-for general panacea, is, in any case, not a viable short- or medium-term option. This is so, without accounting for education's dubious effectiveness—in general because of ideology's self-validating and corrective-resistant power, and in particular when the education originates outside a country. Even when efficacious, which it has been on occasion in unusual circumstances after national or regional trauma and effective occupation (Germany and Japan after World War II), the benefits appear only after assiduous application lasting years, decades, or generations.[16]

Eliminationist politics' constituent features—initiation, institutional freedom to act, and implementation—can each be addressed. Even though the prejudices and hatreds, the conceptions of groups and peoples that dehumanize or demonize them, that typically move political leaders to slaughter or eliminate large population groups, are in their essence irrational, the first constituent feature of eliminationist politics, the leaders' decisions to initiate such programs, are still overwhelmingly clearheaded, calculated, and purposeful, in other words rational in rationality's instrumental sense. In most instances, political leaders opt for such politics only when the opportunity appears propitious for success and to offer *substantially* more political and social benefits than costs. The international community can profoundly affect this calculus.

If eliminationist politics' projected cost-benefit ratio became systematically weighted so the costs overwhelmingly outweighed the benefits, then such politics' incidence would decline enormously. If we focus on increasing the probability not that perpetrators would actually fail to kill or expel their victims but that they would lose power and their lives, then several paths open up. A guarantee should exist that any political leader initiating a mass slaughter or elimination faces severe punishment. A guarantee should exist that his country's membership in all international institutions is immediately suspended, and a total economic embargo is placed upon it. These would end only when the eliminationist assault ends *and* the country's and the armed forces' leaders are dead or surrender themselves to the competent international authorities.

Just as a conception of targeted groups as pernicious and deserving of elimination has been a prerequisite for eliminationist politics, so has such politics' second constituent feature: the institutional freedom to act, more specifically a domestic politics making eliminationist programs possible to plan, enact, and carry out. Institutionally, such a politics' foundation is the absence of democratic institutions, checks, and controls. The past century's record is clear. Whatever a society's and its leaders' passions, prejudices, hatreds, a democratic political dispensation is a powerful brake on their being translated into action. Genuinely democratic institutions (inauthentic exceptions proving the rule) create strong safeguards, including ideological ones, against eliminationist politics and violence. Given that in our time democratic regimes—including in countries that had previously seen mass murder, notably across Latin America—rarely resort domestically to eliminationist politics, and given democracy's representative mechanisms, a world of democracies would be a safer world. Enormously fewer mass murders, expulsions, incarcerations, and other associated violence would blight the globe.

The international community could easily do much more to affect eliminationist politics' second constituent feature—by focusing on transforming tyrannies into democracies. If the international community withdrew the broad and substantial legitimacy it bountifully confers on tyrants, dictators, nondemocratic leaders of all stripes, stopped treating them as though they legitimately represent their countries and peoples, it would both delegitimize these leaders and regimes domestically, and tangibly pressure them to change. The mechanisms and further arguments for doing this I discuss below.

The third constituent feature in the eliminationist political complex is implementation, which revolves around political leaders' followers being willing to become perpetrators. The international community's capacity to directly influence perpetrators or would-be perpetrators— those physically rounding up, expelling, torturing, and killing the victims—is limited. Often outsiders have little access. The perpetrators' or would-be perpetrators' prejudices and hatreds, confirmed and legitimized by their country's political leadership, are often so consuming that they wholeheartedly accept the wisdom and necessity of slaughtering or eliminating their targeted enemies. Still, we should try low-cost interventions. When mass murder or mass expulsions are under way, or it becomes obvious such politics may be imminent, the country should be bombarded with radio broadcasts, leaflets dropped from airplanes, and Internet postings of all kinds and e-mail messages informing its people that (1) mass murder and elimination are immoral and illegal assaults against *all* humanity, (2) the international community condemns them, and (3) anyone participating or abetting these deeds is liable to prosecution when the perpetrating regime falls, WHICH IT WILL. The broadcasts, transmissions, and leaflets should emphasize the international community's commitment to toppling the mass-murdering regime, and underline emphatically that "following orders" will be no defense, legally or morally. Examples of perpetrators from other countries having paid dearly for their mass murdering and associated acts would be added.

Such informational barrages' advantages are several. Many people among the groups from which the perpetrators are drawn need a reality check, a wake-up call revealing that the international community, world of neutral outsiders, condemns critical aspects of their worldviews, including the rightness of brutalizing, expelling, or slaughtering others. Some, perhaps many, would reconsider the eliminationist policies (others would not). Furthermore, when facing prosecution, no perpetrator could plausibly claim he was ignorant his deeds were prosecutable transgressions or use following orders as a viable defense.

One highly critical subset of followers is far more prone to international persuasion: the political leaders' lieutenants and high-ranking subordinates. It should be made emphatically and indisputably clear to them that holding leadership positions in the government or in military or police or administrative bodies initiating or carrying out eliminationist assaults makes them automatically liable for guaranteed punishment when the regime falls, WHICH IT WILL, *even if they as individuals do not transmit eliminationist orders or perpetrate violence.* In other words, it should be communicated to all high-level officials that by not opposing eliminationist politics they endanger themselves. They should resist such politics and if, despite their resistance, mass murder or elimination begins, they must resign or leave (surreptitiously) their positions immediately. Without this second and third tier of political, military, police, and administrative leaders and officers, a country's leadership will be substantially more reluctant to practice mass elimination.

All relevant international institutions—the United Nations or any successor organization, regional political entities including the European Union, African Union, Association of Southeast Nations, and Organization of American States, international military and security associations including NATO, international trade institutions, chiefly the World Trade Organization, international law enforcement and criminal justice institutions, including Interpol and the International Criminal Court, among others—should produce a handbook or series of handbooks spelling out high officeholders' responsibilities to prevent and resist eliminationist politics, and their culpability and penalties for failure. Such handbooks should be sent in every conceivable way—regular mail, e-mail, through international institutions, disseminated to local media—to every relevant officeholder in every country of the world, the moment a new government is formed or an individual takes office or gets promoted to specified political, administrative, military, and security offices. These officeholders' and officers' senior staff should be held similarly responsible and receive the same information, which would also spur them to inform their superiors. Every senior political, administrative, military, or police leader will know he will not be able to claim ignorance of his legal responsibility and culpability, or, through the means mentioned above, of the legal prohibition on such acts. The absolving cover that a perpetrator merely was following orders will dissolve as a rationale bolstering criminal cooperation or, after the fact, as an exculpatory option.

A robust prevention regime combating eliminationist and mass-murdering politics ought to do two things. The first, and most effective, component creates conditions preventing political leaders from even considering such politics. Changing political regimes from tyrannies to democracies would remove the principal institutional conditions permissive toward and even promoting eliminationist politics. It would also immediately or gradually change political leaders' mindset toward seeing eliminationist measures as part of an actual, practical, or sensible political repertoire. Genuine democracy's institutional checks against such politics would radically alter the cost-benefit analysis of leaders daring to contemplate murdering or eliminating hated or unwanted groups. This can be conceived as deterrence, in fact the most effective deterrence, because it essentially takes the acts off the table.

An effective prevention regime's second component addresses those instances when political leaders—whether in tyrannies or democracies—do contemplate eliminationist programs. It makes the costs so overwhelming that even these political leaders will ultimately opt for a noneliminationist path. This is deterrence of a more conventional and obvious kind. It changes the international political regime's aspects permissive toward and even promoting eliminationist politics. Deterrence works by changing the cost-benefit analysis of the wholly or mainly rational, potential mass-murdering and eliminationist leaders, and of the followers at all levels, especially in command positions. If they, particularly the leaders, know that acting upon their eliminationist desires will almost certainly lead to their loss of power and imprisonment or death, choosing an eliminationist solution will not make practical sense.

Each principal component of a prevention regime—increasing the number of democratic countries and creating a resistant international environment—could by itself make mass murder and eliminationist politics all but a thing of the past. Each is feasible or at least reasonably feasible. Still, a fully robust anti-eliminationist regime would include other features, especially more intensive interventionist measures to make eliminationist politics too costly and more difficult to pursue successfully.

Leaders initiating mass murder and eliminations know that if they *fail* they will likely be deposed or worse. But because the condition of their embarking on such an inherently dangerous enterprise is their belief in their impunity and confidence of success, fear for their own power or safety hardly comes into play. Throughout our age, mass-murdering leaders have shown contempt for the international community's capacities. When American Ambassador to Turkey Henry Morgenthau reacted to Mehmet Talât's declaration in 1915 that his regime would follow through on its decision to eliminate the Armenians by telling Talât that "they would be condemned by the world," Talât responded (in Morgenthau's words) that "they would know how to defend themselves; in other words, he does not give a damn."[17] Three-quarters of a century later, Ali Hasan al-Majid, Saddam's cousin and the organizer and commander of the exterminationist assault upon Iraq's Kurds, which earned him the moniker "Chemical Ali," indicated how little had changed. He, more colorfully, conveyed the international community's ineffectiveness in deterring our age's mass murderers. Speaking of the Kurds who would refuse to be deported, Hasan al-Majid declared: "I will kill them all with chemical weapons! Who is going to say anything? The international community? Fuck them! The international community, and those who listen to them!"[18]*

This long-standing, well-founded sense of impunity from the international community must be changed. Eliminationist politics' political leaders and principal perpetrators must be told that—even if eliminationist assaults succeed—they will be severely punished. They then must actually be punished. Several steps would accomplish this simply and effectively.

An authoritative international watchdog organization should be created to identify mass murder and eliminations wherever they are practiced. The organization's membership should be restricted to genuine democracies. Obviously, dictatorships (and sham democracies), by definition criminal and illegitimate, cannot have a say in an organization's operations meant to prevent exactly such regimes in particular from becoming even worse transgressors and more murderous. The criteria for a state to be deemed engaging in eliminationist politics should be minimal. Let's face it: Today it is usually easy to determine when a government, using its own formal security forces or its thinly disguised surrogates, is slaughtering or expelling or incarcerating groups of people or at least to have reason to suspect it is, and therefore have good cause to investigate the situation. Widespread reports of mass murder come first from surviving victims. Large population shifts suddenly occur. Refugees stream into neighboring countries (without credible evidence the refugees are fleeing conventional military operations). "Disappearances" of large numbers of people, including family and friends, become known. The perpetrating state closes the country or certain regions to outside media. Aerial and satellite imagery nonetheless provides pictorial evidence of despoliation and destruction. If the watchdog organization deems an investigation necessary, suspected countries' noncooperation should be taken as prima facie indication of guilt.

---

*Hasan al-Majid was tried and convicted for his mass murders only twenty years later, after the United States and Britain defeated Saddam for reasons that had nothing to do with the eliminationist assaults on the Kurds or others.

When this organization decides an eliminationist program is under way, it automatically triggers certain interventionist measures to stop the eliminationist assault. From the moment the watchdog organization learns of a possible new mass murder or elimination program, the organization must issue its ruling speedily; in a week's time at most. Remember: Perpetrators can brutalize and kill thousands, tens of thousands of people every day.

International law ought to be changed to buttress other measures to combat the most devastating complex of transgressions in existence, for which it currently is all but ineffectual. I say this without great regard for international law, as its relationship to domestic law in democracies is in name more than substance. This is so for two main reasons. The international society or community in the sense of being a real society or community—according to the nature of domestic societies, such as Italy, Japan, or Canada, or even the hybrid European Union—is mainly a fiction. The international community is really a loose collection of individual states—not even the societies and peoples they rule—that come together to agree or disagree, and work or more often not work together, on only a limited range of matters when convenient. There is little sense of actual community. People's density of relations, mutual dependence, and sense of identity within their own societies, as members of a people or a nation, or as sharing in a political compact as citizens, are all missing from the international community. Existing international law is very much detached from any grounding in the actual practices and concerns of the people inhabiting this international noncommunity. Those making international law, such as the genocide convention, exacerbate this condition enormously. The lawmakers include multiple criminal entities, the world's tyrannical regimes. Thus, international law floats above the world's societies so no democratic accountability exists. The international law that gets made emerges through high-level bargaining among states, many of which should be likened to domestic crime syndicates.

Still, international law and treaties are all we have, and so we must work to some extent within their parameters. But we should not fetishize this law as sacrosanct, or even treat it with the ordinary respect democratic countries' law receives. Given international law's near-total inadequacy regarding humanity's greatest offenses—worse, given its enabling quality for the world's mass murderers and eliminators—we should not treat it as a guide to right action. Certainly better international law is preferable, as is following it when possible, but if international law inhibits a country or group of countries (or even individuals) from intervening to stop a state program of mass slaughter or elimination because no legal provision authorizes such intervention, then we should treat this body of law with the contempt it calls upon itself.

International law has codified "crimes against humanity" as well as the "crime of genocide," and "war crimes." They are part of the UN genocide convention (and the International Criminal Court's statutes). In addition to the many other disqualifying problems of this convention and its treatment of mass murder and elimination, conceiving of these acts as *crimes* erects the inadequate frame for understanding and responding to them: law enforcement. *Crime against humanity* sounds grave, but crime does not convey the transgression's enormity, the situation's emergency, and the utterly urgent need to respond. Crime is dealt with by law enforcement, in an orderly way, and people feel little responsibility for crime and law enforcement in foreign countries. *Leave it to them.* Crime is also not inherently political—indeed, it usually is *not* political—and therefore understood not to be of national and international consequence or relevance. If instead eliminationist politics were conceptualized and legally codified as what it much more resembles, and what its own perpetrators think of it as, killing and population expulsion on war's massive scale, and for its same ends—power, territory, domination, scarce resources, national and communal defense, and vanquishing a hated or feared enemy—such politics would be more appropriately and adequately framed and understood as a particular and particularly acute form of war. A new legal concept and law proscribing it would follow, called *war against humanity.* The advantages of this, beyond semantic preference, are several. *War against humanity* more accurately characterizes the magnitude and character of the phenomena currently falling under the rubrics of *crimes against humanity* and the *crime of genocide. War against humanity* characterizes them more accurately according to the perpetrators' conception—throughout our time and around the world—of what they do, which is not anything that could be remotely related to crime, but clearly a war against a dangerous or recalcitrant enemy. *War against humanity* also characterizes them more accurately according to the deeds' objective character: War's scope is vast. Crime's scope is small. States wage war. (Starting recently so do state-like entities, such as Hezbollah, from non-state-controlled areas.) Crimes are committed in defiance of the state. Wars are systematic, mobilize an enormous number of people and institutions, have leaders and followers, and are pursued for political ends. Most crimes have none of these qualities—of particular note is crime's generally apolitical character. Wars threaten everyone in their way. Crimes selectively victimize. Wars require countermobilization, that states and peoples make immense efforts to resist the enemy. Responsible law enforcement professionals deal with crime. Warmakers must be defeated. Crimes must be solved and punished. War must be eradicated from human relations. Crimes are something we will always live with.

Crimes against humanity, bad as it sounds, has an oxymoronic quality. (Even its conceptualization as a plural—crimes—an agglomeration of individual acts, rather than an integral extreme violent political program, reveals its foundational misguidedness.) This is particularly so in our time, which has progressively seen war itself steadily metamorphose from opposing military forces mainly engaging each other to outright slaughters (and expulsions) of unarmed civilians. The ratio of military to civilian deaths and injuries during war was ten military casualties for every civilian casualty during World War I. Even in World War II, which became infamous for the Germans' slaughter of civilians, the ratio was one to one. Since 1945, in more than two hundred civil wars—most wars have been fought *within* countries—the civilian to military casualty ratio has nearly reversed. Civilian deaths and injuries now outstrip military ones, by more than nine to one.[19] War's relationship to mass murder and eliminationist politics more broadly—as we now know from examining many eliminationist assaults and as the death figures powerfully show—is *not* that mass murder is war's byproduct. Mass murder and eliminationist campaigns against targeted civilian groups or peoples have been ever more the reason for, and goal of, war, ever more what war is. If Carl von Clausewitz is correct that war is politics' continuation by other means, today we must say that *that* politics is substantially the politics of elimination and extermination. (That this politics of war has emerged and come to predominate should not be surprising. Its causes are the same conditions of modernity that produce our time's mass eliminationist politics.) Once we recognize that (1) such politics' practice constitutes *war* and not a collection of crimes, and (2) what has been considered those crimes' object—not individual people but *humanity*—is correctly understood as exterminationist and eliminationist assaults' objects, then (3) the justification of reconceptualizing mass murder and other eliminations as *war against humanity* becomes even more compelling.

Unlike *crimes* against humanity, *war against humanity* precisely captures the character and magnitude of perpetrators' onslaughts in another fundamental way. When someone says that entire classes of people do not deserve to live, or live among us, he essentially declares war on a part of humanity, which qualifies, and should legally qualify, as war on humanity in general. How can we know the perpetrators will stop after completing their eliminationist assault on the first group or groups they target, or in the first country they target? The Turks did not. The Germans during the Nazi period did not. The Japanese did not. The Soviets did not. Where would Pol Pot have ended had he stayed in power or had somehow been able to conquer other countries? The Serbs went from area to area in the former Yugoslavia on their mass-murderous and eliminationist drives. Had they not been stopped, they likely would have gone still further. The Hutu mass murderers, defeated by the invading Tutsi army, retreated to neighboring Democratic Republic of the Congo, where they plunged that vast country and people further into chaos, slaughtering people, creating famine conditions, and raping women on a vast scale. Saddam's mass murdering might have expanded exponentially had he defeated Iran or gained the nuclear weapons he was seeking in the 1980s with enormous determination and resources (nearly completing a nuclear facility before the Israelis destroyed it in 1981). The Political Islamists today slaughtered millions in Southern Sudan and then, almost predictably, started a subsequent and ongoing exterminationist and eliminationist drive in the country's Darfur region. Political Islamists have genocide bombers active around the Middle East, in Europe, in Asia, and in the United States. Hezbollah's Hassan Nasrallah, perhaps the most influential and inspirational suicide bombing leader within Political Islam, has openly declared the advisability of striking everywhere. At a rally in Lebanon's

Bekaa Valley, broadcast on Hezbollah's television network, he urged Palestinians: "Martyrdom operations—suicide bombings—should be exported outside Palestine," Nasrallah declared. "I encourage Palestinians to take suicide bombings worldwide. Don't be shy about it."[20] While Hamas, Islamic Jihad, and other Palestinian genocide bombing groups have not yet acted upon this, their and other Political Islamists' potential to carry out Nasrallah's hortatory threat exists. Political Islamists, especially Mahmoud Ahmadinejad, have regularly issued such threats, to strike everywhere with hundreds of "martyrs," during moments of political tension. This is a small but significant part of Political Islamists' more general calls to slaughter millions. And they have been spearheaded by the Iranian regime's highly aggressive orientation toward many countries, bankroll, and drive to acquire nuclear weapons. Political Islamists have regional, continental, and, for some, even global eliminationist ambitions. At any moment, any Jew, any Dane, even the pope can become their target, just for being a Jew, a Dane, or speaking one's mind, or for not wanting a country and its people to be annihilated, for just being a country's citizen where political cartoons are permitted, for remarking that one religion is superior to another or insulting the Prophet Muhammad. Eliminationist perpetrators' unmistakable record is that once conducting an exterminationist and eliminationist war against one part of humanity, their eliminationist aspirations frequently expand, imperiling other, often many, parts of humanity.

War against humanity conveys the alarming threat mass murderers and eliminationist perpetrators pose, and countries' and peoples' urgent need to mobilize themselves to fight it. Theirs is a war against everyone or potentially everyone. It must be met with single-minded effort and full force. It must be defeated. It is an emergency situation entailing sacrifice, including individual sacrifice for greater good. That is why, in principle, none of us is a bystander. We are all implicated in the war itself. Humanity must engage a *war against humanity* with all possible military means to safeguard itself, and its every part.

All humanity, all states, all political leaders, may and should seek to immediately defeat those waging *war against humanity*. This would empower and legitimize any state or group of states or, for that matter, nonstate groups or individuals to take conventional military action or covert measures against the perpetrators, who in conducting a war against *humanity* imperil everyone, making killing the perpetrators a defensive act. War's permissive rules would apply instead of law enforcement's highly restrictive rules, which ordinarily disallow cross-border activity. Neighboring states, alliances such as NATO, and powers that can conduct out-of-area operations such as the United States, France, and Britain would need no further justification for acting to stop mass murder or expulsions or incarcerations. All the alibis for inaction the United Nations' multiple failures provide would disappear. Relevant states and their leaders would face increased pressure to act, because everyone would know of their authority and their presumptive duty to act. Beyond conventional military intervention, such arrangements would have two additional extremely powerful effects.

Once they have initiated a *war against humanity*, the perpetrators remain in a state of war even if their eliminationist assault ends for whatever reason. The perpetrators would fall under the international legal doctrine Hostis Humani Generis, *enemies of humanity*, until now applied to pirates. This would mean the perpetrators would never have peace or immunity because, in a perpetual state of war, and as *enemies of humanity*, they could always be legally killed or captured, by open or covert means. Moreover, just as the Nuremberg International Military Tribunal held the members of the German cabinet, the Nazi Party Leadership Corps, the entire SS and SA (the Nazis' paramilitary), the Gestapo, and the General Staff and High Command of the German armed forces "criminal" groups and organizations, so too this new anti-eliminationist international regime would recognize and define the offending country's government, governing political parties, armed forces, police and security forces, and paramilitary forces (in their entirety or just their leaderships) as what they are: vast criminal organizations, and their members part of criminal conspiracies making "aggressive war," in this case a *war against humanity*.[21] This would make the perpetrating regime's leaders and members of its governmental and state institutions legally culpable for their institutions' mass-murdering, expulsion, and associated eliminationist acts, which they would know to be the case because they would have been forewarned of this, and of their duty to immediately resign from their state and governmental (now criminal) organizations upon eliminationist attacks' initiation—in the aforementioned educational handbooks and other materials given to them in multiple forms upon taking office. This material would also inform them of additional perils they face, including the following.

A further crucial measure of placing bounties on these leading perpetrators, namely all these institutions' leaders and close subordinates, would ensure they would never again sleep peacefully. The sums, substantial enough to make a person in a poor society wealthy, would all be easily fundable for wealthy countries: something on the order of $10 million for killing or delivering the perpetrating regime's leader or top leaders, $1 million for every cabinet minister, military or police general-staff member, $100,000 for their assistants would provide powerful incentives for others to hunt down or remove these people from power. How many political leaders, particularly of tyrannies, could be sure even their own bodyguards would not turn on them for such (or even lesser) sums? How many cabinet ministers, high-level advisers, and others, who would not even have the protection a regime's leader enjoys, would feel or be safe? More important, all these measures, particularly the bounties, would prospectively bear heavily upon them, as the leaders, their staff, advisers, and high-level subordinates weigh initiating and implementing an eliminationist program against the substantial prospect of making themselves hotly sought-after, million-dollar targets? How many such people would choose to pass a high probability of a death sentence upon themselves? Power and the good life are typically paramount among political leaders' and their lieutenants' goals, so why would they guarantee any person in their country or in the world $100,000, $1 million, or $10 million for killing them?

Singly or together, countries or international bodies, Germany, France, or Japan or the European Union or NATO, could offer such bounties. For the United States this would not entail a wholly new initiative but a small though enormously efficacious alteration in its current policy, as it has long had its Rewards for Justice program in place targeting those wanted for terrorism. The program, established in 1984 and further enhanced after 9/11, has led to the killing and apprehension of major terrorists, including Saddam's mass murdering sons Uday and Qusay, and Ramzi Yousef, the mastermind of the first World Trade Center bombing in February 1993. Its payouts, as high as $1 million or

$5 million for most major terrorists, and $25 million for Osama bin Laden and Ayman al-Zawahiri, have totaled $77 million to more than fifty people. The program, which rewards information about impending terrorist attacks, has also led to the prevention of major attacks. The program has been expanded to cover certain people wanted for participating in the Rwandan and Yugoslavian genocides, and has led to major perpetrators' apprehension, including Tharcisse Renzaho, Jean-Baptiste Gatete, and Yusuf John Munyakazi, currently awaiting trial at the International Criminal Tribunal for Rwanda. Yet, for statutory reasons, the program applies only to those few people the Rwandan and Yugoslavian tribunals have already *indicted,* and not more generally to the many people wanted for participating in mass murder and elimination.

The United States, the Europeans, and others could use this already effective program as a foundation, though they must expand it considerably to have the desired effects. From a program that, regarding mass murder and elimination, is retrospective and ad hoc (only to Rwanda and Yugoslavia) and narrow (targeting only people already indicted), it would need to resemble more the antiterrorism component, which targets those *wanted* for their crimes and *promises to target* future terrorists. But in working to prevent the much more massive eliminationist assaults, with many more masterminds and high-level participants, it must also go beyond the antiterrorist program by covering a much wider range of people and not only seeking their arrest but also authorizing their killing. And, unlike the International Criminal Court, it must not use law enforcement and criminal justice's cumbersome and enormously difficult standards of criminal trial proof that has led the court's prosecutor to take five years even to get to recommending an arrest warrant for al-Bashir, all the while—with every passing day—the Sudanese regime slaughtered and eliminated people, totaling millions. Thus, an anti–mass murder and elimination monetary prevention program would:

1. *Automatically* apply to those perpetrating *wars against humanity* so all those considering mass murder and elimination *know* they will become targets.
2. Target people *wanted* for such offenses, and not only those indicted.

3. Substantially expand the program's universe of people *automatically* deemed culpable and therefore wanted and therefore targeted to include all state or governmental institutions' high officeholders, their subordinates, and prominent perpetrators.
4. Pay the substantial rewards not only for information leading to the arrest or conviction of the culpable but also for killing them, which is necessary because many people would be able to kill perpetrators inaccessible to the international community.

If such a program is justified (as it is) and cost effective (as it is) for preventing terrorist attacks that might kill a few dozen or hundreds, it is certainly justified and cost effective for preventing mass murders and eliminations of tens of thousands or hundreds of thousands, and that produce untold suffering for hundreds of thousands or millions more.* A further incentive to countries to establish such a program, and the other preventive measures proposed here, is that their costs are massively outweighed by the costs to the international community of even one humanitarian mission or nation-building endeavor or attempt to bring eliminationist perpetrators to justice after the fact, which often, as it does in Darfur, costs *billions*. (Just the U.S. government's aid to pick up only some of the pieces after the Serbs' eliminationist assault on just Bosnia was $1.35 billion in the first ten years. The cost of justice at the International Criminal Tribunal for the former Yugoslavia alone has topped $1.5 billion.)[22]

The state of war with the perpetrators would end only with their deaths, capture, or surrender to the International Criminal Court, where the only two sentences for conviction of *war against humanity* ought to be life in prison or death. People differ enormously on the death penalty's morality and wisdom. I will not join the debate in full force. Philosophically, I am not opposed to it, though as public policy it has deeply problematic, often disqualifying aspects. Given current international jurisprudence, the death penalty's abolition throughout the European Union and its absence from the current international tribunals' and the

---

*The massive publicizing of this program—in handbooks, Internet postings, e-mails, radio transmissions, etc.—would make it that much more effective than Rewards for Justice, which has worked despite its enormous underpublicizing in the relevant regions.

International Criminal Court's statutes, no international court will soon sentence people to death. So life imprisonment should be the default jurisprudential penalty for those conducting *war against humanity*.

Whatever one's stance toward a jurisprudential death penalty, it has no bearing (except for the rare philosophical pacifists) on the rightfulness of killing those waging *war against humanity* so long as they do so, or are in the position to continue or renew such a war, and therefore an ongoing threat. So long as people wage *war against humanity*, killing those people is a defensive act that protects and preserves that part of humanity under attack or directly imperiled. Perpetrators could stop others from trying to kill them (and from attacking their country and their forces) and remove the bounty on their heads only by surrendering themselves unconditionally to the International Criminal Court or its agents.*

No one should doubt such measures' potential efficacy. No one wants to be "Wanted Dead or Alive." Guaranteed punishment—the certainty you will be hunted until your last day, likely coming decades earlier than your natural end—would powerfully deter all but the most ideologically besotted. Bosnia and Herzegovina's President Silajdžić was the country's foreign minister and then prime minister during the Serbs' eliminationist assault. He knew Milošević well. Agreeing that Milošević was a rational and cunning calculator of advantage, banking on attaining permanent territorial gains, Silajdžić said, when asked whether Milošević would have ever initiated the slaughter of Bosnians if Milošević had known for sure he would be hunted down till his last day: "I don't think he would."[23] Rwandan Minister of Justice Tharcisse Karugarama has steeped himself, as much if not more than just about any of our time's public figures, in the problems of genocide, including preventing and combating the scourge. When I asked him whether a *guarantee* that anyone initiating genocide would be hunted down until killed would have prevented the Rwandan genocide and would be effective in preventing future mass slaughters, he replied with enormous emphasis: "Definitely, definitely, definitely, definitely, many times definitely."

---

*Though a life sentence likely deters less than the death penalty, it might save some innocent people's lives by inducing perpetrators to surrender to the court rather than continue with the eliminationist assaults and risk someone collecting on the substantial "dead or alive" bounty.

Haris Silajdžić, Srebrenica, Bosnia and Herzegovina, July 2008

Tharcisse Karugarama, Kigali, Rwanda, May 2008

Karugarama then explained, "If people knew that at the end of the day they'll be the losers, they'd never invest in a losing enterprise. Because genocide as you correctly pointed out is a political enterprise, it's a political game. But again, it's a power play, it's wealth, it's everything. So if people involved knew at the end of the day they'd be the losers, they would not play the game. That's for sure."[24]

Even if such a guarantee would not completely end eliminationist assaults—and it likely would not prevent every last one—it would reduce them substantially. That would save innumerable future victims' lives and prevent the expulsion and brutalizing of countless more. It would prevent incalculable suffering of still so many others—relatives, friends, community members. It would prevent the deformation of so many countries' polities, societies, and cultures. And it would lift the threat under which so many millions live. And if ever a country's political leaders would not be warded off from implementing their eliminationist desires, and these political, legal, and martial countermeasures were triggered and put into effect, then all other potential mass murderers and eliminationist perpetrators would unmistakably see what awaits them should they war on humanity. One of the international arena's most powerful, underappreciated influences is *learning*. This, of course, is understood for economic matters, but less so for politics. To date, about *eliminationist* politics, political leaders have learned they can kill, expel, or incarcerate hated or unwanted groups, including their children, with impunity. They must now learn the opposite, which they quickly will if it turns out to be true: Impunity is over, and the opposite—guaranteed, uncompromising punishment—prevails.

The prevailing state of affairs, impunity for the perpetrators on the ground and in the halls of power, is illustrated poignantly in Guatemala. Despite the military and paramilitary's vast participation in the "scorched earth" policy against the Maya, the government's term for its eliminationist assault, to date only ten of the genocide's material authors (as the actual killers are called) have been brought to justice. In Guatemala, I heard again and again from survivors that most of all they want Ríos Montt and the other "intellectual authors" of the "genocide" put on trial. In CALDH (Center for Human Rights Legal Action), the oldest, largest, and most prominent human rights organization in Guatemala, unofficial "wanted" posters of Ríos Montt adorn

Nun carrying unofficial Ríos Montt "wanted" poster in front of the Public Ministry, Guatemala City, Guatemala, June 2001

doors and hallways. Furthermore, Guatemala's official Commission for Historical Clarification report named Ríos Montt as responsible for the "genocide," and Guatemala is now a tolerably well–working democracy. So where is he, the mastermind of the eliminationist assault on the Mayan people? Where is Ríos Montt that he has eluded the punishment that should come to him as surely as the sun came today to Guatemala from the east? In Guatemala, untouched, free, and living the good life. What's more, he is a member of Congress. What's still more, as recently as 2005, twenty-three years after his stewardship of the mass murder and elimination ended, Ríos Montt was nothing less than the Congress' president, having in 2003 been a losing candidate to be Guatemala's president.

Sitting across from Ríos Montt at one end of the horseshoe that is the seating arrangement in Congress is Otilia Lux de Coti, an author of the very Commission for Historical Clarification report that demonstrates beyond any doubt Ríos Montt's authorship of Guatemala's largest spate of exterminationist and eliminationist assaults on the Maya, making it clear he is among our time's worst mass murderers. When I asked de Coti in her office how she, a Maya, feels having to see him every day in Congress, she did not answer the question as it was put about her feelings, but eloquently conveyed the reality of the impunity that contemporary politics offers the leaders guilty of exterminationist and eliminationist politics. "It is a political matter, Daniel," she explained, setting the frame for her answer, the frame of politics. "I have to speak with God and the devil. To negotiate a law, I must speak with them all."[25]

In saying this, she revealed her bottled-up feelings and why they must remain corked. After talking to de Coti, I walked with her to Congress, where from the press gallery I watched Ríos Montt talk amiably with his fellow legislators, vote, occupy his honored place in the august chamber. There with a film crew preparing the documentary grounded in this book, I confronted him as he emerged from the chamber into the hallway and pursued him as he walked by without answering the question I posed. To my surprise, as we emerged from the passageway into the Congress building's entrance hall, Ríos Montt stopped, turned to me, and indicated he would speak. I asked: "Was there genocide in Guatemala and were you responsible?" Ríos Montt tried to exonerate himself by falsely stating the genocide convention's definition of genocide, which I immediately corrected, and then after he, somewhat flustered, accepted what I said, I asked him again whether he agrees he is responsible for the genocide. His reply, perhaps rhetorically powerful to the innocent, was to anyone informed, a laugher: "If I was responsible, I would be in jail." As I laid out the charges against him, he said, "Show me the proof and accuse me before any court." So I asked him whether he would go to Spain to face an indictment against him for genocide. He replied that his lawyers will not let him go. In this surrealistic discussion with the Hitler of Guatemala, I said, "There's nothing preventing you from getting on a plane with a passport and going to Spain." Telling me he has already lived in Spain long enough, Ríos Montt, the genocidal mastermind, knows that after more than a quarter-century of immunity he can thumb his nose at justice, even mocking it by saying that if he were guilty he would be in jail.[26]

José Efraín Ríos Montt in discussion with Daniel Jonah Goldhagen, Guatemala City, Guatemala, June 10, 2008

Every democracy has laws, police forces, courts, and prisons to punish criminals and to deter its citizens and others within the country from committing crimes. Without these institutions, criminality would be far greater, so rampant as to render democracy, civil life, even society itself impossible. Everyone recognizes this explicitly or implicitly for his or her own society. Yet internationally, analogous robust institutions that potential exterminationist and eliminationist perpetrators know put them automatically in a determined international community's crosshairs do not exist. No wonder eliminationist assaults have been so frequent. Anyone scoffing at efforts to create such analogous, effective international institutions to deter perpetrators—rulers of countries, state and governmental officials, and the killing fields' executioners—from initiating and participating in exterminationist and eliminationist assaults, to deter them from conducting *war against humanity,* must be moved by something other than regard for future victims' lives. He either does not genuinely want to reduce such colossal atrocities' incidence or privileges his other priorities, such as safeguarding his own personal or parochial political or academic aspirations. To be sure, domestic institutions meant to prevent crime are imperfectly effective. Crime exists. The international institutions and measures proposed here to prevent eliminationist attacks would also sometimes fail. But there is every reason to believe such measures would often work, just as the analogous domestic institutions do that prevent the incalculably vast amount of crime people would commit without them. No one would opt to reduce his own society's law enforcement to the crippled state of the international community's means for preventing, stopping, and punishing genocide (let alone for eliminationism's all but ignored other forms, including non-"genocidal" mass murders), so why should anyone pretend this current international state of affairs is anything but ineffective and undesirable—and scandalous?

If somehow these preventive measures fail, or seem about to fail, then the new antigenocide, anti-eliminationist, international dispensation, codified among other places in a revised genocide convention and revised International Criminal Court, should provide member states standing authorization, alone or in concert, to intervene in the ways discussed here. In addition to its many other problems, the genocide convention does not currently empower such intervention, permitting member states only to refer the problem to the United Nations in the hopeless hope an institution set up to do nothing might do something.

These prescriptions do not include an obligation to intervene. This is not because I oppose one. To the contrary, I think the duty to intervene exists as a moral principle and would support such an obligation wholeheartedly as a political and legal principle. But such an obligation is less likely to be enshrined in law and international institutions than the enabling measures suggested here. Pragmatically, it is wiser to work toward institutions and laws demanding less of participating states, particularly when they are almost as likely to work, as the preventive measures outlined here would. Nevertheless, it is worth laying out more robust contours of prevention, intervention, and justice regimes.

The international watchdog organization would monitor the world for signs an eliminationist onslaught may be on the way, identify when it looks possible, and trigger preventive intervention to forestall it. Some signs are well known: the declaration of a state of emergency or martial law, the suspension of civil liberties, restrictions placed on foreign diplomats and international organizations' representatives, the widespread closing down of media outlets or access, and intensified fanning of hatred and fear of an ethnic, religious, linguistic, or political group by government-controlled or -inspired media. The watchdog organization and independent member states would adopt well-established and -publicized procedures and measures that every country's political leaders and elites would already know.* They would formally warn the threatening country—especially its political, security, and business leaders—that the international community will respond to any eliminationist measures with all its means and power. The warning would further clearly convey that the threatening country's political leadership, including all cabinet ministers and high officials in military and police organizations, will be declared in a state of *war against humanity* and will be hunted down until killed or arrested, with a bounty on their heads ranging from $100,000 to $10 million dollars. The country would be bombarded with radio broadcasts, Internet postings, e-mail, voice mails, and leaflets warning its people against participating in or supporting any such violent measures. The country would also be required to permit the international rapid-deployment force to enter and act freely to ensure no eliminationist violence occurs. If it refuses, then such troops could be forcibly inserted, with participating countries' naval, air, and ground forces' further mobilization, which might also mean deposing the country's leadership.

If a country's political leaders deem the new preventive, interventionist, and punishment regime's practices and past successes insufficiently persuasive, and if their followers—in high political and military positions—are equally blithe about their own safety and futures, and manage to take the international watchdog organization unawares and initiate mass murder, expulsion, or incarceration, then that organization would immediately notify the relevant international institutions and the world community, triggering the interventionist measures to stop it as quickly as possible. A bombing campaign to destroy the country's military infrastructure would immediately commence. Only military targets, including airfields, depots, bases, and ships would be

---

*Diplomatic and other aid would simultaneously be offered to help the threatening leadership defuse the situation, but with an effective and universally known preventive system of this sort in place, any country that would go so far as to trigger its robust anti-eliminationist measures would likely be well past the point where conventional diplomacy would work.

CHANGING THE FUTURE

attacked to minimize civilian deaths and damage to the country's general infrastructure. Such bombing's purpose, as it effectively was against the Serbs, is more to raise the costs to the eliminationist regime's political and military leaders (it would often threaten their hold on power) than to weaken their capacity to proceed, because, as we and they know, perpetrators can quickly slaughter people by the tens of thousands without sophisticated weaponry. Military ground intervention would begin quickly to stop the killing and eliminationist violence, and to topple the enemies of humanity constituting the outlaw regime.*

Complex and difficult nation-building measures would need to follow, ideally under international supervision. Varying enormously from instance to instance, they would include providing justice, with all its complexities, impossibilities, and unhappy choices and compromises.

All these measures to intervene to stop eliminationist assaults are unlikely to occur. Only a naïf would expect that in the foreseeable future, say, the next five to fifteen years, such robust antigenocide, let alone anti-eliminationist, pro-human, institutions and laws will be created, actors lined up, and policies enacted, and then, when necessary, be used appropriately. Many might say that, given the international state system, fifty years would not be enough. States, governed by self-interested political leaders and responsive to publics concerned overwhelmingly with their own countries, are unlikely to intervene to stop mass murder, let alone lesser eliminations, costing substantial sums and the lives of their country's soldiers. And it is difficult to see the United Nations, the leading and currently unavoidable international institution, facilitating such morally positive developments.

That is why focusing on preventive measures is more likely to succeed and (for the other reasons discussed here) be more efficacious. Cynics, many thinking themselves hardheaded realists, might say the proposed preventive measures are equally unlikely to be enacted. To

---

*The possible rejoinder that this will empower states to use the right to intervene against eliminationism as a flimsy pretext to invade other countries is not well grounded. States wishing to invade others will do so regardless, and the powerful reasons preventing states from doing so—deterrence, international interventionist measures, and the many costs war entails, which inherently destabilizes tyrannies making war—will operate forcefully and effectively, just as it otherwise does.

this there are several rejoinders. Such preventive measures, demanding less and requiring less coordination, are by definition easier to bring about. Even if not, those wishing to reduce eliminationist politics' incidence and vast toll should lay out a feasible pathway while recognizing that gathering support will take time. If only in one instance bounties work or *one country intervenes,* saving thousands or tens of thousands, and giving pause to future potential perpetrators, it will be worth it. And here reason for hope exists. Just as one political leader or a small group of political leaders initiates eliminationist onslaughts, so too can one political leader or a small number of leaders, in one country or a cooperating few, initiate measures to prevent or stop a mass extermination or elimination. Even if only one powerful country's leader did so once, the success would be enormous, providing an example, an unmistakable challenge, a model for others.

In thinking about ways to combat eliminationist politics, especially mass murder, we are blinded by misleading analyses and overwhelmed by the problem's colossal scope. We do not see two facts: one moral person, the president of the United States, or a few such people leading a few countries in Europe or elsewhere, can positively change forever the eliminationist equation; and even if he or they are not such moral leaders, they, their advisers, and American congresspersons and other countries' parliamentarians should be politically pressured so their political and reputational interests will be to do the right thing. Second, succeeding *in just one place* would produce enormous positive aspects (save and prevent the ruination of lives) and effects (a demonstration to future potential perpetrators and possible interveners). If we enacted a policy reducing an American city's murder rate by 50 percent, saving in one year four hundred lives in New York, or even fifty-five in Atlanta or forty in Boston, we would declare it an enormous achievement. Studies would be done so the effective methods could be applied elsewhere. Its architects would be celebrated. But if an imperfect but genuine anti-eliminationist regime prevented only one mass murder of tens of thousands but not others, or cut one short while others went on, cynics and critics would scoff at its failures, even as they have for decades failed, every day, to take the obvious feasible steps to save lives, typically of Africans and Asians and Latin Americans. Similarly, even if one nation is rebuilt, even if only some eliminationist assaults are stopped, then such a policy's success would be historic, dwarfing the many bally-hooed initiatives marginally improving life in industrialized democracies. Anyone saying that intervention in Rwanda would have been "folly," no matter that the United Nations was obstructionist and international law provided no other clear mechanism for sanctioning intervention, ought to be condemned.

Implementing *any* of these provisions, especially the preventive ones, would be progress. If international law is not appropriately changed, then the signatories to the convention establishing the international watchdog organization to stop exterminationist and eliminationist onslaughts could still act upon its provisions. The convention's signatories (it can be two or five or fifty) ought to operate under the obvious humanitarian and humane principle moving NATO in Bosnia and Kosovo: Eliminationist onslaughts—mass murders, expulsions, incarcerations, and rapes—must be stopped. They should invoke and further the developing norm of *responsibility to protect,* which the UN Security Council, and therefore international law, at least implicitly recognizes. No real adverse international consequences will befall states acting to save innocents' lives. Even without such an international watchdog organization, single states or supranational entities (certainly the United States or the European Union), or small ad hoc groups (the United Kingdom, France, Germany), can save lives by preventing or stopping *wars against humanity.*

The second necessary preventive measure is reducing the number of regimes with strong tendencies to practice eliminationist politics and replace them with the democratic institutions that rob political leaders of the ready institutional and cultural means to initiate domestic slaughters or eliminations. Many political leaders pay lip service to increasing democratic governance but do little to bring it about. That topic also deserves a separate book.

The problem's crux is twofold: the United Nations, and sovereignty. The United Nations, as we now know, enables, even legitimizes dictatorships. Freedom House, a nongovernmental organization, assesses every country's degree of freedom, using two major dimensions: political rights (including a functioning electoral democracy) and civil liberties. In 2009 out of 193 countries, only 89 are free, while more than half, 104, are partly free (62) or not free (42). Only 119, 62 percent, are electoral democracies. So more than a third of the current UN membership consists of nondemocratic regimes, namely criminal regimes. By broader measures of freedom, more than half the UN membership is tyrannies, committing substantial or colossal crimes and human rights violations against their own peoples.[27]

Imagine your country was run with more than one-third, perhaps even more than half, of the voters hardened, felonious criminals. Your laws are made with their participation. Your enforcement of legal measures depends on their agreement or participation, with their representatives staffing much of the enforcement mechanisms' implementation. Imagine they controlled, absolutely and with utter impunity, not just their own households, but entire towns, cities, and regions. Such is the United Nations.

This immense international problem is barely mentioned and is effectively not part of international or domestic political discourse, let alone where it should be—at the center of concern, thinking, and policy development. Many American commentators, predominantly Republican in orientation, despise the United Nations, mainly because it is the principal international forum and instrument for contesting and constraining American power. They disdain multilateralism in general and the undeniable hostility the United Nations mobilizes against the United States. Similarly, those suspicious of and seeking a counterweight to American power, or simply hoping the international community can become an actual community, reflexively support and wish to expand the United Nations' power. The United Nations (aside from the World Trade Organization for economic matters) is the major overarching international institution and forum for the world's countries to cooperate and solve disputes peacefully. This—in addition to the enormous good its agencies, such as the World Health Organization, perform—is the principal point in its favor. For these reasons the United Nations' fundamentally illegitimate nature and its enabling of tyranny remain world politics' dirty secrets, barely an issue in Europe and the industrial world, let alone in the developing world, home to scores of criminal regimes and tyrants, which look to the United Nations to give their voices weight and support their illegitimate claims to legitimacy. The United Nations is treated more as a revered institution and model for the world than as the fundamentally corrupt, undemocratic, and antidemocratic institution it is. This alone (aside from its administration's additional corrupt aspects) ought to disqualify democrats and people of goodwill from supporting it, no matter the good it may perform.

We should do away with the United Nations and replace it with a powerful international institution carrying out many of its current duties and functions but not suffering its disqualifying deformities. We should do this not because the United Nations constrains American power or is hostile to many American positions, but because it is illegitimate, and ineffectual, and corrupt, and does far too little to coordinate the world's countries to alleviate misery, including to fight against exterminationist and eliminationist politics. The United Nations sits on a conceptual foundation, its charter, that for the foreseeable future all but guarantees its continuing enabling of mass murder, other eliminations, mass brutality, denial of basic democratic and civil libertarian rights to billions, and slowed economic development. The United Nations should be replaced with an institution without foundational principles and membership promoting these horrors and abominations. *This* institution could therefore be true to the United Nations' name (and ignored conceptual foundation), namely the second part of its name: *nations*—not *states* sitting above, often tyrannically, the people, but the people composing each nation.

This leads to the second problem, state sovereignty. Sovereignty exists not for nations or countries' peoples. It exists for states. The notion of sovereignty came into being, law, and international politics beginning with the Peace of Westphalia in 1648, a nondemocratic age of monarchs ruling peoples, not of self-governing citizens. International politics deems states, no matter how atrocious their rulers, sovereign. This unjustifiable conception of international relations made some sense so long as war was a common option, thus rightly orienting the beneficent impulses in international politics toward reducing its incidence. State sovereignty contributed to this by constraining states' capacities to intervene in other states' affairs, diminishing conflict points, and contributing to a more ordered, predictable, and stable international environment.

But today *state* (or rulers') sovereignty—as opposed to national or people's sovereignty—is indefensible. Interstate war and its threat has declined considerably. Respecting the sovereignty of criminal states, namely nondemocracies and tyrannies, does not reduce war but promotes it: It is nondemocratic states and leaders that still use war to aggrandize territory, expand power, seek glory, and accrue economic gains. Furthermore, given the great emerging eliminationist danger of nuclear weapons' proliferation to nondemocratic rogue states or non-state actors finding safe harbor in such states, the threat tyrannies pose to peoples outside their borders is growing exponentially. And because it is indisputable that (absent emergency circumstances or a governing party's eliminationist conduct) a country's people should determine their government, the indefensibility of respecting, legitimizing, and supporting dictators, tyrants, and murderers becomes absolute.

The world's democracies must stop promoting and safeguarding the world's tyrants, including their capacity to practice eliminationist politics, from mass murder to mass expulsions to violently repressing those not conforming to their narrow ethnocentric, ideological, or religious prescriptions. Democratic leaders and the world's peoples should stop perpetuating this legal, institutional, and political fiction, most glaringly at the United Nations, that tyrannical regimes and leaders represent anything aside from their own criminal, warmaking, and eliminationist interests. Democracies should assiduously work to reduce the number of such regimes, which, as we now know, are inherently unstable and weak (being actually or potentially threatened by the demands of their countries' peoples to be represented and treated fairly) and inherently prone to eliminationism. (Creating a world of democracies is the only effective long-term strategy to prevent nuclear weapon use.) Democratic leaders and peoples should replace the United Nations with a new United Democratic Nations that admits only democracies, an idea John McCain also floated while running for the American presidency. But instead of his "league" of democracies, it should be democracies united *against* tyranny, genocide, and all eliminationist politics, and united *for* the world's people. Democracies should similarly make membership in other international political and economic organizations open only to democracies. They should place prohibitions on their companies doing business in nondemocratic countries. There will be short-term costs—acrimony, tension, and harm done to the people under tyrannical regimes refusing to relinquish their antihuman power. Yet many nondemocratic regimes and their sustaining economic elites will see tyranny's continuing costs as prohibitive. Most tyrants and the supporting elites follow calculations of power and advantage. Making democracy a much better cost-benefit option will powerfully appeal to their cherished values and interests, and further create within their countries self-reinforcing societal and economic pressure and support for democracy. Such incentives' power to induce political and economic elites and countries' peoples to opt for democracy is more than a logical conclusion. The evidence for democratizing political and economic pressure's enormous effectiveness exists. The European Union has required countries seeking membership to meet genuine democratic and other criteria, in Freedom House's terms, political rights and civil liberties (NATO has further contributed to this pressure). Consequently, Central and Eastern European countries, as well as Turkey, which otherwise might not have embraced democracy, or fallen away from it, saw democracy as the only option. Quickly, despite a highly unpromising starting point, the region transformed from wholly undemocratic and unfree into an almost wholly democratic and free one.

Freedom in the World 2008 (legend on page 595)

Similarly, when in the late 1980s the United States stopped supporting Latin American tyrannies, making it clear that the military overthrow of

Freedom Status	Country Breakdown	Population Breakdown (in billions)
FREE	90 (47%)	3.03 (46%)
PARTLY FREE	60 (31%)	1.19 (18%)
NOT FREE	43 (22%)	2.39 (36%)
TOTAL	193 (100%)	6.61 (100%)

Freedom in the World 2008

democracy—the previous decades' common occurrence—would lead to political and economic isolation, Latin America (except the communist anachronism Cuba) became near-wholly democratic and mainly free.

Establishing and governing a United Democratic Nations would meet some problems. What actually qualifies as a genuine democracy or a free country, rather than a sham democracy such as Robert Mugabe's

Zimbabwe, even before the fraudulently overturned 2008 election? Dealing with the nondemocratic colossus China and the ever more problematic democracy and increasingly authoritarian Russia is a substantial stumbling block. Identifying sham democracies, as Freedom House shows, is not difficult. Still, some judgment calls would be necessary and likely imperfect. Nevertheless, the difficulty of getting every case right does not justify getting all the obvious ones wrong by maintaining the tyrannical status quo. And there is no reason to succumb to carping holier-than-thous, cynics, or the illegitimate and injurious status quo's dissimulating defenders who would maintain that admitting partly or wholly fake democracies and unfree countries into the United Democratic Nations would poison and therefore nullify the entire project. With China, the largest problem, the diplomatic thing to do, in both senses of diplomacy, is to make an exception. If necessary, the same should be done with Russia. Practical principles' occasional compromise to further other far more important practical principles is preferable to the alternative of sacrificing them all—in this case, supporting all the world's tyrants and brutes. Noble inconsistency, including not applying an operative principle to a few cases, trumps consistently applying the principle to no one, therefore standing by as tyrants brutalize, expel, and kill millions, and repress and suppress hundreds of millions more. To be sure, it would be better if the international system were not the anarchic and essentially lawless place it is, and we could devise a set of solutions to the problems of its governance that are desirable *and* doable. But as the treacherous and difficult international system is the real context for our making choices about how to proceed, the urgent need to save lives and improve the horrifying conditions under which so many people live powerfully argues for these proposals, which are superior to all others.

Democracy is no panacea. Yet, in sum, it is human existence's boon. Democracy should be a prerequisite for deeming a country's government legitimate. Those attacking this approach, arguing that insistently promoting democracy, and political and civil rights, as ineffective or dangerous, ignore the facts. When it has been tried, such as in Western Europe after World War II, by the European Union in Southern, Central, and Eastern Europe, and by the United States in Latin America, *it has worked brilliantly.*

The final substantial hurdle is to motivate the world's democracies to organize themselves to create a more democratic, secure, and prosperous world. The cost would not be great. Praise would likely far exceed criticism. Over time, international governance's and then steadily national governance's reordering would enhance democratic countries' security and lower their costs—including the colossal direct and indirect economic costs—of dealing with the human and economic destruction the world's many undemocratic and tyrannical regimes cause.

A serious *international prevention, intervention, and punishment regime* to stop mass-murderous and eliminationist states and leaders from warring on their peoples and humanity, and a devoted *international push for democratizing more countries* to remove the institutional and political and cultural basis for political leaders to even see eliminationist politics as an option, are the basis for a more secure, more global structure that would greatly end eliminationist politics' mass violence and vast destructiveness. Even if both are not simultaneously brought about, or achieved only in part, establishing just one will save the lives and prevent the misery of untold millions of men, women, and children.

The alternative is to wait around, yet again, to wait as today's mass exterminations and eliminations go on day after day, and to wait until one or another, and then another, and then another of the manifestly proto-eliminationist regimes governing more than half the world's countries decide to enact an elimination or genocide, and slaughters, expels, or incarcerates, and inflicts countless other cruelties on masses of people. How can we, in good faith as moral beings, as citizens of our countries, and as human beings belonging to a common humanity, *choose* to permit this to happen? How can we *choose* not to take simple and effective steps to prevent future wars against humanity?

NOTES

CHAPTER ONE

1. See Gar Alperovitz, *The Decision to Use the Atomic Bomb* (New York: Vintage, 1996), p. 513.

2. J. Samuel Walker, the U.S. Nuclear Regulatory Commission's chief historian, explains: "Careful scholarly treatment of the records and manuscripts opened over the past few years has greatly enhanced our understanding of why the Truman administration used atomic weapons against Japan. Experts continue to disagree on some issues, but critical questions have been answered. The consensus among scholars is that the bomb was not needed to avoid an invasion of Japan. It is clear that alternatives to the bomb existed and that Truman and his advisers knew it." See Nuclear Age Peace Foundation, "U.S. Responses to Dropping the Bomb," NuclearFiles.Org, www.nuclearfiles.org/menu/key-issues/nuclear-weapons/history/pre-cold-war/hiroshima-nagasaki/us-responses-to-bomb.htm for other leading American military men and advisers' views.

The American government's own authoritative immediate postwar *United States Strategic Bombing Survey,* which assessed the effects of bombing on Japan, confirmed that annihilating the people of Hiroshima and Nagasaki was militarily superfluous: "It seems clear that, even without the atomic bombing attacks, air supremacy over Japan could have exerted sufficient pressure to bring about unconditional surrender and obviate the need for invasion.

"Based on a detailed investigation of all the facts, and supported by the testimony of the surviving Japanese leaders involved, it is the Survey's opinion that certainly prior to 31 December 1945, and in all probability prior to 1 November 1945, Japan would have surrendered even if the atomic bombs had not been dropped, even if Russia had not entered the war, and even if no invasion had been planned or contemplated." See *United States Strategic Bombing Survey,* Summary Report (Pacific War), Washington, D.C., 1 July 1946, http://www.anesi.com/ussbs01.htm#jstetw.

3. Dwight D. Eisenhower, *Mandate for Change, 1953–1956: The White House Years* (Garden City, NY: Doubleday, 1963), pp. 312–313.

4. Draft of a White House press release, "Statement by the President of the United States," ca. August 6, 1945, www.trumanlibrary.org/whistlestop/study_collections/bomb/small/mb10.htm.

5. The public opinion data are from J. Samuel Walker, *Prompt and Utter Destruction: Truman and the Use of Atomic Bombs Against Japan,* rev. ed. (Chapel Hill: University of North Carolina Press, 2004), pp. 98 and 5.

6. William D. Leahy, *I Was There: The Personal Story of the Chief of Staff to Presidents Roosevelt and Truman* (New York: Whittlesey House, 1950), pp. 440–441.

7. Norimitsu Onishi, "Okinawans Protest Japan's Plan to Revise Bitter Chapter of World War II," *New York Times,* October 7, 2007, p. 8.

8. Kate Doyle, "The Atrocity Files: Deciphering the Archives of Guatemala's Dirty War," *Harper's Magazine,* December 2007, p. 61.

9. Samantha Power, *"A Problem From Hell": America and the Age of Genocide* (New York: Basic Books, 2002), p. 307.

10. Eberhard Jäckel, ed., *Hitler: Sämtliche Aufzeichnungen 1905–1924* (Stuttgart, Germany: Deutsche Verlags-Anstalt, 1980), pp. 119–120.

11. Homer, *The Iliad,* trans. by Robert Fitzgerald (New York: Everyman's Library, 1992), Book IV, p. 93.

12. Alisa Muratčauš, author interview, Sarajevo, Bosnia and Herzegovina, July 12, 2008.

13. Vahakn N. Dadrian, "The Secret Young-Turk Ittihadist Conference and the Decision for the World War I Genocide of the Armenians," *Holocaust and Genocide Studies* (Fall 1993): 173–175.

14. For a partial historical inventory of expulsions, ghettoizations, and mass murders of Jews, see Paul E. Grosser and Edwin G. Halperin, *Anti-Semitism: The Causes and Effects of a Prejudice* (Secaucus, NJ: Citadel, 1979); and Martin Gilbert, *The Dent Atlas of Jewish History,* 5th ed. (London: JM Dent, 1993).

15. Daniel Jonah Goldhagen, "Foreword to the German Edition," *Hitlers Willige Vollstrecker: Ganz gewöhnliche Deutsche und der Holocaust* (Berlin: Siedler, 1996), reprinted in *Hitler's Willing Executioners: Ordinary Germans and the Holocaust* (New York: Vintage, 1997), p. 480.

16. See Anthony Giddens, *The Nation-State and Violence,* Volume 2 of *A Contemporary Critique of Historical Materialism* (Berkeley: University of California Press, 1987).

17. For this point I am in debt to Stanley Hoffmann.

18. *Frontline,* "Ghosts of Rwanda," www.pbs.org/wgbh/pages/frontline/shows/ghosts/viewers/.

19. Rithy Uong, author interview, April 11, 2008, Lowell, Massachusetts.

20. For a methodological exception (whatever its deterministic shortcomings), see Barbara Harff, "No Lessons Learned from the Holocaust? Assessing Risks of Genocide and Political Mass Murder since 1955," *American Political Science Review* (2003): 57–73.

21. Daniel Jonah Goldhagen, *A Moral Reckoning: The Role of the Catholic Church in the Holocaust and Its Unfulfilled Duty of Repair* (New York: Knopf, 2002).

CHAPTER TWO

1. Quoted in Horst Drechsler, *"Let Us Die Fighting": The Struggle of the Herero and Nama Against German Imperialism (1884–1915)* (London: Zed, 1980), pp. 156–157. By saying "shots to be fired at them," von Trotha had informed his troops that they should fire over the heads of the women and children so they would flee. He was explicit that no male prisoners should be taken, but it should not "give rise to atrocities committed on women and children." He admonished his soldiers to "always bear in mind the good reputation that the German soldier has acquired." But this was clearly salve for their consciences (or a deliberate falsehood entered into the historical record), as the Germans had been mercilessly slaughtering Herero women and children all along—which they continued to do after this order's promulgation. Even if they had not themselves slaughtered the women and children, their formal order was to drive them into the desert where the Herero would all but surely die.

2. Kevork B. Bardakjian, *Hitler and the Armenian Genocide* (Cambridge, MA: The Zoryan Institute, 1985), p. 1.

3. Drechsler, *"Let Us Die Fighting,"* pp. 215–216.

4. *Report on the Natives of South-West Africa and Their Treatment by Germany*, presented to both houses of Parliament by Command of His Majesty, August 1918 (London: H.M. Stationery Office, 1918), p. 65.

5. James Bryce and Arnold Toynbee, *The Treatment of Armenians in the Ottoman Empire, 1915–1916. Documents Presented to Viscount Grey of Falloden by Viscount Bryce* (Princeton, NJ: Gomidas Institute, 2000), Account 65, pp. 290–291.

6. Quoted in Donald E. Miller and Lorna Touryan Miller, *Survivors: An Oral History of the Armenian Genocide* (Berkeley: University of California Press, 1993), p. 80.

7. Ibid., p. 84.

8. Matthias Bjørnlund, "'A Fate Worse Than Dying': Sexual Violence during the Armenian Genocide," in Dagmar Herzog, ed., *Brutality and Desire: War and Sexuality in Europe's Twentieth Century* (New York: Palgrave Macmillan, 2009), p. 34.

9. Vahakn N. Dadrian, *The History of the Armenian Genocide: Ethnic Conflict from the Balkans to Anatolia to the Caucasus,* 3rd rev. ed. (Providence, RI: Berghahn Books, 1997), pp. 347–361.

10. Johannes Lepsius, ed., *Deutschland und Armenien, 1914–1918: Sammlung Diplomatischer Aktenstücke* (Bremen, Germany: Donat & Temmen, 1986), p. 84.

11. Ulrich Trumpener, *Germany and the Ottoman Empire, 1914–1918* (Princeton, NJ: Princeton University Press, 1968), p. 127; and Dadrian, *The History of the Armenian Genocide,* p. 207.

12. Cited in Jeremy Noakes and Geoffrey Pridham, eds., *Nazism: A History in Documents and Eyewitness Accounts,* vol. 2 (New York: Schocken, 1988), p. 1004.

13. U.S. Department of State, "Ethnic Cleansing in Kosovo: An Accounting" (Washington, DC: U.S. State Department Report, 1999).

14. I first demonstrated these views' hollowness in *Hitler's Willing Executioners* and wrote more generally about them in "The Paradigm Challenged, Victim Testimony, Critical Evidence, and New Perspectives in the Study of the Holocaust," *Tikkun,* July–August 1998, pp. 40–47.

15. For a discussion of the complexity and difficulty in arriving at figures, see Matthew White, "Deaths by Mass Unpleasantness: Estimated Totals for the Entire 20th Century," *Historical Atlas of the Twentieth Century,* http://users.erols.com/mwhite28/warstat8.htm. White includes in his compilation the figures from other sources providing estimates for many mass slaughters, as well as estimates of individual mass murders contained in monographs, reports, and journalistic accounts.

16. Robert K. Hitchcock and Tara M. Twedt, "Physical and Cultural Genocide of Various Indigenous Peoples," in Samuel Totten, William S. Parsons, and Israel W. Charny, eds., *Genocide in the Twentieth Century: Critical Essays and Eyewitness Accounts* (New York: Garland, 1995), pp. 493–497; and Jason Clay, "Genocide in the Age of Enlightenment," *Cultural Survival Quarterly* 12, no. 3: 1.

17. For one tabulation of mass murders according to regime type, see R. J. Rummel, "20th Century Democide," www.mega.nu/ampp/rummel/sod.tab16a.1.gif.

18. Quoted in R. J. Rummel, *China's Bloody Century: Genocide and Mass Murder Since 1900* (New Brunswick, NJ: Transaction, 1991), p. 216.

CHAPTER THREE

1. Stacie E. Martin, "Native Americans," *Encyclopedia of Genocide and Crimes Against Humanity* (Farmington Hills, MI: Thomson Gale, 2005), p. 744.

2. Daniel Jonah Goldhagen, "Foreword to the German Edition," *Hitlers Willige Vollstrecker: Ganz gewöhnliche Deutsche und der Holocaust* (Berlin: Siedler, 1996), reprinted in *Hitler's Willing Executioners: Ordinary Germans and the Holocaust* (New York: Vintage, 1997), p. 480. For the development of Hitler's political views, strategies, and policies regarding the Jews, see "The Nazis' Assault on the Jews: Its Character and Evolution," chapter 4 of *Hitler's Willing Executioners*. My general argument made there, that it is an individual or a small political leadership that initiates mass murder, was picked up by Benjamin A. Valentino, *Final Solutions: Mass Killing and Genocide in the 20th Century* (Ithaca, NY: Cornell University Press, 2004), as part of his otherwise wrongheaded and reductionist account of mass murder.

3. See Taner Akçam, *A Shameful Act: The Armenian Genocide and the Question of Turkish Responsibility* (New York: Metropolitan, 2006), pp. 155–156.

4. For an account of what is known of this meeting, see Ben Kiernan, *The Pol Pot Regime: Race, Power, and Genocide in Cambodia under the Khmer Rouge, 1975–79* (New Haven, CT: Yale University Press, 1996), pp. 55–59.

5. Dawit Wolde Giorgis, *Red Tears: War, Famine and Revolution in Ethiopia* (Trenton, NJ: Red Sea, 1989), pp. 290–291.

6. Vahakn N. Dadrian, "The Secret Young-Turk Ittihadist Conference and the Decision for the World War I Genocide of the Armenians," *Holocaust and Genocide Studies* 7, no. 2 (Fall 1993): 173–175.

7. Henry Morgenthau, *Ambassador Morgenthau's Story* (Garden City, NY: Doubleday, Page, 1919), p. 342.

CHAPTER FOUR

1. Daniel Jonah Goldhagen, "The 'Cowardly' Executioner: On Disobedience in the SS," *Patterns of Prejudice* (April 1985): 19–32.

2. Michael T. Kaufman, "Doing Their Part: Looking for the Line Between Patriotism and Guilt," *New York Times,* April 11, 1999, http://query.nytimes.com/gst/fullpage.html?res=9506E0DB1038F932A25757C0A96F958260&scp=2&sq=goldhagen+serbs.

3. Brent Beardsley, *Frontline: Ghosts of Rwanda,* www.pbs.org/wgbh/pages/frontline/shows/ghosts/interviews/beardsley.html.

4. Scott Straus, "How Many Perpetrators Were There in the Rwandan Genocide? An Estimate," *Journal of Genocide Research* (March 2004): 93.

5. Rwandan Minister of Justice Tharcisse Karugarama, author interview, Kigali, Rwanda, May 9, 2008.

6. Quoted in Peter Balakian: *The Burning Tigris: The Armenian Genocide and America's Response* (New York: HarperCollins, 2003), p. 236.

7. Quoted in Vahakn Dadrian, "The Role of the Special Organisation in the Armenian Genocide during the First World War," in Panikos Panayi, ed., *Minorities in Wartime: National and Racial Groupings in Europe, North America and Australia during the Two World Wars* (Oxford, UK: Berg, 1993), p. 57.

8. Quoted in African Rights, *Rwanda: Death, Despair and Defiance* (London: African Rights, 1994), p. 89.

9. Elie Ngarambe, author interview, Kigali, Rwanda, May 8, 2008.

10. Jean Pierre Nkuranga, author interview, Kigali, Rwanda, May 6–7, 2008.

11. Daniel Jonah Goldhagen, *Hitler's Willing Executioners: Ordinary Germans and the Holocaust* (New York: Knopf, 1996), pp. 212–214.

12. Ibid., pp. 344–363, quotation on p. 361.

13. Jean-Paul Nyirindekwe, executive secretariat of TIG, personal communication with author, Kigali, Rwanda, May 7, 2008.

14. Quoted in Jean Hatzfeld, *Machete Season: The Killers in Rwanda Speak* (New York: Farrar, Straus and Giroux, 2005), pp. 110–112.

15. Armen Hairapetian, "'Race Problems' and the Armenian Genocide: The State Department File," *Armenian Review* (Spring 1984): 44–45, 49, 50, 58.

16. Quoted in Vahakn N. Dadrian, *The History of the Armenian Genocide: Ethnic Conflict from the Balkans to Anatolia to the Caucasus,* 3rd rev. ed. (Providence, RI: Berghahn Books, 1997), p. 243.

17. Youkimny Chan, "One Spoon of Rice," in *Children of Cambodia's Killing Fields: Memoirs by Survivors,* compiled by Dith Pran, Kim DePaul, ed. (New Haven, CT: Yale University Press, 1997), pp. 20–21.

18. Edward Kissi, *Revolution and Genocide in Ethiopia and Cambodia* (Lanham, MD: Lexington Books, 2006), p. 127.

19. Quoted in Aleksandr M. Nekrich, *The Punished Peoples: The Deportation and Fate of Soviet Minorities at the End of the Second World War* (New York: Norton, 1978), p. 111.

20. Seyss-Inquart report, November 20, 1939, Nur. Doc. 2278-PS in *Trial of the Major War Criminals Before the International Military Tribunal, Nuremberg, 14 November 1945–1 October 1946* (Nuremberg, Germany, 1947), vol. 30, p. 95.

21. This reproduces a passage from Goldhagen, *Hitler's Willing Executioners,* p. 146.

22. Dawit Wolde Giorgis, *Red Tears: War, Famine and Revolution in Ethiopia* (Trenton, NJ: Red Sea, 1989), p. 301.

23. See Dadrian, *The History of the Armenian Genocide,* pp. 236–243.

24. Kissi, *Revolution and Genocide in Ethiopia and Cambodia,* p. 121.

25. "Conclusions and Recommendations," *Guatemala: Memory of Silence, Report of the Commission for Historical Clarification*, paragraph 42, http://shr.aaas.org/guatemala/ceh/report/english/toc.html.

26. Norman M. Naimark, *Fires of Hatred: Ethnic Cleansing in Twentieth-Century Europe* (Cambridge, MA: Harvard University Press, 2001), pp. 129–130.

27. Quoted in Robert Conquest, *Kolyma: The Arctic Death Camps* (Oxford, UK: Oxford University Press, 1979), p. 134.

28. Quoted in Conquest, *Kolyma*, p.128.

29. Falk Pingel, *Häftlinge unter SS-Herrschaft: Widerstand, Selbstbehauptung und Vernichtung im Konzentrationslager* (Hamburg, Germany: Hoffmann und Campe, 1978), p. 186.

30. R. J. Rummel, *China's Bloody Century: Genocide and Mass Murder Since 1900* (New Brunswick, NJ: Transaction, 1991), pp. 229–232.

31. The camp figures come from Gudrun Schwarz, *Die nationalsozialistischen Lager* (Frankfurt, Germany: Fischer Taschenbuch Verlag, 1990), pp. 72 and 222.

32. Quoted in Liisa H. Malkki, *Purity and Exile: Violence, Memory, and National Cosmology Among Hutu Refugees in Tanzania* (Chicago: University of Chicago Press, 1995), pp. 89–90.

33. Chhun Von, author interview, April 11, 2008, Lowell, Massachusetts. Many Khmer Rouge believed human bladders had great medicinal powers.

34. Quoted in Ben Kiernan, "The Cambodian Genocide—1975–1979," in Samuel Totten, William S. Parsons, and Israel W. Charny, eds., *Genocide in the Twentieth Century: Critical Essays and Eyewitness Accounts* (New York: Garland, 1995), p. 474.

35. James Ron, "Territoriality and Plausible Deniability: Serbian Paramilitaries in the Bosnian War," in Bruce B. Campbell and Arthur D. Brenner, eds., *Death Squads in Global Perspective: Murder with Deniability* (New York: St. Martin's, 2000), pp. 303–304.

36. John Hughes, *Indonesian Upheaval* (New York: David McKay, 1967), p. 181.

37. Quoted in Hughes, *Indonesian Upheaval*, p. 160.

38. Quoted in Jean Hatzfeld, *Machete Season: The Killers in Rwanda Speak* (New York: Farrar, Straus and Giroux, 2005), p. 112.

39. Quoted in Malkki, *Purity and Exile*, p. 98.

40. Hans Frank, *Das Diensttagebuch des deutschen Generalgouverneurs in Polen, 1939–1945*, ed. by Werner Präg and Wolfgang Jacobmeyer (Stuttgart, Germany: Deutsche Verlags-Anstalt, 1975), entry of May 30, 1940, p. 212.

41. See Michael A. Sells, "Kosovo Mythology and the Bosnian Genocide," in Omer Bartov and Phyllis Mack, eds., *In God's Name: Genocide and Religion in the Twentieth Century* (New York: Berghahn, 2001), pp. 187–188.

42. Timothy Longman, "Christian Churches and Genocide in Rwanda," in Bartov and Mack, eds., *In God's Name*, p. 156.

43. Michael A. Sells, *The Bridge Betrayed: Religion and Genocide in Bosnia* (Berkeley: University of California Press, 1996), pp. 1–2.

44. Mary Craig, *Tears of Blood: A Cry for Tibet* (London: HarperCollins, 1992), pp. 123–124.

45. Kiernan, "The Cambodian Genocide—1975–1979,", p. 436.

46. Dawa Norbu, *Red Star Over Tibet* (New Delhi, India: Sterling, 1987), p. 220.

CHAPTER FIVE

1. Daniel Jonah Goldhagen, *Hitler's Willing Executioners: Ordinary Germans and the Holocaust* (New York: Knopf, 1996), pp. 379–381.

2. Mahmood Mamdani, *When Victims Become Killers: Colonialism, Nativism, and the Genocide in Rwanda* (Princeton, NJ: Princeton University Press, 2001), p. 224.

3. See Goldhagen, *Hitler's Willing Executioners*, pp. 116–120, 3–4, and 381–383.

4. For a discussion of the German scholars' tainted pasts and influences, see Götz Aly, "Willige Historiker—Bemerkung in eigener Sache" in *Macht—Geist—Wahn: Kontinuitäten deutschen Denkens* (Berlin, Germany: Argon, 1997), pp. 153–83.

5. See Christopher R. Browning, *Ordinary Men: Reserve Police Battalion 101 and the Final Solution in Poland* (New York: HarperCollins, 1992); for a critique, see Daniel Jonah Goldhagen's review of *Ordinary Men* by Christopher R. Browning, *New Republic* 207, nos. 3 and 4 (1992): 49–52; for a subsequent exchange see Christopher R. Browning, "Ordinary Germans or Ordinary Men? A Reply to the Critics," and Daniel Jonah Goldhagen, "Ordinary Men or Ordinary Germans?" in Michael Berenbaum and Abraham J. Peck, eds., *The Holocaust and History: The Known, the Unknown, the Disputed, and the Reexamined* (Bloomington: Indiana University Press, 1998), pp. 252–265 and 301–307.

6. Jacob Robinson, *And the Crooked Shall Be Made Straight: The Eichmann Trial, the Jewish Catastrophe, and Hannah Arendt's Narrative* (New York: Macmillan, 1965), pp. 34 and 37.

7. Hans Safrian, *Eichmann und seine Gehilfen* (Frankfurt, Germany: Fischer Taschenbuch Verlag, 1995), pp. 15–16.

8. *The Good Man of Nanking: The Diaries of John Rabe*, ed. by Erwin Wickert (New York: Knopf, 1998), p. 101.

9. Quoted in Roy Gutman, "The Rapes of Bosnia," *A Witness to Genocide: The 1993 Pulitzer Prize–Winning Dispatches on the "Ethnic Cleansing" of Bosnia* (New York: Macmillan, 1993), p. 76.

10. Quoted in African Rights, *Rwanda: Death, Despair and Defiance* (London: African Rights, 1994), p. 219.

11. *Guatemala: Memory of Silence, Report of the Commission for Historical Clarification*, "Conclusions and Recommendations," paragraph 87, http://shr.aaas.org/guatemala/ceh/report/english/toc.html.

12. Goldhagen, *Hitler's Willing Executioners*, p. 234.

13. See Joel D. Aberbach, Robert D. Putnam, and Bert A. Rockman, *Bureaucrats and Politicians in Western Democracies* (Cambridge, MA: Harvard University Press, 1981).

14. Felicien Sekamandwa, author interview, Kigali, Rwanda, May 7, 2008; Elie Ngarambe, author interview, Kigali, Rwanda, May 7, 2008; and others.

15. Quoted in Jean Hatzfeld, *Machete Season: The Killers in Rwanda Speak* (New York: Farrar, Straus and Giroux, 2005), p. 11.

16. Quoted in Jean Hatzfeld, *Into the Quick of Life: The Rwandan Genocide—The Survivors Speak* (London: Serpent's Tail, 2005), p. 137.

17. Ibid., p. 146.

18. Quoted in Charles K. Mironko, "Ibitero: Means and Motive in the Rwandan Genocide," in Susan E. Cook, ed., *Genocide in Cambodia and Rwanda: New Perspectives* (New Brunswick, NJ: Transaction, 2006), p. 182.

19. Quoted in Hatzfeld, *Machete Season*, p. 12.

20. Henry Orenstein, *I Shall Live: Surviving Against All Odds, 1939–1945* (New York: Touchstone, 1989), pp. 86–87.

21. Esperance Nyirarugira, Concessa Kayiraba, and Veronique Mukasinafi, author interview, Rwamagana District, Eastern Province, Rwanda, May 6, 2008.

22. Julian Sher and Benedict Carey, "Debate on Child Pornography's Link to Molesting," *New York Times*, July 19, 2007. Presumably, these perpetrators would have hidden still more had they been able to, since many of the seventy-five victims known at the time of sentencing and the 26 percent of the men known to have sexually abused them were probably not known by the legal authorities from perpetrators' confessions but from victims' or their families' accusations.

23. Sabaheta Fejzíc, author interview, Srebrenica, Bosnia and Herzegovina, June 10, 2008.

24. Emmanuel Gatali, author interview, Kigali, Rwanda, May 10, 2008.

25. Mukasinafi, author interview.

26. This is what Browning does in *Ordinary Men*, which treats but one single unit of German perpetrators, and Scott Straus does in *The Order of Genocide*, a study of a sampling of Rwandan perpetrators that is unsalvageable because its findings and conclusions are much more an artifact of his flawed methodology and data set than they are about the reality of the Hutu's slaughter of Tutsi. When Straus (mimicking Browning) justifies his methodology of essentially taking the perpetrators' self-exonerating claims both about the extent of their killing and about their reasons for killing *at face value*, he pens a sentence that reveals his effective repudiation of any realistic, critical stance toward their self-exonerations. When he asked the perpetrators to tell him how many people they themselves killed, Straus informs us, "most respondents appeared not to be deliberately lying" (p. 111). So Straus' standard for skepticism about the self-exonerations of people convicted of perpetrating mass murder is: They must *appear* to Straus himself in a formal interview setting about their crimes to be *deliberately* lying. How many people in general, let alone those practiced in the art of trying to get themselves exonerated from, or as little punishment as possible for, the worst crimes, lie in a transparently obvious and deliberate manner? And lie so transparently and obviously that Straus, who does not speak their language, Kinyarwanda, can tell! Does Straus mean that the more than 70 percent who flat-out denied direct culpability in killing anyone failed to wink at him when they simply said, *I killed no one*, and therefore must have been telling the truth?

27. This in part reproduces a section from Goldhagen, *Hitler's Willing Executioners*, pp. 467–468.

28. Quoted in Hatzfeld, *Machete Season*, pp. 120 and 194.

29. Quoted in Goldhagen, *Hitler's Willing Executioners*, pp. 393–394.

30. Marcel Munyabugingo, author interview, Kigali, Rwanda, May 7, 2008.

31. Quoted in Hatzfeld, *Machete Season*, pp. 163–164.

32. *Report on the Natives of South-West Africa and Their Treatment by Germany* (presented to both Houses of Parliament by Command of His Majesty, August 1918) (London: H. M. Stationery Office, 1918), pp. 64–65.

33. Ibid., p. 102.

34. Quoted in Matthias Bjørnlund, "'A Fate Worse Than Dying': Sexual Violence during the Armenian Genocide," in Dagmar Herzog, ed., *Brutality and Desire: War and Sexuality in Europe's Twentieth Century* (New York: Palgrave Macmillan, 2009), p. 22.

35. "From the War Diary of Blutordenstraeger Felix Landau," in Ernst Klee, Willi Dressen, and Volker Riess, eds., *"The Good Old Days": The Holocaust as Seen by Its Perpetrators and Bystanders* (Old Saybrook, CT: Konecky & Konecky, 1991), p. 91.

36. Quoted in Goldhagen, *Hitler's Willing Executioners*, pp. 219–220.

37. Quoted in Caroline Elkins, *Imperial Reckoning: The Untold Story of Britain's Gulag in Kenya* (New York: Henry Holt, 2005), p. 257.

38. Robert Cribb, "The Indonesian Massacres," in Samuel Totten, William S. Parsons, and Israel W. Charny, eds., *Genocide in the Twentieth Century: Critical Essays and Eyewitness Accounts* (New York: Garland, 1995), pp. 319–320.

39. Quoted in Amita Malik, *The Year of the Vulture* (New Delhi, India: Orient Longman, 1972), pp. 102–103.

40. Quoted in Liisa H. Malkki, *Purity and Exile: Violence, Memory, and National Cosmology Among Hutu Refugees in Tanzania* (Chicago: University of Chicago Press, 1995), p. 95.

41. Sophea Mouth, "Imprinting Compassion," in Kim DePaul, ed., *Children of Cambodia's Killing Fields: Memoirs by Survivors*, compiled by Dith Pran (New Haven, CT: Yale University Press, 1997), pp. 179–180.

42. Quoted in Alexander Laban Hinton, *Why Did They Kill? Cambodia in the Shadow of Genocide* (Berkeley: University of California Press, 2005), p. 266.

43. Tomasa Osorio Chen, author interview, Panchook, Guatemala, June 9, 2008.

44. Alexandra Stiglmayer, "The Rapes in Bosnia-Herzegovina," in Alexandra Stiglmayer, ed., *Mass Rape: The War Against Women in Bosnia-Herzegovina* (Lincoln: University of Nebraska Press, 1994), pp. 120–121.

45. Quoted in Hatzfeld, *Machete Season*, p. 132.

46. Quoted in African Rights, *Rwanda*, p. 347.

47. Quoted in Amnesty International Report, "Darfur: Rape as a Weapon of War: Sexual Violence and Its Consequences," July 19, 2004, www.amnesty.org/en/library/info/AFR54/076/2004/en.

48. Quoted in Goldhagen, *Hitler's Willing Executioners*, pp. 280–281. Erwin Graffman is a pseudonym, as mandated by German law.

49. *Report on the Natives of South-West Africa and Their Treatment by Germany*, pp. 66–67.

50. Quoted in Elkins, *Imperial Reckoning*, p. 252.

51. Jesús Tecú Osorio, author interview, Rabinal, Guatemala, June 8, 2008.

52. Rithy Uong, author interview, Lowell, Massachusetts, April 11, 2008.

53. Alisa Muratčauš, author interview, Sarajevo, Bosnia and Herzegovina, July 12, 2008.

54. *Shattered Lives: Sexual Violence During the Rwandan Genocide and Its Aftermath* (New York: Human Rights Watch, 1996), p. 52.

55. Ngarambe, author interview.

56. Haruko Taya Cook and Theodore F. Cook, *Japan at War: An Oral History* (New York: New Press, 1992), p. 5.

57. See Goldhagen, *Hitler's Willing Executioners*, pp. 245–247.

58. See Klaus-Michael Mallmann, Volker Rieß, and Wolfram Pyta, eds., *Deutscher Osten 1939–1945: Der Weltanschauungskrieg in Photos und Texten* (Darmstadt, Germany: Wissenschaftliche Buchgesellschaft, 2003), pp. 31 and 42.

59. Alison Des Forges, *Leave None to Tell the Story: Genocide in Rwanda* (Human Rights Watch, 1999), www.hrw.org/en/reports/1999/03/01/leave-none-tell-story.

60. Quoted in Hatzfeld, *Machete Season*, pp. 94–95.

61. See Goldhagen, *Hitler's Willing Executioners*, pp. 451–453.

62. Michael A. Sells, "Kosovo Mythology and the Bosnian Genocide," in Omer Bartov and Phyllis Mack, *In God's Name: Genocide and Religion in the Twentieth Century* (New York: Berghahn, 2001), p. 190.

63. It is no coincidence that writers such as Browning, *Ordinary Men*, and Straus, *The Order of Genocide*, who choose to present the perpetrators' self-exonerations at face value also systematically downplay or ignore the perpetrators' cruelty and other acts that degraded the victims, as well as the voluminous victim testimony that tells a far more complete story of the multiple brutal and cruel ways the perpetrators generally treated them.

64. Quoted in Goldhagen, *Hitler's Willing Executioners*, p. 452. Many other studies and much published documentary evidence have since confirmed the book's conclusions. See, for example, Mallmann, Rieß, and Pyta, eds., *Deutscher Osten 1939–1945*.

65. Oscar Pinkus, *The House of Ashes* (Cleveland, OH: World Publishing Company, 1964), p. 119.

66. Quoted in Hatzfeld, *Machete Season*, p. 157.

67. Ngarambe, author interview.

68. Ibid.

69. Quoted in Hatzfeld, *Machete Season*, p. 120.

70. Quoted in Goldhagen, *Hitler's Willing Executioners*, p. 280.

71. Pipit Rochijat, "AM I PKI OR NON-PKI?" *Indonesia* 40 (October 1985), p. 45.

72. Ibid., p. 43.

73. See Helen Fein, *Accounting for Genocide: National Victimization and Jewish Responses During the Holocaust* (New York: Free Press, 1979).

74. Quoted in Jeremy Noakes and Geoffrey Pridham, eds., *Nazism: A History in Documents and Eyewitness Accounts, 1919–1945*, vol. 2 (New York: Schocken, 1988), p. 1132.

75. See Daniel Jonah Goldhagen, *A Moral Reckoning: The Role of the Catholic Church in the Holocaust and Its Unfulfilled Duty of Repair* (New York: Knopf, 2002), for an extensive discussion of these themes.

76. See Yuki Tanaka, *Hidden Horrors: Japanese War Crimes in World War II* (Boulder, CO: Westview, 1996), pp. 201–206.

77. See John W. Dower, *War Without Mercy: Race and Power in the Pacific War* (New York: Pantheon, 1986), pp. 53–55.

78. J. Samuel Walker, *Prompt and Utter Destruction: Truman and the Use of Atomic Bombs Against Japan*, rev. ed. (Chapel Hill: University of North Carolina Press, 2004), pp. 105–106.

79. Dwight D. Eisenhower, *Mandate for Change, 1953–1956: The White House Years* (Garden City, NY: Doubleday, 1963), pp. 312–313; and William D. Leahy, *I Was There: The Personal Story of the Chief of Staff to Presidents Roosevelt and Truman* (New York: Whittlesey House, 1950), p. 441.

80. All quoted in Benjamin Lieberman, *Terrible Fate: Ethnic Cleansing in the Making of Modern Europe* (Chicago: Ivan R. Dee, 2006), p. 233.

81. Ibid., p. 234.

82. Quoted in Norman M. Naimark, *Fires of Hatred: Ethnic Cleansing in Twentieth-Century Europe* (Cambridge, MA: Harvard University Press, 2001), p. 118.

83. Quoted in Jung Chang and Jon Halliday, *Mao: The Unknown Story* (New York: Knopf, 2005), p. 545.

84. Suleiman Abu Gheith, "In the Shadow of Lances," posted at *MEMRI Special Dispatch Series—No. 388*, June 12, 2002, www.memri.org/bin/articles.cgi?ID=sp38802#_edn1.

85. Jon Bridgman and Leslie J. Worley, "Genocide of the Hereros," in Samuel Totten, William S. Parsons, and Israel W. Charny, eds., *Century of Genocide: Critical Essays and Eyewitness Accounts*, 2nd ed. (New York: Routledge, 2004), p. 20.

86. Ibid., p. 27.

87. Peter Balakian, *The Burning Tigris: The Armenian Genocide and America's Response* (New York: HarperCollins, 2003), p. 223.

88. Henry Morgenthau, *Ambassador Morgenthau's Story* (Garden City, NY: Doubleday, 1919), pp. 162–170.

89. Vahakn N. Dadrian, "The Secret Young-Turk Ittihadist Conference and the Decision for the World War I Genocide of the Armenians," *Holocaust and Genocide Studies* 7, no. 2 (Fall 1993): 173–175.

90. Charlotte Kechejian, author interview, Flushing, New York, April 9, 2008.

91. Quoted in Tim Judah, *The Serbs: History, Myth and the Destruction of Yugoslavia* (New Haven, CT: Yale University Press, 1997), pp. 132–133; see also p. 127.

92. Quoted in Martin Bell, *In Harm's Way* (London: Hamish Hamilton, 1995), p. 132.

93. Yasmin Khan, *The Great Partition: The Making of India and Pakistan* (New Haven, CT: Yale University Press, 2007), pp. 79 and 85.

94. Quoted in Robert K. Hitchcock and Tara M. Twedt, "Physical and Cultural Genocide of Various Indigenous Peoples," in Totten, Parsons, and Charny, eds., *Genocide in the Twentieth Century*, p. 494.

95. Quoted in Goldhagen, *Hitler's Willing Executioners*, p. 280.

96. Geert Platner und Schüler der Gerhart-Hauptmann-Schule in Kassel, eds., *Schule im Dritten Reich: Erziehung zum Tod* (Cologne, Germany: Paul-Rugenstein, 1988).

97. Roger Fry, "An Essay in Aesthetics," in Craufurd D. Goodwin, ed., *Art and the Market: Roger Fry on Commerce in Art: Selected Writings* (Ann Arbor: University of Michigan Press, 1998), p. 80.

98. Melita Maschmann, *Account Rendered: A Dossier of My Former Self* (London: Abelard-Schuman, 1964), p. 56.

99. Quoted in Jean Hatzfeld, *Machete Season*, pp. 10–11.

100. This reproduces a section from Goldhagen, *A Moral Reckoning*, pp. 82–83. For these and other passages from *Civiltà cattolica*, see Georges Passelecq and Bernard Suchecky, *The Hidden Encyclical of Pius XI* (New York: Harcourt Brace, 1997), pp. 123–136.

101. Bridgman and Worley, "Genocide of the Hereros," pp. 21 and 29–30.

102. Mamdani, *When Victims Become Killers*, p. 220.

103. For a discussion of how to analyze these issues, see Goldhagen, *A Moral Reckoning*, pp. 120–121.

104. For a discussion of why the notion of collective guilt is to be rejected, of the nature of individual culpability, and of the various kinds of culpability, see Daniel Jonah Goldhagen, "Foreword to the German Edition," *Hitlers Willige Vollstrecker: Ganz gewöhnliche Deutsche und der Holocaust* (Berlin: Siedler, 1996), reprinted in *Hitler's Willing Executioners: Ordinary Germans and the Holocaust* (New York: Vintage, 1997), pp. 481–482, and Goldhagen, *A Moral Reckoning*, pp. 4–5, 9, and 124–131.

105. "Ceausescu's Absolute Power Dies in Rumanian Popular Rage," *New York Times*, January 7, 1990, quoted in James C. Scott, *Domination and the Arts of Resistance: Hidden Transcripts* (New Haven, CT: Yale University Press, 1990), p. 204.

106. Quoted in Hatzfeld, *Machete Season*, p. 219.

107. Ibid., pp. 58–59.

CHAPTER SIX

1. "Convention on the Prevention and Punishment of the Crime of Genocide," adopted by Resolution 260 (III) A of the UN General Assembly on

December 9, 1948, reproduced at Prevent Genocide International, www .preventgenocide.org/law/convention/text.htm.

2. Nicolas D. Kristof, "A Wimp on Genocide," *New York Times,* September 18, 2005.

3. "Convention on the Prevention and Punishment of the Crime of Genocide."

4. Daniel Jonah Goldhagen, *A Moral Reckoning: The Role of the Catholic Church in the Holocaust and Its Unfulfilled Duty of Repair* (New York: Knopf, 2002).

5. Robert Cribb, "The Indonesian Massacres," in Samuel Totten, William S. Parsons, and Israel W. Charny, eds., *Genocide in the Twentieth Century: Critical Essays and Eyewitness Accounts* (New York: Garland, 1995), p. 310.

6. William J. Clinton, "Remarks at the United States Naval Academy Commencement Ceremony in Annapolis, Maryland," May 25, 1994, www.presidency.ucsb.edu/ws/index.php?pid=50236.

7. Quoted in David Remnick, "The Wanderer," *New Yorker,* September 18, 2006, www.newyorker.com/archive/2006/09/18/060918fa_fact1.

8. Quoted in *Frontline: The Triumph of Evil: How the West Ignored Warnings of the 1994 Rwanda Genocide and Turned Its Back on the Victims,* www.pbs.org/wgbh/pages/frontline/shows/evil/etc/slaughter.html.

9. Quoted in Samantha Power, *"A Problem from Hell": America and the Age of Genocide* (New York: Basic Books, 2002), pp. 310–311.

10. Quoted in René Lemarchand, "Burundi," *Encyclopedia of Genocide and Crimes Against Humanity* (Farmington Hills, MI: Thomson Gale, 2005), pp. 133–134.

11. Quoted in Baroness Emma Nicholson of Winterbourne, "The Human Rights of the Sukan Al-ahwar (Marsh Arabs of Iraq)," speech delivered at the Mesopotamian Marshes Conference, October 30, 2004, Harvard University, www.cceia.org/resources/transcripts/5135.html.

12. Reported by BBC News, March 26, 2004, http://news.bbc.co.uk/2/hi/africa/3573229.stm.

CHAPTER SEVEN

1. See "The Cuban Missile Crisis, 1962: The 40th Anniversary," at the National Security Archive, The George Washington University, www.gwu .edu/~nsarchiv/nsa/cuba_mis_cri/audio.htm.

2. Jeremy Noakes and Geoffrey Pridham, eds., *Nazism: A History in Documents and Eyewitness Accounts, 1919–1945,* vol. 2 (New York: Schocken, 1988), p. 1130.

3. Quoted in François Ponchaud, *Cambodia: Year Zero* (New York: Holt, Rinehart and Winston, 1977), p. 50.

4. See Ulrich Trumpener, *Germany and the Ottoman Empire, 1914–1918* (Princeton, NJ: Princeton University Press, 1968), p. 127.

5. Quoted in African Rights, *Rwanda: Death, Despair and Defiance* (London: African Rights, 1994), pp. 54–55.

6. Quoted in African Rights, *Rwanda,* p. 57.

7. Quoted in Gérard Prunier, *The Rwanda Crisis: History of a Genocide* (New York: Columbia, 1995), p. 222.

8. Quoted in Caroline Elkins, *Imperial Reckoning: The Untold Story of Britain's Gulag in Kenya* (New York: Henry Holt, 2005), p. 42; see also pp. 38–46.

9. Quoted in Jean Hatzfeld, *Machete Season: The Killers in Rwanda Speak* (New York: Farrar, Straus and Giroux, 2005), p. 219.

10. These examples come from Amartya Sen, whose pioneering work shows these essential facts about famine. See "Public Action to Remedy Hunger," (August 2, 1990), posted at Global Policy Forum, www.global policy.org/socecon/hunger/general/1990/0802public.htm (accessed May 13, 2009).

11. Quoted in Elkins, *Imperial Reckoning,* pp. 259 and 262.

12. Quoted in Taner Akçam, *A Shameful Act: The Armenian Genocide and the Question of Turkish Responsibility* (New York: Metropolitan Books, 2006), p. 156.

13. Quoted in Robert Melson, "Provocation or Nationalism: A Critical Inquiry into the Armenian Genocide of 1915," in Frank Chalk and Kurt Jonassohn, eds., *The History and Sociology of Genocide: Analyses and Case Studies* (New Haven, CT: Yale University Press, 1990), pp. 282–283.

14. Quoted in David Chandler, *Voices from S-21: Terror and History in Pol Pot's Secret Prison* (Berkeley: University of California Press, 1999), p. 76.

15. Quoted in Lemarchand, *Burundi,* p. xvii.

16. World Health Organization, "Smallpox: Historical Significance," www.who.int/mediacentre/factsheets/smallpox/en/.

17. *Hitler's Secret Conversations, 1941–1944* (New York: Farrar, Straus and Young, 1953), entry of February 22, 1942, pp. 269–270.

18. Quoted in Noakes and Pridham, eds., *Nazism,* p. 1131.

CHAPTER EIGHT

1. James C. Scott, *Domination and the Arts of Resistance: Hidden Transcripts* (New Haven, CT: Yale University Press, 1990), p. 221.

2. Elie Ngarambe, author interview, Kigali, Rwanda, May 8, 2008.

3. Alison Des Forges, *Leave None to Tell the Story: Genocide in Rwanda* (Human Rights Watch, 1999), www.hrw.org/legacy/reports/1999/rwanda/.

4. Augustin Bazimaziki, author interview, Kigali, Rwanda, May 8, 2008.

5. Quoted in Jean Hatzfeld, *Machete Season: The Killers in Rwanda Speak* (New York: Farrar, Straus and Giroux, 2005), pp. 167–168 and 173–174.

6. William Pierce, *The Turner Diaries,* 2nd ed. (Hillsboro, WV: National Vanguard Books, 1978), pp. 42 and 59.

7. Cited in Jeremy Noakes and Geoffrey Pridham, eds., *Nazism: A History in Documents and Eyewitness Accounts,* vol. 2 (New York: Schocken, 1988), pp. 998–999.

8. Quoted in Tetsuo Najita and H. D. Harootunian, "Japanese Revolt Against the West: Political and Cultural Criticism in the Twentieth Century," in Peter Duus, ed., *The Cambridge History of Japan,* vol. 6, *The Twentieth Century* (Cambridge, UK: Cambridge University Press, 1988), p. 770.

9. Rithy Uong, author interview, Lowell, Massachusetts, April 11, 2008.

10. Quoted in Mark Hillel and Clarissa Henry, *Of Pure Blood* (New York: Pocket Books, 1976), p. 26.

11. Quoted in Ernst Klee, Willi Dressen, and Volker Rieß, eds., *"Schöne Zeiten": Judenmord aus der Sicht der Täter und Gaffer* (Frankfurt, Germany: S. Fischer Verlag, 1988), p. 203.

12. Josef Ackermann, *Heinrich Himmler Als Ideologue* (Göttingen, Germany: Musterschmidt, 1979), p. 160.

13. Adolf Hitler, *Mein Kampf* (New York: Houghton Mifflin, 1971), p. 65. In the first edition from 1925 it said "thousands." In the second edition from 1926, it was changed to "millions."

14. Paul Mahehu, author interview, Nyeri District, Kenya, May 1, 2008.

15. John Nottingham, author interview, Nairobi, Kenya, May 4, 2008.

16. Quoted in Caroline Elkins, *Imperial Reckoning: The Untold Story of Britain's Gulag in Kenya* (New York: Henry Holt, 2005), pp. 113–114.

17. See Elkins, *Imperial Reckoning,* pp. 246, 106, and 47.

18. Ibid., p. 49.

19. Nottingham, author interview.

20. For a further discussion of these dimensions, see Daniel Jonah Goldhagen, *Hitler's Willing Executioners: Ordinary Germans and the Holocaust* (New York: Knopf, 1996), pp. 35–37.

21. David P. Chandler, *The Tragedy of Cambodian History: Politics, War, and Revolution Since 1945* (New Haven, CT: Yale University Press, 1991), p. 249.

22. Teeda Butt Mam, "Worms from Our Skin," in Kim DePaul, ed., *Children of Cambodia's Killing Fields: Memoirs by Survivors,* compiled by Dith Pran (New Haven, CT: Yale University Press, 1997), pp. 12–13.

23. Quoted in Adam Hochschild, *King Leopold's Ghost: A Story of Greed, Terror, and Heroism in Colonial Africa* (Boston: Houghton Mifflin, 1998), pp. 119–120.

24. Heinrich Himmler, "Speech of the *Reichsführer-SS* at the SS Group Leader Meeting in Posen (Poznan)," Nuremberg Doc. 1919-PS, reproduced at www.holocaustresearchproject.org/holoprelude/posen.html.

25. Central Intelligence Agency, secret cable, *Counterinsurgency Operations in El Quiché* (February 1982), in the National Security Archive, *The Guatemalan Military: What the U.S. Files Reveal, Volume II, Documents,* Document 20, www.gwu.edu/~nsarchiv/NSAEBB/NSAEBB32/vol2.html.

26. Klaus-Michael Mallmann, Volker Rieß, and Wolfram Pyta, eds., *Deutscher Osten 1939–1945: Der Weltanschauungskrieg in Photos und Texten* (Darmstadt, Germany: Wissenschaftliche Buchgesellschaft, 2003), p. 28.

27. Himmler, "Speech of the *Reichsführer-SS.*"

28. Quoted in Gerald Fleming, *Hitler and the Final Solution* (Berkeley: University of California Press, 1984), p. 17.

29. For a discussion of the evolution of Hitler's thinking and Nazi anti-Jewish policy, see Goldhagen, *Hitler's Willing Executioners,* pp. 131–163, especially pp. 134–136.

30. R. J. Rummel, *China's Bloody Century: Genocide and Mass Murder Since 1900* (New Brunswick, NJ: Transaction, 1991), p. 223.

31. Branimir Anzulovic, *Heavenly Serbia: From Myth to Genocide* (New York: New York University Press, 1999), pp. 51–52.

32. Ibid., pp. 114–116.

33. Ibid., p. 129.

34. Ibid., pp. 138–139.

35. Jacob Robinson, *And the Crooked Shall Be Made Straight: The Eichmann Trial, the Jewish Catastrophe, and Hannah Arendt's Narrative* (New York: Macmillan, 1965), p. 37.

36. Quoted in Elkins, *Imperial Reckoning,* p. 3.

37. Ibid., p. 48.

38. Cvijeto Job, *Yugoslavia's Ruin: The Bloody Lessons of Nationalism, A Patriot's Warning* (Lanham, MD: Rowman & Littlefield, 2002), pp. 167–168.

39. Louis Sell, *Slobodan Milosevic and the Destruction of Yugoslavia* (Durham, NC: Duke University Press, 2002), p. 34.

40. Esperance Nyirarugira, Concessa Kayiraba, and Veronique Mukasinafi, author interview, Rwamagana District, Eastern Province, Rwanda, May 6, 2008.

41. Ngarambe, author interview.

42. Quoted in Hatzfeld, *Machete Season,* p. 218.

43. Ngarambe, author interview.

44. Yeoshua Gertner and Danek Gertner, *Home Is No More: The Destruction of the Jews of Kosow and Zabie* (Jerusalem: Yad Vashem, 2000), pp. 72–73.

CHAPTER NINE

1. Sergei Khrushchev, ed., *Memoirs of Nikita Khrushchev: Volume 2: Reformer, 1945–1964* (University Park: Pennsylvania State University Press, 2006), pp. 158–159.

2. Elie Ngarambe, author interview, Kigali, Rwanda, May 8, 2008.

3. Quoted in Gerald Reitlinger, *The House Built on Sand: The Conflicts of German Policy in Russia, 1941–1945* (London: Weidenfeld & Nicolson, 1960), p. 200.

4. See Daniel Jonah Goldhagen, "There Is No Hierarchy Among Victims," *New York Times*, January 18, 1997.

5. Heinrich Himmler's speech of October 6, 1943, in Posen to the leaders of the Nazi Party in Erich Goldhagen, "Albert Speer, Himmler, and the Secrecy of the Final Solution," *Midstream*, October 1971, p. 46.

6. See Daniel Jonah Goldhagen, "The Globalization of Antisemitism" (republished under "Hate Turns from Shylock to Rambo"), *Sunday Times*, May 11, 2003, www.timesonline.co.uk/tol/news/article884975.ece.

7. Anna Pawełczy ska, *Values and Violence in Auschwitz: A Sociological Analysis* (Berkeley: University of California Press, 1979), pp. 54–55.

8. Quoted in Raul Hilberg, *The Destruction of the European Jews* (New York: New Viewpoints, 1973), p. 149. The final sentence is my translation.

9. "'The Lesser Evil': An Interview with Norodom Sihanouk," *New York Review of Books*, March 14, 1985, p. 24.

10. Quoted in François Ponchaud, *Cambodia: Year Zero* (New York: Holt, Rinehart and Winston, 1977), pp. 50–51.

11. Arn Yan, "My Mother's Courage," in Kim DePaul, ed., *Children of Cambodia's Killing Fields: Memoirs by Survivors*, compiled by Dith Pran (New Haven, CT: Yale University Press, 1997), p. 141.

12. From Ben Kiernan, *The Pol Pot Regime: Race, Power, and Genocide in Cambodia under the Khmer Rouge, 1975–79* (New Haven, CT: Yale University Press, 1996), p. 458. Used with permission. The figures here and in this section are taken from Ben Kiernan, "The Cambodian Genocide—1975–1979," in Samuel Totten, William S. Parsons, and Israel W. Charny, eds., *Genocide in the Twentieth Century: Critical Essays and Eyewitness Accounts* (New York: Garland, 1995), pp. 436–441.

13. Chhun Von, author interview, Lowell, Massachusetts, April 11, 2008.

14. Teeda Butt Mam, "Worms from Our Skin," in DePaul, ed., *Children of Cambodia's Killing Fields*, pp. 13–14.

15. Moly Ly, "Witnessing the Horror," in DePaul, ed., *Children of Cambodia's Killing Fields*, p. 61.

16. Quoted in Kiernan, *The Pol Pot Regime: Race, Power, and Genocide in Cambodia under the Khmer Rouge, 1975–79*, p. 2.

17. Ponchaud, *Cambodia*, pp. 50–51.

18. Quoted in Jean Hatzfeld, *Machete Season: The Killers in Rwanda Speak* (New York: Farrar, Straus and Giroux, 2005), p. 96.

19. John Hughes, *Indonesian Upheaval* (New York: David McKay, 1967), p. 175.

20. Alisa Muratčauš, author interview, Sarajevo, Bosnia and Herzegovina, July 12, 2008.

21. Hatzfeld, *Machete Season*, p. 9.

22. Ibid., p. 93.

23. BA Koblenz, ZSg. 101 Sammlung Brammer zur Pressepolitik des NS-Staates, no. 41, pp. 55–57.

24. Quoted in Alf Lüdtke, "The Appeal of Exterminating 'Others': German Workers and the Limits of Resistance," in Michael Geyer and John W. Boyer, eds., *Resistance Against the Third Reich, 1933–1990* (Chicago: University of Chicago Press, 1994), p. 73.

25. Ngarambe, author interview.

26. Hatzfeld, *Machete Season*, pp. 71 and 219.

27. Daniel Jonah Goldhagen, *Hitler's Willing Executioners: Ordinary Germans and the Holocaust* (New York: Knopf, 1996), especially pp. 450–454.

28. Hatzfeld, *Machete Season*, pp. 219 and 170.

29. Max Weinreich, *Hitler's Professors: The Part of Scholarship in the Germany's Crimes Against the Jewish People* (New York: YIVO, 1946); Léon Poliakov and Joseph Wulf, eds., *Das Dritte Reich und seine Denker* (The Third Reich and Its Thinkers) (Frankfurt, Germany: Ullstein, 1983); Robert Jay Lifton, *The Nazi Doctors: Medical Killing and the Psychology of Genocide* (New York: Basic Books, 1986); Ingo Müller, *Hitler's Justice: The Courts of the Third Reich* (Cambridge, MA: Harvard University Press, 1991); and Paul Lawrence Rose, *Revolutionary Antisemitism in Germany from Kant to Wagner* (Princeton, NJ: Princeton University Press, 1990).

30. Quoted in Hatzfeld, *Machete Season*, pp. 153–154.

31. Quoted in Goldhagen, *Hitler's Willing Executioners*, p. 115.

32. Quoted in Hatzfeld, *Machete Season*, p. 68.

33. Lucy Ngima Wahome, author interview, Nyeri District, Kenya, May 1, 2008; Paul Mahehu, author interview, Nyeri District, Kenya, May 1,

2008; and John Nottingham, author interview, Nairobi, Kenya, May 4, 2008.

34. Nottingham, author interview.

35. Josiah Mwangi Kariuki, *"Mau Mau" Detainee: The Account by a Kenya African of His Experiences in Detention Camps, 1953–1960* (London: Oxford University Press, 1963), p. 81.

36. Mahehu, author interview.

37. Much of this paragraph closely follows a paragraph from Goldhagen, *Hitler's Willing Executioners*, p. 459. For Frank's statements, see Poliakov and Wulf, eds., *Das Dritte Reich und seine Denker*, pp. 503–504. For Himmler's statement, see "Indictment against R.R., M.B., and E.K.," StA Regensburg I 4 Js 1495/85, p. 36.

38. See Goldhagen, *Hitler's Willing Executioners*, "The Nazi German Revolution," pp. 455–461.

39. Otto-Ernst Duscheleit, author interview, Berlin, Germany, July 19, 2008.

40. The last few sentences mainly reproduce a section from Goldhagen, *Hitler's Willing Executioners*, p. 171.

41. Galician Kalinnikovich, author interview, St. Petersburg, Russia, June 26, 2008.

42. Ukhnalev Ilyich, author interview, St. Petersburg, Russia, June 26, 2008.

43. Kalinnikovich, author interview.

44. Ilyich, author interview.

45. Quoted in Anne Applebaum, *Gulag: A History* (New York: Anchor Books, 2003), p. 241.

46. R. J. Rummel, *China's Bloody Century: Genocide and Mass Murder Since 1900* (New Brunswick, NJ: Transaction, 1991), p. 214.

47. Henry Morgenthau, *Ambassador Morgenthau's Story* (Garden City, NY: Doubleday, Page, 1919), pp. 338 and 348; Davis quoted in Peter Balakian, *The Burning Tigris: The Armenian Genocide and America's Response* (New York: HarperCollins, 2003), p. 236.

48. Goldhagen, *Hitler's Willing Executioners*, pp. 289–290; and Albert Speer, *The Slave State: Heinrich Himmler's Masterplan for SS Supremacy* (London: Weidenfeld & Nicolson, 1981), pp. 281–282.

49. Jeremy Noakes and Geoffrey Pridham, eds., *Nazism: A History in Documents and Eyewitness Accounts*, vol. 2 (New York: Schocken, 1988), p. 1131.

50. Applebaum, *Gulag*, pp. 29–30, 108–110, and 471–472.

51. *Guatemala: Memory of Silence, Report of the Commission for Historical Clarification*, "Conclusions and Recommendations," paragraphs 72 and 73, http://shr.aaas.org/guatemala/ceh/report/english/toc.html.

52. Quoted in Applebaum, *Gulag*, p. 271.

53. Ratha Duong, "Hurt, Pain, and Suffering," in DePaul, ed., *Children of Cambodia's Killing Fields*, p. 96.

54. Quoted in Kiernan, "The Cambodian Genocide—1975–1979," p. 478.

55. S. A. Malsagoff, *An Island Hell: A Soviet Prison in the Far North* (London: A. M. Philpot, 1926), p. 174.

56. Quoted in Jung Chang and Jon Halliday, *Mao: The Unknown Story* (New York: Knopf, 2005), p. 325.

57. Ly, "Witnessing the Horror," pp. 63–64.

58. Elizabeth Becker, *When the War Was Over: Cambodia's Revolution and the Voices of Its Rebirth* (New York: Touchstone, 1986), pp. 41–42.

59. Eugon Kogan, *The Theory and Practice of Hell* (New York: Berkeley Medallion Books, 1968), p. 90.

60. *Report on the Natives of South-West Africa and Their Treatment by Germany,* (presented to both houses of Parliament by Command of His Majesty, August 1918) (London: H. M. Stationery Office, 1918), p. 100.

61. Armen Hairapetian, "'Race Problems' and the Armenian Genocide: The State Department File," *Armenian Review* (Spring 1984): 57.

62. Quoted in Caroline Elkins, *Imperial Reckoning: The Untold Story of Britain's Gulag in Kenya* (New York: Henry Holt, 2005), p. 257.

63. Rithy Uong, author interview, April 11, 2008, Lowell, Massachusetts.

64. Joseph Schupack, *Tote Jahre: Eine jüdische Leidensgeschichte* (Tübingen, Germany: Katzmann, 1984), p. 138.

65. Uong, author interview.

66. Quoted in Robert Conquest, *Kolyma: The Arctic Death Camps* (Oxford, UK: Oxford University Press, 1979), p. 132.

67. Savuth Penn, "The Dark Years of My Life," in DePaul, ed., *Children of Cambodia's Killing Fields*, p. 48.

68. Quoted in Elkins, *Imperial Reckoning*, p. 166.

69. Chang and Halliday, *Mao*, p. 106.

70. Quoted in Jasper Becker, *Hungry Ghosts: Mao's Secret Famine* (New York: Free Press, 1996), p. 146.

71. Chang and Halliday, *Mao*, p. 421.

72. Navy Dy, "The Tragedy of My Homeland," in DePaul, ed., *Children of Cambodia's Killing Fields*, pp. 89–90.

73. Charles Karumi, interview with Caroline Elkins, Westlands, Nairobi, Kenya, August 9, 2003.

74. Wolfgang Gust, ed., *Der Völkermord an den Armeniern 1915/16: Dokumente aus dem Politischen Archiv des deutschen Auswärtigen Amts* (Springe, Germany: zu Klampen, 2005), p. 262.

75. Fredy Peccerelli, author interview, Guatemala City, Guatemala, June 5, 2008.

76. Quoted in Elkins, *Imperial Reckoning*, pp. 256–257.

77. Quoted in Hatzfeld, *Machete Season*, pp. 132–133.

78. See Daniel Jonah Goldhagen, "There Is No Hierarchy Among Victims," *New York Times*, January 18, 1997.

79. See Goldhagen, *Hitler's Willing Executioners*, pp. 295–300, from which the passage here reproduces some sections.

80. Quoted in Applebaum, *Gulag*, p. 270.

81. Ilyich, author interview.

82. Jasper Becker, *Hungry Ghosts: Mao's Secret Famine* (New York: Free Press, 1996), p. 194.

83. Quoted in Hatzfeld, *Machete Season*, p. 131.

84. Von, author interview.

85. Uong, author interview.

86. See Norman M. Naimark, *The Russians in Germany: A History of the Soviet Zone of Occupation, 1945–1949* (Cambridge, MA: Harvard University Press, 1995), pp. 72–74.

87. See Daniel Gilbert, "He Who Cast the First Stone Probably Didn't," *New York Times*, July 24, 2006.

88. Roeun Sam, "Living in the Darkness," in DePaul, ed., *Children of Cambodia's Killing Fields*, pp. 76–77.

89. Quoted in Jean Hatzfeld, *Into the Quick of Life: The Rwandan Genocide—The Survivors Speak* (London: Serpent's Tail, 2005), p. 75.

90. Ibid.

91. See Goldhagen, *Hitler's Willing Executioners*, p. 307.

92. Yuki Tanaka, *Hidden Horrors: Japanese War Crimes in World War II* (Boulder, CO: Westview, 1996), p. 204.

93. Erwin Wickert, ed., *The Good Man of Nanking: The Diaries of John Rabe* (New York: Knopf, 1998), p. 173.

94. Quoted in Roy Gutman, "The Rapes of Bosnia," in *A Witness to Genocide: The 1993 Pulitzer Prize–winning Dispatches on the "Ethnic Cleansing" of Bosnia* (New York: Macmillan, 1993), pp. 69–70.

95. Quoted in Alexandra Stiglmayer, "The Rapes in Bosnia-Herzegovina," in Alexandra Stiglmayer, ed., *Mass Rape: The War against Women in Bosnia-Herzegovina* (Lincoln: University of Nebraska Press, 1994), p. 92.

96. Ibid., p. 85.

97. Quoted in Human Rights Watch, *Kosovo: Rape as a Weapon of "Ethnic Cleansing,"* 2000, www.hrw.org/reports/2000/fry/Kosov003-02.htm#P155_28604.

98. Ibid.

99. Quoted in Rounaq Jahan, "Genocide in Bangladesh," in Samuel Totten, William S. Parsons, and Israel W. Charny, eds., *Genocide in the Twentieth Century: Critical Essays and Eyewitness Accounts* (New York: Garland, 1995), p. 398.

100. Susan Brownmiller, *Against Our Will: Men, Women and Rape* (Harmondsworth, UK: Penguin, 1976), pp. 85 and 81–82.

101. Ibid., pp. 60–61.

102. See Julie Mertus, "Women in Kosovo: Contested Terrains," in Sabrina P. Ramet, ed., *Gender Politics in the Western Balkans: Women and Society in Yugoslavia and the Yugoslav Successor States* (University Park: Pennsylvania State University Press, 1999), p. 178.

103. Human Rights Watch, *Kosovo.*

104. Amnesty International Report, "Darfur: Rape as a Weapon of War: Sexual Violence and Its Consequences," July 19, 2004, http://web.amnesty .org/library/index/engafr540762004.

105. Médecins Sans Frontières, "The Crushing Burden of Rape: Sexual Violence in Darfur," March 8, 2005, www.genocideinterventionfund.org/ educate/reports/others/crushing_burden_of_rape.pdf.

106. Benjamin Joffe-Walt, "Arab Militia Use 'Rape Camps' for Ethnic Cleansing of Sudan," *Daily Telegraph,* May 29, 2004, www.telegraph .co.uk/news/main.jhtml?xml=/news/2004/05/30/wdarf30.xml.

107. Quoted in Regina Mühlhäuser, "Between 'Racial Awareness' and Fantasies of Potency: Nazi Sexual Politics in the Occupied Territories of the Soviet Union, 1942–1945," in Dagmar Herzog, ed., *Brutality and Desire: War and Sexuality in Europe's Twentieth Century* (New York: Palgrave Macmillan, 2009), p. 198.

108. *Guatemala: Memory of Silence*, "Conclusions and Recommendations," paragraph 91.

109. Elkins, *Imperial Reckoning*, pp. 247 and 254.

110. Ibid., p. 257.

111. Quoted in Hiroko Tabuchi, "Japan's Abe: No Proof of WWII Sex Slaves," *Washington Post,* March 1, 2007, www.washingtonpost.com/ wp-dyn/content/article/2007/03/01/AR2007030100578.html.

112. *Report on the Natives of South-West Africa and Their Treatment by Germany*, p. 65.

113. James Bryce and Arnold Toynbee, *The Treatment of Armenians in the Ottoman Empire, 1915–1916. Documents Presented to Viscount Grey of Falloden by Viscount Bryce* (Princeton, NJ: Gomidas Institute, 2000), Account 24, p. 128.

114. Stiglmayer, "The Rapes in Bosnia-Herzegovina," pp. 108–109.

115. Quoted in Gutman, "Victims Recount Nights of Terror at Makeshift Bordello," in *A Witness to Genocide*, p. 76; and in Stiglmayer, "The Rapes in Bosnia-Herzegovina," p. 121.

116. Amnesty International Report, "Darfur: Rape as a Weapon of War."

117. Ibid.

118. Tharcisse Karugarama, author interview, Kigali, Rwanda, May 9, 2008.

119. *Shattered Lives: Sexual Violence during the Rwandan Genocide and Its Aftermath* (New York: Human Rights Watch, 1996), pp. 54–56.

120. Ibid., pp. 63–64.

121. Ibid., pp. 62–63.

122. Concessa Kayiraba, author interview, Rwamagana District, Eastern Province, Rwanda, May 6, 2008.

123. Ngarambe, author interview.

124. Muratčauš, author interview.

125. Samuel Totten and Eric Markusen, "Moving into the Field and Conducting the Interviews: Commentary and Observations by the Investigators," in Samuel Totten and Eric Markusen, eds., *Genocide in Darfur: Investigating the Atrocities in the Sudan* (New York: Routledge, 2006), pp. 95–96.

126. Nottingham, author interview.

127. *Guatemala: Never Again!*, REMNI, Recovery of Historical Memory Project, the Official Report of the Human Rights Office, Archdiocese of Guatemala (New York: Orbis, 1999), pp. 31 and 29.

128. Peccerelli, author interview.

129. See Vahakn N. Dadrian, "The Secret Young-Turk Ittihadist Conference and the Decision for the World War I Genocide of the Armenians," *Holocaust and Genocide Studies* (Fall 1993): 174.

130. Heinrich Himmler, "Speech of the *Reichsführer-SS* at the SS Group Leader Meeting in Posen (Poznan)," Nuremberg Doc. 1919-PS, reproduced at www.holocaustresearchproject.org/holoprelude/posen.html.

131. Quoted in Ernst Klee, Willi Dressen, and Volker Rieß, eds., *"The Good Old Days": The Holocaust as Seen by Its Perpetrators and Bystanders* (New York: Free Press, 1991), pp. 54 and 56.

132. Quoted in Liisa H. Malkki, *Purity and Exile: Violence, Memory, and National Cosmology Among Hutu Refugees in Tanzania* (Chicago: University of Chicago Press, 1995), p. 91.

133. African Rights, *Rwanda: Death, Despair and Defiance* (London: African Rights, 1994), pp. 463–464.

134. Quoted in Hatzfeld, *Machete Season*, pp. 131–132.

135. Nottingham, author interview.

136. Malkki, *Purity and Exile*, pp. 92–93.

137. Oscar Pinkus, *The House of Ashes* (Cleveland, OH: World Publishing Company, 1964), p. 36.

CHAPTER TEN

1. Quoted in Orly Halpern, "Exiled Hamas Leader Gives Interview," *Jerusalem Post,* February 26, 2006, www.jpost.com/servlet/Satellite?cid=1139 395452922&pagename=JPost%2FJPArticle%2FShowFull; and "Hamas Pushes for Sharia Punishments," *Jerusalem Post,* December 24, 2008, www .jpost.com/servlet/Satellite?pagename=JPost%2FJPArticle%2FShowFull&cid= 1229868840606. An earlier version of my treatment of Political Islam appeared in Daniel Jonah Goldhagen, "The New Threat: The Radical Politics of Islamic Fundamentalism," *New Republic*, March 13, 2006, pp. 15–27.

2. "To the Americans" Internet posting of October 6, 2002, in Bruce Lawrence, ed., *Messages to the World: The Statements of Osama bin Laden* (London: Verso, 2005), pp. 166–171.

3. Steven Stalinsky, "Dealing in Death: The West Is Weak Because It Respects Life? Too Bad," *National Review Online,* May 24, 2004, www .nationalreview.com/comment/stalinsky200405240846.asp.

4. Quoted in Richard Stengel, "Osama bin Laden and the Idea of Progress," *Time,* December 21, 2001, www.time.com/time/columnist/stengel/article/ 0,9565,189648,00.html.

5. Quoted in Stalinsky, "Dealing in Death."

6. "MEMRI TV Monitor Project—Hizbullah Leader Hassan Nasrallah: 'The American Administration Is Our Enemy . . . Death to America,'" *MEMRI Special Dispatch Series—No. 867,* February 22, 2005, http:// memri.org/bin/articles.cgi?Page=archives&Area=sd&ID=SP86705.

7. For examples from Hamas and the Palestinian Authority more generally, see "PA Indoctrination of Children to Seek Heroic Death for Allah—*Shahada*," *TV Archives—Video Library,* www.pmw.org.il/tv%20part1 .html.

8. "Somali Cleric Calls for Pope's Death," *The Age,* September 17, 2006, www.theage.com.au/news/world/somali-cleric-calls-for-popes-death/2006/ 09/16/1158334739295.html.

9. "Al Qaeda Threat to 'Slit Throats of Worshippers of the Cross,'" *Daily Mail,* September 18, 2006, www.dailymail.co.uk/news/article=405758/Al-Qaeda-threat-slit-throats-worshippers-cross.html.

10. "The Charter of Allah: The Platform of the Islamic Resistance Movement (Hamas)," *www.palestinecenter.org/cpap/documents/charter.html.*

11. *Messages to the World.*

12. Quoted in Amal Saad-Ghorayeb, *Hizbu'llah: Politics and Religion* (London: Pluto, 2002), p. 170.

13. "Terror for Terror" interview of October 21, 2001, for Al-Jazeera (first aired on January 31, 2002), and "To the Americans" Internet posting of October 6, 2002, in *Messages to the World*, pp. 108 and 162.

14. BBC Monitoring: Al-Manar, September 27, 2002, cited in Deborah Passner, "Hassan Nasrallah: In His Own Words," *CAMERA,* July 26, 2006, www.camera.org/index.asp?x_context=7&x_issue=11&x_article=1158.

15. Mahmoud Ahmadinejad, speech at "World without Zionism" Conference, posted at *MEMRI Special Dispatch Series—No. 1013,* October 28, 2005, http://memri.org/bin/articles.cgi?Page=archives&Area=sd&ID=SP101305.

16. "Iran: President Wants to 'Annihilate Corrupt Powers,'" *AKI,* www.adnkronos.com/AKI/English/Security/?id=1.0.2058939507.

17. Ahmadinejad, speech at "World without Zionism" Conference; and "Text of Mahmoud Ahmadinejad's Speech," *New York Times*, October 30, 2005, www.nytimes.com/2005/10/30/weekinreview/30iran.html?ex=11612 30400&en=26f07fc5b7543417&ei=5070.

18. Suleiman Abu Gheith, "In the Shadow of Lances," posted at *MEMRI Special Dispatch Series—No. 388*, June 12, 2002, www.memri.org/bin/articles .cgi?ID=sp38802#_edn1; and Nasir bin Hamid al-Fahd, "A Treaties on the Legal Status of Using Weapons of Mass Destruction Against Infidels," May 2003, p. 8, posted at http://www.carnegieendowment.org/static/npp/fatwa.pdf.

19. Jane Perlez, "From Finding Radical Islam to Losing an Ideology," *New York Times,* September 12, 2007, www.nytimes.com/2007/09/12/world/ europe/12britain.html?_r=1&oref=slogin&pagewanted=print.

20. Colin Freeman and Philip Sherwell, "Iranian Fatwa Approves Use of Nuclear Weapons," *Daily Telegraph,* February, 19, 2006, www.telegraph .co.uk/news/main.jhtml?xml=/news/2006/02/19/wiran19.xml.

21. Owen Bowcott, "Arrest Extremist Marchers, Police Told," *Guardian,* February 6, 2006, www.guardian.co.uk/uk/2006/feb/06/raceandreligion .muhammadcartoons; "London Protests: Call for Arrests," CNN.com, February 7, 2006, http://edition.cnn.com/2006/WORLD/europe/02/06/london .cartoon.protests/; and Ian Fisher, "Tens of Thousands Protest Cartoon in Gaza," *New York Times*, February 3, 2006, www.nytimes.com/2006/02/03/ international/middleeast/03cnd-mide.html?_r=1&scp=1&sq=will%20 not%20accept%20less%20than%20severing%20the%20heads%20of%20t hose%20responsible&st=cse.

22. "Hamas Leader Khaled Mash'al at a Damascus Mosque: The Nation of Islam Will Sit at the Throne of the World and the West Will Be Full of Remorse—When It's Too Late," *MEMRI Special Dispatch Series—No.*

1087, February 7, 2006, www.memri.org/bin/articles.cgi?Area=sd&ID=SP 108706&Page=archives.

23. Itamar Marcus and Barbara Crook, "Hamas Video: We will drink the blood of the Jews," *Palestinian Media Watch,* February 14, 2006, www.pmw .org.il/Latest%20bulletins%20new.htm#b140206.

24. See Matthias Küntzel, "Ahmadinejad's Demons," *New Republic,* April 24, 2006.

25. Quoted in Matthias Küntzel, "From Khomeini to Ahmadinejad," *Policy Review* (December 2006), reproduced at www.matthiaskuentzel.de/ contents/from-khomeini-to-ahmadinejad.

26. "Mashaal: Talks with Israel a Waste of Time," *YNET,* February 21, 2006, www.ynetnews.com/articles/0,7340,L-3219163,00.html; and Ahmadinejad, speech at "World without Zionism" Conference.

27. "Text of Mahmoud Ahmadinejad's Speech," *New York Times,* October 30, 2005, www.nytimes.com/2005/10/30/weekinreview/30iran.html? ex=1161230400&en=26f07fc5b7543417&ei=5070.

28. "Terror for Terror" interview of October 21, 2001, for Al-Jazeera (first aired on January 31, 2002) in *Messages to the World,* pp. 108–109.

29. Quoted in Lawrence Wright, *The Looming Tower: Al-Qaeda and the Road to 9/11* (New York: Knopf, 2006), p. 187.

30. Quoted in Husain Haqqani, "The Ideologies of South Asian Jihadi Groups," *Current Trends in Islamist Ideology,* vol. 1 (Hudson Institute, 2005), www.futureofmuslimworld.com/research/pubID.30/pub_detail.asp.

31. "Hamas Leader Khaled Mash'al at a Damascus Mosque."

CHAPTER ELEVEN

1. Haris Silajdžić, author interview, Srebrenica, Bosnia and Herzegovina, July 11, 2008.

2. For a discussion of the issues, see Jeffrey D. Sachs, *The End of Poverty: Economic Possibilities for Our Time* (New York: Penguin, 2005).

3. Norimitsu Onishi, "Released from Rigors of a Trial, a Nobel Laureate's Ink Flows Freely," *New York Times,* May 17, 2008, www.nytimes .com/2008/05/17/world/asia/17oe.html?scp=1&sq=Norimitsu%20 Onishi,%20?Released%20From%20Rigors%20of%20a%20Trial,%20a% 20Nobel%20Laureate?s%20Ink%20Flows%20Freely&st=cse.

4. For an explanation of the somewhat singular and positive way Germans have dealt with their past's horrific part, see Daniel Jonah Goldhagen, "*Modell Bundesrepublik:* National History, Democracy, and Internationalization in Germany," in Robert R. Shandley, ed., *Unwilling Germans? The Goldhagen Debate* (Minneapolis: University of Minnesota Press, 1998), pp.

275–285; and Daniel Jonah Goldhagen, *A Moral Reckoning: The Role of the Catholic Church in the Holocaust and Its Unfulfilled Duty of Repair* (New York: Knopf, 2002), pp. 282–288. Also, see my open letter to the Turkish government, "Turkey After Pamuk," *New York Sun,* January 24, 2006, for a discussion of how Turkey should emulate Germany in dealing with its past. (It was published in German in *Die Welt.*)

5. See, for example, for Belgium, Rudi Van Doorslaer et al., *Gewillig België: Overheid en Jodenvervolging tijdens de Tweede Wereldoorlog* (Antwerp/Amsterdam: Meulenhoff/Manteau, 2007); for Switzerland, "Independent Commission of Experts Switzerland—Second World War," www.uek.ch/en/index .htm; and for the Northern Protestant State Church in Germany, "Kirche, Christen, Juden in Nordelbien 1933–1945," www.kirche-christen-juden.org/.

6. Quoted in Samantha Power, *"A Problem from Hell": America and the Age of Genocide* (New York: Basic Books, 2002), p. 307.

7. Freedom House, *Freedom in the World 2009,* www.freedomhouse .org/template.cfm?page=445.

8. "African Union in a Nutshell," www.africa-union.org/root/au/About Au/au_in_a_nutshell_en.htm.

9. *International Commission on Intervention and State Sovereignty, The Responsibility to Protect: Report of the International Commission on Intervention and State Sovereignty* (December 2001), available at the Responsibility to Protect Web site, www.responsibilitytoprotect.org/index.php/pages/2.

10. UN Security Council Resolution 1706, August 31, 2006, reproduced at the *Responsibility to Protect* Web site, www.responsibilitytoprotect.org/ index.php/united_nations/792?theme=alt1.

11. Thomas Patrick Melady, *Burundi: The Tragic Years* (Maryknoll, NY: Orbis, 1974), p. 83. Melady stunningly comments, just one page before his apologetics about U.S. inaction: "The UN posture on the Burundi matter gave the impression that while the UN would exercise great energy to protest the violations of human rights, in various parts of the world, it would not do so in regard to Burundi. Such a double standard only brings into disrepute the universal mandate of the United Nations to protect human rights everywhere" (p. 82).

12. See the *Responsibility to Protect* Web site, www.responsibilityto protect.org/.

13. Bush on ABC-TV interview, January 23, 2000, reported in *Washington Post,* August 11, 2000. In the first presidential debate of the fall 2000 election campaign, Bush used the term "vital national interests," saying, "that means," when "our territory is threatened or [our] people could be harmed," when "our defense alliances are threatened" or "our friends in the Middle East are threatened." See Anthony Lewis, "Milosevic and Bush," *New York*

Times, http://query.nytimes.com/gst/fullpage.html?res=9C02E7DD153CF934 A35753C1A9669C8B63.

14. Quoted in Michael A. Sells, *The Bridge Betrayed: Religion and Genocide in Bosnia* (Berkeley: University of California Press, 1996), p. 115.

15. Quoted in Paul Hollander, "The Distinctive Features of Repression in Communist States," in Paul Hollander, ed., *From the Gulag to the Killing Field: Personal Accounts of Political Violence and Repression in Communist States* (Wilmington, DE: ISI, 2007), p. 1.

16. See Goldhagen, *"Modell Bundesrepublik."*

17. Quoted in Taner Akçam, *A Shameful Act: The Armenian Genocide and the Question of Turkish Responsibility* (New York: Metropolitan, 2006), p. 155.

18. Human Rights Watch/Middle East, *Iraq's Crime of Genocide: The Anfal Campaign Against the Kurds* (New Haven, CT: Yale University Press, 1995), p. 254.

19. Richard Goldstone, "Preventing and Prosecuting Crimes Against Humanity in the 21st Century," lecture delivered in Abuja, Nigeria, February 14, 2005, www.iccnow.org/documents/GoldstoneAbuja_14Feb05.pdf.

20. Quoted in Paul Martin, "Hezbollah Calls for Global Attacks: Wants to Export Suicide Bombings," *Washington Times,* December 4, 2002, http://nl.newsbank.com/nl-search/we/Archives?p_action=doc&p_docid=0F7B8 C916BDA6AFE&p_docnum=5&s_accountid=AC0108052114304131874 &s_orderid=NB0108052114301531762&s_dlid=DL01080521143049319 08&s_ecproduct=DOC&s_ecprodtype=&s_username=dgoldhagen&s_ accountid=AC0108052114304131874&s_upgradeable=no.

21. *Trial of the Major War Criminals Before the International Military Tribunal, Nuremberg, 14 November 1945–1 October 1946* (Nuremberg, Germany, 1947), "Indictment," vol. 1, pp. 28–34 and 80–84; available also at http://avalon.law.yale.edu/imt/count.asp.

22. U.S. Department of State, Bureau of European and Eurasian Affairs, "Fact Sheet: U.S. Assistance to Bosnia and Herzegovina, Fiscal Years 1995–2005," November 18, 2005, www.america.gov/st/washfile-english/2005/November/20051212172624xlrennef0.6925623.html.

23. Silajdžić, author interview.

24. Tharcisse Karugarama, author interview, Kigali, Rwanda, May 9, 2008.

25. Otilia Lux de Coti, author interview, Guatemala City, Guatemala, June 10, 2008.

26. José Efraín Ríos Montt, author interview, Guatemala City, Guatemala, June 10, 2008.

27. Freedom House, *Freedom in the World 2009.*

CREDITS

Every reasonable effort has been made to secure required permissions to use all images, maps, and other art included in this volume.

PHOTOGRAPHS

395 National Archives and Records Administration, College Park, courtesy of U.S. Holocaust Memorial Museum
402 GARF
407 Memorial Society
410 GARF
424 Ron Haviv/VII
465 Courtesy of JTN Productions
531 Courtesy of JTN Productions
542 Copyright © PersianEye/Corbis
581 Courtesy of JTN Productions
583 AP/Jaime Puebla
585 Courtesy of JTN Productions

MAPS

594 Courtesy of Freedom House, www.freedomhouse.org
595 Courtesy of Freedom House, www.freedomhouse.org

THOUGHTS AND THANKS

I started working on this book close to thirty years ago, without knowing it, when in college, as with so many of my other beginnings, I began to study genocide with my father, Erich Goldhagen, a man of magisterial character and intellect. Then about twenty years ago I started picking it up again, also unknowingly, when I began working in earnest on my doctoral dissertation, which would become the basis for *Hitler's Willing Executioners: Ordinary Germans and the Holocaust. Hitler's Willing Executioners* was conceptually, empirically, and theoretically embedded in a broad and thorough understanding of mass murder more generally, even though I brought this in manifest form into the book only in glimpses. In the aftermath of that book's publication, I decided to convey to others all I had learned about mass murder in yet another book that was, intellectually, a natural successor to the one focused on the Holocaust.

I still had much to work out about how to analyze certain aspects of mass murder and eliminationist assaults more generally, and how to present such a vast subject in a way that would be faithful to the highest standards of social analysis *and* would be inviting to the general reader. Nevertheless, I had already developed most of this book's fundamental ideas. That eliminationism, not genocide, was the master category became clear to me during my study of the Holocaust, when I was working to create the concept of *eliminationist antisemitism* to capture the particular character of the antisemitism that prevailed in Germany and in other parts of Europe: Conceiving of the antisemitism as "eliminationist" was critically important for analyzing the Germans' persecution of the Jews, precisely because it links the *content* of the prejudice directly to the perpetrators' *treatment* of Jews, showing that the antisemitism had the potential for multiple courses of related actions, leading to a variety of roughly functionally equivalent *eliminationist* policies, culminating in the Germans' attempted total annihilation of the Jews. That any serious study of mass murder had to concentrate on human beings—taking seriously their agency and views of the world—and not abstract structures and institutions also emerged directly from my study of the Holocaust's perpetration. That political leaders were the prime movers of eliminationist assaults was to me as self-evidently true of Mehmet Talât, Joseph Stalin, Mao Zedong, Pol Pot, and others, as it was (and as I analyzed at length in

Hitler's Willing Executioners) for Adolf Hitler. That an understanding of genocide, mass murder, and eliminationist programs had to be embedded in a general understanding of politics was as obvious to me then—after all, I was a professor of political science—as it was surprising to me that, except in the most superficial manner, it had not been treated in this way. Finally, it was also clear to me then that all this knowledge, the ways in which it and other aspects of my thinking repositioned our understanding of mass murder, necessitated a different political and policy approach to reducing the incidence of mass murder and elimination, one that held out the promise of actually being effective.

I was ready with all these ideas in 1997, yet it took much longer than I expected for them to emerge in book form. Not only did the aftermath of the publication of *Hitler's Willing Executioners* occupy me for much longer than expected, but then, when it subsided enough for me to move on, I put aside this book after working on it for a few years, in order to write a book on another topic, this time moral philosophical, that seemed to me badly in need of exploration: moral repair. After writing, publishing, and dealing with the considerable aftermath of that book, *A Moral Reckoning: The Role of the Catholic Church in the Holocaust and Its Unfulfilled Duty of Repair*, I picked up this book yet again. Finally, three years before finishing it, I picked its themes up yet again, or rather anew, this time using the book as the basis for making a feature-length documentary of the same name for PBS together with Jay Sanderson and Mike DeWitt of JTN Productions, and with the support of Stephen Segaller of WNET.org, who when we first met zeroed in on a phrase in a memo I had written to explain the project and said, "There's your title: 'Worse Than War.'" The film is the first cinematic general treatment of the phenomenon of genocide, or as you now know it, eliminationism. As I am about to send the manuscript to my publisher for its final stages of production, we are also in film's final stages of postproduction. Doing the film took me around the world to the sites of barbarities I had long studied from afar, and allowed me to interview many people well situated to impart facts and truths about eliminationist assaults—the powerful and peasants, perpetrators, victims, and bystanders, those dedicated to uncovering the truth, including forensic experts and human rights and legal activists, and those dedicated to obscuring it. The rich interviews yielded abundant, powerful new testimony about many of eliminationist assaults' central features, enriching this book enormously.

I write books with different people in mind: the general public, scholars, religious and other institutional leaders, myself, and, with this book, politicians and policy-makers. The weight that each of these different kinds of people have in my mind vary from book to book, and within each book from one section to the next. To spend a moment on myself, I find it odd I am sometimes accused of hubris or arrogance for daring to say things others have not said—though these charges are also perfectly understandable, as my books have been treated and responded to, also by so many so-called scholars, as political events, especially but not only by those feeling threatened by the truths they contain. I say this because it seems odd to me that anyone would expend the enormous time and energy it takes to write and publish a book unless believing he had original and important things to say. I write books only on topics I think are important and about which I think I have something fundamentally new, different, and right to convey to others, and not just something or any old thing, but enough or perhaps more than enough to change the understanding of the book's subject and themes. Then I endeavor to write the books in ways that adhere to or even push forward the best current understanding of scholarly analysis, and to do so in a way that every engaged citizen, not just the social scientific cognoscenti, can read. Then I let the chips fall. It turns out I have written on grim topics, topics of life and death, topics of sweeping importance and scope, topics that engage or inflame people's minds and hearts. I do so always with what Max Weber discussed in another context, a sense of *calling*, and always, ever more here, with a dual sense of vocation, which in this instance are not in tension: the vocation of science or scholarship, which is the ethic of ultimate ends, and the vocation of politics, which is the ethic of responsibility. As a devotee of the ethics of ultimate ends, I write to the best of my understanding and with all my intellectual care and might (whatever that might be) what is true. As a devotee of the ethics of responsibility, I seek to impart these truths to all who care and, as much as possible, to all who do not, and especially to those who can influence others and the world's events—in order to shape the world, the worlds of people's understanding and actions, and thus to improve people's lot however much a man, or this man, sitting at his computer keyboard and then taking to the media pages and airwaves, can.

As in my other books, I do all this in this book by asking questions that differ markedly from the questions others have asked who have addressed genocide. It is my thinking through of the problem from the beginning, rethinking both what we need to study, namely what the object of study is—both in kind and in size, and its various dimensions (even dispensing with the analytically problematic term *genocide*)—how to organize and present the analysis, how to explain and interpret virtually every aspect of eliminationist assaults, and then, of course, how to stop them. The analysis I present is therefore about mass murder, more broadly, about mass elimination, and not about other authors' work. It is my attempt to substantially recast our understanding of the phenomenon, and not to engage in debates with writer

X or writer Y about what he or she has said on point A or point B. Obviously, I differ from many other authors on how to understand many aspects of mass murder and elimination, from conceptualizing mass murder and other eliminationist measures as being cut from the same cloth, to embedding them in a broader understanding of eliminationist politics and politics more broadly. Carrying on debates on these points is of interest mainly or perhaps only to those authors. For readers, including other scholars, the critical issue is understanding eliminationist assaults, destroyers of so many people and breakers of so many societies past, present, and potentially future. Eliminationist assaults' basic contours are known with many useful and fine books presenting the individual narratives, and as this book is not about those narratives but instead seeks to explore the whys and wherefores neglected or treated in inadequate ways, I have also resisted the fetish of citing sources and loading the book with such unnecessary heft because once one gets into this, the vast monographic sources just on many individual mass murders are shoreless.

This book is not about other people's interpretations. It is not meant to be an exhaustive documentation of any individual mass murder, let alone a history of our time's sweep of mass murders, let alone eliminations. The facts, in any case, are generally straightforward. This book rather seeks to reconceptualize, understand anew, interpret differently, explain adequately, and to propose workable responses to this catastrophic and systematic problem of eliminationism. This book is about our, or more specifically, my ability to do or propose all these in fresh, compelling, and correct ways. *That* is what I present. *That* is what you will judge.

For the general reader, I recommend several general sources dealing with the essential contours of our time's mass murders that contain much of the basic historical material mentioned in this book: *Encyclopedia of Genocide and Crimes Against Humanity*; Samuel Totten, William S. Parsons, and Israel W. Charny, eds., *Genocide in the Twentieth Century* and their subsequent *Century of Genocide*; Frank Chalk and Kurt Jonassohn, eds., *The History and Sociology of Genocide*; Paul Hollander, ed., *From the Gulag to the Killing Fields*; Ben Kiernan, *Blood and Soil*; R. J. Rummel, *Death By Government*; and Matthew White, "Deaths by Mass Unpleasantness: Estimated Totals for the Entire 20th Century," *Historical Atlas of the Twentieth Century,* http://users.erols.com/mwhite28/warstat8.htm. The monographic literature on individual mass murders is often large. On the Holocaust alone, it would fill a decent-sized library. Mentioning here just a few extremely helpful works in no way implies there are not many, many others that could also be cited for other eliminationist assaults or for the ones the works themselves treat: on the Turks' slaughter of the Armenians, Vahakn N. Dadrian,

The History of the Armenian Genocide; on the Holocaust, my own *Hitler's Willing Executioners*; on the Soviet gulag, Anne Applebaum, *Gulag*; on Cambodia, Ben Kiernan, *The Pol Pot Regime*; on Rwanda, Jean Hatzfeld, *Machete Season*; and on the U.S. response to exterminationist assaults, Samantha Power, *A Problem from Hell*. In addition to the historical treatments themselves, many of these sources present excellent selections of witness testimony. It is important, however, to understand that just because these and other publications contain facts and figures that provide the foundation for an analysis of exterminationist and eliminationist assaults, it does not mean that I agree or disagree with any of the specific or many interpretations and explanations they offer.

Not merely other people's books, but other people have also been indispensable for this book. For their comments and support, I am thankful to Clive Priddle, Mustafa Emirbayer, Esther Newberg, Peter Osnos, Paul Pierson, Thane Rosenbaum, and Susan Weinberg. I am also thankful, and more, to my mother and father, Norma Goldhagen and Erich Goldhagen, for all they have singly and together done to make this book possible. My father continues to provide me unending intellectual companionship and inspiration. His appearance in the film, for which he accompanied me, or rather I him, on his first trip back to where he survived the Holocaust, provides only a small, though to me a cherished, part of the recognition he deserves for his own seminal thinking and for his incalculable contributions to my intellectual formation and work.

Most of all, I want to thank Sarah Williams Goldhagen for everything, a slight but enormous portion of which is the many, many improvements she has made to this book owing to her skilled editing hand and still more skilled mind.

INDEX

Locators in italics indicate figures or tables.

Until devoting himself full time to writing, Daniel Jonah Goldhagen taught political science for many years at Harvard University. He is also the prize-winning author of the international number one bestseller *Hitler's Willing Executioners* and *A Moral Reckoning* and contributes to major newspapers and magazines around the world.

Please visit www.goldhagen.com

Portland Community College